Studies in Classification, Data Analysis, and Knowledge Organization

T0135030

Springer
Berlin
Heidelberg
New York
Barcelona
Hong Kong
London
Milan
Paris
Tokyo

Titles in the Series

Wolfgang Gaul · Gunter Ritter (Eds.)

Classification, Automation, and New Media

Proceedings of the 24th Annual Conference of the Gesellschaft für Klassifikation e.V., University of Passau, March 15–17, 2000

With 101 Figures and 57 Tables

Springer

Professor Dr. Wolfgang Gaul
University of Karlsruhe
Institute for Decision Theory
and Operations Research
Kaiserstraße 12
76128 Karlsruhe
Germany
wolfgang.gaul@wiwi.uni-karlsruhe.de

Professor Dr. Gunter Ritter
University of Passau
Department of Mathematics and Informatics
Innstraße 33
94030 Passau
Germany
ritter@fmi.uni-passau.de

ISBN 3-540-43233-7 Springer-Verlag Berlin Heidelberg New York

Classification, automation, and new media: University of Passau, March 15–17, 2000, with 57 tables / Wolfgang Gaul; Gunter Ritter (ed.). – Berlin; Heidelberg; New York; Barcelona; Hong Kong; London; Milan; Paris; Tokyo: Springer, 2002
   (Proceedings of the ... annual conference of the Gesellschaft für Klassifikation e.V.; 24)
   (Studies in classification, data analysis, and knowledge organization)
   ISBN 3-540-43233-7

Springer-Verlag Berlin Heidelberg New York
a member of BertelsmannSpringer Science+Business Media GmbH

http://www.springer.de

© Springer-Verlag Berlin · Heidelberg 2002
Printed in Germany

Softcover-Design: Erich Kirchner, Heidelberg

SPIN 10864600   43/2202-5 4 3 2 1 0 – Printed on acid-free paper

Preface

This volume of the "Studies in Classification, Data Analysis, and Knowledge Organization" contains elaborate versions of selected papers presented at the 24th *Annual Conference of the German Classification Society GfKl* (Gesellschaft für Klassifikation), held at the University of Passau in March 2000.

As in previous years, also this annual conference of GfKl supported interdisciplinary research, stimulated innovative directions, and strengthened the exchange of new ideas and of hitherto unknown results in areas where the need for handling data problems has been recognized. In Passau, special emphasis was put on the interplay of classification with automation and the New Media. Automation, as opposed to manual or cerebral work, is one of the big challenges today. Knowledge discovery in the huge amount of information in the internet and in practically every domain of knowledge that we are facing today calls for automation. Application of methods from classification and data analysis is an effective response to this rapidly growing demand.

Since many contributions tackle diverse aspects of data treatment at the same time, an unambiguous assignment of results is sometimes difficult. The editors grouped the papers in a way they found appropriate. The following chapter headings were chosen:

Data Analysis, Statistics, and Classification

Pattern Recognition and Automation

Data Mining, Information Processing, and Automation

New Media, Web Mining, and Automation

Applications in Management Science, Finance and Marketing

Applications in Medicine, Biology, Archaeology, and Others

Within chapters, the presentations are listed in alphabetical order with respect to first authors' names; papers of plenary and semiplenary speakers are marked with asterisks * at their titles.

The organizers gratefully take the opportunity to acknowledge support by

- Deutsche Forschungsgemeinschaft Bonn

as well as by

- BMW AG München

- DaimlerChrysler AG Stuttgart

- Loher AG Ruhstorf/Rott

- OBAG Regensburg

- Siemens AG München

- Sparkasse Passau

- Stadtwerke Passau GmbH

- SUN Microsystems GmbH Grasbrunn

- Vogt electronic AG Obernzell

- Volksbank-Raiffeisenbank Passau-Freyung eG

Finally, we thank all authors for their contributions and many colleagues who reviewed papers, chaired sessions, and helped in various ways with respect to the organization of the conference. Special thanks are due to Drs. Christoph Pesch and Gernot Schreib for their efficient assistance with the hard– and software necessary for running the conference and to Frau Prof. Moosmüller for her support. Frau Ingrid Winter did an excellent job with the bookkeeping.

Last but not least we mention Springer Verlag and, here, Dr. Bihn and her colleagues for their excellent cooperation in publishing this volume.

Karlsruhe   Wolfgang Gaul
Passau   Gunter Ritter

Contents

Data Analysis, Statistics, and Classification

Part I

Data Analysis, Statistics, and
Classification

Clustering and Models *

Christophe Ambroise[1], Gerard Govaert[1]

[1]UMR CNRS 6599, Université de Technologie de Compiègne,
F60200 Compiègne, France

Abstract: Basing cluster analysis on mixture models has become a classical and powerful approach. It proves to be useful for understanding and suggesting significant criteria. With Gaussian clustering models, for instance, the parametrization of the variance matrix of a cluster in terms of its eigenvalue decomposition allows to propose many general clustering criteria from the simplest (k-means criterion) to the most complex. Mixture models can also deal with very different situations such as quantitative data, binary data, spatial data, missing data, partially classified samples, order constraints on clusters or outliers. This paper intends to illustrate the application of mixture models to various clustering situations from classical Gaussian models to multivariate binary observation vectors located at neighboring geographic sites.

1 Introduction

Cluster analysis has been developed mainly through the invention and empirical investigation of ad hoc methods using metric criteria. The k-means and Ward algorithms which optimize the inertia criterion are best representative of this approach. In this context, it is often difficult to justify the metric and criterion choices. In recent years, replacing algorithmic and geometric approaches by a statistical approach, has shown that a probabilistic model can be useful both for understanding when methods are likely to be successful, and for suggesting new methods.

In this approach, the intuitive idea of "natural cluster" is formalized by means of probabilistic models. More precisely, the objects to classify are assumed to be an i.i.d. sample of a random vector and a cluster structure is sought by analyzing the density of this random vector.

Different probabilistic models for clustering have been proposed : mode clusters (Hartigan (1975)), high-density clusters (Wong (1982)), random graphs (Ling (1973)), link likelihood (Lerman (1981)), finite mixture distribution,... The interested reader may refer to an exhaustive review by Bock (1996).

In this paper, we will consider only the mixture model (Titterington et al. (1985), McLachlan and Basford (1988)). Its main advantages consist in explaining some metric criteria (i.e. trace(W), $|W|$), and giving a strategy for defining new criteria when facing new problems. It also

---

*Invited lecture

gives a theoretical framework for answering difficult questions such as the number of clusters or the relevance of the resulting clusters. Another interest of the mixture approach of clustering is its capacity to treat different situations as quantitative data, binary data, spatial data, missing data, partially classified samples, order constraints on clusters, outliers (uniform distribution and median) and in this paper we wish to illustrate these properties by a number of examples.

The paper is organized as follows. In Section 2, we recall the mixture model and the EM algorithm. In Section 3, we outline the two classical approaches in competition to estimate the parameters of a mixture. In Section 3, we present the Gaussian mixture models specifying different clustering situations from the eigenvalue decomposition of the variance matrices Σ_k of the mixture components. Section 4 is devoted to the treatment of binary spatial data and Section 5 to the treatment of missing spatial data.

2 Finite Mixture Models

We assume that the n objects to classify are vectors in $\mathbb{R}^d$ defining the data matrix $X = (\mathbf{x}_1, \ldots, \mathbf{x}_n)$.

Knowing the proportions $\pi_1, \ldots, \pi_q$ and the distribution $p_1, \ldots, p_q$ of the q components of the mixture, data are supposed to be generated according to the following process: each object is assigned to a class according to a multinomial distribution with parameters $\pi_1, \ldots, \pi_q$ and its characteritic vector $\mathbf{x_i}$ originates from the probability density function corresponding to its class.

More formally, data $\mathbf{x}_1, \ldots, \mathbf{x}_n$ are assumed to arise from a random vector with probability density function

$$p(\mathbf{x}, \theta) = \sum_{k=1}^{q} \pi_k p_k(\mathbf{x}; \mathbf{a}_k) \tag{1}$$

where p_k denotes a distribution in $\mathbb{R}^d$, $\theta = (\Pi, \mathbf{a})$ are the model parameters with the mixing proportions $\Pi = (\pi_1, \ldots, \pi_q)$ ($0 < p_k < 1$ for all $k = 1, \ldots, q$ and $\sum_k p_k = 1$) and $\mathbf{a} = (\mathbf{a}_1, \ldots, \mathbf{a}_q)$ denote class density parameters.

The problem consists in estimating the parameter θ knowing the data matrix $\mathbf{x}_1, \ldots, \mathbf{x}_n$. Various approaches, i.e. method of moments (Karl Pearson (1894)), minimum chi-square and least square approaches, have been used while a classical method consists in maximizing the log-likelihood

$$L(\theta) = L(\Pi, \mathbf{a}) = \ln\left(\prod_{i=1}^{n} p(\mathbf{x}_i; \theta)\right) = \sum_{i=1}^{n} \ln\left(\sum_{k=1}^{q} \pi_k p_k(\mathbf{x}_i; \mathbf{a}_k)\right). \tag{2}$$

Generally, there is no analytical solution and a usual solution is the EM algorithm: starting from an initial parameter $\theta^0 = (\pi^0, \mathbf{a}^0)$, an iteration of the EM algorithm consists in

1. (E-step): computing the current conditional probabilities $t_{ik}^h = P(\mathbf{x}_i \in P_k | \pi^h, \mathbf{a}^h)(1 \leq i \leq n, 1 \leq k \leq q)$ that $\mathbf{x}_i$ arises from the k-th mixture component for the current value of θ, according to the equation

$$t_{ik}^h = \frac{\pi_k^h p_k(\mathbf{x}_i; \mathbf{a}_k^h)}{\sum_{\ell=1}^q \pi_\ell^h p_k(\mathbf{x}_i; \mathbf{a}_\ell^h)}; \qquad (3)$$

2. (M-step): then the m.l. estimates $\hat{p}_k, \hat{\mu}_k, \hat{\Sigma}_k$ are computed using the conditional expectation of the log-likelihood (knowing the t_{ik}^h): $\pi_k^{h+1} = \frac{1}{n} \sum_{i=1}^n t_{ik}^h$ and $\mathbf{a}_k^{h+1}$ will be obtained by solving the likelihood equations.

The EM algorithm is generally easy to implement, leads to a local optimization of the log-likelihood, has a good practical behavior but may be slow to converge, for instance, when clusters are very mixed.

3 Model-Based Clustering

Many authors (Scott et Symons (1971), Marriott (1975),...) have considered non-hierarchical clustering methods where a mixture of distributions is used as a statistical model. In this context, two common approaches have been proposed: the mixture approach and the classification approach.

3.1 Mixture Approach

Roughly speaking, the mixture approach aims at estimating the parameter θ from the available sample. The mixture component from where each $\mathbf{x}_i$ originates is then estimated using the maximum a posteriori probabilities $(t_{ik}(\hat{\theta}))$ (MAP).

3.2 Classification Approach

The classification approach aims at estimating simultaneously the parameter θ and the partition P by maximizing the classification likelihood criterion $CL(P, \theta)$ (Scott et Symons (1971), (Symons (1981))

$$CL(P, \theta) = \sum_{k=1}^q \sum_{\mathbf{x}_i \in P_k} \ln \pi_k p_k(\mathbf{x}_i, \mathbf{a}_k). \qquad (4)$$

Let $\mathbf{z}_i = (z_{i1}, \ldots, z_{iq})'$ denote the identifying labels, where $z_{ik} = 1$ if $\mathbf{x}_i$ belongs to the k-th cluster and 0 otherwise. Thus, these n vectors in $\mathbb{R}^q$ define a classification matrix $Z = (\mathbf{z}_1, \ldots, \mathbf{z}_n)$ verifying $z_{ik} \in \{0, 1\}$ and $\forall i, \sum_{k=1}^{q} z_{ik} = 1$.

The classification likelihood criterion can also be considered as the log-likelihood of the *complete data* $p(X, Z)$.

To maximize this criterion, the CEM Algorithm (Celeux and Govaert (1992)) can be used. This algorithm, which is an alternate optimization of the classification likelihood criterion CL can be viewed as a modified version of the EM algorithm which computes an extra classification step between the E-step and the M-step:

1. (E-Step): computation of the t_{ik}^h;

2. (C-step): computation of the partition $P^{h+1} = \text{MAP}(t_{ki}^h)$ (the t_{ki}^h are replaced by 1 or 0);

3. (M-step): maximization or $CL(P^{h+1}, .)$:

   (a) $\pi_k^{h+1} = \frac{\#P_k^{h+1}}{n}$, where $\#P_k^{h+1}$ is the number of objects of cluster k;

   (b) $\mathbf{a}_k^{h+1}$: estimation of m.l. using the sample P_k^{h+1}.

In this way, we obtain a very general classification algorithm.

3.3   Relation Between the Two Approaches

The classification likelihood criterion can be written

$$CL(P, \theta) = CL(Z, \theta) = \sum_{i=1}^{n} \sum_{k=1}^{q} z_{ik} \ln \pi_k p_k(\mathbf{x}_i; \mathbf{a}_k). \qquad (5)$$

If $C = (c_{ik})$ denotes a fuzzy classification matrix ($c_{ik} \in [0, 1]$ and $\forall i$, $\sum_{k=1}^{q} c_{ik} = 1$), the classification likelihood criterion can be extended to

$$CL(C, \theta) = \sum_{i=1}^{n} \sum_{k=1}^{q} c_{ik} \ln \pi_k p_k(\mathbf{x}_i; \mathbf{a}_k). \qquad (6)$$

but its maximization leads to a hard partition. A fuzzy classification likelihood can be proposed

$$FCL(C, \theta) = CL(C, \theta) + E(C) \quad \text{where } E(C) = -\sum_{i=1}^{n} \sum_{k=1}^{q} c_{ik} \ln c_{ik} \quad (7)$$

and Hathaway (1986) showed that an alternate optimization of $FCL(C, \theta)$ corresponds exactly to the EM algorithm: the EM algorithm can thus be considered as a fuzzy clustering algorithm. Moreover, he obtained the relation

$$L(\theta) = FCL(T(\theta), \theta) = CL(T(\theta), \theta) + E(T(\theta)) \qquad (8)$$

where $T(\theta)$ is the fuzzy classification matrix defined by the $t_{ik}(\theta)$: the differences between the two criteria is a term of entropy and if the fuzzy partition $T(\theta)$ is well-separated, the two criteria $L(\theta)$ and $CL(P, \theta)$ are similar. This property can be viewed as a posterior justification of the classification likelihood criterion which searchs for well-separated components.

4 Gaussian Mixture

4.1 The Model

When data is quantitative, the Gaussian mixture model is the usual approach. In this situation, the pdf of each component takes the form

$$p_k(\mathbf{x}; a_k) = p_k(\mathbf{x}; (\mu_k, \Sigma_k)) = \frac{1}{(2\pi)^{\frac{d}{2}} |\Sigma_k|^{\frac{1}{2}}} \exp\{ -\frac{1}{2}(\mathbf{x} - \mu_k)' \Sigma_k^{-1} (\mathbf{x} - \mu_k) \}$$

$$(9)$$

where μ_k is the mean vector and Σ_k is the variance matrix.

The form of the mixture model is defined by parameterizing the variance matrix Σ_k in terms of its eigenvalue decomposition, as developed by Banfield and Raftery (1993) and Celeux and Govaert(1995),

$$\Sigma_k = \lambda_k D_k A_k D_k' \qquad (10)$$

where $\lambda_k = |\Sigma_k|^{\frac{1}{d}}, D_k$ is the matrix of eigenvectors of Σ_k and A_k is a diagonal matrix, such that $|A_k| = 1$, with the normalized eigenvalues of Σ_k on the diagonal in a decreasing order. The parameter $\lambda_k = |\Sigma_k|^{\frac{1}{d}}$ determines the volume of the k-th group, D_k its orientation and A_k its shape.

We want to stress the differences between the size and the volume of a cluster to avoid a possible confusion between these two notions. For example, Banfield and Raftery designated the parameter λ as the size of a cluster. In fact, the size of a cluster P_k is $\#P_k$ and is proportional to p_k. Size and volume are not directly related: a small (resp. large) size cluster can occupy a large (resp. small) volume.

By allowing some but not all of these quantities to vary between groups, we obtain easily interpretable models appropriate to describe various clustering situations. We denote conventionally those models as exemplified hereby: $[p_k \lambda D_k A D_k']$ indicates the model with different proportions and orientations and equal volumes and shapes. Moreover we can assume diagonal variance matrices, we denote B a diagonal variance matrix and, for instance, $[p\lambda_k B]$ indicates the model with equal proportions, different volumes, equal shapes and diagonal orientations. Finally, models can constrain shapes to be spherical : they are denoted $[p\lambda I]$, $[p\lambda_k I]$, $[p_k \lambda I]$, and $[p_k \lambda_k I]$.

4.2 CEM Algorithm

The E and the C steps do not need further explanation. Let us just remark that these 2 steps produce a partition defined by minimizing the distance

$$d^2_{\Sigma_k^{-1}}(\mathbf{x}_i, \mu_k) + \ln|\Sigma_k| - 2\ln\pi_k. \tag{11}$$

The M step consists in maximizing according to θ the function

$$-\frac{1}{2}\sum_{k=1}^{q}\sum_{\mathbf{x}\in P_k}(\mathbf{x}-\mu_k)'\Sigma_k^{-1}(\mathbf{x}-\mu_k)-\frac{1}{2}\sum_{k=1}^{q}\#P_k\ln|\Sigma_k|+\sum_{k=1}^{q}\#P_k\ln\pi_k. \tag{12}$$

We obtain $\pi_k = \frac{\#P_k}{n}$ for the models $[\Pi_k]$ and $p_k = \frac{1}{q}$ for the models $[\Pi]$. Considering the mean, all the models leads to $\mu_k = \overline{\mathbf{x}}_k$ (center of gravity of the class k).

The updated formulas for the variance matrices depend on the considered mixture model but in all the cases, they are obtained by minimizing the function

$$F(\Sigma_k) = \sum_{k=1}^{q}\text{trace}(W_k\Sigma_k^{-1}) + \sum_{k=1}^{q}\#P_k\ln|\Sigma_k| \tag{13}$$

where $W_k = \sum_{\mathbf{x}\in P_k}(\mathbf{x}-\overline{\mathbf{x}}_k)(\mathbf{x}-\overline{\mathbf{x}}_k)'$.

For instance, for the Model $[\Pi, \Sigma_k = \lambda I]$, the E-C step corresponds to the assignment of objects to classes by minimizing the euclidean distance $d^2(\mathbf{x}_i, \mu_k)$. In the M-step, the function F takes the form $F(\lambda) = \frac{1}{\lambda}\text{trace}(W) + nd\ln(\lambda)$ where $W = \sum_{k=1}^{q}W_k$ which gives $\lambda = \frac{\text{trace}(W)}{nd}$. The likelihood expression takes the form $F(\lambda) = nd + nd\ln\frac{\text{trace}(W)}{nd}$ and in this case, the maximization of the classification likelihood is equivalent to the minimization of the inertia criterion $\text{trace}(W)$. Moreover, the CEM algorithm is exactly the k-means algorithm. Finally, the fact of considering the inertia criterion, implicitly assumes that classes are spherical, mixed in same proportions and have the same volume.

Similar results obtained with other interesting models (among the 16 possible models described in Section 4.1) are presented in Table 1 references.

Model	distance	criterion	Remarks
$\Pi, \lambda I$	$d^2(\mathbf{x}_i, \mu_k)$	trace(W)	CEM = k-means
$\Pi, \lambda_k I$	$\frac{1}{\lambda_k} d^2(\mathbf{x}_i, \mu_k) + d \ln(\lambda_k)$		separ. surf. : hyperspheres
$\Pi, \lambda B$	$d^2_{B^{-1}}(\mathbf{x}_i, \mu_k)$	diag(W)	classification + weights
Π, Σ	$d^2_{\Sigma^{-1}}(\mathbf{x}_i, \mu_k)$	$|W|$	

Table 1: Examples of variance matrix parametrization and their corresponding classification assumptions

5   Binary Spatial Data

In this section, we consider the problem of partitionning a set of n binary observations $\mathbf{x}_1, \ldots, \mathbf{x}_n$, ($\mathbf{x}_i \in \{0,1\}^d$, $1 \le i \le n$) located at neighboring geographic sites. For instance, it may be applied in biogeography to cluster n contiguous quadrats over which the occurrences of d animal species have been recorded. The aim is twofold: produce clusters that are homogeneous in the feature space, and account for some a priori hypothesis of spatial smoothness.

5.1   Clustering Based on Bernoulli Mixture

In the case of binary data, a mixture of q multivariate Bernoulli laws comes as a natural assumption. Following Govaert (1990) and Celeux and Govaert (1991), distribution p_k is characterized by its centers $m_k \in \{0,1\}^d$ and its dispersion $\varepsilon_k \in]0; \frac{1}{2}[^d$ so that any observation $\mathbf{x} \in \{0,1\}^d$ belonging to group k occurs with probability

$$p_k(\mathbf{x}; (\mathbf{m}_k, \varepsilon_k)) = \prod_{j=1}^{d} \varepsilon_{kj}^{|x_j - m_{kj}|} (1 - \varepsilon_{kj})^{1 - |x_j - m_{kj}|}. \qquad (14)$$

Expression (14) means that given class k, observation $\mathbf{x}$ arises from independent drawings of d univariate Bernoulli laws with parameters $1 - \varepsilon_{kj}$ if $m_{kj} = 1$, or ε_{kj} if $m_{kj} = 0$ ($1 \le j \le d$). Thus, given class k, for each variable j, m_{kj} represents the value that occurs with highest probability, while ε_{kj} represents the probability that observations x_j differs from m_{kj}, thence the terminology of center m_k and dispersion for ε_k.

As in the Gaussian approach, we obtain various models making constraints on the mixing proportions and on the ε_{kj}. Thus, we obtain the model $[\varepsilon]$ if the dispersion is the same for all variables and all classes, the model $[\varepsilon_k]$ if the dispersion is the same for all classes, the model $[\varepsilon_j]$ if the dispersion is the same for all variables and in the more general case the model $[\varepsilon_{kj}]$. We can remark that this last Bernoulli mixture is exactly the mixture associated with the general latent class model.

The mixture approach and the clustering approach described in Section 2 can be applied without any problem to these binary models. For the model having equal proportions and dispersions, the criterion $-CL(P, \theta)$ is akin to a sum of intraclass inertia with a L_1 norm, so that its alternate optimization yields a k-means like algorithm using L_1 distance and binary kernels.

5.2   Spatial Classification

The fuzzy classification likelihood criterion $FCL(C, \theta)$ (Equation 7) optimized by EM favors the homogeneity of the clusters in the variable space, but does not take into account the spatial information of the data. This second point can be addressed by adding the following spatial regularizing term to $FCL(C, \theta)$ (Ambroise (1996)), Ambroise et al. (1997))

$$G(C) = \frac{1}{2} \sum_{k=1}^{q} \sum_{i=1}^{n} \sum_{j=1}^{n} c_{ik} c_{jk} v_{ij} \qquad (15)$$

where v_{ij} are the weights of the geographic neighborhood system ($v_{ij} > 0$ if observation i is neighbor of observation j, $v_{ij} = 0$ otherwise). $G(C)$ is an increasing function of the number of neighbor pairs having the same label. The degree of spatial smoothing is controlled via a weighting coefficient β, so that the new criterion to be optimized is defined as

$$W(C, \theta) = FCL(C, \theta) + \beta.G(C). \qquad (16)$$

Optimizing alternatively criterion $W(C, \theta)$ over C and θ yields an iterative algorithm having the same structure as EM, called Neighborhood EM (NEM). The calculation is then initialized by choosing arbitrary initial values for the parameters of the mixtures, θ^0, and the classification matrix, C^0. The two following steps are then iteratively repeated until convergence is reached ($h + 1$ denotes the current iteration):

1. E-step:
$$C^{h+1} = \arg\max_{C} W(C, \theta^h).$$

The following equations are obtained, for $1 \le i \le n$ and $1 \le k \le q$:

$$c_{ik}^{h+1} = g_{ik}(C^{h+1}) = \frac{\pi_k^h p_k(\mathbf{x}_i; \mathbf{a}_k^h).\exp\{\beta \sum_{j=1}^{n} c_{kj}^{h+1} v_{ij}\}}{\sum_{\ell=1}^{q} \pi_\ell^h p_\ell(\mathbf{x}_i; \mathbf{a}_\ell^h).\exp\{\beta \sum_{j=1}^{n} c_{\ell j}^{h+1} v_{ij}\}}$$
$$(17)$$

suggesting an iterative computing algorithm of the form $C = g(\tilde{C})$, where $\tilde{C}$ is the old classification matrix. The convergence of this fixed point procedure can be proved under a bounding condition on β (Ambroise and Govaert (1998));

2. M-step: identical to the M step of EM.

It can be shown that this algorithm carries out the same calculations as the application of the mean field approximation to a particular hidden Markov random field model (Dang and Govaert (1998)).

5.3 Simulated Example

The simulated example of this paragraph illustrates the behavior of the NEM algorithm with respect to its underlying Markov and Bernoulli hypotheses. The $n = 400$ observation vectors consist in $d = 6$ binary values and are located on a square grid of 20 by 20 pixels. The classes of the observations were first randomly generated according to a Markov Random field distribution with $q = 5$ classes and $\beta = 1.2$, using a Gibbs sampler. The observations (Figure 1 (a)) were then randomly generated according to Bernoulli class distribution. The result of applying the EM algorithm to partition this simulated dataset is displayed in Figure 1 (b) and the result of applying the NEM algorithm is displayed in Figure 1 (c). This small example illustrates clearly the advantages of considering the spatial information.

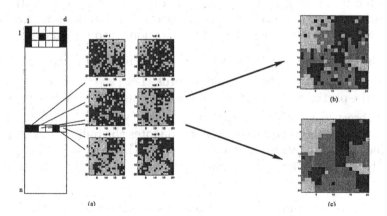

Figure 1: Example of application of EM and NEM algorithms to simulated spatial binary data.

5.4 Discussion

The spatial clustering method presented in this section takes into account the spatial relationship between the geographical units without imposing any *ad hoc* contiguity constraint in order to obtain a legible map. It is worth noting that the algorithm may lead to a legible map according to the underlying structure of the dataset. Thus, if the degree of mappability of the data is low, then there is logically no reason to obtain a legible map.

The spatial fuzzy clustering procedure discussed here should not be run without using the tools dedicated to provide some guidance about the parameters. Some heuristics to choose the number of clusters and the the degree of spatial smoothness which show interesting performance can be proposed.

This algorithm has the advantage of exhibiting a computable criterion that allows to choose among different local optima. Notice that the classification approach if applied to the method presented above, generally achieves a quicker convergence, without, however, producing results of the same quality.

6 Spatial Data and Missing Data

This study has been motivated by the following application: climatic annual measures such as minimum and maximum temperature or rainfall data have been collected at various meteorological stations, ecologists are interested in defining groups of stations that have similar climatic characteristics. At several stations, only a part of the measures are available, but it would be desirable to include all stations into the analysis.

Let n be the number of records (the stations in this example), d be the number of variables of the complete records. Let $(x_1^{\{o_1\}}, \ldots, x_n^{\{o_n\}}) = x^{\{o\}}$ denote the partially observed records, where the set o_i denotes the indices of the observed variables for the i-th record, $(x_1^{\{m_1\}}, \ldots, x_n^{\{m_n\}}) = x^{\{m\}}$ denote the unobserved values where m_i denotes the indices of the missing variables for that record, and $x = (x^{\{o\}}, x^{\{m\}})$ the completed data. Let r be the $n \times d$ binary matrix such that $r_{id} = 1$ if x_{id} is observed and $r_{id} = 0$ otherwise.

With such a problem, we have two kinds of observations at hand: the observed values themselves $x^{\{o\}}$ and the missingness pattern r. It is usually convenient to decompose the model using the mechanism that generates the complete data x and the mechanism that generates the missingness pattern r given the complete data. We propose to model the generation of the complete data by using a hidden Markov random field, and the missingness pattern by assuming that the data are missing at random.

6.1 Missing Data

To solve the problem of missing data, different solutions have been proposed: delete incomplete observations, replace missing values by some plausible data or make use of a method which takes missing data into account. In this work, we have considered this last alternative.

It is proposed to model the mechanism leading to missing data by using a simple missing at random (MAR) model (see e.g. Little and Rubin 1987). This means that, after conditioning on the observed data, the missingness pattern is independent of the unobserved data:

$$p(\mathbf{r}|\mathbf{x}, \mathbf{z}) = p(\mathbf{r}|\mathbf{x}^o).$$

The mixture approach leads to maximizing the associated log-likelihood $L(\theta) = \ln \left(\prod_{i=1}^{n} p(\mathbf{x}_i^0; \theta) \right)$ with the EM algorithm. The h-th iteration of the EM algorithm, which is defined by

$$\theta^{h+1} = \arg\max_{\theta} \left(Q(\theta, \theta^h) = E\left[\log p(\mathbf{x}^o, \mathbf{x}^m, \mathbf{z}; \theta)|\mathbf{x}^o; \theta^h\right] \right)$$

consists in the two following steps:

- E Step: computation of the $t_{ik}^{(h+1)} = p(z_{ik} = 1|\mathbf{x}^o; \theta^h)$

$$t_{ik}^{(h+1)} = \frac{\pi_k^h p_k^{o_i}(\mathbf{x}_i^{o_i}; \mu_k^{(h)}, \Sigma_k^{(h)})}{\sum_{\ell=1}^{q} \pi_\ell^h p_\ell^{o_i}(\mathbf{x}_i^{o_i}; \mu_\ell^{(h)}, \Sigma_\ell^{(h)})}$$

- Step M (for the mean vector computation assuming a Gaussian model i.e.)

$$\mu_{kj}^{h+1} = \frac{\sum_{i=1}^{n} t_{ik}^{(h+1)}\left(r_{ij}x_{ij} + (1 - r_{ij})\mu_{kj}^h\right)}{\sum_{i=1}^{n} t_{ik}^{(h+1)}}$$

We can obtain similar results for the CEM algorithm.

6.2 Spatial missing data

The basic idea is to integrate the missing data in the NEM algorithm of Section 5.2 as done in Section 6.1.

Simulation have been carried out (Dang and Govaert (1999) in order to evaluate the behavior of this method with respect to its underlying hidden Markov random field model. An example of simulated dataset and its processing are shown in Figure 2.

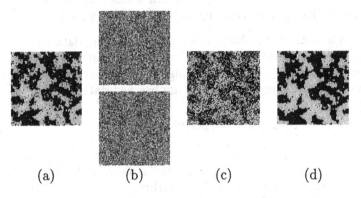

(a)   (b)   (c)   (d)

Figure 2: Example of simulation of spatial incomplete data. (a) Unobserved 2-class label field $z^{sim} \sim$ Markov random field with $\beta = 1$. (b) Incomplete data simulated (40 % missing) (c) Blind (non spatial) classification : error rate = 22%. (d) Spatial classification : error rate = 7%.

The results of this simulation showed, as is apparent from this figure, that using the spatial information improves notably the partition in comparison with blind partition. In comparison with the EM algorithm for this model, the proposed method yields somewhat simpler computations, the missing statistics being simply ignored instead of being replaced by their expectation. Experiments show that both approaches provides almost identical estimates and error rates.

7 Conclusion

This paper is a partial review of mixture models for clustering. Even if this statistical framework for clustering does not solve all problems, it allows to develop highly flexible criteria and algorithms. Some complex problems as the choice of the model and number of clusters have not been dealt with this paper, but may also find solutions or heuristics in this context.

The two alternatives presented here, i.e. mixture approach and classification approach, can be applied indifferently to all presented problems :

missing data, spatial data, Bernoulli models. On the one hand, the classification approach converges generally in a shorter time, but on the other
hand it suffers from several disadvantages : the resulting estimates are
inconsistents (number of parameter increasing with n), and are biased.
Actually, the classification approach is searching for separated classes
and could thus be advantageously used once this prior assumption has
been ascertained.

References

AMBROISE, C., DANG, D. and GOVAERT, G (1997): Clustering of
spatial data by the em algorithm. In: A. Soares, J. Gumez-Hernandez,
and F. Froidevaux (eds.): geoENV1-Geostatistics for Environmental Applications, volume 9 of Quantitative Geology and Geostatistics, 493–504.
Kluwer Academic Publisher, Dordrecht.

AMBROISE, C. (1996): Approche probabiliste en classification automatique et contraintes de voisinage. PhD thesis, Université de Technologie de Compiègne.

AMBROISE, C. and GOVAERT, G (1996): Constrained clustering and
kohonen self-organizing maps. *Journal of Classification, 13(2), 299–313.*

AMBROISE, C. and GOVAERT, G: Convergence of an em-type algorithm for spatial clustering. *Pattern Recognition Letters, 19, 919–927.*

BANFIELD, J. and RAFTERY, A. (1993): Model-based gaussian and
non-gaussian clustering. *Biometrics, 49, 803-821.*

BOCK, H. (1996): Probability models and hypothesis testing in partitioning cluster analysis: In: P. Arabie, L. J. Hubert, and G. De Soete
(eds.): Clustering and Classification, 377–453. World Scientific Publishing, River Edge, N. J.

CELEUX, G. (1992): Modèles probabilistes en classification. In: B. Droes-
beke, J. Fichet and P. Tassi (eds.): Modèles pour l'analyse de données
multidimensionnelles, 165–211. Economica, 1992.

CELEUX, G. and GOVAERT, G (1992): Clustering criteria for discrete
data and latent class models. *Journal of Classification, 8(2),157–176.*

CELEUX, G. and GOVAERT, G (1995): Gaussian parsimonious clustering models. *Pattern Recognition, 28(5), 781–793.*

DANG, D. and GOVAERT, G (1998): Spatial Fuzzy Clustering using
EM and Markov Random Fields. *System Research and Info. Systems,
8,183-202.*

DANG, D. and GOVAERT, G (1999): Clustering of spatial incomplete
data using a fuzzy classifying likelihood. In: A. Friedl, A. Berghols,
and G. Kauermann (eds.): 14th International Workshop on Statistical
Modelling, 150–157, Graz (Austria), July, 19-23 1999.

GOVAERT, G (1992): Classification binaire et modéles. *Rev. Statistique Appliquée, XXXVIII(1), 67–81.*

HARTIGAN, J. (1975): Clustering Algorithms. Wiley, New York.

HATHAWAY, R (1986): Another interpretation of the em algorithm for mixture distributions. *Statistics & Probability Letters, 4, 53–56.*

LERMAN, I. (1981) : Classification automatique et analyse ordinale des données. Dunod, Paris.

LING, R. (1973): A probability theory for cluster analysis. *J. Am. Statis. Assoc., 68, 159–164.*

LITTLE, J. and RUBIN, D. (1987): Analysis with Missing Data. Wiley, New York.

MARRIOTT, F. (1975): Separating mixtures of normal distributions. *Biometrics, 31, 767–769.*

MCLACHLAN, G. and BASFORD, K. (1988) : Mixture Models, Inference and applications to clustering. Marcel Dekker, New York.

PEARSON, K. (1894): Contributions to the mathematical theory of evolution. *Phisosophical Transactions of the Royal Society of London, Series A, (185), 71–110.*

SCOTT, A. and SYMONS, J. (1971): Clustering methods based on likelihood ratio criteria. *Biometrics, 27, 387–397.*

SYMONS, J. (1971): (1981): Clustering criteria and multivariate normal mixtures. *Biometrics, 37, 35–43.*

TITTERINGTON, D., SMITH, A. and MAKOV, U. (1985): Statistical Analysis of Finite Mixture Distributions. Wiley, New York.

WONG, A. (1982): A hybrid clustering method for identifying high-density clusters. *J. Am. Statis. Assoc., 77, 841–847.*

Some New and Some Old Results for the Polytomous Rasch Model *

Erling B. Andersen

University of Copenhagen
Institute of Economics
1455 Copenhagen,Denmark

Abstract: In the first part, the polytomous Rasch model is discussed as it was presented by Rasch at the Berkeley Symposium in 1960, and published in the Proceedings from the Symposium in 1961. I shall then discuss what was achieved in the next 10 to 15 years as regards estimation and check of the model. As Georg Rasch himself never learned to program a computer, this work was carried out by a handful or so statisticians, who worked on the model. In the next 10 to 15 years much work was done on the polytomous Rasch model in many directions. But I shall skip this period. In the second part, I shall present a quite recent result for the estimates in the polytomous Rasch model, which is extremely simple and require only very few elementary combinations of quantities already computed. In addition it solves the problem of identifying significant points on the graphs suggested by Rasch.

1 Introduction

The polytomous Rasch model was first presented by Georg Rasch, at the Berkeley Symposium on Mathematical Statistics and Probability Theory in the summer of 1960. Later published in the proceedings from the Symposium in 1961 (Rasch (1961)). See also Fischer (1995) and Andersen (1997). It was a model for

$$P_{ni}(j) = P(\text{response } j \text{ on item } i \mid \text{person parameter } \theta_n),$$

with $i = 1, \ldots, k$ items, $j = 1, \ldots, m$ response categories and $n = 1, \ldots, N$ individuals.

Rasch claimed, that in order to estimate the item characteristics and the individual characteristics by sufficient statistics, these probabilities must have the form

$$P_{ni}(j) = \frac{1}{C(\theta_n, \varepsilon_i, \phi, \psi, \chi, \omega)} e^{\phi_j \theta_n + \psi_j \varepsilon_i + \chi_j \theta_n \varepsilon_i + \omega_j}$$

He, however, soon discarded the multiplicative term and actually never reintroduced it. He also, which came to play an important role later

---

*Invited lecture

on, required φ_j and ψ_j to be equal if the item parameters ε_i and the individual parameters were to be measured independently of each other. He, thus, arrived at the polytomous Rasch model, version 1:

$$P_{ni}(j) = \frac{e^{(\theta_n+\varepsilon_i)c_j+\omega_j}}{1+\sum_{q=1}^{m-1} e^{(\theta_n+\varepsilon_i)c_q+\omega_q}} \qquad \text{for } j = 1,\ldots,m-1 \qquad (1)$$

and

$$P_{ni}(m) = \frac{1}{1+\sum_{q=1}^{m-1} e^{(\theta_n+\varepsilon_i)c_q+\omega_q}},$$

where

θ_n is the person parameter for individual n
c_j the scoring of response category j
ε_i the item parameter for item i

After 1961, when Rasch analysed real data in Denmark, using the model, he was much concerned about the item and individual parameters being one-dimensional, as assumed in (1). For the applications of his model he, therefore, used the polytomous Rasch model, version 2.

$$P_{ni}(j) = \frac{e^{\theta_{nj}+\varepsilon_{ij}}}{1+\sum_{q=1}^{m-1} e^{\theta_{nq}+\varepsilon_{iq}}} \qquad \text{for } j = 1,\ldots,m-1 \qquad (2)$$

and

$$P_{ni}(m) = \frac{1}{1+\sum_{q=1}^{m-1} e^{\theta_{nq}+\varepsilon_{iq}}}$$

Here $\{\theta_{nj}\}$ is a matrix of individual parameters and $\{e_{ij}\}$ a matrix of item parameters.

2   Early attempts to estimate the parameters of the model and check the fit of the model to the data

For model (2) Rasch derived the conditional likelihood equations (see Section 3), but he was not able to solve them numerically. Basically such solutions required computer calculations. Although a few mainframe computers were available in the early 1960's in Denmark, Rasch never mastered this new essential tool for statisticians.

At this point we need to introduce some notations. Write the response of individual n as $(a_{ni}^{(1)},\ldots,a_{ni}^{(m)}) = (0,\ldots,1,\ldots,0)$, where $a_{ni}^{(j)} = 1$ if individual n responds on item i with a response in category j, and $a_{ni}^{(q)} = 0$ for $q \neq j$.

The complete set of responses for individual n can then be collected in the matrix

$$A_n = \begin{bmatrix} a_{n1}^{(1)} & \cdots & a_{n1}^{(m)} \\ a_{n2}^{(1)} & \cdots & a_{n2}^{(m)} \\ \cdots & \cdots & \cdots \\ a_{nk}^{(1)} & \cdots & a_{nk}^{(m)} \end{bmatrix}$$

The m-dimensional **score vector** for person number n is then defined as

$$(s_{n1}, \ldots, s_{nm}) = \left(a_{n\cdot}^{(1)}, \ldots, a_{n\cdot}^{(m)} \right)$$

A simple example may clarify the concepts. The response of individual θ_n is a sequence of numbers. For example for $k = 8$ and $m = 5$

$$(2\,4\,3\,5\,1\,1\,2\,5).$$

This is equivalent to the 8 selection vectors.

$$\begin{array}{ccccc}
(0 & 1 & 0 & 0 & 0) \\
(0 & 0 & 0 & 1 & 0) \\
(0 & 0 & 1 & 0 & 0) \\
(0 & 0 & 0 & 0 & 1) \\
(1 & 0 & 0 & 0 & 0) \\
(1 & 0 & 0 & 0 & 0) \\
(0 & 1 & 0 & 0 & 0) \\
(0 & 0 & 0 & 0 & 1)
\end{array}$$

The matrix A_n then becomes

$$A_n = \begin{bmatrix} a_{n1}^{(1)} & \cdots & a_{n1}^{(m)} \\ a_{n2}^{(1)} & \cdots & a_{n2}^{(m)} \\ \cdots & \cdots & \cdots \\ a_{nk}^{(1)} & \cdots & a_{nk}^{(m)} \end{bmatrix} = \begin{bmatrix} 0 & 1 & 0 & 0 & 0 \\ 0 & 0 & 0 & 1 & 0 \\ \cdots & \cdots & \cdots & \cdots & \cdots \\ 0 & 0 & 0 & 0 & 1 \end{bmatrix}$$

For this matrix, the score vector is

$$(s_{n1}, s_{n2}, s_{n3}, s_{n4}, s_{n5}) = (2, 2, 1, 1, 2)$$

To estimate the parameters and check the model, Rasch used an 'ad hoc' method based on the assumption, that individuals with the same sufficient statistic, i.e. the same score vector, had the same vector of individual parameters $(\theta_{n1}, \ldots, \theta_{nm})$.

Let thus $\theta_{nj} = \theta_{gj}$ for all individuals with the same score vector, i.e. if for a given score vector $(s_{g1}, \ldots, s_{gm})$

$$(s_{g1}, \ldots, s_{gm}) = \left(a_{n\cdot}^{(1)}, \ldots, a_{n\cdot}^{(m)} \right).$$

We then say that individual n belongs to group S_g. If there are G possible score vectors, i.e. G m-dimensional vectors with integer components that sum to k, then there are $g = 1, \ldots, G$ groups.

Then, under the assumption that Rasch made,

$$P_{ni}(j) = \frac{e^{\theta_{gj} + \varepsilon_{ij}}}{1 + \sum_{q=1}^{m-1} e^{\theta_{gq} + \varepsilon_{iq}}} \quad \text{for } n \in S_g \quad (3)$$

$$P_{ni}(m) = \frac{1}{1 + \sum_{q=1}^{m-1} e^{\theta_{gq} + \varepsilon_{iq}}} \quad \text{for } n \in S_g. \quad (4)$$

These equations made it possible for Rasch to make the numerical computations by hand in the following way: Let N_g be the number of individuals in group S_g. Then

$$a_{gi}^{(j)} = \sum_{n \in S_g} a_{ni}^{(j)},$$

such that

$$h_{gi}^{(j)} = \frac{a_{gi}^{(j)}}{N_g},$$

and, by estimating probabilistics by their relative frequences,

$$h_{gi}^{(j)} \approx \frac{e^{\theta_{gj} + \varepsilon_{ij}}}{1 + \sum_{q=1}^{m-1} e^{\theta_{gq} + \varepsilon_{iq}}}, \quad \text{for all } g, i \text{ and } j.$$

Thus he arrived at

$$\ln h_{gi}^{(j)} \approx \theta_{gj} + \varepsilon_{ij} - C_{gi}$$

where C_{gi} is independent of j.

Since $\theta_{gm} = \varepsilon_{im} = 0$, as can be seen from the formula (4), he then got

$$L_{gi}^{(j)} = \ln h_{gi}^{(j)} - \ln h_{gi}^{(m)} \approx \theta_{gj} + \varepsilon_{ij}, \quad (5)$$

and, accordingly,

$$\overline{L}_{\cdot i}^{(1)} \approx \overline{\theta}_{\cdot j} + \varepsilon_{ij}$$

$$\overline{L}_{g \cdot}^{(j)} \approx \theta_{gj} + \overline{\varepsilon}_{\cdot j},$$

where a subscript "·" means a summation and a "bar", as usually, stands for an average.

Rasch obtained graphs for checking the model in the following way: Plot for fixed value of g and for each value of j

$$L_{gi}^{(j)} \text{ against } \overline{L}_{\cdot i}^{(1)} \quad i = 1, \ldots, k.$$

This should result in points clustering around straight lines with slope 1. Then plot for fixed value of i and for each value of j,

$$L_{gi}^{(j)} \text{ against } \overline{L}_{g\cdot}^{(j)} \quad g = 1, \ldots, G.$$

This should result in points clustering around straight lines with slope 1.

For the first data set with polytomous responses that Rasch analysed, Figure 1 and Figure 2 show the results for selected score groups and selected items.

Using the same technique, Rasch obtained "ad hoc" estimates of the item parameters as follows.

Estimates for θ_{gj} and ε_{ij} are easily derived from (5). For example the ε_{ij}'s can, for each fixed score group g, be estimated as

$$\hat{\varepsilon}_{ij}^{(g)} = L_{gi}^{(j)} - \overline{L}_{g\cdot}^{(j)} \approx \varepsilon_{ij} - \overline{\varepsilon}_{\cdot j} = \varepsilon_{ij}, \tag{6}$$

since we can always constrain the ε_{ij}'s, such that $\overline{\varepsilon}_{\cdot j}$ for all categories. This gives, of course, one set of estimates for each group g. The over-all estimate is obtained by averaging

$$\hat{\varepsilon}_{ij} = \overline{L}_{\cdot i}^{(j)} - \overline{L}_{\cdot \cdot}^{(j)} \approx \varepsilon_{ij} \tag{7}$$

So Rasch could as well have plotted the score group estimates (6) against the over-all estimates (7) for each score group.

3 Conditional ML-estimation of the item parameters

The distribution of the matrix of responses A_n **given** the response vector $(s_{n1}, \ldots, s_{nm})$ is

$$P(A_n | s_{n1}, \ldots, s_{nm}) = \frac{\exp\left\{\sum_i \sum_j \varepsilon_{ij} a_{ni}^{(j)}\right\}}{\gamma(s_{n1}, \ldots, s_{nm}; \varepsilon_{11}, \ldots, \varepsilon_{km})},$$

where

$$\gamma(s_1, \ldots, s_m; \varepsilon_{11}, \ldots, \varepsilon_{km}) = \sum_{\{\sum_i a_{ij} = s_j, \text{ all } j\}} \exp\left\{\sum_i \sum_j \varepsilon_{ij} a_{ij}\right\}.$$

The CML (Conditional Maximum Likelihood) estimates are then derived from the conditional likelihood function

$$L_C(\varepsilon_{11}, \ldots, \varepsilon_{km}) = \prod_{n=1}^{N} P(A_n | s_{n1}, \ldots, s_{nm})$$

22

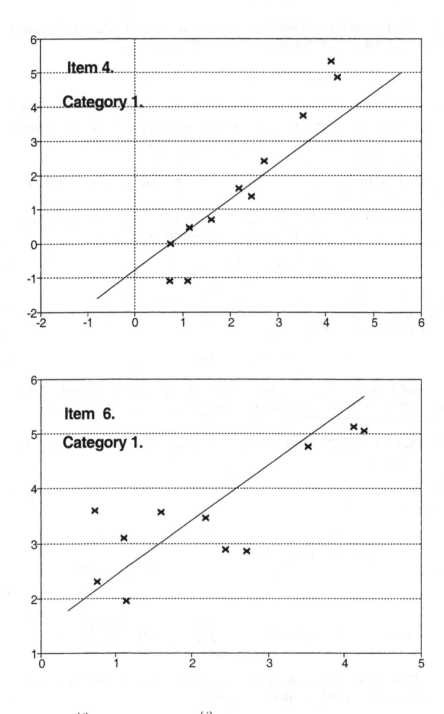

Figure 1: $L_{gi}^{(j)}$ plotted against $\overline{L}_{g.}^{(j)}$ for all i, for selected score groups and categories

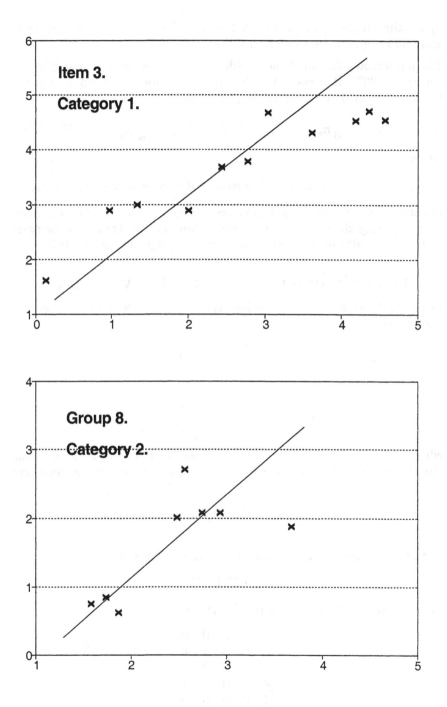

Figure 2: $L_{gi}^{(j)}$ plotted against $\overline{L}_i^{(j)}$ for all g, for selected items and categories,

by maximalization. The solution of the likelihood equations thus in the early 60's depended on mastering the γ-functions.

The numerical solution of the likelihood equations became possible in the spring of 1967. It turned out that the conditional likelihood equations for the estimation of $(\varepsilon_{11}, \ldots, \varepsilon_{km})$ became

$$a_{\cdot i}^{(j)} = \sum_{(s_1, \ldots, s_m)} n_{s_1}, \ldots, n_{s_m} \frac{\gamma(s_1, \ldots, s_{j-1}, s_{j+1} \ldots, s_m; \varepsilon_{11}, \ldots, \varepsilon_{i-1m}, \varepsilon_{i+11}, \ldots, \varepsilon_{km})}{\gamma(s_1; \ldots; s_m; \varepsilon_{11}, \ldots, \varepsilon_{km})},$$

where

$$n_{s_1}, \ldots, n_{s_m} = \text{numbers of persons with score vector } (s_1, \ldots, s_m).$$

Obviously to solve such equations, one needs reliable iterative algorithms for computing the γ-ratios. Such algorithms were obtained in the spring of 1967 and fully implemented in computer programs before 1970.

4 The polytomous Rasch model, version 3

In the early 70's, when Rasch had retired, his co-workers worked with the model

$$P_{ni}(j) = \frac{e^{\theta_n c_j + \varepsilon_{ij}}}{1 + \sum_{q=1}^{m-1} e^{\theta_n c_q + \varepsilon_{iq}}}, \quad \text{for } j = 1, \ldots, m-1 \tag{8}$$

and

$$P_{ni}(m) = \frac{1}{1 + \sum_{q=1}^{m-1} e^{\theta_n c_q + \varepsilon_{iq}}},$$

where the individual parameter θ_n, is assumed to be one-dimensional. For this model the sufficient statistic for θ_n is the uni-dimensional score

$$t_n = \sum_{i=1}^{k} \sum_{j=1}^{m} a_{ni}^{(j)} c_j.$$

In our example with $k = 8$ and $m = 5$, the responses

$$(2\,4\,3\,5\,1\,1\,2\,5)$$

were equivalent to the 8 selections vectors

$$
\begin{array}{ccccc}
(0 & 1 & 0 & 0 & 0) \\
(0 & 0 & 0 & 1 & 0) \\
(0 & 0 & 1 & 0 & 0) \\
(0 & 0 & 0 & 0 & 1) \\
(1 & 0 & 0 & 0 & 0) \\
(1 & 0 & 0 & 0 & 0) \\
(0 & 1 & 0 & 0 & 0) \\
(0 & 0 & 0 & 0 & 1).
\end{array}
$$

The score with equidistant category scores $c_1 = m - 1, \ldots, c_{m-1} = 1$, $c_m = 0$, then becomes

$$t_n = 2 \cdot 4 + 2 \cdot 3 + 1 \cdot 2 + 1 \cdot 1 + 2 \cdot 0 = 17.$$

For model (7), the conditional likelihood is

$$L(\varepsilon_{11}, \ldots, \varepsilon_{km}) = \prod_{n=1}^{N} f(A_n | t_n) = \frac{\exp\left\{\sum_i \sum_j \varepsilon_{ij} a_{\cdot i}^{(j)}\right\}}{\prod_t (\gamma(t; \varepsilon_{ij}, \ldots, \varepsilon_{km}))^{n_t}},$$

where n_t is the number of persons with $t_n = t$, and

$$\gamma(t; \varepsilon_{11}, \ldots, \varepsilon_{km}) = \sum_{"S"} \exp\left\{\sum_i \sum_j \varepsilon_{ij} a_{ij}\right\},$$

where $S = \left\{\sum_i \sum_j a_{ij} c_j = t\right\}$.

The over-all CML-estimates are obtained as

$$L(\hat{\varepsilon}_{11}, \ldots, \hat{\varepsilon}_{km}) = \max L(\varepsilon_{11}, \ldots, \varepsilon_{km}),$$

while score group CML-estimates are obtained as

$$L_g(\hat{\varepsilon}_{11}^{(g)}, \ldots, \hat{\varepsilon}_{km}^{(g)}) = \max L_g(\varepsilon_{11}, \ldots, \varepsilon_{km}),$$

where

$$L_g(\varepsilon_{11}, \ldots, \varepsilon_{km}) = \prod_{t_n \in S_g} f(A_n | t_n) = \frac{\exp\left\{\sum_i \sum_j \varepsilon_{ij} a_{gi}^{(j)}\right\}}{(\gamma(t; \varepsilon_{ij}, \ldots, \varepsilon_{km}))^{n_t}},$$

and - as we may recall

$$a_{gi}^{(j)} = \sum_{n \in S_g} a_{ni}^{(j)}.$$

A graphical test for the model, essentially suggested by Rasch, is then for each score group to plot

$$\left(\hat{\varepsilon}_{11}^{(g)}, \ldots, \hat{\varepsilon}_{km}^{(g)}\right)$$

against

$$(\hat{\varepsilon}_{11}, \ldots, \hat{\varepsilon}_{km}).$$

If the model holds, these points should cluster at random around straight lines through the origin with slope 1.

26

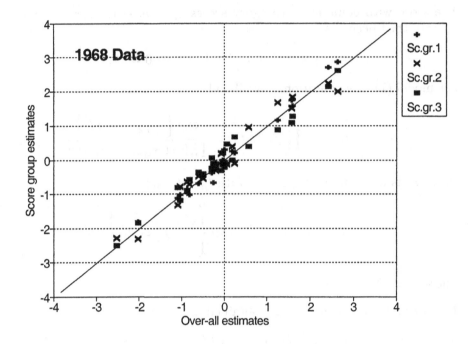

Figure 3: Score group estimates plotted against over-all estimates

For the 1968 data the graph is shown as Figure 3. A numerical goodness of fit test was suggested by Andersen (1973). He considered the test statistics

$$Z = -2\sum_{g=1}^{G} \ln L_g(\hat{\varepsilon}_{11}^{(g)}, \ldots, \hat{\varepsilon}_{km}^{(g)}) + 2\ln L(\hat{\varepsilon}_{11}, \ldots, \hat{\varepsilon}_{km}) \sim \chi^2(df)$$

with

$$df = (k(m-1)(M-1).$$

5 Item residuals as tools for model check

In 1997 Andersen proved the following theorem (Andersen (1997))

$$\left(\hat{\sigma}_{ij}^{(g)}\right)^2 = \text{var}\left[\hat{\varepsilon}_{ij}^{(g)} - \hat{\varepsilon}_{ij}\right] = \text{var}\left[\hat{\varepsilon}_{ij}^{(g)}\right] - \text{var}\left[\hat{\varepsilon}_{ij}\right].$$

Hence, standardized item residuals for each score group t, given by

$$r_{ij}^{(g)} = \frac{\hat{\varepsilon}_{ij}^{(g)} - \hat{\varepsilon}_{ij}}{\hat{\sigma}_{ij}^{(g)}}$$

follow asymptotically a $N(0,1)$ distribution. They can, thus, be used for a graphical check of the model, since all residuals $r_{ij}^{(g)}$ should, if the model holds, stay inside approximately -2 and $+2$.

For the 1968 data these graphs are shown in Figure 4.

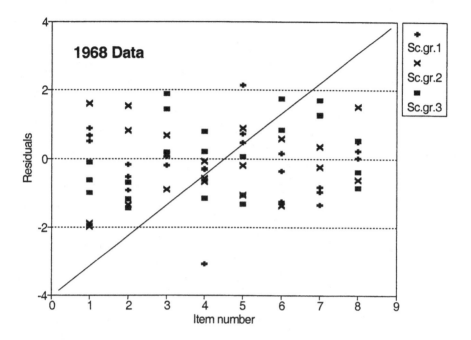

Figure 4: Standardized item residuals plotted against item number

References

ANDERSEN, E. B.(1973) A goodness of fit test for the Rasch model. *Psychometrika, 38, 123-139.*

ANDERSEN, E. B.(1995) Residualanalysis in the Polytomous Rasch model. *Psychometrika, 60, 375-393.*

ANDERSEN, E. B.(1997) The rating scale model. In: van den Linden, W.J. and Hambleton, R.K., Handbook of Modem Item Response Theory. Springer, New York.

FISCHER, G. H.(1995) The derivations of polytomous Rasch models. In: Fischer, G.H. and Molenaar, I.W., Rasch Models: Foundations, Recent Developments and Applications.

RASCH, G.(1961) On general laws and the meaning of measurement in psychology. Proceedings of the Fourth Berkeley Symposium on Mathematical Statistics and Theory of Probability, IV, 321-333.

Some Basic Results on the Extension of Quasi-likelihood Based Measurement Error Correction to Multivariate and Flexible Structural Models

T. Augustin

Seminar für Ökonometrie und Statistik
Universität München
D 80799 München, Germany

Abstract: Quasi-score equations derived from corrected mean and variance functions allow for consistent parameter estimation under measurement error. However, the practical use of some approaches relying on this general methodological principle was strongly limited by the assumptions underlying them: only one covariate was allowed to be measured with non-negligible error, and, additionally, this covariate had to be conditionally independent of the other covariates. This paper extends basic principles of this method to multivariate and flexible models in a way that, on the one hand, retains the neat statistical properties, but on the other hand, manages to do without the restrictive assumptions needed up to now.

1 Introduction

A typical problem in regression analysis is the presence of covariate measurement error. Often there are covariates X ('latent variables') of particular interest, which cannot be directly observed or measured correctly. However, if one ignores the measurement error by just plugging in substitutes or incorrect measurements W instead of X ('naive estimation'), then all the parameter estimates may be severely biased. *Error-in-variables modeling* develops procedures to adjust for the measurement error. For the linear model many basic results had already been achieved until the eighties. They are summarized in the books by Schneeweiß, Mittag (1986) and by Fuller (1987). Recent developments in that area are covered by Cheng, van Ness (1999). Caroll et. al. (1995) present the state of the art in nonlinear models up to the middle of the nineties.[1]

One general and powerful methodological principle to deal with measurement error is structural, quasi-likelihood based measurement error correction: corrected mean and variance functions can be used to construct

---

[1]According to the literature the term 'measurement error' is only applied to continuous variables. The corresponding problem for discrete variables (' misclassification') is not addressed here. This paper will also concentrate on *covariate measurement* error by assuming that the dependent variables are measured without error.

a measurement error corrected quasi-score equation which produces consistent parameter estimates. In particular this idea underlies the work of Armstrong (1985), Liang, Lu (1991), Caroll et al. (1995, Section 7.8 and Appendix A.4), and also the papers of Thamerus (1998A, 1998B) and Augustin (2001).

The present paper discusses basic ingredients of this method in an extended context which does not suffer from severe restrictions inherent to some former approaches. Section 2 recalls a few essentials of the problem of measurement error and then states the error model used throughout the paper. Special attention is paid to the question how to model the distribution of the unknown variables with sufficient flexibility. Section 3 is devoted to measurement error corrected quasi-likelihood estimation and demonstrates how the requirements of this technique can be satisfied by the model introduced.

2 Measurement Error

2.1 Some Basic Considerations

Measurement error occurs in very different areas of application: often for all (or some of the) units $i = 1, \ldots, n$ variables X_i of primary interest are not observable. One has to be satisfied with so called surrogates W_i, i.e. with somehow related, but different variables. For instance, in physics or medical science these surrogates are typically inexact measurements of X_i. In social science insufficiency of operationalizations of complex theoretic constructs gives rise to measurement error.

As symbolized in Figure 1, the problem caused by measurement error is that one is interested in estimating effects of the variable X_i, while the data are realizations of a different variable W_i. In estimating regression parameters, however, this difference has to be taken into account: neglecting it by just plugging in W_i instead of X_i in the estimating procedures will typically lead to estimates with a considerable bias.

The theory of *measurement error correction* or *error-in-variables modeling* provides a framework which aims at deriving consistent parameter estimates for the effects of $X_1, \ldots, X_n$. As is also suggested by Figure 1, this can only be possible if one takes some relationship between the Xs and the Ws into account. In the case of validation data, i.e. simultaneous observation of the Ws and the Xs in a sub-sample, this relationship can be estimated from the data. Otherwise, one has to model it as flexible as possible. Here the following flexible model is used.

2.2 The Error Model I – Basic Assumptions

- All covariates X_i, $i = 1, \ldots, n$, are continuous.

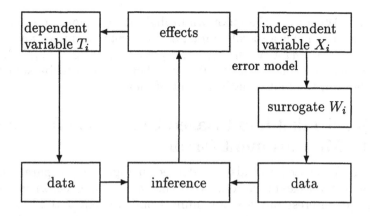

Figure 1: Regression under covariate measurement error:

- Additive measurement error:[2] $W_i = X_i + U_i$.
- U_i is independent of T_i, X_i and U_j, $j \neq i$.
- Normal measurement error: $U_i \sim \mathcal{N}(0, \Sigma_U)$ with Σ_U known.
- Structural model: X_i is stochastic. $X_1, \ldots, X_n$ are independently and identically distributed.

These assumptions imply that the measurement error is *nondifferential*: T_i and W_i are conditionally independent given X_i, i.e. W_i possesses no information which is not contained in X_i. So, knowing X_i would make knowledge of W_i superfluous.

2.3 The Error Model II – the Distribution of X

In addition to the assumptions listed above, an appropriate class of parametric distributions for X has to be chosen. For sake of mathematical convenience there is a strong temptation to take a normal distribution as the distribution law P_X of X. Then also the W_is would be normal. However, in many applications the empirical marginal distributions of W are heavily skewed and/or possess several modes, which makes the assumption of normality for P_X rather questionable.

To account for multi-modality and skewness turning to *mixtures of normals* proves to be successful. The main idea is to allow for heterogeneity: one takes the population to be divided into m different groups, where, in principle, m need not to be known a priori. For the elements of every group j normality with group specific parameters is assumed: $X_i \sim$

---

[2]Note that this formulation also covers the case of correctly measured components of the vector of covariates. If $X_i[j]$ is correctly measured then one puts $U_i[j] \equiv 0$.

$\mathcal{N}(\mu_j, \Sigma_j)$. With κ_j as the unknown probability to belong to group j the overall distribution is a so-called *mixture of normals* or *mixed normal distribution*: $X_i \sim \mathcal{MIXN}(m; \kappa_1, \ldots, \kappa_m; \mu_1, \ldots, \mu_m; \Sigma_1, \ldots, \Sigma_m)$. This model is very flexible[3], but it will nevertheless prove to be sufficiently tractable from the mathematical point of view.

3 Quasi-Likelihood Based Correction for Covariate Measurement Error

As already discussed and also illustrated in Figure 1 the parameter estimation has to take into account that the data are not realizations of the variables of interest but are stemming from different variables. So the likelihood relevant for parameter estimation is the *data-based likelihood*, i.e. the likelihood $\mathrm{Lik}(\theta \| T_i, W_i)$ of the unknown parameter vector θ given $W_1, \ldots, W_m$. For many models of interest it is however not manageable to calculate this expression from the *ideal likelihood*, i.e. the likelihood $\mathrm{Lik}(\theta \| T_i, X_i)$ derived from the regression model formulated in terms of the unobservable quantities $X_1, \ldots, X_n$.

Therefore one is forced to search for another general estimation principle. Here a successful choice will be quasi-score estimation based on mean and variance functions. The basic ideas of this approach were introduced in Wedderburn (1974) and developed further especially by McCullagh (1983, 1991). In the meanwhile they are embedded into the extended framework of general estimation functions (see Heyde (1997) for a comprehensive monograph on this topic).

The quasi-score function which will prove to be successful in the context considered here uses the data-based means $\mathbb{E}[T_i|W_i; \theta]$ and (co)variances $\mathbb{V}[T_i|W_i; \theta]$. In contrast to the full data-based likelihood these quantities will prove to be obtainable from the ideal model formulated in terms of the unobservable variables. The resulting quasi-score equation is

$$\sum_{i=1}^{n} \frac{\partial\, \mathbb{E}[T_i|W_i; \theta]}{\partial\, \theta} \cdot \mathbb{V}[T_i|W_i; \theta]^{-1} \cdot \{T_i - \mathbb{E}[T_i|W_i; \theta]\} = 0. \quad (1)$$

To the author's knowledge, Armstrong (1985) was the first to recognize the power of this principle for measurement error correction. Also Caroll et. al. (1995; Section 7.8 and Appendix A.4) briefly mention the importance of this idea. Thamerus (1998A, 1998B) and Augustin (2001) worked with much simpler versions of the model used here. For modeling the distribution of the latent variable, Thamerus (1998B) and Augustin (2001) do only allow for a single normal distribution, but not for mixtures.

---

[3]See, for instance, Everitt & Hand (1981, p. 28f.), who give an impression of the quite different shapes which can be produced by even only the mixture of two normals.

Even more important, all three papers just quoted had to concentrate on the case where only one dimension, $X_i[1]$ say, of the covariate vector is measured with error. This assumption may not only be unrealistic in many empirical situations, but it is also responsible for an additional requirement which may be even more tricky: to enable the calculation of measurement error corrected mean and covariance functions along the lines below, the conditional distribution of $X_i[1]$ given the surrogate $W_i[1]$ and other dimensions $X_i[2], X_i[3], \ldots$ of the vector of covariates de facto was taken to be independent of $X_i[2], X_i[3], \ldots$.

The central observation of quasi-likelihood based measurement error correction is that, via the theorem of iterated expectation and the nondifferentiality of the measurement error, the conditional moments $\mathbb{E}\left(T_i^r | W_i; \theta\right)$ with respect to the observable quantities can be derived from their counterparts $\mathbb{E}\left(T_i^r | X_i; \theta\right)$ based on the unobservable quantities:

$$\mathbb{E}\left[T_i^r | W_i; \theta\right] = \mathbb{E}\left(\mathbb{E}\left[T_i^r | X_i, W_i; \theta\right] \middle| W_i; \theta\right) = \mathbb{E}\left(\underbrace{\mathbb{E}\left[T_i^r | X_i; \theta\right]}_{\text{ideal model}} \middle| \underbrace{W_i}_{\text{observable}}; \theta\right)$$

This relation is very helpful for calculating the corrected mean and variance functions. It separates the problem into two distinct steps:

- Firstly, determine the 'ideal moments' of first and second order of the ideal model.
- Secondly, integrate with respect to the conditional distribution of X_i given W_i.

The first step is an easy exercise for most models.[4] The second step is prepared by the following proposition applying some basic properties of mixtures of normals in the context under consideration.

Prop. 1. Let $X_i \sim \mathcal{MIXN}\left(m; \kappa_1, \ldots, \kappa_m; \mu_1, \ldots, \mu_m; \Sigma_1, \ldots, \Sigma_m\right)$, and denote the density of the $j - th$ component by $\varphi(\cdot \| \mu_j, \Sigma_j)$. Furthermore, let $U_i \sim \mathcal{N}(0, \Sigma_U)$, and U_i be independent of X_i. Define $W_i := X_i + U_i$. Then

a) $W_i \sim \mathcal{MIXN}\left(m; \kappa_1, \ldots, \kappa_m; \mu_1, \ldots, \mu_m; \Sigma_1 + \Sigma_U, \ldots, \Sigma_m + \Sigma_U\right)$.

b) $X_i \mid W_i \sim \mathcal{MIXN}\left(m; \bar{\kappa}_{i,1}, \ldots, \bar{\kappa}_{i,m}; \bar{\mu}_{i,1}, \ldots, \bar{\mu}_{i,m}; \bar{\Sigma}_1, \ldots, \bar{\Sigma}_m\right)$

with $(j = 1, \ldots, m)$

$$\bar{\kappa}_{i,j} = \frac{\kappa_j \cdot \varphi(W_i \| \mu_j, \Sigma_j + \Sigma_U)}{\sum_{l=1}^{m} \kappa_l \cdot \varphi(W_i \| \mu_l, \Sigma_l + \Sigma_U)}$$

$$\bar{\mu}_{i,j} = \mu_j + \Sigma_j \cdot \left(\Sigma_j + \Sigma_U\right)^{-1} \cdot \left(W_i - \mu_j\right)$$

$$\bar{\Sigma}_j = \Sigma_j - \Sigma_j \cdot \left(\Sigma_j + \Sigma_U\right)^{-1} \Sigma_j.$$

[4]One interesting exception is the case of censored survival times, see Augustin (2001, Section 6) for details.

According to Part a) of this proposition, $W_1, \ldots, W_n$ follow a mixture of normals with the same set of parameters as $X_1, \ldots, X_n$. Therefore, these unknown nuisance parameters can be estimated from the observable quantities $W_1, \ldots, W_n$ and then be plugged in to obtain (an estimate for) the conditional distribution of X_i given W_i along the lines of Part b). Another basic result from the theory of mixture distributions tells that an expectation with respect to a mixture is just a weighted average of the expectations with respect to the single components. Therefore, integration with respect to the conditional distribution of X_i given W_i consists only of the evaluation of m integrals with respect to multivariate normals. Then they have to be summed up, weighted by the $\bar{\kappa}_j$s derived in Part b) of this proposition. Finally, solving the corresponding quasi-score equation (1) yields the measurement error corrected quasi-likelihood estimates.

4 On the Estimation Procedure

Proposition 1 allows to split estimation into two steps — the estimation of the nuisance parameters and the estimation of the regression parameters. For the first step note that Part a) of Proposition 1 isolates the problem from the error-in-variables context. Since every W_i again follows a mixture of normals, in principle, any algorithm for estimating mixtures of normals[5] could be used to determine the nuisance parameters. The concrete choice of the algorithm and its implementation, however, needs much care. Estimating multivariate mixtures of normals is still a demanding issue, inducing a plenty of vivid research in different fields. For example, Robert (1996) studies the topic in the Bayesian framework. Coming from multivariate latent variable modelling, Arminger, Stein, Wittenberg (1999) discuss the estimation of mixture distributions with an underlying regression structure for the mean — an approach which additionally looks promising to handle also generalizations of the error models described in Section 2.2.

Plugging in the estimates for the nuisance parameter, (estimates for) the measurement error corrected moments can be calculated. They are used to estimate the regression parameters by solving Relation (1). This can be done by iteratively reweighted least squares (see, e.g., Appendix A4 of Caroll, Ruppert, Stefanski (1995).)[6] Assuming the (maximal) number of components to be apriori known, the results of Kukush, Schneeweiß (2000) can be extended to show that consistency of the quasi-likelihood estimates is preserved under plug-in-estimates for the nuisance parameters; the bias caused by measurement error is eliminated.

---

[5]See, e.g., the references in Titterington's (1997) survey.

[6]Note, however, that in some situations a reparametrization will be necessary to ensure identifiability of parameter estimates (c.f. Augustin (2001, Section 4)).

5 Concluding Remarks

The paper prepared the basis for extending quasi-likelihood based measurement correction to avoid severe restrictions of previous approaches. Firstly, more flexible models for the covariate distribution can be dealt with. Secondly, the approach allows to handle multivariate error-prone variables. Finally, as a technical side-effect but of high practical importance, some odd requirements on conditional independence are not needed any more. At least in the extended version presented here, quasi-likelihood provides an easy to handle framework to adjust for measurement error; it promises to be widely applicable in many different models. An area where the approach is particularly elegant is the case of parametric duration models without censoring. The concept of accelerated failure time models can serve as a superstructure which enables one to handle the commonly used models in a unified way. The approach can be extended to cover also the case of measurement error in the dependent variables, i.e. in the lifetimes themselves. The arguments given in Augustin (2001) carry over to the extended situation studied here.

Acknowledgements. I'm very grateful to Helmut Küchenhoff, Hans Schneeweiß and Roland Wolf for many stimulating discussions and comments on a previous version. I'm also indebted to an anonymous referee for valuable remarks. In particular, (s)he pointed out the relation to multivariate latent variable models with normal mixtures. Part of this research was supported by the Deutsche Forschungsgemeinschaft (DFG).

References

ARMINGER, G., STEIN, P. and WITTENBERG, J. (1999): Mixtures of conditional mean- and covariance-structure models. *Psychometrika, 64, 475-494.*

ARMSTRONG, B. (1985): Measurement error in the generalized linear model. *Communications in Statistics, Part B – Simulation and Computation, 14, 529–544.*

AUGUSTIN, T. (2001): Correcting for measurement error in parametric duration models by quasi-likelihood. Accepted for publication in *Biometrical Journal.*

CAROLL, R. J., RUPPERT, D. and STEFFANSKI, L. A. (1995): Measurement Error in Nonlinear Models. Chapman and Hall, London.

CHENG, C.-L. and VAN NESS, J.W (1999): Statistical Regression with Measurement Error. Arnold, London.

EVERITT, B. S. and HAND, D. J. (1981): Finite Mixture Distributions. Chapman and Hall, London.

FULLER, W. A. (1987): Measurement Error Models. Wiley, New York.

HEYDE, C. F. (1997): Quasi-Likelihood and its Application. A General Approach to Parameter Estimation. Springer, New York.

KUKUSH, A., SCHNEEWEISS, H. (2000). An asymptotic comparison of a structural least squares estimator and an adjusted least squares estimator in a polynomial errors-in-variables model. *SFB Discussion Paper*, 218, University of Munich. Submitted.

LIANG, K.-Y. and LIU, X.-H. (1991): Estimating equations in generalized linear models with measurement error. In: Godambe, V. P. (ed.): Estimating Functions. Clarendon Press, Oxford, 47–63.

McCULLAGH, P. (1983): Quasi-likelihood functions. *The Annals of Statistics*, *11, 59–67*.

McCULLAGH, P. (1991): Quasi-likelihood and estimating functions. In: Hinkley, D. V., Reid, N. and Snell, E. J. (eds.): Statistical Theory and Modelling. Chapman and Hall, London, 265–286.

ROBERT, C.P. (1996): Inference in mixture models. In: W.R. Gilks, S. Richardson, and D.J. Spiegelhalter (eds.): Markov Chain Monte Carlo in Practice, Chapman and Hall, London, 441-464.

SCHNEEWEISS, H. and MITTAG, H. J. (1986): Lineare Modelle mit fehlerbehafteten Daten. Physica, Heidelberg.

THAMERUS, M. (1998A): Nichtlineare Regressionsmodelle mit heteroskedastischen Meßfehlern. Logos, Berlin.

THAMERUS, M. (1998B): Different nonlinear regression models with incorrectly observed covariates. In: Galata, R. and Küchenhoff, H. (eds.): Econometrics in Theory and Practice. Physika. Heidelberg.

TITTERINGTON, D.M. (1997): Mixture distributions (update). In: S. Kotz, C.B.Read, and D. Banks (eds.): Encyclopedia of Statistical Sciences, Update Volume 1, Wiley, New York, 399-407.

WEDDERBURN, R. W. M. (1974): Quasi-likelihood functions, generalised linear models and the Gauss-Newton method. *Biometrika, 61, 439–447*.

On the Optimal Number of Clusters in Histogram Clustering

J. M. Buhmann[1], M. Held[1]

[1]Institut für Informatik III,
Universität Bonn, D-53117 Bonn, Germany

Abstract: Clusters in data clustering should be robust to sample fluctuation, i.e., the estimate of cluster parameters on a second sample set should yield qualitatively similar results. This robustness requirement can be quantified by large deviation arguments from statistical learning theory. We use the principle of *Empirical Risk Approximation* to determine an optimal number of clusters for the case of histogram clustering. The analysis validates stochastic approximation algorithms like Markov Chain Monte Carlo which maximize the entropy for fixed optimization costs.

1 Introduction

Learning algorithms are designed to extract structure from data, e.g., information on data clusters. This paper applies statistical learning theory to study the robustness of cluster inference in histogram clustering (Pereira at al. (1993), Hofmann, Puzicha (1998)) and to derive error bounds as a safeguard against overfitting. Our theoretical results support the use of *deterministic annealing* as a continuation method which yields robustness of the learning process in the sense of statistical learning theory. The computational temperature of annealing algorithms plays the role of a control parameter regulating the complexity of the learning machine.

To provide a mathematical framework we assume that a hypothesis class $\mathcal{H}$ of loss functions for histogram clustering is given. These loss functions measure the quality or risk of cluster structures in data. The complexity of $\mathcal{H}$ is controlled by coarsening, i.e., we define a γ-cover of $\mathcal{H}$. The inference principle which we advocate in this paper performs learning by the following two inference steps:

1. *Determine the optimal approximation level γ for consistent learning (in the sense of a large deviation theory).*

2. *Given the optimal approximation value γ average over all hypotheses in a γ-neighborhood of the empirical minimizer.*

The reader should note that the learning algorithm has to return a structure which is *typical* in a γ-cover sense but it is not required to return the structure with *minimal empirical risk* as in Vapnik's "Empirical Risk Minimization" (ERM) induction principle for classification and regression (Vapnik (1998)). The loss function with minimal empirical risk is usually a structure with maximal complexity, since clustering cost functions usually decrease monotonically with a growing number of clusters.

2 Empirical Risk Approximation Principle

The data samples $\mathcal{Z} = \{\mathbf{z}_r \in \Omega, \ 1 \leq r \leq l\}$ which have to be analyzed by the clustering algorithm are elements of a suitable object (resp. feature) space Ω. The samples are distributed according to a probability distribution μ which is not assumed to be known for the analysis.[1] The quality of structures extracted from the data set $\mathcal{Z}$ is evaluated by the *empirical risk* of a structure α given the training set $\mathcal{Z}$

$$\hat{R}(\alpha; \mathcal{Z}) = \frac{1}{l} \sum_{r=1}^{l} \mathbf{h}(\mathbf{z}_r; \alpha). \qquad (1)$$

$\mathbf{h}(\mathbf{z}; \alpha)$ is known as the *loss function* for datum $\mathbf{z}$ being clustered by model α. The set of all loss functions is denoted as the hypothesis class $\mathcal{H} = \{\mathbf{h}(\mathbf{z}; \alpha)\}$. This paper is concerned with the class of *unbounded nonnegative functions* since we are particularly interested in logarithmic loss functions $- \log p(\mathbf{z})$ as they occur in maximum likelihood approaches. The relevant quality measure for clustering is the expectation value of the loss or *expected risk*

$$\mathcal{R}(\alpha) = \int_{\Omega} \mathbf{h}(\mathbf{z}; \alpha) \, d\mu(\mathbf{z}). \qquad (2)$$

The distribution μ is assumed to decay sufficiently fast such that all rth moments $(r > 2)$ of $\mathbf{h}(\mathbf{z}; \alpha)$ are bounded by $\mathbf{E}_{\mu}\{|\mathbf{h}(\mathbf{z}; \alpha) - \mathcal{R}(\alpha)|^r\} \leq r! \tau^{r-2} \mathbf{V}_{\mu}\{\mathbf{h}(\mathbf{z}; \alpha)\}, \forall \mathbf{h} \in \mathcal{H}$. $\mathbf{E}_{\mu}\{.\}$ and $\mathbf{V}_{\mu}\{.\}$ denote expectation and variance of a random variable, respectively. τ is a constant which depends on the distribution μ .

ERA requires the learning algorithm to select a hypothesis on the basis of the finest consistently learnable cover of the hypothesis class, i. e. given an approximation accuracy γ we can define a subset of loss functions $\mathcal{H}_{\gamma} = \{\mathbf{h}(\mathbf{z}; \alpha) : \alpha = \alpha_1, \ldots, \alpha_{\tilde{n}}\}$ such that the hypothesis class $\mathcal{H}$ is covered by the spheres

$$\mathcal{B}_{\gamma}(\mathbf{h}(\mathbf{z}; \alpha)) := \left\{ \mathbf{h}(\mathbf{z}; \alpha') : \int_{\Omega} |\mathbf{h}(\mathbf{z}; \alpha') - \mathbf{h}(\mathbf{z}; \alpha)| \, d\mu(\mathbf{z}) \leq \gamma \right\} \qquad (3)$$

---

[1]Knowledge of covering numbers is required in the following analysis which is a weaker type of information than complete knowledge of the probability distribution μ.

with $\mathcal{H} \subset \bigcup_{\mathbf{h} \in \mathcal{H}_\gamma} \mathcal{B}_\gamma(\mathbf{h})$. The empirical minimizer

$$\hat{\alpha}^\perp := \arg \min_{\mathbf{h} \in \mathcal{H}} \hat{\mathcal{R}}(\alpha; \mathcal{Z})$$

is assumed to be an element of the cover $\mathcal{H}_\gamma$.

Here we are interested in averaging over hypotheses which are statistically indistinguishable from the empirical minimizer $\hat{\alpha}^\perp$. The optimal structure is denoted by $\alpha^\perp := \arg \min_{\mathbf{h} \in \mathcal{H}} \mathcal{R}(\alpha)$. Large deviation theory is used to determine the approximation accuracy γ for learning a hypothesis from the hypothesis class $\mathcal{H}$. Using the cover property of the γ-cover yields the chain of bounds (Vapnik (1971))

$$
\begin{aligned}
\mathcal{R}(\hat{\alpha}^\perp) - \inf_{\mathbf{h} \in \mathcal{H}} \mathcal{R}(\alpha) \;\leq\;& \mathcal{R}(\hat{\alpha}^\perp) - \inf_{\mathbf{h} \in \mathcal{H}_\gamma} \mathcal{R}(\alpha) + \gamma \\
\leq\;& \mathcal{R}(\hat{\alpha}^\perp) - \hat{\mathcal{R}}(\hat{\alpha}^\perp) + \sup_{\mathbf{h} \in \mathcal{H}_\gamma} |\hat{\mathcal{R}}(\alpha) - \mathcal{R}(\alpha)| + \gamma \\
\leq\;& 2 \sup_{\mathbf{h} \in \mathcal{H}_\gamma} |\hat{\mathcal{R}}(\alpha) - \mathcal{R}(\alpha)| + \gamma.
\end{aligned}
\tag{4}
$$

Deviations of the empirical risk from the expected risk are measured on the scale $\sigma^\top := \sup_{\mathbf{h} \in \mathcal{H}_\gamma} \sqrt{\mathbf{V}\{\mathbf{h}(\mathbf{x}; \alpha)\}}$. The expected risk of the empirical minimizer exceeds the global minimum of the expected risk by $\epsilon \sigma^\top$ with a probability bounded by Bernstein's inequality (Vaart, Wellner (1996))

$$
\begin{aligned}
\mathbf{P}\left\{\mathcal{R}(\hat{\alpha}^\perp) - \mathcal{R}(\alpha^\perp) > \epsilon \sigma^\top\right\} \;\leq\;& \mathbf{P}\left\{\sup_{\mathbf{h} \in \mathcal{H}_\gamma} |\hat{\mathcal{R}}(\alpha) - \mathcal{R}(\alpha)| \geq \frac{1}{2}\left(\epsilon \sigma^\top - \gamma\right)\right\} \\
\leq\;& 2|\mathcal{H}_\gamma| \exp\left(-\frac{l\left(\epsilon - \gamma/\sigma^\top\right)^2}{8 + 4\tau\left(\epsilon - \gamma/\sigma^\top\right)}\right) \equiv \delta.
\end{aligned}
\tag{5}
$$

The complexity of the considered ϵ-cover $|\mathcal{H}_\gamma|$ of the hypothesis class $\mathcal{H}$ has to be small enough to guarantee with high confidence small ϵ-deviations.

This large deviation inequality weighs two competing effects in the learning problem, i. e. the probability of a large deviation exponentially decreases with growing sample size l, whereas a large deviation becomes increasingly likely with growing cardinality of the γ-cover of the hypothesis class. According to eq. (5) the sample complexity $l_0(\gamma, \epsilon, \delta)$ is defined by

$$\log|\mathcal{H}_\gamma| - \frac{l_0\left(\epsilon - \gamma/\sigma^\top\right)^2}{8 + 4\tau\left(\epsilon - \gamma/\sigma^\top\right)} + \log\frac{2}{\delta} = 0. \tag{6}$$

Equation 6 relates the precision ϵ and the coarsening of the hypothesis class γ to the sample size l_0 with $\epsilon^{\text{opt}} := \min_\gamma \epsilon(\gamma, l_0, \delta)$ and $\gamma^{\text{opt}} :=$

$\arg\min_\gamma \epsilon(\gamma, l_0, \delta)$. With probability $1 - \delta$ the deviation of the empirical risk $\hat{\mathcal{R}}(\alpha)$ from the expected risk $\mathcal{R}(\alpha)$ is bounded by $\frac{1}{2}\left(\epsilon^{\mathrm{opt}}\sigma^\top - \gamma^{\mathrm{opt}}\right) =: \gamma^{\mathrm{app}}$. Averaging over a function sphere with radius $2\gamma^{\mathrm{app}}$ around the empirical minimizer yields a hypothesis corresponding to a statistically significant structure in the data, i.e., $\hat{\mathcal{R}}(\alpha^\perp) - \hat{\mathcal{R}}(\hat{\alpha}^\perp) \leq \mathcal{R}(\alpha^\perp) + \gamma^{\mathrm{app}} - (\mathcal{R}(\hat{\alpha}^\perp) - \gamma^{\mathrm{app}}) \leq 2\gamma^{\mathrm{app}}$ since $\mathcal{R}(\alpha^\perp) \leq \mathcal{R}(\hat{\alpha}^\perp)$. The key task in the following remains to calculate an upper bound for the cardinality $|\mathcal{H}_\gamma|$ of the γ–cover.

3   A model for clustering histogram data

The following model for clustering histogram data was developed for grouping objects which are characterized by their co–occurrence with certain features (Pereira at al. (1993), Hofmann, Puzicha (1998)). Application domains for this explorative data analysis approach can be found for example in texture segmentation (Puzicha et al. (1999)), in statistical language modeling (Pereira et al. (1993)) or in document retrieval.

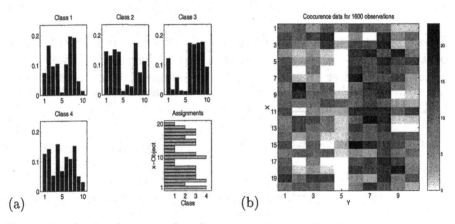

Figure 1: A simple example of a generative model for co–occurrence data. Depicted are the class–conditional distributions $q_{j|\nu}$, $\nu = 1, \ldots 4$, the assignments of the objects $\mathbf{x}_i$, $i = 1, \ldots, 20$ to classes (part a) and an example of co–occurrence data (part b) which is the only information the data analyst has at hand. The absolute frequencies are encoded by gray values.

The model for clustering histogram data can be stated formally in the following way: Denote by $\Omega = \mathcal{X} \times \mathcal{Y}$ the product space of objects $\mathbf{x}_i \in \mathcal{X}, 1 \leq i \leq n$ and features $\mathbf{y}_j \in \mathcal{Y}, 1 \leq j \leq m$. The $\mathbf{x}_i \in \mathcal{X}$ are characterized by observations $\mathcal{Z} = \{\mathbf{z}_r\} = \{\mathbf{x}_{i(r)}, \mathbf{y}_{j(r)}, 1 \leq r \leq l\}$. The set of frequencies $\{n_{ij} :$ number of observations $(\mathbf{x}_i, \mathbf{y}_j)/$ total number of observations$\}$ how often the object–feature pair $(\mathbf{x}_i, \mathbf{y}_j)$ occurs in the data set $\mathcal{Z}$ defines a sufficient statistics (Duda, Hart (1973)). Derived measurements are the frequency $n_i = \sum_j n_{ij}$ of observing object $\mathbf{x}_i$ and the frequency $n_{j|i} = n_{ij}/n_i$ of observing $\mathbf{y}_j$ given object $\mathbf{x}_i$.

The clustering model for histogram data (Pereira et al. (1993), Hofmann98 and Puzicha (1998) defines a generative model of a finite mixture of component probability distributions in feature space, i. e. data are generated by the following steps:

1. select an object $\mathbf{x}_i \in \mathcal{X}$ with uniform probability $1/n$,

2. choose the cluster C_ν according to the cluster membership $\nu = c(\mathbf{x}_i)$,

3. select $\mathbf{y}_j \in \mathcal{Y}$ from a class–conditional distribution $q_{j|\nu}$.

A toy example for this generative model is given in figure 1. The structure of the model is similar to k–means clustering where each object, i. e. data point $\mathbf{x}_i$, should be assigned to a prototypical centroid. In histogram clustering the objects $\mathbf{x}_i$ should be assigned to a class specific feature histogram $q_{j|\nu}$. These prototypes $\vec{q} = (q_{j|\nu})$ are defined as generators for class–specific feature distributions in the space of discrete distributions. Class membership of object $\mathbf{x}_i$ is denoted by the indicator variables $\mathbf{M}_{i\nu} \in \{0,1\}$, where $1 \le \nu \le k$ indexes the cluster. $\sum_{\nu=1}^{k} \mathbf{M}_{i\nu} = 1 \, \forall i : 1 \le i \le n$ enforces the unique assignment constraint. Using these variables the observed data $\mathcal{Z}$ is distributed according to the generative model over $\mathcal{X} \times \mathcal{Y}$:

$$\mathbf{P}\left\{\mathbf{x}_i, \mathbf{y}_j | \mathbf{M}, \vec{q}\right\} = \frac{1}{n} \prod_{\nu=1}^{k} (q_{j|\nu})^{\mathbf{M}_{i\nu}} = \frac{1}{n} \sum_{\nu=1}^{k} \mathbf{M}_{i\nu} q_{j|\nu}. \tag{7}$$

For the analysis of the unknown data source — characterized (at least approximatively) by the empirical data $\mathcal{Z}$ — a structure $\alpha = (\mathbf{M}, \vec{q})$ ($\mathbf{M} \in \{0,1\}^{n \times k}$) has to be inferred. The log–likelihood function is given by

$$\mathcal{L} = \sum_{r=1}^{l} \log\left(\mathbf{P}\left\{\mathbf{x}_{i(r)}, \mathbf{y}_{j(r)} | \alpha\right\}\right) = \sum_{r=1}^{l}\sum_{\nu=1}^{k} \mathbf{M}_{i(r)\,\nu} \log q_{j(r)|\nu} - l \log n. \tag{8}$$

The maximization of the log–likelihood is equivalent to the minimization of the KL–divergence between the empirical distribution of $\mathbf{z}$ and the model distribution $\mathbf{P}\left\{\mathbf{x}_i, \mathbf{y}_j | \alpha\right\}$. A good approximation for the empirical distribution, therefore, should in principle yield a good approximation for the true distribution of the unknown data source. The conditions for this property to generalize with respect to unknown observations are formulated in the context of uniform convergence results from statistical learning theory and will be examined in the following.

Using the sufficient statistics $\tilde{\mathcal{Z}} = (n_{ij})$ and the *loss function* $\mathbf{h}(\mathbf{x}_i, \mathbf{y}_j; \alpha) = \log n - \sum_\nu \mathbf{M}_{i\nu} \log q_{j|\nu}$ the maximization of the likelihood can be formulated as minimization of the *empirical risk*

$$\hat{\mathcal{R}}(\alpha; \mathcal{Z}) = \sum_{i=1}^{n} \sum_{j=1}^{m} n_{ij} \mathbf{h}(\mathbf{x}_i, \mathbf{y}_j; \alpha). \tag{9}$$

Replacing n_{ij} by $\mathbf{P}^{\text{true}} \{\mathbf{x}_i, \mathbf{y}_j\}$ yields the expected risk.

Minimization of (9) using differentiation and the method of Lagrange parameters to ensure proper normalization of the model parameters yields the stationary equations for the empirical estimates of $\hat{q}$ resp. $\mathbf{M}$:

$$\hat{q}_{j|\nu} = \frac{\sum_{i=1}^{n} \hat{\mathbf{M}}_{i\nu} n_{ij}}{\sum_{i=1}^{n} \hat{\mathbf{M}}_{i\nu}} = \sum_{i=1}^{n} \frac{\hat{\mathbf{M}}_{i\nu} n_i}{\sum_{h=1}^{n} \hat{\mathbf{M}}_{h\nu}} n_{j|i}, \tag{10}$$

$$\hat{\mathbf{M}}_{i\nu} = \begin{cases} 1 & \text{if } \nu = \arg\min_\mu \left\{ -\sum_{j \leq m} n_{j|i} \log \hat{q}_{j|\mu} \right\} \\ 0 & \text{else} \end{cases}. \tag{11}$$

A local minimum for the minimization of (9) (local maximum of 8) is obtained by alternating these equations until a fixed point is found. It is worth mentioning, that (10) generalizes the centroid term of the k-means algorithm and (11) is a nearest neighbor rule for histogram clustering.

4   Bound on Approximation Accuracy

Due to the limited precision of the observed data it is natural to study histogram clustering as a learning problem with the hypothesis class

$$\mathcal{H} = \left\{ -\sum_{\nu=1}^{k} \mathbf{M}_{i\nu} \log q_{j|\nu} : \forall i \forall \nu \, \mathbf{M}_{i\nu} \in \{0, 1\} \wedge \sum_{\nu=1}^{k} \mathbf{M}_{i\nu} = 1 \right.$$
$$\left. \forall j \, q_{j|\nu} \in \{1/l, 2/l, \dots, 1\}, \, \sum_{j=1}^{m} q_{j|\nu} = 1 \right\} \tag{12}$$

The limited number of observations causes a limited precision of the frequencies $n_{j|i}$. The value $q_{j|\nu} = 0$ has been excluded since it gives rise to infinite expected risk for $\mathbf{P}^{\text{true}} \{\mathbf{y}_j | \mathbf{x}_i\} > 0$.

The size of the regularized hypothesis class $\mathcal{H}_\gamma$ can be upper bounded by the cardinality of the complete hypothesis class divided by the minimal cardinality of a γ function ball, i. e.

$$|\mathcal{H}_\gamma| \leq |\mathcal{H}| \Big/ \min_{\tilde{\mathbf{h}} \in \mathcal{H}} \left| \mathcal{B}_\gamma(\tilde{\mathbf{h}}) \right|. \tag{13}$$

The cardinality of a function sphere with radius γ can be approximated by adopting techniques from statistical physics and asymptotic analysis (de Bruijn (1958))

$$
\begin{aligned}
\left|\mathcal{B}_\gamma(\tilde{\mathbf{h}})\right| &= \sum_{\mathcal{M}} \sum_{\{q_{j|\alpha}\}} \Theta\left(\gamma - \sum_{i=1}^n \sum_{j=1}^m \frac{1}{n} \mathbf{P}^{\text{true}}\{\mathbf{y}_j\,|\mathbf{x}_i\}\left|\log\frac{q_{j|m(i)}}{\tilde{q}_{j|\tilde{m}(i)}}\right|\right) \quad (14)\\
&= \frac{k^n l^{k(m-1)}}{(2\pi)^k} \int_0^1 \prod_{j=1}^m \prod_{\nu=1}^k dq_{j|\nu} \int_{-i\infty}^{+i\infty} dQ_\nu \int_{-i\infty}^{+i\infty} \frac{d\beta}{2\pi\beta} \exp\left(nS\left(\vec{q},\mathbf{Q},\beta\right)\right),
\end{aligned}
$$

with $\left(\Theta(x) = \left\{{1 \atop 0}\right.\text{ for } x{\geq\atop<}0\right)$[2]. The entropy S is given by

$$
\begin{aligned}
S\left(\vec{q},\mathbf{Q},\beta\right) &= \beta\gamma - \sum_{\nu=1}^k Q_\nu\left(\sum_{j=1}^m q_{j|\nu} - 1\right) + \\
&\quad \frac{1}{n}\sum_{i=1}^n \log \sum_{\rho=1}^k \exp\left(-\beta\sum_{j=1}^m \mathbf{P}^{\text{true}}\{\mathbf{y}_j\,|\mathbf{x}_i\}\left|\log\frac{q_{j|\rho}}{\tilde{q}_{j|\tilde{m}(i)}}\right|\right). \quad (15)
\end{aligned}
$$

The auxiliary variables $\mathbf{Q} = \{Q_\nu\}_{\nu \in \{1,\dots,k\}}$ are Lagrange parameters to enforce the constraints $\sum_{j=1}^m q_{j|\nu} = 1$, $\forall i$. The cardinality $\left|\mathcal{B}_\gamma(\tilde{\mathbf{h}})\right|$ can be calculated by saddle point methods which yields a bound on the complexity of the coarsened hypothesis class $\mathcal{H}_\gamma$. Inserting this complexity in equation (6) yields a functional relationship between the precision ϵ and the approximation quality γ for fixed sample size l_0 and confidence δ, i. e.

$$
\epsilon = \frac{\gamma}{\sigma^\top} + \frac{2}{l_0}\left[\sqrt{2l_0 C + \tau^2 C^2} + \tau C\right], \quad (16)
$$

using the abbreviation $C = \log|\mathcal{H}_\gamma| + \log\frac{2}{\delta}$. The minimum of the function $\epsilon(\gamma)$ defines a compromise between uncertainty originating from empirical fluctuations and the loss of precision due to the approximation by a γ–cover. Differentiating with respect to γ and setting the result to zero yields an upper bound for β at the saddle point, i.e.,

$$
\beta \leq \frac{1}{\sigma^\top}\frac{l_0}{2n}\left(\tau + \frac{l_0 + C\tau}{\sqrt{2l_0 C + \tau^2 C^2}}\right)^{-1}. \quad (17)
$$

The variable $1/\beta$ is also known as computational temperature in annealing algorithms which are frequently used in optimization problems. A

---

[2]The Fourier transform of the Heaviside function with integration variable β is used.

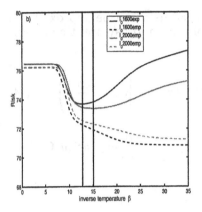
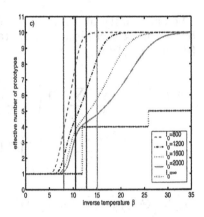

Figure 2: Comparison between theoretically derived upper bound on the optimal temperature and the observed critical temperatures (minimum of the β vs. expected risk curve). The bold (dashed) lines denote expected (empirical) risk averaged over 2000 i.i.d. sample sets. Depicted are the plots for $l_0 = 1600, 2000$. Vertical lines indicate the predicted critical temperatures. In addition the average effective number of clusters is drawn in part c).

decrease in temperature allows us to infer an increasing number of components of our mixture, revealing finer and finer details of the data set. The critical β^{opt} defines the resolution limit below which details can not be resolved in a reliable fashion on the basis of the sample size l_0.

5   Empirical Results

For the evaluation of the derived theoretical result a series of Monte–Carlo experiments on artificial data has been performed for the histogram clustering model. Given the number of objects $n = 30$, the number of groups $k = 5$ and the size of the histograms $m = 15$ the generative model for this experiments was created randomly. In figure 2a,b the predicted temperatures (vertical lines) are compared to the empirically observed critical temperatures (minima of the expected risk), which have been estimated on the basis of 2000 different samples of randomly generated co–occurrence data for each l_0. The expected risk (solid) and empirical risk (dashed) of these 2000 inferred models are averaged.

Figure 2c indicates that on average the minimal expected risk is assumed when the effective number is smaller than or equal five, i. e. the number of clusters of the true generative model. Therefore predicting the right computational temperature also enables the data analyst to solve the cluster validation problem for the histogram clustering model. Especially for $l_0 = 800$ these results suggest that in the light of such a small training set five clusters normally can not be estimated in a reliable way. On the other hand for $l_0 = 1600$ and $l_0 = 2000$ the stop temperature prevents the algorithm to infer too many clusters and, thereby, to overfit. At this point we conclude, that the ERA principle solves the problem of model validation for the case of histogram clustering, i. e. choosing the right number of clusters.

References

DUDA, R.O. and HART, P.E. (1973): Pattern Classification and Scene Analysis. Wiley, New York.

DE BRUIJN, N.G.(1958): Asymptotic Methods in Analysis. North-Holland Publishing Co., (repr. Dover), Amsterdam.

HOFMANN, T. and PUZICHA, J. (1998): Statistical models for co-occurrence data. *AI–MEMO 1625, Artifical Intelligence Laboratory.* Massachusetts Institute of Technology.

PEREIRA, F.C.N., TISHBY, N.Z. and LEE, L (1993): Distributional clustering of english words. In *30th Annual Meeting of the Association for Computational Linguistics, Columbus, Ohio*, pages 183–190.

PUZICHA, J., HOFMANN, T. and BUHMANN, J.M. (1999): Histogram Clustering for Unsupervised Segmentation and Image Retrieval. *Pattern Recognition Letters, 20, 135–142.*

VAN DER VAART, A.W. and WELLNER, J.A. (1996): Weak Convergence and Empirical Processes. Springer-Verlag, New York.

VAPNIK, V.N. and CHERVONENKIS, A.Ya. (1971): On the uniform convergence of relative frequencies of events to their probabilities. *Theory of Probability and its Applications, 16, 264–280.*

VAPNIK, V. N. (1998): Statistical Learning Theory. Wiley–Interscience, New York.

The Dual Dynamic Factor Analysis Models *

R. Coppi P. D'Urso

Department of Statistics, Probability and Applied Statistics
University of Rome "La Sapienza", Rome, Italy

Abstract: An exploratory methodology for analyzing three-way arrays of the type "Units ×Variables ×Times" is described. This is based on the decomposition of the total variation in the array into three components and their modelling by means of a joint utilization of regression and principal components analyses. An extension of this methodology, denominated "dual" approach, is developed, based on interchanging the roles of units w.r.t. variables and times w.r.t. units and variables. An illustration is provided, with reference to the analysis of data concerning the problem of deforestation in Latin America.

1 Introduction

Dynamic Factor Analysis (DFA), originally introduced by Coppi and Zannella (1978) and further developed by Coppi et al. (1996) and Corazziari (1999a, 1999b), is an exploratory methodology for analyzing three-way arrays of the type "Units ×Variables ×Times", where the variables are quantitative. Let us denote by x_{ijt} the generic element of this array related to unit i $(i = 1, \ldots, I)$, variable j $(j = 1, \ldots, J)$, time t $(t = 1, \ldots, T)$. In its three-dimensional form this array is represented by $\mathbf{X}(I, J, T)$. However, two of the indices may be collapsed into one dimension in 3 different ways. The original proposal by Coppi and Zannella (1978) is based on pooling together units and times along the rows, while associating the variables with the columns of a two-way array. This can be done in two different ways according to whether T is nested within I, thus defining the array $\mathbf{X}(IT, J)$ where t is an index of groups of units, or vice versa I is nested within T, thus defining the array $\mathbf{X}(TI, J)$ where i becomes an index of groups of times. The DFA approach (and related models) referred to $\mathbf{X}(IT, J)$ or $\mathbf{X}(TI, J)$ is called "direct". Following this line of reasoning we can define two new DFA approaches. The first one, referred to the structures $\mathbf{X}(JT, I)$ or $\mathbf{X}(TJ, I)$, may be defined "dual", emphasizing the exchange of roles between units and variables. The second one, concerning the structures $\mathbf{X}(IJ, T)$ or $\mathbf{X}(JI, T)$, may be denominated "tridual", pointing out its "twofold duality" with respect to each of the previous approaches, as will be explained later on. In the following Section we shall give a general description of the methodological bases of DFA, including the direct approach. The dual perspective in DFA is examined in Sec. 3, while Sec. 4 is devoted to an empirical illustration concerning the problem of deforestation in Latin America.

---

*Invited lecture

2 Methodological bases of Dynamic Factor Analysis

Before applying any DFA model, the raw data x_{ijt} are normalized in the following way:

$$z_{ijt} = \frac{x_{ijt}}{\bar{x}_{.j.}}, \quad i = 1, \ldots, I; \quad j = 1, \ldots, J; \quad t = 1, \ldots, T \qquad (1)$$

where $\bar{x}_{.j.}$ denotes the overall mean of variable j. Different normalizations might be considered (e.g. dividing each variable by the overall median or standard deviation). Transformation (1) seems to perform well in most situations, eliminating the effects due to different units of measurement and sizes of the characters while preserving the information related to variation, which is a key concept in DFA. In what follows we shall refer to the normalized arrays $\mathbf{Z}(I, J, T)$, $\mathbf{Z}(IT, J)$ and so forth. The general methodological bases of DFA, common to all approaches and models, are:

1. The decomposition of the overall variation of $\mathbf{Z}(I, J, T)$ into three components;

2. The modelisation and analysis of these components by means of a joint utilization of Singular Value Decomposition (SVD) and Regression analysis with respect to time (when applicable).

We shall first illustrate this methodology in connection with the direct approach. In this case the overall variation of $\mathbf{Z}(I, J, T)$ refers to the collapsed arrays $\mathbf{Z}(IT, J)$ or $\mathbf{Z}(TI, J)$, for which the operator $\mathbf{S} = \{s_{jj'}\}$, $j, j' = 1, \ldots, J$, is defined, where

$$s_{jj'} = \frac{1}{IT} \sum_{i,t} \left(z_{ijt} - \bar{z}_{.j.} \right) \left(z_{ij't} - \bar{z}_{.j'.} \right)$$

is the overall covariance between variables j and j'.
The basic decomposition of $\mathbf{S}$ is as follows:

$$\mathbf{S} = {}^*\mathbf{S}_I + {}^*\mathbf{S}_T + \mathbf{S}_{IT} \qquad (2)$$

where the generic elements of ${}^*\mathbf{S}_I$, ${}^*\mathbf{S}_T$ and $\mathbf{S}_{IT}$ are respectively:

$$ {}^*_I s_{jj'} = \frac{1}{I} \sum_i \left(\bar{z}_{ij.} - \bar{z}_{.j.} \right) \left(z_{ij'.} - \bar{z}_{.j'.} \right) $$

$$ {}^*_T s_{jj'} = \frac{1}{T} \sum_t \left(\bar{z}_{.jt} - \bar{z}_{.j.} \right) \left(\bar{z}_{.j't} - \bar{z}_{.j'.} \right) $$

$$\overset{*}{IT} s_{jj'} = \frac{1}{IT} \sum_{i,t} \left(z_{ijt} - \bar{z}_{ij.} - \bar{z}_{.jt} + \bar{z}_{.j.} \right) \left(z_{ij't} - \bar{z}_{ij'.} - \bar{z}_{.j't} + \bar{z}_{.j'.} \right)$$

$^*\mathbf{S}_I$ describes the "synthetic structure" of the units, independently of time; $^*\mathbf{S}_T$ measures the variation due to the "average time evolution" of the variables (for the whole set of units) and, finally, $\mathbf{S}_{IT}$ assesses the residual variation due to the "differential time evolution" of the units (interaction between units and times). With reference to $\mathbf{Z}(IT, J)$ and $\mathbf{Z}(TI, J)$ respectively, we establish the two following decompositions:

$$\mathbf{S} = \bar{\mathbf{S}}_T + {}^*\mathbf{S}_T \tag{3}$$

$$\mathbf{S} = \bar{\mathbf{S}}_I + {}^*\mathbf{S}_I \tag{4}$$

where

$$\bar{\mathbf{S}}_T = {}^*\mathbf{S}_I + \mathbf{S}_{IT}$$

measures the "global structure" of the units (including their differential time evolution) and

$$\bar{\mathbf{S}}_I = {}^*\mathbf{S}_T + \mathbf{S}_{IT}$$

measure the "global dynamics" of the system (average evolution of variables+differential evolution of units).

Two basic DFA models can now be defined.

Model 1 (direct approach)

This is based on decomposition (3). Notice that

$$\bar{\mathbf{S}}_T = \frac{1}{T} \sum_t \mathbf{S}(t) \tag{5}$$

where $\mathbf{S}(t)$ is the covariance matrix at time t. Thus, expression (3) may be interpreted as a classical decomposition of the total variation in the array into "within times" + "between times" variation. The "within times" variation identifies the "global structure" of the units. The corresponding operator, $\bar{\mathbf{S}}_T$, is analyzed by means of a SVD. This is equivalent to carrying out a Principal Components analysis of T clouds of points in R^{J+1}, where the t-th cloud (along the time axis) represents the I units centered with respect to their barycenter

$$\bar{\mathbf{u}}'_{.t} = (\bar{z}_{.1t}, \ldots, \bar{z}_{.Jt}, t) \tag{6}$$

This analysis provides:

a. Component scores for each unit (along the h-th principal axis): F_{ih}. The scores F_{ih} ($i = 1, \ldots, I$) allow us to represent the synthetic structure of the units, related to the variation of the vectors

$$(z_{i1.}, \ldots, z_{iJ.}), \quad t = 1, \ldots, T$$

b. Factorial "trajectories" of each unit, given by the component scores $F_{iht} (t = 1, \ldots, T)$, obtained by applying the h-th eigenvector of $\bar{\mathbf{S}}_T$ to vectors $(\bar{z}_{i1t}, \ldots, \bar{z}_{iJt})$, $i = 1, \ldots, I$. These trajectories represent the differential time evolution of the units.

The "between times" variation, measured by $^*\mathbf{S}_T$, is analyzed by means of a polynomial Time Regression model for the components of $\bar{\mathbf{u}}_{.t}$ [see (6)]:

$$\bar{z}_{.jt} = b_{0j} + b_{1j}t + \ldots + b_{kj}t^k + e_{jt} \qquad j = 1, \ldots, J \qquad (7)$$

where the residuals e_{jt} verify the following conditions:

$$cov\left(e_{jt}, e_{j't'}\right) = \begin{cases} w_j \geq 0, & j = j', t = t' \\ 0, & otherwise \end{cases}$$

The parameters matrix $\mathbf{B} = (\mathbf{b}_1, \ldots, \mathbf{b}_J)$ in model (7) is estimated by Least Squares:

$$\hat{\mathbf{B}} = (\mathbf{A}'\mathbf{A})^{-1}\mathbf{A}'\,{}^*\mathbf{Z}_I$$

where $^*\mathbf{Z}_I = \{\bar{z}_{.jt}\}, t = 1, \ldots, T, j = 1, \ldots, J$ and $\mathbf{A}$ is the design matrix associated with model (7). This model accounts for the average time evolution of the set of variables. Model 1 of DFA may also be interpreted in terms of an "optimal" fitting of the array $\mathbf{Z} = \{z_{ijt}\}$. In fact we can write

$$z_{ijt} = (z_{ijt} - \bar{z}_{ij.} - \bar{z}_{.jt} + \bar{z}_{.j.}) + (\bar{z}_{ij.} - \bar{z}_{.j.}) + \bar{z}_{.jt}$$

and look for theoretical values $\hat{z}_{ijt}$ such that

$$\Phi = \sum_{i,j,t} \left(z_{ijt} - \hat{z}_{ijt}\right)^2 = min$$

within a class of possible models. If we assume the form

$$\hat{z}_{ijt} = \sum_h a_{jh}F_{iht} + {}_jf(t)$$

we may write

$$\Phi = \sum_{i,j,t} \left\{ \left[(z_{ijt} - \bar{z}_{ij.} - \bar{z}_{.jt} + \bar{z}_{.j.}) + (\bar{z}_{ij.} - \bar{z}_{.j.}) - \sum_h a_{jh}F_{iht} \right] + \left[\bar{z}_{.jt} - {}_j f(t) \right] \right\}^2 = min \qquad (8)$$

Since the cross product in (8) can be shown to vanish, the minimum is achieved by: $a_{jh} = j$-th element of the h-th eigenvector of $\bar{\mathbf{S}}_T$, i.e. $\mathbf{a}_h$; $F_{iht} =$ factorial coordinate of unit i at time t on the h-th axis: ${}_jf(t) =$ time regression estimate of the mean value of variable j at time t. The

SOURCE	REFERENCE (A)	ACCOUNTED (B)	INDICATOR (B:A)
Global structure of units	$tr\bar{S}_T$		I_T
Synthetic structure of units	$tr\,{}^*\bar{S}_I$	$\sum_h a'_h\,{}^*S_I a_h + tr\hat{S}_{IT}$ $\sum_h a'_h\,{}^*S_I a_h$	${}^*I_I$
Differential evolution of units	$tr S_{IT}$	$tr\hat{S}_{IT}$	I_{IT}
Average evolution of variables	$tr\,{}^*\bar{S}_T$	$tr\,{}^*\hat{S}_T$	${}^*I_T$
Total	$tr S$	$\sum_h a'_h\,{}^*S_I a_h + tr\hat{S}_{IT} + tr\,{}^*\bar{S}_T$	I

Table 1: Indicators of Quality of Representation (Model 1 - Direct approach)

quality of representation pertaining to Model 1 can be assessed by means of specific indicators summarized in Table 1. where

$$
{}^*\hat{S}_T = \frac{1}{T}\left[{}^*Z'_I \left(I - \frac{1}{T}11' \right) A\left(A'A\right)^{-1} A'{}^*Z_I \right]
$$

$$
\hat{S}_{IT} = S - \left(\sum_h \lambda_h a_h a'_h + {}^*\hat{S}_T \right)
$$

λ_h are the eigenvalues of $\bar{S}_T$ and $\sum_h$ is extended over the set of components retained in the analysis. In addition, the usual PCA measures of quality of representation for the individual units (such as the squared cosine) can be adopted in the context of the analysis of their synthetic structure. When looking at their evolutive configuration in terms of factorial trajectories, the quality of representation can be assessed by means of a Minimum Spanning Tree visualization (see, e.g., Jolliffe, 1984), computed in R^{J+1} and mapped onto the selected factorial space. It should also be underlined that by introducing appropriate dissimilarity measures in the set of trajectories, these can undergo suitable cluster analysis procedures in order to determine useful classifications of the units (Coppi and D'Urso, 1999; D'Urso, 2000).

Model 2 (direct approach)
This is based on decomposition (4). Notice that

$$
\bar{S}_I = \frac{1}{I} \sum_i S(i)
$$

where $S(i)$ is the covariance matrix for unit i, letting t play the role of individuals. In this respect, (4) may be interpreted as a decomposition of the total variation of the array into "within units" and "between units" variation.The "within units" variation, measured by $\bar{S}_I$, identifies the "global structure" of times corresponding to the variation due to the overall dynamics of the array. In this case the two sources of dynamics, namely the average evolution of variables and the differential evolution of units, are simultaneously analyzed by means of a polynomial time Regression model for each unit and variable:

$$z_{ijt} = b_{0ij} + b_{1ij}t + \ldots + b_{kij}t^k + e_{ijt} \qquad i = 1, \ldots, I, \; j = 1, \ldots, J \quad (9)$$

where

$$cov\left(e_{ijt}, e_{i'j't'}\right) = \begin{cases} w_{ij} \geq 0, & i = i', j = j', t = t' \\ 0, & otherwise \end{cases}$$

Least squares estimation of the parameters in (9) provides a way of studying the time evolution of the units for each single variable. For given k, it can be shown that models (7) are the average (over the units) of models (9), for each variable. The differential dynamics of the units can be analyzed by comparing the equations (9) and the corresponding equations (7) (looking at the differences between the homologous parameters). The "between units" variation, measured by $^*S_I$, identifies the "synthetic structure" of the units and is analyzed by a SVD of $^*S_I$. Differently from Model 1, in the present case the factorial approach refers only to the mean values $\bar{z}_{ij}$ which do not contain information related to time evolution.

3 The "dual" perspective in Dynamic Factor Analysis

We now take into consideration the arrays $\mathbf{Z}(JT, I)$ or $\mathbf{Z}(TJ, I)$, on one side, and the arrays $\mathbf{Z}(IJ, T)$ or $\mathbf{Z}(JI, T)$ on the other side. In the former case we may look at the total "Proximity Operator" between units:

$$\mathbf{P} = \left\{ \frac{1}{JT} \sum_{j,t} \left(z_{ijt} - \bar{z}_{i..}\right)\left(z_{i'jt} - \bar{z}_{i'..}\right) \right\}_{i,i' \in I} \qquad (10)$$

In the latter case we may focus our interest on the total "Proximity Operator" between times:

$$\mathbf{Q} = \left\{ \frac{1}{IJ} \sum_{i,j} \left(z_{ijt} - \bar{z}_{..t}\right)\left(z_{ijt'} - \bar{z}_{..t'}\right) \right\}_{t,t' \in T} \qquad (11)$$

Operators (10) and (11) match the previously considered matrix $\mathbf{S}$, which can be interpreted as a "Proximity Operator" between variables. It should be noticed that all quantities in (10) and (11) bear a statistical meaning, since the data z_{ijt} are normalized according to (1) and can be dealt with as "index numbers". Comparing $\mathbf{P}$ with $\mathbf{S}$ we realize that the role of units and variables is permuted. Dual DFA is defined by the application of the DFA machinery to $\mathbf{P}$, instead of $\mathbf{S}$. When considering $\mathbf{Q}$, the "time dimension" looses its characteristic of being an ordered set and is treated in the same way as I and J respectively in $\mathbf{P}$ and $\mathbf{Q}$. The reference arrays of operator $\mathbf{Q}$, namely $\mathbf{Z}(IJ,T)$ and $\mathbf{Z}(JI,T)$, differ from the previous ones in that their rows are not related to ordered sets (as it happens, on the contrary, for the set T in the direct and dual approaches). As a consequence, the time regression component of DFA is meaningless in this context. Nonetheless, it makes sense to apply the factorial component of the DFA machinery when considering $\mathbf{Q}$. This defines what we may call the "tridual" DFA. We start our illustration by examining in some detail the dual DFA, whereas we shall limit ourselves to giving just a hint to the tridual approach.

Dual Dynamic Factor Analysis
It can easily been shown that the basic decomposition of type (2) holds true also for $\mathbf{P}$:

$$\mathbf{P} = {}^{*}\mathbf{P}_J + {}^{*}\mathbf{P}_T + \mathbf{P}_{JT} \tag{12}$$

where

$$ {}^{*}\mathbf{P}_J = \left\{ \frac{1}{J} \sum_j \left(\bar{z}_{ij.} - \bar{z}_{i..} \right) \left(z_{i'j.} - \bar{z}_{i'..} \right) \right\}_{i,i' \in I} \tag{13}$$

measures the "synthetic structure" of the variables, independently of time,

$$ {}^{*}\mathbf{P}_T = \left\{ \frac{1}{T} \sum_t \left(\bar{z}_{i.t} - \bar{z}_{i..} \right) \left(z_{i'.t} - \bar{z}_{i'..} \right) \right\}_{i,i' \in I} \tag{14}$$

represents the variation due to the "average time evolution" of the units (over the whole set of variables), and

$$ \mathbf{P}_{JT} = \left\{ \frac{1}{JT} \sum_{j,t} \left(z_{ijt} - \bar{z}_{ij.} - \bar{z}_{i.t} + \bar{z}_{i..} \right) \times \right.$$
$$ \left. \times \left(z_{i'jt} - \bar{z}_{i'j.} - \bar{z}_{i'.t} + \bar{z}_{i'..} \right) \right\}_{i,i' \in I} \tag{15}$$

is a measure of the "residual" variation due to the "differential evolution" of the variables (interaction between variables and times). The two decompositions, matching (3) and (4) of the direct approach, are as follows:

$$\mathbf{P} = \bar{\mathbf{P}}_T + {}^{*}\mathbf{P}_T \tag{16}$$

$$\mathbf{P} = \bar{\mathbf{P}}_J + {}^{*}\mathbf{P}_J \tag{17}$$

where

$$\bar{\mathbf{P}}_T = {}^{*}\mathbf{P}_J + \mathbf{P}_{JT} \tag{18}$$

measures the "global structure" of the units (including their differential time evolution) and

$$\bar{\mathbf{P}}_J = {}^*\mathbf{P}_T + \mathbf{P}_{JT} \qquad (19)$$

measures the "global dynamics" of the system (given, in this case, by the sum of the average evolution of units and the differential evolution of variables, as compared with the corresponding matrix $\bar{\mathbf{S}}_I$ of the direct approach). In connection with decompositions (18) and (19) respectively, the following two dual DFA models can be set up.

Model 1 (dual approach)
This is based on decomposition (18). In this respect we get

$$\bar{\mathbf{P}}_T = \frac{1}{T} \sum_t \mathbf{P}(t) \qquad (20)$$

where $\mathbf{P}(t)$ is the proximity matrix between units at time t. In this case the "within+between times" interpretation of (18) refers to the variation of units instead of variables (as in the direct approach). The "within times" variation of units identifies the "global structure" of variables and is studied by means of a SVD, providing:

a. Component scores for each variable (along the h-th principal axis): F_{hj}. These scores allow us to represent the synthetic structure of the variables, related to the variation of the vectors

$$\left(\bar{z}_{1j.}, \dots, \bar{z}_{Ij.}\right), \ \ j = 1, \dots, J$$

b. Factorial "trajectories" of each variable, given by the component scores $F_{hjt}(t = 1, \dots, T)$, obtained by applying the h-th eigenvector of $\bar{\mathbf{P}}_T$ to vectors $(z_{1jt}, \dots, z_{Ijt})$, $t = 1, \dots, T$. These trajectories represent the differential time evolution of the variables.

The "between times" variation, measured by ${}^*\mathbf{P}_T$, is analyzed by means of a Time Regression of the following type:

$$\bar{z}_{i.t} = b_{0i} + b_{1i}t + \dots + b_{ki}t^k + e_{it} \qquad i = 1, \dots, I \qquad (21)$$

with the conditions

$$cov\left(e_{it}, e_{i't'}\right) = \begin{cases} w_i \geq 0, & i = i', t = t' \\ 0, & otherwise \end{cases} \qquad (22)$$

Model (21) represents the average time evolution of the units and is estimated by Least Squares, in the same way as illustrated for the corresponding model (7) in the direct approach. The same analogy exists concerning the "reconstruction" of the data z_{ijt} on the basis of Model 1 in the dual version, and the possibility of setting up a similar system of indicators for assessing the quality of representation.

Model 2 (dual approach)
We refer now to decomposition (19), where

$$\bar{\mathbf{P}}_J = \frac{1}{J} \sum_j \mathbf{P}(j) \qquad (23)$$

where $\mathbf{P}(j)$ is the proximity matrix between units calculated for variable j with reference to the values observed over the entire period. Therefore, in this case, we get a decomposition of the overall variation into "within variables+between variables" variation. The former component is measured by (23) and identifies the "global dynamics" of the system from the viewpoint of proximity between units (instead of proximity between variables, as in the direct approach). The latter component, $^{*}\mathbf{P}_J$, characterizes the "synthetic structure" of variables, in terms of proximity between units, independently of time. Model 2, in the dual version, utilizes a Time Regression model for $\bar{\mathbf{P}}_J$, which coincides with model (9) of the direct approach. Thus we are using the same model for explaining the global dynamics of the system, looking on one side at the proximity between variables and, on the other side, at the proximity between units. The "synthetic structure" of the variables is analyzed by means of a SVD of $\bar{\mathbf{P}}_J$. Also Model 2, in the dual version, lends itself to an interpretation in terms of data reconstruction. Moreover, the usual indicators of quality of representation can be computed.

Relationships between direct and dual DFA
The above illustration of the dual approach makes it clear that interchanging the roles of units and variables, passing from the direct to the dual DFA models, provides a useful integration as to the information embodied in the array $\mathbf{Z}(I, J, T)$. Looking for instance at Model 1, the direct approach allows us to compute component scores and factorial trajectories for each unit, whereas the same information concerning the variables is only given by the dual approach. It should be underlined, in this connection, that there does not exist an explicit algebraic relationship between the SVD's of matrices $\bar{\mathbf{S}}_T$ and $\bar{\mathbf{P}}_T$. In fact, considering expressions (5) and (20), we notice that

$$\begin{aligned}
\mathbf{S}(t) &= \mathbf{Z}_t'\mathbf{Z}_t - I\left(_J\bar{\mathbf{z}}_t \,_J\bar{\mathbf{z}}_t'\right) \\
\mathbf{P}(t) &= \mathbf{Z}_t\mathbf{Z}_t' - J\left(_I\bar{\mathbf{z}}_t \,_I\bar{\mathbf{z}}_t'\right)
\end{aligned}$$

where $_J\bar{\mathbf{z}}_t$ and $_I\bar{\mathbf{z}}_t$ are, respectively, the column and row centers of $\mathbf{Z}_t$. Therefore, due to different centerings of the component matrices, the eigenvectors of $\bar{\mathbf{S}}_T$ and $\bar{\mathbf{P}}_T$ do not necessarily define the same latent dimensions (as it happens in classical PCA). However, empirical studies confirm that the principal axes drawn from the two matrices have similar interpretations. This is witnessed, for instance, by the fact that the correlations between the variables and the component scores of the units in the direct approach, show the same pattern as the component scores of the variables in the dual approach.

Tridual Dynamic Factor Analysis
We give just a hint to this case, emphasizing the specificity due to the treatment of Times as columns of the array $\mathbf{Z}(IJ, T)$, which prevents us from using a regression approach in this framework. In any case, using a notation already introduced in the direct and dual models, we get the following decompositions:

$$
\begin{aligned}
\mathbf{Q} &= {}^{*}\mathbf{Q}_I + {}^{*}\mathbf{Q}_J + \mathbf{Q}_{IJ} & (24) \\
&= \bar{\mathbf{Q}}_I + {}^{*}\mathbf{Q}_I & (25) \\
&= \bar{\mathbf{Q}}_J + {}^{*}\mathbf{Q}_J & (26)
\end{aligned}
$$

All of these operators can be analyzed by means of SVD providing, in particular, additional information on the role of time with respect to the units and the variables. For example, the SVD of $\bar{\mathbf{Q}}_I$ gives, among other things, the component scores of the times (w.r.t. the whole set of units) and their differential scores across the different units. In this way, we obtain a dual perspective as compared to the component scores and factorial trajectories of the units provided by the SVD of $\bar{\mathbf{S}}_T$ in Model 1 (direct approach). The two perspectives can be matched in order to cast more light on the complex relationship between units and times. Similar considerations can be made for the SVD of the remaining $\mathbf{Q}$-operators (in particular, concerning the duality w.r.t. the dual models). Summing up, it is suggested that the integration of the direct DFA approach with the dual and tridual models greatly improves the capability of the method in drawing information from the original 3-way array and opens up the way to the formulation of appropriate strategies of analysis in this framework.

4 Application

We illustrate, in an extremely concise way, an application of DFA to a 3-way array which has been set up within a study of deforestation in Latin America (see Corazziari, 1999b). The data refer to 19 Countries in Latin America; 27 variables concerning the proportion of different types of land use, the population densities w.r.t. areas differently characterized from the viewpoint of land use, wood production and commerce, gross domestic product (GDP); 24 years (1961, 1970-1992). A specific software for DFA, written in Xlisp-Stat, has been utilized (Corazziari,

1999b). The data have been normalized according to (1). We limit our comments here to the application of Model 1, in both the direct and the dual versions. In both cases a three-dimensional solution has been chosen for the factorial part of the models. The global Quality Indicators for the two models are reported in Table 2: A common interpretation of

SOURCE	DIRECT	DUAL
Global Structure	0.74	0.76
Synthetic Structure	0.72	0.73
Differential Dynamics	0.89	0.83
Average Evolution	0.79	0.80
Total	0.74	0.76

Table 2: Global Quality Indicators for Model 1 (direct and dual versions)

the factorial structure in the two models is possible, taking into account the correlations of the variables (units) with the component scores of the units (variables) as previously underlined. In fact the first factorial dimension, accounting for nearly 40% of the variation due to the global structure in both models, is connected with the degree and type of agricultural exploitation of the land, while the second dimension ($\simeq20\%$) is linked with the import/export of industrial wood and GDP. The third dimension ($\simeq15\%$) enhances the opposition between the extension of forests and the extension of lands devoted to permanent pasture. Specific groups of Countries (direct analysis) and of variables (dual analysis) can be singled out on the three principal planes. A few Countries lie apart from the others, showing specific features on the various factorial axes, namely Belize, Chile, Guyana, Surinam and Uruguay. Similarly, a few variables seem to have the major impact on the global structure: Forest surface, Total Agricultural surface, Permanent Pasture surface, Farmers density, Production and Import of Industrial Wood, GDP. These results are also reflected by the clusters obtained from the analysis of trajectories of the units and variables. As to the time regression analyses of the operators $^*\mathbf{S}_T$ and $^*\mathbf{P}_T$, it can be observed that for most of the variables the average evolution is linear but for the production of fuel and coal wood, which show a cyclical component acting together with an increasing trend. A linear trend is also suitable for describing the average evolution of the Countries, although a more detailed analysis for the group of variables related to wood production and commerce and to GDP points out nonlinear trends for many Countries. We shall not dwell, in this paper, on the other results of the analysis, as well as on the detailed examination of the features emphasized in the previous brief comment. We just remark the usefulness of DFA, in its extended form, as a sensitive filter capable to translate the complexity of the data into systematic information concerning the structure and the dynamics of the array $\mathbf{Z}(I, J, T)$.

58

References

COPPI, R.; BLANCO, J.; CAMAÑO, G. and CORAZZIARI, I. (1996): Descomposicin Factorial y Regresiva de la Variabilidad de un Array a tres Vias. In Seminario de Capacitación y Investigación, Bogotà, Colombia, 355-392. Also published in Quantum, vol. 4, 10, 1999, Montevideo, Uruguay, 81-107.

COPPI, R. and D'URSO, P. (1999): The Geometric Approach to the Comparison of Multivariate Time Trajectories. *Proceedings of CLADAG 99, Rome, Italy, 177-180.*

COPPI, R. and ZANNELLA, F. (1978): L'Analisi Fattoriale di una Serie Temporale Multipla relativa allo stesso Insieme di Unità Statistiche. *Proceedings of the XXIX Scientific Meeting of the Italian Statistical Society (SIS), Bologna, Italy, 61-77.*

CORAZZIARI, I. (1999a): Dynamic Factor Analysis. In: Vichi M. and Opitz O. (eds.): Classification and Data Analysis. Theory and Application, Springer-Verlag, Heidelberg, 171-178.

CORAZZIARI, I. (1999b): Analisi di dati Longitudinali Multivariati. Unpublished doctoral dissertation, University of Naples "Federico II", Naples, Italy.

D'URSO, P. (2000): Classificazione Fuzzy per Matrici a Tre Vie Temporali. Unpublished doctoral dissertation, University of Rome "La Sapienza", Rome, Italy.

JOLLIFFE, I.T. (1985): Principal Component Analysis. Springer-Verlag, New York.

Joint Non-symmetrical Correspondence Analysis with Ordered Categories

L. D'Ambra[1], R. Lombardo[2], P. Amenta[3]

[1]Department of Mathematic and Statistics,
University of Naples, via Cinzia-Monte S. Angelo, 80126 Napoli, Italy
E-Mail: dambra@unina.it

[2]Department of Accounting and Quantitative Methods,
II University of Naples, P.zza Umberto I,81043 Capua (CE),Italy.
E-Mail: lombardo@unina2.it

[3]Department of Economics, Mathematic and Statistics,
University of Lecce, via Monteroni, 73100 Lecce, Italy
E-Mail: amenta@economia.unile.it

Abstract: In this paper we study the dependence relationship among a response and two or more predictor variables in a flattened contingency table. Considering ordinal categorical variables, the main aim is to preserve the ordinal compliance of categories by using a monotone function and optimal scaling for the first axis and Partial Least Squares for the remaining ones.

1 Introduction

When dealing with categorical variables, we can distinguish between techniques in which all the variables play the same role (Analysis of Interdependence, Greenacre (1984)) and those in which one or more variables are thought to be logically dependent on the other ones (Israël (1997)). Non-Symmetrical Correspondence Analysis (NSCA) (D'Ambra et al. (1988), (1992)) is primarily an exploratory tool, whenever it is based on a characteristic index which measures the relative increase in predictability of a response variable given the knowledge of the predictor variable group. The index, known in literature as the intra-class correlation measure for categorical data, is the Goodman & Kruskal'sτ (1954).

When the number of categorical variables increases, it becomes more difficult to investigate all the possible higher-order associations in the style of three-way NSCA (D'Ambra et al. (1989), (1992); Lombardo et al. (1996)) and it is very hard to represent individuals. As a compromise, all possible 2-way associations between the response and predictor variables are jointly explored (JNSCA). JNSCA aims at evaluating the dependence structure of variables with ordered categories and representing not just the variables but also the individuals. When the categorical variables are ordinal, we preserve this order also in the representations. Our method will be based on two specific algorithms "optimal scaling" to preserve the order of the column categories on the first axes, and

"Partial Least Squares" (PLS) (Wold (1966)) to detect the remaining orthogonal axis. Other approaches which use order constraints on the first space dimension, imply different transformation of the original data matrix (Nishisato 1980, Nishisato and Arri 1975) more or less evident. Clearly whenever the order constraint is imposed on all the other dimensions it is hard to obtain orthogonal axis. Nishisato proposed to modify the columns of the original data matrix when the order relations of the first axes are broken, consequently he implicitly modifies the original frequency marginals. In this paper we proposed to transform directly the first axis when the order relations are not respected, without modifying the frequency marginals. The first axes is of maximum inertia, ordered with respect to the Weighted Least Squares criterion so it results of minimum distance with respect to the original principal one. The index, computed with respect to the flattened contingency table, is shown to be the weighted mean of the τ indices referring to each sub-table.

2 Joint Non-Symmetrical Correspondence Analysis

The analysis of the dependence structure among categorical variables, observed on the same individual set, can be properly studied referring to a table crossing the set of categories of the response variable with that of the predictor group. Let Y and $X = [X_1|..|X_M]$ be the disjunctive complete matrices associated to one response and M predictor variables, respectively. Let $C = Y'X$ be the flattened contingency table (Leclerc (1975)). The dimension of the table C is $I \times J$ where I is the number of categories of the response variable, and $J = \cup_{m=1}^{M} J_m$ is the category number of all predictors with $I < J$. Let n be the individual number of C, n_{im} the number of units of the sub-table of order $I \times J_m$, with J_m the category set of the $m.th$ predictor variable. Let $P = C/n$ be the relative frequency matrix and $p_{i.} = \sum_{j=1}^{J} c_{ij}/n$ and $p_{.j} = \sum_{i=1}^{I} c_{ij}/n$ the row and column margins, respectively, where $p_{i.}$, i.e. the marginal profile, represents the estimated probability that an individual is in row i independently on the column it belongs to.

In this paper we focus our attention on the JNSCA to evaluate the centered column profile matrix $\Pi = (\pi_{ij})$ whenever the variables have ordered category values. The generic element of Π is $\pi_{ij} = \frac{p_{ij}}{p_{.j}} - p_{i.}$ where the marginal profile $p_{i.}$ is the weighted average of the column profiles. JNSCA maximizes the inertia or Euclidean norm of the flattened contingency table Π, with the relative frequency that an individual belongs to column $j.th$ as weight $(p_{.j})$, i.e. the numerator of the tau index

$$N_\tau = \sum_{i=1}^{I} \sum_{j \in J} \pi_{ij}^2 = \sum_{i=1}^{I} \sum_{m=1}^{M} \sum_{j \in J_m} p_{.j} (\frac{p_{ij}}{p_{.j}} - p_{i.})^2$$

which represents the absolute increase in predictability of a response variable given the knowledge of the predictor variable group. As a compromise, all possible 2-way associations between the response and predictor variables in the multi-way data are jointly explored . By a generalization of the Singular Value Decomposition (GSVD), the (full) rank representation of the columns and rows of Π is found:

$$\pi_{ij} = \sum_{s=1}^{I} \lambda_s a_{is} b_{js}$$

where the scalar λ_s is the singular value, and $a_s = (a_{is})$, $b_s = (b_{js})$ are orthonormal singular vectors in an unweighted and weighted metric, respectively:

$$\sum_{s=1}^{I} a_{is} a_{is'} = \sum_{s=1}^{I} p_{.j} b_{js} b_{js'} = \{ \begin{array}{ll} 0 & (\text{if } s \neq s') \\ 1 & (\text{if } s = s') \end{array}$$

All the classical formulas of NSCA are verified, just the interpretation will differ, in relation with the different nature of the contingency table (simple or flattened). The rows have standard coordinates and the columns have principal coordinates (Column Isometric Biplot, Greenacre (1984)). We define $r_{is} = a_{is}$ and $z_{js} = \lambda_s b_{js}(p_{.j})^{-1/2}$ the rows and columns coordinates and the transition formulas $r_{is} = \sum_j p_{.j} \pi_{ij} z_{js}$ and $z_{js} = (1/\sqrt{\lambda_i}) \sum_i \pi_{ij} r_{is}$, respectively.

3   Properties of JNSCA

•The N_τ can be expressed as the mean of inertias of sub-tables which are part of the flattened table.
Let $p'_{ij} = \frac{c_{ij}}{n_{im}} = \frac{c_{ij}}{n/M} = p_{ij} M$ be the relative frequency of a generic sub-table and $p'_{i.} = \frac{c_{i.}}{M n_{im}} = \frac{c_{i.}}{M n/M} = p_{i.}$ and $p'_{.j} = \frac{c_{.j}}{n_{im}} = \frac{c_{.j}}{n/M} = p_{.j} M$ the marginal frequency of a sub-table. The generic contingency sub-matrix of relative frequencies is characterized by the row and column marginals equal to $p_{i'} = p_{..}$ and $p_{.j'} = M p_{.j}$, respectively. Expressing the inertia in terms of the frequencies of a sub-table ($p_{i.} = p'_{i.}$ and $p_{.j} = 1/M p'_{.j}$), we show that

$$N_\tau = \frac{1}{M} \sum_{i \in I} \sum_{j \in J} p_{.j} \pi_{ij}^2 = \frac{1}{M} \sum_{j=1}^{M} \sum_{j \in J_m} [p_{.j} (\frac{p_{ij}}{p_{.j}} - p_{i.})^2] = \frac{1}{M} \sum_{j=1}^{M} \sum_{j \in J_m} \tau_j$$

• The inertia, as sum of eigenvalues, can be decomposed in order to know the contribution of a generic column category or of a variable. An eigenvalue of the flattened matrix is the mean of the respective M eigenvalues of each sub-table.

• We can compute the predictive power of a generic column category or of a variable. The contribution of a variable to the explanation of a factor (absolute contribution) and the contribution of a factor to the representation of a variable (relative contribution) are easily calculated.

• It is possible to investigate all two-way dependence relationships between pairs of variables in a single joint representation. JNSCA allows an average view of all pairwise dependence associations.

• The origin of representation is the gravity centre not only for the set J of categories, but also for each sub-set J_m.

The interpretation rules to understand biplots in JNSCA can be found (Kroonenberg et al. (1999), Lombardo et al.(2000))

4 The computational procedure

In this section we describe the computational procedure of JNSCA. Compute row and column coordinates from the JNSCA of the matrix $C = X'Y$. If the order of the column coordinates reflect the ordinal compliance of the original variable categories then exit. Otherwise, apply the regression monotone fitting and the optimal scaling procedures(§4.1) to order the predictor categories on the first axis, and the PLS algorithm for the remaining axes (§4.2).

4.1 Monotone Regression Fitting and Optimal Scaling

The algorithm is presented supposing that the column variables are ordinal, clearly when the response variable is ordered too, the following steps should be repeated for the row coordinates.

Let $z = [z_1|..|z_m|..|z_M]$ be the column coordinates, where z_m concerns the coordinates of the mth variable.

Step 1 Compute the new column coordinates z_m^+, replacing them by the theoretical values of a rank regression function (weighted least squares fitting) or of a non-linear monotone regression fitting.

Step 2 Normalize the new coordinates $z_m^+ = z_m^+/\sqrt{(z_m^+)'D_c^+ z_m^+}$ where $D_c^+ = (p_{\cdot j})$ is the weight matrix of the mth variable.

Step 3 Compute the standard row coordinates by using z^+ (normalized):

$r^+ = (1/\sqrt{\lambda^+})\Pi D_c z^+$ where $\lambda^+ = \sqrt{z^{+\prime} D_c^{1/2}\Pi'\Pi D_c^{1/2} z^+}$

Step 4 By transition formula, compute the corresponding column coordinates $z^* = \Pi' r^+$ and go to step 1 until the inertia $r^{+\prime} r^+$ does not increase and the vector z^+ changes a little.

Step 5 Set the new coordinates $z^{(1)} = z^+$ and $r^{(1)} = r^+$ so that the first axis column coordinates satisfy the ordinal compliance.

5 Partial Least Squares of the remaining axes

The PLS method is useful in situations where the ratio of observations to variables is small and predictors are highly correlated. It constructs a sequence of uncorrelated explanatory variables (called latent variables or components) to predict the responses in a linear fashion. It allows the representation not only of the variable categories, but whenever it makes sense, also of the individuals. In this framework, thinking at the remaining components as explanatory variables of the centered column profile residual matrix, by means of PLS components, we estimate the remaining axes to display the individuals and the dependence relationship of variables. Consider the disjunctive matrices Y and X.

Step 1: Set the first component $F^{(1)} = X(D_c)^{-1}z^{(1)}$ and compute the orthogonal projector $P_{F^{(1)}} = F^{(1)}(F^{(1)'}F^{(1)})^{-1}F^{(1)'}$ set $k = 2$
Step 2: Compute the residual matrix
$X^{(k)} = X^{(k-1)}(D_c)^{-1} - P_{F^{(k-1)}}X^{(k-1)}(D_c)^{-1}$
Step 3: GSVD of $Y'X^{(k)}$ with weight (D_c) and let $b^{(k)}$ be the right singular vector associated to the greatest singular value.
Step 4: Compute the components $F^{(k)} = X^{(k)}D_c b^{(k)}$ and the column coordinates $z^{k+1} = \lambda_s D_c^{-1/2}b^{(k)}$
Step 5: Increase k by one and go to step 1, repeat for $k = 3, \ldots, (I-1)$ until the maximum number of axes is computed.

Remark 1: It can be shown that the described computational procedure is equivalent whenever we compute the residual matrix from the contingency table Π. The residual matrix is $\hat{\Pi}^{(k+1)} = \Pi - \hat{\Pi}^{(k)}$ where $\hat{\Pi}^{(k)} = \Pi z^k(z^{(k)'}D_c z^{(k)})^{-1}z^{(k)'}D_c$
Remark 2: Furthermore, it can be checked that the components $F^{(k)}$ are mutually orthogonal as well as the coefficients $z^{(k)}$ by the weight matrix D_c.

6 An example of Ordered JNSCA

In this section we present an example to study the dependence relationship of a response and three predictor variables. The data are taken from the Italian magazine "Quattroruote" (May, 97). The data refer to the contingency table crossing 6 class prices per three explanatory variables. The response is the **Price** ($\times$ 1.000): **P1** ($<$£18.800), **P2** (£18.800-25.600), **P3** (£25.600-32.400), **P4** (£32.400-39.200), **P5** (£39.200-46.000) and **P6** ($>$£46.000). The predictors are **Displacement Piston** with four categories: **D1** ($<$1.300), **D2**, (1.300-1.600), **D3**, (1600-1900) and **D4** ($>$1.900); **Maximum speed** with four categories: **S1** ($<$160),**S2** (160-190),**S3** (190-210) and **S4**($>$210); **Expenditures of Exercise** with six categories: **E2** (500-630), **E3** (630-760), **E4** (760-890), **E5** (890-1020) and **E6** (1020-1150). The disjunctive matrices associated to the variables

	e1	e2	e3	e4	e5	e6	s1	s2	s3	s4	d1	d2	d3	d4
P1	32	-7	-7	-7	-7	-7	36	-7	-7	-7	41	-7	-7	-7
P2	5	38	-8	-21	-21	-21	22	7	-21	-21	31	16	-17	-19
P3	-3	-24	49	24	-33	-33	-29	8	6	-15	-33	11	26	-8
P4	-16	1	-20	22	24	-20	-11	-3	10	7	-20	-7	7	11
P5	-12	-3	-12	-12	43	18	-12	-5	6	33	-12	-7	-3	13
P6	-6	-6	-2	-6	-6	64	-6	-2	6	3	-6	-6	-6	11

Table 1: Centered Column Profile

	d1	s1	e1	e2	d2	s2	e3	d3	e4	s3	d4	e5	e6	s4
P2	31	22	5	38	16	7	-8	-17	-21	-21	-19	-21	-21	-21
P1	41	36	32	-7	-7	-7	-7	-7	-7	-7	-7	-7	-7	-7
P3	-33	-29	-3	-24	11	8	49	26	24	6	-8	-33	-33	-15
P6	-6	-6	-6	-6	-6	-2	-2	-6	-6	6	11	-6	64	3
P4	-20	-11	-16	1	-7	-3	-20	7	22	10	11	24	-20	7
P5	-12	-12	-12	-3	-7	-5	-12	-3	-12	6	13	43	18	33

Table 2: Centered Column Profile by Ordered JNSCA

list the unluckily anonymous car vehicles with these characteristics. Observe that the predictors are all ordinal, for each of them the order compliance will be preserved in the graphical display. The tau index with

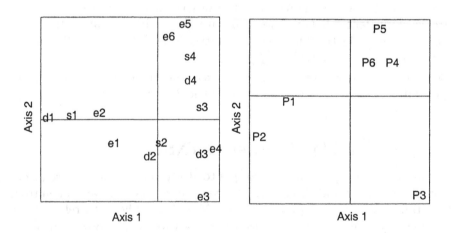

Figure 1: Joint Non Symmetrical Correspondence Analysis

respect to the flattened contingency table is equal to 0.16, concerning the three single sub-tables are $\tau_1 = 0.27$, $\tau_2 = 0.089$ and $\tau_3 = 0.13$. The dependence structure among the four variables clearly shows that car **Price** class is to be predicted from **Speed max**, **Exercise Expenditure**, and **Displacement Piston** variables. The central question is whether there are differences in price distribution for the various predictor category variables. The key information comes from the centered column profile matrix, which contains the information on how the prices of the different cars differ from the row marginal distribution, i.e. irrespective of Speed max, Exercise Expenditure, and Displacement Piston. This information is in Table 1. From the varying sizes of the difference between the column profile and the marginal row distribution, it is clear that different price groups have different distributions. After using the rows and columns JNSCA coordinates both for the ordering of the centered column profile and for constructing the column isometric biplot, we show in Table 2 the clearer structure resulting from the rearrangement of the centered column profiles (the higher the values, the stronger the importance of the predictors). It is clear that there is a first dimension dominated by the contrast between **D1**, **S1** and **S4**, **E6** which are the column categories explanatory of **P1**, **P2**, and of **P6**, **P5**, **P4**, respectively, while the predictor category **E3** strongly influences the category response **P3**. The biplots display the deviations from the marginal profile which is located at the origin. In Figure 1 the biplot refers to the results of JNSCA before the re-ordering of the first axis, while Figure 2 shows the results after the optimal scaling of the first axis and PLS for the remaining ones.

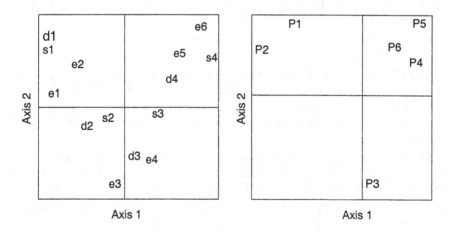

Figure 2: Ordered Joint Non Symmetrical Correspondence Analysis

7 Conclusion

In order to study the dependence relationship among a response variable and a large number of predictor variables, JNSCA has been proposed. As a compromise, all possible 2-way associations between the response and predictor variables have been jointly explored . Furthermore, when some variables are ordinal, to preserve the ordinal compliance in the graphical display, we have proposed the linear monotone regression fitting of the first component, but clearly non-linear monotone functions (for example monotone cubic spline functions) could be also properly considered. The new ordered component is an optimal scaled component, while the remaining ones are found by PLS Regression which guarantees the orthonormality of the components but no the order of categories.

Acknowledgments. The authors are grateful to the anonymous referee for his comments and suggestions. This paper has been supported with a grant from MURST "Multidimensional Statistical methods to evaluate efficacy and efficiency of the professional training courses" 1999, (L. D'Ambra)

References

D'AMBRA, L. and LAURO, N.C. (1989): Non symmetrical analysis of three-way contingency tables. In: Coppi, R. and Bolasco S. (eds.) Multiway Data Analysis.Elsevier, Amsterdam.

D'AMBRA, L. and LAURO, N.C. (1992): Non symmetrical exploratory data analysis. In Statistica Applicata,4, 511-529.

GREENACRE, M.J. (1984): Theory and Applications of Correspondence Analysis. (eds.) Academic Press.

GOODMAN, L. and KRUSKAL, N.C. (1954): Measures of Association for cross classifications. JASA, 49,732-764.

ISRAEL, A. (1997): Eigenvalue techniques for qualitative data. The Netherlands, DSWO press.

LECLERC, A. (1975): L'Analyse des Correspondences sur Juxtaposition de Tableaux de Contingence. Revue de Statistique Appliquèe vol.XXIII,3.

LOMBARDO, R. CARLIER, A. and D'AMBRA, L. (1996): Nonsymmetric Correspondence Analysis for three-way contingency tables. In Methodologica, n.4 pp.59-80.

KROONENBERG, P. LOMBARDO, R. (1999) Nonsymmetric Correspondence Analysis: A Tool for Analysing Contingency Tables with a Dependence Structure. Multivariate Behavioral Research Journal n.34 (3) p.367-396.

NISHISATO, S. (1980): Analysis of Categorical Data: Dual Scaling and its applications. University of Toronto Press.

NISHISATO, S.and ARRI, P. S. (1975): Non linear Programming approach to optimal scaling of partially ordered categories. Psychometrika, 40, 525-48.

WOLD, H. (1966): Estimation of principal components and related models by iterative least squares. In Multivariate Analysis, (eds.) P.R. Krishnaiah, New York: Academic Press, 391-420.

Regression Analysis of Extremely Multicollinear Data

Norman Fickel

Wirtschafts- und Sozialwissenschaftliche Fakultät,
Universität Erlangen-Nürnberg, D-90403 Nürnberg, Germany

Abstract: Regression analysis tries to measure the influences of independent variables on a dependent variable. This can be achieved by partial coefficients if there is not too much multicollinearity. A new method provides alternative coefficients which can be interpreted for every degree of multicollinearity.

1 Introduction

Regression analysis is a statistical tool for analyzing data sets which consist of several variables. One of these variables (the so-called regressand) is regarded as being dependent on the other variables (the regressors). The aim is to measure the influences of the regressors on the regressand. It can be achieved by the partial coefficients of a multiple regression if the regressors are not too much correlated. The partial coefficient of a regressor describes the average change of the regressand when the regressor is varied by one unit on condition that the remaining regressors are held constant. However, this interpretation critically relies on the assumption that holding other regressors constant is a plausible condition. As a result, a partial coefficient does not have any substantial meaning if the regressors are extremely multicollinear.

Literature knows a lot of approaches for handling multicollinearity categorized as follows (cf. Draper, Smith (1998); Miller (1990)):

Classifying Regressors. Algorithms divide the regressors into two types according to a significant or insignificant influence on the regressand. Standard algorithms are forward selection and backward elimination. Regression analysis gives a coefficient for the significant regressors only and neglects the influence of insignificant regressors.

Suppressing Variance. Artificial variables are constructed in order to explain variance of the regressors. The omission of some of those artificial variables provides changed coefficients. Known methods are the partial least squares method and principal components regression (Wold (1966); Hawkins (1973)).

Modifying Coefficients. Multicollinearity often causes partial coefficients to have an absolute value which is unplausibly high. Some shrinkage methods produce smaller values via a penalization parameter that controls the extend of modification. Examples are ridge regression, the garotte and the lasso method (Hoerl, Kennard (1970); Breiman (1995), Tibshirani (1996)). Unfortunately, in real situations one scarcely knows how to choose an appropriate parameter.

All known approaches either use changed regressors or assume certain conditions. However, this paper follows up a completely different approach in order to measure the direct influences of the given regressors. A first step chooses an ordering of the regressors and employs sequential instead of partial coefficients (section 2). The second step uses these sequential coefficients to determine an alternative to the partial coefficients which can be interpreted for every degree of multicollinearity (section 3).

2 Sequential Regression

The basic idea of sequential regression is to consider a sequence of the given regressors. The regressors can have a natural ordering such as questions in a questionnaire. This natural ordering, however, is not absolutely necessary. The data analyst can choose an arbitrary ordering as a tool to get a first insight into the data. A known method is the sequential sum of squares (in some statistical software packages also called "hierarchical" sum of squares), which describes how the explained variance of the regressand increases with more regressors taken into account (cf. Morrow-Howell (1994: 250f)). By dividing the increments by the total sum of squares the analyst gets a partition of the coefficient of determination, which shows the percentages of variance every regressor can explain additionally (cf. equation 10).

Some textbooks use a sequential approach to make the idea of multiple regression clear, as, for example, Ezekiel, Fox (1959: 169ff); Sen, Srivastava (1994: 243) and Draper, Smith (1998: 151f). However, I feel that a sequential approach can accomplish more than that. By using it, the data analyst is directly able to understand a data set even if multiple regression fails. On that score, the methodology of "neodescriptive" statistics, as defined by Kruskal (1987: 6), sets an appropriate framework, which, in the terminology of Mosteller, Tukey (1977: 21f), comprises the levels of indication and determination. It allows the development of new methods without requiring the assumptions of statistical inference.

Increments of explained variance measure the determination of influences. So the question arises how to measure the indication of those influences. A suitable coefficient should be interpreted as an average change of the regressand and should be zero if the regressor adds no explained variance. To achieve this, this paper proposes a "sequential coefficient" constructed in three steps (cf. table 2):

1. The regressor is *adjusted* for the influences of all regressors which stand before that regressor with respect to the ordering chosen. One adjusts the regressor by replacing its values by its residuals of a (multiple) regression.

2. The adjusted regressor is *synchronized* with its original form by multiplying all values with a certain constant. This constant is chosen so that a unit change of the regressor on average comes along with a unit change in its adjusted and synchronized form.

3. The *sequential coefficient* is the average change of the regressand, when the adjusted and synchronized regressor is varied by one unit.

As a result, the sequential coefficient describes the *additional* change in the regressand when the regressor is varied by one unit on condition that the first regressors are held constant. In particular the first sequential coefficient is the slope of a simple regression. The sequence of all sequential coefficients describes the structure of a data set as a whole.

There is another way to determine the sequential coefficient of a regressor which uses its tolerance. The tolerance is the percentage of its variance not explained by the first regressors. The sequential coefficient is the product of its tolerance and its partial coefficient (cf. equation 12). In this case the partial coefficient belongs to the regression which omits the regressors behind the actual regressor in the ordering.

Since high multicollinearity shows up in small tolerances, it also leads to small sequential coefficients. This is plausible, because a correlated regressor only gives a small piece of additional information on the regressand. So an extremely correlated regressor has a vanishing sequential coefficient.

3 Averaging Over Orderings

Every ordering provides a vector of sequential coefficients. For a very small number of regressors, say two or three, one can consider the sequential coefficients of all possible orderings as a description of the data set. However, even for only three regressors, there is a total of six possible orderings and therefore of six different coefficients. This number of coefficients is the factorial function of the number of regressors and so increases rapidly.

That is why the coefficients of each regressor need be aggregated. To achieve this, an appropriate mean value of the sequential coefficients has to be chosen. Every coefficient is an average change of the regressand. So it is obvious to take the average of these average changes. In this paper, the resulting measure is called "averaged coefficient", whose computation is summarized as follows (cf. table 2):

1. For every ordering of the regressors their *sequential coefficients* are computed.

2. For every regressor its *averaged coefficient* is the arithmetic mean of all its sequential coefficients.

An averaged coefficient can be interpreted as the average change in the regressand (when the regressor is varied by one unit) on condition that the other regressors are held constant *on average*. The averaged coefficient measures the influence of a regressor. A different measure is necessary to measure the determination of this influence. By analogy with the procedure described, the averages of the sequential sum of squares can be taken for each regressor. These values sum up to the total sum of squares and result in percentages of the total coefficient of determination. Clearly, these averages of determination lie between zero and one (cf. equations 10 and 11).

Kruskal (1987) employs those averages of determination to assess the *relative importance* of regressors, and Chevan, Sutherland (1991) and Fickel (2000) present methods for a more detailed examination. A discussion of alternative measures, such as standardized coefficients, can be found in Darlington (1990: 217ff) and Bring (1994). Finally, both the methods of 'sequential regression' and of 'averaging over orderings' can be extended to more general settings, like generalized linear models, if appropriate concepts of adjustment and synchronization are used. To stress this point, the abstract mathematical object 'adjustment space' is introduced in section 5.

4 Real-World Example

The price of a product as well as the prices of rival products influence the demand. Bowerman, O'Connell (1993: 142) discuss a data set containing demands for the product "Fresh Detergent" in 30 periods. They use three variables for explanation: the price of Fresh Detergent (no. 1), the average price of rival products (no. 2) and the resulting price difference (no. 3). Multiple regression achieves a coefficient of determination of 0.83, that is, it explains 83% of the observed demand's variance. The three variables are extremely multicollinear since there is an exact linear relationship between them. Two variables always fix the values of the third one. Clearly, partial coefficients cannot be employed. Please note that this property is not specific for small data sets and also occurs with

ordering	price no. 1	rival price no. 2	difference no. 3
1–2–3	-3.55	2.45	0.00
1–3–2	-3.55	0.00	-2.21
2–1–3	-3.98	2.34	0.00
2–3–1	0.00	2.34	-0.63
3–1–2	-1.38	0.00	-2.67
3–2–1	0.00	-0.24	-2.67
averaged coefficient	**-2.08**	**1.15**	**-1.36**
average of determination	13%	29%	41%

Table 1: Sequential coefficients for the demand of Fresh Detergent in 100,000 bottles per US-dollar

very large data sets analogously. Yet the used small data set is easy to get and to handle.

In any case, sequential coefficients, as shown in table 1 for each ordering of the three regressors, help to understand the data set. The sequential coefficient of the last regressor is always zero due to the perfect multi-collinearity. (Obviously, this coefficient can substantially differ from zero if the regressors are less correlated.) The price of Fresh Detergent has an averaged coefficient of -2.08, that is, the demand decreases by 2,080 bottles when the price varies by 1 US-cent. The rival price and the price difference are held constant *on average*.

The analogous averaging of the increments of determination gives averaged percentages of variance explained. (Table 1 omits the individual increments.) This method assigns 41% of the observed variance to the price difference, which so appears to be the most important regressor. It accounts for about half of the total coefficient of determination of 83%.

5   Mathematical Theory of Adjustment

An appropriate mathematical object called "adjustment space" makes the ideas of the previous sections clear. The proofs of the formulated theorems use only textbook results on linear algebra and can be found in Fickel (1999).

Definition 1 *A triple* (N, B, E) *is called an* adjustment space, *if* N *is a set,* $B : N \times \wp(N) \to N$ *a mapping such that for some* $0 \in N$ *(with* $\tilde{x} := B(x, M)$*)*

$$B(\tilde{x}, M) = \tilde{x} \qquad \textit{for all} \quad x \in N, M \subseteq N \tag{1}$$

as well as $\tilde{x} = 0$ if $x \in M$ is satisfied. The symbol $E : N \times N \to \mathbb{R}$ is a mapping such that for all $x \in N$ it holds $E(x,x) = 1$ if $B(x, \emptyset) \neq 0$.

Clearly, from $0 \in N$ follows $N \neq \emptyset$. The element 0 is also uniquely determined, because $B(0, \{0\}) = 0$.

In the following let n be a natural number. One defines an operator $B_n : \mathbb{R}^n \times \wp(\mathbb{R}^n) \to \mathbb{R}^n$ by

$$B_n(x, M) = x - X(X'X)^{-1}X'x \qquad \text{for all} \quad x \in \mathbb{R}^n, M \subseteq \mathbb{R}^n \qquad (2)$$

where the columns of X are a basis of the vector space $\text{span}(\{1_n\} \cup M)$. A mapping $E_n : \mathbb{R}^n \times \mathbb{R}^n \to \mathbb{R}$ is also defined for all $x, y \in \mathbb{R}$ by

$$E_n(x, y) := \frac{\sum_{i=1}^n (x_i - \bar{x})(y_i - \bar{y})}{\sum_{i=1}^n (x_i - \bar{x})^2} \qquad (3)$$

if $\sum_{i=1}^n (x_i - \bar{x})^2 \neq 0$ and $E_n(x, y) := 0$ else. Further, a mapping $R_n : \mathbb{R}^n \times \mathbb{R}^n \to \mathbb{R}$ is defined by

$$R_n(x, y) := E_n(x, y) \cdot E_n(y, x) \qquad \text{for all} \quad x, y \in \mathbb{R}^n \qquad (4)$$

For any $M \subseteq \mathbb{R}^n$ and $y \in \mathbb{R}$ the coefficient of determination $R^2(M, y)$ has the property $R^2(M, y) = 1 - R_n(y, \tilde{y})$ where $\tilde{y} := B(y, M)$. One has $R^2(\{x\}, y) = R_n(x, y)$ for all $x, y \in \mathbb{R}^n$.

Theorem 1 (Adjustment Spaces in $\mathbb{R}^n$) *The triples $(\mathbb{R}^n, B_n, E_n)$ and $(\mathbb{R}^n, B_n, R_n)$ are adjustment spaces.*

For a finite set M let $|M|$ be its number of elements and S_M be the set of bijections from $\{1, \ldots, |M|\}$ onto M. It holds $|S_M| = |M|!$. For $\sigma \in S_M$ and $x \in M$ let $M_x^\sigma := \{\sigma(l) | l = 1, \ldots, \sigma^{-1}(x)\}$.

Definition 2 *Let (N, B, E) be an adjustment space, M be a finite subset of N, $y \in N$ and $\sigma \in S_M$. Then one defines a vector $(a_x)_{x \in M}$ of type (i), (ii) or (iii) by*

$$\text{(i)} \qquad a_x := E(B(x, M \setminus \{x\}), y) \qquad (5)$$

$$\text{(ii)} \qquad a_x := E(B(x, M_x^\sigma \setminus \{x\}), y) \qquad (6)$$

$$\text{(iii)} \qquad a_x := \frac{1}{|S_M|} \sum_{\tau \in S_M} E(B(x, M_x^\tau \setminus \{x\}), y) \qquad (7)$$

Definition 3 *An adjustment space (N, B, E) is called synchronized if for all $x \in N$ and $M \subseteq N$ the element $\tilde{x} := B(x, M)$ fulfills the condition*

$$E(x, \tilde{x}) = 1 \qquad \text{if} \quad \tilde{x} \neq 0 \qquad (8)$$

symbol	coefficient	adjustment space	type
p_x	partial coefficient	$(\mathbb{R}^n, B_n, E_n)$	i
R_x^σ	increment of determination	$(\mathbb{R}^n, B_n, R_n)$	ii
s_x^σ	sequential coefficient	$(\mathbb{R}^n, B_n^s, E_n)$	ii
$\bar{R}_x$	average of determination	$(\mathbb{R}^n, B_n, R_n)$	iii
$\bar{s}_x$	averaged coefficient	$(\mathbb{R}^n, B_n^s, E_n)$	iii

Table 2: Coefficients in Regression Analysis

None of the adjustment spaces $(\mathbb{R}^n, B_n, E_n)$ and $(\mathbb{R}^n, B_n, R_n)$ is synchronized. One defines $B_n^s : \mathbb{R}^n \times \wp(\mathbb{R}^n) \to \mathbb{R}$ by

$$B_n^s(x, M) := \frac{1}{E_n(x, \tilde{x})} B_n(x, M) \qquad \text{if} \quad E_n(x, \tilde{x}) \neq 0 \qquad (9)$$

and $B_n^s(x, M) := 0$ else (where $\tilde{x} := B_n(x, M)$).

Theorem 2 (Synchronized Adjustment) *The triple $(\mathbb{R}^n, B_n^s, E_n)$ is a synchronized adjustment space.*

Theorem 3 (Coefficients in Regression Analysis) *For $y \in \mathbb{R}^n$, a finite subset $M \subseteq \mathbb{R}^n$ and (if applicable) $\sigma \in S_M$ the characterizations of table 2 hold.*

The notation of table 2 allows the formulation of statements mentioned in sections 2 and 3:

$$\Sigma_{x \in M} R_x^\sigma = \Sigma_{x \in M} \bar{R}_x = R^2(M, y) \qquad (10)$$
$$0 \leq R_x^\sigma \leq 1, \qquad 0 \leq \bar{R}_x \leq 1 \qquad (11)$$
$$s_x^\sigma = T_x \cdot p_x \qquad \text{if} \quad M_x^\sigma = M \qquad (12)$$

where $T_x := 1 - R^2(M \setminus \{x\}, x)$ is the tolerance of x.

References

BOWERMAN, Bruce L. and O'CONNELL, Richard T. (1993): Forecasting and Time Series. 3rd edition. Duxbury, Belmont (California).

BREIMAN, Leo (1995): Better Subset Regression Using the Nonnegative Garrote. Technometrics, 37, 373-384.

BRING, Johan (1994): How to Standardize Regression Coefficients. The American Statistician, 48, 209–213.

CHEVAN, Albert and SUTHERLAND, Michael (1991): Hierarchical Partitioning. The American Statistician, 45, 90–96.

DARLINGTON, Richard B. (1990): Regression and Linear Models. McGraw-Hill, New York.

DRAPER, Norman R. and SMITH, Harry (1998): Applied Regression Analysis. 3rd edition. Wiley, New York.

EZEKIEL, Mordecai and FOX, Karl A. (1959): Methods of Correlation and Regression Analysis. 3rd edition. Wiley, New York.

FICKEL, Norman (2000): Partition of the Coefficient of Determination in Multiple Regression. In: Inderfurth, K. et al. (eds.): Operations Research Proceedings 1999. Springer, Berlin. 154–159.

FICKEL, Norman (1999): Sequential Regression: A Neodescriptive Solution of the Multicollinearity Problem Using Stepwisely Adjusted and Synchronized Variables (German). Habilitationsschrift University of Erlangen-Nuremberg. Unpublished manuscript. Nuremberg.

HAWKINS, Douglas M. (1973): On the Investigation of Alternative Regressions by Principal Component Analysis. *Applied Statistics, 22, 275–286.*

HOERL, Arthur E. and KENNARD, Robert W. (1970): Ridge Regression: Biased Estimation for Non-orthogonal Problems. *Technometrics, 12, 55–67.*

KRUSKAL, William H. (1987): Relative Importance by Averaging Over Orderings. *The American Statistician, 41, 6–10.*

MILLER, Alan J. (1990): Subset Selection in Regression. Chapman and Hall, London.

MORROW-HOWELL, Nancy (1994): The M Word: Multicollinearity in Multiple Regression. *Social Work Research, 18, 247–251.*

MOSTELLER, Frederick and TUKEY, John W. (1977): Data Analysis and Regression. Addison-Wesley, Reading (Massachusetts).

SEN, Ashish and SRIVASTAVA, Muni (1994): Regression Analysis: Theory, Methods, and Applications. 2nd edition. Springer, New York.

TIBSHIRANI, Robert (1996): Regression Shrinkage and Selection via the Lasso. *Journal of the Royal Statistical Society, Series B, 58, 267–288.*

WOLD, Herman (1966): Nonlinear Estimation by Iterative Least Squares Procedures. In: David, F. N. (ed.): Research Papers in Statistics: Festschrift for J. Neyman. Wiley, New York. 411–444.

Modern Data Analysis: A Clash of Paradigms *

David J. Hand

Department of Mathematics
Imperial College of Science, Technology, and Medicine
180 Queen's Gate, London SW7 2BZ, United Kingdom
E-mail: d.j.hand@ic.ac.uk

Abstract: Several distinct intellectual communities are involved in modern developments in data analysis. Of these, perhaps the most important are statistics and computing science. These two disciplines have different emphases, different strengths, and different weaknesses. Statistical data analysis has the merit of a clear and principled theoretical base, but this has been earned at the cost of restricting the class of problems to which the methods may be applied. In contrast, data analysis derived from a computing science background often lacks a sound theoretical base, but this frees it to tackle a wider range of problems. This talk looks at the historical contexts from which the two approaches arose, and examines some of the similarities and differences between them.

1   Introduction

In this paper, I shall define data analysis as *what we do when we turn data into information*. There are various technical definitions of 'information', but here I intend it to convey the implication of shedding light on some stated question or purpose. By analysing data, then, we produce something which can help us answer specific questions.

Modern data analysis is very much a new technological discipline, formed from the merger of several other disciplines. In particular, the disciplines of statistics, pattern recognition, artificial intelligence, and machine learning play fundamental roles. What is interesting here is that these parental disciplines fall naturally into two groups. On the one hand we have statistics, a discipline which many see as a branch of mathematics and which is certainly a mathematical discipline. I shall return to this point below. On the other hand, pattern recognition, artificial intelligence, and machine learning are very much computational disciplines. The fact that there are these two groups, the mathematical and the computational, has led to certain tensions, and it is these which I wish to explore in this paper. As with any technical or scientific area, tensions stimulate development, and it is clear that benefits have resulted in data analysis from the different perspectives brought to the area. At its simplest, the fact that the different disciplines are often conducting

---

*Invited lecture

parallel work on similar problems, though each with their own unique emphasis, has led to synergy developing.

Perhaps I should say at the start that what is in the rest of this paper is false. But it is not false because I am lying. It is false because in the few pages I have available I necessarily have to simplify. This means that what I say about the various disciplines I discuss is inevitably a caricature or cartoon of the real thing. I hope that these simplifications are not so great as to falsify the overall conclusions I draw.

2 The history of statistics

The roots of any discipline or development can be traced as far back as one likes - there is, as they say, nothing new under the sun. Certainly statistical ideas appeared millennia ago. For example, King David I of Scotland, in 1150 AD, defined the inch as the *average* of the widths of the thumbs of a big man, a medium man, and a small man, measured at the base of the thumbnail (Klein, 1974). Likewise, according to an account written in the Sixteenth Century, the old British unit of measurement, the rood, is determined as follows: 'the surveyor should station himself by a church door on Sunday. When the service ends, he should "bid sixteen men to stop, tall ones and short ones, as they happen to come out..."... The chosen sixteen should be made to stand in line with "their left feet one behind the other". The resulting sum of the sixteen actual left feet constituted the length of "the right and lawful rood" and the sixteenth part of it constituted "the right and lawful foot".' (Klein, 1974). Here we have notions of averaging and of random sampling being used.

If one foot on which statistics stands is data, the other is uncertainty, with probability being the science of understanding and manipulating uncertainty.

Formal probability theory is often dated from the middle of the 17th Century, when a revolution in understanding seemed to occur (Hacking, 1975). This revolution is generally attributed to thinkers such as Pierre de Fermat (1601-1665), Blaise Pascal (1623-1662), Christian Huygens (1631-1699), and Gottfried Leibniz (1646-1716). From these beginnings, a deluge of ideas and understanding resulted. The names of Abraham de Moivre (1667-1754), Thomas Bayes (1702-1761), Pierre Simon Laplace (1749-1827), and Karl Friedrich Gauss (1777-1855) spring to mind.

Moving on to the 19th Century, we find statistical things beginning to hot up. The Royal Statistical Society (then the London Statistical Society) was founded in 1834. What is particularly interesting in the present context is that almost no mathematical papers appeared in its journals for the first fifty years. This is in total contrast to the appearance of today's journals. Then, in 1885, a paper by Edgeworth appeared which included

(Hill, 1984) discussion of 'probability, the normal curve, use of the modulus $(=\sqrt{2}\sigma)$, and the fluctuation $(= 2\sigma^2)$, discusses n or $n-1$ as divisor, divides by $\sqrt{n}$ for modulus of the mean, discusses significance tests, use of the median, parametric versus non-parametric tests, describes normal and Poisson approximations to the binomial, deals with the modulus of a sum or difference, and with the tendence of a mean towards normality.' Then there was something of a gap until 1893, when three mathematical papers appeared, one, again, by Edgeworth, discussing the bivariate normal distribution, one by Galton on the correlation coefficient, and one by Pearson on standard deviation and skewness. After that point, as we head towards the turn of the century, more and more mathematical papers begin to appear, and, in 1888, the *Journal of the American Statistical Association* was launched.

As we progress into the 20th Century we find more and more major developments, produced by such luminaries as Fisher, Jeffreys, Keynes, Ramsey, Savage, de Finetti, Neyman, and many others.

From this, one is tempted to draw the conclusion that statistical science as we know it today is very much a child of the 20th Century: its roots predate that period, but almost all the development of significant tools has gone on since the end of the 19th Century.

Looking back over the last century, it is clear that much of the development of statistics has been motivated by the domains in which it was applied. It is presumably no coincidence that many of the early researchers in statistical methodology were also experts in some application domain. Fisher was also well-known for his expertise in genetics, Jeffreys in geology, and Keynes in economics. The development of experimental design was driven by agricultural application, though the methods are now applied much more widely (in manufacturing industry, for example). Likewise, survival analysis and conditional independence graphs owe much to medical applications. Factor analysis, linear structural relational models, and item response theory owe much to psychology. Ordination and multidimensional scaling owe much to ecological applications. In each case, of course, once developed, the ideas were then applied and developed even further in other areas.

More recently, the power of the computer as a tool through which to apply statistical methods has itself led to the development of new methods. Resampling methods, such as the bootstrap, and practical application of Bayesian methods through Markov chain Monte Carlo are only feasible (or perhaps even only conceivable) thanks to the computer.

3 The history of computational data analysis

The roots of modern computers, ideas which lie behind the modern tools, can also be traced back as far as one likes, although mechanical devices only go back a few hundred years and electronic ones even less far. In 1614, John Napier developed the ideas of logarithms and in 1623 William Schickard devised a mechanical calculator. In 1801 Jacquard built a loom controlled by punched cards, often regarded as the first example of a machine which followed a 'program'. Babbage produced the design for his Difference Engine in 1822 and his Analytical Engine in the 1830s, though practical construction was stymied by the inadequacies of the manufacturing processes of the time. Herman Hollerith used punched cards as memory devices in the US census of 1890, and Alan Turing devised what is often regarded as the theoretical foundations of modern computing in the 1930s. A young German engineer, Konrad Zuse, produced the first programmable calculator - what many regard as the first computer - in 1938. And then the flood gates opened: Colossus (1943), ENIAC (1945), Manchester University Mark I (1948), magnetic core memory (1953), FORTRAN (1957), integrated circuits (1958), the first microprocessor, the Intel 4004 (1970), the CLIP-4 parallel architecture (1974), the first personal computer, the Altair 8800 (1975), the first WIMPS system (1981), and so on.

Computers are the stratum on which computational data analysis exists, but what can one say about the history of computational approaches to data analysis themselves? At this stage, perhaps the best that can be said is that it is too early to write a history: things are changing too fast. What is interesting is that, whereas statistics approached data analysis from the data and from notions of uncertainty, computational work approached it from a different perspective. In particular, much emphasis was placed on the artificial intelligence viewpoint(s). Expert systems were models of how a human expert might perform, with the emphasis on rule-based architectures, following the seminal work of Newell and Simon. And instead of being concerned with 'analysing data' per se, the aim was to build a model of the brain, to build a device which could 'learn', producing such things as the perceptron - in fact a simple linear decision surface but with an adaptively updating estimation algorithm.

4   Why another area?

If statistics already existed and provided a set of tools for data analysis, one is naturally led to pose the question of why other areas grew up. One possible explanation lies in misunderstandings of statistics.

Was statistics seen as concerned only with a narrow range of problems? Certainly, study of the texts may give the impression that it is concerned with idealised, and hence unrealistic problems. For example, normally distributed data, when any practical experience soon reveals that *no* natural data are normally distributed. Or iid data, when a huge number of problems involve clear correlations between observations or distributions which evolve over time.

Were there simply misconceptions of what statistics was all about? A glance in any statistics text shows the tremendous emphasis on inference, almost to the exclusion of all else. And in contrast, the lay view doubtless still owes something to those first fifty years of the Royal Statistical Society: an apparent belief that statistics is all about producing table after tedious table of numbers. I think the public attitude is illustrated in the following anecdote: *she was studying birth and death statistics. Suddenly she turned to a man near her and said, 'Do you know that every time I breath a man dies?' 'Very interesting,' he replied. 'Have you tried toothpaste?'* Firstly, this looks boring. Who on earth would want to read birth and death statistics? Secondly, there is the translation into something familiar in an attempt to make it comprehensible: the matching of the rate of breathing and the rate of dying. And thirdly, there is the misinterpretation and misunderstanding.

The fact that there is lay suspicion of statistics is nicely conveyed by the following:

Stekel (1931): *Statistics is the art of lying by means of figures.*

Belloc (1940): *Before the curse of statistics fell upon mankind we lived a happy, innocent life, full of merriment and go, and informed by fairly good judgement.*

Baudrillard (1987): *Like dreams, statistics are a form of wish fulfillment.*

At a more sophisticated level, concern that statisticians may not be able to come up with the goods is conveyed by Seaton (1948): *'...as the job of finding the truth and explaining it continues to become more complex and more difficult, management again casts a doubtful eye at the statistician, for a different reason. Management's big question is no longer "What can the statistician do for us that we can't do just as well ourselves?'; the question now is, 'Do our statisticians have the tools and the capacity and the experience and the persistence and the breadth of vision to seek the truth and to know it when they have found it?"*

5   A clash of paradigms

My title is intended to convey the sense that the two types of discipline which have grown up for analysing data - statistics on the one hand and the computational on the other - have significant differences, and that we can learn from identifying and understanding these differences. I shall examine just four of these aspects: emphasis on models or on algorithms, the role of mathematics and the role of computing, exploratory data analysis and graphical procedures, and the data.

5.1 Models versus algorithms

A glance in any modern statistics text book will show that the discipline is 'model-centric': the notion of a model is what underlies almost all of modern statistics. There are different kinds of models - such as descriptive models and iconic models (Hand, 1998) - but they are still models, and this is true for both Bayesian and frequentist perspectives. The aim of data analysis, from the statistical viewpoint, is to summarise the data, describe it, or construct a mathematical structure which would lead to data of very similar form to that observed if it was used to generate new data. This mathematical structure is a model.

There are only a handful of exceptions in the statistical literature. One exception is the Gifi school of nonlinear multivariate analysis. In the preface to Gifi (1990), the authors say: 'In this book we adopt the point of view that, given some of the most common MVA [multivariate analysis] questions, it is possible to start either from the model or from the technique. .... classical multivariate statistical analysis starts from the model. In many cases, however, the choice of the model is not at all obvious, choice of a conventional model is impossible, and computing optimum procedures is not feasible. In order to do something reasonable in these cases we start from the other end, with a class of techniques designed to answer the MVA questions, and postpone the choice of model and of optimality criterion.' This is particularly interesting, since it conveys the idea that something other than the model, and in particular, the algorithm, could be the central focus of attention. This viewpoint is uncomfortable, even an anathema, to most statisticians. It certainly represents a different paradigm for data analysis.

However, this Gifi perspective is very much in tune with the computational viewpoint, which is clearly 'algorithm-centric'. Perhaps this is not surprising, given the central role that the computer plays in such forms of data analysis. Whereas statistics developed before the computer, and many modern statistical methods can be applied, if with some pain, by hand, the computational approaches required the computer from the start, and no-one would try to apply them by hand.

The emphasis on models or algorithms is very nicely demonstrated by the titles of the two leading books on recursive partitioning methods. The CART book by Breiman *et al* (1984) has the title *Classification and Regression Trees*. It is about 'trees' - that is, structures, shapes, or models. In contrast, the C4.5 book by Quinlan (1993) has the title *C4.5: Programs for machine learning*. It is about 'programs' - that is, recipes or algorithms.

5.2 Mathematics versus computing

There can be no doubt whatsoever that modern statistics is perceived to be a mathematical discipline. A glance in any modern statistical journal will demonstrate this and it is certainly true that it has mathematics at its roots (in a technical if not historical sense - see above). On the other hand, this does not really justify regarding statistics as a branch of mathematics: engineering, surveying, and other disciplines are also mathematical disciplines, but they are certainly not regarded as branches of mathematics.

Of course, not everyone thinks of statistics as mathematics. Some are aware of its other properties, and have drawn attention to the importance of an understanding of the application domains, of the impact of computer power on statistical ideas and methodology, and of the different objectives of statistics and mathematics. Thus, for example, George Box (1996) wrote 'this mathematical strait-jacket is of little use for scientific learning because it requires the investigator to provide a priori all the things he doesn't know.' John Nelder commented (Nelder, 1986) 'The main danger, I believe, in allowing the ethos of mathematics to gain too much influence in statistics is that statisticians will be tempted into types of abstraction that they believe will be thought respectable by mathematicians rather than pursuing ideas of value to statistics. One origin of this temptation is undoubtedly the siting of statisticians working in universities in departments of mathematics; the pressure on the statisticians to develop their researches in directions thought to be acceptable to mathematicians may then become too strong to be easily resisted. However, there is little doubt that it ought to be resisted, for the two disciplines have very different objectives.' Leo Breiman (Breiman, 1995) commented 'As a result of the would-be mathematicians in statistics, it has been dominated by useless theory and fads ... If statistics is an applied field and not a minor branch of mathematics, then more than 99% of the published papers are useless exercises. (The other colleagues in statistics I have spoken to say this is an exaggeration and peg the percentage at 95%. Either way it is significant.) The result is a down grading of sensibility and intelligence....But among all of the trash, there are a few places where theory has been useful.'

It is important to understand that I am not arguing that mathematics is bad. On the contrary, mathematics is undoubtedly good, for it brings rigour to one's thinking. On the other hand, it is also conducive to a cautious and risk averse approach to science. Thus one is encouraged not to publish one's algorithm until one can prove convergence, not to publish a proposed theorem until one can prove it, and so on.

In contrast to the above, the computational disciplines—machine learning, database technology, pattern recognition, and so on—have a more pragmatic, adventurous, even risk taking orientation. This means that they may well try to tackle a problem which the more mathematically oriented statisticians would be wary of attempting. This could mean they waste their time, but it could also mean that they solve a problem others had considered intractable. One important consequence is that the computational data analytic literature is full of algorithms with relatively little theoretical underpinning, and with little critical comparison. It is easy to invent an algorithm, but less easy to invent one which is *provably* good.

Further comments about the relationship between mathematics and statistics is given in Sprent (1998), Hand (1998b), Senn (1998), Bailey (1998), and in the discussion following those papers.

5.3   EDA and data mining

I noted above how central were notions of inference to classical statistics. These are embedded in tools for testing, for model building, and in model diagnostics, for example. Modern statistics, however, is broader than this. In particular, thanks in large part to the imagination of John Tukey (Tukey, 1977), the notion of *exploratory data analysis* (EDA) has gained legitimacy. EDA stresses the role of informal graphical procedures to gain insight into the structure of data. Much EDA work has been focused— in a classical statistical way—on relatively small data sets, even though computers were often necessary to produce the graphical displays. Some powerful and relatively easy to use statistical tools (such as Splus) owe at least some of their design philosophy to the ideas of EDA.

In contrast, the computational schools of data analysis have also developed graphical tools, but theirs have emphasised colour, dynamic interaction, and often the analysis of large data sets (as in data mining, for example). Indeed, sometimes these tools are not regarded as having any inheritance from statistics (some of the geographical ones, for example), and often the term *visualisation* is used to describe the process (though some statisticians think this more properly describes the intellectual effort of imagining the data structure underlying the graphical display).

5.4   The data

One of the earliest and most important books on classical multivariate statistics was that of Anderson (1958). It was largely concerned with multivariate normal data and it was not until twenty years later that Bishop, Fienberg, and Holland's (1978) book on discrete multivariate analysis— chiefly about loglinear models—appeared. This is but one illustration of the fact that statistics has had a narrow view of data. Other examples include the traditional emphasis on single data sets (look at most applied papers), on small data sets (look in most text books), on clean data sets, and the hesitancy to apply methods to data which are not a random sample (with justification, since such sampling mechanisms underlie the probabilistic theory of inference, but implying serious limitations for the scope of the methods, since so many data sets are not random samples).

In contrast, the computational disciplines, right from the start, have emphasised categorical data, logical as well as numerical analytic methods, algorithms which improve as more data accumulates, and real time analysis, so that estimation and induction is very much viewed as a *process* and not a one-off exercise. The process view is more in tune with a great many situations (e.g., business applications, where similar data sets are analysed day after day or month after month). Of course, I am aware that the Bayesian perspective is essentially an updating strategy, but even within this framework the commitment to process does not seem very widespread. The computational disciplines have also tended to ignore the fact that data are often contaminated or weak in other ways. It is no accident that the acronym GIGO—Garbage In, Garbage Out—was coined in a computational context.

6   New tools for data analysis

Researchers from the mathematical and computational sides of the divide are beginning to come together—though sociological and cultural pressures often work against this. For example, criticism of one camp by the other is not conducive to easy working relationships, and the media tend to favour terms such as 'expert systems' and 'neural networks' rather than conditional independence graphs or projection pursuit regression, even though these may be just as powerful. It is interesting that the new tools that have emerged in recent years have tended to come from one side or the other: hidden Markov models, generalised additive models, and MCMC have come from the statistical camp; rule based systems, and optimisation algorithms such as genetic algorithms and simulated annealing have come from the computational camp.

7   Conclusion

I opened this paper by arguing that modern statistics essentially began at around the beginning of the Twentieth Century. In view of the above, I would now like to argue further that it ended at around the end of the Twentieth Century. What we are currently witnessing is a broadening perspective on data analysis, involving a synthesis of ideas from different backgrounds. Two significantly distinct schools are involved here, the statistical and the computational, each with its own strengths and weaknesses. They have very significant overlap in their objectives, but with differences in emphasis. Inevitably, in situations like this, tensions arise. But a productive synergy can emerge from this. In the early 1990s I invited leading thinkers in the area of data analysis to contribute to a special issue of the journal *Statistics and Computing* on the future of data analysis. A fitting way to conclude this article is to quote from the contribution made by John Chambers (1993). He wrote: 'Greater statistics can be defined simply, if loosely, as everything related to learning from data, from the first planning or collection to the last presentation or report. Lesser statistics is the body of specifically statistical methodology that has evolved within the profession—roughly, statistics as defined by texts, journals, and doctoral dissertations. Greater statistics tends to be inclusive, eclectic with respect to methodology, closely associated with other disciplines, and practiced by many outside of academia and often outside of professional statistics. Lesser statistics tends to be exclusive, oriented to mathematical techniques, less frequently collaborative with other disciplines, and primarily practiced by members of university departments of statistics.'

References

BAILEY, R. A.(1998) Statistics and mathematics: the appropriate use of mathematics within statistics. *Journal of the Royal Statistical Society, Series D, The Statistician, 47, 261–271.*

BAUDRILLARD, J.(1987) Cool memories. Galilee, Paris.

BELLOC, H.(1940) The silence of the sea. Sheed and Wood, New York.

BOX, G.(1996) Scientific statistics, teaching, learning and the computer. In *Proc. Computational Statistics*, ed. A.Prat, Physica, Heidelberg, 3-10.

BREIMAN, L.(1995) Reflections after refereeing papers for NIPS. In *The Mathematics of Generalization*, ed. D.H.Wolpert, Addison-Wesley, Reading, Mass., 11-15.

BREIMAN, L., FREIDMAN, J. H., OLSHEN, R. A. AND STONE, C. (1984) Classification and regression trees. Wadsworth: Belmont, California.

CHAMBERS, J. M.(1993) Greater or lesser statistics: a choice for future research. *Statistics and Computing, 3, 182-184.*

GIFI, A.(1990) Nonlinear Multivariate Analysis. Chichester: Wiley.

HACKING, I.(1975) The Emergence of Probability. Cambridge University Press, Cambridge.

HAND, D. J.(1998) Data mining: statistics and more? *The American Statistician, 52, 112-118.*

HAND, D. J.(1998b) Breaking misconceptions—statistics and its relationship to mathematics. *Journal of the Royal Statistical Society, Series D, The Statistician, 47, 245-250.*

HILL, I. D.(1984) Statistical Society of London—Royal Statistical Society, the first 100 years: 1834-1934. *Journal of the Royal Statistical Society, Series A, 147, 130-139.*

KLEIN, H.A. (1974) The Science of Measurement. Dover: New York.

NELDER, J. A.(1986) Statistics, science, and technology. *Journal of the Royal Statistical Society, Series A, 144, 289-297.*

QUINLAN, J. R. (1993) C4.5: Programs for machine learning. Morgan Kaufmann: San Mateo, California.

SEATON, G. L.(1948) The statistician and modern management. *The American Statistician, 2, No. 6.*

SENN, S.(1998) Mathematics: governess or handmaiden? *Journal of the Royal Statistical Society, Series D, The Statistician, 47, 251-259.*

SPRENT, P.(1998) Statistics and mathematics–trouble at the interface? *Journal of the Royal Statistical Society, Series D, The Statistician, 47, 239-244.*

STEKEL, W.(1931) Marriage at the crossroads. W.Godwin, Inc., New York.

Two-mode Clustering with Genetic Algorithms

J. Hansohm

Lehrstuhl für Methodengestützte Planung,
Universität der Bundeswehr München, 85577 Neubiberg, Germany
Juergen.Hansohm@UniBw-Muenchen.de
http://www.UniBw-Muenchen.de/Campus/WOW/Hansohm.html

Abstract: In contrast to one-mode clustering, the objective of two-mode clustering is to cluster objects **and** variables of a datamatrix simultanously so that the elements of a cluster are more similar than elements of different clusters. Since the use of genetic algorithms was very successfull for one-mode clustering, one may assume that this will also be true for two-mode clustering problems. In the following paper a genetic algorithm is proposed which takes the special structure of two-mode clustering into account. This algorithm is moreover compared with the Alternating Exchanges (AE) algorithm proposed by Gaul and Schader (1996). The comparison is done by testdata as well as by real life data.

1 Introduction

The objective of one-mode partitioning is to cluster objects so that there is a high similarity between elements of the same cluster whereas elements of different clusters should have a high dissimilarity (Opitz (1980), S. 65). In contrast to this, it exists a relationship between objects and their variables in a two-mode partitioning problem. In a production problem for example, there is a relation between the variants of a good *(objects)* and the parts which are necessary to assemble these variants *(variables)* (v. Strauch (1979)).

In general, two-mode clustering problems are described by a matrix of the form

$$\mathbf{X}_{n \times m} = (x_{ij})_{n \times m} = \begin{pmatrix} x_{11} & \cdots & x_{1m} \\ \vdots & \ddots & \vdots \\ x_{n1} & \cdots & x_{nm} \end{pmatrix} \tag{1}$$

where x_{ij} describes the relationship between mode1 *(rows, objects)* and mode2 *(columns, variables)*.

This could be

- an **association** (x_{ij} is the value of object i at variable j) or

- a **confusion** (x_{ij} is the number of assignments of object i to attribute j) or

- a **fluctuation** (x_{ij} is interpreted as the number or the percentage of persons who preferred object i in the first time and later object j)

(Schwaiger (1999)).

As mentioned before, the objective of two-mode clustering problems is to cluster the rows and columns of **X** simultanously. For the production problem mentioned above, for example, one may cluster variants *(mode1)* in a way that they can be produced by preassembled parts *(cluster of mode2) (see below)*.

2 Description of the Problem and Notation

Starting from a two-mode data matrix $\mathbf{X}_{n \times m}$, the objective is to find a classification

$$\mathcal{K} = \{K_1, \ldots, K_k\} \subseteq \mathcal{P}(\{1, \ldots, n\})$$

and a classification

$$\mathcal{L} = \{L_1, \ldots, L_l\} \subseteq \mathcal{P}(\{1, \ldots, m\})$$

so that

$$b = \sum_{i=1}^{n} \sum_{j=1}^{m} (x_{ij} - \hat{x}_{ij})^2 \to min \qquad (2)$$

where $\hat{\mathbf{X}}_{n \times m} = (\hat{x}_{ij})_{n \times m} = \mathbf{PWQ}^{\mathbf{T}}$ with $\mathbf{P}_{n \times k}, \mathbf{W}_{k \times l}, \mathbf{Q}_{m \times l}$

Depending on the conditions on **P** and **Q**, one gets the formulation for partitioning or overlapping clustering, hard partitioning or fuzzy clustering (see Gaul, Schader (1996). Other models, especially hierarchical two-mode classification problems, are beyond the scope of this paper (see Schwaiger (1997, 1999) for more details).

3 Known Solution Methods

As mentioned before, Gaul, Schader (1996) proposed a *penalty algorithm* and a so-called *alternating exchange algorithm* (AE) to minimize (2). Baier et. al. (1997) use a successive alternating minimization of (2) with fixed **Q** and variable **P** and **W** and then with fixed **P** and variable **Q** und **W** to approach the minimum (2). Trejos, Castillo (2000) on the other hand uses the method of *simulated annealing* to minimize (2).

4 Genetic Algorithms

Originally introduced by Holland (1975), the genetic algorithms try to adapt the natural process of evolution and selection for optimization. These algorithms are stochastical search methods to find a global optimum of an objective function even in cases of local optima (Goldberg (1989), Michalewicz (1992)). In contrast to conventional search methods, genetic algorithms are working with a lot of points simultanously and compute the objective function - also called *fitness* in the terminology of the evolution - for all these points.

There are a lot of papers dealing with one-mode clustering using genetic algorithms (Krovi (1992); Tagami et al. (1993); Murthy, Chowdhury (1996); Tianzi, Song (1996); Hauke, Paul (1999); Hansohm (1999)). In most cases the method of genetic algorithm was compared with hierarcical clustering, exchange methods, TABU search, simulated annealing, etc. Some authors used genetic algorithms also for fuzzy cluster analysis (Srikanth et al. (1995); Nascimento et al. (1997)). The genetic algorithms outperformed in most cases the other methods or they were at least as good as the others, but the degree of superiority was depending on the kind of the objective function (Hansohm (1999)).

Obviously, in cases of two- or n-mode data one will use a genetic algorithm which has one chromosome for each mode. For the classifications $\mathcal{K}$ and $\mathcal{L}$ (see (2)) on a two-mode partitioning problem one would use two chromosomes α and β which are strings of the following form[1]:

$$\alpha = (\alpha_1, \ldots, \alpha_n) \text{ with } \alpha_i = j \Leftrightarrow i \in K_j$$

respectively

$$\beta = (\beta_1, \ldots, \beta_m) \text{ with } \beta_i = j \Leftrightarrow i \in L_j$$

Starting population, selection in the pool of the individuals, recombination, mutation and survival of the fittest may be used in an analogous way as for one-mode clustering with genetic algorithms. The fitness for a two-mode classification *(hard partition)* is derived from (2) by

$$b(\mathcal{K}, \mathcal{L}) = \sum_{i=1}^{n} \sum_{j=1}^{m} (x_{ij} - \sum_{r=1}^{k} \sum_{s=1}^{l} p_{ir} w_{rs} q_{js})^2 \tag{3}$$

where (see Gaul, Schader (1996))

$$p_{ir} = \begin{cases} 1 & \text{for } i \in K_r \\ 0 & \text{otherwise} \end{cases} \quad q_{js} = \begin{cases} 1 & \text{for } j \in L_s \\ 0 & \text{otherwise} \end{cases} \quad w_{rs} = \frac{\sum_{i=1}^{n} \sum_{j=1}^{m} p_{ir} x_{ij} q_{js}}{\mid K_r \mid \mid L_s \mid}$$

---

[1] about the questionability of this coding, which is used by all authors, see Hauke, Paul (1999) und Hansohm (1999).

Obviously, being a disadvantage of this approach, the two classifications $\mathcal{K}$ and $\mathcal{L}$, represented by their chromosomes, have no relationship between each other. A "good" classification $\mathcal{K}$ for the first mode should be "marriaged" with a "good" classification $\mathcal{L}$ of the second mode. In order to get this, the selection of two individuals depends on the value of $b(\mathcal{K}^u, \mathcal{L}^v)$, resp. $b(\mathcal{K}^v, \mathcal{L}^u)$ in comparison to $b(\mathcal{K}^u, \mathcal{L}^u)$, resp. $b(\mathcal{K}^v, \mathcal{L}^v)$ where u is represented by the two classifications $\mathcal{K}^u$, $\mathcal{L}^u$, v by $\mathcal{K}^v$, $\mathcal{L}^v$ and b is the objective function from (2).

4.1 Problems for Testing the Algorithms

In order to compare the genetic algorithm with the AE algorithm on a two-mode partitioning problem, ten test problems are used. These ten test problems are desribed by the following data matrices $\mathbf{X}_{100n \times 100n} = (x_{ij})_{100n \times 100n}$ where

$$x_{ij} = \begin{cases} 1 & \text{if } i - 10nk \in [1, 10n] \text{ and } j - 10nk \in [1, 10n] \text{ for a } k \in [0, 9] \\ 0 & \text{otherwise} \end{cases}$$

where $n = 1, \dots, 10$.

For the test problems the optimal solution is obviously the perfect classification $\{1, \dots, 10n\}, \{10n+1, \dots, 20n\}, \dots \{90n+1, \dots, 100n\}$ for mode1 and mode2. It was tested how the genetic algorithm and the exchange algorithm will recover this classification.

Because the objective function b from (2) is zero in its minimal point, the value of b, reached by an algorithm is a direct measure of the quality. For $n = 1$ *(that is a 100×100-matrix)* the genetic algorithm with a population of 50 classifications reached the optimal value of 0 after 100 iterations. The same was true for the exchange algorithm (AE) with a multistart[2] method after 100 iterations for each starting classification.

If n grows the difference between the AE algorithm and the genetic algorithm was marginal if both methods had no upper limits of iterations. If there was an upper limit on iterations, the genetic algorithm was sligthly better in most cases but the quality of the classifications decreased rapidly if n grows. For $n = 10$, corresponding to a 1000×1000 matrix, both methods were inadequate.

---

[2]50 starting classifications according to the number of the population of the genetic algorithm

4.2 Case Study - Continuous Data

In this case study - published by Schwaiger (1999) - the objects *(rows of the data matrix, mode1)* are brands of cars and their advertises, described by pairs of opposite attributes. The variables *(columns of the data matrix, mode2)* of this association got their values on a seven points rating scale[3].

The author used the method of hierarcical two-mode clustering (ESO-CLUS) to get a classification. With the elbow criteria he got four classes for each mode. *The variable M_{11} - not described detailled by the author - was assumed to build an own class.*

The classifications, found by the genetic algorithm, the exchange algorithm (AE) and with ESOCLUS *(see above)* have nearly the same values respective to the objective function b from (2) *(see table below)*

b	
22.051394	genetic algorithm with a population of 50 classifications
26.971738	AE with multistart method
29.159813	ESOCLUS

The crucial point is the fact that the classifications found by the different methods are nearly the same. Indeed, all classifications are identical in respect to mode2 *(variables)*. Concerning to mode1, the brands of cars and their advertises *(objects)*, there are of course minor differences but the interpretation of the classes together with the relation to the classes of mode2 is identical with the interpretation given by the author (see Schwaiger (1999)).

4.3 Real Life Study - Binary Data

This confusion problem consists of 95 objects described by 54 variables. The 95 objects are variants of a electric stove described by parts necessary to assemble the different variants of this electric stove. The 54 variables correspond to all possible individual parts with the binary value 1 if this single component is necessary for this variant and 0 if not. The objective is to cluster objects *(=variants)* **and** variables *(=individual parts)* so that it hints at preproduced assemblies in order to get more flexibility on production (see v. Strauch (1979)).

---

[3]to be correct, the data were originally on an ordinal scale but because the aggregated data matrix **X** consists of the mean values of the sample, the data were used as continuous data.

Obviously, minimizing (2) is equal to maximize

$$\sum_{r=1}^{k}\sum_{s=1}^{l}\hat{x}_{K_r L_s}^2 \to max \text{ where } \hat{x}_{K_r L_s} = \frac{\sum_{i \in K_r}\sum_{j \in L_s} x_{ij}}{\mid K_r \parallel L_s \mid} \qquad (4)$$

(see also (3))

The two-mode classification given by v. Strauch (1979) has a value of 1445.440073. The exchange algorithm, repeated with different starting classifications, reached as its highest value 1496.158102. The above described genetic algorithm with a population of 100 classifications leads to a value of 1498.303144 - which is nearly the same value. The classifications, computed by the different algorithms, are of course slightly different, but the interpretation of the classes are virtually the same.

5 Conclusions and Remarks

It can be stated that for two-mode partitioning problems the method of genetic algorithm is not superior as it is for one-mode clustering *(see above)*. One reason for this may be that the variance criteria is a smooth objective function. Small changes in a classification by an exchange algorithm will change the value of the objective function in most cases. For one-mode partitioning problems, the use of genetic algorithms leads to better results if the objective function is more "flat"[4] (see Hansohm (1999)).

References

BAIER, D., GAUL, W., SCHADER, M. (1997): Two-Mode Overlapping Clustering With Applications to Simultaneous Benefit Segmentation and Market Structuring. In: Klar, R., Opitz, O. (eds.): Classification and Knowledge Organization, Springer, Berlin, 557-566.

GAUL, W., SCHADER, M. (1996): A New Algorithm for Two-Mode Clustering. In: Bock, H., Polasek, W. (eds.): Data Analysis and Information Systems, Springer, Berlin, 15-23.

GOLDBERG, D. E. (1989): Genetic Algorithms in Search, Optimization and Machine Learning. Addison Wesley, Reading, MA.

HANSOHM, J. (1999): Clusteranalyse mit Genetischen Algorithmen. In: Gaul, W., Schader, M. (eds.): Mathematische Methoden der Wirtschaftswissenschaften, Physica, Heidelberg, 57-66.

HAUKE, W., PAUL, H. (1999): Evolutionäre Algorithmen zur Clusteranalyse. In: Gaul, W., Schader, M. (eds.): Mathematische Methoden der Wirtschaftswissenschaften, Physica, Heidelberg, 67-75.

---

[4]Roughly speaking, this means that the maximum function is in any way part of the objective function measuring the classification (see Opitz (1980)).

HOLLAND, J. H. (1975): Adaption in Natural and Artifical Systems. University of Michigan Press, Ann Arbor, USA.

KROVI, R. (1992): Genetic Algorithms for Clustering: A Preliminary Investigation. *Proceedings of the twenty-fifth Hawaii International Conference on System Sciences, 4, Information Systems, 540-544.*

MICHALEWICZ, Z. (1992): Genetic Algorithms + Data Structures = Evolution Program. Springer, Berlin.

MURTHY, C. A., CHOWDHURY, N. (1996): In Search of Optimal Clusters using Genetic Algorithms. *Pattern Regcognition Letters 17, 825-832.*

NASCIMENTO, S., MOURA-PIRES, F. (1997): A Genetic Approach to Fuzzy Clustering with a Validity Measure Fitness Function. In: Lin, X., Cohen, P., Berthold, M. (eds.): Advances in Intelligent Data Analysis, Springer, 325-335.

OPITZ, O. (1980): Numerische Taxonomie. UTB 918, Gustav Fischer, Stuttgart, NY.

SCHWAIGER, M. (1997): Multivariate Werbewirkungskontrolle, Konzepte zur Auswertung von Werbetests, Gabler, Wiesbaden.

SCHWAIGER, M. (1999): Zweimodale Klassifikationsverfahren: Top oder Flop? In: Gaul, W., Schader, M. (eds.): Mathematische Methoden der Wirtschaftswissenschaften, Physica, Heidelberg, 85-96.

SRIKANTH, R., GEORGE, R., WARSI, N., PRABHU, D., PETRY, F. E., BUCKLES, B. P. (1995): A Variable-length Genetic Algorithm for Clustering and Classification. *Pattern Recognition Letters 16, 789-800.*

VON STRAUCH, R. (1979): Variantenanalyse und ihre Anwendung in der Montage bei Serienfertigung. *Proceedings in Operations Research 8, Würzburg-Wien, Physica, 1979, 207f.*

TAGAMI, T., MIYAMOTO, S., MOGAMI, Y. (1993): Application of Genetic Algorithms to Cluster Analysis. *Proceedings of the 32nd SICE Annual Conference, International Session, Japan, 1115-1118.*

TIANZI, T., SONG DE MA (1996): Cluster Analysis using Genetic Algorithms. *3rd International Conference on Signal Processing Proceedings, 2, USA, 1277-1279.*

TREJOS, J., CASTILLO, W. (2000): Simulated Annealing Optimization for Two-Mode Partitioning. In: Decker, R. (eds.): Classifikation and Information Processing at the Turn of the Millennium, Springer, Berlin,.

Exact Tests for the Comparison of Binary Data Structures in Time

J. Krauth

Department of Psychology,
University of Düsseldorf, D–40225 Düsseldorf, Germany

Abstract: The occurrence/non-occurrence of an event is being observed at equidistant points of time. This yields a sequence of binary variables which are assumed to form a stationary time series. A second stationary binary sequence is observed independently of the first one. Four exact tests are proposed for the comparison of the two sequences. The four tests differ with respect to the parameters which are compared and the assumed dependence structure. Similar problems were considered by Sim and Johnson (1998) for dichotomous spatial data. However, due to the complexity of the spatial models only Markov chain Monte Carlo approximations were considered by these authors. We illustrate our exact tests by comparing the structure of two epidemiological data sets.

1 Introduction

Assume m equidistant points of time. At each point of time (i) a certain event (A_i) occurs with probability $P(A_i)$ or does not occur with probability $(1 - P(A_i))$ for $1 \leq i \leq m$. This yields a sequence of m binary variables $X_1, \ldots, X_m$, where $X_i = 1$ if A_i occurs and $X_i = 0$ otherwise for $1 \leq i \leq m$. The joint distribution of $X_1, \ldots, X_m$ can be written as

$$
\begin{aligned}
&P(X_1 = x_1, \ldots, X_m = x_m) \\
&= P(X_1 = x_1) \prod_{i=2}^{m} P(X_i = x_i \mid X_{i-1} = x_{i-1}, \ldots, X_1 = x_1).
\end{aligned}
$$

If $X_1, \ldots, X_m$ are independent this yields

$$
\begin{aligned}
P(X_1 = x_1, \ldots, X_m = x_m) &= \prod_{i=1}^{m} P(X_i = x_i) \\
&= \prod_{i=1}^{m} P(X_i = 1)^{x_i} P(X_i = 0)^{1-x_i} = \exp \left\{ \alpha^{(0)} + \sum_{i=1}^{m} \beta_i^{(0)} x_i \right\},
\end{aligned}
$$

where

$$
\alpha^{(0)} = \sum_{i=1}^{m} \ln P(X_i = 0), \quad \beta_i^{(0)} = \ln \frac{P(X_i = 1)}{P(X_i = 0)} \text{ for } 1 \leq i \leq m.
$$

If a first–order dependence is assumed, i.e. if

$$P(X_i = x_i \mid X_{i-1} = x_{i-1}, \ldots, X_1 = x_1)$$
$$= \quad P(X_i = x_i \mid X_{i-1} = x_{i-1}) \qquad \text{for } 2 \le i \le m$$

for an arbitrary choice of $(x_1, \ldots, x_m)$, the joint distribution of $X_1, \ldots, X_m$ can be written in the following form

$$P(X_1 = x_1, \ldots, X_m = x_m) = \exp \left\{ \alpha^{(1)} + \sum_{i=1}^{m} \beta_i^{(1)} x_i + \sum_{i=1}^{m-1} \beta_{i,i+1}^{(1)} x_i x_{i+1} \right\},$$

where

$$\alpha^{(1)} = \ln P(X_1 = 0) + \sum_{i=1}^{m-1} \ln \frac{P(X_i = 0, X_{i+1} = 0)}{P(X_i = 0)},$$

$$\beta_1^{(1)} = \ln \frac{P(X_1 = 1, X_2 = 0)}{P(X_1 = 0, X_2 = 0)},$$

$$\beta_i^{(1)} = \ln \frac{P(X_{i-1} = 0, X_i = 1)P(X_i = 1, X_{i+1} = 0)P(X_i = 0)}{P(X_{i-1} = 0, X_i = 0)P(X_i = 0, X_{i+1} = 0)P(X_i = 1)}$$
$$\text{for } 2 \le i \le m - 1,$$

$$\beta_m^{(1)} = \ln \frac{P(X_{m-1} = 0, X_m = 1)}{P(X_{m-1} = 0, X_m = 0)},$$

$$\beta_{i,i+1}^{(1)} = \ln \frac{P(X_i = 1, X_{i+1} = 1)P(X_i = 0, X_{i+1} = 0)}{P(X_i = 0, X_{i+1} = 1)P(X_i = 1, X_{i+1} = 0)}$$
$$\text{for } 1 \le i \le m - 1.$$

This kind of reparametrization was called auto–logistic model by Besag (1972, 1974) or first–order auto–logistic model by Sim and Johnson (1998).

If a second–order dependence is assumed, i.e. if

$$P(X_i = x_i \mid X_{i-1} = x_{i-1}, \ldots, X_1 = x_1)$$
$$= \quad P(X_i = x_i \mid X_{i-1} = x_{i-1}, X_{i-2} = x_{i-2}) \qquad \text{for } 3 \le i \le m,$$

the joint distribution of $X_1, \ldots, X_m$ can be written in the following form

$$P(X_1 = x_1, \ldots, X_m = x_m)$$
$$= \quad \exp \left\{ \alpha^{(2)} + \sum_{i=1}^{m} \beta_i^{(2)} x_i + \sum_{i=1}^{m-1} \beta_{i,i+1}^{(2)} x_i x_{i+1} + \sum_{i=1}^{m-2} \beta_{i,i+1,i+2}^{(2)} x_i x_{i+1} x_{i+2} \right\},$$

where the parameters $\alpha^{(2)}$, $\beta_i^{(2)}$, $\beta_{i,i+1}^{(2)}$, and $\beta_{i,i+1,i+2}^{(2)}$ have to be defined in an appropriate way. It is obvious (Besag (1974)) that the reparametrization of the joint distribution of $X_1, \ldots, X_m$ can be written analogously for an arbitrary dependence structure.

Sim and Johnson (1998) considered two independent samples $(X_1, \ldots, X_m)$ and $(Y_1, \ldots, Y_n)$ from first–order auto–logistic models which were observed on equilateral two–dimensional sample grids. They considerably reduced the number of unknown parameters using the joint distributions

$$P(X_1 = x_1, \ldots, X_m = x_m) = \exp\left\{ \alpha_x^{(2)} + \beta_x^{(2)} \sum_{i=1}^{m} x_i + \gamma_x^{(2)} \sum_{i=1}^{m-1} x_i x_{i+1} \right\},$$

$$P(Y_1 = y_1, \ldots, Y_n = y_n) = \exp\left\{ \alpha_y^{(2)} + \beta_y^{(2)} \sum_{i=1}^{n} y_i + \gamma_y^{(2)} \sum_{i=1}^{n-1} y_i y_{i+1} \right\}.$$

These authors studied the test problem

H_0: $\beta_x^{(2)} = \beta_y^{(2)}$ versus H_1: $\beta_y^{(2)} > \beta_x^{(2)}$

under the constraint $\gamma_x^{(2)} = \gamma_y^{(2)}$ and the test problem

H_0: $\gamma_x^{(2)} = \gamma_y^{(2)}$ versus H_1: $\gamma_x^{(2)} \neq \gamma_y^{(2)}$.

By means of Theorem 3 in Lehmann (1986, p. 147) they derived UMPU (uniformly most powerful unbiased) tests as the joint distribution of the samples $(X_1, \ldots, X_m)$, $(Y_1, \ldots, Y_n)$ is a member of a multiparameter exponential family.

The authors observe for both test problems "that the evaluation of the exact test can be computationally excessive" and "that a standard Monte Carlo test is not easily implemented". Therefore, they use Markov chain Monte Carlo tests for both problems.

Since it is certainly true that it is difficult to express the conditional distributions in a compact functional form if we consider grids of two or more dimensions, we consider here a one–dimensional equilateral grid. We were able to derive the conditional distributions in this case in an explicit form in four different situations. The corresponding exact tests are applied to two data sets from epidemiology.

2 Exact tests for comparing univariate data structures

Consider a sample of m binary variables $(X_1, \ldots, X_m)$ with the joint distribution

$$P(X_1 = x_1, \ldots, X_m = x_m) = \exp\left\{ \alpha_x^{(k)} + \sum_{j=0}^{k} \beta_{xj}^{(k)} u_j \right\},$$

where

$$u_j = \sum_{i=1}^{m-j} \prod_{s=i}^{i+j} x_s \qquad \text{for } 0 \le j \le k$$

and an independent sample $(Y_1, \ldots, Y_n)$ of n binary variables with the joint distribution

$$P(Y_1 = y_1, \ldots, Y_n = y_n) = \exp\left\{ \alpha_y^{(l)} + \sum_{j=0}^{l} \beta_{yj}^{(l)} v_j \right\},$$

where

$$v_j = \sum_{i=1}^{n-j} \prod_{s=i}^{i+j} y_s \qquad \text{for } 0 \le j \le l.$$

Here, the fixed numbers $k \in \{0, 1, \ldots, m-1\}$ and $l \in \{0, 1, \ldots, n-1\}$ describe the degree of dependence within the X and Y samples.

The joint distribution of $(X_1, \ldots, X_m, Y_1, \ldots, Y_n)$ is given by

$$P(X_1 = x_1, \ldots, X_m = x_m, Y_1 = y_1, \ldots, Y_n = y_n)$$
$$= \exp\left\{ \alpha_x^{(k)} + \alpha_y^{(l)} + \sum_{j=0}^{k} \beta_{xj}^{(k)} u_j + \sum_{j=0}^{l} \beta_{yj}^{(l)} v_j \right\}.$$

First, we consider the test problem
$$\text{H}_0^{(1)}: \beta_{x0}^{(k)} \ge \beta_{y0}^{(l)} \text{ versus } \text{H}_1^{(1)}: \beta_{x0}^{(k)} < \beta_{y0}^{(l)}.$$

Here, we admit an arbitrary dependence structure which may be different for both samples and we compare the parameters associated with U_0 and V_0.

Because of

$$P(X_1 = x_1, \ldots, X_m = x_m, Y_1 = y_1, \ldots, Y_n = y_n)$$
$$= \exp\left\{ \alpha_x^{(k)} + \alpha_y^{(l)} + \left(\beta_{y0}^{(l)} - \beta_{x0}^{(k)}\right) v_0 + \beta_{x0}^{(k)}(u_0 + v_0) + \sum_{j=1}^{k} \beta_{xj}^{(k)} u_j + \sum_{j=1}^{l} \beta_{yj}^{(l)} v_j \right\}$$

a UMPU test is based on the conditional distribution of V_0 for fixed values of $w_0 = u_0 + v_0$, $u_1, \ldots, u_k$, $v_1, \ldots, v_l$. This distribution can be computed, if the following quantities have been determined:

$v_0, w_0 = u_0 + v_0, u_1, v_1,$

$b_x = $ length of the longest 1–run in $(x_1, \ldots, x_m)$,

$b_y = $ length of the longest 1–run in $(y_1, \ldots, y_n)$,

m_i = number of 1–runs of length i in $(x_1, \ldots, x_m)$ for $1 \le i \le b_x$,
$m_1 = 0$ for $b_x = 0$,

n_i = number of 1–runs of length i in $(y_1, \ldots, y_n)$ for $1 \le i \le b_y$,
$n_1 = 0$ for $b_y = 0$.

Next, we compute

$$v_{\min}^{(1)} = v_0 - n_1 + \max \left\{ n_1 - \left\lfloor \frac{m - 2w_0 + 2v_0 + 1 + u_1}{2} \right\rfloor, 0 \right\},$$

$$v_{\max}^{(1)} = v_0 + \min \left\{ \left\lfloor \frac{n - 2v_0 + 1 + v_1}{2} \right\rfloor, m_1 \right\},$$

and

$$a_i^{(1)} = \binom{n - i + 1}{n - 2i + 1 + v_1} \binom{m - w_0 + i + 1}{m - 2w_0 + 2i + 1 + u_1} \times$$

$$\frac{\left(i - \sum_{j=2}^{b_y}(j-1)n_j \right)!}{\left(i - \sum_{j=2}^{b_y} jn_j \right)! \prod_{j=2}^{b_y}(n_j!)} \frac{\left(w_0 - i - \sum_{j=2}^{b_x}(j-1)m_j \right)!}{\left(w_0 - i - \sum_{j=2}^{b_x} jm_j \right)! \prod_{j=2}^{b_x}(m_j!)}$$

for $v_{\min}^{(1)} \le i \le v_{\max}^{(1)}$. Then the upper P–value of the exact test for $H_0^{(1)}$ versus $H_1^{(1)}$ is given by

$$P_1$$
$$= P(V_0 \ge v_0 \mid W_0 = w_0, U_1 = u_1, \ldots, U_k = u_k, V_1 = v_1, \ldots, V_l = v_l)$$
$$= \sum_{i=v_0}^{v_{\max}^{(1)}} a_i^{(1)} / \sum_{j=v_{\min}^{(1)}}^{v_{\max}^{(1)}} a_j^{(1)}.$$

In the application of this test it is not necessary to know the orders of dependence k and l. We have a significant result for $P_1 \le \alpha$, where α is the given significance level.

Second, we consider the test problem

$$H_0^{(2)} : \beta_{x0}^{(1)} \ge \beta_{y0}^{(1)} \quad \text{versus} \quad H_1^{(2)} : \beta_{x0}^{(1)} < \beta_{y0}^{(1)}.$$

Here, in contrast to the first test problem, only a first–order dependence is allowed, i.e. we assume $k = l = 1$. A UMPU test is based on the conditional distribution of V_0 for fixed values of $w_0 = u_0 + v_0, u_1$, and v_1 as can be concluded from

$$P(X_1 = x_1, \ldots, X_m = x_m, Y_1 = y_1, \ldots, Y_n = y_n)$$
$$= \exp \left\{ \alpha_x^{(1)} + \alpha_y^{(1)} + \left(\beta_{y0}^{(1)} - \beta_{x0}^{(1)} \right) v_0 + \beta_{x0}^{(1)} (u_0 + v_0) + \beta_{x1}^{(1)} u_1 + \beta_{y1}^{(1)} v_1 \right\}.$$

We compute

$$
\begin{aligned}
d_x &= u_1 + 1 \text{ for } u_1 \geq 1, \quad d_x = 0 \text{ for } u_1 = 0, \\
d_y &= v_1 + 1 \text{ for } v_1 \geq 1, \quad d_y = 0 \text{ for } v_1 = 0, \\
v_{\min}^{(2)} &= d_y + \max\left\{ v_0 - d_y - \left\lfloor \frac{m + u_1 - 2w_0 + 2v_0 + 1}{2} \right\rfloor, 0 \right\}, \\
v_{\max}^{(2)} &= v_0 + \min\left\{ \left\lfloor \frac{n + v_1 - 2v_0 + 1}{2} \right\rfloor, w_0 - v_0 - d_x \right\}, \\
f_{iy}^{(2)} &= \binom{i-1}{v_1} \text{ for } i \geq 1 \text{ and } v_{\min}^{(2)} \leq i \leq v_{\max}^{(2)}, f_{0y}^{(2)} = 1, \\
f_{ix}^{(2)} &= \binom{w_0 - i - 1}{u_1} \text{ for } i \leq w_0 - 1 \text{ and } v_{\min}^{(2)} \leq i \leq v_{\max}^{(2)}, f_{w_0 x}^{(2)} = 1, \\
a_i^{(2)} &= \binom{n-i+1}{n-2i+1+v_1}\binom{m-w_0+i+1}{m-2w_0+2i+1+u_1} f_{iy}^{(2)} f_{ix}^{(2)}
\end{aligned}
$$

for $v_{\min}^{(2)} \leq i \leq v_{\max}^{(2)}$. Then, the upper P–value of the exact test for $\mathrm{H}_0^{(2)}$ versus $\mathrm{H}_1^{(2)}$ is given by

$$
P_2 = P\left(V_0 \geq v_0 \mid W_0 = w_0, U_1 = u_1, V_1 = v_1\right) = \sum_{i=v_0}^{v_{\max}^{(2)}} a_i^{(2)} \Bigg/ \sum_{j=v_{\min}^{(2)}}^{v_{\max}^{(2)}} a_j^{(2)}.
$$

We have a significant result for $P_2 \leq \alpha$, where α is the given significance level.

Third, we consider the test problem

$$
\mathrm{H}_0^{(3)}: \beta_{x0}^{(1)} \geq \beta_{y0}^{(1)} \text{ versus } \mathrm{H}_1^{(3)}: \beta_{x0}^{(1)} < \beta_{y0}^{(1)}
$$

under the constraint $\beta_{x1}^{(1)} = \beta_{y1}^{(1)} =: \beta_1^{(1)}$.

Here, as in the second test problem, only a first–order dependence with $k = l = 1$ is allowed, but in addition the parameters $(\beta_{x1}^{(1)}, \beta_{y1}^{(1)})$ associated with U_1 and V_1 are assumed to be identical. This test problem corresponds to the first test problem considered by Sim and Johnson (1998). Contrary to these authors we consider a simpler one–dimensional grid and not a two–dimensional grid. Because of

$$
\begin{aligned}
&P(X_1 = x_1, \ldots, X_m = x_m, Y_1 = y_1, \ldots, Y_n = y_n) \\
&= \exp\left\{ \alpha_x^{(1)} + \alpha_y^{(1)} + \beta_{x0}^{(1)} u_0 + \beta_{y0}^{(1)} v_0 + \beta_1^{(1)}(u_1 + v_1) \right\} \\
&= \exp\left\{ \alpha_x^{(1)} + \alpha_y^{(1)} + \left(\beta_{y0}^{(1)} - \beta_{x0}^{(1)}\right) v_0 + \beta_{x0}^{(1)}(u_0 + v_0) + \beta_1^{(1)}(u_1 + v_1) \right\}
\end{aligned}
$$

a UMPU test is based on the conditional distribution of V_0 for fixed values of $w_0 = u_0 + v_0$ and $w_1 = u_1 + v_1$.

We compute

$$v_{\min}^{(3)}$$
$$= w_0 - \left\{ \min\{w_1 + 1, m\} + \min\left\{ \max\left\{ \left\lfloor \frac{m - w_1 - 1}{2} \right\rfloor, 0 \right\}, w_0 - w_1 - 1 \right\} \right\},$$

$$v_{\max}^{(3)} = \min\{w_1 + 1, n\} + \min\left\{ \max\left\{ \left\lfloor \frac{n - w_1 - 1}{2} \right\rfloor, 0 \right\}, w_0 - w_1 - 1 \right\}$$

$$k_{i,\min} = \max\{0, w_0 - 2 - w_1 - \min\{m - w_0 + i, w_0 - i - 1\}\}$$

for $v_{\min}^{(3)} \leq i \leq v_{\max}^{(3)}$ and $1 \leq i \leq w_0$,

$$k_{i,\max} = \min\{w_0 - 2 - w_1, \min\{n - i, i - 1\}\}$$

for $v_{\min}^{(3)} \leq i \leq v_{\max}^{(3)}$ and $1 \leq i \leq w_0$,

$$k_{0,\min} = k_{0,\max} = -1$$
$$f_{i,k_i,y} = \binom{i-1}{k_i} \qquad \text{for } i \geq 1, \, f_{0,k_0,y} = 1$$
$$f_{i,k_i,x} = \binom{w_0 - i - 1}{w_0 - 2 - k_i - w_1} \qquad \text{for } i \leq w_0 - 1, \, f_{w_0,k_{w_0},x} = 1$$
$$a_{i,k_i} = \binom{n - i + 1}{n - i - k_i}\binom{m - w_0 + 1 + i}{m - 2w_0 + i + 2 + k_i + w_1} f_{i,k_i,y} f_{i,k_i,x}$$

for $v_{\min}^{(3)} \leq i \leq v_{\max}^{(3)}$, $k_{i,\min} \leq k_i \leq k_{i,\max}$,

$$a_i^{(3)} = \sum_{k_i = k_{i,\min}}^{k_{i,\max}} a_{i,k_i} \qquad \text{for } v_{\min}^{(3)} \leq i \leq v_{\max}^{(3)}.$$

The upper P–value of the exact test for $H_0^{(3)}$ versus $H_1^{(3)}$ is given by

$$P_3 = P\left(V_0 \geq v_0 \mid W_0 = w_0, W_1 = w_1\right) = \sum_{i=v_0}^{v_{\max}^{(3)}} a_i^{(3)} \Big/ \sum_{j=v_{\min}^{(3)}}^{v_{\max}^{(3)}} a_j^{(3)}.$$

We have a significant result for $P_3 \leq \alpha$, where α is the given significance level.

Last, we consider the test problem

$H_0^{(4)} : \beta_{x1}^{(1)} \geq \beta_{y1}^{(1)}$ versus $H_1^{(4)} : \beta_{x1}^{(1)} < \beta_{y1}^{(1)}$.

Here, as in the second and third test problem, only a first–order dependence is allowed. However, not the parameters associated with U_0 and V_0 but those associated with U_1 and V_1 are being compared. This test problem corresponds to the second test problem considered by Sim and Johnson (1998). Again, contrary to these authors we consider only a one–dimensional grid. Because of

$$P(X_1 = x_1, \ldots, X_m = x_m, Y_1 = y_1, \ldots, Y_n = y_n)$$
$$= \exp\left\{ \alpha_x^{(1)} + \alpha_y^{(1)} + \beta_{x0}^{(1)} u_0 + \beta_{y0}^{(1)} v_0 + \left(\beta_{y1}^{(1)} - \beta_{x1}^{(1)} \right) v_1 + \beta_{x1}^{(1)} (u_1 + v_1) \right\}$$

a UMPU test is based on the conditional distribution of V_1 for fixed values of $u_0, v_0,$ and $w_1 = u_1 + v_1$.

We compute

$$v_{\min}^{(4)} = \max\left\{ w_1 - \min\left\{ u_0 - 1, w_1 \right\}, \max\left\{ 0, 2v_0 - n - 1 \right\} \right\}$$

for $u_0 \geq 1, v_{\min}^{(4)} = v_1$ for $u_0 = 0,$

$$v_{\max}^{(4)} = \min\left\{ \min\left\{ v_0 - 1, w_1 \right\}, w_1 - \max\left\{ 0, 2u_0 - m - 1 \right\} \right\}$$

for $v_0 \geq 1, v_{\max}^{(4)} = 0$ for $v_0 = 0,$

$$f_{iy}^{(4)} = \binom{v_0 - 1}{i} \text{ for } v_0 \geq 1, \ f_{iy}^{(4)} = 1 \text{ for } v_0 = 0, \text{ for } v_{\min}^{(4)} \leq i \leq v_{\max}^{(4)}$$

$$f_{ix}^{(4)} = \binom{u_0 - 1}{w_1 - i} \text{ for } u_0 \geq 1, f_{ix}^{(4)} = 1 \text{ for } u_0 = 0, \text{ for } v_{\min}^{(4)} \leq i \leq v_{\max}^{(4)},$$

$$a_i^{(4)} = \binom{n - v_0 + 1}{n - 2v_0 + 1 + i} \binom{m - u_0 + 1}{m - 2u_0 + 1 + w_1 - i} f_{iy}^{(4)} f_{ix}^{(4)}$$

for $v_{\min}^{(4)} \leq i \leq v_{\max}^{(4)}$.

The upper P–value of the exact test for $H_0^{(4)}$ versus $H_1^{(4)}$ is given by

$$P_4 = P\left(V_1 \geq v_1 \mid U_0 = u_0, V_0 = v_0, W_1 = w_1 \right) = \sum_{i=v_1}^{v_{\max}^{(4)}} a_i \bigg/ \sum_{j=v_{\min}^{(4)}}^{v_{\max}^{(4)}} a_j.$$

We have a significant result for $P_4 \leq \alpha$, where α is the given significance level.

The proofs for the four results given above are based on elementary combinatorics. In all four cases the conditional distribution of a statistic V

is to be derived under the condition (say C) that certain other statistics have given values. In a first step we determine the range of possible values of V given the condition C. This range is defined by the two bounds $v_{\min}$ and $v_{\max}$. Next, for each possible value (i) of V we derive the number (a_i) of those ($m + n$)–dimensional vectors with components 0 and 1 for which $V = i$ and condition C hold at the same time. From this, the conditional probability

$$P(V = i \mid C) = a_i / \sum_{j=v_{\min}}^{v_{\max}} a_j$$

can be computed.

3   Interpretation of test results

In contrast to Sim and Johnson (1998) we see some problems with respect to the interpretation of test results. First, the assumption of stationarity of the binary sequences is not very realistic in many applications, where clusters in time are expected. If we have, e.g., a cluster of events in the first sequence at the beginning of the time period and in the second sequence at the end of the time period, none of the four tests will detect this difference in the data structure if the two clusters are similar in their structure. However, if we have only one cluster in one sequence and two or more clusters in the other sequence this might be detected by the tests.

A second problem is the reduction of the number of unknown parameters made by Sim and Johnson (1998) and also by us. In our presentation of the first–order auto–logistic model we observe that the definition of the two parameters $\beta_1^{(1)}$ and $\beta_m^{(1)}$ differs considerably from that of $\beta_i^{(1)}$ for $2 \le i \le m - 1$. Similar effects occur for second–order dependence structures and for dependence structures of an even higher order. From this one can conclude that the present formulation of the model does not only require stationary sequences but also that the orders of dependence should be small in comparison with the lengths of the two sequences.

However, the most problematical issue seems to be the interpretation of significant results for the single tests in terms of the original parameters. In our first three tests we considered the same parameters (associated with U_0 and V_0) as Sim and Johnson (1998) in their first test. If independence of the observations is assumed, a significant result means that $\beta_{x0}^{(0)} < \beta_{y0}^{(0)}$ holds and this is equivalent with $P(X = 1) < P(Y = 1)$, i.e. the probability of the occurrence of an event is smaller in the first sequence. This follows immediately from the relation

$$\beta_{x0}^{(0)} = \ln\{P(X = 1)/P(X = 0)\}$$

given in the introduction.

If first–order dependence is allowed, we can conclude from the expressions for $\beta_i^{(1)}$ for $1 \leq i \leq m$ given in the introduction that such a straight-forward interpretation is no longer possible if we try to transform the relation $\beta_{x0}^{(k)} < \beta_{y0}^{(l)}$ into the corresponding relation for $P(X = 1)$ and $P(Y = 1)$, even if we assume $k = l = 1$.

In our fourth test we considered the same parameters (associated with U_1 and V_1) as Sim and Johnson (1998) in their second test. A significant result means that $\beta_{x1}^{(1)} < \beta_{y1}^{(1)}$ holds. From the introduction we can see from the formulas for $\beta_i^{(1)}$ (for $1 \leq i \leq m$) and $\beta_{i,i+1}^{(1)}$ (for $1 \leq i \leq m - 1$) that the interpretation of the result with respect to the original parameters is difficult.

4   Application

The data of our example consist of two data sets which were first published by Knox (1959) and reanalyzed by Weinstock (1981) and Krauth (1998, 1999). The data are given in all three references. The first data set gives the exact dates (dates of birth) of the occurrence of congenital oesophageal atresia or tracheo-oesophageal fistula observed in a hospital in Birmingham, U. K., between 1 January 1950 and 31 December 1955. Altogether thirty–five cases were observed on thirty–five different days, i.e. the assumption of binary variables seems justified on a daily basis. This data set was also reported and analyzed by Nagarwalla (1996).

The second data set gives the exact dates (dates of birth) of the occurrence of congenital oesophageal atresia or tracheo-oesophageal fistula observed in several hospitals in Newcastle, U. K., between 1 January 1950 and 31 December 1958. Altogether sixty–three cases were observed at sixty–three different days. Again, on a daily base binary variables can be assumed.

In the articles mentioned above one tried to detect clusters or change–points in time separately for the two data sets. Here, we intend to test for differences between the two data sets.

On a daily basis we have for the first data set:

$m = 2191$ days, $u_0 = 35$ cases, $u_1 = 1$ pair of cases on two successive days, $m_1 = 33$ cases on isolated days, $m_2 = 1$ isolated pair of successive days where cases occurred on each day.

For the second data set we find:

$n = 3287$ days, $v_0 = 63$ cases, $v_1 = 3$ pairs of cases on two successive days, $n_1 = 57$ cases on isolated days, $n_2 = 3$ isolated pairs of successive days where cases occurred on each day.

For the four exact tests we get

$$P_1 = .290, \quad P_2 = .287, \quad P_3 = .227, \quad P_4 = .627.$$

Because the lengths of the time periods differ for the two data sets by three years, we performed a second evaluation, where we did not consider the years 1956–1958 in the second data set. Thus, we considered the same time period at two different locations. For the Newcastle data this resulted in the modified frequencies

$n^\star = 2191$ days, $v_0^\star = 33$ cases, $v_1^\star = 1$ pair of cases on two successive days, $n_1^\star = 31$ cases on isolated days, $n_2^\star = 1$ isolated pair of successive days where cases occurred on each day.

Comparing the first data set with the modified second data set, we find

$$P_1 = .649, \quad P_2 = .649, \quad P_3 = .641, \quad P_4 = .727.$$

In most applications it is not realistic to assume that only one event is observed for each time unit. If the total numbers of events had been higher in the data sets above, the probability that two or more events occur at the same day would have been increased. In addition, usually many epidemiological data are reported not on a daily basis but on a monthly or even yearly basis, where more than one case is recorded at many time units.

To simulate these more realistic situations we consider not a time unit of one day but of one week using the data sets above. As a consequence we observe now time units with more than one event, i.e. we no longer have binary variables and our tests cannot be used. One way to overcome this difficulty is to define a threshold and to set for a particular time unit a binary variable to 1 if a frequency larger than the threshold is observed and to 0 otherwise. This proceeding was also used by Sim and Johnson (1998) in their snowfall example. We consider the threshold .5, i.e. for one or more events in a week the binary variable is set to 1, in case of no event to 0.

For the first data set this yields:

$m = 313$ weeks, $u_0 = 30$ weeks with events, $u_1 = 7$ situations with events in two successive weeks, $m_1 = 18$ isolated weeks with events, $m_2 = 3$ isolated pairs of successive weeks with events in both weeks, $m_3 = 2$ isolated triples of successive weeks with events in all three weeks.

For the second data set we find:

$n = 469$ weeks, $v_0 = 54$ weeks with events, $v_1 = 6$ situations with events in two successive weeks, $n_1 = 42$ isolated weeks with events, $n_2 = 6$ isolated pairs of successive weeks with events in both weeks.

For these aggregated data our tests yield:

$$P_1 = .056, \quad P_2 = .040, \quad P_3 = .245, \quad P_4 = .989.$$

Again, if we consider the same time periods for both locations, we have for the reduced second data set

$n^* = 313$ weeks, $v_0^* = 29$ weeks with events, $v_1^* = 4$ situations with events in two successive weeks, $n_1^* = 21$ isolated weeks with events, $n_2^* = 4$ isolated pairs of successive weeks with events in both weeks.

The comparison of this reduced data set with the first data set yields

$$P_1 = .387, \quad P_2 = .330, \quad P_3 = .597, \quad P_4 = .912.$$

The data structures do not seem to be different, if comparable time periods are being considered.

References

BESAG, J. E. (1972): Nearest–neighbour Systems and the Auto–logistic Model for Binary Data. *Journal of the Royal Statistical Society, Series B, 34, 75–83.*

BESAG, J. (1974): Spatial Interaction and the Statistical Analysis of Lattice Systems (with Discussion). *Journal of the Royal Statistical Society, Series B, 36, 192–236.*

KNOX, G. (1959): Secular Patterns of Congenital Oesophageal Atresia. *British Journal of Preventive Social Medicine, 13, 222–226.*

KRAUTH, J. (1998): Upper Bounds for the P–values of a Scan Statistic with a Variable Window. In: I. Balderjahn, R. Mathar, and M. Schader (eds.): *Classification, Data Analysis, and Data Highways.* Springer, Berlin, Heidelberg, New York, 155–163.

KRAUTH, J. (1999): Discrete Scan Statistics for Detecting Change-points in Binomial Sequences. In: W. Gaul, and H. Locarek-Junge (eds.): *Classification in the Information Age.* Springer, Berlin, Heidelberg, New York, 196–204.

LEHMANN, E. L. (1986): *Testing Statistical Hypotheses.* Second Edition. John Wiley & Sons, New York, Chichester, Brisbane, Toronto, Singapore.

NAGARWALLA, N. (1996): A Scan Statistic with a Variable Window. *Statistics in Medicine, 15, 845–850.*

SIM, S. and JOHNSON, R. A. (1998): Comparisons of Spatially Correlated Binary Data. *Statistics & Probability Letters, 39, 81–87.*

WEINSTOCK, M. A. (1981): A Generalized Scan Statistic Test for the Detection of Clusters. *International Journal of Epidemiology, 10, 289–293.*

Connected Maximum Split Clustering of Ladder Graphs

I. Lari

Dipartimento di Statistica, Probabilità e Statistiche Applicate, Università di Roma "La Sapienza," Piazzale Aldo Moro 5, I-00185 Roma, Italy.

Abstract: The clustering problem with relational constraints can be formulated as an optimal graph partitioning problem. The complexity of this latter problem depends on the graphs and on the objective function. In particular the problem of maximizing the split of a connected partition is solvable in polynomial time on complete graphs (DELATTRE and HANSEN 80) and trees (HANSEN et al. 93), and is NP-hard on grid graphs (HANSEN et al. 93, GAREY and JOHNSON 77). In this paper an algorithm that solves in $O(N^2 \log N)$ time the Maximum Split problem on a grid graph with two rows and N columns (a *ladder graph*) is presented. Ladder structures naturally arise whenever there are two parallel ways connected by several "bridges" or "connectors" (for instance, river banks, assembly lines, processes).

1 Introduction

In many applications, the clustering problem requires that the clusters are subject to relational constraints (FERLIGOJ and BATAGELJ 82, LEFKOVITCH 80). A usual approach to deal with constrained classification is to define a graph $G = (V, E)$, where the vertex set V is the set of n objects to be classified and the edge set E represents a symmetric and reflexive relation defined on pairs of objects $i, j \in V$. A *connected* partition $\pi = \{C_1, \ldots, C_p\}$ of G is a partition of V into p classes such that the subgraphs induced by the classes of π are connected. Moreover let $d_{i,j}$ be the dissimilarity between the objects i and j, with $i, j \in V$, $d_{i,j} = 0$ if $i = j$ and $d_{i,j} = d_{j,i}$. The clustering problem with relational constraints can be stated as follows: find a connected partition of G into p classes that maximizes (minimizes) a given function that measures the separation between clusters (the dissimilarity within clusters). Given a partition $\pi = \{C_1, \ldots, C_p\}$, three common such functions are:

$$\text{inner dissimilarity} \quad \text{ind}(\pi) = \sum_{k=1}^{p} \sum_{i,j \in C_k} d_{i,j}$$

$$\text{maximum diameter} \quad \text{diam}(\pi) = \max_{k=1,\ldots,p} \left(\max_{i,j \in C_k} d_{i,j} \right)$$

$$\text{split} \quad \text{split}(\pi) = \min_{k,h=1,\ldots,p:k\neq h} \left(\min_{i \in C_h, j \in C_k} d_{i,j} \right)$$

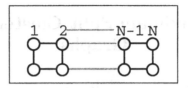

Figure 1: A ladder graph

The computational complexity of such constrained problems depends on the graph G and on the objective function. In fact minimizing the inner dissimilarity and minimizing the maximum diameter are NP-hard problems even when G is a tree (MARAVALLE et al. 97), while maximizing the split is NP-hard on grid graphs (HANSEN et al. 93, GAREY and JOHNSON 77) and is solvable in polynomial time on complete graphs (DELATTRE and HANSEN 80) and trees (HANSEN et al. 93).

In this paper we present a $O(N^2 \log N)$ time algorithm that finds an optimal solution to the Maximum Split (for short Max-Split) problem on ladder graphs, where a *ladder graph* is a grid graph with 2 rows and N columns (see Figure 1). Ladder structures naturally arise whenever there are two parallel ways connected by several "bridges" or "connectors" (for instance, river banks, assembly lines, processes).

The paper is organized as follows: in Section 2 we briefly show how, in HANSEN et al. 93, the Maximum Split problem has been reduced to the Forest Wrapping problem and we present a polynomial time algorithm for this latter problem; in Section 3 we show an example of working of the algorithm described in Section 2.

2 An algorithm for the Max-Split problem on ladder graph

2.1 Combinatorial formulation of the Max-Split problem

Given a graph $G = (V, E)$ with n vertices, let $G_V = (V, E_V)$ be the complete graph on the vertex set V, and let the dissimilarity $d_{i,j}$ be the weight of the edge (i, j), for each $(i, j) \in E_V$. Let $T = (V, E_T)$ be a minimum weight spanning tree of G_V. T can be easily found in $O(n^2 \log n)$. Let S be the set of the weights of the edges of T ordered by increasing values and let π^s be the partition obtained by joining each pair of vertices with dissimilarity less than s in a unique class. S and π^s can be found in $O(n \log n)$ and $O(n^2)$, respectively. Moreover, we say that a partition π of G *wraps* a partition π' of G if each class of π' is included in some class of π. In DELATTRE and HANSEN 80 it is proved that the split of an arbitrary partition of G is always equal to the weight of

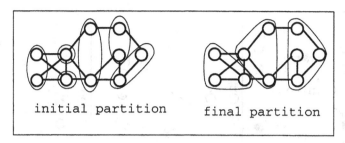

Figure 2: The Forest Wrapping problem

some edge of T. As a consequence of this result, in HANSEN et al. 93, it is shown that, in order to find the maximum split partition of a given cardinality p, one has to perform a binary search on the set S and, for each encountered weight s, solve the following problem:

Forest Wrapping Problem Find a connected partition π of G that wraps the partition π^s and has maximum number $m(s)$ of classes.

In Figure 2 an example of Forest Wrapping problem in which the initial and the final partition have six and three classes, respectively, is given.

The maximum value $s^* \in S$ such that $m(s^*) \geq p$ is the maximum split of a connected partition of G into p classes.

2.2 An algorithm for the Forest Wrapping problem on ladder graphs

In the following we describe a polynomial time algorithm for the Forest Wrapping problem on ladder graphs. Given a ladder graph $G = (V, E)$ with N columns, we denote by (i, j) the vertex at row i and column j. Given a set $C \subseteq V$, let (i, r) and (j, s) be the vertices in C with minimum and maximum column indices, respectively. We say that C *starts* at column r and *ends* at column s, and we use the notations $I(C) = r$ and $T(C) = s$.

A partition π of G is *h-feasible* if: (i) the classes obtained from the classes of π by deleting the vertices in columns $h + 1, \ldots, N$, are connected; (ii) all the classes having at least one element in columns $1, \ldots, h - 1$ and at least one element in columns $h + 1, \ldots, N$, have at least one element in column h. The *initial partition* π^s of the Forest Wrapping Problem is 1-feasible. Any N-feasible partition is a connected partition of G.

The basic idea of the algorithm for the Forest Wrapping problem on ladder graphs is to scan the columns of the ladder from 1 to $N - 1$ and, at each iteration h, merge some pairs of classes in such a way that

110

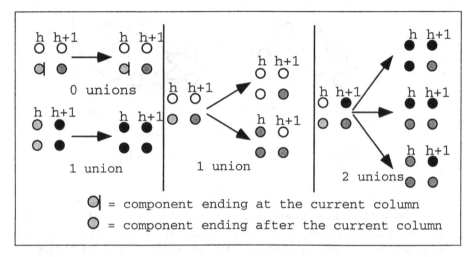

Figure 3: Feasible moves minimizing the number of unions

the obtained partition is $h + 1$-feasible. At a given iteration h of the algorithm, we will call *expanding class* a class having at least one element in column h and at least one element in columns $h + 1, \ldots, N$ and such that if it contains the vertex (k, h) then it does not contain the vertex $(k, h + 1)$. Moreover, a *feasible move* is the union of pairs of classes having elements in column h and/or $h + 1$, such that the new partition is $h + 1$-feasible. For each connected partition of G that wraps π^s, there exists at least one sequence of feasible moves producing it. A suitable criterion for choosing among feasible moves, is to minimize the number of unions at each iteration. In Figure 3 some examples of feasible moves with the minimum number of unions are given, where vertices with the same color belong to the same class.

Proposition 2.1 *Given two feasible moves m and m' at iteration h, let q and q' be the minimum number of unions required to obtain a connected partition after m and m', respectively. Then $|q - q'| < 1$.*

Proof. Suppose that $q' > q$. This occurs only if the vertices in column $h + 1$ belong to two different classes after the move m'. If after the move m', one merge these two classes, the minimum number of unions required to get a connected partition is at most q. $\qquad\square$

Proposition 2.1 ensures that a move that makes the minimum number of unions at the current iteration can increase the number of unions during the next iterations at most by one; hence the previous criterion is correct. However, as shown in Figure 3, in some cases there are two or three feasible moves minimizing the number of unions at the current iteration.

This occurs only when in column h there is at least one expanding class and in column $h + 1$ there are two different classes.

The following algorithm minimizes the number of unions at each iteration and, if suitable hypothesis hold, minimizes the number of unions in the next iterations.

algorithm SCAN
input: a ladder $G = (V, E)$ with N columns and a partition π^s of G
output: a connected partition G wrapping π^s
begin
   for $h := 1$ **to** $N - 1$ **do**
      if there is at least one expanding class **then**
         let C be the union of the expanding classes
         let C_1 be the class containing the vertex $(1, h + 1)$
         let C_2 be the class containing the vertex $(2, h + 1)$
         if $C_1 = C_2$ **then**
            merge C and C_1
         else
           let $j := h$
           repeat
              let B_1 be the class containing the vertex $(1, h + 1)$
              let B_2 be the class containing the vertex $(2, h + 1)$
              let $j := \min\{T(B_1), T(B_2)\}$
           until $(B_1 = C)$ or $(B_2 = C)$ or $(T(B_1) \neq T(B_2))$ or $(B_1 = B_2)$
           if $B_1 = B_2$ **then** merge C with C_1 or C_2 (it is the same)
           else if $(T(B_1) > T(B_2))$ or $(B_1 = C)$ **then** merge C and C_1
           else merge C and C_2
end

Remark 2.2 *Algorithm SCAN minimizes the number of unions at the current iterations.*

Let B_1' and B_2' be the classes B_1 and B_2 at the end of the REPEAT cycle of algorithm SCAN and let N_C be the minimum index greater than h of a column containing an element of C. The following proposition holds.

Proposition 2.3 *If $N_C > \min\{T(B_1'), T(B_2')\}$, then algorithm SCAN minimizes the number of unions in the next iterations.*

Proof. Let j' be the value of j at the end of the REPEAT cycle. The number of unions in iterations $h + 1, \ldots, j' - 1$ does not depend on the move at iteration h since C has not elements in these columns. Algorithm SCAN minimizes the number of expanding classes at iteration j', hence it minimizes the minimum number of unions in the iterations $j', \ldots, N - 1$. $\square$

In the case where $N_C \leq \min\{T(B_1'), T(B_2')\}$, the algorithm SCAN is not guaranteed to produce an optimal solution. In Figure 4 the gray and the black classes are included in the same class in any connected partition. In this case move (b) is better than move (a) (that is the move done by

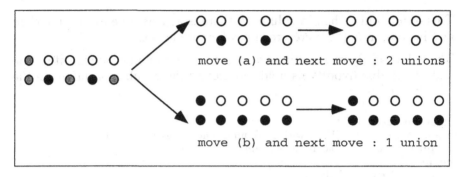

Figure 4: Application of algorithm SCAN

algorithm SCAN). The following definitions include all the cases in which $N_C \leq \min\{T(B_1'), T(B_2')\}$.

Given a partition π of $G = (V, E)$, a *monolevel class* C is a class having all vertices in the same row. A monolevel class on row i, starting at column r and ending at column s, is denoted by $C_i^{r,s}$. A *bilevel class* is a class containing vertices of both the rows of the ladder. Given a bilevel class C, there always exist two monolevel classes $C_1^{r_1,s_1}$ and $C_2^{r_2,s_2}$ such that $C = C_1^{r_1,s_1} \cup C_2^{r_2,s_2}$; C will be denoted as $C(r_1, s_1, r_2, s_2)$.

Overlapping of two monolevel classes. Two monolevel classes $C_i^{r,s}$ and $C_i^{r',s'}$ such that $r < r'$ *overlap* if there exists at least one vertex $(i, q) \in C_i^{r,s}$ such that $r' < q < s'$ (Figure 5 (a)).

Overlapping of a monolevel class and a bilevel class. A monolevel class $C_i^{r,s}$ and a bilevel class C *overlap* if there exists at least one vertex $(i, q) \in C$ such that $r < q < s$ (Figure 5 (b)).

Overlapping of two bilevel classes. Two bilevel classes $C(a_1, b_1, a_2, b_2)$ and $C(r_1, s_1, r_2, s_2)$ such that $\min\{a_1, a_2\} < \min\{r_1, r_2\}$ *overlap* if $r_1 < b_1$ or $r_2 < b_2$ (Figure 5 (c) and (d)).

Remark 2.4 *Two overlapping classes of π^s are included in the same class in any feasible partition of the Forest Wrapping Problem.*

Remark 2.5 *If at a given iteration of algorithm SCAN the current parti-*

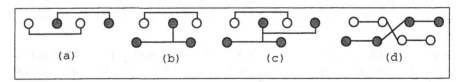

Figure 5: Overlapping classes

*tion has not overlapping classes, then the case $N_C \leq \min\{T(B_1'), T(B_2')\}$
cannot occur.*

Remark 2.6 *If π^s has no overlapping classes, then the partitions generated during algorithm SCAN have no overlapping classes.*

From the previous remarks it follows that, if the initial partition does not have overlapping classes, algorithm SCAN produces an optimal partition. Hence we add a preprocessing phase in which all pairs of overlapping classes are merged. This can be accomplished by a scanning of the columns of the ladder.

Although a trivial $O(N^2)$ time complexity would be enough to show our results, the preprocessing phase and algorithm SCAN can be easily implemented with time complexity $O(N \log N)$.

In the binary search over S, for a given $s \in S$, the most expensive operation is finding the initial partition π^s in $O(N^2)$ time. Since the binary searcho iterates $O(\log N)$ times, the overall time complexity of the algorithm for the Max-Split problem on ladder graphs is $O(N^2 \log N)$.

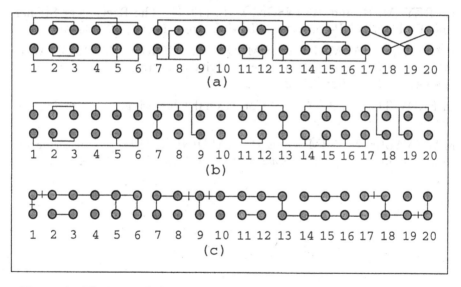

Figure 6: Working of the algorithm for the Forest Wrapping problem

3 An example

In this Section we find a solution to the Forest Wrapping problem on a ladder with 20 columns, by using the algorithm described in Section 2. In Figure 6 (a) the initial partition is given, where vertices belonging to the the same class are joined by lines. The initial partition has 21 classes and there are 5 pairs of overlapping classes. During the preprocessing phase, for each pair C and C' of overlapping classes, a class C'' has been obtained by merging C and C'. As shown in Figure 6 (b), the resulting partition has 16 non overlapping classes. In Figure 6 (c) the working of the algorithm SCAN starting from this partition is shown. The final partition is represented by a forest and each marked edge indicates a union between classes. The final number of classes is 10. At iterations 1 and 9 there were 3 and 2 moves, respectively, minimizing the number of unions. At iteration 1 the two expanding classes have been merged with the class containing vertex (1,2), whereas at iteration 9 the unique expanding class has been merged with the class containing vertex (1,10).

References

DELATTRE, M. and HANSEN, P. (1980): Bicriterion Cluster Analysis. *IEEE Transactions on Pattern Analysis and Machine Intelligence, PAMI-2(4), 277–291.*

FERLIGOJ, A. and BATAGELJ, V. (1982): Clustering with relational constraints. *Psychometrika, 47, 413–426.*

GAREY, M. R. and JOHNSON, D. S. (1977): The Rectilinear Steiner Tree Problem is NP-complete. *SIAM J. Appl. Math., 32, 826-834.*

HANSEN, P., JAUMARD B., SIMEONE, B., DORING, V. (1993): Maximum Split Clustering Under Connectivity Constraints. *Les Cahiers du GERARD, Tech. Rep. G-93-06.*

LEFKOVITCH, L.P. (1980): Conditional Clustering. *Biometrics, 36, 43–58.*

MARAVALLE M., SIMEONE B., NALDINI R. (1997): Clustering on Trees. *Computational Statistics and Data Analysis, 24, 217–234.*

A Generalization of Two-mode Three-way Asymmetric Multidimensional Scaling

A. Okada[1], T. Imaizumi[2]

[1]Department of Industrial Relations, School of Social Relations
Rikkyo (St. Paul's) University, 3 Nishi Ikebukuro
Toshima-ku Tokyo, JAPAN 171-8501

[2]Tama University, Hijirigaoka, Tama city Tokyo, JAPAN 206-0022

Abstract: A model and an associated nonmetric algorithm for multidimensional scaling of two-mode three-way asymmetric proximities or a set of proximity matrices, where each matrix can be asymmetric, is presented. The present model is extended from that of Okada and Imaizumi (1997), and can represent differences among sources both in symmetric and in asymmetric proximity relationships along each dimension. An application to intergenarational occupational mobility is presented.

1 Introduction

To analyze two-mode three-way proximities INDSCAL (Carroll, Chang (1970)) has been frequently used. INDSCAL model represents individual differences, or differences among sources, in proximity relationships by a set of weights given to each source. A set of weights given to a source consists of weights each of which shows the salience of dimensions in proximity relationships among objects along each dimension for the source. INDSCAL implicitly assumes that proximity relationships for a source are symmetric or each proximity matrix is symmetric, and cannot represent differences among sources in asymmetric proximity relationships.

There are several procedures of two-mode three-way asymmetric MDS (DeSarbo et al. (1992); Okada, Imaizumi (1997); Zielman (1991); Zielman, Heiser (1993)) which can represent individual differences or differences among sources both in symmetric and in asymmetric proximity relationships. Each of them adopts different approach to deal with differences among sources in symmetric and in asymmetric proximity relationships. Only the model of Zielman (1991) can represent differences among sources in symmetric and in asymmetric proximity relationships separately along each dimension. But the model cannot represent proximity values as distances in the object configuration for each source. It seems important that the asymmetric MDS model for two-mode three-way proximities is based on distance (Bove, Rocci (1999); Okada, Imaizumi (1997)), because many researchers have been familiarized with the model where interpoint distances represent proximity values. The model of Okada and Imaizumi (1997) is fully based on distance. Although the model can represent differences among sources in asymmetric proximity relationships along each dimension, it cannot represent differences among sources in symmetric proximity relationships along each dimension but only in magnitude. The purpose of the present paper is to develop a model and an associated algorithm which represent differences among sources in symmetric and in asymmetric proximity relationships separately along each dimension based on the model of Okada and Imaizumi (1997) or the predecessor model.

2 The Model and the algorithm

The present model is extended from the predecessor model. The present model consists of the common object configuration, the symmetry weight configuration, which replaced the symmetry weights of the predecessor model, and the asymmetry weight configuration. The common object configuration and the asymmetry weight configuration are identical with those of the predecessor model. The common object configuration represents the proximity relationships among objects which are common to all sources. In the common object configuration, object j is represented as a point $(x_{j1}, x_{j2}, \cdots, x_{jp})$ and a circle (sphere, hypershpere) of radius r_j in a multidimensional Euclidean space, where x_{jt} is the coordinate of object j on dimension t, and p is the dimensionality of the space. Radii are normalized so that the smallest one is zero. The symmetry weight configuration represents differences among sources in symmetric proximity relationships. In the symmetry weight configuration, source i is represented as a point $(w_{i1}, w_{i2}, \cdots, w_{ip})$ in a multidimensional space, where w_{it} ($w_{it} \geq 0$) represents the salience of symmetric proximity relationships along dimension t for source i. The asymmetry weight configuration represents differences among sources in asymmetric proximity relationships. In the asymmetry weight configuration, source i is represented as a point $(u_{i1}, u_{i2}, \cdots, u_{ip})$ in a multidimensional space, where u_{it} ($u_{it} \geq 0$) represents the salience of asymmetric proximity relationships along dimension t for source i (Okada, Imaizumi (1997)).

Each source has its own configuration of objects. In the configuration of objects for source i, object j is represented as a point $(w_{i1}x_{j1}, w_{i2}x_{j2}, \cdots, w_{ip}x_{jp})$ and an ellipse (ellipsoid, hyperellipsoid) of the length of semi axes $(u_{i1}r_j, u_{i2}r_j, \cdots, u_{ip}r_j)$. The object configuration for source i is derived by applying the symmetry weight w_{it} to dimension t of the configuration of points in the common object configuration in order to stretch or shrink each dimension differentially, and by applying the asymmetry weight u_{it} to the radius of the circle along dimension t in order to transform a circle into an ellipse. In the predecessor model, all dimensions of the common object configuration are uniformly stretched or shrunk, because the symmetry weight w_i is applied to the common object configuration in order to obtain the configuration of objects for source i. While in the predecessor model each source has the geometrically similar configuration of points, in the present model the configuration of points for each source is not geometrically similar. Let s_{jki} be the observed similarity from objects j to k for source i. It is assumed that s_{jki} is monotonically decreasingly related to m_{jki}, which is defined as

$$m_{jki} = d_{jki} - \frac{d_{jki}r_j}{\sqrt{\sum_{t=1}^{p}\left[(x_{jt} - x_{kt})/u_{it}\right]^2}} + \frac{d_{kji}r_k}{\sqrt{\sum_{t=1}^{p}\left[(x_{kt} - x_{jt})/u_{it}\right]^2}}, \quad (1)$$

where d_{jki} is the distance between objects j and k in the configuration of objects for source i, and is defined as

$$d_{jki} = \sqrt{\sum_{t=1}^{p} w_{it}^2 (x_{jt} - x_{kt})^2}. \quad (2)$$

Let n be the number of objects, and N be the number of sources. A nonmetric iterative algorithm to derive the common object configuration $(x_{jt}; j = 1, \cdots, n; t = 1, \cdots, p : r_j; j = 1, \cdots, n)$, the symmetry weight configuration $(w_{it}; i = 1, \cdots, N; t = 1, \cdots, p)$, and the asymmetry weight configuration $(u_{it}; i = 1, \cdots, N; t = 1, \cdots, p)$ from observed proximities s_{jki} was extended from the one for the predecessor model. The badness of fit measure called stress

$$S = \sqrt{\frac{1}{N} \sum_{i=1}^{N} \left[\sum_{\substack{j=1 \\ j \neq k}}^{n} \sum_{k=1}^{n} (m_{jki} - \hat{m}_{jki})^2 \Big/ \sum_{\substack{j=1 \\ j \neq k}}^{n} \sum_{k=1}^{n} (m_{jki} - \bar{m}_i)^2 \right]}, \quad (3)$$

is defined, where $\hat{m}_{jki}$ is the monotone transformed s_{jki}, and $\bar{m}$ is the mean of m_{jki} for source i. The common object configuration, the symmetry weight configuration, and the asymmetry weight configuration which minimize the stress are sought for a given dimensionality.

3   The application

The present model and the associated algorithm of two-mode three-way asymmetric proximities were utilized to analyze the intergenerational occupational mobility among eight occupational categories for four years

(Seiyama et al. (1990)). The data consist of four 8×8 tables, where the (j, k) element of the i-th table represents the number of sons whose occupations are in occupational category k and whose fathers' occupations are(were) in occupational category j in year i. Each of the four tables corresponds to year 1955, 1965, 1975 or 1985. The eight occupational categories are: (a) *Professional* occupations; (b) *Non-manual* occupations employed by *large* enterprises; (c) *Non-manual* occupations employed by *small* enterprises; (d) *Non-manual self*-employed occupations; (e) *Manual* occupations employed by *large* enterprises; (f) *Manual* occupations employed by *small* enterprises, (g) *Manual self*-employed occupations, and (h) *Farm* occupations. Emboldened word(s) will be used hereafter to represent each occupational category. The data were rescaled to remove the differences in the share of manpower among the eight occupational categories (Harshman et al. (1982)). The rescaled data, shown in Okada and Imaizumi (1997), were analyzed in the present study.

The smallest stress obtained by analyzing the 8×8×4 two-mode three-way asymmetric proximities for five-through unidimensional spaces were 0.312, 0.312, 0.322, 0.348, and 0.431 respectively. These figures suggest adopting the two-dimensional result as the solution. They are smaller than corresponding stress values obtained by the analysis using the predecessor model (Okada, Imaizumi (1997)). This solution was validated by executing the analyses using 20 different two-dimensional random initial common object configurations having the same r_j of this preferred solution as the initial radius with initial $u_{it} = 1$, and $w_{it} = 1$ (Carroll (1985)). The analyses resulted in the smallest stress of 0.396, suggesting the validity of the preferred solution.

The common object configuration is shown in Figure 1. The common object configuration inherited the uniqueness of the orientation of dimensions of the common object configuration up to reflections and permutations from the predecessor model. The configuration is similar to that derived by Okada and Imaizumi (1997). The vertical Dimension 2 of the configuration represents the difference between non-manual and manual occupations, and the horizontal Dimension 1 corresponds to the difference among the self-employed, the employed by large enterprises, the employed by small enterprises, and the professional or the farm.

Each occupational category is represented as a point and a circle centered at that point. A larger radius means that sons of fathers in the corresponding occupational category have the larger tendency of moving out from that occupational category and entering into another occupational categories. The farm has the largest radius. This is compatible with the shrinkage of the farm occupational categories from 1960s (Seiyama et al. (1990)). The non-manual small has the smallest radius (the radius is zero), and is represented only by a point in Figure 1. Two self-employed occupational categories have larger radii than the employed occupational categories have. This is compatible with the moving out of manpower from self-employed occupational categories into employed occupational categories (Seiyama et al. (1990)).

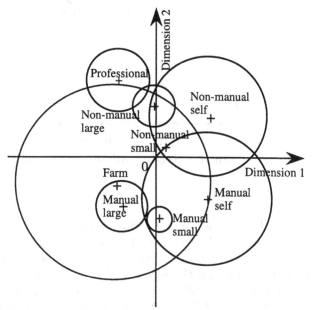

Figure 1: The common object configuration of eight occupational categories.

Figure 2 shows the symmetry weight configuration, and Figure 3 shows the asymmetry weight configuration. Each year is represented as a point in Figures 2 and 3. The symmetry weight along Dimension 2 is larger than that along Dimension 1 except for year 1985, suggesting the salience of symmetric proximity relationships between non-manual and manual occupational categories was relatively larger than that within non-manual and manual occupational categories except for 1985. The symmetry weight decreased along Dimension 2 from 1955 through 1985, and increased along Dimension 1 from 1975 to 1985. This suggests that the salience of symmetric proximity relationships between non-manual and manual occupational categories decreased from 1955 through 1985, and that the salience of symmetric proximity relationships within non-manual and manual occupational categories increased from 1975 to 1985.

The asymmetry weight along Dimension 1 is larger than that along Dimension 2, suggesting the salience of asymmetric proximity relationships within non-manual and manual occupational categories was relatively larger than that between non-manual and manual occupational categories. The asymmetry weight increased along Dimension 2 from 1955

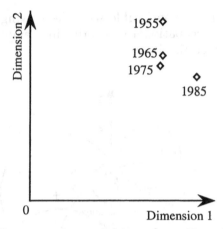

Figure 2: The symmetry weight configuration of four years.

through 1975, and decreased along Dimensions 1 and 2 from 1975 to 1985. This suggests that the salience of asymmetric proximity relationships between non-manual and manual occupational categories increased from 1955 through 1975, and the salience of asymmetric proximity relationships both between and within non-manual and manual occupational categories decreased from 1975 to 1985. Both symmetry and asymmetry weights varied mainly along Dimension 2. This means that the occupational mobility between non-manual and manual occupational categories, upon which occupational mobility studies have especially focussed their attention (Lipset, Bendix (1959)), has changed more than the mobility within non-manual and manual occupational categories has.

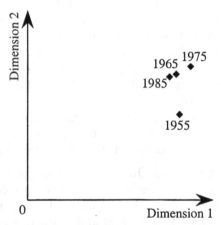

Figure 3: The asymmetry weight configuration of four years.

4 Discussion

A model and an associated nonmetric algorithm for MDS of two-mode three-way asymmetric proximities were introduced, and were applied successfully to analyze intergenerational occupational mobility. The present model is characterized that it can represent differences among sources both in symmetric and in asymmetric proximity relationships along each dimension.

The common object configuration shown in Figure 1 is very similar to that obtained by the analysis using the predecessor model. But the symmetry weight configuration, which has been newly introduced in the present model, revealed that the symmetry weight decreased along Dimension 2 from 1955 through 1985 and that increased along Dimension 1 from 1975 to 1985. These cannot be disclosed from the analysis using the predecessor model. In the asymmetry weight configuration 1975 has the largest asymmetry weight along both Dimensions 1 and 2, and in the symmetry weight configuration 1975 has the smallest symmetry weight along both Dimensions 1 and 2. This shows that the largest occupational mobility in 1975, suggested by Seiyama et al. (1990), was due to the asymmetric component of proximity relationships among occupational categories and was not due to the symmetric component (cf. Okada, Imaizumi (1997)).

The present model represents differences among sources in symmetric and in asymmetric proximity relationships along each dimension. Although different weights were used, common dimensions were used to represent differences among sources in symmetric and in asymmetric proximity relationships. This mean that the orientation of dimensions is determined by differences among sources both in symmetric and in asymmetric proximity relationships. One interesting possible model is that allows different orientations of dimensions for symmetric and for asymmetric proximity relationships (Okada, Imaizumi (1997)).

References

BOVE, G. and ROCCI, R. (1999): Methods for Asymmetric Three-way Scaling. In: M. Vichi and O. Opitz (eds.): Classification and Data Analysis: Theory and Application (pp. 131–138). Springer, Berlin.

CARROLL, J. D. (1985): [Review of Multidimensional Scaling]. *Psychometrika, 50, 111–113.*

CARROLL, J. D. and CHANG, J. J. (1970): Analysis of Individual Differences in Multidimensional Scaling via an N-way Generalization of "Eckart-Young" Decomposition. *Psychometrika, 35, 283–319.*

DeSARBO, W. S., JOHNSON, M. D., MANRAI, A. K., MANRAI, L. A., and EDWARD, E. A. (1992): TSCALE: A New Multidimensional Scaling

Procedure Based on Tversky's Contrast Model. *Psychometrika, 57, 43–69.*

HARSHMAN, R. A., GREEN, P. E., WIND, Y., and LUNDY, M. E. (1982): A Model for the Analysis of Asymmetric Data in Marketing Research. *Marketing Science, 1, 205–242.*

LIPSET, S. M. and BENDIX, R. (1959): Social Mobility in Industrial Society, University of California Press, Berkeley, CA.

OKADA, A. and IMAIZUMI, T. (1997): Asymmetric Multidimensional Scaling of Two-Mode Three-Way Proximities. *Journal of Classification, 14, 195–224.*

SEIYAMA, K., NAOI, A., SATO, Y., TSUZUKI, K., and KOJIMA, H. (1990): Stratification Structure of Contemporary Japan and its Trend. In: A. Naoi and K. Seiyama (eds.): Social Stratification in Contemporary Japan Vol. 1. Structure and Process of Social Stratification (pp. 15–50). Tokyo University Press, Tokyo.

ZIELMAN, B. (1991): Three-Way Scaling of Asymmetric Proximities. Research Report RR91-01, Department of Data Theory, University of Leiden.

ZIELMAN, B. and HEISER, W. J. (1993): Analysis of Asymmetry by a Slide-Vector. *Psychmetrika, 58, 101–114.*

Central Limit Theorem for Probabilities of Correct Classification

Wolf-Dieter Richter

Fachbereich Mathematik, Universität Rostock,D-18051 Rostock

Abstract: A minimum-distance classification rule studied in Krause and Richter (1994) for measurements from spherical distributions will be used here for allocating measurements from distributions being unspecified but having finite second order moments. The derivation of a representation formula for exact probabilities of correct classification similar to that derived in Richter (2000) for measurements from spherical distributions will be the first step of proving a central limit theorem for probabilities of correct classification.

1 Introduction

A minimum-distance classification rule for measurements from spherical distributions was derived in Krause and Richter (1994) based upon a certain non classical linear model approach. This rule will be used here for allocating measurements from distributions being unspecified but having finite second order moments. Probabilities of correct classification will be analysed in two steps. A representation formula for exact probabilities of correct classification similar to that derived in Richter (2000) for measurements from spherical distributions will be checked in a first, vector algebraic, step. This representation formula will be the starting point for proving in a second, analytical, step a central limit theorem for probabilities of correct classification. To this end, the law of large numbers for the three dimensional vector of measurement means in the three populations and the corresponding central limit theorem will be combined with the help of the well known delta method.

2 Exact probabilities of correct classification

Let an investigator draw n_i independent measurements from three populations $\Pi_i, i = 1, 2, 3$. Denote the over all sample size by $n, n = n_1 + n_2 + n_3$ and assume that the over all sample vector follows an unspecified distribution having finite variances σ_i^2 and expectations $\mu_i, i = 1, 2, 3$:

$$Y_{(n)} = \begin{pmatrix} Y_{(n_1)}^1 \\ Y_{(n_2)}^2 \\ Y_{(n_3)}^3 \end{pmatrix} \sim \begin{pmatrix} V_1(\mu_1, \sigma_1^2)^{\times n_1} \\ V_2(\mu_2, \sigma_2^2)^{\times n_2} \\ V_3(\mu_3, \sigma_3^2)^{\times n_3} \end{pmatrix}.$$

We shall not demand that the distribution V_3 of the third population coincides with one of the distributions V_1 and V_2 but that

$$\sigma_3^2 = \sigma_i^2 \text{ holds iff } \mu_3 = \mu_i, \ i \in \{1, 2\}. \tag{*}$$

The problem of interest here is to decide between two hypotheses:

$$H_{1/3} : \mu_3 = \mu_1 \quad \text{and} \quad H_{2/3} : \mu_3 = \mu_2 \,,$$

where it is natural to assume that

$$\mu_1 \neq \mu_2.$$

Hence, the statistical structure under consideration is

$$S_n = \left(R^n, \mathcal{B}^n, \{V_{(\mu, \Sigma)}, \mu \in \mathfrak{M}, \Sigma \in \Theta, (*)\} \right).$$

Here, $V = V_1^{\times n_1} \times V_2^{\times n_2} \times V_3^{\times n_3}$ denotes a product measure, μ belongs to the model space $\mathfrak{M}$,

$$\mathfrak{M} = \{\mu = \mu_1 1^{+00} + \mu_2 1^{0+0} + \mu_3 1^{00+}, (\mu_1, \mu_2) \in R^2, \mu_3 \in \{\mu_1, \mu_2\}\},$$

$$1^{+00} = \begin{pmatrix} 1_{n_1} \\ 0_{n_2+n_3} \end{pmatrix}, 1^{0+0} = \begin{pmatrix} 0_{n_1} \\ 1_{n_2} \\ 0_{n_3} \end{pmatrix}, 1^{00+} = \begin{pmatrix} 0_{n_1+n_2} \\ 1_{n_3} \end{pmatrix},$$

$$1_{n_i} = (1, \ldots, 1)^\top \in R^{n_i}, 0_{n_i} = (0, \ldots 0)^\top \in R^{n_i}$$

and Σ belongs to the space of disturbing parameters

$$\Theta = \left\{ \Sigma = \begin{pmatrix} \sigma_1^2 I_{n_1} & & \\ & \sigma_2^2 I_{n_2} & \\ & & \sigma_3^2 I_{n_3} \end{pmatrix}, (\sigma_1^2, \sigma_2^2) \in R^+ \times R^+, \sigma_3^2 \in \{\sigma_1^2, \sigma_2^2\} \right\},$$

with I_{n_i} being the $n_i \times n_i$ - unit matrix.

Remarks

- The model space $\mathfrak{M}$ is not a linear space.

- We do not assume that V_3 belongs to $\{V_1, V_2\}$.

- Moments of higher than second order are not assumed to exist.

- The case that the over all sample vector $Y_{(n)}$ follows an elliptically contoured distribution $V(\mu, \Sigma) = EC_n(\mu, \Sigma_i; g)$ with density generating function g has been dealt with in Krause and Richter (1994). Note that the function g makes it possible to reflect the influence of heavy or light distribution tails, respectively.

The hypotheses $H_{1/3}$ and $H_{2/3}$ can be reflected in the hypotheses spaces

$$\mathfrak{M}_{1/3} = \mathcal{L}(1^{+0+}, 1^{0+0}) \text{ and } \mathfrak{M}_{2/3} = \mathcal{L}(1^{0++}, 1^{+00}),$$

respectively, where $\mathcal{L}(.)$ denotes the linear space spanned up by the vectors standing within the brackets. Note that $\mathfrak{M}_{1/3}$ and $\mathfrak{M}_{2/3}$ are linear subspaces of R^n with

$$1^{+0+} = 1^{+00} + 1^{00+} \text{ and } 1^{0++} = 1^{0+0} + 1^{00+}.$$

Recognize further that

$$\mathfrak{M}_{1/3} \cap \mathfrak{M}_{2/3} = \mathcal{L}(1^{+++})$$

is a discrimination free space, where $1^{+++} = 1^{+0+} + 1^{0+0}$. The smallest linear subspace $\widetilde{\mathfrak{M}}$ of R^n including the model space $\mathfrak{M}$ is called extended model space. Obviously,

$$\widetilde{\mathfrak{M}} = \mathcal{L}(1^{+00}, 1^{0+0}, 1^{00+}).$$

Another basis representation for this space is given by

$$\widetilde{\mathfrak{M}} = \mathcal{L}(1^{+++}, 1^{-0+}, 1^{0-+}),$$

where

$$1^{-0+} = -\frac{1}{n_1}1^{+00} + \frac{1}{n_3}1^{00+}, 1^{0-+} = -\frac{1}{n_2}1^{0+0} + \frac{1}{n_3}1^{00+}.$$

Let us call

$$\mathfrak{W} = \mathcal{L}(1^{-0+}, 1^{0-+})$$

the action space, or, alternatively, effect or decision space. The effects reflected therein are

$$\Pi_{1^{-0+}}\mu = \frac{n_1 n_3}{n_1 + n_3}(\mu_3 - \mu_1)1^{-0+}$$

and

$$\Pi_{1^{0-+}}\mu = \frac{n_2 n_3}{n_2 + n_3}(\mu_3 - \mu_2)1^{0-+}.$$

The least squares estimates for the effects $\mu_3 - \mu_1$ and $\mu_3 - \mu_2$ can be derived from the relations

$$\widehat{\Pi_{1^{-0+}}\mu} = \Pi_{1^{-0+}}Y_{(n)} = \frac{n_1 n_3}{n_1 + n_3}(\overline{Y}_{3\cdot} - \overline{Y}_{1\cdot})1^{-0+}$$

and

$$\widehat{\Pi_{1^0-+}\mu} = \Pi_{1^0-+}Y_{(n)} = \frac{n_2 n_3}{n_2 + n_3}(\overline{Y}_{3\cdot} - \overline{Y}_{2\cdot})1^{0-+}.$$

It follows that

$$\widehat{\mu_3 - \mu_i} = \overline{Y}_{3\cdot} - \overline{Y}_{i\cdot}, i = 1, 2.$$

A generalized minimum-distance classification rule $d_c | R^n \to \{1, 2\}$ studied in Krause and Richter (1994) is defined as

$$d_c(y_{(n)}) = 2 - I\{\widehat{CC}_1(c)\}, c > 0,$$

where

$$\widehat{CC}_1(c) = \left\{ y_{(n)} \in R^n : \|\Pi_{1-0+}y_{(n)}\| < c\|\Pi_{1^0-+}y_{(n)}\| \right\}$$

$$= \left\{ y_{(n)} \in R^n : |\overline{y}_{3\cdot} - \overline{y}_{1\cdot}| < c\sqrt{\frac{1 + n_3/n_1}{1 + n_3/n_2}} \cdot |\overline{y}_{3\cdot} - \overline{y}_{2\cdot}| \right\}.$$

If $Y_{(n)}$ is Gaussian distributed and $c = 1$ then this decision rule coincides with the maximum likelihood rule. The event of correct classification is $CC_i(c)$ if $H_{i/3}$ is true, $i \in \{1, 2\}$, where

$$CC_1(c) = Y_{(n)}^{-1}\left(\widehat{CC}_1(c)\right), CC_2(c) = \overline{CC_1(c)}.$$

The probability of correct classification is under $H_{1/3}$ therefore

$$P(CC_1(c)) = P\left(\frac{\|\Pi_{1-0+}\Pi_{\mathfrak{W}}Y_{(n)}\|}{\|\Pi_{1^0-+}\Pi_{\mathfrak{W}}Y_{(n)}\|} < c \right).$$

Note that

$$\Pi_{\widetilde{\mathfrak{W}}}Y_{(n)} = \overline{y}_{1\cdot}1^{+00} + \overline{y}_{2\cdot}1^{0+0} + \overline{y}_{3\cdot}1^{00+}.$$

Hence,

$$\Pi_{\mathfrak{W}}y_{(n)} = a\left(\overline{y}_{1\cdot}, \overline{y}_{2\cdot}, \overline{y}_{3\cdot}\right)1^{-0+} + b\left(\overline{y}_{1\cdot}, \overline{y}_{2\cdot}, \overline{y}_{3\cdot}\right)1^{0-+},$$

for suitably defined functions $a\left(\overline{y}_{1\cdot}, \overline{y}_{2\cdot}, \overline{y}_{3\cdot}\right)$ and $b\left(\overline{y}_{1\cdot}, \overline{y}_{2\cdot}, \overline{y}_{3\cdot}\right)$ given in Richter (2000). The latter equation can be rewritten as

$$\Pi_{\mathfrak{W}}y_{(n)} = \eta_1(y_{(n)})B_1 + \eta_2(y_{(n)})B_2$$

or

$$\Pi_{\mathfrak{W}}y_{(n)} = \sqrt{\frac{n_1 n_3}{n_1 + n_3}}(\overline{y}_{3\cdot} - \overline{y}_{1\cdot})B_1 + \sqrt{\frac{n_2(n_1 + n_3)}{n}}\left(\overline{y}^{(1/3)} - \overline{y}_{2\cdot}\right)B_2,$$

where

$$B_1 = \frac{1^{-0+}}{\|1^{-0+}\|} \quad \text{and} \quad B_2 = \frac{1^{0-+} - \Pi_{1-0+}1^{0-+}}{\|1^{0-+} - \Pi_{1-0+}1^{0-+}\|}$$

are orthogonal unit vectors and

$$\bar{y}^{(1/3)} = \frac{n_1\bar{y}_{1.} + n_3\bar{y}_{3.}}{n_1 + n_3}.$$

Notice that the corresponding representation formula for $\Pi_{\mathfrak{W}}\mu$,

$$\Pi_{\mathfrak{W}}\mu = \sqrt{\frac{n_1 n_3}{n_1 + n_3}}(\mu_3 - \mu_1)B_1 + \sqrt{\frac{n_2(n_1 + n_3)}{n}}\left(\bar{\mu}^{(1/3)} - \mu_2\right)B_2,$$

reflects a certain reparametrisation based upon orthogonalisation and that

$$\Pi_{\mathfrak{W}}\mu|_{H_{1/3}} = \sqrt{\frac{n_2(n_1 + n_3)}{n}}(\mu_1 - \mu_2)B_2.$$

The new parameter

$$\bar{\mu}^{(1/3)} = \frac{n_1\mu_1 + n_3\mu_3}{n_1 + n_3}$$

depends on the sample sizes n_1 and n_3 and can therefore not easily be interpreted within the original problem. Let

$$\Pi_{\mathfrak{W}}Y_{(n)} = H_1 B_1 + H_2 B_2.$$

As a consequence from the above vector algebraic consideration, we have the following dimension reduction formula.

Theorem 1 With

$$\chi = \sqrt{n_3(n_1 + n_2 + n_3)/(n_1 n_2)}$$

and

$$\zeta = 1/\sqrt{(1 + n_3/n_1)(1 + n_3/n_2)}$$

it holds that

$$P\left(CC_1(c)\right) = P^{H_1 B_1 + H_2 B_2}\left(\{\eta_1 B_1 + \eta_2 B_2 \in R^n : |\eta_1| < |\eta_1 + \chi\eta_2|c\zeta\}\right)$$

$$= P^{(H_1, H_2)^\top}\left(\left\{\begin{pmatrix}\eta_1 \\ \eta_2\end{pmatrix} \in R^2 n : |\eta_1| < |\eta_1 + \chi\eta_2|c\zeta\right\}\right).$$

3 Central limit theorem

In this section, we exploit the well known delta method. Notice that

$$\begin{pmatrix} H_1 \\ H_2 \end{pmatrix} = \sqrt{n_1} f_{n_1}(\overline{Y}_{1\cdot}, \overline{Y}_{2\cdot}, \overline{Y}_{3\cdot}), \qquad (**)$$

where

$$f_{n_1}(x, y, z) = \left(\frac{z - x}{\sqrt{n_1}\|1 - 0 + \|}, \frac{1}{\sqrt{n_1}\|1^{0-+} - \Pi_{1-0+}1^{0-+}\|} \left[\frac{n_1 x + n_3 z}{n_1 + n_3} - y \right] \right)^{\mathsf{T}}.$$

In what follows we shall assume that the condition of asymptotically comparable sample sizes will be fulfilled:

$$\frac{n_i(n_1)}{n_1} \to \lambda_i, \; n_1 \to \infty, \; i \in \{2, 3\}. \qquad (***)$$

If condition (***) is satisfied then

$$f_{n_1}(x, y, z) \to f(x, y, z) = \begin{pmatrix} f_1(x, y, z) \\ f_2(x, y, z) \end{pmatrix},$$

where

$$f_1(x, y, z) = \frac{z - x}{\sqrt{1 + 1/\lambda_3}}, f_2(x, y, z) = \sqrt{\frac{\lambda_2(1 + \lambda_3)}{1 + \lambda_2 + \lambda_3}} \left(\frac{x + \lambda_3 z}{1 + \lambda_3} - y \right).$$

The law of large numbers ensures that under (***) a.s.

$$\begin{pmatrix} \overline{Y}_{1\cdot} \\ \overline{Y}_{2\cdot} \\ \overline{Y}_{3\cdot} \end{pmatrix} \longrightarrow \begin{pmatrix} \mu_1 \\ \mu_2 \\ \mu_3 \end{pmatrix}, n_1 \to \infty.$$

From the central limit theorem and assumption (***) it follows that

$$\mathcal{L} \left(\sqrt{n_1} \left[\begin{pmatrix} \overline{Y}_{1\cdot} \\ \overline{Y}_{2\cdot} \\ \overline{Y}_{3\cdot} \end{pmatrix} - \begin{pmatrix} \mu_1 \\ \mu_2 \\ \mu_3 \end{pmatrix} \right] \right) \Longrightarrow \Phi_{O_3, \Lambda} \text{ as } n_1 \to \infty,$$

where

$$\Lambda = \begin{pmatrix} \sigma_1^2 & & \\ & \sigma_2^2/\lambda_2 & \\ & & \sigma_3^2/\lambda_3 \end{pmatrix}.$$

Recall that the delta method applies commonly with a fixed function f, say. We must switch therefore from the sequence of functions f_{n_1} in relation (**) to the fixed function f. The following lemma proves then what we need:

$$\left(f_{n_1}(\overline{Y}_{1\cdot}, \overline{Y}_{2\cdot}, \overline{Y}_{3\cdot}) - f(\mu_1, \mu_2, \mu_3)\right)\sqrt{n_1} = o_P(1) \text{ as } n_1 \to \infty.$$

Lemma If (x, y, z) belongs to a sufficiently small neighbourhood of (μ_1, μ_2, μ_3) then

$$\left(f_{n_1}(x, y, z) - f(x, y, z)\right)\sqrt{n_1} = o(1) \text{ as } n_1 \to \infty.$$

Theorem 2 If condition (***) is satisfied then

$$\mathcal{L}\left(\left(f_{n_1}(\overline{Y}_{1\cdot}, \overline{Y}_{2\cdot}, \overline{Y}_{3\cdot}) - f(\mu_1, \mu_2, \mu_3)\right)\sqrt{n_1}\right) \Longrightarrow \Phi_{O_2, \Gamma},$$

where

$$\Gamma = \frac{1}{\lambda_3 + 1}\begin{pmatrix} \lambda_3\sigma_1^2 + \sigma_3^2 & \dfrac{\sqrt{\lambda_2\lambda_3}[\sigma_3^2 - \sigma_1^2]}{\sqrt{1 + \lambda_2 + \lambda_3}} \\ & \dfrac{\lambda_2\sigma_1^2 + (1 + \lambda_3)^2\sigma_2^2 + \lambda_2\lambda_3\sigma_3^2}{1 + \lambda_2 + \lambda_3} \end{pmatrix}.$$

Approximation Formula 1 If sample sizes are sufficiently large then

$$P\left((H_1, H_2) \in A\right) \approx \Phi_{\sqrt{n_1}f(\mu_1, \mu_2, \mu_3), \Gamma}(A).$$

Remarks

- If $H_{1/3}$ is true then

$$f_1(\mu_1, \mu_2, \mu_3) = 0 \text{ and } f_2(\mu_1, \mu_2, \mu_3) = \sqrt{\frac{\lambda_2(1 + \lambda_3)}{1 + \lambda_2 + \lambda_3}}(\mu_1 - \mu_2)$$

  as well as

$$\Gamma = \Gamma_0 = \begin{pmatrix} \sigma_1^2 & 0 \\ & \dfrac{\lambda_2\sigma_1^2 + (1 + \lambda_3)\sigma_2^2}{1 + \lambda_2 + \lambda_3} \end{pmatrix}.$$

- The parameters χ and ζ from the definition of the set $CC_1{}^0(c)$ depend on the sample size n_1. Hence, the central limit theorem and Approximation Formula 1 do not immediately apply for this set. However, the dependence of χ and ζ on n_1 is not very strong as can be seen from the following asymptotic relations which hold for $n_1 \to \infty$:

$$\zeta = \zeta(n_1) = \sqrt{\lambda_2(1+\lambda_3)^{-1}(\lambda_2+\lambda_3)^{-1}} + 0\left(\frac{1}{\sqrt{n_1}}\right),$$

$$\chi = \chi(n_1) = \sqrt{\lambda_3(1+\lambda_2+\lambda_3)/\lambda_2} + 0\left(\frac{1}{\sqrt{n_1}}\right).$$

As a consequence, we can derive the Approximation Formula 2 which is, from an applied point of view, the main result of the present paper.

Approximation Formula 2 If $H_{1/3}$ is true and the sample sizes are sufficiently large then

$$P\left(CC_1(c)\right) \approx \Phi\left(\begin{array}{c} 0 \\ \sqrt{n_1}f_2 \end{array}\right), \Gamma_0 \quad \left(CC_1^\circ(c)\right),$$

where

$$CC_1^\circ(c) = \left\{ \begin{pmatrix} \eta_1 \\ \eta_2 \end{pmatrix} \in R^2 : |\eta_1| < |\eta_1 + \chi\eta_2|c\zeta \right\}.$$

References

KRAUSE, D. and RICHTER, W.-D. (1994): Geometric Approach to Evaluating Probabilities of Correct Classification into two Gaussian or Spherical Categories. In : Bock, H. H.,Lenski, W. and Richter, M. (eds.): Information Systems and Data Analysis, 242 - 250. Springer-Verlag, Berlin.

RICHTER, W.-D. (2000): Representation Formulae for Probabilities of Correct Classification. In: Charalambides,Ch.A., Koutras,M.V. and Balakrishnan,N. (eds.): Probability and Statistical Models with Applications, 517-536.

A New Model for the Analysis of Multitrait-multimethod Data

R. Rocci[1], G. Bove[2]

[1]Department SEGeS,
University of Molise, Campobasso, Italy

[2]Department of Educational Sciences,
University of Roma Tre, Rome, Italy

Abstract: The composite direct product model proposed by Browne (1984) is one of the most important models for the analysis of multitrait-multimethod matrices. In this paper the model is extended to attempt to overcome lack-of-fit problems. The usefulness of the proposal is demonstrated by an application to an exemplary MTMM matrix.

1 Introduction

Measurement of educational and psychological attributes of individuals has gained increasing importance in recent years, particularly for educational and job evaluation, where the attributes refer to specific abilities required of the subjects. The measures defined for the attributes have to be reliable and effective in order to assess correctly personal abilities. This calls for adequate studies investigating their construct validity. Campbell and Fiskes's (1959) multitrait-multimethod (MTMM) correlation matrix is one of the most important tools to evaluate this aspect. It is a correlation matrix between measurements obtained by a crossed two-facet design in which each condition of one facet, usually named T facet, is combined with each condition of the other facet, M facet. A typical example is when the T facet refers to traits of personality and the M facet refers to different methods of measuring those traits. Campbell and Fiske (C&F) suggested some criteria to evaluate the construct validity of measures defining an MTMM matrix:

i) Correlations between the same trait under different methods should be positive and substantial;

ii) Correlations between the same trait under different methods should exceed corresponding correlations between different traits under different methods; i.e.

$$\rho(T_i M_r, T_i M_s) \geq \rho(T_i M_r, T_j M_s) \tag{1}$$

iii) Correlations between the same trait under different methods should exceed corresponding correlations between different traits under the same method; i.e.

$$\rho(T_i M_r, T_i M_s) \geq \rho(T_i M_r, T_j M_r) \tag{2}$$

iv) All blocks of correlations between traits, under the same method or under different methods, should exhibit the same pattern.

Since these four requirements were suggested, several procedures were proposed in order to detect this structure in the data (see Schmitt and Stults, 1986). In practice, the approach most often applied is to use a latent variate model to examine the construct validity of the measures, taking into account different sources of random measurement error. This paper focuses on this approach. First the two most relevant models, composite direct product (CDP) and restricted factor analysis (RFA), are reviewed as special cases of a general model introduced by Browne (1989). Finally, a new model, which include the CDP as a constrained variant, is proposed.

2 The general model

Following Browne (1989), a latent variable model for MTMM matrices can be formulated as

$$\mathbf{x} = \mathbf{D}(\boldsymbol{\xi} + \boldsymbol{\delta}) \tag{3}$$

where $\mathbf{x}' = [x_{11}, ..., x_{t1}, ..., x_{1m}, ..., x_{tm}]$ is the $p \times 1$ ($p = tm$) random vector of observed variables, $\boldsymbol{\xi}' = [\xi_{11}, ..., \xi_{t1}, ..., \xi_{1m}, ..., \xi_{tm}]$ is the $p \times 1$ random vector of "common scores", $\boldsymbol{\delta}$ is the $p \times 1$ random vector of "unique scores", uncorrelated with $\boldsymbol{\xi}$, and $\mathbf{D}$ is a positive definite diagonal $p \times p$ matrix of scale factors. Assuming all random vectors to be centred around the mean and $\boldsymbol{\xi}$ to have unit variances, the covariance matrix of $\mathbf{x}$ can be written as

$$\Sigma_{\mathbf{x}} = \mathbf{D}(\mathbf{R} + \boldsymbol{\Psi})\mathbf{D} \tag{4}$$

denoting the $p \times p$ correlation matrix of common scores by $\mathbf{R}$ and the $p \times p$ diagonal matrix of unique variances by $\boldsymbol{\Psi}$. The elements of $\mathbf{R}$ represent correlations corrected for distortions due to differences among variables in their level of reliability. Thus the degree of construct validity of the measures should be assessed according to the C&F requirements on the matrix $\mathbf{R}$ rather than on observed correlations.

To separate method and trait variance it is usually assumed that $\boldsymbol{\xi}$ is a function f of $\boldsymbol{\xi}_T$ and $\boldsymbol{\xi}_M$, i.e. $\boldsymbol{\xi} = f(\boldsymbol{\xi}_T, \boldsymbol{\xi}_M)$, where the $t \times 1$ random vector $\boldsymbol{\xi}_T$ and the $m \times 1$ random vector $\boldsymbol{\xi}_M$ represent respectively trait and method factors having zero means and unit variances. In the following sections we review the CDP and RFA models which are special cases of (3) having particular specifications of the function f.

3 Composite Direct Product model

Early in the study of MTMM matrices it was remarked by Campbell and O'Connell (1967) that in many applications the effect of the methods was multiplicative rather than additive. In fact they plotted observed heteromethod correlation values against corresponding monomethod values and noted that invariably the linear regression curve passes through the origin with a slope greater than unity. Motivated by these results Browne (1984) proposed a composite direct product model possessing the multiplicative structure required. It is based on the assumption that the latent factors for traits and methods are independently distribuited and such that

$$\boldsymbol{\xi} = \boldsymbol{\xi}_M \otimes \boldsymbol{\xi}_T \qquad (5)$$

where $\otimes$ refer to the (right)Kronecker product, with, for example,

$$\begin{bmatrix} a_{11} & a_{12} \\ a_{21} & a_{22} \end{bmatrix} \otimes \mathbf{B} = \begin{bmatrix} a_{11}\mathbf{B} & a_{12}\mathbf{B} \\ a_{21}\mathbf{B} & a_{22}\mathbf{B} \end{bmatrix}. \qquad (6)$$

Equation (5) implies the following multiplicative correlational structure for the common scores

$$\mathbf{R} = \boldsymbol{\Phi}_M \otimes \boldsymbol{\Phi}_T. \qquad (7)$$

The CDP model can be considered as the scale invariant version of the direct product model proposed by Swain (1975). Similar to Swain's model, it provides information relevant to the C&F requirements. In fact, it is possible to check if those requirements are satisfied by $\mathbf{R}$ simply by evaluating and comparing the parameters contained in $\boldsymbol{\Phi}_M$ and $\boldsymbol{\Phi}_T$; namely: (i) is satisfied whenever all elements of $\boldsymbol{\Phi}_M$ are positive and large; (ii) is satisfied if and only if all elements of $\boldsymbol{\Phi}_M$ are positive; (iii) is satisfied if and only if no off-diagonal element of $\boldsymbol{\Phi}_T$ is larger than an off diagonal element of $\boldsymbol{\Phi}_M$; (iv) holds if and only if all elements of $\boldsymbol{\Phi}_M$ are positive.

The CDP model has a structure simple and meaningful but a certain lack-of-fit was noted by Browne (1984) even in cases of meaningful summaries of the data. In the next section we introduce the restricted factor analysis model which usually provides a better fit.

4 Restricted Factor Analysis

The application of standard unrestricted factor analysis to the MTMM correlation matrix does not guarantee that the effects of traits and methods will be separated. For this reason Jöreskog (1974) proposed a linear latent model called restricted factor analysis (RFA) which can be written in scalar notation as

$$x_{ir} = \beta_{M,ir}\xi_{M,r} + \beta_{T,ir}\xi_{T,i} + \delta_{ir}. \qquad (8)$$

This model has been reparameterized by Dudgeon (1994) as a special case of model (3) where

$$\xi_{ir} = \lambda_{M,ir}\xi_{M,r} + \lambda_{T,ir}\xi_{T,i} \tag{9}$$

with $\lambda_{M,ir}^2 + \lambda_{T,ir}^2 = 1$. In matrix notation (9) can be written as

$$\boldsymbol{\xi} = \boldsymbol{\Lambda}_M\boldsymbol{\xi}_M + \boldsymbol{\Lambda}_T\boldsymbol{\xi}_T \tag{10}$$

implying the following structure for $\mathbf{R}$

$$\mathbf{R} = \boldsymbol{\Lambda}_M\boldsymbol{\Phi}_M\boldsymbol{\Lambda}_M' + \boldsymbol{\Lambda}_T\boldsymbol{\Phi}_T\boldsymbol{\Lambda}_T' \tag{11}$$

since the trait factors are assumed uncorrelated with the method factors. The RFA model usually provides a better fit than the CDP model but the interpretation can be rather cumbersome. In fact, the influence of traits and methods cannot be completely separated since the loadings are a combination of both. Another difficulty is that in general the RFA model does not enable us to verify directly if the C&F requirements are met (e.g. Browne 1984, pp. 4-5). To overcome these difficulties, Dudgeon (1994) proposes to impose on (9) the following constraints

$$\lambda_{M,ir} = \lambda_{M,r}; \lambda_{T,ir} = \lambda_{T,r}. \tag{12}$$

In this way the C&F requirements can be checked by means of the following conditions: (i) is satisfied if all the $\lambda_{T,r}$ are near to $\sqrt{.5}$; (ii) is satisfied if and only if all products $\lambda_{T,r}\lambda_{T,s}$ are positive; (iii) is satisfied if no off-diagonal element of $\boldsymbol{\Phi}_T$ is larger than the products $\lambda_{T,r}\lambda_{T,s}$ provided that $\lambda_{M,r}\phi_{M,rs}\lambda_{M,s} \geq 0$; (iv) holds if and only if all the products $\lambda_{T,r}\lambda_{T,s}$ are positive. The constraints (12) simplify the interpretation but imply the non-identifiability of the model (see Grayson and Marsh, 1994). To solve this problem the user should add some constraints to ensure identification, for instance by setting to zero some of the elements of $\boldsymbol{\Phi}_T$ and $\boldsymbol{\Phi}_M$.

5   An additive multiplicative model

In practical applications the CDP model often fails to describe adequately MTMM matrices satisfying the C&F requirements. This suggests to seek adequate extensions of this model. Our proposal is to incorporate an additive term related to the trait factors. For this purpose, we consider the trait factors as the sum of two components: $\boldsymbol{\xi}_T = \boldsymbol{\xi}_{T_a} + \boldsymbol{\xi}_{T_m}$, where only $\boldsymbol{\xi}_{T_m}$ is influenced by the multiplicative effects of method factors. In formulas

$$\xi_{ir} = \xi_{T_a,i} + \xi_{M,r}\xi_{T_m,i}. \tag{13}$$

Assuming the three latent vectors $\boldsymbol{\xi}_{T_a}, \boldsymbol{\xi}_{T_m}, \boldsymbol{\xi}_M$ to be independently distribuited with zero means, we obtain

$$\mathbf{R} = \mathbf{1}_m \mathbf{1}'_m \otimes \boldsymbol{\Phi}_{T_a} + \boldsymbol{\Phi}_M \otimes \boldsymbol{\Phi}_{T_m} \tag{14}$$

where $\boldsymbol{\Phi}_{T_a} = E(\boldsymbol{\xi}_{T_a}\boldsymbol{\xi}'_{T_a}), \boldsymbol{\Phi}_{T_m} = E(\boldsymbol{\xi}_{T_m}\boldsymbol{\xi}'_{T_m})$ and $\boldsymbol{\Phi}_{T_a} + \boldsymbol{\Phi}_{T_m} = \boldsymbol{\Phi}_T = E(\boldsymbol{\xi}_T\boldsymbol{\xi}'_T)$. This model will be referred to henceforth as additive multiplicative (AM). It is important to note that in this case the correlations among the common scores of the traits measured by methods r and s can be written as

$$\boldsymbol{\Phi}_{T_a} + \phi_{M,rs}\boldsymbol{\Phi}_{T_m} \tag{15}$$

or, after some elementary algebra,

$$\phi_{M,rs}\boldsymbol{\Phi}_T + (1 - \phi_{M,rs})\boldsymbol{\Phi}_{T_a}. \tag{16}$$

On the basis of the parameters contained in $\boldsymbol{\Phi}_T, \boldsymbol{\Phi}_{T_a}$ and $\boldsymbol{\Phi}_M$ we could formulate necessary and sufficient conditions for the C&F requirements. However, these conditions can not be checked simply evaluating and comparing the parameters as in the CDP model. For this reason we propose to use the following conditions when method correlations are positive: (i) is satisfied whenever all elements of $\boldsymbol{\Phi}_M$ and/or the diagonal elements of $\boldsymbol{\Phi}_{T_a}$ are large; (ii) is satisfied if all the diagonal elements of $\boldsymbol{\Phi}_{T_a}$ are greater than the corresponding off-diagonal elements; (iii) is satisfied if no off-diagonal element of $\boldsymbol{\Phi}_T$ is larger than an off diagonal element of $\boldsymbol{\Phi}_M$ and/or the corresponding diagonal element of $\boldsymbol{\Phi}_{T_a}$; (iv) is satisfied if $\boldsymbol{\Phi}_T$ and $\boldsymbol{\Phi}_{T_a}$ have the same pattern. Our suggestion, which seems to be useful in practice, is: first verify if the four conditions are satisfied or not; secondly examine in detail the situations where they do not hold, taking into account that the above conditions are sufficient but not necessary. For sake of parsimony and to avoid non-identification of the model, we suppose that the trait factors $\boldsymbol{\xi}_T$ are linear combinations of t second order trait factors $\boldsymbol{\eta}$ independent of $\boldsymbol{\xi}_M$. That is

$$\begin{cases} \boldsymbol{\xi}_{T_a} = [\boldsymbol{\Theta}_a | \mathbf{0}]\boldsymbol{\eta} \\ \boldsymbol{\xi}_{T_m} = [\mathbf{0} | \boldsymbol{\Theta}_m]\boldsymbol{\eta} \end{cases} \Rightarrow \boldsymbol{\xi}_T = \boldsymbol{\Theta}\boldsymbol{\eta} \tag{17}$$

where $\boldsymbol{\Theta}_a$ and $\boldsymbol{\Theta}_m$ are upper triangular matrices and $\boldsymbol{\Theta}$ is such that

$$\boldsymbol{\Theta} = [\boldsymbol{\Theta}_a | \boldsymbol{\Theta}_m] = [\boldsymbol{\Theta}_a | \mathbf{0}] + [\mathbf{0} | \boldsymbol{\Theta}_m]. \tag{18}$$

The factors $\boldsymbol{\eta}$ are also assumed independent with zero means and unit variances. This implies

$$E(\boldsymbol{\xi}_T\boldsymbol{\xi}'_T) = \boldsymbol{\Theta}\boldsymbol{\Theta}' = \boldsymbol{\Theta}_a\boldsymbol{\Theta}'_a + \boldsymbol{\Theta}_m\boldsymbol{\Theta}'_m = \boldsymbol{\Phi}_{T_a} + \boldsymbol{\Phi}_{T_m} = \boldsymbol{\Phi}_T. \tag{19}$$

Model	G^2	d.f.	p-value	AIC	BIC
CDP	115.8	77	0.0028	-38.2	-255.4
RFA* (eq. 8)	61.5	64	0.5654	-66.5	-247.0
RFA (eqs. 9 20)	76.4	68	0.2269	-59.6	-251.4
RFA (eqs. 9 20 12)	120.7	78	0.0014	-35.3	-255.3
AM	81.6	73	0.2296	-64.4	-270.3

*under the constraints: $\phi_{M,13} = 1, \phi_{M,12} = \phi_{M,23}$.

Table 1: Summary fitting results

6 An example

The statistical models considered in the previous sections are now illustrated in the analysis of a multitrait-multimethod matrix taken from the clinical psychology literature (Campbell & Fiske, 1959, tab.12). The data concern five personality traits: Assertive (A), Cheerful (C), Serious (S), Unshakeable Poise (U) and Broad Interests (B) measured by three raters: Assessment Staff (a), Teammates (t) and Self (s) in a sample of 124 students in clinical psychology. Previous analyses of these data were reported in Browne (1984) and Dudgeon (1994). The first author showed the limits of the standard RFA approach (8) that in spite of an acceptable fit provides misleading estimates for method correlations and factor loadings. The application of the CDP model gave a solution in which heteromethod trait correlations involving staff and teammate tended to be higher than corresponding correlations involving self, a feature also observed in the data. This pattern was also present in the method correlations. A problem of the CDP solution is that it was rejected by the likelihood ratio test, although the model provided a meaningful summary of the data. Reparameterized RFA models were applied by Dudgeon (1994) under the following constraints

$$\begin{aligned} \phi_{M,31} &= \phi_{M,32} = 0, \\ \phi_{T,54} &= \phi_{T,53} = \phi_{T,52} = \phi_{T,43} = 0. \end{aligned} \tag{20}$$

In this way he obtained an acceptable solution avoiding the misleading estimates noted by Browne. However, for this model the C&F requirements cannot be assessed easily. Constraints (12) simplify their analysis but make the model unacceptable for this data. In order to overcome the previous problems we applied the AM model with Θ_a and Θ_m of order 5×4 and 5×1, respectively. The parameters, as for the other models, were estimated by maximum likelihood under the multinormality assumption.

		Φ_T					Φ_M	
	A	C	S	U	B		a	t	s
A	1	0.58	-.30	0.35	0.50	a	1	0.60	0.10
C	0.58	1	-.27	0.66	0.38	t	0.60	1	0.22
S	-.30	-.27	1	0.24	0.23	s	0.10	0.22	1
U	0.35	0.66	0.24	1	0.63				
B	0.50	0.38	0.23	0.63	1				

		Φ_{T_a}			
	A	C	S	U	B
A	0.99	0.53	-.37	0.26	0.40
C	0.53	0.86	-.50	0.36	0.09
S	-.37	-.50	0.63	-.26	-.26
U	0.26	0.36	-.26	0.33	-.03
B	0.40	0.09	-.26	-.03	0.36

Table 2: AM model: parameter estimates

From table 1 it is possible to compare the fit obtained by the different models. AM and RFA (eqs. 9 20) have an equivalent acceptable fit but AM had less parameters. In fact, the AM model gave a better value of the Akaike's Information Criterium, named AIC, and Schwarz's Bayesian Information Criterium, denoted by BIC (see Bollen and Long 1993 for detailed discussions about these criteria). The parameters of the AM model are represented in table 2. It is interesting to note that the correlations between the methods reflects the expected pattern, without imposing any constraint on the model. We can also verify whether the C&F requirements are satisfied. For instance, to check (i) we analyse the three correlations of Φ_M and the five diagonal elements of Φ_{T_a}. It is easy to observe that the condition is always satisfied for traits A, C and S. A more detailed examination is required for U and B when method correlations are low, i.e. heteromethod correlations involving self. Conditions (ii) and (iii) are also easily checked comparing the size of the diagonal elements of Φ_{T_a} with the corresponding extra-diagonal elements in Φ_{T_a} and Φ_T . Condition (ii) is almost completely satisfied with only two minor deviations concerning again the U and B traits. More relevant are the deviations of U and B respect to condition (iii). Finally, condition (iv) is not completely satisfied because Φ_T and Φ_{T_a} have not exactly the same pattern and there are some method correlations very low. Examining the matrix Φ_M we see that the main difference regards the pattern of the monomethod blocks and the pattern shared by the two heteromethod blocks involving self.

Acknowledgements. This research has been supported by a grant of the National Research Council of Italy.

138

References

BOLLEN, K. A. and LONG J. S. (eds.)(1993): Testing structural equation models. Sage, Newbury Park, California.

BROWNE, M. W. (1984): The decomposition of multitrait-multimethod matrices. *British Journal of mathematical and Statistical Psychology, 37, 1-21.*

BROWNE, M. W. (1989): Relationships between an additive model and a multiplicative model for multitrait-multimethod matrices. In: Coppi R. and Bolasco S. (eds.): Multiway data analysis. North - Holland, Amsterdam. 507-520.

CAMPBELL, D. T. and FISKE, D. W. (1959): Convergent and discriminant validation by the multitrait-multimethod matrix. *Psychological Bulletin, 56, 81-105.*

CAMPBELL, D. T. and O'CONNELL, E. J. (1967): Method factors in multitrait-multimethod matrices: multiplicative rather than additive? *Multivariate Behavioral Research, 2, 409-426.*

DUDGEON, P. (1994): A reparametrization of the restricted factor analysis model for multitrait-multimethod matrices. *British Journal of mathematical and Statistical Psychology, 47, 283-308.*

GRAYSON, D. and MARSH, H. W. (1994): Identification with deficient rank loading matrices in confirmatory factor analysis: multitrait-multimethod models. *Psychometrika, 59, 1, 121-134.*

JÖRESKOG, K. G. (1974): Analysing psychological data by structural analysis of covariance matrices. In: D.H. Krantz et al. (eds.): Contemporary developments in mathematical psychology: Measurement, Psychophysics and Neural Information Processing, W.H. Freeman, San Francisco, 1-56.

SCHMITT, N. and STULTS, D. M. (1986): Methodology review: analyses of multitrait-multimethod matrices. *Applied Psychological Measurement,10, 1-22.*

SWAIN, A. J. (1975): Analysis of parametric structures for variance matrices. Unpublished doctoral dissertation, University of Adelaide, Australia.

Discrete and Continuous Models for Two-way Data *

Maurizio Vichi

Università "La Sapienza" di Roma, P.le A.Moro 5, I-00185, Roma Italy.
e-mail:maurizio.vichi@uniroma1.it

Abstract: A continuous factorial model together with a discrete clustering one are fitted simultaneously to two-way data, with the aim to identify the best partition of the objects and the best partition of the variables, according to a least-squares loss function. In addition, the proposed methodology allows to detect simultaneously, factors describing classes of variables and centroids characterizing classes of objects.

The continuous and discrete models are fitted to two-way data by solving a least-squares modeling problem, mathematically restated as a quadratic constrained program with mixed variables.

An iterative alternating least-squares algorithm is proposed to give an efficient solution of the NP-hard minimization problem: starting from clusters centroids, in a number of reduced dimensions, a constrained orthogonal rotation allows to highlight classes of variables that better identify the classification of the objects; then new cluster centroids are computed and the partition of the objects is given by solving an assignment problem. At each step of the alternating least-squares algorithm the objective function is not increased, thus the algorithm converges to at least a local optimal solution of the problem.

1 Introduction

In some multivariate statistical analyses classes of objects (sometimes variables) are synthesized fitting exploratory discrete models such as partitions, n-trees, hierarchies to the observed two-way data, via nonparametric techniques of clustering. In other statistical analyses continuous exploratory models (e.g., MDS or factor analysis) are fitted to two way-data, in order to detect non-observable dimensions summarizing the common information among the variables considered in the analyses. Frequently, these continuous and discrete models are sequentially applied with the aim to synthesize data in direction relating to variables and objects, defining classes of homogeneous objects and classes (as a matter of fact, coverings) of variables with common information. However, the approach of using a factorial analysis followed by a clustering algorithm has some drawbacks, since continuous models do not always identify factors that help to perceive the clustering structure in the data.

---

*Invited lecture

To overcome these inconsistencies of the sequential approach some authors have developed simultaneous discrete and continuous models.

De Sarbo, Howard and Jedidi (1991) developed MULTICLUS a maximum likelihood based method for simultaneously performing multidimensional scaling and cluster analysis on two-way data. MULTICLUS utilizes mixtures of multivariate conditional normal distributions to estimate a space of reduced dimensions for the objects and a set of vectors in a space of reduced dimensions for the clusters. An EM algorithm was introduced for the parameter estimation of the model.

De Soete and Carroll (1994) developed a procedure for clustering objects in a low r-dimensional subspace requiring that the centroids lie in this subspace. This was accomplished by imposing in the k-means algorithm (MacQueen, 1967) the constraint to assign objects to the best rank approximation of order r of the centroids, given according to their singular value decomposition. Thus, at each step of the k-means algorithm before assigning objects, centroids are approximated according their rank r truncated SVD. At the end a representation of objects, variables and centroids is given by a *biplot* representation (Gabriel, 1971) based on the SVD of the final centroids.

In this paper we propose a new model that simultaneously detects the best partition of objects and the best partition of variables minimizing a single loss function. Further, the proposed methodology allows the identification of a factor for each class of variables that best describes, according to the loss function, the classification of objects. These factors help to discriminate between original variables selecting those that have largely contributed to the definition of the classification.

The methodology is statistically formalized as a least-squares fitting problem and mathematically restated as a quadratic constrained problem with continuous and discrete variables. Sections 2 and 3 provide the new model and an alternating least-squares algorithm. The results of the model applied on macroeconomic data are given in section 4. Some conclusions follow in section 5.

2 A Discrete and Continuous Model for Two-way Data

Let $\mathbf{X} = [x_{ip}]$ be a $(n \times k)$ two-way two-mode (objects and variables) data matrix, describing the k-variate profiles of n objects.

Without loss of generality we suppose that the variables are standardized in order to exclude, in the application of the continuous and discrete models, problems connected with different units of measurements of variables. For the convenience of the reader the terminology used in this paper is listed here:

n	number of objects to be partitioned:
k	number of variables to be partitioned;
$I = \{o_1, \ldots, o_n\}$;	set of n objects to be partitioned;
$V = \{v_1, \ldots, v_k\}$	set of k variables to be partitioned;
$P = \{P_1, \ldots, P_c\}$	partition of I into c classes, where P_j is the jth class of P;
$Q = \{Q_1, \ldots, Q_m\}$	partition of V into m classes, where Q_l is the lth class of Q;
$\mathbf{U} = [u_{ij}]$	$n \times c$ matrix specifying for each o_i the membership to class P_j, i.e., $\mathbf{u}_{ij} = 1$ if o_i belongs to P_j, $\mathbf{u}_{ij} = 0$ otherwise;
$\mathbf{Y} = [y_{il} = \sum_{p=1}^{k} a_{pl} x_{ip}]$	$n \times m$ factor matrix, where y_{il} is the value of o_i for the lth factor y_l; synthesizing the common information of the set of variables Q_l;
$\mathbf{A} = [a_{pl}]$	$k \times m$ columnwise orthonormal matrix of the coefficients of the linear combination, with $\sum_p (a_{pl} a_{pl'})^2 = 0$, for any l and $l'(l \neq l')$;
$\overline{\mathbf{Y}} = [\sum_{i=1}^{n} \mathbf{u}_{ij})^{-1} \sum_{i=1}^{n} y_{il} \mathbf{u}_{ij}]$	$c \times m$ matrix containing centroids $\overline{y}_{jl}$ of P_j based on factors y_l. Matrix $\overline{\mathbf{Y}}$ can be rewritten: $\overline{\mathbf{Y}} = (\mathbf{U}'\mathbf{U})^{-1}\mathbf{U}'\mathbf{X}\mathbf{A}$.

The discrete and continuous model, proposed in this paper, detects an optimal partition P of I into c classes $P_j (j = 1, \ldots, c)$ and, simultaneously, an optimal partition Q of V into m classes $Q_l (l = 1, \ldots, m)$. For each class Q_l a factor y_l, which is the best linear combination of the variables in the class, according to the minimized LS loss function, is identified; while for each class P_j the centroid of the variables $y_l (l = 1, \ldots, m)$ is obtained allowing, in this way, to detect a class of the "closest" (similar) objects.

The model is mathematically specified as follows:

$$\mathbf{XA} = \mathbf{U}\overline{\mathbf{Y}} + \mathbf{E},$$

that is,

$$\mathbf{XA} = \mathbf{U}(\mathbf{U}'\mathbf{U})^{-1}\mathbf{U}'\mathbf{XA} + \mathbf{E} \qquad (1)$$

with variables $\mathbf{A}$ and $\mathbf{U}$, while $\mathbf{E}$ is the matrix of the error components.

The least-squares fit of the model leads to identification of the binary u_{ij} and continuous variables a_{pl} that minimize the following quadratic convex objective function subject to the sets of linear and non-linear constraints:

$$\min \sum_{j=1}^{c} \sum_{i=1}^{n} \sum_{l=1}^{m} (y_{il} - \bar{y}_{jl})^2 \mathbf{u}_{ij} = \tag{2}$$

$$= \min \|\mathbf{XA} - \mathbf{U}\bar{\mathbf{Y}}\|^2 = \min \|(\mathbf{I} - \mathbf{U}(\mathbf{U}'\mathbf{U})^{-1}\mathbf{U}')\mathbf{XA}\|^2 \tag{P1}$$

subject to constraints

$$\mathbf{u}_{ij} \in \{0, 1\}, \quad i = 1, \ldots, n, j = 1, \ldots, c; \tag{3}$$

$$\sum_{j=1}^{c} \mathbf{u}_{ij} = 1, \quad i = 1, \ldots, n; \tag{4}$$

$$\sum_{p=1}^{k} a_{pl}^2 = 1, \quad l = 1, \ldots, m; \tag{5}$$

$$\sum_{p=1}^{k} (a_{pl} a_{pl'})^2 = 0, \quad l = 1, \ldots, m-1; l' = l+1, \ldots, m; \tag{6}$$

The sets of constraints (3) and (4) define a partition P of I, while constraints (5) normalize matrix $\mathbf{A}$ and constraints (6) allow to define a partition Q of V, so as to have $\mathbf{A}$ orthogonal. Partition Q may have a class of unassigned variables for which $\sum_l a_{pl}^2 = 0$, i.e., these variables do not contribute to define the partition of I.

Remark 1. An optimal trivial solution of [P1] is given when $c = n$ and therefore $\mathbf{U} = \mathbf{I}$, i.e., the set I of n objects is partitioned into n classes, independently from the partition Q of variables, and consequently whatever matrix $\mathbf{A}$ is $\Diamond$

Remark 2. If $m = k$ problem [P1] degenerates into the k-means algorithm solution MacQueen (1967), since the set V is partitioned into k classes and therefore $\mathbf{A}$ degenerates into the identity matrix of order k $\Diamond$

In order to obtain in [P1] factors y_l with variability comparable with the components of maximum variance defined by the PCA on $\mathbf{X}$, we can require to normalize y_l by redistributing the variance explained by the first m components, according to the following ratio:

$$\left(\frac{\sum_{l=1}^{m} \lambda_l}{\sum_{l=1}^{m} \sum_{i=1}^{n} y_{il}^2} \right)^{\frac{1}{2}} \tag{7}$$

where $\lambda_l (l = 1, \ldots, m)$ are the largest eigenvalues of the correlation matrix of $\mathbf{X}$. Alternatively we can standardize y_l, and compare the results with the standardized components obtained by the PCA.

3   An Alternating Least-Squares Algorithm

Problem [P1] can be minimized using a constrained alternating least-squares (ALS) approach, that is, the objective function $F(\mathbf{A},\mathbf{U},\overline{\mathbf{Y}}) = \|\mathbf{XA} - \mathbf{U}\overline{\mathbf{Y}}\|^2$ is minimized with respect to: 1) $\mathbf{U}$, given the current estimate of $\mathbf{A}$ and $\overline{\mathbf{Y}}$, subject to the constraints on $\mathbf{U}$; then: 2) updating $\overline{\mathbf{Y}}$, given current $\mathbf{A}$ and $\mathbf{U}$; and finally minimizing with respect to: 3) $\mathbf{A}$, given $\mathbf{U}$ and $\overline{\mathbf{Y}}$, subject to the constraints on $\mathbf{A}$. Note that point 2 is just an updating of the solution since when $\mathbf{A}$ and $\mathbf{U}$ are given, also $\overline{\mathbf{Y}}$ can be computed. We are now in position to specify the algorithm for solving efficiently [P1].

Alternating Least-Squares Algorithm

Step a	Given the estimates of $\mathbf{A}$ and $\overline{\mathbf{Y}}$, new values $\mathbf{U} = [\mathbf{u}_{ij}]$ are given for $i = 1,\ldots,n$, by $\mathbf{u}_{ij} = 1$, if $F(\mathbf{A},[\mathbf{u}_{ij}],\overline{\mathbf{Y}}) = \min\{F(\mathbf{A},[\mathbf{u}_{iv}],\overline{\mathbf{Y}}) : v = 1,\ldots,m,(v \neq j)\}$; $\mathbf{u}_{iv} = 0$ otherwise;
Step b	given $\mathbf{A}$ and $\mathbf{U}$, matrix $\mathbf{Y} = \mathbf{XA}$ is computed and also $\overline{\mathbf{Y}}$ by: $\left(\sum_{i=1}^n \mathbf{u}_{ij}\right)^{-1} \sum_{i=1}^n y_{il}\mathbf{u}_{ij};$
Step c	given $\mathbf{U}$ and $\overline{\mathbf{Y}}$ the following sub-problem is solved with respect to $\mathbf{A}$: $$\begin{cases} \min \|\mathbf{XA} - \mathbf{U}\overline{\mathbf{Y}}\|^2 \\ \text{subject to constraints} \\ \sum_{p=1}^k a_{pl}^2 = 1, l = 1,\ldots,m; \qquad\qquad [P2]\quad (5)\\ \sum_{p=1}^k (a_{pl}a_{pl'})^2 = 0, l = 1,\ldots,m; l' = l+1,\ldots,m. \quad(6) \end{cases}$$

Remark 3. Problem [P2] can be considered a particular orthogonal procrustes model, even thought it is more restrictive than the classical one, since $\mathbf{A}$ is orthonormal and a partition of variables is also required. Problem [P2] is solved with a sequential quadratic programming algorithm (SQP). The SQP algorithm is known to solve efficiently constrained non linear problems with a linear rate of convergence $\Diamond$

Remark 4. The ALS algorithm starting from initial $\overline{\mathbf{Y}}$ in an m-dimensional space, orthogonally projects $\mathbf{X}$ onto the m-dimensional space and rotates projections to better fit centroids. Then centroids and the partition are updated. The process continues until it monotonically converges to at least a local optimum, since each of the three steps does not increase and generally decreases the objective function $\Diamond$

Remark 5. To run the algorithm, an initial $\overline{\mathbf{Y}}$ is needed, i.e., an initial partition of the objects and an initial matrix $\mathbf{A}$. The partition of the objects can be obtained using the k-means algorithm. An unfeasible orthogonal matrix $\mathbf{A}$ is given by the eigenvectors associated with the largest eigenvalues of the correlation matrix of $\mathbf{X}$ $\Diamond$

Remark 6. The initial partition of the objects can be randomly generated. The orthogonal pattern of matrix $\mathbf{A}$ can be defined partitioning the variables into m groups by using the k-means algorithm. Then, to satisfy constraints (5), for each column of $\mathbf{A}$, random values between $[-1, 1]$ are given to at most $k - 1$ rows (variables) that belongs to the lth class defined by the k-means; 0 otherwise. The kth values of each column is determined by difference so as to satisfy constraint (5). By using a large number of random initial estimates and retaining the best solution the probability of obtaining a global minimum is increased $\Diamond$

4 Macroeconomic Performance of Industrialized Countries

The proposed methodology was used to analyze the average macroeconomic performances of G7 most industrialized countries: France (FRA), Germany (GER), Great Britain (GB), Italy (ITA), United States of America (USA), Japan (JAP), Canada (CAN), plus Spain (SPA), according to 7 variables: Gross Domestic Product (GDP), Inflation (INF), Budget deficit/gdp (DEF)*, Public debt/gdp (DEB)*, Long term interest rate (INT), Trade balance/gdp (TRB)*, unemployment rate (UNE) - most of these considered in the Maastrich treaty - in the period 1980-1990. This data set has been studied also by Rizzi & Vichi (1995), using a factorial three-way technique, to observe the convergence of the countries' trajectories.

In the present analysis variables were standardized in order to allow the cross-sectional and time series comparison. On the 8×7 standardized data matrix, principal component analysis (PCA) was applied to identify two dimensions explaining 84% total variance. In table 1, the correlation between components and variables is shown. The first factor is correlated positively with inflation, long term interest rate, unemployment rate; while it is correlated negatively with trade balance and gross domestic product. Thus, the first factor shows the economic performances of the countries (countries with the best performances have negative scores on the first component). The second factor is mainly linked with public debt (countries with high debts have large positive scores on the second component). Budget deficit is correlated negatively with the bisecting line of the two factors. On the scores of the first two principal components the k-means clustering algorithm was applied. The partition of the countries into three classes is:

$$P = \{(FRA, GB, SPA), (GER, USA, JAP, CAN), (ITA)\} \quad (8)$$

---

*both aggregates measured in domestic currency and at current price

	GDP	INF	DEF	DEB	INT	TRB	UNE
Factor 1	-0.578	0.987	-0.687	0.093	0.958	-0.813	0.901
Factor 2	0.273	0.113	-0.684	0.952	0.081	0.348	-0.340

Table 1: PCA of the macroeconomic data. Correlation between variables and components

In Figure 1 the representation of the countries according to the first two components does not show three well-separated classes, since the two factors maximize the total explained variance, but do not select variables that may better separate the three classes present in the data. Partition (8) into three classes is also obtained directly classifying countries on the basis of the 8×7 standardized data matrix, thus, confirming that PCA this time did not distort much the distances among objects (even though this may happen), and consequently the corresponding classification. However, k-means on the first two PCA components does not detect well-separated classes and therefore does not identify factors formed by variables that better explain partition (8).

The alternating least squares algorithm used for solving [P1] converged after only two iterations, starting from the k-means algorithm solution and using for $\mathbf{A}$ the eigenvectors of the correlation matrix of $\mathbf{X}$.

The sequential quadratic algorithm used for solving [P2] converged after 504 and 1077 function evaluations, respectively (requiring the termination tolerance for variables and objective function to be 10^{-4} and for constraint violation to be equal to 10^{-6}). The variance of the first two principal components was redistributed to the two factors $y_l(l = 1, 2)$ using formula (7) to allow the comparison with PCA results. The partition of the objects, given by solving [P1], is shown in Figure 2. It can be clearly noted that the second analysis improves interpretability of results. The two factors in this case produce a partition into three classes equal to the previous analysis, but this time the three classes are well-separated. The partition of the variables into two classes defining the two factors plotted in Figure 2 is:

$$Q = \{(\text{INF,DEB,TRB,UNE}),(\text{GDP,DEF,INT})\}. \tag{9}$$

This is obtained by the orthonormal matrix $\mathbf{A}$ in Table 2. This partition highlights two factors: the first is mainly linked to inflation and unemployment rate; the second is primarily associated with public deficit and long term interest rate. Even though [P1] obtained the same partition given by the k-means on the first two principal components, here we have the advantage toof obtaining the best partition of the variables that explains the best partition of the countries.

146

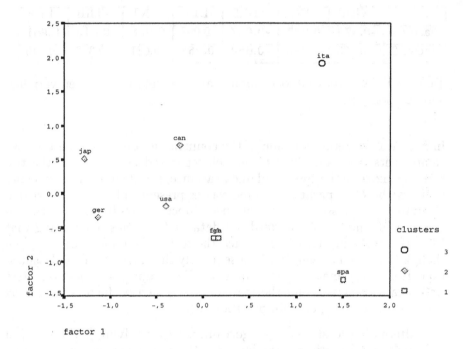

Figure 1: PCA and cluster analysis on first two components

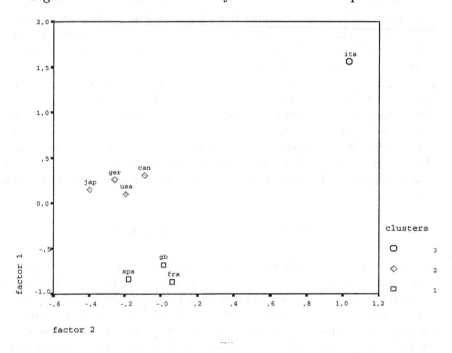

Figure 2: Simultaneous partitioning of units and variables according [P1]

$$A' = \begin{bmatrix} 0.00 & 0.85 & 0.00 & -0.12 & 0.00 & 0.24 & -0.46 \\ 0.15 & 0.00 & -0.84 & 0.00 & -0.52 & 0.00 & 0.00 \end{bmatrix}$$

Table 2: Orthonormal matrix defined solving [P1]

5 Discussion

In this paper a model for simultaneous classification of the units and variables of a two-way data set is presented. The methodology proposed is statistically formalized as a least-squares fitting problem formed by an exploratory discrete (partitioning) model and a continuous factorial one. This last, in practice, is transformed into the combinatorial problem to identify a partition of variables that best describes the optimal partition of objects. The mathematical restatement of the methodology leads to a constrained quadratic minimization problem, which is hard to solve since already the partitioning of the objects can be proved to be an NP-hard problem. For this reason, a direct solution of [P1] is disregarded. An alternating least-squares algorithm is given. This splits the problem into three simpler parts whose optimal solution is easier to obtain.

References

DESARBO, W., S. and HOWARD, D., J. and JEDIDI, K.(1991): MULTICLUS: A new method for simultaneously performing multidimensional scaling and clustering, *Psychometrika, 56, 121-136.*

DE SOETE G. and CARROLL, J. D.(1994): K-means clustering in a low-dimensional Euclidean space. In: Diday et al. (eds): *New approaches in classification and data analysis*, Springer, Heidelberg, 212-219.

GABRIEL, K. R.(1971): The biplot graphic display of matrices with application to principal component analysis, *Biometrika, 58, 453-467.*

GOWER, J.(1987): Procrustes Analysis. In: B. Fichet and C. Lauro (eds.): *Methods for Multidimensional Data Analysis*, ECAS, 247-258.

MACQUEEN, J.(1967): Some Methods for Classification and Analysis of Multivariate Observations. *Proceedings of the Fifth Berkeley Symposium on Mathematical Statistics and probability*, Volume 1 Statistics, L.M. Le Cam and J. Neyman (eds.), Berkeley CA: University of California Press, 281-297.

RIZZI, A. and VICHI, M.(1995): Three-way Data Set Analysis. In: A. Rizzi (ed.) *Some relations between matrices and structures of multidimensional data analysis*, 93-166.

Part 2

Pattern Recognition and Automation

Towards Feature Fusion – A Classifier on the Basis of Automatically Generated Significant Contour Sections

D. Pechtel, K.-D. Kuhnert

Fachbereich Elektrotechnik und Informatik,
Universität Siegen, D-57068 Siegen, Germany

Abstract: An intelligent method in the field of object recognition should be able to work in the real world, i.e. the objects could be complex and deformed. Such a method consists of two main parts: Generating automatically the characteristics of object classes from known samples of objects and classifying unknown objects with the help of the learnt characteristics.

The presented method is based on our work introduced in Pechtel, Kuhnert (2000) where important contour sections are detected in order to distinguish between contours.

Our further developments contain (un)supervised learning of a knowledge base consisting of Significant Contour Sections of complex, deformed and discrete contours and a hierarchical classification method for unknown contours based on this knowledge base. The classifier does not need feature vectors of an equal number of elements.

1 Introduction

Variable objects belong to specific classes due to their appearance (this article) or to the task. E.g. different birds belong to the bird class or different fishes belong to the fish class. The objects in one class can be interpreted as small deformations of each other. Among a multiplicity of similarity analysis methods of object contours (Loncaric (1998)) there are different approaches, which deal with contour deformation. In these cases often some cost function is minimized. The cost is defined as *elastic energy* (Basri et al. (1998)) needed to transform one contour to the other, or the contour is interpreted as a string, in which contour points are replaced (shifted), inserted and deleted, respectively (Pechtel, Kuhnert (2000), Sankoff, Kruskal (1983)). We do not make a psychophysical or part based approach as Siddiqi, Kimia (1995), Latecki, Lakämper (1999) and our method is also no pure alignment approach (Ullman (1996)). The main ideas of our work were developed in Pechtel, Kuhnert (2000). Here we concentrate on the generation (fusion) of significant local contour sections for recognition. The present method is a first complete approach for classifying 2D-object contours into their classes, using only Significant Contour Sections *SCS*. *SCS* are local contour sections that distinguish a specific contour of a specific class from the contours of other classes in a learning sample. In a complex learning process successive contour points are fused to SCS of a contour (section 2) and serve as a basis of a comparatively simple hierarchical classifier (section 3). The SCS can be regarded as a special case of local feature fusion.

2   Generating significant contour sections

In Pechtel, Kuhnert (2000) we presented a method for the determination of global similarity of two different 2D-object contours. Here our method is briefly recapitulated and the interested reader is referred to Pechtel, Kuhnert (2000) for details. Our method is based on a systematic similarity analysis of local contour sections of the same **constant length** l. Here, that method is presented in a little changed form. We now use a **variable** l.

$a = \{a_0, .., a_i, .., a_{p-1}\}$, $b = \{b_0, .., b_j, .., b_{q-1}\}$ are two discrete closed 2D-object contours consisting of p contour sections $S_i^a = \{a_{i-l_i}, .., a_i, .., a_{i+l_i}\}$ and q contour sections $S_j^b = \{b_{j-l_j}, .., b_j, .., b_{j+l_j}\}$ respectively with $l_i = l_j = L_{ij}(\epsilon)$, $L_{ij} \in N$, $\epsilon \le E$, $E \in R^+$, $R^+ = \{x | x \ge 0; x \in R\}$. E is the maximum permitted error (distance, dissimilarity) of 2 contour sections. It is presupposed that successive contour points have all equal Euclidean distances and the contour point indices have to be calculated modulo p and q, respectively, because the contours are closed. Calculating the L_{ij} of all pairs of contour sections around a_i, b_j results in a $p \times q$ - matrix $L^{a,b} = [L_{ij}]$ of local similarities. The elements L_{ij} in $L^{a,b}$ represent the maximum length of the contour sections S_i^a and S_j^b around the contour points a_i and b_j, that have a local dissimilarity (distance) lower or equal a given maximum dissimilarity E. In other words, L_{ij} gives the osculating length of two contour sections that can be treated equal in respect to a fixed maximum error E.

Now, one has to determine exactly one **monotone** discrete path (list of neighbored elements) $Q_{t^0}^{a,b}$ in $L^{a,b}$, that possesses minimum cost for the deformation (transformation) from a to b. For that, the objective function

$$g^{a,b} = \sum_{z=0}^{Z-1} Q_{t_z}^{a,b} \ , \forall\, t \in \{0, 1, \ldots, t^0, \ldots, \psi - 1\} \quad \rightarrow \max \ ; \quad \psi = min(p,q) \quad (1)$$

with $max(p,q) \le Z < (p+q)$ is maximized with the help of some *dynamic programming technique* (e.g. Sankoff, Kruskal (1983)). p (in the first column of $L^{a,b}$) or q (in the first row of $L^{a,b}$) possible start elements for $Q_t^{a,b}$ exist. We calculate all pathes starting in the first column ($p \le q$) or row ($q < p$) and select the path $Q_{t^0}^{a,b}$ over all t causing the lowest cost. Because of that the method is invariant against rotation. Sections of $Q_{t^0}^{a,b}$ that contribute only a little to $g^{a,b}$, i.e. the osculating length is short, map those contour sections of a and b onto each other, that are dissimilar. Thus, those contour sections are **Important Contour Sections** ICS for the distinction of the contours a and b.

Classes are built supervised, or unsupervised using cluster analysis based on global similarities $g^{a,b}$ as shown in Pechtel, Kuhnert (2000). Now the generation of **Significant Contour Sections** SCS for a specific contour A, belonging to a specific contour class K_i, from all ICS that came from the comparison with all contours b of the other classes $K_j, j \neq i$ is explained. First, all similarity matrices $L^{A,b}$ and paths $Q_{t0}^{A,b}$ have to be calculated. Those contour sections of A which belong to elements z of $Q_{t0}^{A,b}$ satisfying the condition

$$Q_{t_z^0}^{A,b} < \Theta \qquad (2)$$

are the ICS of A. Θ is constant for all ICS and is called **importance value**. I.e., now there is a list of all ICS of the contour A with respect to all contours b. In general, this list includes ICS that overlap each other, i.e. they have also equal contour points, and ICS that do not overlap each other, i.e. they do not have a single contour point in common.

m_r overlapping $ICS_k, 1 \leq k \leq m_r$ are combined to one SCS_r with the following one-standard-deviation method that obtains the best results among the tested methods. The method calculates the arithmetic means $\bar{s}_r$, $\bar{e}_r$ and the variances $\bar{\bar{s}}_r$, $\bar{\bar{e}}_r$ of the m_r starting point and ending point indices s_k, e_k of all overlapping ICS_k. This results in the following starting and ending point indices S_r, E_r of the SCS_r:

$$S_r = \bar{s}_r - \sqrt{\bar{\bar{s}}_r} \quad , \quad E_r = \bar{e}_r + \sqrt{\bar{\bar{e}}_r} \qquad , 0 \leq r \leq R-1. \qquad (3)$$

An example of such a combination (fusion) is shown in Fig.1. Since contour A could have R SCS_r it's reasonable to define a **significance measure** σ_r:

$$\sigma_r = \frac{m_r^\alpha \, d_r^\beta}{1 + v_r^\gamma} \quad , \quad \alpha, \beta, \gamma \in R^+ \qquad (4)$$

with m_r as number of overlapping ICS_k and

$$v_r = \bar{\bar{s}}_r + \bar{\bar{e}}_r \qquad (5)$$

$$d_r = \frac{1}{m_r} \sum_{k=0}^{m_r-1} \frac{1}{w_k} \quad , \quad w_k = \sum_{z=s_k}^{e_k} Q_{t_z^0}^{A,b}. \qquad (6)$$

This is a first simple approach to define a significance measure that combines the following dependencies: the bigger the number m_r of overlapping ICS_k and the smaller the variation v_r of the starting and ending

154

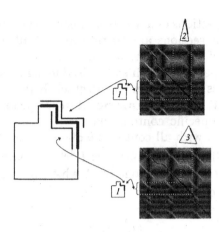

Figure 1: Example for the fusion of 2 Important Contour Sections ICS_k to 1 Significant Contour Section SCS_r of a sketched bottle with respect to a class consisting of 2 triangles. The elements of the similarity matrices $L^{1,2}$ and $L^{1,3}$ are scaled between 0 and 255. Thus the matrices can be visualized as an image. Dark areas map dissimilar contour sections onto each other. Paths are marked in black. Important path sections and corresponding Important Contour Sections ICS are marked bold.

point indices of the m_r overlapping ICS_k and the bigger the mean of the sum of dissimilarities d_r with similarity w_k between the m_r individual overlapping ICS_k and the m_r corresponding contour sections of the contours b, *the bigger is the significance* σ_r. α, β, γ are exponential weights for each dependency of σ_r and it seems to be good if the weighting of m_r is high with respect to d_r, v_r.

The contour A possesses R Significant Contour Sections SCS_r with $0 \leq r \leq R - 1$. The SCS_r of contour A with the biggest significance is called **Most Significant Contour Section** $MSCS$ of contour A.

3 Hierarchical classifier

The Most Significant Contour Sections $MSCS$ of all contours in the learning sample are the knowledge base of a hierarchical classifier. The hierarchy is constructed with a **reliability** measure, where reliability means the reliability of a $MSCS$ for a correct classification result. For deriving the reliability measure the following notations are introduced for the learning sample: Class K_i consists of n_i contours $C_{i,k}$ with $p_{i,k}$ points:

$$K_i = \{C_{i,0}, C_{i,1}, \ldots, C_{i,k}, \ldots, C_{i,(n_i-1)}\}. \tag{7}$$

$MSCS_{i,k}$ is the $MSCS$ of contour $C_{i,k}$ and the classes K_i are equal to the classes that are fixed for the determination of the $MSCS$.

First of all the most similar contour section of a contour $C_{j,l}$, consisting of $p_{j,l}$ contour points with regard to a $MSCS_{i,k}$, consisting of $\lambda_{i,k}$ contour points, is determined. For that, orientation vectors $o_{i,k}$ of the $MSCS_{i,k}$ and o_{j,l_s} of contour sections $C_{j,l_s}, 0 \leq s \leq (p_{j,l} - 1)$ of $C_{j,l}$, also with $\lambda_{i,k}$ points, are constructed by the starting and ending points of the contour sections. Now $MSCS_{i,k}$ and C_{j,l_s} are translated and rotated, so that their orientation vectors start in the origin of the coordinate system and coincide with the positive x-axis. This results in $MSCS_{i,k}^{**}$ and C_{j,l_s}^{**}. Now the means of the minimal sums $d_{(i,k),(j,l_s)}, 0 \leq s \leq (p_{j,l} - 1)$ of squared Euclidean distances of corresponding contour points are calculated for the specific $MSCS_{i,k}^{**}$ and all $p_{i,k}$ contour sections C_{j,l_s}^{**} with the following equation:

$$
d_{(i,k),(j,l_s)} = \frac{1}{\lambda_{i,k}} \sum_{r=0}^{\lambda_{i,k}-1} \left(\left(MSCS_{i,k_{r_x}}^{**} - \overline{MSCS_{i,k_x}^{**}} - (C_{j,l_{(s+r)_x}}^{**} \right. \right.
$$
$$
\left. \left. - \overline{C_{j,l_{s_x}}^{**}} \right) \right)^2 + \left(MSCS_{i,k_{r_y}}^{**} - C_{j,l_{(s+r)_y}}^{**} \right)^2 \right) \quad (8)
$$

where r is the starting point index of the $MSCS_{i,k}^{**}$, s is the starting point index of the contour sections C_{j,l_s}^{**}, and x, y are the x, y-coordinates of the points. $\overline{MSCS_{i,k_x}^{**}}, \overline{C_{j,l_{s_x}}^{**}}$ are the means of the x-coordinates of the contour sections. The distance of the most similar contour section is now:

$$
d_{(i,k),(j,l)}^{min} = \min\{d_{(i,k),(j,l_0)}, \ldots, d_{(i,k),(j,l_s)}, \ldots, d_{(i,k),(j,l_{(p_{j,l}-1)})}\} \quad (9)
$$

This is done with all $MSCS_{i,k}$ and all $C_{j,l}$. With N classes this results in distance vectors $D_{i,k}$ for each $MSCS_{i,k}$:

$$
D_{i,k} = \begin{pmatrix} d_{(i,k),(0,0)}^{min} \\ \vdots \\ d_{(i,k),(0,n_0-1)}^{min} \\ \vdots \\ d_{(i,k),(j,0)}^{min} \\ \vdots \\ d_{(i,k),(j,l)}^{min} \\ d_{(i,k),(j,n_j-1)}^{min} \\ \vdots \\ d_{(i,k),(N-1,0)}^{min} \\ \vdots \\ d_{(i,k),(N-1,n_{(N-1)}-1)}^{min} \end{pmatrix} \quad (10)
$$

If $(i = j) \wedge (k = l)$ then $d_{(i,k),(i,k)}^{min} = 0$ because $MSCS_{i,k}$ is compared to itself. This is the case for exactly one element in each $D_{i,k}$.

If n_i is the total number of $MSCS_{i,k}$ in class K_i and m is the number of the most similar contours $C_{i,l}$ from the same class K_i among the first n_i

most similar contours, then we can define now the **reliability** measure $\rho_{i,k}$ for each $MSCS_{i,k}$ with the help of $D_{i,k}$:

$$\rho_{i,k} = \frac{m}{n_i} \qquad (11)$$

I.e., the bigger the number m of correct classification results with respect to n_i within the learning sample, the higher the reliability of this $MSCS_{i,k}$.

The $MSCS_{i,k}$ in the knowledgebase of the hierarchical classifier are ordered with respect to their reliability. During classification of a contour T from the test sample the classifier calculates in succession the minimal distance $d^{\min}_{(i,k),T}$ between T and the ordered $MSCS_{i,k}$ with translation, rotation, and equations 8, 9. After each comparison of T with a $MSCS_{i,k}$ it is decided with a rejection threshold $\tau_{i,k}$ if the minimal distance $d^{\min}_{(i,k),T}$ is sufficient to assign T to the class of the $MSCS_{i,k}$ or not. Each $MSCS_{i,k}$ has its own threshold $\tau_{i,k}$ which is defined as:

$$\tau_{i,k} = \min\{d^{\min}_{(i,k),(0,0)}, ..., d^{\min}_{(i,k),(j,l)}, ..., d^{\min}_{(i,k),(N-1,n_{(N-1)}-1)} \mid i \neq j\}. \qquad (12)$$

If for the calculated minimal distance

$$d^{\min}_{(i,k),T} < \tau_{i,k} \qquad (13)$$

then T is assigned to the class K_i of $MSCS_{i,k}$. If not, T is compared with the next most reliable $MSCS_{i,k}$ etc.. The algorithm of such a hierarchical classification is shown in Fig.2.

T =*contour from test sample to be classified*
Initialize classmembership of T to the rejection class
M =*number of MSCS in the knowledge base*
$c = 0$ //Initialize index of the $MSCS$ according their reliabilities
while $c \leq M - 1$
    Calculate $d^{\min}_{(i,k),T}$ of T and the **cth most reliable** $MSCS_{i,k}$
    if $d^{\min}_{(i,k),T} <$ ($\tau_{i,k}$ *of the cth most reliable $MSCS_{i,k}$*)
        T is predicted as a member of class K_i
        break
    else
        $c = c + 1$
    end
end

Figure 2: Algorithm of the hierarchical classification. Comments are marked with //.

The method was tested with a learning sample consisting of the contours

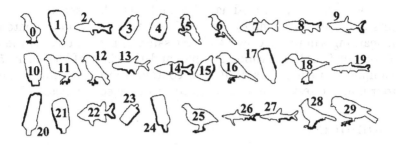

Figure 3: Learning sample: Most Significant Contour Sections $MSCS$ are marked bold.

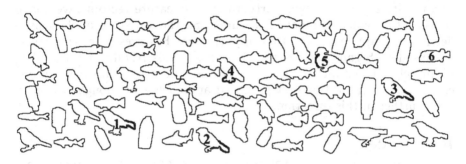

Figure 4: Test sample: most similar contour sections of the wrong predicted contours are marked bold.

of 10 birds, 10 bottles, and 10 fishes. Fig.3 shows the contours ordered according to the reliability of their Most Significant Contour Sections (marked bold). In Fig.4 the contours of the test sample (16 birds, 22 bottles, and 36 fishes) different from the learning sample are shown. Finally Tab.1 shows the resulting confusion matrix.

predicted → actual ↓	birds	bottles	fishes	rejection	correct
birds	11	1	4	-	0.69
bottles	-	22	-	-	1.00
fishes	-	-	35	1	0.97
correct	1.00	0.96	0.90	-	total: 0.92

Table 1: Confusion matrix.

It turns out that the proposed classification method has a high total accuracy. The $MSCS_{i,k}$ in the learning sample have on average 100 contour points. The average number of comparisons of one test contour with the ordered $MSCS_{i,k}$ is 5. This results in a classification time of a contour with 500 points of 0.15s on average (Pentium III, 450MHz; C).

Only a few birds are predicted as fishes and a bottle respectively. 3 tail feathers (1,2,3 in test sample) are predicted as the tail fin of contour 2 in the learning sample, 1 claw (4 in test sample) is predicted as the tail fin of contour 9 in the learning sample, and the chest of the duck (5 in test sample) is predicted as $MSCS$ of contour 4 in the learning sample. Contour 6 in the test sample is assigned to the rejection class.

4 Summary

We presented a hierarchical classifier based on nearly automatically generated Most Significant Contour Sections $MSCS$. Since the learning sample is small and the test objects are quite variable the classification results are remarkable. Furthermore the feature vectors have not to consist of an equal number of features. So the structure of the classifier is easily applicable to other applications. Features (contour points) are fused to Significant Contour Sections. This results in a complex, intuitively understandable learning process and a comparatively simple classifier. We think this first proposed approach give enough reason to work further in this direction.

References

BASRI, R., COSTA, L., GEIGER, D., and JACOBS, D. (1998): Determining the Similarity of Deformable Shapes. *Vision Research, 38,* 2365-2385.

LATECKI, L. and LAKÄMPER, R. (1999): Convexity Rule for Shape Decomposition Based on Discrete Contour Evolution. *Computer Vision and Image Understanding (CVIU), 73 (3), 441-454.*

LONCARIC, S. (1998): A Survey of Shape Analysis Techniques. *Pattern Recognition, Vol. 31, No. 8, 983-1001.*

PECHTEL, D. and KUHNERT, K.-D. (1999): Automatic Generation of Significant and Local Feature Groups of Complex and Deformed Objects, Proc. of ICIAP'99, Venice, Italy, 340-345.

PECHTEL, D. and KUHNERT, K.-D. (2000): Generating Automatically Local Feature Groups of Complex and Deformed Objects. In: Gaul, W. and Decker, R. (eds.): Classification and Information Processing at the Turn of the Millenium. Springer, Heidelberg, 237-244.

SANKOFF, D. and KRUSKAL, B. (eds.) (1983): Time Warps, String Edits, and Macromolecules. Addison-Wesley, Reading, Massachusetts.

SIDDIQI, K. and KIMIA, B.B. (1995): Parts of Visual Form: Computational Aspects. *IEEE Transactions PAMI, 17, 239-251.*

ULLMAN, S. (1996): High-level Vision. A Bradford Book, MIT Press, Cambridge, Massachusetts

Convex Discriminant Analysis Tools for Non Convex Pattern Recognition

M. Rémon

Département de Mathématique,
Facultés Universitaires Notre-Dame de la Paix,
Rempart de la Vierge, 8, B-5000 Namur (Belgium)
(e-mail:marcel.remon@fundp.ac.be)

Abstract: The estimation of convex sets when inside and outside observations are available is often needed in current research applications.

The key idea of this paper is to propose a solution based on convex and discriminant analysis tools, even when non convex domains are considered. Simulations are done and comparisons are made with respect to a natural candidate for estimation of non convex bodies, based on the Voronoi tessellation.

A part of this paper is devoted to a theoretical framework showing how convex sets can be used to approximate non convex sets in $\mathbb{R}^2$.

1 A discriminant analysis algorithm for convex bodies

Suppose that X is a Poisson point process within a fixed finite window $F \subset \mathbb{R}^d$. In F, we have a compact convex domain D. We suppose that the Poisson process X is homogeneous on F, with density λ. We observe a number $t \geq 1$ of realizations of X in F, from which n turn out to be inside the domain D and m outside D ($t = n + m$). We want to estimate the unknown convex domain D.

The solution we propose in Rémon (1996) is the modification of a classical discriminant analysis criterion developed by Baufays and Rasson (1985) to distinguish between two disjoint convex domains. The situation here is quite similar as we have two disjoint domains, D and its complement $\sim D = F \setminus D$. The main difference lies in the non convexity of $\sim D$.

Here we note $(x, y) = \{x_1, y_1, \ldots, x_{n+m}, y_{n+m}\}$ the realizations of the homogeneous Poisson process X and the labeling variable $Y : y_i = 1$ if $x_i \in D$ and $y_i = 2$ otherwise. Suppose $y_i = 1$ for $i = 1, \ldots, n$ and $y_i = 2$ for $i = n + 1, \ldots, n + m$, without loss of generality.

Conditionally on n and m fixed, the likelihood function for (x, y) is

$$L(x, y) = \left(\frac{1}{m(D)^n} \prod_{i=1}^{n} \mathbf{1}_{[x_i \in D]} \right) \left(\frac{1}{m(\sim D)^m} \prod_{i=n+1}^{n+m} \mathbf{1}_{[x_i \in \sim D]} \right)$$

$$= \left(\frac{1}{m(D)} \right)^n \left(\frac{1}{m(\sim D)} \right)^m \times$$

$$\mathbf{1}_{[H(x_1,...,x_n) \subseteq D]} \, \mathbf{1}_{[J(x_{n+1},...,x_{n+m}|x_1,...,x_n) \subseteq \sim D]}$$

where $m(C)$ is the Lebesgue measure of C, $\mathbf{1}_{[A]} = 1$ if A is true and 0 otherwise, $H(x_1, ..., x_n)$ is the convex hull statistic of $\{x_1, ..., x_n\}$ and $J(x_{n+1}, ..., x_{n+m}|x_1, ..., x_n)$ is the "shadow" statistic defined in Hatchel et al. (1981) as:

$$J(x_{n+1}, ..., x_{n+m}|x_1, ..., x_n) =$$
$$\bigcup_{i:y_i=2} \{x_i + \lambda(x_i - b) \in I\!\!R^d | \lambda \geq 0, b \in H(x_1, ..., x_n)\}.$$

$(H(.), J(.|.))$ is a minimal sufficient statistic for the estimation of D. It

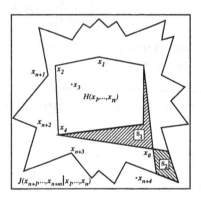

Figure 1: Discriminant rule for convex domains

is known that $J(x_{n+1}, ..., x_{n+m}|x_1, ..., x_n)$ has similar properties as the convex hull statistic $H(x_1, ..., x_n)$. It is a consistent estimate of $\sim D$. It is robust with respect to small changes in the location of the data points and it satisfies the equivariance requirement (see Rémon (1994)).

One then gets that the following boundary of the allocating regions for D and $\sim D$ is the set of points x_0 such that:

$$\frac{1}{m(H(x_1, ..., x_n, x_0)) + m(J(x_{n+1}, ..., x_{n+m}|x_1, ..., x_n))}$$

$$= \frac{1}{m(H(x_1, ..., x_n)) + m(J(x_{n+1}, ..., x_{n+m}, x_0|x_1, ..., x_n))}$$

i.e.

$$S_1(x_0) = S_2(x_0)$$

where

$$S_1(x_0) \equiv m(H(x_1, ..., x_n, x_0)) - m(H(x_1, ..., x_n))$$

and

$$S_2(x_0) \equiv$$
$$m(J(x_{n+1}, ..., x_{n+m}, x_0 | x_1, ..., x_n)) - m(J(x_{n+1}, ..., x_{n+m} | x_1, ..., x_n)).$$

This boundary gives us a practical and easily computable estimate $\hat{D}$ for the unknown domain D.

2 The Voronoi solution to the inside/outside problem for non convex bodies in $I\!\!R^2$

Let the notation be the same as before except that the unknown domain D is no longer required to be convex. The Voronoi estimation is a very natural one. It allocates any new point x_o to D if

$$\min_{1 \leq i \leq n} d(x_o, x_i) \leq \min_{n+1 \leq i \leq n+m} d(x_o, x_i)$$

where $d(.,.)$ is the Euclidean distance in $I\!\!R^2$. The set of all these points will be the estimate $\hat{D}$. If one computes the Voronoi cell V_i associated to each point x_i of the training set, i.e.

$$V_i = \{x_o \in I\!\!R^2 : d(x_o, x_i) \leq \min_{j \neq i} d(x_o, x_j)\},$$

then $\hat{D} = \bigcup_{1 \leq i \leq n} V_i$, as showed in Figure 2. The problem with such a solution is the non smoothness of the result. This irregularity of $\hat{D}$ is not reduced by increasing the size of the observed training set. One could think of a smoothing algorithm applied in a second stage to the border of $\hat{D}$, but this leads to a "smooth estimate" incompatible with the observed data (especially when the data are numerous). The question of how to get a smooth estimate of the unknown non convex domain D is the core of this research.

3 A discriminant analysis algorithm for non convex domains

Let the notation be the same as for the Voronoi estimation. The algorithm is the following.

162

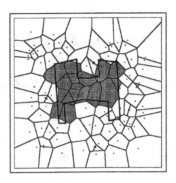

Figure 2: Voronoi estimation for non convex domains

It first labels the observed points as $x_1^1, \ldots, x_{n_1}^1, x_{n_1+1}^1, \ldots, x_{n_1+m_1}^1$. By convention, the first n_j points are considered as inside points while the m_j following ones are outside points. Here the algorithm takes j as 1.

In the second step, it takes the convex hull statistic of the inside points $H(x_i^j : 1 \leq i \leq n_j)$, and disregards the outside points in it. Let us denote these disregarded points $x_1^{j+1}, x_2^{j+1}, \ldots, x_{n_{j+1}}^{j+1}$. With the remaining points, it performs the discriminant algorithm for convex domains, as explained in Section 1. This gives an estimating domain $\hat{D}^j$.

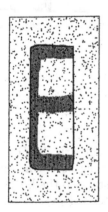 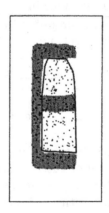 

Figure 3: Letter E recognition. From left to right, $H(x_1^1, \ldots, x_{n_1}^1)$, $H(x_1^2, \ldots, x_{n_2}^2)$ and $H(x_1^3, \ldots, x_{n_3}^3)$.

The next step consists in relabeling the inside points :

$$x_1^j, \ldots, x_{n_j}^j \rightarrow x_{n_{j+1}+1}^{j+1}, \ldots, x_{n_{j+1}+m_{j+1}}^{j+1} \qquad \text{with} \qquad m_{j+1} = n_j.$$

Then, considering $\{x_1^{j+1}, \ldots, x_{n_{j+1}}^{j+1}\}$ as our new set of inside points and

$\{x_{n_{j+1}+1}^{j+1}, \ldots, x_{n_{j+1}+m_{j+1}}^{j+1}\}$ as our set of outside points, the algorithm goes back to the second step with $j := j + 1$. See Figure 3.

The algorithm stops as soon as no outside points can be found within the convex hull $H(x_i^j : 1 \le i \le n_j)$. The final solution is then :

$$\hat{D} = \hat{D}^1 \setminus (\hat{D}^2 \setminus (\hat{D}^3 \setminus (\hat{D}^4 \ldots))).$$

In fact, the algorithm tries first to estimate the unknown domain D by $\hat{D}^1$, an element of $\mathcal{C}_1$, then by $\hat{D}^1 \setminus \hat{D}^2$, an element of $\mathcal{C}_2$, and so forth, where $\mathcal{C}_1$ and $\mathcal{C}_2$ are defined in the theoretical section of this paper (see Section 5). If the algorithm requires more than three recursive calls, it divides the original figure in two, works on each half figure separately, and combines the results together. The division follows the first principal component axis of the inside points.

4 Examples and comparison with Voronoi solution

Figure 4 is an example of letter recognition with inside and outside points from an homogeneous Poisson point process. Figure 5 is the result of

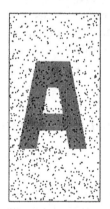

Figure 4: Example with $n = 201$, $m = 799$ and $m(D) = 0.102$. Voronoi solution (in the center) yields $m(\hat{D}) = 0.101$ and $m(D \triangle \hat{D}) \equiv m(D \cup \hat{D} \setminus D \cap \hat{D}) = 0.015$, while the discriminant algorithm (on the right) yields $m(\hat{D}) = 0.104$ and $m(D \triangle \hat{D}) = 0.008$.

our algorithm for a chromosome picture with very low resolution : the original image is 25 by 46 pixels, with 22 different grey values. Thanks to Prof. Dr. G. Ritter for the chromosone picture. We have taken three thresholds to estimate the contours of the chromosome. The point process was no longer an homogeneous Poisson one. The point were

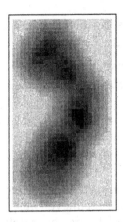 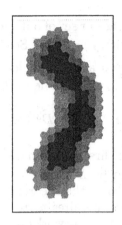 

Figure 5: Estimation of the density of a chromosome : on the left, the original image (25 × 46 pixels), in the center, the Voronoi estimation based on a grid (13 × 26) point process and on the left, the discriminant estimation based on exactly the same grid point process.

generated from a grid of 13 × 26 nodes, with small random deviation to avoid strict linearity between points.

The results of 100 comparisons with Voronoi are published in Rémon (2000). In all cases, the discriminant analysis algorithm gives better estimation for D. The results show a gain of more than 40 percent with respect to the symmetric difference criterion for our solution.

In future researches, we hope to apply this algorithm to spatial non parametric density estimation.

5 A hierarchy of non convex domains in terms of complexity

5.1 Grenander's feature logic of p-order

The aim of pattern recognition is to recover structured figures which are in some sense "simple". We look for smooth estimates of unknown domains. Grenander (1976), in his lectures in Pattern Theory, proposed to define a *feature logic of p-order* as an image

$$I = \bigcap_{\alpha=(\alpha_1,...,\alpha_p)\in A} (g_{\alpha_1} \cup g_{\alpha_2} \cup ... \cup g_{\alpha_p})$$

where g_α belongs to some set G of generators.

For instance, if G is the set of all half plans of $\mathbb{R}^2$ having index α, $I = \bigcap_{\alpha \in A} g_\alpha$ may represent any convex set in $\mathbb{R}^2$, depending on the choice of A.

He suggested to measure the numerical complexity of an image by the power of the index set A (rectangles have finite numerical complexity while ellipsoides have infinite complexity) and the structural complexity by the number of maximum conjunction needed to obtain the image (any convex set is of structural complexity one). Grenander proved that any (topologically) closed subset E can be approximated by a sequence of feature logics of p-order with p increasing to infinity (see Grenander (1976), Section 3.9, for more details).

5.2 A "fractal" classification of non convex sets in $I\!\!R^2$

We propose here a different way of measuring the structural complexity of a figure in $I\!\!R^2$, which is closely related to the algorithm presented above. The hierarchy is based on a zooming process.

Let C_1 be the class of all compact convex sets in the window F in $I\!\!R^2$. Consider the recursive definition ($k \geq 2$) :

$$C_k = C_{k-1} \cup \{D \subseteq F :$$
$$H(D) \setminus D \text{ is a finite union of a.e. disconnected elements of } C_{k-1}\}.$$

In this definition, $H(D)$ is the convex hull of the (non convex) set D, and two elements are said to be a.e. disconnected if they are connected by at most a finite number of points. In the class C_2, one can find figures like moon quadrants, annulus, some capital letters (A, D, E, ...), and biological cells. In most of our applications, the unknown domain D belongs to C_1, C_2 or C_3. The index k of C_k is a good measure of the structural simplicity of a body.

Figure 6 is an example of a fractal set belonging to $C_k \setminus C_{k-1}$. Such a fractal figure can only be estimated through a very large amount of observed inside/outside points. Let us consider an alternate sequence of union and disjunction of discs. Let $D[z; r]$ denote a disc with center $(z, 0)$ and radius r.

Consider :

$$A_0 = D[0; 1] \quad , \quad A_1 = D[\frac{1}{2}; \frac{1}{4}] \quad , \quad A_i = D[\sum_{j=1}^{i} \frac{1}{2^{2j-1}}; \frac{1}{2^{2i}}]$$

and :

$$B_0 = D[1; \frac{1}{2}] \quad , \quad B_1 = D[\frac{3}{4}; \frac{1}{8}] \quad , \quad B_i = D[1 - \sum_{j=1}^{i} \frac{1}{2^{2j}}; \frac{1}{2^{2i+1}}]$$

Then,

$$C = \bigcup_{i=0}^{k} (A_i \setminus B_i) \in C_{2(k+1)} \quad \text{and} \quad C = \bigcup_{i=0}^{k-1} (A_i \setminus B_i) \cup A_k \in C_{2k+1}$$

In Rémon (1997), we prove that any finite union or intersection of convex

Figure 6: Example of a fractal non convex domain.

sets in $I\!R^2$ belongs to some C_k. As Grenander proved that any closed set can be approximated by a sequence of $\bigcap_{i=1}^{I}(\bigcup_{j=1}^{J} A_{ij})$ with I and J growing to infinity, it follows that any closed set in the plane can be approximated by a set in C_k with k large enough.

Thus, our algorithm should correctly estimate any non convex set D as long as enough inside and outside points are available. However, for a given number of inside and outside points, our algorithm will try to find the "simplest" (in the sense of our fractal classification) estimate of D.

References

BAUFAYS, P. and RASSON, J.-P. (1985) : A new geometric discriminant rule. *Computational Statistics Quarterly, 2, 15–30.*

GRENANDER, U. (1976) : Pattern Synthesis : Lectures in Pattern Theory, vol.1, Springer Verlag, New York.

HACHTEL, G.D. , MEILIJSON, I. and NADAS, A. (1981) : The estimation of a convex subset of $I\!R^k$ and its probability content, IBM research report, Yorktown Heights N.Y.

REMON, M. (1994) : The estimation of a convex domain when inside and outside observations are available, *Supplemento ai Rendiconti del Circolo Matematico di Palermo, 35, 227–235.*

REMON, M. (1996) : A discriminant analysis algorithm for the inside/outside problem, *Comput. Stat. and Data Analysis, 23, 125–133.*

REMON, M. (1997) : Utility of discriminant analysis in pattern recognition, *Supplemento ai Rendiconti del Circolo Matematico di Palermo, 50, 335–345.*

REMON, M. (2000) : Discriminant analysis tools for non convex pattern recognition. In: Kiers, H.A.L. et al. (eds.), Data Analysis, Classification, and Related Methods, Springer Verlag, Berlin, 241–246.

Sparse Kernel Feature Analysis *

Alex J. Smola[1], Olvi L. Mangasarian[2], Bernhard Schölkopf[3]

[1]RSISE, Australian National University, Canberra, ACT 0200, Australia

[2]CS Department, University of Wisconsin, Madison, WI 53705, USA

[3]Biowulf Technologies, Broadway 305, Floor 7, New York, NY 10007, USA

Abstract: Kernel Principal Component Analysis (KPCA) has proven to be a versatile tool for unsupervised learning, however at a high computational cost due to the dense expansions in terms of kernel functions. We overcome this problem by proposing a new class of feature extractors employing ℓ_1 norms in coefficient space instead of the Reproducing Kernel Hilbert Space in which KPCA was originally formulated in. Moreover, the modified setting allows us to efficiently extract features which maximize criteria other than the variance in a way similar to projection pursuit.

1 Introduction

Supervised learning is typically concerned with finding an estimate that maps observations x into corresponding labels y, based a 'training sample' $\{(x_1, y_1), \ldots, (x_m, y_m)\}$ drawn from some underlying distribution $\Pr(x, y)$. The main distinction in unsupervised learning is that we are only given a set of observations $\{x_1, \ldots, x_m\}$, drawn from $\Pr(x)$, with the additional goal to extract *some* useful information from the dataset, and if possible, perform inference about $\Pr(x)$ as well.

This means that we have to begin unsupervised learning by defining the question we are going to ask. One possibility is to strive for features that *describe* the observations x_i well. Another possibility is to seek "properties of the data that may be extracted with high confidence." In other words, we look for *simple* feature extractors among a given class of functions with, say, unit variance and zero mean. Examples of this *feature extracting* approach of unsupervised learning are Principal Component Analysis (PCA) (see e.g., Jolliffe (1986)), or Kernel-PCA, as proposed by Schölkopf et al. (1998) in the case of nonlinear functions.

For $x \in \mathbb{R}^n$ and $n \ll m$, computational cost is not a major concern in PCA, since the covariance matrix C, whose eigensystem has to be computed, is in $\mathbb{R}^{n \times n}$. Things change dramatically in Kernel-PCA, where $n \gg m$. This may be due to the inherently high dimensionality of x (e.g., high resolution images) or due to the fact that x is mapped into a *feature space* via the map $\Phi : \mathcal{X} \to \mathcal{F}$. What is done in such a case is to look

---

*Invited lecture

for the eigensystem of the Gram matrix, i.e. the matrix of dot products between observations x_i and subsequently express the eigenvectors of C by a linear combination of observations x_i. The computational cost of diagonalizing C is $O(m^3)$, the cost for obtaining C is typically $O(m^2 N)$ where $N \leq n$.

Besides the significantly increased cost of *obtaining* the feature extractors, i.e., directions to project on, *application* of the latter to new observation is much more costly, too. It is roughly m times more costly than in PCA (details follow in the next section). Several approaches tried to alleviate these problems, either by computation of a compact representation as done by Burges, Schölkopf (1997), or by the heuristic of selecting a subset of basis functions at random. Whilst leading to computationally more favourable expansions in the end, the process is still rather time consuming.

In this paper we propose a new approach which uses an ℓ_1 penalty on the expansion coefficients of the approximate eigenvectors to obtain computationally more favourable expressions. This is similar to a method proposed by Mangasarian (1965) in the context of supervised learning, where the ℓ_1 norm was used as a regularization term. The advantage of this setting is that we need only l terms to extract l features, unlike in Kernel-PCA, where m terms are required regardless of the number of features.

2 Kernel Feature Analysis

The common property of the feature extractors $f_i : \mathcal{X} \to \mathbb{R}$ in this section is to yield meaningful features on the data (e.g., large variance, kurtosis, bimodality) while maintaining a certain degree of simplicity in f_i itself. The latter may be given by a small RKHS norm or a small ℓ_1 norm of the expansion coefficients.

Principal Component Analysis (PCA) The first principal component of a sample is given by the direction with maximum variance. More formally, for centered data $\tilde{X} := \left\{ \tilde{x}_i | \tilde{x}_i = x_i - \frac{1}{m} \sum_{j=1}^{m} x_j \right\}$ the first eigenvector v_1 can be obtained as

$$v_1 = \underset{\|v\|^2 \leq 1}{\operatorname{argmax}} \frac{1}{m} \sum_{i=1}^{m} |\langle v, \tilde{x}_i \rangle|^2. \tag{1}$$

The successive eigenvectors $v_2, \ldots v_d$ are chosen satisfy (1) under the constraint to be orthogonal to the previous ones. This optimization problem is typically solved by computing the eigensystem of C.

Let us proceed to a nonlinear generalization of PCA. This is particularly useful if data is abundant ($m \gg n$). Here one may want to capture more information about the distribution of the data than the n projections onto the principal directions.

Kernel PCA Schölkopf et al. (1998) proposed to map the data into some feature space $\mathcal{F}$ and perform PCA there, following the pioneering work of Aizerman et al. (1964). For this purpose define a map

$$\Phi : \mathcal{X} \to \mathcal{F} \tag{2}$$

into some Hilbert space $\mathcal{F}$, whose purpose it is to "preprocess" data suitably such that nonlinear features can be obtained. Such a mapping could, for instance, map x into its pth order monomials. Typically, the dimensionality of $\mathcal{F}$ is too large to compute Φ explicitly. Aizerman et al. (1964) introduced a method to circumvent this problem, and applied it in a convergence proof for the potential function method. It is applicable whenever an algorithm can be formulated in terms of dot products and does not require explicit knowledge of $\Phi(x)$. Just as Support Vector Machines, Kernel PCA satisfies this condition.

Denote by $\mu := \frac{1}{m} \sum_{i=1}^{m} \Phi(x_i)$ the empirical mean of X mapped in feature space $\mathcal{F}$. Then the covariance 'matrix' C is given by

$$C = \frac{1}{m} \sum_{i=1}^{m} \tilde{\Phi}(x_i)\tilde{\Phi}^{\top}(x_i) \text{ where } \tilde{\Phi}(x) = \Phi(x) - \mu. \tag{3}$$

To compute the eigensystem (v_i, λ_i) of C we have satisfy

$$Cv_i = \lambda_i v_i \text{ for all } 1 \le i \le m. \tag{4}$$

Since we may not want to (or we even may be unable to) compute the covariance matrix C explicitly, we resort to an implicit representation of v_i in terms of the mapped patterns $\Phi(x_i)$. This can always be done since the image of C is contained in the span of $\{\tilde{\Phi}(x_1), \dots \tilde{\Phi}(x_m)\}$ (cf. Schölkopf et al. (1998)). This allows us to rewrite (4) as

$$\frac{1}{m} \sum_{j,j'}^{m} \langle \tilde{\Phi}(x_i), \tilde{\Phi}(x_j) \rangle \langle \tilde{\Phi}(x_j), \tilde{\Phi}(x_{j'}) \rangle \alpha_{j'}^l = \lambda_l \frac{1}{m} \sum_{j}^{m} \langle \tilde{\Phi}(x_i), \tilde{\Phi}(x_j) \rangle \alpha_j^l \tag{5}$$

where $v_l = \sum_{i=1}^{m} \tilde{\Phi}(x_j)\alpha_j^l$ and consequently $\langle v_l, x \rangle = \sum_{i=1}^{m} \alpha_j^l \langle \Phi(x_j), \Phi(x) \rangle \alpha_j^l$.

Note that the new formulation does not require explicit computation of $\Phi(x)$ anymore. Instead, only dot products of the mapped patterns into $\mathcal{F}$ appear. This allows us to introduce kernels.

Kernels Denote by $k(x, x') := \langle \Phi(x), \Phi(x') \rangle$ a kernel corresponding to Φ. Typically, k is much cheaper to compute than Φ. Rewriting (5) in terms of kernels (see Schölkopf et al. (1998), for details) we obtain

$$\tilde{K}\tilde{K}\alpha^l = \lambda_l \tilde{K}\alpha^l \tag{6}$$

where $\tilde{K} = (1 - 1_m)K(1 - 1_m)$, $K_{ij} = k(x_i, x_j)$, 1 is the identity matrix, and $1_m \in \mathbb{R}^{m \times m}$ is the matrix with all entries set to $\frac{1}{m}$. Furthermore $\alpha^l \in \mathbb{R}^m$ and $1 \leq l \leq m$. Since we are not interested in the null-space of $\tilde{K}$, (6) can be solved by diagonalizing $\tilde{K}$ and keeping the eigenvectors corresponding to nonzero eigenvalues.

Examples of kernels include the dot product of all monomial features of order d generated from x, given by $k(x, x') = \langle x, x' \rangle^d$. Similar relations hold for inhomogeneous polynomials $k(x, x') = (\langle x, x' \rangle + 1)^d$. In general, any kernel corresponding to a positive integral operator, i.e.

$$\int k(x, x')f(x)f(x') \, dx \, dx' \geq 0 \text{ for all } f \in L_2, \tag{7}$$

corresponds to dot products in some feature space $\mathcal{F}$. A popular example of this class are Gaussian radial basis functions

$$k(x, x') = \exp\left(-\frac{\|x - x'\|^2}{2\sigma^2}\right) \text{ for some } \sigma > 0. \tag{8}$$

Constrained Maximization By the above reasoning one may reformulate Kernel PCA as follows: define the set of admissible weight vectors

$$V_{\text{RKHS}} := \left\{ v \middle| v = \sum_{i=1}^{m} \alpha_i \Phi(x_i) \text{ with } \|v\|^2 = \sum_{i,j}^{m} \alpha_i \alpha_j k(x_i, x_j) \leq 1 \right\}.$$

Now the problem of finding the first principal component (4) (i.e. the direction of projection with maximum variance) may be transformed into

$$v_1 = \underset{v \in V_{\text{RKHS}}}{\text{argmax}} \frac{1}{m} \sum_{i=1}^{m} \left| \langle v, \tilde{\Phi}(x_i) \rangle \right|^2 \text{ where } \tilde{\Phi}(x) = \Phi(x) - \mu. \tag{9}$$

In other words, we seek the function $f(x) = \langle v, \Phi(x) \rangle + \mu$ with zero mean and maximal empirical variance on $\{x_1, \ldots, x_m\}$, while restricting the complexity of f to those functions allowed by V_{RKHS}. Depending on the choice of the kernel k this may mean that we seek f among all polynomials of bounded degree ($k(x, x') = \langle x, x' \rangle^d$), among functions of bounded variation ($k(x, x') = \exp(-\|x - x'\|)$), or functions with general smoothness constraints ($k(x, x') = \exp(-\|x - x'\|^2)$). See Smola et al. (1998), for more details on kernels.

Sparse Kernel PCA This leads to the question whether sets V other than V_{RKHS} might lead to useful feature extractors, too. In particular, one could choose

$$V_{\text{LP}} := \left\{ v \middle| v = \sum_{i=1}^{m} \alpha_i \Phi(x_i) \text{ with } \sum_{i} |\alpha_i| \leq 1 \right\}. \tag{10}$$

This constraint is popular in supervised learning for both classification Mangasarian (1965), and regression Chen et al. (1999), . The best orthogonal basis algorithm is an example thereof. In those algorithms, rather than specifying the function class via (10) directly, an ℓ_1 penalty is added to the data-dependent term. One may show that these two formulations are equivalent.

By the above reasoning we just obtained a new way of defining feature extractors: we maximize the variance of $\langle v, \Phi(x)\rangle + \mu$ under the constraint that $v \in V_{\mathrm{LP}}$. This gives us the definition of the first "principal vector" in the ℓ_1 context.

$$v_1 = \operatorname*{argmax}_{v \in V_{\mathrm{LP}}} \frac{1}{m} \sum_{i=1}^{m} \left| \langle v, \tilde{\Phi}(x_i)\rangle \right|^2 \text{ where } \tilde{\Phi}(x) = \Phi(x) - \mu. \tag{11}$$

As before with PCA, subsequent "principal vectors" v_i can be defined by enforcing optimality with respect to (11) while enforcing orthogonality to all v_j with $j < i$.

The solution of (11) has the nice property of being sparse in terms of the expansion coefficients α_i, due to the ℓ_1 constraint (the coefficients may be chosen from the "hyperdiamond-shaped" ℓ_1 ball).* In fact, as we shall show in section 3, the optimal solution is found by picking the direction $\Phi(x_i)$ corresponding to a single pattern, i.e. the solution lies on one of the vertices of the ℓ_1 ball.

Kernel Projection Pursuit The second modification regarding (9) is to choose a *contrast* function other than the variance, that should be optimized. Hence one obtains solutions of the following type of problems

$$v_1 = \operatorname*{argmax}_{v \in V} \frac{1}{m} \sum_{i=1}^{m} q(\langle v, \Phi(x_i)\rangle) \text{ or } \operatorname*{argmax}_{v \in V} Q\left(\{\langle v, \Phi(x_i)\rangle, \ldots\}\right), \tag{12}$$

where $q(\cdot)$ and $Q(\cdot)$ are functions which are maximized for an "interesting" function $f(x) = \langle v_1, \Phi(x)\rangle$. This leads to methods which are quite similar to projection pursuit, however with the novelty that they act in feature space rather than in input space (one can easily check that both methods coincide for $\Phi(x) = x$).

Common contrast functions regard directions as interesting, if projection on the latter yields features which are "least Gaussian," have several modes, maximize the Fisher Information, the negative Shannon entropy, or other quantities of interest. A possible function q would be $q(\xi) = \xi^4$ — a function that favours projections with non–Gaussian distributions and high kurtosis (see e.g., Klinke (1995)).

---

*Note that the requirement of $\|v\|^2 = 1$ or the corresponding ℓ_1 constraint are necessary — the value of the target function might increase without bound otherwise simply by rescaling v.

3 Algorithms

Convex Maximization Solving a general feature extraction problem, as defined by (12), is often prone to local minima and thus difficult to achieve, be it numerically or explicitly. However, under certain conditions, the optimal solution can be found easily in quadratic or even linear time. The key idea is based on a theorem of Rockafellar (1970).

Theorem 1 (Rockafellar (1970), Cor. 32.3.4)
The problem of globally maximizing a convex function on $\mathbb{R}^m$ bounded above on a polyhedral set not containing straight lines that go to infinity in both directions has a vertex solution.

This means that we may obtain solutions of convex maximization problems efficiently, if the domain of optimization is chosen such that the number of vertices is small (otherwise such problems can be NP-hard). To make Theorem 1 more amenable to our analysis we prove:

Corollary 2 (Vertex Solutions for Kernel Feature Analysis)
The optimization problem $v_1 = \underset{v \in V_{\mathrm{LP}}}{\mathrm{argmax}}\, Q\left(\{\langle v, \Phi(x_1) \rangle, \ldots, \langle v, \Phi(x_m) \rangle\}\right)$
has a vertex solution if Q is convex and bounded above on V_{LP}.

Proof. Clearly the ℓ_1 ball (and thus V_{LP}) is a compact polyhedral set and Q is convex and bounded on V_{LP} by construction. Hence Theorem 1 applies and an optimal solution can be found at one of the vertices $(0, \ldots, 0, 1, 0, \ldots, 0) \in \mathbb{R}^m$ of the ℓ_1 ball. In other words, the solution can be found by simply picking the direction of projection $v_1 = \Phi(x_i)$ with largest Q value. $\square$

This allows us to compute the first component of interest v_1 by evaluating the terms $Q\left(\{k(x_i, x_1), \ldots, k(x_i, x_m)\}\right)$ for all $1 \leq i \leq m$ and picking the one with the largest value. We assume that projections onto v and $-v$ yield the same Q value (i.e. are equally interesting), thus we may limit ourselves to the positive orthant.

Sequential Decompositions We proceed to finding v_i (with $i \geq 2$). In the following denote by V^{i-1} the space of directions to select from in the i-th round; in particular, $V^0 := V$. The vectors spanning V^i will be denoted by Φ_j^i. We start with $\Phi_j^0 := \Phi(x_j)$ and obtain

$$V^i := \left\{ w \,\middle|\, w = \sum_{j=1}^m \alpha_j^i \Phi_j^{i-1} \text{ with } \sum_{j=1}^m |\alpha_j^i| \leq 1 \right\}. \tag{13}$$

To obtain orthogonality of v_i we have several options. We might cut the polyhedral set V_{LP} with a plane orthogonal to the first chosen basis function. Unfortunately this may up to double the number of vertices. The following strategy is numerically more efficient:

As stated above, we want that each direction v_i be orthogonal to all previous directions, i.e. $\langle v_i, v_j \rangle = 0$ for all $i \geq j \geq 1$. This is clearly the case if for all $v \in V^i$ we have $\langle v, v_j \rangle = 0$ for all $i > j \geq 1$. Assuming that this holds for some $i - 1$, we can satisfy the constraint for V^i by projecting all Φ_j^i (which span V^i) on the space orthogonal to v_i. This yields

$$\Phi_j^i := \Phi_j^{i-1} - \frac{v_i}{\|v_i\|^2} \langle \Phi_j^{i-1}, v_i \rangle = \Phi_j^i - \frac{v_i}{\|v_i\|^2} \langle \Phi_j^0, v_i \rangle. \tag{14}$$

For the last equality note that $\Phi_j^i - \Phi_j^0$ is spanned by v_l with $l \leq i-1$ and therefore $\langle \Phi_j^i - \Phi_j^0, v_i \rangle = 0$. This is crucial for practical implementations, since the second formulation of (14) requires only i kernel computations: v_i is a linear combination of i vectors chosen from Φ_l^0. Moreover, (14) reduces the set of vectors spanning V^i by 1, as v_i is chosen among Φ_j^{i-1}. Of course, we compute $\|v_i\|^2$ beforehand since it is identical for all Φ_j^i.

Since Φ_j^i is not necessarily in V_{LP}, we will call this approach *unnormalized* Kernel Feature Analysis. Clearly we might also choose to normalize Φ_j^i back to V_{LP} before extracting more features. This is achieved by

$$\tilde{\Phi}_j^i := \left(\sum_{l=1}^{i} |\alpha_{jl}^i| \right)^{-1} \Phi_j^i, \text{ where } \Phi_j^i = \sum_l \alpha_{jl}^i \Phi(x_l).$$

We will call this approach *normalized* Kernel Feature Analysis. For the sake of simplicity we only discuss the unnormalized case below.

A Quantile Trick The algorithms presented so far have the advantage of providing an optimally sparse decomposition for feature extraction, however they still require a maximum search over all possible directions of projection and their respective Q values. It means that (in the "training" stage) an implementation will be bound to have $O(m^2)$ cost per iteration which is as bad as what one can expect from implementations of principal component analysis. This is clearly not satisfactory.

We can address this problem by relaxing the requirements of optimality slightly: typically one is not interested in the *best* n feature extractors but would already be content to obtain feature n extractors which are *among the best* ones obtainable. For instance, for preprocessing it might be sufficient if with high probability each selected feature was among the best 5% obtainable. The following strategy addresses this problem: compute a subsample of $\tilde{m}$ directions from all m available ones and choose the largest Q–value amongst them. Such a subsampling approach leads on average to values in the $\frac{\tilde{m}}{\tilde{m}+1}$ quantile range:

Lemma 3 (Quantiles and Subsampling) *Taking the maximum element of an $\tilde{m}$ subsample of numbers ξ_i with $i \leq m$ leads on average* to an element above the $\frac{\tilde{m}}{m+1}$ quantile range of the whole set and with probability $1 - \eta$ to a quantile of at least $\eta^{(1/\tilde{m})}$.

Proof. Denote by ν the rank of the random variable ξ then $F(\nu) = \nu$ is a lower bound on the staircase-shaped cumulative distribution of ranks (for m observations), with $\nu \in [0, 1]$. We know that consequently the cumulative distribution of ranks for $\hat{\xi} := \max(\xi_1, \ldots, \xi_{\tilde{m}})$ is lower-bounded $\xi^{\tilde{m}}$. Therefore the expected rank of $\hat{\xi}$ is lower-bounded by $\int \xi (\partial_\xi \xi^m) d\xi = 1 - \frac{1}{\tilde{m}+1}$. This proves the first statement.

For a single observation, the probability of being in the top $1 - \varepsilon$ quantile is ε. Therefore, for the maximum of $\tilde{m}$ random variables to be in the top $1 - \varepsilon$ quantile is $1 - (1 - \varepsilon)^{\tilde{m}}$. Solving for $\eta = (1 - \varepsilon)^{\tilde{m}}$ give the second part of the lemma. $\qquad\square$

Algorithm 1 Sparse Kernel Feature Analysis

---

input: Data $x_1, \ldots, x_m$, I (# of features to extract), $\tilde{m}$ (random subset)
  [a] initialize idx $= \{\}$ (empty list), $n = 0$
  for $i = 1$ **to** I **do**
    [b] Pick random subset $S \subset \{1, \ldots m\}\backslash$idx with $|S| = \tilde{m}$.
    [c] Compute $\langle \Phi_j^{i-1}, \Phi(x_l) \rangle = K_{jl} - \left(K^{m,i-1}(K^{i-1,i-1})^{-1} K^{m,i-1\top} \right)_{jl}$
    for all $j \in S$ and $1 \leq l \leq m$, i.e. the features.
    [d] Compute $Q_j := Q(\langle \Phi_j^{i-1}, \Phi(x_1) \rangle, \ldots \langle \Phi_j^{i-1}, \Phi(x_m) \rangle$ for all $j \in S$ and pick the maximum $Q\hat{j}$.
    [e] Add $\hat{j}$ to the index list idx and store $(\alpha_{\hat{j},1}^{i-1}, \ldots, \alpha_{\hat{j},i-1}^{i-1})$ for the expansion coefficients of v_i.
    [f] Obtain K^{mi} by adding the corresponding row and K^{ii} by adding the corresponding row and column.
    [g] Perform rank-1 update for the pre-computed value of $\alpha^i = K^{mi}(K^{ii})^{-1}$ (this can be done using the matrix inversion lemma).
  end for
output: Index vector idx, decomposition vector $\alpha = K^{mi}(K^{ii})^{-1}$

For instance, in order to obtain a $\eta^{(1/\tilde{m})} \hat{=} 95\%$ quantile with $1 - \eta \hat{=} 95\%$ percent probability one has to consider a subset of only $\tilde{m} = 59$ samples. This leads to a considerable speedup in computing feature extractors since in general m is several orders of magnitude larger than that. Note that this only ensures that we will obtain *one* of the best feature extractors, but no guarantee can be given in terms of its *absolute distance* to the best extractor (since this depends on the tails of the distribution). Thus unless the *best* feature extractors are needed subsampling should be the method of choice.

The previous considerations lead to the following simple Algorithm 1 to compute sparse kernel feature analyzers. The key point is that computation of only $\tilde{m}$ instances of Q at iteration i is of cost $O(\tilde{m}im)$ which is considerably less than $O(m^2)$ which is required for PCA (in addition to an $O(m^2)$ storage requirement which may be prohibitive in most cases).

Whilst the computation of i features on new data requires only $O(M \cdot i \cdot m)$ operations, extraction of the principal directions themselves is still an $O(m^2)$ operation. The constants, however, are significantly smaller than when computing the eigenvectors of a matrix (the latter requires several passes over the matrix K_{ij}). This is the case since finding the direction with maximum Q value still requires computation of all dot products between all possible directions of projection and the actual patterns to be analyzed.

Numerical Details To compute the projections $\langle \Phi^i_j, \Phi(x_l) \rangle$ we use

$$
\begin{aligned}
\langle \Phi^i_j, \Phi(x_l) \rangle &= \langle \Phi^i_j, \Phi^0_l \rangle = \langle \Phi^0_j, \Phi^0_l \rangle + \langle \Phi^i_j - \Phi^0_j, \Phi^0_l \rangle \\
&= \langle \Phi^0_j, \Phi^0_l \rangle - \langle \Phi^i_j - \Phi^0_j, \Phi^i_l - \Phi^0_l \rangle + \langle \Phi^i_j - \Phi^0_j, \Phi^i_l \rangle \\
&= \langle \Phi^0_j, \Phi^0_l \rangle - \langle \Phi^i_j - \Phi^0_j, \Phi^i_l - \Phi^0_l \rangle = K_{jl} - \bar{K}_{jl}.
\end{aligned}
$$

The last equality holds due to the orthogonality of Φ^i_l with respect to $v_1, \ldots, v_i$. Here $K_{jl} := k(x_j, x_l)$ and $\bar{K}_{jl}$ is the matrix of dot products between the projections of Φ^0_j, Φ^0_l onto the space spanned by $v_1, \ldots, v_i$. $\bar{K}_{jl}$ is obtained by $\bar{K} = K^{mi}(K^{ii})^{-1}K^{mi\top}$, where K^{mi} is the $m \times i$ submatrix $K^{mi}_{jl} = k(x_j, x_{\mathrm{idx}(l)})$, spanned by the dot product between the data and the so-far chosen vectors $\Phi(x_{\mathrm{idx}(1)}), \ldots, \Phi(x_{\mathrm{idx}(i-1)})$ for the expansion of the v_j. Likewise K^{ii} is the $i \times i$ submatrix given by the dot product between the so-far chosen vectors $\Phi(x_{\mathrm{idx}(1)}), \ldots, \Phi(x_{\mathrm{idx}(i-1)})$ on their own.

To show the explicit form for $\bar{K}$ we follow Smola, Schölkopf (2000). Without loss of generality (and to simplify the notation) we assume that $\mathrm{idx}(j) = j$, i.e. that K^{ii} is simply the upper leftsubmatrix of K (and K^{mi} the left submatrix, analogously). The orthogonal projection $\Phi^i_l - \Phi^0_l$ of $\Phi(x_l)$ onto $\Phi(x_1), \ldots, \Phi(x_i)$ minimizes $\|\Phi(x_l) - \sum_{j=1}^i \beta_j \Phi(x_j)\|^2$. Therefore $\beta \in \mathbb{R}^i$ is given by $\beta = (K^{ii})^{-1}\kappa$, where $\kappa = (k(x_l, x_1), \ldots, k(x_l, x_i))$. Now α^i is the matrix of all coefficients such that all $\Phi(x_j)$ are projected onto the space spanned by $\Phi(x_1), \ldots, \Phi(x_i)$. Therefore it must be given by $\alpha^i \in \mathbb{R}^{i \times m}$ where $\alpha^i = (K^{ii})^{-1}K^{mi\top}$.

4   Experiments

We show that on 2D toy examples, Kernel Feature Analysis provides features qualitatively similar to Kernel Principal Component Analysis.

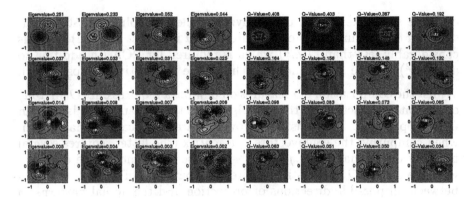

Figure 1: Left: Contour plots of first 16 feature extractors of Kernel-PCA for a Gaussian RBF Kernel ($\sigma^2 = 0.05$) and a dataset of 120 samples. The small dots denote data. Right: Contour plots of first 16 feature extractors of Sparse Kernel Feature Analysis. Note that every additional feature needs only one more kernel function to be computed. Observe how KFA first selects the cluster centers, then starts splitting the clusters, next splits them orthogonally, with much fewer kernel functions than Kernel-PCA. The Q-value denotes the variance of the projected-out feature.

Figure 1 displays features extracted by both types of algorithms (the results obtained by the quantile trick are virtually identical and are thus omitted).

Note that the main difference lies in the first few features. For instance, KFA is using only one basis function for the first feature (due to the built-in sparsity), which enforces a feature extractor sitting on one of the three clusters. Kernel PCA, on the other hand, will typically have contributions of all basis functions already for the first feature.

In both cases, it can be seen that the features are meaningful in that they discover nontrivial structure. The first features identify the cluster structure in the data set, while the higher order ones analyze the individual clusters in more detail.

As a real world example we used the NIST database of handwritten digits (Fig. 2). Due to memory constraints (the whole database is 0.5 GB in MATLAB) we used a subset of $m = 10.000$ samples. As default option a kernel of width $\sigma^2 = 0.5 \cdot 28^2$ was chosen to account for the image size of 28×28 pixels. Randomization was set to a subset of $\tilde{m} = 59$ in order to ensure that in at least $1 - \eta = 95\%$ of all cases we found one of the 5% best feature extractors.

One can clearly see that all digits appear at least once among the first 15 feature extractors. Moreover, note the repeated occurence of the digit 1. This is so since the latter appears almost orthogonal to the kernel, when shifted, even by only a few pixels (the overlap is zero in this case). Hence they can be considered independent feature extractors.

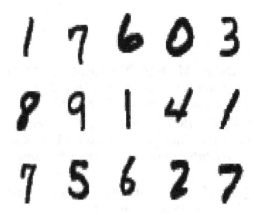

Figure 2: The first 15 patterns (top left to lower right) from a reduced NIST database (10.000 samples) corresponding to the first 15 feature extractors. We used a Gaussian RBF kernel with the width $2\sigma^2$ chosen to be $0.5 \times n$ (here $n = \mathrm{Dim}(x)$).

5 Discussion and Outlook

Sparse Kernel Feature Analysis provided us with a means to obtain results similar to Kernel-PCA, however, with much lower memory and time requirements. Therefore it is ideally suited for feature extraction and data description in lower dimensional subspaces. In fact, it is a drop-in replacement for Kernel-PCA in all its applications.

Furthermore we believe that the feature extraction framework as stated in (12) will provide a large class of useful algorithms in the future. However, the crucial point will be, which sets of hypotheses can be found such that (1) the solution can be computed with little computational cost, (2) the features can be extracted rapidly, (3) the class of functions is interesting for the user.

Finally, despite the rather simple algorithmic rule:

(1) find the function with the maximum Q–value
(2) project $\Phi(x_i)$ out
(3) repeat

Kernel feature analysis has interesting theoretical properties such as a close resemblance with clustering, wavelet techniques proposed by Mallat, Zhang (1993) (Matching Pursuit), and reduced set algorithms for Support Vector machines as the one by Schölkopf et al. (1999). The main difference to the two latter methods is that there exists not only one target function that needs to be well approximated, but that the class of functions itself is the object of the investigation.

Intermediate versions may provide a means to design algorithms that combine the domains of supervised and unsupervised learning, or to include prior knowledge, e.g. by leading to feature extractors that are particularly good for a specific set of estimates. This will be the topic of further research.

References

AIZERMAN, M. A., BRAVERMAN, É.. M., ROZONOÉR, L. I. (1964): Theoretical foundations of the potential function method in pattern recognition learning. *Automation and Remote Control*, *25*, 821–837.

BURGES, C. J. C., SCHÖLKOPF, B. (1997): Improving the accuracy and speed of support vector learning machines. In: M. Mozer, M. Jordan, T. Petsche (eds.), *Advances in Neural Information Processing Systems 9*, 375–381, Cambridge, MA. MIT Press.

CHEN, S., DONOHO, D., SAUNDERS, M. (1999): Atomic decomposition by basis pursuit. *Siam Journal of Scientific Computing*, *20*(1), 33–61.

JOLLIFFE, I. T. (1986): Principal Component Analysis. Springer-Verlag, New York, New York.

KLINKE, S. (1995): Exploratory Projection Pursuit - The multivariate and discrete case. Discussion Paper 70, SFB 373, Humboldt-University of Berlin.

MALLAT, S., ZHANG, Z. (1993): Matching Pursuit in a time-frequency dictionary. *IEEE Transactions on Signal Processing*, *41*, 3397–3415.

MANGASARIAN, O. L. (1965): Linear and Nonlinear Separation of Patterns by Linear Programming. *Operations Research*, *13*, 444–452.

ROCKAFELLAR, R. T. (1970): Convex Analysis, vol. 28 of *Princeton Mathematics Series*. Princeton University Press.

SCHÖLKOPF, B., MIKA, S., BURGES, C., KNIRSCH, P., MÜLLER, K.-R., RÄTSCH, G., SMOLA, A. (1999): Input Space vs. Feature Space in Kernel-Based Methods. *IEEE Transactions on Neural Networks*, *10*(5), 1000–1017.

SCHÖLKOPF, B., SMOLA, A., MÜLLER, K.-R. (1998): Nonlinear component analysis as a kernel Eigenvalue problem. *Neural Computation*, *10*, 1299–1319.

SMOLA, A., SCHÖLKOPF, B., MÜLLER, K.-R. (1998): The Connection between Regularization Operators and Support Vector Kernels. *Neural Networks*, *11*, 637–649.

SMOLA, A. J., SCHÖLKOPF, B. (2000): Sparse Greedy Matrix Approximation for Machine Learning. In: P. Langley (ed.), *Proceedings of the 17th International Conference on Machine Learning*, 911–918, San Francisco. Morgan Kaufman.

Part 3

Data Mining, Information Processing, and Automation

Exploring Association Rules by Interactive Graphics

H. Hofmann, A. Wilhelm

Institut für Mathematik,
Universität Augsburg, D-86135 Augsburg, Germany

Abstract: Data Mining (DM) works with very computer-intensive methods and uses automated techniques from various fields of data analysis. Getting some results is a (comparatively) fast process, yet, filtering the results in terms of their usefulness and importance is not quite as straightforward. It has been already proposed in the DM literature, to analyse the full $X - Y$ data table, whenever a rule $X \to Y$ has been found (Kardaun and Alanko, 1999). *Mosaicplots* provide analysts with exactly this possibility in a graphical way. Enhanced with standard interactive features they represent a powerful tool to "look at" multidimensional categorical data. It will be shown in this paper, how Association Rules and a variation of Mosaicplots, the so-called Doubledecker plots, fit together, and, how visualization techniques can be used to filter interesting rules.

1 Association Rules

Association Rules are a typical data mining procedure and aim to describe correlations between items that occur together. They have been proposed by Agrawal et al. (1993) in the context of market basket analysis to provide an automated process, which could find connections among items, that were not known before. In market basket analysis the data or *database* D is a set of *transactions*, every transaction T being a subset of the set of possible items $\mathcal{I} = \{i_1, i_2, \ldots, i_p\}$. Each transaction is identified by a unique number, the *transaction identification (TID)*. An *association rule* is an implication of the form $X \to Y$, where X and Y are mutually exclusive itemsets (i.e. $X, Y \subset \mathcal{I}$ and $X \cap Y = \emptyset$).

An association rule $X \to Y$ holds with *confidence* $c = c(X \to Y)$, if $c\%$ of transactions in D that contain X also contain Y. The rule $X \to Y$ has *support* s in the database D, if $s\%$ of transactions in D contain $X \cup Y$. Discovery of association rules is based on the frequent item set approach and typically some variation of the a priori algorithm (Agrawal et al., 1993) is used in this process. These methods aim to generate all association rules that pass some user-specified thresholds for support (*minsup*) and confidence (*minconf*). The problem is, that depending on the specified thresholds for confidence and support a vast amount of rules may be generated. However, only a small fraction of the rules found are of economical value which means that the rules are previously unknown, are explicable, and actionable.

Instead of concentrating on each transaction and the items bought in it, we prefer the statistical approach and concentrate on the items themselves. We identify every transaction according to its TID with a positive integer. Thus, the sample space Ω is a subset of the set of positive integers and the probability space $(\Omega, \mathcal{P}(\Omega), P)$ is given by the power set $\mathcal{P}(\Omega)$ and some probability measure P on $(\Omega, \mathcal{P}(\Omega))$. Every item i_j is then represented by a random variable $X_j : \Omega \rightarrow \{0, 1\}$ $(1 \leq j \leq p)$, taking ones and zeroes for "bought" and "not bought" respectively. We are interested in the events that certain items are bought together. We say that an event $X = (X_{j_1}, \ldots, X_{j_\ell})$ occurs in the database $\mathcal{D}$ if there exists some $\omega \in \Omega$ such that the variables $X_{j_1}, \ldots, X_{j_\ell}$ take the value 1 for this particular ω. The *frequency* of an event X is then the number of ω's for which the event X occurs. The support $s(X \cap Y)$ of a rule then corresponds to the frequency with which two events X and Y occur together and the *conditional frequency* of event Y given event X corresponds to the confidence $c(X \rightarrow Y)$.

In classical data analysis the frequency and the conditional frequency are maximum likelihood estimators of the probability of $X \cap Y$ and the conditional probability of Y given X, respectively. The conditions for an association rule given above can therefore be re-formulated as. Let X and Y be two events, then $X \rightarrow Y \iff P(X \cap Y) \geq s, P(Y|X) \geq c$ where s and c have the same meaning as before.

2 Visualisation of Association Rules

Confidence and support are important characteristics of association rules. Visualization should display both criteria in one display. In addition, visualization should provide insight into the full contingency table of the involved variables and not only into one particular combination of these variables. *Mosaic Plots* were introduced by Hartigan and Kleiner (1981) as a graphical display of multivariate contingency tables and an interactive version has been implemented in MANET (Unwin et al., 1996). A more detailed description of the interactive facilities for mosaic plots is given in Hofmann (2000). One way to visualize an association rule $X \rightarrow Y$ is, to combine all variables involved in X as *explanatory* variables and draw them within one mosaicplot. Visualize the *response* Y by highlighting the categories of interest in a barchart (or a second mosaic plot, if Y consists of more than one variable). Then, the highlighted area in a bin in a mosaic plot gives a visual measure for the frequency $S(X \cap Y)$, highlighting heights relative to the bin's height give the conditional frequency $S(X \cap Y)/S(X)$.

In order to be able to compare the proportions of highlighting heights more easily, only mosaics of the following form, called double-decker plots, are used: Starting from the basic rectangle, the width is divided according to the first variable's categories and their numbers of entries. Each of these bins is divided again and again horizontally in the same way according to the other variables. Highlighting, however, splits the bins vertically, see Figure 1. This has two advantages: firstly, all bins are of the same height now. Highlighting heights are directly comparable - the vertical axis on the left of the double-decker plot in Figure 1 shows percentages of highlighting heights. Secondly, these plots can easily be labelled. By falling the perpendicular from a bin through the labels below, the exact combination a bin represents can be read from. Each

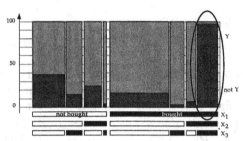

Figure 1: Double-decker plot representing a three-way contingency table. A response variable is added by highlighting.

row corresponds to one variable, the white rectangles stand for "0"s, the blacks for "1"s.

The encircled bin on the right of fig. 1 therefore represents the combination $X_1 = 1 \cap X_2 = 1 \cap X_3 = 1$. Highlighting shows the cases $Y = 1$. The highlighted area in the encircled bin thus gives an estimate of the support of the rule $X_1 = 1 \cap X_2 = 1 \cap X_3 = 1 \to Y = 1$ (ca. 12.5%), the height of highlighting gives its confidence (ca. 95%).

2.1 Pruning Sequences

Agrawal et al. (1995) exploit metainformation to define expected confidence and support of rules based upon an ancestor/successor structure imposed by a taxonomy. Rules are pruned according to the result of comparing expected and observed values. Let us assume, we are dealing with a *sequence of association rules for* Y of the following form:

$$X_1 \to Y, \qquad X_1 \cap X_2 \to Y, \qquad X_1 \cap X_2 \cap X_3 \to Y$$

Goal of the analysis is to decide, which rules are essential to explaining the data and which rules may be pruned from the set. It is obvious, that each item we add to the left-hand-side of a rule reduces the support of it. But what do we gain in exchange? A rule $X \to Z$ is called *ancestor* of $Y \to Z$, if Y contains X, i.e. the items of X form a subset of the items in Y. Accordingly, $Y \to Z$ is called the *successor* of $X \to Z$.

Method 1: Comparing with Ancestor Rules (Bing et al., 1999)

Bing et al. based the decision, whether to accept a rule or not, on expectations founded on information, which has already been mined before - a rule is being judged according to the expectations derived from its ancestor rule. If a rule provides significantly higher values than expected, it will be accepted, since it provides additional information about the data. Let $X \to Z$ be an ancestor rule of $X \cap Y \to Z$.

The *expected support* of a rule $X \cap Y \to Z$ given $X \to Z$ is defined as

$$sup_{X \to Z}(X \cap Y \to Z) = sup(X \to Z) \cdot sup(Y)$$

the *expected confidence* is defined as

$$conf_{X \to Z}(X \cap Y \to Z) = conf(X \to Z).$$

From a statistical point of view the above definition of expected support coincides with the assumption of statistical independence of $X \cap Z$ and Y, this leads to a first method for testing a rule w.r.t its ancestor.

$$
\begin{array}{ll}
p_1 = P(Z|X,Y) & p_2 = P(Z|X) \\
n_1 = n \cdot P(X \cap Y) & n_2 = n \cdot P(X) \\
H_o : p_1 = p_2 \quad \text{vs.} & H_1 : p_1 < p_2
\end{array}
$$

$$\text{test-statistic: } T_1 = \frac{\widehat{p_1} - \widehat{p_2}}{\sqrt{\widehat{p}(1 - \widehat{p})}} \sqrt{\frac{\widehat{n_1 n_2}}{\widehat{n_1} + \widehat{n_2}}},$$

with $p = \frac{P(X \cap Y \cap Z) + P(X \cap Z)}{P(X \cap Y) + P(X)}$ and $1 - p = \frac{P(X \cap Y \cap \neg Z) + P(X \cap \neg Z)}{P(X \cap Y) + P(X)}$.

If p_1 and p_2 were independent, the above test statistic, T_1 would be approximately standard normal distributed. Unfortunately, p_1 and p_2 are not independent, since a subgroup of the data is being compared to its total (including the subgroup).

The problem here is that in practice a situation like this is quite common and often is handled in exactly the same way as described above. Moreover, this method proves to provide sensible results in a lot of examples. As a satisfying solution we therefore have to provide a procedure that is statistically sound and not inferior to the approach above.

In the following lines we will therefore further discuss the approach above, in order to be able to give an appropriate alternative for it later. The procedure of pruning according to method 1 is the following: Accept the association rule, if the alternative gets accepted and the support of $X \cap Y \to Z$ is still larger than *minsup*. Thus, only if the null hypothesis is rejected (on a specified level of significance α), the rule is accepted and vice versa. We assume (this is the illegal part of it), that T_1 is approximately standard normally distributed. Critical values for T_1 are therefore 1.96, 1.65 and 1.29 for levels of 0.025, 0.05 and 0.1 respectively. Of course, we still only accept rules which have sufficient support.

No	rule		confidence	support
1	olives	→ bourbon	51.80	24.48
2	olives & coke	→ bourbon	73.65	10.89
3	olives & heineken	→ bourbon	65.52	13.29
4	olives & cracker	→ bourbon	70.81	13.09
5	olives & heineken & coke	→ bourbon	61.22	3.00
6	olives & heineken & cracker	→ bourbon	77.86	10.89

Table 1: Six rules from the SAS Assocs Data.

Let us consider the rules from table 1. Table 2 gives the results from evaluating the rules with respect to their ancestor structures. The numbers given in it are the value from the incorrect test statistic T_1 and the value of the proper $N(0,1)$-test statistic T_2 which will be discussed later. An overview of the results is given in figure 2. Crossed out arrows indicate, that the corresponding rule has been rejected w.r.t. its ancestor using test statistic T_1 on a significance level of 5% . One problem is, that

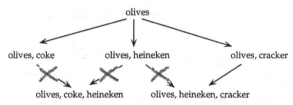

Figure 2: Summary of the left-hand-sides of the rules listed above. Crossed out arrows indicate, that the correponding rule has been rejected w.r.t. its ancestor on a significance level of 5% .

different ancestors lead to different expected values. This opens the way to situations like the one sketched in fig. 2, where a rule is rejected w.r.t one ancestor but accepted w.r.t another (rule 6).

The obvious solution to this is, to reject a rule, if it is not significant w.r.t at least **one** of its ancestor rules.

We still have to deal with the problem that the test-statistic T_1 is **not** normally distributed. We now want to modify the problem slightly and give a statistically sound testing procedure for it. Consider again the values p_1 and p_2 we want to compare: $p_1 = P(Z \mid X, Y)$ and $p_2 = P(Z|X)$. Let $p_3 = P(Z \mid X, \neg Y)$. From $p_2 = P(Y)p_1 + (1 - P(Y))p_3$ follows:
$$p_2 < p_1 \iff (p_3 - p_1) \cdot (1 - P(Y)) < 0. \tag{1}$$
This leads us to an alternative method of pruning sequences.

Method 2: Comparing neighbouring Splits

Instead of testing the confidence of $X \cap Y \to Z$ vs. the confidence of $X \to Z$, we propose to use the confidence of $X \cap \neg Y \to Z$ as test alternative.

This results in a test statistic, which is approximately $N(0,1)$:

$$p_1 = P(Z|X,Y) \qquad p_3 = P(Z|X,\neg Y)$$
$$n_1 = n \cdot P(X \cap Y) \qquad n_3 = n \cdot P(X \cap \neg Y)$$
$$H_o : p_1 = p_3 \qquad \text{vs.} \qquad H_1 : p_1 < p_3$$

$$\text{test-statistic: } T_2 = \frac{\widehat{p_1} - \widehat{p_3}}{\sqrt{\widehat{p}(1-\widehat{p})}} \sqrt{\frac{\widehat{n_1 n_3}}{\widehat{n_1 + n_3}}} \sim N(0,1),$$

with $p = P(Z|X)$. T_2 is equivalent to

$$\frac{P(\widehat{Z \cap Y}|X) - \widehat{P(Z|X)}\widehat{P(Y|X)}}{\sqrt{\widehat{P(Z|X)}\widehat{P(\neg Z|X)} \cdot \widehat{P(Y|X)}\widehat{P(\neg Y|X)}}} \sqrt{n \cdot \widehat{P(X)}} \sim N(0,1),$$

which tests the conditional independence of Y and Z given X.

Let us consider again the rules from table 1. Comparing neighbouring splits is a less strict test than comparing the confidence of a rule with its ancestor rule. Table 2 shows the results from testing these rules according

rule	T_1		T_2	
test with respect to rule 1				
olives & coke → bourbon	*4.690*		*6.418*	
olives & cracker → bourbon	*4.420*		*6.633*	
olives & heineken → bourbon	*3.290*		*5.179*	
test with respect to rule 2				
olives & heineken & coke → bourbon	*-1.650*	*X*	*-2.417*	*X*
test with respect to rule 3				
olives & heineken & coke → bourbon	*-0.560*	*X*	*-0.728*	*X*
olives & heineken & cracker → bourbon	*2.460*		*5.513*	
test with respect to rule 4				
olives & heineken & cracker → bourbon	*1.430*	*X*	*3.719*	

Table 2: Test statistics for the rules from table 1 based on different ancestor rules.

to methods 1 and 2. The crosses after some of the test results indicate, that the rule is rejected because of the result on a significance level of 5%. Since we are dealing with a special case of intersecting rules, we can use a similar technique to visually explore them. For this, we can order the left-hand side items according to their appearance in the sequence and start with a Double-decker plot regarding only $X_1 \to Y$ (see figure 3, left most plot). After that, we add the second item, X_2, to the display and look at the effect. The tile of X_1 is split in two, namely $X_1 \cap X_2$ and $X_1 \cap \neg X_2$. The support of the resulting rule $X_1 \cap X_2 \to Y$ is still relatively high and, as we had hoped, the split gives us more confidence. Splitting

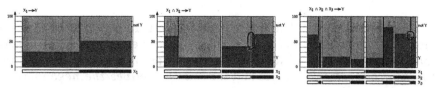

Figure 3: Three Double-decker Plots of the rules 1, 3 and 5 of the table.

a second time into the combinations $X_1 \cap X_2 \cap X_3$ and $X_1 \cap X_2 \cap \neg X_3$ gives a different result (cf. fig. 3, rightmost plot). Here, the support shrinks drastically and at the same time even the confidence is lowered.

Inspecting the left-hand-sides of the rules in table 1 more closely, several questions arise: *Is any of the 3-item rules better (or worse) than the others? How do the 3-item rules affect the 4-item rules?* and *Why has the fifth rule less confidence than either of its ancestor rules, 2 and 3 ?* For

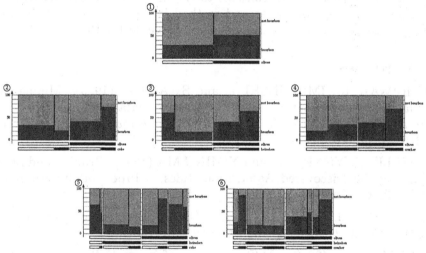

Figure 4: Double-decker plots corresponding to the rules in table 1.

answers to these questions - and to a lot more, we did not even think of asking - have a look at figure 4. Here, all Double-decker plots corresponding to the rules of the table are shown. Plots number 2 and 4 show similar behaviour: rules where both items have been bought together show the highest confidence, while all other rules show relatively low confidences. Plot no. 3 looks more suspicious: here, two combinations have high confidences (above 60%): *olives&heineken* → *bourbon* has confidence 65.52 and support 13.29 and not*olives&*not*heineken* → *bourbon* has confidence 60.90 and support 13.09. Any left hand side, which includes the same items, will show the same behaviour. This becomes very obvious in plot no. 6. This plot has exactly two combinations with very high confidence ($\approx$ 80%). Plot no. 5 shows two groups of combinations with

188

rel. high confidences. The important feature here is, however, that the intersection of *olives&heineken* *&coke* itself is very small. That means, that we, again, deal with two disjoint groups of bourbon buyers: the *bourbon&olives&coke* buyers and the *bourbon&olives&heineken* buyers.

3 Conclusion

Filtering association rules is possible by using ancestor structure in sequences and by looking at neighbouring splits. Two methods have been proposed and their visualization using double-decker plots have been demonstrated. Statistically, the second method is less strict than the first (cf. equation (1)): Method 2 is based on comparing the differences $P(Z|X,Y)$ and $P(Z|X,\neg Y)$, whereas the first method multiplies this difference with the factor $1-P(Y)$ additionally. The first approach therefore has always a smaller absolute value than the second. On the other hand, the second approach is in contrast to the first one statistically correct. Another advantage of the second method is that the values of its test statistic can be visually estimated in a Double-decker Plot.

References

AGRAWAL, R., IMIELINSKI T. and SWAMI A. (1993): Mining Associations between Sets of Items in Massive Databases. In: *Proc. of the ACM-SIGMOD 1993 Int'l Conference on Management of Data*, 207 - 216, Washington D.C.

BING LIU, WYNNE HSU and YIMING MA (1999): Pruning and Summarizing the Discovered Association Rules, Proc. of the 5th ACM SIGKDD Conference: KDD99, pp.125-134.

HARTIGAN, J. and KLEINER, B. (1981): Mosaics for Contingency Tables, *Computer Science and Statistics, 13, 268–273*.

HOFMANN, H. (2000). Different levels of interactivity — Interactive mosaic plots. *Metrika*, (forthcoming).

KARDAUN J., V.D. WAETEREN-DE HOOG B., KAPER E. LAAKSONEN S., ALANKO T., LEHTINEN H., MATTSSON C., V.D. HEYDE C., POTAMIAS G. DOUNIAS G., and MOUSTAKIS V. (1999): KESO - User's Evaluation Report, *Centraal Bureau voor de Statistiek, Research paper no. 9925*.

KARDAUN J. and ALANKO T. (1999): Exploratory Data Analysis and Data Mining in the setting of National Statistical Institutes. *in Kardaun et al.*

UNWIN A., HAWKINS, G., HOFMANN, H. and SIEGL, B.(1996): Interactive graphics for data sets with missing values — MANET, *Journal of Computational and Graphical Statistics, 5, 113–122*.

Classification of Texts with Support Vector Machines: An Examination of the Efficiency of Kernels and Data-transformations

Jörg Kindermann, Edda Leopold

GMD German National Research Center for Information Techonology
Institute for Autonomous intelligent Systems
Schloss Birlinghoven; D-53754 Sankt Augustin

Abstract: It is known that Support Vector Machines (SVM) provide a fast and powerful means for the classification of documents. In this paper we examine how different representations of documents effect the performance of SVM in different text classification tasks . We discuss the role of importance-weights (inverse document frequency and redundancy) and we show that time consuming lemmatization can be avoided even when classifying a highly inflectional language like German.

1 Introduction

Support vector machines (SVM) recently gained popularity in the learning community. An overview can be found in Schölkopf, Burges, Smola (eds.) (1998). Several authors have shown, that SVM provide an effective means for text categorization tasks (Joachims,1998a,b; Dumais et al 1998; Leopold & Kindermann forthcoming). This paper describes how different combinations of linguistic preprocessing, frequency transformations and kernel-functions affect the performance of support vector machines in text categorization tasks. A central issue of this paper is the representation of texts in input space. In information retrieval "stemming" refers to a process which strips affixes from word-forms and returns their stems. The term "lemmatization" refers to a procedure which maps word-forms to a standardized lexicon entry (lemma) and performs a morphological analysis (Manning & Schütze 1999). Thoughout the paper the lexical units under consideration are called "types". As we study the effect of lemmatization, types may be either word-forms, lemmas or tagged word-forms. Tagged word-forms are word-forms with a number of tags, provided by the lemmatizer, which indicate their grammatical function.

Texts differ in their length. Long texts contain several thousands of words whereas short texts consist of some dozen words. Type-frequencies have to be normalized in order to make texts of different length comparable. From the standpoint of quantitative linguistics this is not a trivial task (Orlov, 1982; Margulis, 1993). The best solution is to devide type-frequency by the total number of tokens in the text. This is equivalent to mapping the type-frequency vector to the unit-sphere in the L_1-sense. From the standpoint of the SVM learning algorithm the best normalization rule is the L_2-normalization because it yields the best error bounds (Vapnik 1998). L_2-normalization has been used by Joachims (1998) and Dumais et al. (1998).

All the text-representations, which we consider in this paper, confirm to the *tf.idf* scheme described by Manning and Schütze (1999). So all representations consist of three parts: the frequencies are transformed by a frequency transformation, then multiplied by a importance weight and finally normalized with respect to L_1 or L_2.

2 Frequency transformations

In small texts type frequencies are confined to a relative small interval. They do not scale to different orders of magnitude. The situation is completely different when it comes to larger texts, where Zipf's law (Zipf 1932) ensures that type frequencies scale to different order of magnitude. Common benchmarks like Reuters, Ohsumed and 20-Newsgroups, however, consist of very small documents, so it is not surprising that even a binary coding of term-frequency vectors yields good results on these corpora as Dumais et al. (1998) report.

For our empirical tests we use two transformations of type frequencies. As the simplest "frequency-transformation" we use is the identity, which maps a document to its type-frequecy vector:

$$\mathbf{f}_i = (f(w_1, d_i), \ldots, f(w_{|V|}, d_i)),$$

where $f(w_k, d_i)$ is the number of occurrences of type w_k in document d_i and $|V|$ is the number of types in the document collection. In the following we refer to $\mathbf{f}_i$ as relative frequencies.

The other frequency transformation, which we examine in this paper is the logarithm. We consider this transform because it is a common approach in quantitative linguistics to study logarithms of linguistic quantities rather than the quantities themselves.

$$\mathbf{l}_i = (\log f(w_1, d_i), \ldots, \log f(w_{|V|}, d_i)).$$

This transformation has also been proposed by Manning and Schütze (1999), but it is novel to SVM text categorization.

3 Importance weights

Importance weights like inverse document frequency (*idf*) originally have been designed for identifying index words (Salton & McGill 1983). And feature extraction in text retrieval is often thought of in terms of reduction of dimensionality of the input space.

However, since SVM can manage high dimensional feature spaces effectively, reduction of dimensionality of input space is not necessary and importance weights can be used to quantify how specific a given type is to the documents of a text collection. A type which is evenly distributed across the document collection is given a low importance weight, because it is judged to be less specific for the documents it occurs in. In contrast a type which is used in only a few documents is given a high importance weight.

Idf is often used when the SVM is applied to text classification. The *idf* of the k-th type in the document collection is defined by

$$idf_k = \log \frac{n}{df_k}, \qquad (1)$$

where n is the number of all documents in the collection and df_k is the number of those documents in the collection, which contain the type w_k. *Idf* has the advantage of being easy to calculate. Its disadvantage is that it disregards the frequencies of the term w_k in each of the documents.

Redundancy quantifies the KL-distance of a probability distribution from the uniform distribution. It is defined by

$$R_k = \log n + \sum_{i=1}^{n} \frac{f(w_k, d_i)}{f(w_k)} \log \frac{f(w_k, d_i)}{f(w_k)}, \qquad (2)$$

where $f(w_k)$ is the total number of occurrence of type w_k in the document collection. R_k is a measure of how much the distribution of a term w_k in the various documents deviates from the uniform distribution. Equation (2) is the usual definition of redundancy. But as far as we know redundancy has never been used in *this* way. A similar weighting scheme has been proposed by Bookstein and Swanson (1974). They used the probability of the classical occupancy problem, in which exactly $f(w_k)$ balls are distributed at random into N urns.

In our experiments redundancy was combined with logarithmic frequency l_i and relative frequency f_i. The *idf* was combined solely with relative frequency. Furthermore we tested l_i and f_i without any importance weight. In each case both L_1-normalization and L_2-normalization was applied. So we obtained 10 different mappings of type-frequency vectors into feature space.

4   Kernel functions

One advantage of SVM is that different kernel functions can be used. The kernel function induces an inner product in the input space. It is well known that the choice of the kernel function is crucial to the efficiency of support vector machines. Therefore the data transformations described above were combined with three different kernel functions:

- linear kernel $\qquad\qquad\qquad\; K(\vec{x}, \vec{x}') \;=\; \vec{x} \cdot \vec{x}'$
- 3rd order polynomial kernel $\; K(\vec{x}, \vec{x}') \;=\; (\vec{x} \cdot \vec{x}')^3$
- Gaussian rbf-kernel $\qquad\qquad K(\vec{x}, \vec{x}') \;=\; e^{-\|\vec{x}-\vec{x}'\|/2}$

Each of the 10 frequency transformations was combined with these three kernels. This yields 30 combinations of kernel functions, frequency-transformations, importance-weights, and text-length-normalization, that were tested in our experiments

5   The role of linguistic preprocessing

Linguistic preprocessing takes the lion's share of computation time when applying SVM to a text classification problem. For our experiments we used the SVM-implementation SVM^{light} written by Thorsten Joachims, which is especially appropriate for sparse input vectors (Joachims 1998b).

Lemmatization and tagging were only performed on the German material. We expected that the of linguistic preprocessing on the accuracy of the learning algorithm would be larger in the case of German, because of the morphological richness of German compared to English. The lemmatizer Morphy (Lezius et al. 1998), which we used, performs a morphological analysis for each word. If there are different readings the most probable is chosen. For about 9% of the word-forms the morphological analysis was not successful. These word-forms were removed from the lemmatized data set. The lemmatization procedure resulted in a reduction of the dimensionality of the input of about 60%. No stemming was performed on the English data. We simply refer to the results obtained by Joachims (1998a).

We generated a further data set where the grammatical tags which resulted from the morphological analysis were appended to the word-forms in order to resolve the ambiguities of grammatically polyfunctional word-forms. So for instance "winde-SUB-AKK-SIN-FEM" (Engl. crane) destinguished from "winde-SUB-DAT-SIN-MAS" (Engl. wind) and "winde-SUB-NOM-PLU-MAS" (Engl. winds). Our hypothesis was that an improvement of performance could be archieved by providing SVM with as much information as possible. Those word-forms which could not be analized by the lemmatizer were used without any tagging information. We obtained some 300000 tagged word-forms.

6   The data

We considered three document collections for empirical tests. The full texts were used as input. Neither stop-words nor low-frequency words were removed from the input. An exception was made in the case of relative frequencies with *idf* normalized with respect to L_2. Here words occurring once or twice were removed in order to make our results comparable to those obtained by Joachims (1998a). Documents shorter than 10 words were discarded. A lemmatized and tagged type-frequency list was drawn from both German document collections.

The first document collection under consideration was the Reuters-21578 data set compiled by David Lewis and originally collected by the Carnegie group from the Reuters newswire in 1987. The "ModApte" split was used leading to a corpus of 9603 training documents, 3299 test documents, and about 1.52 million running words.

The second data collection was obtained from the German daily newspaper "Frankfurter Rundschau" (FR). We considered the issues of July 1998 which consists of 12079 documents and about 3.47 million running words. Training set and test sets were obtained randomly. The training set consisted of 8018 documents (7976 in the lemmatized material) and the test set consisted of 3954 documents (3932 in the lemmatized material). Classes were provided by respective topics in the document collection. We used the five most frequent of the 41 topics in the material. These classes covered nearly 75% of the data.

	tokens (*1000)	types (*1000)	percent hapaxes	# of texts	av. doc. length
Reuters	1520	28.2	24.4	12902	117.8
Taz: lemmas	2890	84.7	50.1	10508	275.0
Taz: word-forms	3200	200.3	53.0	10539	303.6
Taz: plus tags	3200	308.4	58.9	10539	303.6
FR: lemmas	3143	86.0	48.2	11908	263.9
FR: word-forms	3472	193.0	49.1	11972	290.0
FR: plus tags	3472	301.0	55.6	11972	290.0

Table 1: Statistics of the corpora under consideration.
See (Leopold & Kindermann forthcoming) for a more detailed discussion.

The third document collection was the German daily newspaper "Die Tageszeitung" (Taz). The issues June 1988, August 1998, and June 1991 consisted of 10539 texts and about 3.2 million running words. In order to test if SVM are capable to classify opaque classes we considered different years of publication. So one class of the newspaper consists of the issues of June and August 1988 and the other class consists of the issues of June 1991. Both training set and test set are obtained randomly from these three months of newspaper. The training set contains 7070 articles (7039 in the lemmatized material) and the test set comprises 3469 articles (3469 in the lemmatized material).

7 Empirical results

For all our experiments we used the SVM-implementation SVM^{light}. Precision/recall break-even points were calculated. The rightmost column of table (2) shows precision/recall break-even points when using lemmatized text, relative frequencies normalized with respect to L_2 with inverse document frequency and rbf-kernel. The values of the second column are obtained with the same kernel and $tf.idf$-weighting scheme, but word-forms instead of lemmas were used as input data. On the Reuters data word-forms lead to slightly worse results than lemmas, whereas word-forms perform better on the German material. Performance on the unlemmatized German material improves further when idf is substituted by redundancy (see column 5).

category	$F_{rel,L2}$ + idf + rbf			$F_{log,L2}$ + red. + rbf		
	lemmas	plain	tagged	lemmas	plain	tagged
earn	98.4	98.27	–	–	98.66	–
acq	95.3	94.87	–	–	94.57	–
money	76.3	73.47	–	–	71.33	–
grain	91.9	89.55	–	–	91.73	–
crude	88.9	86.42	–	–	84.71	–
LOK	80.88	85.82	84.82	79.58	86.12	87.25
LRL	90.02	90.85	90.25	90.24	92.04	91.72
NAC	81.07	82.85	82.37	84.24	84.44	84.20
SPO	86.93	89.12	86.36	87.32	89.89	87.06
WIR	81.55	88.97	80.47	85.03	86.31	81.66
Taz	75.71	75.16	75.38	76.44	82.01	79.12

Table 2: The effect of lemmatization on the performance.
The precision/recall break-even for Gaussian rbf-kernels and different frequency transformation are displayed. The upper box in the first column shows the results obtained by Joachims (1998a).

The columns 4 to 6 of table (2) were obtained by using logarithmic frequencies with L_2-normalization ($F_{rel,L2}$) and redundancy . It can be seen that on the Reuters data and on the German lemmas there is no great difference in performance between logarithmic frequencies with L_2 normalization ($F_{log,L2}$) and redundancy on the one hand and and relative frequencies with L_2-normalization and inverse document frequency on the other hand. This examplifies a general tendency found in our experiments: Logarithmic frequency and redundancy perform the better the longer the documents and the more skewed the type-frequency distributions. Comparing the fifth with the first column of table (2) we observe a considerable improvement on the newspaper material (about 4% average) and especially on the Taz newspaper, which was the most opaque classification task and yields the highest number of support vectors. Table (3) shows that on the Taz-newspaper redundancy performs better than *idf* regardless of kernels and frequency transformations.

	no importance			redundancy			idf		
	rbf	poly	lin.	rbf	poly	lin.	rbf	poly	lin.
$F_{log,L1}$	75.8	63.8	76.1	80.2	79.8	81.2	-	-	-
$F_{log,L2}$	77.2	77.9	77.4	82.0	81.9	81.9	-	-	-
$F_{rel,L1}$	74.8	75.0	76.0	80.2	79.8	81.2	71.6	71.1	74.4
$F_{rel,L2}$	76.3	76.4	76.2	81.3	81.0	80.6	75.2	75.1	73.9

Table 3: The performance of different importance weights. Only the Taz classification task is considered. For each combination the median of precision/recall break-even over all classification tasks is displayed.

From table (3) one can see that the kernel functions do not have a large influence on the accuracy of the learning algorithm. We have made this observation in a series of experiments (Leopold & Kindermann forthcoming). This is remarkable because in most applications of SVM the kernel function is crucial to the classification performance. One explanation is that the occurrence of two types in a document does not consist a special quality which could be captured by the geometry which is induced by a kernel. A word occuring in the beginning of a text does not (or at most weakly) influence the meaning of another word occuring at the end of the document. We suppose that the "bag-of-words" representation can be improoved when the co-occurrences of words within a sentence are represented in input space.

8   Conclusion

The most important result obtained from our experiments performed on the Reuters data set and on two German newspaper corpora is that lemmatization in most cases leads to a loss of performance in terms of precision and recall and can be omitted. There are however some few exceptions where word-forms lead to worse results.

Importance weights improve the performance significantly. Redundancy defined in equation (2) is a better importance weight than the inverse document frequency. The advantage of redundancy over inverse document frequency seems to be greater for larger documents.

Support vector machines are capable to efficiently process a very high number of dimensions, when vectors are sparse. We have used more than 300 000 types in the tagged Taz and FR corpus. Even opaque classes, like newspaper issues of different years, can be classified by support vector machines. Deletion of rare words and stop-words is not necessary when applying SVM to text classification.

Acknowlegements. We thank Prof. Dr. Köhler (Dept. of Computational Linguistics, University of Trier) who contributed the frequency data of "Die Tageszeitung" and "Frankfurter Rundschau". We also thank Gerhard Paaß (GMD-AiS) and Thorsten Joachims (GMD-AiS) for fruitful discussions on the topic.

References

DUMAIS, S. and PLATT, J. and HECKERMAN, D. and SAHAMI, M. (1998): Inductive Learning Algorithms and Representations for Text Categorization. *Proceedings of CIKM-98; 7th International Conference on Informationretrieval and Knowledgemanagement, 148–155.*

JOACHIMS, T. (1998a): Text categorization with support vector machines: learning with many relevant features. *Proceedings of ECML-98, 10th European Conference on Machine Learning, Lecture Notes in Computer Science, Number 1398, 137–142, Springer, Heidelberg.*

JOACHIMS, T. (1998b): Making Large-scale Support Vector Machine Learning Practical *B. Schölkopf and C. J. C. Burges and A. J. Smola (eds.) Advances in Kernel Methods, MIT Press: Cambridge MA, London, 169–184.*

JOACHIMS, T.: SVM^{light} http://ais.gmd.de/~thorsten/svm_light/

LEOPOLD, E. and KINDERMANN, J. (forthcoming): Text Categorization with Support Vector Machines. How to Represent Texts in Input Space? *Machine Learning.*

LEZIUS, W. and RAPP, R. and WETTLER, M. (1998): A Freely Available Morphological Analyzer, Disambiguator and Context Sensitive Lemmatizer for German. *Proceedings of the COLING-ACL 1998.*
(Morphy is available at http://www-psycho.uni-paderborn.de/lezius/)

MANNING, C. D. and SCHÜTZE, H. (1999): Foundations of Statistical Natural Language Processing; MIT-Press: Cambridge, London.

ORLOV, Ju. K.(1982): Linguostatistik: Aufstellung von Sprachnormen oder Analyse des Redeprozesses? (Die Antinomie 'Sprache-Rede' in der statistischen Linguistik) *Ju. K. Orlov and M. G. Boroda and I. S. Nadarejčvili (eds.) Sprache, Text, Kunst. Quantitative Analysen; (QL 15); Brockmeyer: Bochum, S. 1–55.*

PORTER, M. F.(1980): An algorithm for suffix stripping *Program (Automated Library and Information Systems) 14 (3), 130–137.*

REUTERS-21578 data set
http://www.research.att.com/~lewis/reuters21578.html)

SALTON, G. and McGILL, M. J. (1983): Introduction to Modern Information Retrieval; McGraw Hill, New York et al.

SIMON, H. A. (1960): Some further notes on a class of skew distribution functions. *Information and Control 3, 80–88.*

SCHÖLKOPF, B. and BURGES, C. J. C. and SMOLA, A. J. (eds.) (1998) Advances in Kernel Methods, MIT Press: Cambridge MA, London.

VAPNIK, V. N.(1998): Statistical Learning Theory, Wiley & sons, New York.

ZIPF, G. K.(1932): Selected studies of the principle of relative frequency in language. Harvard University Press, Cambridge MA.

Text Mining with the Help of Cohesion Trees

A. Mehler

Linguistische Datenverarbeitung,
Universität Trier,
D-54286 Trier, Germany

Abstract: In the framework of automatic text processing, *semantic spaces* are used as a format for modeling similarities of natural language texts represented as vectors. They prove to be efficient in divergent areas, as information retrieval (Dumais 1995), computational psychology (Landauer, Dumais 1997), and computational linguistics (Rieger 1995; Mehler 1998). In order to group semantically similar texts, cluster analysis is used. A central problem of this method relates to the difficulty to name clusters, whereas lists neglect the poly-hierarchical structure of semantic spaces. This paper introduces the concept of *cohesion tree* as an alternative tool for exploring similarity relations of texts represented in high dimensional spaces. Cohesion trees allow the perspective evaluation of numerically represented text similarities. They depart from minimal spanning trees (MST) by context-sensitively optimizing path costs. This central property underlies the linguistic interpretation of cohesion trees: instead of manifesting context-free associations, they model context priming effects.

1 Introduction

Because of the increase of documents available online, the significance of natural language texts as the prime informational unit for the management of knowledge is increasing. To make relevant documents available depending on varying tasks in different contexts is decisive for efficient task completion. The realization of this demand requires the automatic, content based processing of texts, which allows to reconstruct or even to explore the connection of tasks and documents. Furthermore, transferability is needed so that the same procedure of text analysis is easily adapted to new tasks, knowledge domains, and information needs. *Text mining* is a technology which intends to solve these problems. Operationally defined, it covers three steps: first occurs the *reconstruction* of knowledge underlying the usage of text components and their intra-, intertextual and exophoric relations. Next, heretofore unknown, task relevant relations, which were not constitutive for the corpus to be analyzed, are *explored*. Finally, implicit relations which were discovered during the first two steps are made explicit with the help of annotation/visualization techniques. Text mining comprises information extraction, text categorization, text summarization and text linkage. The latter task deals with the automatic exploration of intertextual, meaning based relations. This paper deals with the problem of text linkage and the annotation of connotative, meaning based relations as typed links in hypertext.

The majority of procedures proposed for hypertext construction is based on the *vector space model* of Salton (1989), which represents texts as term vectors. In this context, the main idea underlying text linkage runs as follows: the more similar two texts, the more they share lexical constituents, the more probably they are linked. Salton et al. (1994) propose several methods for the generation of hypertexts. For example, the so called *breadth m-depth n*-search starts with adding the m nearest neighbors in the vector space as the immediate successors of the root text. This procedure is repeated for all successors until the tree has a depth of n levels. Similarity thresholds restrict the set of texts to be inserted. Although the vector space model proves to be efficient in information retrieval, a formal model for hypertext authoring and a theoretical justification for the usage of similarity thresholds is missing. This paper aims at outlining a theoretical framework for text linkage, which is formalized with the help of graph theory. In this context, the linguistic concept of *cohesion* is used as a basic criterion for text linkage.

2 Cohesive Hypertexts

Cohesion forms an aspect of *textuality*. It comprises a system of text-forming resources which are used to connect text components in order to express *semantic continuity*. Halliday, Hasan (1976) distinguish four types of such resources: reference, ellipsis/substitution, conjunction, and lexical cohesion, which is based on the repetition of lexical items sharing *sense relations* or *paradigmatic usage regularities*. The latter type of cohesion is based on the fact that words which tend to occur in similar contexts generate a cohesive force, if they co-occur.

The view is taken that cohesion also applies to hypertext: given a chain of texts, the question arises, whether it forms a *cohesive whole*. The importance of cohesion can be exemplified with reference to semantic discontinuity as a result of purely associative links. Suppose a hypertext, in which (A, B, C) is a text chain. For example, A deals with the *concept of information in economics*, B with *computer simulations in information science*, and C with the *simulation of physical systems*. Although these units can be seen to justify associative links, a strong change in topic is detected: there is a high risk that A and C do not form a cohesive whole. This *thematic diversification* results from intransitive meaning relations: A and B are semantically similar for other reasons than B and C. To connect A and C via B can produce an incohesive chain of texts. In order to reduce this risk of thematic diversification, the concept of cohesion is applied to whole paths of links: any link is evaluated in the context of the paths into which it enters. This can be illustrated as follows: suppose that the path $(R, \ldots, A, C)$ is more cohesive than $(R, \ldots, B, C)$, while texts B and C are more similar than A and C. From the perspective of optimizing associativity of immediately linked texts, a link between B and C is expected to be created. But linking A and C allows to reduce the risk of incohesive topic change, because in this case semantic relationships of indirectly linked texts are reflected, too. The more cohesive path $(R, \ldots, A, C)$ causes a weaker change of topic. To follow this premise means to optimize global aspects of cohesive paths instead of local, associative text-to-text similarities. Furthermore, two types of links are distinguished: (i) *cohesive hierarchical links* underlying cohesive paths and (ii) *associative cross-reference links*, as in the case of linking B and C additionally.

Cohesion does not only apply to single texts, but serves as a *linguistic* source for text linkage in hypertext. The *cohesiveness* of link candidates serves as a necessary condition for linkage. Consequently, not only are direct text-to-text dependencies reflected, but *also* cohesion relations of indirectly linked units. Applying the concept of cohesion thus shifts the perspective from binary text links to whole paths of such links. In the following, cohesion is only analyzed in terms of *lexical cohesion*.

3 Semantic Spaces

In order to explore lexical cohesion as a source for text linkage, *semantic spaces* are used, which consider signs to be semantically similar to the extent that they enter into semantically similar contexts. Semantic spaces are computed in three steps: (i) for measuring syntagmatic regularities of words observed in a corpus C, Rieger (1996) uses a correlation coefficient. The correlations are used to map words onto the corpus space $C \subset \mathbb{R}^n$, whose dimensions are defined by the set W of n words. Similarities of syntagmatic regularities are mapped by an Euclidian metric δ_1 operating on C. (ii) The resulting distance values are used for the generation of a semantic space $S \subset \mathbb{R}^n$. The meaning point $m(a_i)$ of word $a_i \in W$ is defined as $m(a_i) = (m_{i1}, \ldots, m_{in})$, where $\forall j \in \{1, \ldots, n\} : m_{ij} = 1 - \delta_1(c_i, c_j)/(2\sqrt{n}) \in [0, 1]$ and c_i, c_j are the corpus points of lexemes $a_i, a_j \in W$. (iii) Mehler (1998) uses a weighted mean for mapping texts onto S: $m(x_k) = \sum_{a_i \in W(x_k)} w_{ik} m(a_i) \in S$ is the meaning point of text $x_k \in C$; w_{ik} is a bias having the same function as the *tfidf*-scores in information retrieval. As a result of mapping texts onto S, they can be compared regarding the similarity of their lexical organization. Semantic similarity of signs is modeled via distance of their meaning points: the more similar their usage regularities, the shorter their points' distances, which represent *semantic similarity* as a result of similar *paradigmatic usage regularities*. As outlined above, this kind of meaning relation underlies lexical cohesion. In the literature, many models of semantic spaces are found. They prove to be efficient in areas like information retrieval (Dumais 1995), computational psychology (Land-auer, Dumais 1997), and computational linguistics (Rieger 1996). The algorithm for hypertext construction, proposed in the following, works on any of these models. It only assumes a complete weighted graph to be derived based on the texts' vector representations.

4 The Formalism

In this section, *cohesion trees* (CT) are introduced as a representational format for hypertexts. CTs are modeled with the help of *order rela-tions* using the following terms: $C = \{x_1, ..., x_n\}$ is a *text corpus*, $W = \{a_1, ..., a_m\}$ the set of *types* occurring in C, $W(x)$ the set of types of $x \in C$, and $Z = C \cup W$ the set of signs. Furthermore, $\leq_z^a \subseteq Z \times Z$ is an alphabetic order with infimum z. Finally, if δ_1 is an Euclidean metric operating on meaning points of the semantic space S, the pseudo metric δ is defined as $\delta(a_i, a_j) = \delta_1(m(a_i), m(a_j))$ for all $a_i, a_j \in W$. The formalism concentrates on links of type $l = \langle x, a, y \rangle$, where the lexical *anchor* a links $x \in C$ as the *reference* with $y \in C$ as the *referent* of l.

Definition 1 Let $z \in Z$ be a sign. $\leq_z \subseteq Z \times Z$ orders signs based on the distances of their meaning points regarding the meaning point of z: $x \leq_z y$ iff $\delta(x, z) < \delta(y, z) \vee (\delta(x, z) = \delta(y, z) \wedge x \leq_z^a y)$.

$x \leq_z y$ states that the meaning point $m(x)$ of x is closer to the meaning point $m(z)$ than $m(y)$, i.e. x and z realize more similar usage regularities, than y and z. z is the infimum of $\leq_z$, which is reflexiv, antisymmetric, transitive, and linear. In the following, *cohesion trees* are introduced based on the concept of *path sensitive distance*:

Definition 2 Let $\langle V, E \rangle$ be a graph, a sequence $P_{v_1 v_n} = (v_1, ..., v_i, ..., v_n)$ of vertices $V(P_{v_1 v_n}) = \{v_1, ..., v_n\} \subseteq V$ is called *path* from v_1 to v_n, if for each consecutive pair of vertices $v_i, v_{i+1} \in V(P_{v_1 v_n})$ there exists a distinct edge $\{v_i, v_{i+1}\} \in E$, $i \in \{1, ..., n-1\}$. v_1 is called *start*, and v_n *end vertex* of $P_{v_1 v_n}$, all other vertices are called *inner*. $P_{v_1 v_n}$ is *cyclic*, if $v_1 = v_n$. $P_{v_1 v_n}$ is called *simple*, if all its inner vertices are distinct.

If G is a tree, the shortest path between any two vertices of G is unique.

Definition 3 Let $G = \langle V, E \rangle$ be a tree and $P = (v_1, ..., v_k)$ a simple path in G. The *path sensitive distance* $\delta^*(P, x)$ of $x \in V$ with re-spect to P is defined as $\delta^*(P, x) = \frac{1}{\sqrt{n}} \sum_{v_i \in V(P)} w_i \delta(x, v_i) \in [0, 1]$, where $\sum_{v_i \in V(P)} w_i \leq 1$ (and $\delta(x, v_i) = \delta_1(m(x), m(v_i))$, $m(x) \in [0, 1]^n$).

Definition 4 Let $G = \langle V, E \rangle$ be a tree. Let $\mathcal{P}$ be the set of all paths in G starting with z and $x \in V$. The well-ordering $\sqsubseteq_x \subseteq \mathcal{P} \times \mathcal{P}$ orders all paths in $\mathcal{P}$ with respect to x: $P_{zv} \sqsubseteq_x P_{zw}$ iff $\delta^*(P_{zv}, x) < \delta^*(P_{zw}, x) \vee (\delta^*(P_{zv}, x) = \delta^*(P_{zw}, x) \wedge v \leq_z^a w)$.

Definition 5 Let $z \in Z$ be a sign. The *cohesion tree* (CT) induced by z is a tree $C(z) = \langle V, E, \omega \rangle$ with vertices $V = Z$ and the set of edges $E = \{\{x, y\} \mid x \leq_z y \wedge \nexists v \in V : v \leq_z y \wedge P_{zv} \sqsubseteq_y P_{zx}\}$. $\omega : E \to [0, 1]$ is a weighting function: $\forall \{x, y\} \in E, x \leq_z y : \omega(\{x, y\}) = 1 - \delta^*(P_{zx}, y)$.

In definition (3) and (5) contextual influences of indirectly linked units are modeled with the help of bias w_i, whose computation includes the following alternative: If w_i is monotone increasing with path length, then the syntagmatic order of P is reflected in the sense that the shorter the distance of vertex x to any vertex in P the more important their similarity measured by δ. Consequently, the descending impact of more distant units allows a weak change of topic as the path grows. A function, which meets this condition, looks as follows: let $P = (v_1, \ldots, v_k)$ be a path of k nodes and $c \in (0, 1]$ a constant, then w_i, $i = 1, \ldots, k$, can be computed as follows (in the following, c is set to 0.5):

$$w_i = \frac{1}{\sum_i c^{k-i+1}} c^{k-i+1} \in [0, 1] \tag{1}$$

Cohesion trees are built with the help of two types of order relations: (i) $\leq_z$ models *root priming*. It determines the order of nodes to be inserted into the tree $C(z)$, which is dependent on their distance to the meaning point $m(z)$. (ii) $\sqsubseteq_y$ models *context priming* by specifying the predecessor of node y to be inserted as the end of the most cohesive path. $\sqsubseteq_y$ is based on δ^* which extends the metric δ in the sense of modeling paradigmatic dissimilarities: δ^* does not only reflect distances of meaning points of pairs of signs, but of *sign sequences*. This is done with the help of a *fish-eye mechanism*: the more distant two signs in a path, the less their mutual impact, the less important their lexical cohesiveness, and consequently, the less their contribution to δ^*. But this negative distance effect can be compensated by higher relatedness, i.e. by shorter distances of meaning points. Thus, the more semantically similar the units the stronger their mutual cohesive force. So far, cohesion trees do not restrict the membership of signs in a path regarding their linguistic resolution. In order to model hypertexts, it is necessary to restrict the edge set of cohesion trees so that lexical anchors are used to link texts:

Definition 6 Let $x \in C$ be a text. The *textual cohesion tree* of x is a cohesion tree $C(x) = \langle V, E, \omega \rangle$ with vertex set $V = C$. The *hierarchical hypertext* $H(x) = \langle V', E' \rangle$ induced by $C(x)$ is defined as follows: for all $\{v, w\} \in E, v \leq_x w$, exist two edges $\{v, a\}, \{a, w\} \in E'$ so that $\delta(v, a) + \delta(a, w) = \min_{b \in W(v)} \{\delta(v, b) + \delta(b, w)\}$. Finally, $V' = \cup_{e \in E'} e$.

In definition (6), $\delta(v, a)$ and $\delta(a, w)$ measure the suitability of the constituent $a \in W(v)$ of text v as a candidate anchor of a link, connecting reference v with referent w. According to definition (6), hierarchical hypertexts allow the ambiguous use of the same word to link a text with different referents. Since $H(x)$ is based on $C(x)$ and the construction of edges in $C(x)$ is determined by δ^*, it is guaranteed that only such links are added to $H(x)$, which fulfill the requirement of *path cohesion*. Definition (6) produces strictly hierarchical hypertexts. Since the *value-added information* of hypertexts lies in the possibility to follow *cross-reference links* breaking down the actual context and following new branches of information, it is necessary to extend it. This is done with the help of a measure κ introduced by Botafogo et al. (1992), which evaluates hypertexts regarding their topology. κ rates hypertexts the more *compact* the fewer links a user needs to follow in order to reach its nodes. κ operates on the converted distance matrix D_{ij} representing the shortest distance between each pair of nodes in the hypertext. In the case of a fully connected hypertext, κ equals 1; in the opposite case, κ equals 0. κ is defined as follows–let H be a hypertext with distance matrix D_{ij}:

$$\kappa(H) = \frac{\max D_{ij} - \sum_i \sum_j D_{ij}}{\max D_{ij} - \min D_{ij}} \in [0,1] , \qquad (2)$$

where $\max D_{ij}$ ($\min D_{ij}$) is the maximum (minimum) distance the converted distance (the sum of all entries of D_{ij}) can assume. κ is used to extend hypertexts as long as a threshold of compactness is not exceeded:

Definition 7 Let $H(x) = \langle V, E \rangle$ be the hierarchical hypertext of text $x \in C$, and $\tau \in (0,1]$ a threshold. The *hypertext* $H_\tau(x) = \langle V_\tau, E_\tau \rangle$ is computed as follows: all tuples $(\{v, a\}, \{a, w\})$, where $v, w \in C, \Delta = \delta(v, a) + \delta(a, w) = \min_{b \in W(v)} \{\delta(v, b) + \delta(b, w)\}$, and $\{v, a\}, \{a, w\} \notin E$, are ranked with decreasing Δ so that each tuple is assigned a unique number coding its rank beginning with 1. Set $i = 0$, $H_0(x) = \langle V_0, E_0 \rangle = H(x)$ and proceed as follows: (i) *Extension:* let $(\{v, a\}, \{a, w\})$ be the tuple of rank $i + 1$. Set $H_{i+1}(x) = \langle V_{i+1}, E_{i+1} \rangle$, where $V_{i+1} = V_i \cup \{a\}$ and $E_{i+1} = E_i \cup \{\{v, a\}, \{a, w\}\}$. (ii) *Termination:* If $\kappa(H_{i+1}) \geq \tau$, then stop, else $i = i + 1$, go to (i). Finally, set $V_\tau = V_i$; $E_\tau = E_i$.

Although hypertexts produced according to definition (7) include cohesion trees as a skeleton, they possibly contain cross-reference links defining circular paths. Definition (7) formally combines the concept of CT with an algorithm for hypertext authoring proposed by Smeaton, Morrissey (1995), *without* facing the problem of producing graphs covering isolated components unreachable from a hypertext's root. Smeaton, Morrissey propose to use indexing techniques as elaborated in information retrieval in order to overcome this deficiency. This problem is avoided by using cohesion trees as a basis for hypertext construction, *since they already link all texts of the corpus to be converted.* Beyond this–and in contrast to the approach of Smeaton, Morrissey–, hypertexts according to definition (7) always include two types of links: (i) hierarchical links belonging to the underlying cohesion tree and (ii) cross-reference links produced according to definition (7).

5 A Sample Analysis

In this section, an example for hypertext authoring is outlined. A corpus C of 502 newspaper articles from the Süddeutsche Zeitung, march/april 1996, was mapped onto a semantic space of 2,058 dimensions. A text–dealing with a football game broadcast in pay tv–was chosen as the root of a CT to be generated out of C–see table (1). Figure (1) shows the MST of the complete weighted graph derived from the semantic space onto which the elements of C were mapped and the corresponding CT. Although the MST starts with semantically similar texts (regarding the text sample), it leads to thematically diverse texts. Furthermore, no text dealing with the broadcast topic is found in the outline of the MST. In contrast to this, the CT in figure (1.b) shows a branching structure with two homogeneous branches: the one comprises texts dealing with *football*, the other covers texts dealing with *broadcasting rights*. This difference results from the fact that in cohesion trees, topic changes are also controlled by cohesion relations of indirectly linked texts. Cohesion trees seem to be more adequate in dealing with similarity relations as represented in semantic spaces.

Nun braucht der FC Bayern einen Auswärts-Sieg: Abwehrfehler der Münchner bescheren Barcelona ein 2:2 im Halbfinale des UEFA-Cup.

München — Fußball vom Feinsten boten der FC Bayern und der FC Barcelona am Dienstagabend, bevor sie sich mit einem leistungsgerechten 2:2 (0:1) trennten. Die Bayern benötigen nun im Rückspiel in 14 Tagen in Spaniens Fußballheiligtum Nou Camp wohl einen Sieg, um in die Endspiele um den UEFA-Cup einziehen zu können. ...

Table 1: Süddeutsche Zeitung, 03.04.96, p. 60.

6 Concluding Remarks

The model presented so far makes use of the concept of *cohesion*. Hypertexts are seen as linguistic units, whose organization is tied to restrictions which already prove to be efficient on the text level. A content based approach is realized: the links produced are interpreted in text linguistic terms. Future work aims at (i) incorporating other types of cohesion, (ii) modeling intratextual cohesion, and (iii) empirically evaluating the usefulness of cohesion trees as a source for hypertext authoring.

206

Nun braucht der FC Bayern einen Auswärts-Sieg [Fußball]
  ⌐ Klinsmann erlöst die Bayern in letzter Minute [Fußball]
    ⌐ Tapferer Optimismus nach dem Spektakel [Fußball]
      ⌐ Münchner Geschenke zu Gladbachs Osterfest [Fußball]
      ⌐ Schaumschläger im Superschlager [Fußball]
        ⌐ Ansturm auf die Klagemauer [Fußball]
        ⌐ Erst Badener Lied, dann Punkt ... [Fußball]
          ⌐ Keine Fortschritte im Flockenwirbel [Fußball]
            ⌐ 1860 und die Not ... [Fußball]
              ⌐ Wirklich kein Anlaß zu eitlem Planspiel [Fußball]
                ⌐ Im Landeanflug auf den Münchner Flughafen
                  ⌐ Massenkarambolagen legen Verkehr lahm
          ⌐ Borussia Dortmund [Fußball]
        ⌐ Meister über Meiers Datenbank [Fußball]
          ⌐ Peter Neururer löst Stefan Engels ab [Fußball]

Nun braucht der FC Bayern einen Auswärts-Sieg [Fußball]
  ⌐ Klinsmann erlöst die Bayern in letzter Minute [Fußball]
    ⌐ Tapferer Optimismus nach dem Spektakel [Fußball]
      ⌐ Münchner Geschenke zu Gladbachs Osterfest [Fußball]
      ⌐ Schaumschläger im Superschlager [Fußball]
        ⌐ Ansturm auf die Klagemauer [Fußball]
        ⌐ Erst Badener Lied, dann Punkt ... [Fußball]
          ⌐ 1:1 bei Feyenoord Rotterdam [Fußball]
          ⌐ Mehmet Scholl (FC Bayern) [Fußball]
          ⌐ Keine Fortschritte im Flockenwirbel [Fußball]
            ⌐ Wirklich kein Anlaß zu eitlem Planspiel [Fußball]
              ⌐ 1860 und die Not ... [Fußball]
            ⌐ Borussia Dortmund [Fußball]
    ⌐ Taktik des Tauschens [Fußball + Fernsehen]
      ⌐ Premiere will [...] Champions League [Fußball + Fernsehen]

Figure 1: The MST (left) and CT (right) of the text sample (table 1).

References

BOTAFOGO, R. A., RIVLIN, E. and SHNEIDERMAN, B. (1992): Structural Analysis of Hypertexts: Identifying Hierarchies and Useful Metrics. *ACM Transactions on Information Systems, 10(2), 142–180.*

DUMAIS, S. T. (1995): Latent Semantic Indexing (LSI): TREC-3 Report. In: Harman (ed.): Overview of the Third Text Retrieval Conference (TREC-3). NIST, Gaithersburg, 219–230.

HALLIDAY, M. A. K. and HASAN, R. (1976): Cohesion in English. Longman, London.

LANDAUER, T. K. and DUMAIS, S. T. (1997): A Solution to Plato's Problem: The Latent Semantic Analysis Theory of Acquisition, Induction, and Representation of Knowledge. *Psychological Review, 104(2), 211–240.*

MEHLER, A. (1998): Toward Computational Aspects of Text Semiotics, in Proceedings of the IEEE ISIC, CIRA, ISAS, Joint Conference on the Science and Technology of Intelligent Systems, Gaithersburg, 807-813.

RIEGER, B. (1995): Situation Semantics and Computational Linguistics: In: Kornwachs, Jacoby (eds.): Information. New Questions to a Multidisciplinary Concept, Akademie-Verlag, Berlin, 285-315.

SALTON, G. (1989): Automatic Text Processing: The Transformation, Analysis, and Retrieval of Information by Computer. Addison-Wesley, Reading.

SALTON, G., ALLAN, J. and BUCKLEY, C. (1994): Automatic Structuring and Retrieval of Large Text Files. *Communications of the ACM, 37(2), 97-108.*

SMEATON, A. F. and MORRISSEY, P. J. (1995): Experiments on the Automatic Construction of Hypertext from Texts. *The New Review of Hypermedia and Multimedia: Applications and Research, 1.*

New Features of Categorical Principal Components Analysis for Complicated Data Sets, Including Data Mining *

J.J. Meulman[1], A.J. van der Kooij[1], A. Babinec[2]

[1]Data Theory Group, Faculty of Social and Behavioral Sciences, Leiden University, P.O. Box 9555, 2300 RB Leiden, The Netherlands

[2]Eucid Inc. & SPSS Inc, Chicago, U.S.A.

Abstract: This paper focuses on a technique to perform principal components analysis with nonlinear scaling of variables, and having correspondence analysis features. Special attention will be given to particular properties that make the technique suited for data mining. In addition to fitting of points for individual objects or subjects, additional points may be fitted to identify groups among them. There is a large emphasis on graphical display of the results in biplots (with variables and objects) and triplots (with variables, objects, and groups). The information contained in the biplots and triplots is used to draw special graphs that identify particular groups in the data that stand out on selected variables. Supplementary variables and objects may be used to link different data sets in a single representation. When a fixed configuration of points is given, the technique may be used for property fitting, i.e., fitting external information into the space. The method can be used to analyze very large data sets by assuming that the variables are categorical; when, however, continuous variables are available as well, these can be made discrete by various optimal procedures. Ordered (ordinal) and non-ordered (nominal) data can be handled by the use of monotonic or non-monotonic (spline) transformations. A state-of-the-art computer program (called CATPCA) is available from SPSS Categories 10.0 onwards.

1   Introduction

A prevalent type of multivariate categorical data consists of a small number of variables with a limited number of categories obtained for a very large number of objects (subjects), presented in the form of a multiway contingency table. Models are fitted to the cell counts, with respect to the margins of the table. Currently, the most popular method to analyze this type of categorical data is loglinear analysis. The information in a multiway contingency table can be efficiently transformed into a profile frequency matrix. Here, a weight is attached to each profile corresponding to the occurrence of the row profile in the data matrix.

---

*Invited lecture

An alternative analysis for loglinear analysis is a multiple correspondence analysis of this profile frequency matrix (Meulman & Heiser, 1997). Multiple correspondence analysis aims at a simple representation of the profiles as a set of profile points in a low-dimensional space; Meulman and Heiser (1997) have shown that this graphical display also contains possible higher order interactions. When the number of categories and/or the number of variables is large, however, the number of profiles becomes large as well. In this case, it is useful to see whether the observed profiles can be classified into a limited number of clusters in the representation. Multiple correspondence analysis only takes the nominal (categorical) information into account. In a lot of cases, we would like to maintain the ordinal information available in the variables. The method discussed presently can be viewed as what has been called a 'forced classification' method (Nishisato, 1984) that can be also be regarded as 'supervised learning' in the analysis of complicated data. The CATPCA method implies a mixture of two different representation models. The first is called the vector model, after Tucker (1960); Kruskal (1978) coined the term bilinear model, and Gabriel (1971) invented the name biplot. The vector model usually represents objects/subjects as points and variables as vectors, but there are exceptions (for instance in preference analysis, where Tucker's vector model originated, and in which subjects are represented as vectors and the stimuli that they have ordered as points; see Carroll, 1972, for an extended treatment of the vector model in the context of preference analysis). In our implementation of the vector/bilinear model, we fit (non)monotonic quantifications to the categories of the variables. The centroid model originates from multiple correspondence analysis, where a nominal variable is represented as a set of category points, which are in the centroids of the associated objects. Unlike the vector model that is based on projection, the centroid model is most easily viewed in terms of distances between object points and category points. Summarizing, using CATPCA, complicated multivariate data (with different scaling levels) are given a simple spatial representation, where different groups of objects can be distinguished without taking 'averages' of categorical data beforehand. The approach will be illustrated by using a large scale data set concerning feelings of national identity from about 28.500 respondents in 23 different countries (ISSP, Zuma, 1995).

2 Special features of the CATPCA method

The special features of the CATPCA method can be described as follows.

a) The bilinear (vector) model and the distance (centroid) model can be fitted for different variables in the same analysis.

b) The method accommodates differential weights for separate variables. In this way, the centroid model can be used for 'forced classification'

(Nishisato, 1984), which can be compared to 'supervised' learning by applying an (infinitely) large weight for the classification variable(s). The latter will cause the object points that belong together according to the specified classification variable to cluster in the low-dimensional space.

c) The algorithm is tuned to the analysis of categorical variables; continuous variables can be introduced into the analysis as well, after they have been made discrete according to a variety of options. The latter are optimal according to a particular distribution, normal or uniform, or according to other choices of grouping objects, like using equal intervals. The properties of a continuous variable can be maintained as closely as possible by a particular linear transformation that transforms the real-valued variable into a discrete variable with N categories, where N denotes the number of objects in the analysis.

d) When it is appropriate to apply the vector model for a particular variable, the choice exists between different nonlinear transformations, being either monotonic with the original order of the categories, or non-monotonic, also called nominal transformations that maintain the class membership only. For both transformations, two options are available, and these are either the use of splines, or the use of optimal functions originating from the multidimensional scaling literature (Kruskal, 1965; Kruskal and Shepard, 1974; Young, De Leeuw and Takane, 1978; Gifi, 1990, to mention some of the more important references). In the latter type of transformations, the numbers of parameters is free. The use of spline transformations in multivariate analysis was introduced in the psychometric literature by Winsberg and Ramsay (1983), see Ramsay (1988) for a nice overview, and 'optimal scaling' was introduced in the mainstream statistical literature through the ACE algorithm proposed by Breiman and Friedman (1985). Given the choice between the different options, the transformation functions are optimized with respect to the central least squares loss function that is minimized to obtain the spatial representation that is the core of the CATPCA method, i.e., representing the objects as points in a low-dimensional space, with some of the variables represented as a set of category points, and the remaining ones as vectors in the same space. Spline transformations require less parameters than least squares (non)monotonic transformations. For splines, the number of parameters is determined by the degree of the spline that is chosen, and the number of interior knots. Because splines use less parameters, they usually will be smoother and more robust, albeit this is at the cost of less goodness-of-fit with respect to the overall loss function that is minimized.

e) To handle incomplete data in the analysis, a sophisticated option is available that only takes into account the nonmissing data when minimizing the loss function (by the use of data weights); alternatively, other straightforward strategies are provided. The first is to exclude objects with missing values; the second provides a very simple imputation method (using the modal category). Also, a separate, additional category can be fitted optimally. If other more advanced missing data strategies would be called for, these would have to be part of a preprocessing process before the actual CATPCA analysis.

f) Different normalization options are provided for the display of objects and variables in the low-dimensional Euclidean space. The standard normalization option in PCA is to display the objects in an orthonormal cloud of object points, where the representation of the variables shows the differential fit in subsequent dimensions, the first dimension accounting for most of the fit, and subsequent dimensions displaying the fit in a decreasing order. An alternative option, is associated with the Principal Coordinates Analysis method of Gower (1966), where the emphasis is on the representation of the objects, and where the cloud of object points displays the differential fit in subsequent dimensions (the cloud is not orthonormal, but shows a definite shape). Interpretation in terms of distances between objects is also given, a.o., in Heiser and Meulman (1983), and Meulman (1986). Whether the object points or the (category points of the) variables are normalized depends algebraically on the allocation of the singular values in the use of the singular value decomposition to represent both sets of entities in the low-dimensional space. The impact of the singular values (symbolizing the fit) can also be distributed symmetrically over objects and variables (enhancing the joint display, especially when the overall fit is small), or handled in a completely customized way to enhance the joint representation.

g) The CATPCA method provides an option for the analysis of supplementary objects and/or variables. In this way, the main analysis can be performed on a subset of the available data, while the remaining (supplementary) objects and/or variables are afterwards fitted into the representation. This feature also provides the possibility to add supplementary data to an existing representation, by specifying a fixed configuration of objects points, so the CATPCA method may be used for so-called property fitting (Meulman, Heiser and Carroll, 1986), i.e., external information on objects is fitted into the representation space by the use of the vector model or the centroid model. The 'supplementary' option accommodates the appropriate scaling levels required (nominal, ordinal, or numerical treatment of variables).

h) For the graphical display of the results, three different biplots are available. The standard biplot visualizes objects as points and variables as vectors in a joint space. Also, we can have objects and their centroids according to a selected (classification) variable as points in the same graph. The third possibility shows groups of objects (as points) and variables (as vectors). Combining these three options reveals relationships between objects, groups of objects, and variables, and we call this display a triplot.

i) The ultimate summary of the analysis represents the information in the biplots and triplots in one-dimensional displays. These are obtained by taking centroids of the objects, according to a particular (classification) variable, and project them on the vectors representing variables of particular interest in the analysis. In this way, the graph identifies particular groups in the data that standout on the selected variables. If a supplementary classification variable is defined in the analysis containing the rank numbers of the objects, the objects themselves can be projected on the selected variables.

3 The joint objective function

In this section we will describe the joint objective function for simultaneous fitting of the vector and the centroid model. We start by defining the following terminology. The $N \times M$ matrix Q contains the scores for the N objects on M variables. The nature of the individual variables q_m will be discussed shortly. The $N \times P$ matrix X contains the coordinates for the N objects in a p-dimensional representation space, and the matrix A (of size $M \times P$) gives the coordinates in the same space for the endpoints of the vectors that are fitted to the variables deemed to be appropriately represented by a bilinear (biplot) model. Thus, a_m contains the coordinates for the representation of the mth variable, $m = 1, ..., M$. Consequently, the part of the objective function that minimizes the value of the objective function with respect to the bilinear/vector model can be written as:

$$\sigma(X; A; Q) = M^{-1} \sum_{m=1}^{M} ||q_m - X a_m||^2. \tag{1}$$

Assuming the data to be categorical, with the q_m discrete variables, we can also write

$$\sigma(X; A; y) = M^{-1} \sum_{m=1}^{M} ||G_m y_m - X a_m||^2, \tag{2}$$

where G_m is an indicator matrix that classifies each of the objects into one and only one category. The optimal category quantifications that will be obtained are contained in the C_m-vector y_m, where C_m denotes the number of categories for the mth variable. The quantifications for the m different variables y_m are collected in the vector y. The projection of the objects points X onto the vector a_m gives the approximation of the transformed (quantified) variable $q_m = G_m y_m$ in p-dimensional Euclidean space. Minimization of the loss function for the bilinear/vector model can be shown to be equivalent to the minimization of

$$\sigma(X; A; y) = M^{-1} \sum_{m=1}^{M} ||X - G_m y_m a'_m||^2, \tag{3}$$

(see Gifi, 1990). Here a p-dimensional matrix X is approximated by the inner product $G_m y_m a'_m$, which gives the coordinates of the categories of the mth variable located on a straight line through the origin in the joint p-dimensional space. The major advantage of this reformulation of the objective function is its capacity of capturing the distance/centroid model in the same framework. The latter can simply be written as

$$\sigma(X; Y) = K^{-1} \sum_{k=1}^{K} ||X - G_k Y_k||^2, \tag{4}$$

where the index k denotes the variables for which a distance model is considered to be appropriate. The $C_k \times P$ matrix Y_k contains the coordinates of the categories in the p-dimensional space. The objective function for the distance/centroid model implies that to obtain perfect fit, an object point in X, say x_i, should coincide with its associated category point y_k of the kth variable. The minimum of the objective function will give each category point in the centroid of the objects that are grouped in the particular category; hence the term centroid model. (In the context of computation, it should be noted that the indicator matrices are only used in the equations and NOT in the computations.)

4 The Geometry of CATPCA

Computationally, we start for each variable with fitting a centroid model according to (4). Next, when the vector model is required, the centroids Y_m are projected on a best fitting line (vector) through the origin. The resulting coordinates $y_m a'_m$ give the category points on this straight line, the vector that represents the variable in the joint space with the objects. The a_m give the component loadings, and these determine geometrically the directions of the vectors in the space. For a variable for which an ordinal scaling level is chosen, the quantifications y_m have to be constrained to be monotonic with the order of the original categories. When we choose the numerical scaling level, distances between the category points have to be equal, and the category quantifications y_m will be equivalent to the original category numbers. The goodness of fit is reflected in the components loadings, and their sum of squares, which gives the variance accounted for (VAF). If the distances between the categories have to be stretched very much to obtain unit variance, the VAF will be very small. It is important to realize, that this also applies to ordinary PCA, with continuous variables (i.e., a categorical PCA where each variable has N categories). When the centroid model has been chosen for particular variables, and when the solution has a decent fit, the category points of different variables that are associated with the same objects will be close together, while categories of the same variables will be far apart. The weighted mean squared distance of the category points towards the origin gives a measure similar to variance accounted for, and is called 'discrimination measure' (Gifi, 1990). In the centroid model, categories partition the objects points into subclouds. Overlapping subclouds correspond to a relatively badly discriminating variable, while well-separated subclouds are associated to a good discriminator.

5 Application

The CATPCA method has been applied to a large multivariate data set concerning feelings of national identity from about 28,500 respondents in 23 different countries all over the world (ISSP, ZUMA, 1995). We included about 60 variables in the analysis, and a very short description is given below. The first block of variables asked (among other things) how important the following aspects of one's country are: To have been born in one's own country; to have citizenship; to have spent most time of one's life there; to be able to speak various languages; religion; respect for institutions and law; to feel a member of one's country. The next block asked how close respondents felt to their: neighborhood; town/city; county; country; continent, and whether to improve upon their living conditions, they would be willing to move to another neighborhood; town/city; county; country; continent. The third block asked respondents whether they agreed or not to the following statements: feeling ashamed about some things; own country better than other countries; one should always support one's country; ...; limit the import of foreign products; schools should teach more languages; take care of only one's own interests; foreigners should not be allowed to buy land; TV/movies should be dubbed in one's own language; foreigners should share traditions; minorities should be helped to preserve traditions; ...; immigrants increase the crime rates; immigrants are good for the economy; immigrants take jobs away; immigrants give new ideas and culture; the number of immigrants should increase. The fourth block contained questions about pride about one's: democracy; political influence; economic achievement; scientific achievement; sports; arts; armed forces; history; treatment of different groups. Finally, the following background variables were considered: how long lived in town; how long stayed in other countries; are parents citizens; sex; age; marital status; education; employment status. The results have been summarized as follows. The following Figure 1 shows 14 transformation plots for different variables in the analysis. Transformations of variables with a favorable statement

214

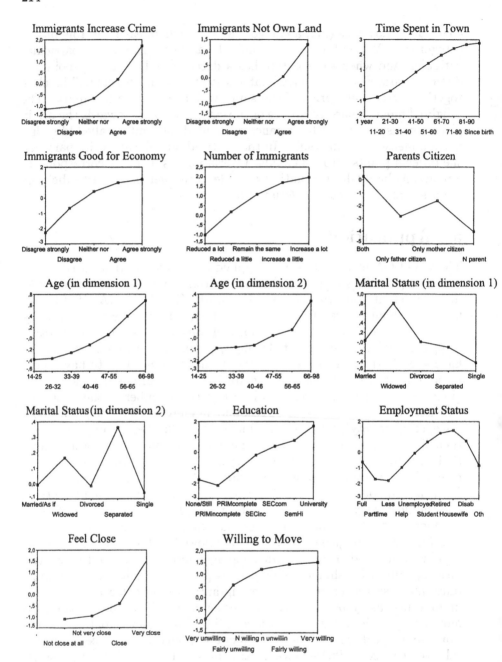

Figure 1: Transformations for selected variables from the National Identity questionnaire.

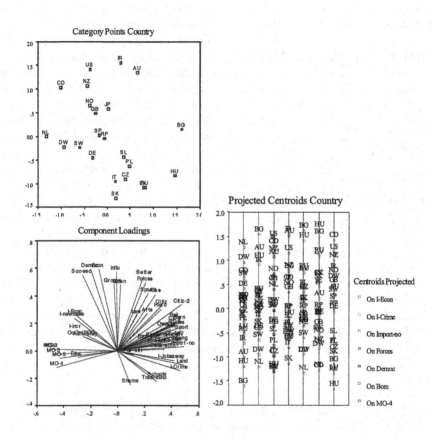

Figure 2: Visualization of the relationships between 23 countries (upper left panel) and 60 variables (lower left panel) from the National Identity study. Projection of the countries on a number of selected variables (right panel), derived from the two-dimensional spaces displayed at the left hand-side.

about immigrants ('Immigrants are good for the economy', 'Number of immigrants should be increased'; row 2, plots 1 and 2) are concave, as is 'Willing to move to another country'; row 5, plot 2). By contrast, transformations of variables unfavorable to immigrants ('Immigrants increase crime', 'Should not own land'; row 1, plots 1 and 2), are convex, as is 'Feel close to neighborhood'; row 5, plot 1). 'Time lived in one's own town' (row 1, plot 3) has been made discrete (and shows an S-shaped function). The variable 'Have parents been citizens?' (row 2, plot 3) was given a nominal scaling level, and shows the optimal order as: 'Both-Only Mother-Only Father-None', and decreasing. Age was fitted by the centroid model and obtained monotonically increasing functions in both dimensions (row 3, plots 1 and 2), and could have been treated as 'vector, with ordinal scaling level'. This is not true for Marital Status (row 3, plot 3, and row 4, plot 1). Figure 2 shows the configuration of the 23 countries separate from the configuration of the variables. The order of the countries from left to right is: Netherlands, Canada, West-Germany, Sweden, New Zealand, United States, Norway, East-Germany, Great Britain, Spain, Philippines, Japan, Italy, Slovakia, Ireland, Slovenia, Czechia, Poland, Australia, Latvia, Romania, Hungary, Bulgaria. The joint representation (the projection of the countries onto the vectors) is given in seven one-dimensional scales. These clearly display particular countries to be outstanding on different variables, from left to right: 'Willing to move to other country' (Netherlands versus Bulgary), 'Important to be born in one's own country' (Bulgaria versus Netherlands), 'Proud on democracy' (United States versus Slovakia), 'Proud on armed forces' (Ireland versus Slovakia), 'No Import foreign products' (Bulgaria versus Netherlands), 'Immigrants increase crime' (Hungary versus Canada), and 'Immigrants good for economy' (Canada versus Hungary).

References

BREIMAN, L. and FRIEDMAN, J.H. (1985): Estimating optimal transformations for multiple regression and correlation (with discussion). *Journal of the American Statistical Association, 80, 580-619.*

CARROLL, J.B. (1972): Individual differences and multidimensional scaling, In: Shepard, R.N., Romney, A.K., and Nerlove, S.B. (eds.): Multidimensional scaling: Theory and applications in the behavioral sciences. Vol I, New York and London: Seminar Press, 105-155.

GABRIEL, K.R. (1971)): The biplot graphic display of matrices with application to principal components analysis. *Biometrika, 58, 453-467.*

GIFI, A. (1990): *Nonlinear multivariate analysis.* Chicester: J. Wiley & Sons.

GOWER, J.C. (1966): Some distance properties of latent roots and vectors methods used in multivariate analysis. *Biometrika, 53, 325-338.*

HEISER, W.J. and MEULMAN, J.J. (1983): Analyzing rectangular tables by joint and constrained multidimensional scaling. *Journal of Econometrics, 22, 139-167.*

KRUSKAL, J.B. (1965): Analysis of factorial experiments by estimating monotone transformations of the data. *Journal Royal Statistical Society, B, 27, 251-263.*

KRUSKAL, J.B. (1978): Factor analysis and principal components analysis: bilinear methods. In: Kruskal, W.H. and Tanur, J.M. (eds.): International Encyclopedia of Statistics. New York: The Free Press, 307-330.

KRUSKAL, J.B. and SHEPARD, R.N. (1974): A nonmetric variety of linear factor analysis. *Psychometrika, 39, 123-157.*

MEULMAN, J.J. and HEISER, W.J. (1997): Visual display of interaction in multiway contingency tables: the 2x2x2x2 case. In: Blasius, J. and Greenacre, M. (eds.): Visualization of categorical data. New York: Academic Press, 277-297.

MEULMAN, J.J., HEISER, W.J. and CARROLL, J.D. (1986): PREFMAP-3 Users' Guide, Murray Hill, NJ: AT&T Bell Laboratories.

MEULMAN, J.J., HEISER, W.J. and SPSS (1999): SPSS Categories 10.0, SPSS Inc, Chicago.

NISHISATO, S. (1984). Forced classification: a simple application of a quantification method. *Psychometrika, 49, 25-36.*

RAMSAY, J.O. (1988): Monotone splines in action. *Stat. Science, 3, 425-441.*

TUCKER, L.R (1960): Intra-individual and inter-individual multidimensionality. In: Gulliksen, H. and Messick, S. (eds.): Psychological Scaling: Theory and applications. New York: Wiley.

WINSBERG and RAMSAY (1983): Monotone spline transformations for dimension reduction. *Psychometrika, 48, 575-595.*

YOUNG, F.W., TAKANE, Y., and DE LEEUW, J. (1978). The principal components of mixed measurement level multivariate data: an alternating least squares method with optimal scaling features. *Psychometrika, 43, 279-281.*

Supplement of Information: Data Integration by Classification of Pairs of Records

M. Neiling[1], H.-J. Lenz[2]

{mneiling,hjlenz}@wiwiss.fu-berlin.de

[1,2]Free University of Berlin, Department of Economics,
Institute of Applied Computer Science

[1]Berlin-Brandenburg Graduate School in Distributed Information Systems
(DFG grant no. GRK 316)

Abstract: Almost everywhere unique identifiers like keys are required for joining data in databases or information systems. If keys are absent or corrupted the supplement of data extracted from different sources is difficult. The question is: *Does the data contained in a single record belong to another record, or not?* This leads to a classification problem with at least two classes: *identical* and *not identical.* Classifying pairs of records needs some preprocessing. The first step is to detect suitable common properties of the different sources. Secondly, to allow comparisons the values of the records are transformed to this common properties. Finally, the classification is performed on an almost finite subset $R \subset \mathbb{R}^k$, the range of an appropriate comparison function. Given two data sets, a random sample of pairs is used for detecting similarities, rules or classification criteria. Different classification techniques can be applied to classify the pairs of the sources in order to link them or not. Unbiased error rates can be estimated by cross validation. The procedure is illustrated by an example of a library database from the internet.

1 Introduction

Assume that there exist two or more accessible data sources containing data on the same universe of objects. Sometimes global identifiers are available like the ISBN for books. But in general identifiers are missing, such that joins may be difficult to be performed.

Example 1 *The next census in Germany, scheduled for 2002, will be of type* administrative record census. *The census data will be collected from local public databases like registration, housing and social insurance databases. These databases contain no global identifier. For identification they store name and address data and sometimes date of birth. The question is: Does the data contained in a single record of data source A belong to any record of source B, or not? Evidently, if both data correspond to the same people, the records belong together. Hence, if we are able to identify people given by their data, we can establish joins. Unfortunately, misprints and obsolete data complicate identification. While a human is being able to decide, which records belong together, this could be difficult for an automatic processor.*

To perform a join the records of A and B are pipelined to output:

$$A, B \implies \textbf{Conversion} \implies \textbf{Comparison} \implies \textbf{Classification} \implies A \bowtie B,$$

where $A \bowtie B$ denotes the FULL OUTER JOIN of A and B w.r.t. the identification process. This JOIN splits into three parts for $a \in A, b \in B$, the NATURAL JOIN with pairs of records $a \bowtie b$ referring to identical objects, containing data from both data sources, and the LEFT and RIGHT OUTER JOIN with records $a \bowtie \emptyset$ and $\emptyset \bowtie b$ containing only data from one origin source A or B, with no counterpart in the other source.

Unfortunately, similarity search is not sufficient to establish this join in general. Typically a distance measure is needed for similarity search, but a meaningful distance measure can not be always performed due to problems like missing values and other irregularities (i.e. nominal comparison cases). We propose a classification approach to handle this, where distance measures are a special case.

The remainder of this paper is organized as follows. In section 2, we introduce the methodological background and annotation. In section 3, the classification is described. Section 4 illustrates the approach by an example of a library database from the Internet. Finally, in section 5, we summarize our results, and outline future work.

2 General Framework

Let U be an universe of distinct real world objects (e.g. people, books or cars). There are data sources A and B over U with attribute sets X and Y, respectively. A record from data source A or B is written $a \in A$, $b \in B$. The domain of possible values of a single attribute e is denoted by $\mathcal{D}_e$; for an attribute set $E = \{e_1, \ldots, e_n\}$ the domain is defined by $\mathcal{D}_E := \prod_{i=1}^{d} \mathcal{D}_{e_i}$.

Definition 1 (DERIVABLE ATTRIBUTE) *An attribute set E is* derivable *from an attribute set X iff there exists a surjective conversion function $\mathbf{h}_X : \mathcal{D}_X \to \mathcal{D}_E$, which maps the domain of X into the domain of E.*

Example 2 *Let A be a data source over a population, containing the attribute A.BirthDate. Then $e = Age$ is derivable using the conversion function $h : DATE \to \{0, 1, 2, \ldots\}$, $h(date) := \mathtt{Year}(today - date)$.*

Definition 2 (COMPARISON FUNCTION) *Let E be a set of d attributes with domain $\mathcal{D}_E$. Then a function $\mathbf{f} : (\mathcal{D}_E)^2 \to R \subset \mathbb{R}^k$ is designated as* comparison function. *R is called* comparison space.

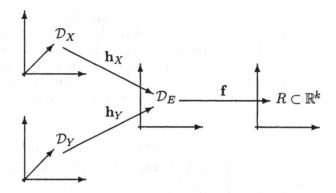

Figure 1: Two-step object identification.

Example 3 *Components of a comparison function can be defined for various data types by*[1]

$$f_1(value_1, value_2) := \begin{cases} 0 & : & value_1 = value_2 \\ 1 & : & otherwise \end{cases}$$

$$f_2(string_1, string_2) := distance_{EDIT}(string_1, string_2)$$

$$f_3(number_1, number_2) := \min\{5, |number_1 - number_2|\}$$

Definition 3 (CLASSIFICATION) *A classification rule on a space V is given by a decision function $\delta : V \to \{1, 2, \ldots, max\}$, which returns for $v \in V$ the index $j = \delta(v)$ of a class c_j.*

V could be equal $V = R$. Let E be a set of d attributes both derivable from X and Y with $\mathbf{h}_X, \mathbf{h}_Y$ and $\mathbf{f}$ a comparison function on E. Then from the definitions 1 – 3 it follows immediately

Proposition 1 *Each classification on R is a classification of $A \times B$, too.*

3 Classification

In Breiman et al. (1984) classification has two objectives:

(*i*) prediction of a response variable for a given measurement vector

(*ii*) exploration of relationships between response and measurements

In our case, the measurement vector is given by the comparison vector $r \in R$ for pairs of records (a, b), and the response variable is the class

---

[1]distance$_{EDIT}()$ is defined as the minimum number of edit operations (insertions, deletions and substitutions) to transform the first into the second string

(*'identical'*, *'not identical'*, etc.). For object identification the prediction of the class-membership is the main goal. On the other hand, if we discover relationships between the variables, prediction may be more understandable. Decision trees and association rules meet both purposes, while the statistical test used for Record Linkage fulfills only prediction. Classification methods can be distinguished by the scaling of the comparison space (compare table 1).

Class. Method	Scales of the Comparison Space[1]			
	nominal	ordinal	cardinal	mixed[2]
Record Linkage	++	+	--	-
Association Rules	++	++	-	-
Decison Tree	++	++	++	++
k-Nearest Neighbor	--	-	++	--
g. D. M. Class.[3]	--	0	++	--

[1]the score ranges from (−−) not suitable, (0) indifferent, up to (++) well suited
[2]mixed scales of nominal and cardinal type
[3]generalized Distance Measure Classification, e.g. $\sum_1^k w_i Dist_i(x_i, y_i)$

Table 1: The Appropriateness of Classification Methods

As is well known, sampling is crucial for supervised learning. A sample of pairs of records corresponding to different objects can be choosen at random from $A \times B$. To get a learning sample of pairs of records corresponding to identical objects is more complicated: Take a random sample S_A of records from source A. Find corresponding records in B and vice versa for a sample S_B from B. Getting a large sample is quite expensive, because it is 'handpicked'. Please note, that the portion of records in S_A and S_B with a counterpart in the other source is an estimator of the overlap of A and B.

If the range $R \subset \mathbb{R}^k$ of the comparison function $\mathbf{f}$ is of finite cardinality, we may assume a multinomial distribution on R. This situation is typical for categorical or ordinal comparison scales.

3.1 Record Linkage

The most common approach is called *Record Linkage*, c.f. Alvey, James (Eds.) (1997). There a function $\gamma : A \times B \to R \subset \mathbb{N}^k$, is to be defined. In our notation, γ is the comparison value r, more formal $\gamma = r = \mathbf{f}(\mathbf{h}_X(a), \mathbf{h}_Y(b))$. Two learning samples are chosen from $A \times B$ at random. The first sample M contains *matched pairs*, where the elements refer to the same object, the second sample N contains *not matched pairs* only.

The conditional probabilities $P(r \mid M)$ and $P(r \mid N)$ can be estimated and the Likelihood Ratio λ can be calculated for all comparison values $r \in R$:

$$\lambda = \lambda(r) := \frac{P(r \mid M)}{P(r \mid N)}. \tag{1}$$

A pair (a, b) with comparison value r and $\lambda(r) < 1$ is deemed not to matched (class *'not identical'*). Conversely, if $\lambda(r) > 1$ for a pair (a, b) we decide for class *'identical'*, since the probability $P(r \mid M)$ is larger than $P(r \mid N)$ here. For $\lambda \approx 1$ we get a third class for undecided cases. If the classes are defined as follows: $c_1 = identical$, $c_2 = critical$ and $c_3 = not\ identical$ a classification rule is given by the decision function $\delta : R \to \{1, 2, 3\}$:[2]

$$\delta\big(\lambda(r)\big) := \begin{cases} 1: & \lambda(r) > \lambda_u \\ 2: & \lambda_l \leq \lambda(r) \leq \lambda_u \\ 3: & \lambda(r) < \lambda_l, \end{cases} \tag{2}$$

Remark 1 *The assumption of the multinomial distribution is fundamental for this approach. Hence the comparison space R has to be finite, with only finite number of comparison cases. Given a learning sample, the distribution function is to be estimated. While the cardinality of R becomes much bigger than the 'handpicked' learning sample M, simplifying assumptions of the distribution are necessary, like the not generally valid conditional independence assumption for the probabilities, that means*

$$P\big(r \mid K\big) = P(\, (r_1, \ldots, r_d) \mid K) = \prod_{i=1}^{k} P(r_i \mid K) \ \textit{for } K = M, N. \tag{3}$$

4 The Library Catalogue

As data source $A = B$ we consider the integrated library catalogue of *GB-Vdirekt*, available at the Internet at `www.gbv.de`, and we try to identify duplicates there.[3]

The universe U is given by editions of books. Derivable attributes are chosen by $E = \{ISBN, Title, Name, Year, Pages\}$. According to the structure of the records, the conversion mappings h_i are simple filters from the origin data source (compare table 2) like

`Extract the page number from the origin record.`

---

[2] i.e. a (two-sided) simple likelihood-ratio test, c.f. Mood et al. (1974), p.410. The lower and upper bounds $\lambda_l, \lambda_u : 0 < \lambda_l \leq 1 < \lambda_u$ are computed according to the 'error of first type' for both incorrect classifications, bounded by a small α. The basic idea is an ordering of the comparison value according to the Likelihood-Ratio. Compare for more details Neiling (1998) or Fellegi et al. (1969).

[3] the example is taken from (Neiling, Lenz (2000))

Titel:	An introduction to database systems / C. J. Date
Verfasser:	C. J. Date
Ausgabe:	6. ed.
Erschienen:	Reading, Mass : Addison-Wesley, 1995
Umfang:	XXIII, 839 S. : graph. Darst. ; 24 cm
Serie:	Addison-Wesley systems programming series
ISBN:	0-201-54329-X

Table 2: The detailed structure of a record from *GBVdirekt*.

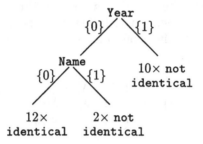

Figure 2: The decision tree for a learning sample.

The comparison function $\mathbf{f} = (f_1, \ldots, f_5)^\mathrm{T}$ can be defined as follows:[4]

$$f_1(ISBN_1, ISBN_2) := \begin{cases} 0 : ISBN_1 = ISBN_2 \\ 1 : ISBN_1, ISBN_2 \text{ are missing} \\ 2 : \text{otherwise} \end{cases}$$

$$f_2(title_1, title_2) := \begin{cases} 0 : title_1 = title_2 \\ 1 : title_1 \neq title_2, \text{ but} \\ \quad SameWords(title_1, title_2) \geq 70\% \\ 2 : \text{otherwise} \end{cases}$$

$$f_i(value_1, value_2) := \begin{cases} 0 : value_1 = value_2 \\ 1 : \text{otherwise}, \end{cases} \quad i = 3, \ldots, 5.$$

From a query result of 30 books a small learning sample of 24 pairs of books is chosen manually (12 pairs refer to identical books and the remaining 12 to different books), and different classification methods are applied (c.f. Neiling, Lenz (2000)). A decision tree technique based on an entropy measure generates the tree shown in fig. 2. Association rules can be derived directly from the comparison table, containing the comparison values of the five attributes for all of the 24 pairs of records, the labeled learning sample used here. The standard algorithm (Agrawal

---

[4]the function *SameWords( )* is defined as the ratio of the count of common words and the smaller total count of words. We only count words with at least three letters.

comparison values r_i	ratio λ_i for the i-th attribute				
	ISBN	Title	Name	Year	Pages
0	9/2	10/6	12/6	12/2	7/4
1	1/2	2/4	0/6	0/10	5/8
2	2/8	0/2			

Table 3: The Likelihood Ratios

et al. (1993)) is slightly modified for our purposes. A rule associates comparison values with the class-membership, e.g.

(R1) **if** comparison values for Pages=0 and for Year=0
        then records refer to the same book
        with **confidence 100%** and **support**[5] **58%**.

To apply Record Linkage we make the conditional independence assumption 3 and compute the Likelihood Ratio by $\lambda(r) = \prod_{i=1}^{5} \lambda_i(r_i)$. For each attribute $e_i \in E$ we calculate the $\lambda_i(r_i)$ separately from the estimations of the conditional probabilities: $\lambda_i(r_i) = \frac{P(e_i=r_i|M)}{P(e_i=r_i|N)}$. We apply the Maximum-Likelihood-Estimator for the multinomial distribution — the relative frequencies of occurrence of $e_i = r_i$ among the learning sample. The values of $\lambda_i(r_i)$ are displayed in table 3. For a pair of records with total agreement $r(a,b) = 0$ we get $\lambda = 157,5 \gg 1$. Therefore we decide on class $c_3 = identical$. If for another pair ISBN and Name disagree, while the others agree, we get $\lambda(2,0,1,0,0) = \frac{2}{8} \cdot \frac{10}{6} \cdot \frac{0}{6} \cdot \frac{12}{2} \cdot \frac{7}{4} = 0 < 1$. In this case we decide that the records refer to different books, class $c_3 = not$ $identical$. Let us finish with a non informative case: $\lambda(2,1,0,0,1) \approx 1$, so we can not decide, whether the two records belong to the same book or not. This pair is allocated to class $c_2 = critical$.

5 Outlook

We showed how several classification methods can be applied for object identification. Some future work remains:

- Further classification methods are to be evaluated for various data sources and learning sets.

- Dependencies between the comparison values of attributes may strongly affect the error rate of a classification. Hence the exploration of these relationships will be useful for identification.

- Since there exist a lot of alternatives of conversions and comparisons, feature selection will play a critical role.

---

[5]the support is related to the positive examples, t.i. **support 58%** is the validity of this rule for 7 out of the 12 positive examples used here.

Thanks to the standard XML (the eXtensible Markup Language recommended by the W3C) integration of data from the Internet will be simplified. Think for instance of XLink, where XML-elements from world-wide distributed XML-files can be embedded in a new document without specified target names. But all the schematic and semantic conflicts known from database integration (c.f. Kashyap, Sheth (1996)) will be complicate the integration of XML-formatted data.

The growth of the Internet requires data integration, that means supplementation of information from various sources. Especially, if they contain data corresponding to identical objects, integration is essential for well-designed future information systems.

References

AGRAWAL, R., IMIELINSKI, T. and SWAMI, A. N. (1993): Mining association rules between sets of items in large databases. ACM SIGMOD Int. Conf. on Management of Data, Washington, DC, pp. 207–216

ALVEY, W. and JAMERSON, B. (eds.) (1997): Record Linkage Techniques — 1997. Int. Workshop and Exposition. Fed. Committee on Stat. Methodology, Off. of Management and Budget, Washington, DC

BREIMAN, L., FRIEDMAN, J., OLSHEN R., and STONE C. (1984): Classification and regression trees. Chapman & Hall.

FELLEGI, I. P. and SUNTER, A. B. (1969): A theory of record linkage. *Journal of the American Statistical Association, 64, 1183–1210.*

KASHYAP, V. and SHETH, A. (1996): Semantic and schematic similarities between database objects: a context-based approach. *The VLDB Journal, 5, 276–304*

MICHIE, D., SPIEGELHALTER, D. J. and TAYLOR, C. C. (1994): Machine learning, neural and statistical classification. Horwood, New York.

MOOD, A. M., GRAYBILL F. A., and BOES, D. C. (1974): Introduction to the Theory of Statistics. McGraw-Hill, Tokyo

NEILING, M. (1998): Data Fusion with Record Linkage. In *3. Workshop "Föderierte Datenbanken", Magdeburg.*

NEILING, M. (1999): Datenintegration durch Objekt-Identifikation. In Kutsche R. et al. *4. Workshop "Föderierte Datenbanken", Berlin.*

NEILING, M. and LENZ, H.-J. (1999): The creation of the register based census for Germany in 2001. Disskusionsbeitrag 1999/34, FB Wirtschaftswissenschaft der FU Berlin.

NEILING, M. and LENZ, H.-J. (2000): Data integration by means of object identification in information systems. *8th Eur. Conf. on Information Systems, Vienna, Austria, July 2000.*

The Completion of Missing Values by Neural Nets for Data Mining

A. Ultsch, S. Rolf

Department of Mathematics and Computer Science,
Philipps-University Marburg, D-35032 Marburg, Germany

Abstract: Missing values are a problem occuring in the analysis of most application datasets. Though the deletion of observations with missing values is common practice, the loss of information in doing so is regrettable. This is even more the case for high-dimensional data, where the structural information in many components of an observation is lost because of few missing values. A new method is suggested for missing value imputation. The basis of the presented approach is an emergent self-organizing neural network that adjusts to the inherent structure of the input data. The technique has been successfully tested on a real-world example of financial data and turned out to be superior to the other methods under consideration.

1 Introduction to the Problem

Data Mining and Knowledge Discovery deal with the analysis of large multivariate datasets with respect to their inherent structure. For this task usually classes of elementary states are sought in the data. The Data Mining tool "Neuro Data Mine" (Ultsch (1999)) has proven to be a valueable tool for Knowledge Discovery in the last years.

A major problem to most Data Mining methods is the problem of missing values within many real-world datasets. Though it is common practice to simply ignore those observations that contain missing values in one or more components, the loss of information in doing so is regrettable. This is especially the case for high-dimensional data, where the information in all other components is left out because of one missing value in a single component. Moreover, if the share of missing values is too high, it is very likely that structural features can no longer be captured by the analyzing algorithms.

Since missing values are a problem which occurs in many real-world data sets, the question of its handling is of high relevance to the Data Mining community (e.g. Lakshmirnarayan et al. (1996); Timm, Klawonn (1998); Ragel (1998)). Two main options for the handling of missing data can be distinguished: On one hand methods are developed that are able to impute missing values such that all following methods are provided with a complete data matrix. The second option is to adapt the used Data Mining techniques such that they can handle incomplete data.

The main objective of this paper is to study the capacity of emergent self-organizing maps (Ultsch (1999)) for the imputation of missing values in comparison to commonly used imputation techniques.

2 Methods for Missing Value Imputation

2.1 Standard-Methods

Bankhofer (1995) distinguishes three major types of imputation techniques for missing data for cases in which the pattern of missingness is not systematic and the scale of the data is metric:

Simple techniques:

Imputation of each missing value by a chosen measure of central tendency as e.g. mean or median. If the underlying distribution of the data is known, the missing values can also be imputed by generating random numbers from that distribution.

Imputation within classes:

If classes of similar objects are known, this information can be used for the imputation of missing values. Within its imputation-class a reference observation is chosen for each incomplete observation The missing values are then replaced by the corresponding values of the reference. The simplest case of imputation within classes is the Nearest Neighbor Imputation (NNI), where for each incomplete observation the most similar observation with respect to all available components is chosen to be the reference vector.

Multivariate techniques:

Multivariate techniques build a multivariate model of the data and estimate the model parameters. On the basis of this model the missing values are estimated.

2.2 Neural Net Methods

The proposed Neural Net methods are based on emergent self-organizing maps (ESOMs) which have proven to be a powerful tool for structure analysis in high-dimensional data sets. ESOMs are Neural Nets with a large number of neurons arranged on a grid. The number of neurons usually exceeds the number of observations in the dataset. In the course of a training phase the map adjusts to the high-dimensional structure of the data and represents it on the two-dimensional grid. Starting from this concept, two methods for missing value imputation are proposed:

IESOM – Imputing emergent self-organizing map

The IESOM method trains an ESOM with all complete observations. Once the IESOM is trained, the most similar neuron (the "best match") is sought. All missing components are then replaced by the corresponding values of the neuron.

IESOM uses the fact that the neurons of an ESOM interpolate between the values presented during the training phase. Therefore not only the values in the data set are substituted for missing values, but also meaningful values between them.

UDnet-Imputation

The UDnet (Ultsch (2000)) is a Neural Net which is able to handle data with skewed distributions and different scales. It adapts itself to the distribution of each variable. After its learning phase a ud-network produces an output that can be interpreted as a 'relative distance' which is close to 1 if two values are rather different and close to 0 if they are very similar. 'Similarity' in a ud-net depends on the underlying distribution of the variables under consideration. It could be demonstrated in (Ultsch(2000)) that this learned distance is reasonably robust against standard types of non-linear transformations.

Since ESOMs are sensitive to skewed distributions as well as to variables on different scales, the combination of the two methods offers an approach to structure analysis that needs no preprocessing.

For the UDnet-Imputation, the data is presented to the ESOMs through the UDnet. In the course of the training, the UDnet learns the different distributions and scales in the dataset and is therefore able to interpret the raw data for the ESOM. The ESOM then adapts to the data-inherent structure as usual. For a more precise definition of the UDnet-method see Ultsch (2000).

3   Comparison of Methods

To assess the quality of the different methods, a dataset was derived form Morningstar™, a Chicago-based company that provides data on the majority of stocks and funds listed on US exchange (Deboeck, Ultsch (1999)). Morningstar™ publishes monthly and quarterly fundamental and technical information on over 7700 stocks listed on the NYSE, AMEX and NASDAQ exchanges. From these 7700 observations, 330 complete observations have been chosen. The 19 variables in the data set have been transformed into a standard-normal distribution using log and sqrt-transformations.

For the experiment, missing values have been inserted into the dataset. The values to be deleted have been chosen randomly over all observations and variables, therefore the missing value mechanism is MCAR (missing completely at random) (Little, Rubin (1987)).

Since one subject of the experiment is the performance in dependence on the number of incomplete cases, four different numbers of missing values (100, 300, 500 and 700) have been inserted. No restrictions on the number of missing values per observation have been introduced. To get more reliable results, 20 data sets have been generated for each number of missing values, such that there are 80 data sets in the experiment. For 100 missing values an average of 26.21% of the observations are incomplete. This value increases to 60.74% for 300 missing values, 79.36% for 500 missing values and reaches 89.33% for 700 missing values.

4 Results

The main aim of the experiment was to assess the quality of the imputation techniques in terms of the error made in substituting missing values. To measure the error, the mean absolute error (mae) (Schwab (1991)) will be used:

$$mae = \frac{1}{20} \sum_{d=1}^{20} \frac{1}{k_d} \sum_{d=1}^{20} \sum_{i=1}^{n} \sum_{j=1}^{m} |x_{ij} - y_{dij}| \tag{1}$$

with k_d no. of missing values in dataset d, n no. of observations, m no. of components, x_{ij} jth component of ith observation in the original dataset, y_{dij} corresponding value in the dth imputed dataset (either the value itself or the substitute for a missing value).

Though the mean absolute error will be considered as the main measurement for quality, some attention should also be given to the distortion of the underlying standard-normal distributions. Therefore the following two additional measures are introduced:

The mean absolute error in estimating the distribution's mean measures the bias in the estimation of the mean introduced by the substitution of the missing values. Since all variables in the 20 datasets follow a standard-normal distribution, the deviation from the true mean is averaged over all datasets and variables.

To measure the deviation from the true variance, the mean error for the estimation of the variance is reported. This error is splitted into the cases of over- and underestimation since – in contrary to the mean value – the direction of the bias is of some interest for the variance. As could be expected, the Mean Imputation (MI) shows the worst result for the mae with errors around 0.75 for all numbers of missing values. This is no surprise, because it is the only method which does not use relationships between the variables. Nevertheless the MI is a widely used technique

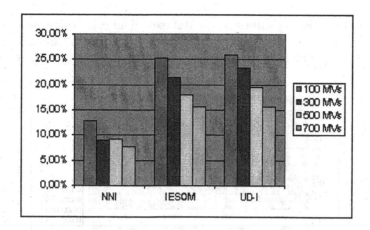

Figure 1: Mean Absolute Error Improvement in Comparison to Mean Imputation

for missing value handling and is therefore used as a reference for this study. Figure 1 therefore shows the improvement on Mean Imputation's *maes* reached by the other three methods under consideration.

It can be seen that the Nearest Neighbor Imputation (NNI) improves the results from MI by about 8% to 13%. The IESOM's *maes* are between 16% and 25% better than the references. Approximately the same holds for the UDnet-Imputation (UD-I), where improvements between 16% and 26% are attained. Considering the error in estimating the distribution's

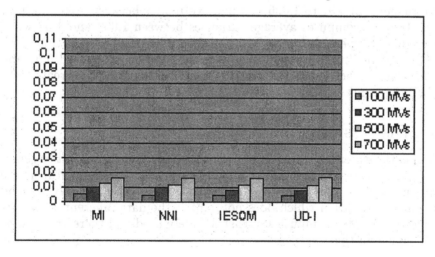

Figure 2: Mean Absolute Error in Estimation of Distribution's Mean

mean, it can be seen from Figure 2 that the methods show nearly the same performance in this respect. All methods generate errors at about

0.005 for 100 missing values in the dataset. The error increases with the number of missing values to up to about 0.016 for 700 missing values. Figure 3 shows the outcomes for the methods concerning variance estim-

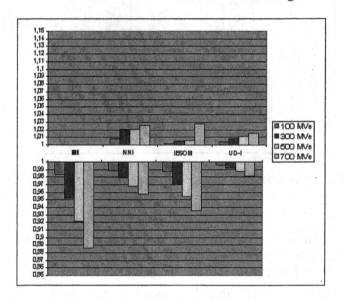

Figure 3: Mean Error in Estimation of Distribution's Variance

ation splitted into under- and overestimation. The MI generates average variances between 0.98 and 0.88. The NNI overestimates the variance in the range from 1.01 to 1.026 and underestimates between 0.99 and 0.96. The IESOM computes average variances between 1.002 and 1.03 when overestimating and between 0.99 and 0.94 when underestimation. The UD-I underestimates variances on average between 0.996 and 0.98 and overestimates between 1.004 and 1.02. All methods show a greater bias when the number of missing values increases.

5 Discussion

Within the experiment the Mean Imputation method turned out to generate the worst results in terms of Mean Absolute Error in substituting the missing values. This result was expected because it is the only method under consideration which does not exploit the data-inherent structure. Nevertheless Mean Imputation is still widely used and therefore used as a reference in this study.

The Nearest Neighbor Imputation could already improve the results attained by Mean Imputation by up to 13%. It also turned out to be the least sensitive to the number of missing values. This observation can be explained by the fact that the Nearest Neighbor Imputation uses all available information in the data by allowing for completed observations to be used as a reference in the further imputation process.

The presented methods based on Neural Nets, IESOM and UD-Imputation, gave better results than Mean Imputation or Nearest Neighbor Imputation. Both methods lowered the values of the Mean Imputation up to 26%. Since both methods rely only on information available in complete observations, their performance decreases with the number of missing values in the dataset. Nevertheless, even for the worst case of 700 missing values the results of the Neural Net methods are still better than the Nearest Neighbor Imputation.

Though the Mean Absolute Error is considered to be the main quality-criterion, some attention should also be given to the distortion of the underlying distributions caused by the imputations. Inspection of the estimated means and variances leads to the following results:

All methods generated nearly the same distortion of the mean value by means of the imputation. However, the measured values between 0.004 and 0.017 do not give rise to concern. As a comparison: A Gauss-test (Hartung(1991), p. 178) with hypothesis "Mean equals zero" would only reject the hypothesis for values larger than 0.1081 at an α-level of 0.05.

In contrary to the mean value, the methods performed quite differently for the variance: The Mean Imputation showed worst results for all numbers of missing values. The Nearest Neighbor Imputation generated clearly better estimates, showing just slight differences in over- and underestimation. The IESOM showed larger distortions in underestimating the variance, still being clearly better than the Mean Imputation. Best performance was shown by the UD-Imputation, average distortions of no more than 0.02 were computed. A two-sided test on "Variance equals 1" (Hartung(1991), p. 179) would not reject the hypothesis in an intervall of [0.8530, 1.1585] at 0.05 α-level. Only the Mean Imputation for 700 missing values comes close to that border with an average estimated variance of 0.89.

6 Conclusion

In this paper two methods for the imputation of missing values based on Emergent Self-Organizing Maps (ESOM) are proposed: IESOM and UD-Imputation. An experiment has been performed on real data which showed that both methods are superior to commonly used methods as Mean Imputation and Nearest Neighbor Imputation. Since the Neural Net methods need no prior information about the data, no interaction with the analyzer and no explicit model building, they can be considered to be well suitable for Data Mining applications.

Unlike Nearest Neighbor Imputation, the Neural Net methods do not use the whole information available in the data. Therefore a Neural Net capable of handling missing values would be expected to perform even better. This is subject to further investigation.

References

BANKHOFER, U. (1995): Unvollständige Daten- und Distanzmatrizen in der Multivariaten Datenanalyse, Verlag Josef Eul, Bergisch Gladbach, Köln.

DEBOECK, G. and ULTSCH, A. (1999): Picking Stocks with Emergent Self-organizing Value Maps, to appear in Proc. PASE 2000.

HARTUNG, J. (1991): Statistik: Lehr- und Handbuch der angewandten Statistik. 8. Auflage, München, Wien, Oldenbourg, 1991.

LITTLE, R. J. A. and RUBIN, D. B. (1987): Statistical Analysis with Missing Data, Wiley, New York.

LAKSHMINARAYAN, K. and HARP, S.A. and GOLDMAN, R. and SAMAD, T. (1996): Imputation of missing data using machine learning techniques, in: Proceedings of the 2nd International Conference on Knowledge Discovery and Data Mining, pp. 140–145.

RAGEL, A. (1998): Preprocessing of Missing Values Using Robust Association Rules, in: Zytkow, J.M. (ed.): Principles of data mining and knowledge discovery, 2nd European Symposium, Lecture Notes in Artificial Intelligence 1510, pp. 414–422.

SCHWAB, G. (1991): Fehlende Werte in der angewandten Statistik, Dt. Univ.-Verl., Wiesbaden.

TIMM, H. and KLAWONN, F. (1998): Classification of Data with Missing Values, in: Proceedings of the 6th European Conference in Intelligent Techniques and Soft Computing, pp. 639–643.

ULTSCH, A. (1999): Data Mining and Knowledge Discovery with Emergent Self-Organizing Feature Maps for Multivariate Time Series, in: Oja, E., Kaski, S. (eds.): Kohonen Maps, Elsevier, pp. 33–46.

ULTSCH, A. (2000): A Neural Network Learning Relative Distances, in: Amari, S., Giles, C., Gori, M., Piuri, V. (eds.): Neural Computing: New Challenges and Perspectives for the New Millennium, 2000 IEEE International Joint Conference on Neural Networks (IJCNN 2000), Vol. V, pp. 553–558, Como, 2000.

Knowledge Landscapes: Clustering Hypermedia Course Content for Efficient Overviews

E. Weippl[1], H. Lohninger[2]

[1]Software Compentence Center Hagenberg
Softwarepark, A-4232 Hagenberg, Austria

[2]Institute of Analytical Chemistry
Vienna University of Technology, A-1060 Vienna, Austria

Abstract: The virtual Knowledge Landscape (KL) simulates a natural cognitive space for users. Visualizing the relationship between educational texts, it helps students when browsing through the data and when studying details. The main objective of the KL is to allow students to quickly gain an overview over a large collection of educational hypermedia materials. Relations between texts are calculated using a SOM after having analyzed the texts' vocabulary. Additional information is derived from the link-structure so that texts can be classified as overview or detailed texts.

1 Introduction

The virtual Knowledge Landscape (KL) simulates a natural cognitive space for users. By visualizing the relationship between educational texts, it helps when browsing through the data and when studying details. Advanced navigational techniques allow for a flight through the virtual 3D space and a multimedia browsing of selected documents. The main objective of the KL is to give students a quick overview over a large collection of educational hypermedia content.

The KL can be characterized by four main facts. (1) It is a combination of extracting relevant information from texts and visualizing the relationship between these (texts). (2) The information is extracted from the full text, which is possible even if authors have not provided keywords. (3) On the user interface (UI) related texts are displayed next to each other in a 2D plane. (4) The third dimension is used to distinguish whether the text contains overviews or detailed information.

In this paper we compare different algorithms (Principal Component Analysis, an Error Backpropagation Network, a Kohonen Net, and a modified Genetic Algorithm) and we explain how to optimize classification based on text data. New research results that rely on link-based algorithms (Terveen 1999), (Chakrabarti 1999), (Kleinberg 1999) can be modified and integrated into the KL. Feedback from students and faculty staff using Teach/Me (Lohninger 1999), a courseware product that offers the KL as a UI, made it possible to further improve it.

2 Related Work

Before implementing the KL, we tried to find tools that could extract relevant information from texts and visualize the relationship between them. What we found is that the efficient tools1 are not readily available. Most tools cover some essential aspects of a KL but lack support of either automatically categorizing or visualizing the content.

2.1 Research Based Approaches

The Scatter/Gather system (Cutting 1992) is an approach that is effective for browsing search results. Every text can be found in a cluster. Compared with our approach, the paper does not describe any form of visualizing the inter-cluster relationship.

Bead (Chalmers 1992) uses multidimensional scaling to calculate a 2D visualization, similar to the approach described by Schoder (1999). However, the main drawback of the MDS based algorithm is that clusters may lie very far apart and the density within a cluster may be very high. Due to this fact the resulting data clouds are hard to visualize. We described (Weippl 1999) a similar situation for a PCA based approach.

The Galaxy of News (Rennison 1994) uses an Associative Relation Network to classify news texts based upon assumptions of which words (keywords, location, time, etc.) are important. This implies that the information in the text body is ignored. For news articles this may not matter but for a general solution this is definitely a drawback.

Fowler (1991) describes a system based on inter-document similarity. The main display shows keywords and in another frame a list of corresponding documents. The keywords are connected to each other so that a Concept Map (or associative term thesaurus) is displayed.

Websom (Lagus 1996) can be used to compute a 2D projection of a document space, but the program only does the computation and provides no form of graphical UI to manipulate the document clustering or to highlight additional information as for example the hyperlink structure.

Lin (1991) uses a SOM for a prototype system in HyperCard. The system uses latent semantic indexing (Furnas 1988) to build the original high-dimensional document space. According to the authors, the extended vector model offers advantages but has not been implemented.

2.2 Commercial Software

As organizing data is a common task so that knowledge can be derived quickly, there is lot of commercial software that supports at least some aspects.

The MindManager[1] is a tool that allows visualizing concepts using a graph structure. Every node can be annotated and hyperlinks can be set to the corresponding documents. However, the MindManager does not support importing data using some form of prestructuring. All the nodes have to be created and linked to the documents.

The Brain[2] is a similar tool. It supports importing data stored in a file system structure and hyperlinked documents. The automatic layout relies on the graph derived from the file structure or the hyperlinks in HTML documents.

Document management tools, like Acrobat[3] are useful to annotate files and embed hyperlinks within these documents. They are often used to create structured overview documents with links to the documents. The drawback, however, is that Acrobat does not provide any form of assistance of how to structure these overviews.

2.3 Link-Based Structure

Cinecat (Dridi 1999) visualizes link-relations of documents that have been accessed recently. Link-structures also play an important role in new algorithms designed to improve Web searching.

Chakrabarti (1999) classifies pages either as hubs or as authorities. A good authority is a page pointed to by many good hubs, while a good hub is a page that points to many good authorities.

They propose an algorithmic formulation of the notion of authority, based on the relationship between a set of authoritative pages and hub pages that are connected via links. Kleinberg (1999) describes the algorithm in detail. Their formulation has connections to the eigenvectors of certain matrices associated with the link graph; these connections in turn motivate additional heuristics for link-based analysis.

For many purposes, the Web page as unit is too small for interaction and analysis. Web sites consist of many pages, and users are interested in topically related sites and not single pages that may even be subframes. The 'auditorium visualization' (Terveen 1999) builds upon these premises to assist users in finding high-quality sites.

3 Creating Knowledge Landscapes

As already stated, we developed an algorithm to position texts automatically in the KL. Analyzing texts provides enough information to build a

---

[1] http://www.mindman.com
[2] http://www.thebrain.com
[3] http://www.adobe.com

thesaurus of keywords. Text chapters that contain similar keywords are placed next to each other.

We start by building a matrix (each row represents a text, each column a keyword), counting how often a keyword appears in each text. The matrix consists of a key-term vector for each text. The term 'key-term vector' refers to 'term vectors' mentioned by Wise (1995).

To decide whether a word is important or not, we do not rely on titles and typographic information. Obviously, titles are important, but a lot of equally important information is often contained in the text bodies. In contrast to previously mentioned systems like "Galaxy of News" (Rennison 1994) our approach does not ignore relationships based on the full text. To reduce the number of different words, i.e. to reduce the dimensionality of the task, we use Porter's stemming algorithm (an overview can be found in Baezo-Yates (1999)) and a stop-word list. Finally we eliminate words that can be found only in few or in nearly all texts.

The rows of the obtained data matrix are vectors in a high dimensional space. Within this space, texts form clusters according to the topics they deal with. As not all words are equally important, each item of the matrix is multiplied by a weight, the so called 'Term Frequency - Inverse Document Frequency' (tf-idf) (Baezo-Yates 1999, Salton 1989). The goal is to find a 2D projection of this high dimensional (typically around 600D) space that preserves the clustering despite of the sparsity structure of the data matrix. Having evaluated different algorithms (PCA, Error Backpropagation Networks, and SOM) (Weippl 1999), the best results have been achieved with a Kohonen net.

We used dendrograms to assess the quality of clustering. Using the x/y coordinates of the texts in the KL, a cluster analysis was performed. The colors of the dendrograms' branches were assigned according to the *real* clustering in the high dimensional space. This means that if colors are clearly separated in the dendrogram, the algorithm preserves the original clustering during the mapping process. If the colors are mixed, the *clustering error* is considered to be big. The clustering error is measured by visually judging how well the colors are separated (see Fig. 1).

The results are influenced by the metric used within the SOM, too. Kohonen (Kohonen 1997, p26) uses the 'pattern vector angle' as a distance measure which is robust concerning outliers. The Euclidean metric is normally considered to deliver poor results when calculating distances between texts. Due to the tf-idf transformation (Baezo-Yates 1999) extreme outliers can be prevented.

The algorithm[4] we used is similar to that employed in the WebSom project (Lagus 1996). There are three important improvements with our

---

[4] After the tf-idf transformation the Euclidean metric can be used.

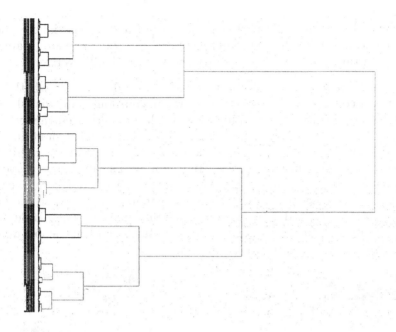

Figure 1: The dendrogram shows that the SOM preserves the original clustering very well.

KL: (1) External texts can be imported into the KL. Placing these texts in the vicinity of related texts is a useful feature if writers need to find texts related to their manuscripts. (2) The visualization of additional structure information improves the possibilities of recognizing relationships. (3) Interactive manipulation of the map allows the user to change it according to his needs.

4   Adding Structure Information

We modify the classification scheme proposed by Chakrabarti (1999), so that every page is assigned a value describing to what extent it is a hub and an authority. A page that is classified to be 0.9 hub is 0.1 authority, i.e. the sum is always 1.0.

Using this classification, the user can set thresholds and map values to glyphs. In Figure 2 each text is represented by one glyph. The lines show the link-structure of some selected texts. The glyph's size gives information whether the corresponding text contains overview or detailed information. The figure shows texts that are hubs, i.e. overview pages as larger box-shaped glyphs. Pages with a hub-value [0;0.4] are mapped to small boxes,]0.4;0.7] to medium-sized boxes and]0.7;1.0] to large boxes.

We also implemented a VRML based 3D KL (see Fig. 3).   The first obvious advantage of 3D is that we now have a third spatial dimension for visualization. Each mountain represents one text. The mountains are placed in the 2D base plane the same way as in the 2D version.

The third dimension, i.e. the mountains' height, depends on whether the mountain contains detailed or overview information. This visual metaphor is very intuitive: In real life everyone has experienced the overview one gets when standing on high mountains. Thus high mountains contain overview information, e.g. a table of contents or an overview over various forms of neural networks. High mountains can easily be spotted from large distances and help people reading detailed information to keep the general concept in mind all the time. Small mountains, on the other hand represent texts dealing with detailed information. These mountains can only be seen in the vicinity of big mountains and thus people are not confused when first entering the 3D KL.

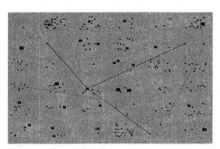

Figure 2: This screenshot shows a 2D view of the KL that has been enriched by structural information.

Figure 3: This screenshot shows a 3D view of the KL (see also Fig. 2).

5 Applications

The underlying computational algorithm is indispensable but not sufficient. Much more is needed for KLs to be useful. The UI has to be designed for the tasks the user wishes to perform. For example, a simpler UI (see Figure 4) has been integrated into Teach/Me (Lohninger 1999). Observations and interviews with more than ninety users (Weippl 1999) helped to optimize the KL for teaching and learning purposes.

We also used the KL to visualize 20000 Newsgroup articles, the Reuters-21578 text collection[5], 1500 medical abstracts[6] and a textbook on mathematics [7].

---

[5]source data available at http://kdd.ics.uci.edu/
[6]source data from ECCO10 conference in Vienna.
[7]STRASSER, H. (1997): Mathematik für Wirtschaft und Management. Management Book Service, Vienna.

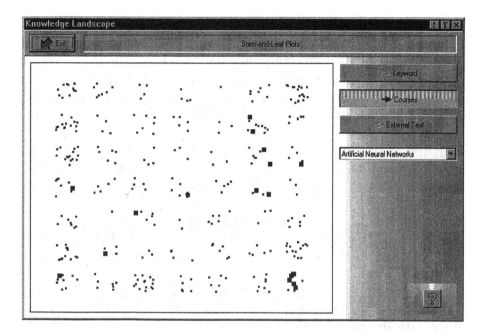

Figure 4: This screenshot shows the KL that has been integrated into Teach/Me (Lohninger 1999). The texts marked by box shaped glyphs are part of a short lecture on Artificial Neural Networks.

6 Outlook and Future Research

Currently several other CBT courses are being developed using the Teach/ Me platform. The algorithms described in this paper work well for small to medium-sized text collections but processing time limits the total number of texts that can be processed. The Reuters-21578 text collection currently is the upper limit[8]. We assume that the training of the SOM can be accelerated by using carefully chosen prototypes and not all texts as training set.

References

BAEZO-YATES, R. and RIBEIRO-NETO, B. (1999): Modern Information Retrieval. Addison-Wesley, Reading Massachusetts.

CARD, S.K., MACKINLAY, J.D. and SHNEIDERMAN, B. (1999): Readings in Information Visualization. Morgan Kaufmann Publishers.

CHAKRABARTI, S. et al. (1999): Mining the Web's Link Structure. *IEEE Computer, 32(8):60-67.*

---

[8]On a Pentium 200MHz/128MB this can be done overnight; depending on the size of the SOM and the degree of stemming performed times may vary from 4 to 12 hours.

242

CHALMERS, M. and CHITSON, P. (1992): Bead: Explorations in Information Visualization. In Proceedings of the Fifteenth Annual International ACM SIGIR Conference. 330–337.

CUTTING, D.R. et al. (1992): Scatter / Gather: A Cluster-based Approach to Browsing Large Document Collections. In Proceedings of the Fifteenth Annual International ACM SIGIR Conference. Copenhagen, Denmark. 318–329.

DRIDI, F., HÜLSBUSCH, T. and NEUMANN, G. (1999): Visualization and Categorization of Cached Hypermedia Data. *Classification in the Information Age*. W. Gaul and H. Locarek-Junge (editors). Springer Heidelberg. 387–394.

FOWLER, R.H. et al. (1991): Integrating Query, Thesaurus, and Documents Through a Common Visual Representation. In Proceedings of the Fourteenth Annual International ACM SIGIR Conference. Chicago, USA, 142–151.

FURNAS, G.W. et al. (1988): Information retrieval using a singular value decomposition model of latent semantic structure. In Proceedings of the 11th International Conference on R&D in Information Retrieval. ACM Press. Grenoble, France. 465–480.

KLEINBERG, J. (1999): Authoritative Sources in a Hyperlinked Environment. *Communications of the ACM, 46(5):604-632.*

KOHONEN, T. (1997): Self–Organizing Maps. Springer, Berlin, Heidelberg, New York, London, Paris, Tokyo.

KÖPPENN, E. and NEUMANN, G. (1999): Visualization of Course Structures Through Adaptive Internet Techniques. *Classification in the Information Age*. W. Gaul and H. Locarek-Junge (editors). Springer Heidelberg. 395–401.

LAGUS, K. et al. (1996): WEBSOM — A Status Report. In Proceedings of STeP'96, Finnish Artificial Intelligence Conference. Finnish Artificial Intelligence Society. Vaasa, Finland.

LIN, X., SOERGEL, D. and MARCHIONINI, G. (1991): A Self-Organizing Semantic Map for Information Retrieval. In Proceedings of the 14th Annual International ACM SIGIR Conference. Chicago, USA. 262–269.

LOHNINGER, H (1999): Teach/Me Data Analysis. Springer, Heidelberg.

RENNISON, E. (1994): Galaxy of News: An Approach to Visualizing and Understanding Expansive News Landscapes. In Proceedings of the UIST 94, ACM Symposium on User Interface Software and Technology. New York, USA. 3–12.

SCHODER, D. (1999): Navigation in Cyperspace: Using Multi-Dimensional Scaling to Create Three-dimensional Navigation Maps. *Classification in the Information Age.* W. Gaul and H. Locarek-Junge (editors). Springer Heidelberg.

TERVEEN, L. and HILL, W. (1999): Constructing, Organizing, and Visualizing Collections of Topically Related Web Resources. *ACM Transactions on Computer-Human Interaction, 6(1):67–94.*

WEIPPL, E. (1999): Integration of Virtual Reality Knowledge Landscapes into Multimedia Teachware for Chemometrics, Doctoral Dissertation, Vienna University of Technology. Vienna, Austria.

WISE, J.A. et al. (1995): Visualizing the Non-Visual: Spatial Analysis and Interaction With Information from Text Documents. In Proceedings of the Information Visualization 95. IEEE Society Press. Los Alamitos. 51–58.

Simplification of Knowledge Discovery using "Structure Classification"

S. Zumpe, W. Esswein

Chair of Business Informatics
esp. System Engineering
Dresden University of Technology
D-01062 Dresden, Germany

Abstract: In order to make pieces of information accessible to a user, they have to be analyzed and structured. Thereby often concepts from the area of Artificial Intelligence (AI), in particular semantic networks, are used. These networks will be extended by using knowledge about meta languages. The paper presents an approach to information structuring. It offers the possibility to cope with highly complex data by using information about the meta-structure of the knowledge base.

1 Introduction

The world could be understood as a market place, where dealers offer their products, services and information. Customers visit the market place in order to gain suitable information. Thereby two customer types could be distinguished. On the one hand they find eligible products and information on their own, because they are well aware of their needs. On the other hand the second type of customers does not know which dealer offers which product, i. e. the desired information. Neither they know how to gain access to information, once they found the correct dealer. Therefore extensive knowledge regarding the market structure as well as the internal structure of offered products is required.

The provision of the user with the desired information is regarded as one of main tasks of information and knowledge systems. Furthermore they have to cope with knowledge complexity, but at the same time need to be accessible to the user (cf. Ferstl, Sinz (1998) pp. 47). If automatic systems aim to deliver information in an excellent way, their knowledge bases have to be perfect. The knowledge structure and accessibility is one of the main prerequisites in order to achieve these goals.

2 Knowledge in Complex Systems

In almost every field of science a variety of information exists, which is regarded useless for itself. Only a purpose-oriented network of these data leads to the development of knowledge. However such networks require knowledge about interdependencies between different pieces of information and their meaningful linkage. Complexity describes the feature of material systems to implement a great variety of feasible internal and external relations between system elements and outside conditions (cf. Grochla (1973) p. 1621).

Complex knowledge in automated systems should be presented in a formal way. Thereby the presentation aims to illustrate each informational unit, its features and relations towards other units as a whole. It is complete, all-embracing, correct, conclusive in itself and consistent. In order to make a problem accessible, the information capacity may not exceed a critical limit. Therefore complexity needs to be restricted. This can be achieved by structuring the given pieces of information (cf. Rosemann (1996) pp. 14).

A reduction in complexity is only attainable by splitting them into smaller units. These sub-units could be processed by humans, since their complexity has to be below the critical limit (cf. Dorn (1989) pp. 9).

Additionally a decision has to be taken between complexity and simplicity. The final answer to this question depends on the information system to be modelled. If the user has detailed ideas about it, highly complex facts could be modelled. Thereby we use the fact, that individuals without precise knowledge of current circumstances do have exact conceptions of the concerned object and its relations. It is able to gain access to relevant knowledge areas very easily and has detailed information about the knowledge meta-structure. In this case the critical limit can be shifted upward. Meta knowledge is defined as knowledge about the current knowledge.

Contradictiously, if the knowledge system is new and the required information amount is not accessible by the user completely, the critical limit must be shifted downward. Subsequently the user has to deal with a knowledge area, which could only be explored by using a simple representation with low complexity.

Basically we can conclude, that highly structured knowledge bases permit a low degree of complexity to be managed by the information system. In contrast, the degree of complexity is very high in weakly structured knowledge bases, whereby the user does only need a small amount of information about the meta-structure.

In order to explain this conclusion, the following examples are given:

Individual information units:

There is a great variety of individual information units, which are characterised by a low content complexity and a weak meta-structure. For instance, individual traffic announcements regarding traffic jams and accidents could be mentioned.

Strongly structured knowledge bases:

Enterprises are characterised by tight organisational structures which are

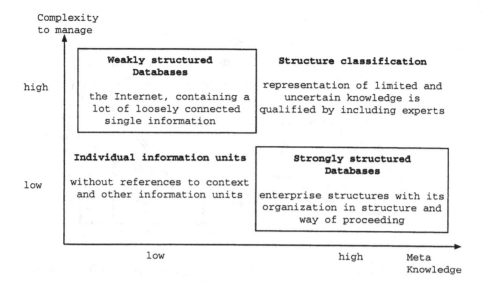

Figure 1: Representation of the complexity in contrast to the accessibility

determined by hierarchical relationships between different units. Therefore the available information of and about them could be understood easily.

Weakly structured knowledge bases:

The amount of separate pieces of information on the World Wide Web can be described as weakly structured, since they are only loosely linked together. Therefore structuring models are rarely used and support systems have to cope with higher complexity.

Structure classification:

The establishment of an information system for existing or future start-up companies serves as a practical example. It should be able to deal with every kind of measures and actions which are linked to the field of business start-ups. Although suitable meta knowledge is available in this field, the complexity to be processed is extremely high (cf. Schäfer (1996) pp. 33). By reducing the complexity, system becomes more understandable and manageable for both, the modeler and the user. An extended structure opens up the possibility to split up an extensive problem area. Therefore well defined sections could be processed by using specialised methods or tools (cf. Eckert (1993) pp. 139). Moreover it can also unveil structural and semantical relations within the knowledge base. Finally, by using different structuring tools and the principle of abstraction a model of the real world could be built.

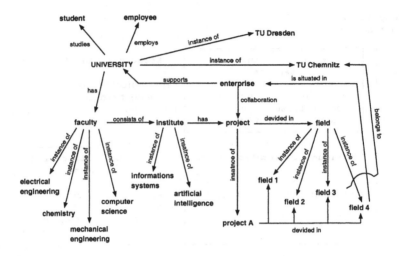

Figure 2: Semantic Network of the Dresden University of Technology

3 Knowledge Representation

With the development of knowledge-based systems, pure Artificial Intelligence systems were evolved to systems possessing knowledge about a certain area of interest (cf. Kurbel (1992) pp. 1). Their knowledge bases could be presented in different forms, so that they could be expanded, exchanged and modified easily. The development of such systems requires some crucial steps. These embrace the identification, classification and structuring of knowledge as well as its representation. In conjunction with the establishment of these systems major concepts for knowledge representation were used, particulary semantic networks, frames, and logic and production rules where knowledge is represented through classes and objects. (cf. Bibel (1993) pp. 32).

Kurbel defines an object as a description of a concrete item, characterised by its features. Given the descriptions, objects could be classified into hierarchies. In order to make them accessible to a user often the concept of semantic networks is used (cf. Reimer (1991) pp. 79). An example is given in figure 2.

Knowledge representation languages are very useful in order to get an overview of relationships and interdependencies in the current field of interest by building a model. Their simple syntax reduces the learning period, so that models could be developed independently after a short time (cf. Lusti (1990) pp. 201).

4 Structure Classification

Common knowledge representation languages are well suited to get an idea of the area to be modelled. However they could only be used within tight limits. For example, if the entire area is modelled, often clarity is reduced. In contradiction if only sections are modelled, complexity will be lost. Furthermore the knowledge base will suffer from a missing focus on individual objects, preventing the identification of relevant objects afterwards.

Given the mentioned problems, a new way of structuring information units was developed. The "Structure Classification" extends common methods of AI knowledge representation languages by taking experiences from the Internet into account. The following figures, figure 3 and figure 4, are representing a different point of view on the same knowledge base. Figure 3 focuses on the Technical University Dresden and figure 4 focuses on Projects in Saxonia.

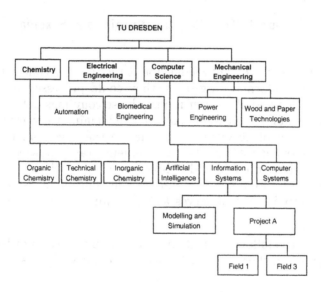

Figure 3: Tree diagram of the selected innovative areas

In order gain an overview of the relationships between individual information units, a semantic network,compare figure 2, is presented as a tree diagram, whereby content complexity was emphasised. Using this approach, limits of hierarchical super- and subordination could be overcome. Additionally both, dependencies as well as relationships, could be visualised by stretching the semantic network. The latter supports the purpose-oriented linkage of information units.

Another important modelling step is the development of major and minor structures. However, the final decision has to be taken by the modeler himself. It requires the extensive use of well-founded knowledge about relationships between individual information objects.

Concerning the core idea, "structure classification" embraces the development of flexible and dynamic structures, permitting different, temporar-

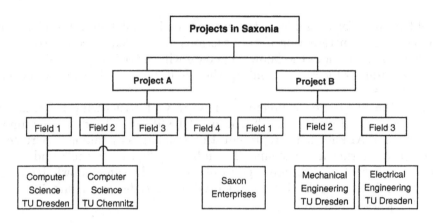

Figure 4: Tree diagram of projects in Saxonia

ily limited views. Given knowledge about relationships and interdependencies between information groups, they could processed by automatic systems. On demand of an user inquiry loose couplings between relevant information units will tightened and relaxed again afterwards.

The involvement of an expert is crucial to the development of such a system. Deploying his experiences supplementary knowledge could be added. This in turn enables the discovery of new relationships and interdependencies. Figure 5 summarises the concept of "structure classification" graphically and serves as an example for the new approach.

In conclusion the following strategy could be suggested in order to structure complex and therefore hardly accessible knowledge bases:

1. Gathering relevant information in the field of interest

2. Arrangement of single information units into consistent groups of certain types

3. Establishment of hierarchical relationships between different groups using meta knowledge

4. Development of major and minor structures

5. Detection of complementary relationships between information groups by taking their content complexity into account

6. Inspection of determined knowledge relationships by experts

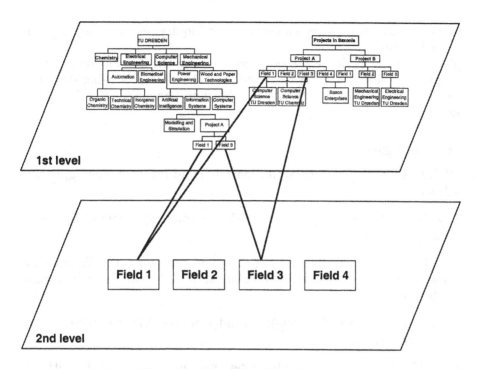

Figure 5: Structure classification

5 Conclusions

The structuring of large knowledge amounts could be supported by the use of methods from the field of Artificial Intelligence (AI), in particular semantic networks, frames and production rules. They provide an easy access to the field of knowledge discovery and related research areas.

Once complexity exceeds a certain level, management of knowledge becomes more and more difficult. Meta knowledge is defined as knowledge about the current knowledge. It is derived from the primary information source by using principles of abstraction. Received data could be used in order to structure the given information source.

The goal of each information system has to be the effective and efficient management of user inquiries. By using meta-structures it will be enabled to cope with highly complex information units, but still provides a fairly simple user interface to them. However, an expert should accompany the derivation of meta knowledge.

Combining methods from AI and the meta knowledge discussions, the model of "structure classification" evolved. It aims for the development of flexible and dynamic structures for knowledge bases, which permit different views on the same information. Thereby all relationships between different knowledge nodes will be realized and managed as loose couplings between them. Given a certain user inquiry relevant couplings will be tightened.

The presented model was used successfully in the development of topic maps. Furthermore it revealed very useful in projects using dedicated meta languages like the "Extensible Markup Language" (XML) and its derivatives.

References

BIBEL, W. (1993): Wissensrepräsentation und Inferenz. Vieweg, Braunschweig.

DORN, J. (1989): Wissensbasierte Echtzeitplanung. Vieweg, Braunschweig.

ECKERT, H. (1993): Ein Konzept zur Unterstützung der Wartung von Expertensystemen. Dissertation. Fakultät für Informatik der Universität Karlsruhe.

FERSTL, O., SINZ, E. (1998): Grundlagen der Wirtschaftsinformatik. Oldenburg, München.

GROCHLA, E. (1973): Handbuch der Organisation. Poeschel, Stuttgart.

KURBEL, K. (1992): Entwicklung und Einsatz von Expertensystemen. Springer, Berlin.

LUSTI, M. (1990): Wissensbasierte Systeme. Institut 6 F.A. Brockhaus AG, Mannheim.

REIMER, U. (1991): Einführung in die Wissensrepräsentation: netzartige und schemabasierte Repräsentationsformate. B.G.Teubner, Stuttgart.

ROSEMANN, M. (1996): Komplexitätmanagement in Prozeßmodellen. Gabler, Wiesbaden.

SCHÄFER, H. (1996): Die Repräsentation von Managementwissen. Peter Lang, Frankfurt.

Part 4

New Media, Web Mining, and Automation

Natural Language-based Specification and Fuzzy Logic for the Multimedia Development Process

Klaus Alfert[1], Matthias Heiduck[2]

[1]Lehrstuhl für Software-Technologie
Universität Dortmund
44221 Dortmund, Germany

[2]SerCon GmbH
44139 Dortmund, Germany

Abstract: Developing large multimedia systems shows problems similar to those of constructing software systems. But specific for multimedia systems is that non-technical people are much more involved in the development process. This leads to a strong demand for communication between developers with very different backgrounds. In the literature, this problem is usually neglected. We present a new approach *Vitruv* dealing with this communication problem. A specification language based on natural language and founded with formal models is our proposed communication platform for participants of the development process.

1 Introduction

Difficulties in the development of large multimedia systems resemble problems in constructing ordinary software systems. The systems grow, they can only be built by teams, they are in use for a longer time, they have to be maintained throughout their lifetime. This indicates that multimedia systems need software engineering methods and practices for their development. But software-engineering generally does not address the requirements for multimedia applications. Thus, we need to adopt software engineering methods for multimedia.

In the Altenberg Cathedral project, the Chair for Software Technology and the Chair for History of Architecture at the University of Dortmund have been working together since 1996, aiming at a multimedia teaching system presenting the period of Gothic architecture at university level. We expected strong communication activities between both project partners only in some clear defined stages, in the very beginning and during the final testing of the development process. But there was a strong demand for communication throughout the entire process. The communication between the partners turned out to be difficult, due to different types of education and knowledge.

The multimedia development process is an augmentation of the ordinary software development process with a strong commitment to content production. The different phases of multimedia development, namely content creation, media creation, media composition and technical realization, are strongly related. This results in a significant volume of retrograde influences to previous phases. Thus, the heterogeneity of working groups and tasks requires a maintenance of communication between all parties involved. This vivifies the need for a common language or form of abstraction but different (educational) backgrounds do not make it easy to find a proper platform.

Experiences in other multimedia projects at our University show that similar problems arose. We think the communication problem mentioned above is a part of the multimedia development process in general. In our project we tried an XML-based approach, which worked in some ways, although our project partners felt very uncomfortable with its formal structure. Therefore, we were encouraged to search for a better solution for the communication problem.

In the following we present our new approach. After discussing the requirements, we take a short look at the literature, followed by the presentation of our approach in some detail. Finally, a conclusion and ideas for further work are given.

2 Requirements

Our aim is a language closing this gap in the multimedia development process. Such a language needs to fit two different kinds of requirements: a) its powers of description and b) style of description. Statement a) can be explained with the question "*What* needs to be described?", while b) can be expressed as "*How* should this be described?". The answer to a) is strongly connected to the possibilities of the multimedia development process, while b) aims at the persons involved in the process.

Considering the common metaphor of multimedia development as movie making, a description in our language should be similar to a movie-script forming the basis of the entire movie making process. Thus, our language should be able to describe media creation, media composition and handling information about the organization of the process, defining who does what at which time. Given the goal of supporting media creation, one needs the power to describe a pool of different media types such as movies, pictures, audio files etc.

Since available media technology is changing fast, extensibility based on supporting the two main categories of discrete and continuous media types is a clear prerequisite. The need to describe the position of media types in time and space derives from the phase of composition during the media development process. Multimedia systems are also programs. They provide interaction with their environment, therefore, descriptions of interactivity and algorithms are needed.

By Partsch (1998), a catalog of requirements is described which a specification language should fulfill to solve the communication problem between developers and clients during requirements engineering. As our problem is an extension of it, this catalog is an important benchmark. The language should be easy to learn and use, processable by machines with exact semantics, and tolerant of partial incompleteness. Documents for the end-user are often written in natural language, then translated by developers to a formal language which forms then the basis of the subsequent developing process. This is not feasible in our domain because of the high communication activity during the entire process. We badly need a language which can be understood easily by everyone such as natural language and yet is formal enough to be used to guide the process automatically.

3   Related Work

In the literature we found several approaches dealing with specifications and models of multimedia systems. We analyzed them with respect to the communication problem.

A lot of formal models have been proposed, including various Petri Nets, temporal logics, process algebras and others (cf. Little (1994), Khalfallah, Karmouch (1995)). Whereas these models are well suited for describing the formal semantics of multimedia systems, they are not very helpful at solving our communication problem. Their need for mathematical knowledge is not acceptable for all project partners.

UML (Scott, Fowler (1997)) is currently the *lingua franca* for design and analysis in object-oriented development. However, as a general language, UML lacks strength in topics required by multimedia applications, such as concurrency and user-interaction.

Last but not least, there exists some hypermedia design methods (e.g., OOHDM by Schwabe, Rossi (1995)). They are direct extensions of database design methods and use as a starting point a conceptual data model. In our application, this is not feasible as nothing like this exists for the domain of Gothic architecture. A second problem with these methods is that they do not consider the temporal composition itself, but focus on the concept of links.

4   Our Approach: Vitruv

After outlining existing approaches we now present *Vitruv*[1] which is intended to bypass some of their shortcomings. It deals with the communication problem at first hand and is supported by formal models.

---

[1]Vitruv was an antique author on Roman architecture, whose work influenced many artists and architects during the Renaissance.

4.1 Analysis and Conceptual Model

Based on the requirements outlined in sec. 2, we analyzed the field of multimedia development (Heiduck (1999)). We used a bottom-up approach,
first analyzing the media types standalone and then the media types in
the context of the multimedia presentation. As a result we obtained a
set of attributes to describe the multimedia process which considers the
aspects of process organization, spatial and temporal position, and interaction. Attributes of process organization are e.g., production process
dependencies, deadlines and personal responsibilities.

One of the main results was that describing contents in a video (e.g.,
appearance of characters etc.) is quite like describing the order and
positioning of media in the context of a multimedia presentation. Thus,
we can use a homogeneous and unified model to describe the content of
media objects and the media composition itself. It even allows computing
positions of one media with respect to one of the content of another
media. For example, during a camera flight through the cathedral, a
certain piece of music can be played when featuring different areas of the
cathedral.

We found it possible to base the whole temporal and spatial positioning
on the two base abstractions of intervals and rectangles (bounding box)
and the relations between them. Allen (1983) and Pribbenov (1991),
resp., developed these temporal and spatial relations in the area of textunderstanding formalized in classical logic. Considering our goal of natural language-based descriptions we enrich these relations with a certain
fuzziness to capture impreciseness and vagueness in a better way. We
allow fuzzy descriptions for the whole set of attributes, which has major
drawbacks for formalizing the conceptual model described later on.

For structuring our model we use the concept of a scene which is based on
the movie metaphor mentioned earlier. For interaction, we only provide
a link model based on media and scenes as anchors and targets, resp..
The composition of scenes is based on the same homogeneous model used
for media description and composition.

4.2 SMP: The natural language implementation

Based on these requirements (using natural language and having a formal
character at the same time), we designed our specification language for
multimedia presentations (SMP). One basic prerequisite was imposed:
natural language readability before writeability. Therefore, we use for
defining SMP a subset of German with an efficiently to parse context-free
grammar. We carefully enriched SMP with elements without formal but
with user-defined semantics such as qualitative media information and
production guidance. SMP strictly translates the concepts mentioned

above into natural language resulting in a wrapping of the conceptual model. More details of SMP are given by Heiduck (1999).

A typical scene which covers most of the formalizable subjects is a multimedia presentation within the context of our Altenberg Cathedral project. Consider an animation presenting different French Gothic cathedrals, e.g. those of Chartres and Amiens. We present here the media composition part (in SMP translated from German to English):

> Description of scene "FrenchCathedrals":
> ... declaring media objects aliased as v, a, b, s...
> Media composition:
> Shortly after the start of content element "chartres" of video "v", the audio "a" is played. During content element "chartres" the button "b" is shown and enabled. If the left mouse button is pressed on link element "b", then the scene "info_chartres" will be shown.

This example is shown in the declarative model in fig. 1 and in the operational model in fig. 2.

4.3 The formal models

In our formal models we focus on the static media composition and their temporal arrangement. The formalization serves two different aims: it defines precisely the formal semantics and is the basis for models establishing different views on the specification. The declarative model emphasizes static structures whereas the operational model focuses explicitly on dynamics. Due to the lack of space, we can only give an overview of formal models and refer for details to the forthcoming phd thesis of Klaus Alfert (2001).

The declarative model

The declarative model is an object-oriented hierarchical composition of scenes consisting of media objects. A scene is a class and is divided in a let-part and a body. The let-part declares a set of local media objects used in the body. The body-part defines the (fuzzy) interval relationships between the local media objects. User interaction is also handled here: a special kind of media object, the *selector*, chooses between different alternative paths through the following media objects. The selection is specified by a (fuzzy) rule set. The special intervals alpha and omega identify start and end of the scene, resp.

Temporal relations between media objects are based on Allen's interval calculus in a fuzzyfied version (Dubois, Prade (1989)), modified further to allow more junctors than only and. Additionally, the selector object enables loops in the otherwise strict acyclic specification. Media objects

```
class FrenchCathedrals extends scene
   let
     v : video_history;
     a : sound;
     b : button;
     s : selector;
     info_chartres : scene;
   body
     alpha starts v.play.
     a.play starts shortly after v.chartres.
     b.enable during v.chartres.
     (b.pressed or v.chartres) meets s.
     s meets (v.amiens or info_chartres) with rules
       on b.pressed do goto(info_chartres).
       on v.chartres.stop do v.amiens.
     end
     v.play meets omega.
   end
end;

class video_history extends video
   exports chartres, amiens;
   body
     alpha before chartres.
     chartres shortly before amiens.
     amiens before omega.
   end
end;
```

Figure 1: The declarative model of our example about the French Gothic cathedrals. The class video_history extends the build-in class video, exporting the specific timed predicates.

are all augmented (fuzzy) intervals and defined by classes. Each class defines a set of temporal predicates, which can be exported. They are formalizations of media object content specifications. In the body of a scene these exported predicates can be used. The temporal arrangement of these predicates is also defined by interval relations.

A natural language specification can translated to the declarative model, e.g., the example above in figure 1, as follows. The hierarchy of scenes, media elements and their content elements is realized as composition of classes. Some element types such as scenes or media objects are identified with the corresponding predefined classes. Identifiers and temporal relationships are taken directly from the natural language model. The definition of the fuzzy sets, realizing the relationships and additional constraints, is separated from the class definitions. This allows to bind several realizations to same declarative model, e.g., after fine-tuning the specification.

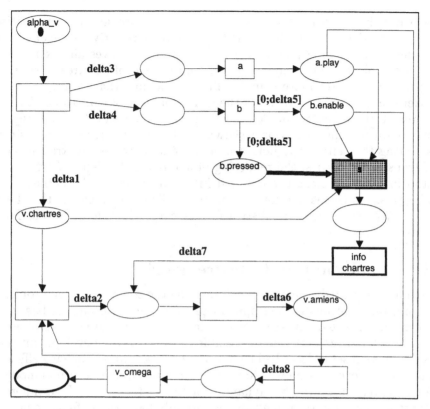

Figure 2: The scene FrenchCathedrals. The arc labels $delta_i$ are fuzzy delays, label $[0; delta5]$ specifies the possibility distribution by intersecting intervals, $[0; +\infty) \cap (-\infty; delta5]$. The length of $delta5$ is defined by the fuzzy subtraction $delta5 := v.chartres \ominus delta4$.

The operational model

In the declarative model the static structure of a scene is explicitly shown. Dynamics are only specified in an implicit way and have to be inferred. In the operational model we reverse this relationship and concentrate on the dynamic behavior. First, we augment Object Composition Petri Nets (Little, Ghafoor (1990)) by fuzzyfied timings (Murata (1996)) capturing the fuzzy interval relationships. The rules of selector objects in the declarative model translate into Petri Nets with fuzzy markings. We combine these two different kinds of Petri Nets in a unified model. Now, we can apply the well-known Petri Nets techniques such as deadlock detection, critical paths estimation, animation etc. for analyzing the behavior of the multimedia presentation.

The translation of the declarative model into an operational model is shown in fig. 2. Each interval is defined as the combination of a transition and an output place, its length defines the relative arrival time of tokens in the corresponding place. A firing transition removes all tokens from its input places. This models the premature end of an already running action. It requires more complex firing behaviors than conjunctions of tokens in input places, defining the usual enabling of transitions. This is similar to token colors in Colored Petri Nets (Jensen (1997)). In fig. 2, the modified firing behavior is shown by the bold input arc of transition s stating that either the bold arc or all others arcs enable transition s. If transition s occurs, the rendering of audio a and video $v.chartres$ will stop in order to start the detailed information about the cathedral of Chartres. As this is another scene, its details are defined in other Petri Nets. We use transition substitution for combining hierarchies of Petri Nets.

5   Conclusion and Future Work

We have presented a new approach tackling the communication problems during the multimedia development process. Our approach is based on a carefully selected subset of natural language as an already well-known common language between all possible partners in the development process. This subset is described by a context-free grammar allowing efficient parsing, its formal semantics are captured in two different formal models, focusing on structure and dynamics of the system, resp. The inherent impreciseness of natural language is formally handled by fuzzy logic.

Currently, the formal models do not deal with spatial specifications. For practical use of our approach, we need a set of tools, working both with SMP and the formal models. At least a syntax-oriented editor for SMP and compilers from SMP into the formal models are needed.

We would like to thank the anonymous referees for their valuable comments.

References

ALFERT, K. (2001): Vitruv: A New Approach for Requirements Engineering of Non-Standard Applications. Ph.D. thesis, Fachbereich Informatik, Universität Dortmund, in preparation.

ALLEN, J. F. (1983): Maintaining Knowledge about Temporal Intervals. *Communications of the ACM, 26*(11).

DUBOIS, D., PRADE, H. (1989): Processing Fuzzy Temporal Knowledge. *IEEE Transactions on Systems, Man, and Cybernetics, 19*(4), 729–744.

HEIDUCK, M. (1999): Konzeption einer Beschreibungssprache für eine eingeschränkte Klasse von Multimedia-Systemen. Diplomarbeit, Universität Dortmund, Fachbereich Informatik, Lehrstuhl für Software-Technologie.

JENSEN, K. (1997): Coloured Petri Nets. Basic Concepts, Analysis Methods and Practical Use. Volume 1. Springer-Verlag, Berlin, 2nd edn.

KHALFALLAH, H., KARMOUCH, A. (1995): An architecture and a data model for integrated multimedia documents and presentation applications. *ACM Multimedia Systems*, *3*(5/6), 238–250.

LITTLE, T. D., GHAFOOR, A. (1990): Synchronization and Storage Models for Multimedia Objects. *IEEE Journal on Selected Areas in Communication*, *8*(3), 413–427.

LITTLE, T. D. C. (1994): Time-Based Media Representation and Delivery. In: J. F. K. Buford (ed.), *Multimedia Systems*, chap. 7, 175–200. ACM-Press, Reading, MA.

MURATA, T. (1996): Temporal Uncertainty and Fuzzy-Timing High-Level Petri Nets. In: J. Billington, W. Reisig (eds.), *Application and Theory of Petri Nets 1996. 17th International Conference*, 11–28. Springer-Verlag.

PARTSCH, H. (1998): Requirements-Engineering systematisch: Modellbildung für softwaregestütze Systeme. Springer-Verlag, Berlin.

PRIBBENOV, S. (1991): Phenomena of Localization. In: O. Herzog, C.-R. Rollinger (eds.), *Textunderstanding in LILOG*, Berlin. Springer-Verlag.

SCHWABE, D., ROSSI, G. (1995): The Object-Oriented Hypermedia Design Model. *Communications of the ACM*, *38*(8), 45–46.

SCOTT, K., FOWLER, M. (1997): UML distilled. Applying the standard object modeling language. Addison-Wesley, Reading, MA.

A Tool System for an Object-oriented Approach to Construction and Maintenance of Hypermedia Documents

Alexander Fronk

Lehrstuhl für Software-Technologie,
Universität Dortmund, D-44221 Dortmund, Germany

Abstract: Construction and maintenance of large hypermedia documents (hyperdocuments, for short) turn out to be fairly awkward and less manageable when HTML paired with proprietary tools is used. Software engineering methods help to reduce the cost of construction and maintenance of hyperdocuments.

In contrast to HTML, the document description language *DoDL*, developed at the Chair for Software-Technology of Dortmund University, yields an object-oriented definition of hyperdocuments. The language regards high-level concepts and a separation of documents' content and link structure. Thus, alternative strategies evolve not just for maintaining hyperdocuments specified in this manner.

In this paper we show a prototypical, yet both explorative and expressive, tool system to support the *DoDL*-based construction and maintenance of hyperdocuments. Our approach encompasses a visual understanding of *DoDL* in the analysis and design of hyperdocuments, as well as automatically generating the documents' linkage. Thus, we enclose and accompany the entire hyperdocuments' life cycle, based on a powerful language.

1 Introduction

Hyperdocuments can be constructed in several ways, accompanied with different tool systems. According to Fünfstück et al. (2000), tools can be classified into two main classes: "document controlled" tools for document and media adaptation, authoring tools and design tools, regarding aspects such as *shaping, arrangement* and *organization* of media; "program controlled" tools aim at *programming* hyperdocuments. The latter class is based on software engineering principles and methods, and subsumes classical CASE-tools like editors, compilers, debuggers, generators, etc.

It is precisely this software engineering topic that our approach substantially exploits. In general, one part of software-technique is to provide principles, methods, and tools for software development, particularly focusing on engineering helpful tools. Hypermedia application development may profit well from this field, as existing hypermedia development tools show.

Our approach concentrates more on hyperdocuments themselves. It requires only little effort to consider hyperdocuments as programs, yet it holds considerable significance for their construction and maintenance. Hyperdocuments can then be treated exactly as programs, managed by software-technical principles, methods, and tools. This is not a new idea (c.f. Reid's page-description language *Scribe*). Nonetheless, due to this point of view, we differ from existing approaches like, for example, OO-HDM by Schwabe, Rossi (1995), where an implemenation is still done by hand though regarding object-oriented descriptions of concepts, navigation, and interaction.

This paper is organized as follows. The next section makes some notes on the document/program-dualism, followed by a brief introduction to our document description language, *DoDL*; section 2.2 sketches a hyperdocument's life cycle and extracts some supporting tools; section 3 discusses our tool system, its data flow and architecture; we finish with a conclusion and further work.

2   A Hyperdocument/program-dualism

Not only in our view, hyperdocuments are programs which allow the opportunity to experience non-linear data. Those data are *media objects* like text, pictures, or videos, and their non-linear cross-referencing called *link structure*. This software is thereby based on a uniform data structure, which contains media objects and operations to build a link structure. The software is subject to frequent data change, one of its most important properties. In general, the link structure, however, must be adapted only to the data used. That is, the description of a link structure may be reused repeatedly, if it can be specified data independently. Collecting media objects and link structures separately allows a high degree of adaption to this change process. We target this goal by providing our object-oriented language *DoDL*, where link structures can be specified with respect to media objects involved, but kept away from those. Not until binding concrete media objects to this specification-like document description, a hyperdocument is encoded automatically.

We clearly distinguish between the specification of a desired link structure, i.e. a *DoDL* specification, and the resulting software product, i.e. the hyperdocument. Changing the media objects involved simply results in automatically encoding the hyperdocument again, leaving its link structure specification untouched. In XML-languages, logical markups can be defined and allow structuring of hyperdocuments. Nonetheless, links must be declared within media objects themselves and cannot be described separately. That is, why XML-based languages do not fulfill our requirements.

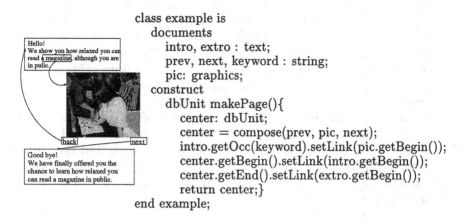

```
class example is
   documents
      intro, extro : text;
      prev, next, keyword : string;
      pic: graphics;
   construct
      dbUnit makePage(){
         center: dbUnit;
         center = compose(prev, pic, next);
         intro.getOcc(keyword).setLink(pic.getBegin());
         center.getBegin().setLink(intro.getBegin());
         center.getEnd().setLink(extro.getBegin());
         return center;}
end example;
```

Figure 1: A *DoDL* Example

2.1   *DoDL* by example

The description language *DoDL* was introduced in Doberkat (1996) the
first time and updated in Doberkat (1998). For the sake of conciseness,
we only sketch the most interesting aspects here.

DoDL provides object-oriented features like classes, attributes, methods,
and object instantiation, as well as class relations like inheritance, aggregation, local and generic classes. The language works like any other object-
oriented language, reducing its constructs to those essentially needed for
hyperdocument description. *DoDL* describes a hyperdocument by structuring it into classes, collecting media objects within class attributes, and
information concerning their link structure within class methods. Here,
DoDL reflects the demanded separation of content and link structure
in a well-structured object-oriented way. Instantiating a class means to
create an object, the methods of which describe a set of possibilities to
build a link structure. Thus, each object may construct a sub-document,
where the *DoDL* specification is structured in accordance with the entire
hyperdocument.

A small, yet expressive, example given in figure 1 may clarify how *DoDL*
works. The hyperdocument shows two texts and a picture with two
strings attached. The contents of the texts are not important for the sake
of this discussion. To describe this hyperdocument, the *DoDL* class introduces two text variables, three string variables, and a picture variable
in its documents-section as attributes. The construct-section contains
a method, makePage, which creates the desired links when executed.
Here, we compose a new media object, center, by amalgamating two

strings and the picture. A link is built (`setLink`) from the occurrence of a given keyword within the text `intro` to the beginning of the picture, `pic.getBegin()`. The other links are created analogously. The method returns the `center` media object. Equally, we may amalgamate the entire document and return it for further use within other methods or classes, where it serves as a sub-document then. Separated from the description of the hyperdocument's link structure, we assign a concrete media object to each of the variables. Such a *binding* is a list of pairs of variable and value. The string *"back"* is assigned to the variable `prev`, *"next"* to `next`, and *"magazine"* to `keyword`. The texts and the picture may be taken from a repository. Whenever the keyword occurs in the text assigned to `intro`, a link starting at this occurrence is drawn to the beginning of the picture.

The advantage of our approach is not only a high-level structuring mechanisms realized through object-oriented classes. Much more, the definition of a link structure is consequently kept away from the media objects involved. This facility strongly adapts hyperdocument development and maintenance to engineering software and thus offers adaption of well-known principles, methods and tools.

2.2 Accompanying the hyperdocument's life cycle

In contrast to some processing models for XML/SGML (c.f. Goldfarb (1999)), our development process is software engineering based and thus adopts its terminology from there. Analogies exist but are not discussed.

DoDL, as the center of our approach, intends a specific design process and tool support throughout the hyperdocument's life cycle. Instantiating class `example` several times results in several objects creating the link structure described, but with variables bound to different texts and pictures. If we may identify such sub-structures occurring more than once within a hyperdocument, modeling them by a class is the choice. Thus, *analyzing* a hyperdocument aims at finding recurrent uniform link structures. *Designing* means modeling those structures as classes and developing algorithms to build them. This phase is supported by a graphic modeling tool, as the next section will show. It hides *DoDL* interna from a designer, so they can concentrate on the creative moment. To reach an *implementation*, a further tool helps to bind concrete media objects to their respective place holders. The hyperdocument is then generated automatically by parts of the tool system. *Testing* will be done by a tool checking the link structure and detecting disagreeable properties. *Maintaining* the hyperdocument is done separately on media objects and *DoDL* specifications, the latter treated like usual program code.

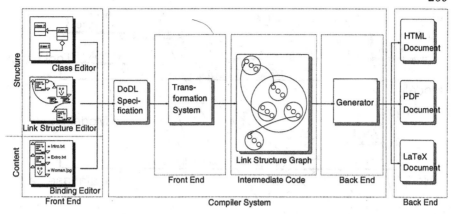

Figure 2: The *DoDL* data flow

3 A Tool System

The tool system, currently under development, is presented here both in a horizontal and vertical view. The former shows how we obtain a hyperdocument, starting with modeling classes and link structures. The latter view shows our architecture on which we base the aforementioned data flow.

3.1 Modeling and data flow

Figure 2 describes the main data flow thread. In the front end, three editors help to design a hyperdocument, trying to integrate both experts in class modeling and experts in hypermedia design into the entire design process. The *class editor* uses a UML-like modeling language to declare classes and their relations, the media objects used and the methods to produce a desired link structure. Providing the class structure, of course, requires some knowledge in object-oriented modeling and design. The methods can be graphically defined within the *link structure editor*, which provides powerful operations a designer may like to use. The media objects involved are automatically transferred from the class editor into both the link structure editor and the binding editor, where they are replaced by icons. Link structure creating operations provided by *DoDL* are graphically offered service as well. A designer is equally free to use them without restrictions, as a computer scientist may wish to write a *DoDL* specification. Finally, we bind concrete media objects to their respective icons in a *binding editor* giving access to a repository.

A compiler system takes the task to create the desired hyperdocument. First, the *DoDL* specification of the hyperdocument is transformed into a directed, attributed graph serving as intermediate code. This graph contains all information necessary to describe the hyperdocument under construction. Second, a generator traverses this graph properly and

270

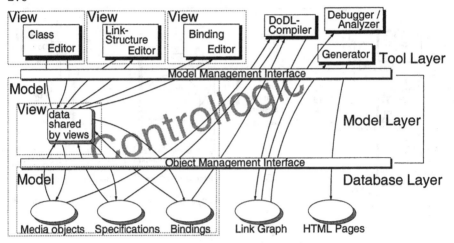

Figure 3: The *DoDL* tool system architecture

transforms it alternatively into various output formats such as HTML, PDF or LaTeX. This process has been worked out in Fronk, Pleumann (1999) and in Pleumann (2000).

3.2 A 3-tier architecture

Figure 3 shows our tool integrating architecture. It is widely discussed in Alfert, Fronk, Doberkat (1999) and provides a foundation for our hypermedia development environment. Arcs denote a directed data flow. The architecture is based on three layers and works as follows. In the upper layer, we collect tools and give them access to a shared data pool, the model layer, via a model management interface. The model layer contains the entire control logic, which consists of operations to be carried out on the shared data. This layer is concealed by the model management interface, such that the tool layer can easily be extended by further tools.

The tools share their data respecting a model-observer strategy. Each tool is a view on a model recursively following this strategy. The shared data serve as a model shared by the tools. For its part, it is a view on the *DoDL* specification, bindings and media objects involved. Those are hidden by an object management interface giving access to any arbitrary and exchangeable repository. Thereby, each layer is exchangeable, extensible and scalable, some of the most important benefits a 3-tier architecture provides.

The data flow shown in the previous subsection can be traced within the architecture as well. The class editor is responsible to create and modify a *DoDL* class structure enriched by documents and methods. Both the class structure and their interiors are stored in a *DoDL* specification of a hyperdocument. The specification is abstractly represented within the shared data. Both the class editor and the link structure editor access this data and display only those parts the editors are adjusted to. Changes within the shared data made by any editor are forwarded to other tools via a notification mechanism, allowing the tools to update their view on the data changed. Due to the model-observer strategy, enriching the shared data for use with further tools does not effect the existing editors' functioning.

The control logic transforms the data into a valid *DoDL* specification and its assigned bindings. The compiler system accesses both them and the media objects involved to create the link structure graph, traversed by the code generator afterwards. Some debugger or analyzer tools work on this graph as well. Finally, HTML pages are generated automatically and written into the repository.

4 Conclusion and Further Work

We have sketched a tool system based on a hyperdocument description language. The tool system aims at two crucial issues, the first and most important of which is to prove the *DoDL* approach applicable to hyperdocument construction. A graphical front end used within the design process displaces a program-based codification of hyperdocuments and thus offers a modeling possibility near to a desired hyper-structural information presentation. The process stands on an object-oriented basis and supports an automatic generation of hyperdocuments. Here, we differ from approaches like OOHDM, or Hyperform by Wiil and Leggett (1997) where the focus lies on the development of hypermedia systems.

Secondly, due to the separation of the hyperdocuments' content and the specification of their link structure, the tool system can easily support maintenance of hyperdocuments. It is no more the hyperdocument itself, which has to be maintained, it is the *DoDL* specification to be treated and thus maintained like a program (Fronk (1999)). Versioning and configuration tools can easily be brought into our architecture and integrated into the hyperdocuments' life cycle. Changing the contents' versions simply results in automatically generating the hyperdocument again; changing the specification does not need to touch the content.

Missing properties mainly concern browsing a hyperdocument. Some basic ideas are given in Doberkat (1996-2), where Feature Logic formally corroborates the use of value-attributed links. The missing properties of our approach include describing how and when an attribute value is changed (dynamic links), describing actions carried out when a link is traversed (operative links), and describing how to browse a hyperdocument context-sensitively (conditional links). Successively, possible answers severely touch synchronization of contents like videos, sound and animations.

Layout is a topic we are only partially concentrating on. Here, our main efforts lie on ordering media objects in space, where both their respective horizontal and vertical position is considered. In Pleumann (2000) we have developed a simple algorithm grouping media objects and placing them within a HTML page.

Work on an algebraic model for *DoDL* is in progress. Thereby, we obtain a formal semantics to forecast both structural properties such as reachability of sub-documents or dangling links, and dynamic properties such as constructibility of a hyperdocument under consideration. We are currently investigating these and other questions to obtain a powerful way to construct and maintain hyperdocuments.

Acknowledgments. We thank the anonymous referees for their constructive remarks and suggestions which very much helped to improve this article.

References

DOBERKAT, E.-E. (1996): A Language for Specifying Hyperdocuments. *Software - Concepts and Tools, 17, 163–172.*

DOBERKAT, E.-E. (1996-2): Browsing a Hyperdocument. *Memorandum 87, Lehrstuhl Software-Technologie, Universität Dortmund.*

DOBERKAT, E.-E. (1998): Using Logic for the Specification of Hypermedia Documents. In: Balderjahn, Mathar, Schader (eds.): Classification, Data Analysis and Data Highways, 205 – 212, Springer.

FRONK, A. (1999): Support for Hypertext Maintenance. *IEEE Computer, June 1999, p. 7 , Letter to the Editor.*

FRONK, A. and PLEUMANN, J. (1999): Der *DoDL*-Compiler. *Memorandum 100, Lehrstuhl Software-Technologie, Universität Dortmund.*

FÜNFSTÜCK, F. and LISKOWSKY, R. and MEISSNER, K. (2000): Softwarewerkzeuge zur Entwicklung multimedialer Anwendungen. *Informatik Spektrum, 23:1, 11–25.*

ALFERT, K. and FRONK, A. and DOBERKAT, E.-E. (Eds.) (1999): Abschlußbericht der Projektgruppe PG-HEU (326). *Memorandum 103, Lehrstuhl Software-Technologie, Universität Dortmund*

GOLDFARB, C. F. and PRESCOD, P. (1999): XML Handbuch. Prentice Hall, 1999.

PLEUMANN, J. (2000): dodl2html - Ein Generator zum Erzeugen von graphspezifizierten Hyperdokumenten. *Diplomarbeit, Lehrstuhl Software-Technologie, Universität Dortmund.*

SCHWABE, D. and ROSSI, G. (1995): The Object-Oriented Hypermedia Design Model. *Communications of the ACM, 38:8, 45 – 46.*

WIIL, U. K. and LEGGETT, J. J. (1997): Hyperform: A Hypermedia System Development Environment. *ACM Transactions on Information Systems, 15:1, 1–31.*

Recommendations for Virtual Universities from Observed User Behavior

A. Geyer-Schulz, M. Hahsler, M. Jahn[1]

[1]Abteilung für Informationswirtschaft
Wirtschaftsuniversität Wien, A-1090 Wien, Austria

Abstract: Recently recommender systems started to gain ground in commercial Web-applications. For example, the online-bookseller *amazon.com* recommends his customers books similar to the ones they bought using the analysis of observed purchase behavior of consumers.

In this article we describe a generic architecture for recommender services for information markets which has been implemented in the setting of the Virtual University of the Vienna University of Economics and Business Administration (http://vu.wu-wien.ac.at). The architecture of a recommender service is defined as an agency of interacting software agents. It consists of three layers, namely the meta-data management system, the broker management system and the business-to-customer interface.

1 Introduction

Recommender services for customer relationship management and one-to-one marketing as offered, e.g., by Net Perceptions, Inc. (Minneapolis) belong to the hottest e-commerce applications today with an estimated market growth rate of more than 40 percent as reported by Selland et al. (2000). Recommender services are at the heart of business-to-customer e-commerce applications, they **are** the information channels of electronic markets.

In this paper we define a distributed, scalable, and flexible architecture for recommender services for information broker systems as an agency of software agents. See Minsky (1988). The recommendations are based on observed user behavior and experience profiles obtained by self-selection. A prototype of a scientific and educational broker system has been implemented and is currently field-tested in the Virtual University of the Vienna University of Economics and Business Administration. In an educational and scientific environment recommender systems have a considerable potential for improving student/teacher communication, reducing information overload, addressing user heterogeneity, and team-building.

We have structured this paper as follows: In section 2 we present an overview of the architecture of an information broker with recommender services, in sections 3, 4, and 5 we describe each type of software agent required for recommender services in more detail. In section 4 we address the problem of generating recommendations for heterogeneous user groups and we propose a solution based on establishing experience profiles by self-assessment.

2 An Architecture for integrating Recommender Services into an Information Broker

In figure 1 we show an architecture for recommender services as an agency of software agents which consists of three layers, namely the meta-data management system, the broker management system, and the business-to-customer interface. See Russel and Norvig (1995). The interactions between persons, software agents and information stores is represented by arrows, where the direction indicates who starts an activity. A name near an arrow states the nature of the activity, if the arrow is unnamed, it means a simple request for information.

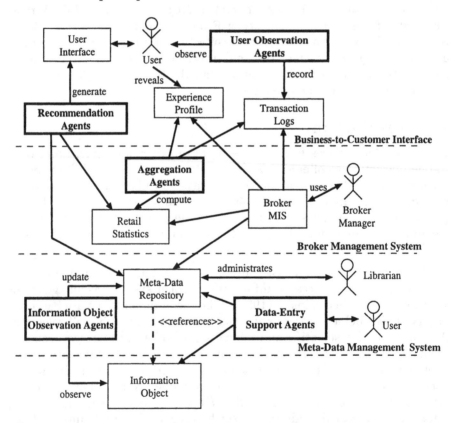

Figure 1: An Architecture for an Information Broker with Recommender Services

On the level of the **meta-data management system** (which can be an instance of a virtual library), every information object (product) is described by its meta-data stored in the repository. Depending on the application area, standards for meta-data may exist, as for example the IEEE P1484.12/D4.0 draft standard for learning object metadata for educational broker systems. See IEEE (2000). However, because the interface to the other layers of this architecture is quite minimal (it requires only a method for retrieving the meta-data by object), the broker management system and the business-to-customer interface are almost completely independent from the database technology used in this layer.

In the meta-data management system we have integrated information object observation agents and data-entry support agents. These are 2 types of software agents which observe, analyze, and classify information objects on the Internet and which update the meta-data periodically. In a virtual university, the main tasks of these agents are to reduce the cost of data entry, administration and maintenance of meta-data, as well as to improve the service quality of the information broker system. Consider, for example, an agent which detects revisions in course material and its application for distributed course-ware versioning control and update systems.

The **broker management system level** and the business-to-customer interface are more tightly coupled. Recommender services are market information services based on observed user behavior. In an information market selecting a recommended information object (e.g. following a link) is considered as a purchase of this information object. Aggregation agents on the broker management system level compute market-baskets, purchase histories and other statistics common in the retail industry (e.g. conditional purchase probabilities from transaction logs and customer experience profiles collected in the business-to-customer interface). Consumer behavior models, diffusion-models and web-mining algorithms are integrated into the broker management information system (broker MIS) which supports the manager of the broker in decision-making about the future development of the information broker system (e.g. decisions on content acquisition, bundling of services, design and placement of user interface elements).

For the recommender agents on the **business-to-customer interface** level the retail statistics provide information on the preferences of users for information objects and for internal broker services which is inferred from observed user behavior recorded in the transaction logs. The user observation agents are also embedded into the business-to-customer interface. Conceptually they observe the behavior of a user and record his transactions. Depending on the degree of anonymity of a user, different methods are applied in order to gain as much information as possible from user transactions. Self-assessment of a user´s experience for the disciplines he is interested in are collected in an experience profile and used to improve the recommender services offered to him. The complete observe - analyze - generate cycle of interacting user observation agents, aggregation agents, and recommendation agents corresponds to an interactive evolutionary algorithm which evolves for each user a personalized user-interface. The user interface contains several market information services (e.g. favorites of a user, lists of information objects used by users with similar experience profiles, ...).

3 User Observation Agents

User observation agents observe the behavior of a user and record relevant transactions of the user. In the left part of figure 2 the cookie mechanism is used to add session identifiers to the stateless http-protocol for anonymous sessions, in the right part of figure 2 anonymous sessions become associated with a pseudo user id, when the user logs into myVU, the personalized Virtual University environment. What is remarkable about this approach is, that it does not matter, when a user logs into myVU. If he uses a myVU service during a session, the whole session is associated with his pseudo user id.

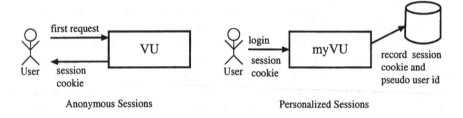

Figure 2: Cookies and Pseudoids

In the following we describe three different user observation agents, namely the VU web transaction log agent, the VU purchase log agent, and the myVU log agent.

```
(1)  aipc14.wu-wien.ac.at - - [25/May/2000:16:10:23 +0200]
(2)  "GET /dyn/virlib?&lib=materials/english&file=wu01_698&
(3)  type=stat HTTP/1.1" 302 226 "myvu=myvuf46e35c7706bb43;
(4)  tempvu=16d3f" 0 "http://vu.wu-wien.ac.at/dyn/virlib?
(5)  type=doquery&errors=0&lib=materials&query=
(6)  CATEGORY:='Artificial+Intelligence+AI/Agents'"
(7)  "Mozilla/4.0 (compatible; MSIE 5.0; Windows 95)"
```

Figure 3: VU Web Transaction Logs

The VU web transaction log agent basically is a reconfigured standard web-server with a modified log format shown in figure 3. The entry shown in figure 3 is the record of the purchase of an information object. Line (1) shows the address of the computer used and the date of the purchase. The purchased object is identified in line (2) by the string `file=wu01_698`. Lines (3) and (4) contain the session cookie (`tempvu=16d3f`) and a cookie for myVU authentification (`myvu=myvuf46e...`). The rest is additional information provided by the web server (the time needed to process the request, the referer and the user agent). Of course, a web server records all requests including images, icons and navigation pages. Therefore, the analysis of such transaction log files requires a considerable amount of preprocessing.

The task of preprocessing transaction log files can be considerably simplified by inserting specialized user observation agents into the mediation mechanism of an information broker. The VU purchase log agent which is integrated into the mediation mechanism of the virtual library system which serves as meta-data repository is an example for this approach.

```
[Thu May  4 13:08:27 2000]
    "wu01_533" "tempvu=1478e" "atisrv2.alcatel.at"
[Thu May  4 13:17:24 2000]
    "wu01_8bd" "tempvu=14793" "proxy.luiss.it"
[Thu May  4 13:19:24 2000]
    "wu01_4cf" "tempvu=1479c" "fsztmss01.tu-graz.ac.at"
```

Figure 4: VU Purchase Logs

The VU purchase log agent records purchase incidents as shown in figure 4. A record of a purchase incident consists of a time stamp, the unique identifier of the purchased information object, the session cookie, and the host name of the computer on which the user works with his browser. Note, that this agent eliminates the need for preprocessing and considerably reduces the amount of data stored.

Next, consider the myVU log agent as yet another representative of the species of user observation agents. This agent is integrated into the user-interface elements of the myVU environment. He tracks all actions of a user within myVU and all purchases of information objects of a user in the myVU environment.

Figure 5 shows such a myVU log which contains the purchase history of a user combined with internal broker services accounting. An entry in the purchase history has three elements, namely a time stamp, the record type (`mediate` for a purchase), and the unique information object id. For an example, see lines 2 and 3 in figure 5. An entry for internal service accounting has at least four elements: time stamp, the record type (`function` for a service), the service name and function with optional arguments. For example, the last line in figure 5 means that the user

```
(1) Tue Mar 21 14:05:55 2000 function bookmarks over
(2) Tue Mar 21 14:06:05 2000 mediate    wu01_eff
(3) Tue Mar 21 14:07:13 2000 mediate    wu01_13ab
(4) Tue Mar 21 14:10:33 2000 function bookmarks over
(5) Tue Mar 21 14:10:48 2000 function bookmarks wu_bookmarks
(6) Tue Mar 21 14:10:51 2000 function bookmarks
        drop_bookmark wu01_2b6c
```

Figure 5: myVU Logs

has deleted the information object wu01_2b6c from his personal myVU bookmark list. Again, the myVU log agent considerably reduces the need for preprocessing and he produces a purchase history for information objects and internal broker services.

4 Aggregation Agents

Aggregation agents compute market baskets, purchase histories, ... and estimate e.g. consumer behavior models from the transaction logs generated by the user observation agents periodically. In general, aggregation agents must address the following problems:

- User heterogeneity.
- Discounting the impact of older information.
- Data representation.
- Update period.

User heterogeneity. Aggregation agents must respect differences in the preferences of non-homogeneous user groups. Therefore, identification of user groups is vital for successful aggregation agents. User groups can be identified by several approaches. For example, a-priori segmentation based on demographic user attributes, or cluster techniques on user purchase histories (for a recent survey, see Jain et al. (1999)), or by the principle of self-selection suggested by Shapiro and Varian (1999). For example, in an educational environment the crucial dimension for grouping users is the user's experience in a discipline. In the myVU virtual university environment the principle of self-selection is used for obtaining user groups by incrementally establishing discipline specific user experience profiles.

Discounting the impact of older information. Information objects as well as the preferences of users for them change over time. Aggregation agents discount older observations in the aggregation process in order to take this non-stationarities into account. The challenge is in finding personalized, context-specific discount rates. Too high discount rates lead to fast changes in the user interface which tend to disorient users. Too small discount rates leads to a user interface which is perceived static.

Data representation. Because of the usually large number of information objects in an information broker, aggregation agents must work efficiently on sparse data structures. For example, the representation of empirical conditional cross-selling distributions for information objects in the VU environment is organized as a list of lists which tends to grow with the order of $O(n)$ with the number of items. Representing this as a $n \times n$ matrix leads to $O(n^2)$ growth in the number of items. The data structure must be suitable to support efficient access by the recommendation agents.

Update period. The aggregation process is a time and computationally intensive task. Therefore, aggregation agents usually process observation logs in the background and update statistics only in regular intervals. The time required for each update grows with the size of the transaction logs.

5 Recommendation Agents

Recommendation agents provide recommendations about information objects to the users. They infer information on the preferences of users for information objects and for internal broker services from the statistics generated by the aggregation agents and they generate and bundle appropriate user-interface elements. These agents must cope with the following problems:

- The influence of the user-interface design on purchase behavior.
- Scalability to large numbers of users.

The influence of the user-interface design on purchase behavior. Empirical evidence exists that the design of the user interface has a strong impact on user behavior. For example, Introna and Nissenbaum (2000) discuss the influence of ranking information objects in search engines and the problem of biased search results which is also present for recommendation agents.

Scalability to large numbers of users. The recommendation agents generating the user-interface and its elements have to process all requests of users within acceptable time. The request, the user's experience profile and the statistics provided by the aggregation agents have to be combined and formatted in real-time. For example, in the myVU environment performance is improved by incremental compilation of user interface elements. Scalability can be achieved by using several servers for the interface and distributing the users among them.

6 Links

The reader is welcome to try the anonymous recommender services integrated in the Virtual Univeristy (http://vu.wu-wien.ac.at) of the Vienna University of Economics and Business Administration and to get a myVU account at (http://myvu.wu-wien.ac.at) for experiencing personalized and group recommendations.

Acknowledgements. This project is financed by the Jubiläumsfonds of the Austrian National Bank under Grant No. 7925.

References

IEEE (2000): Draft Standard for Learning Object Metadata (IEEE P1484.12/D4.0). IEEE Standards Department, Piscataway, 5 February 2000. http://ltsc.ieee.org/doc/wg12/LOM_WD4.htm

INTRONA, L. and NISSENBAUM, H. (2000): Defining the Web: The politics of search engines, *IEEE Computer*, 33(1), 54–62.

JAIN, A. K., MURTY, M. N. and FLYNN, P. J. (1999): Data Clustering: A Review, *ACM Computing Surveys*, 31(3), 264–323.

MINSKY, M. L. (1988): *The Society of Mind*. Simon & Schuster, New York.

RESNICK, P. and VARIAN, H.R. (1997): Recommender Systems. *Communications of the ACM*, 40(3), 56–58.

RUSSEL, S. and NORVIG, P. (1995): *Artificial Intelligence – A Modern Approach*. Prentice Hall, Upper Saddle River.

SELLAND, C., ANDERSON, H. and the YANKEE GROUP (2000): E-Biz 150: E-Business Winners and Loosers: Trends to Watch. *UpsideToday*, February 18th, 2000.
http://www.upside.com/texis/mvm/ebiz/story?id=38a1ee130

SHAPIRO, S. and VARIAN, H.R. (1999): *Information Rules: A Strategic Guide to the Network Economy*. Harvard Business School Press, Boston.

Virtual Dialect Areas in the Internet: "Townchats"

Bernhard Kelle

Deutsches Seminar I, Arbeitsbereich Geschichtliche Landeskunde,
Universität Freiburg, D-79085 Freiburg, Germany

Abstract: The new text types e-mail and chat have some remarkable features both in communicative intent and in linguistic expression. While e-mail has established itself in areas previously dominated by the conventional letter, the chat is a completely new, technologically induced text type. The fact that this is "uncharted territory" means that norms of appropriateness have yet to be established, in part independently of or in intentional opposition to the norms of the standard variety. This paper is concerned especially with the geographical factor in the "city chats" that are used to a certain extent by people who are actually from the city for which a chat channel is named. This results in a language style that reflects – phonetically, lexically and pragmatically – the regular regional variety. An interaction of language economical factors with group dynamics can be observed when regional and dialectal variants are used in the chats. For this study, 26 city chats, their linguistic peculiarities and their regional distribution were observed.

1 Arrangement of data

After I was able to show, in a first study (Kelle (2000)), that German language chats exhibit a great diversity in the use of regional and dialect features, the present study intends to demonstrate that the regional linguistic competence of chat participants is manifested in their language usage in the chats and that this regional usage can be traced cartographically. Two basic characteristics of the chat make an analysis on regional grounds difficult.

- The anonymity of the participants: The identities of the chatters are shielded to a great extent, so that long-standing dogmas of dialect research are of no use. It cannot be determined whether a chat participant is male or female, 17 or 65 years old, a CEO (=chief executive officer) or an unskilled worker. What's more – and this is the tricky part for the analysis at hand – it cannot be determined whether a chatter participating in a certain city chat is actually from that city (including his parents and grandparents up to the third degree, according to the traditional criteria). Thus the control of independent variables that is obligatory in dialectology and sociolinguistics fail to apply in this situation.

- The "camouflage" of participants: Besides anonymity, there is a second characteristic of the chat situation that makes arrangement of the data difficult. Chatter often play roles in order to make the dialogue with other participants more interesting. They disguise themselves as someone of the opposite sex, or they conceal who they are and where they come from. The use of regional language can be a part of this role-playing, and thus camouflage. It cannot be decided with any certainty whether linguistic group pressure comes into play at this stage. There are indications that chatters who challenge or reject the regional nature of a chat in fact later face sanctions by the dominant chatters.

At this point it is necessary to clarify the difference between the terms "regional variety" and "dialect". The discipline of linguistics has great difficulties finding terms for the many varieties that are determined by the regional, social and functional dimensions. Even today, the triad standard – colloquial speech – dialect has not yet been stamped out, although we know by now that, depending on factors like topic, emotionality and connotation, the means of expression in a conversation can be mixed with or dominated by regional and dialectal features to greatly varying degrees. So when we speak of a "dialect", this does not refer to a specific form normally used by the oldest speakers of an out-of-the-way village, but instead to a manifestation of language which regionally is defined by a small geographical area, which socially obligates speakers to group loyalty, and which is organized functionally. The dialect is as variable as a regional or a standard language depending on which type of communicative function forms the background for an utterance. A dialect is less elaborate in certain areas (institutional or technical jargon, etc.) in comparison to the standard language, which has the greatest geographical extension of all varieties of a language and is probably also best developed for all communication types. A regional variety is between standard and dialect on the scales of geographic and social range. It is instable, as it is used for the different degrees of communicational intent in a wider radius of interaction than just the village or hometown; when speakers return to their central private spheres, their speech tends to lose the regional characteristic that is manifested in the reduction of the use of dialect features (Jakob (1984)). This phenomenon was explored by Bellmann (1994ff.) in his "double layer" atlas. He too sees commuting as an important aspect of regional speech. In the chat setting, most chatters are probably commuters to the chat – from near or farther away. Whether or not a regional style with its geographic differences is perceptible, alongside other linguistic idiosyncrasies, is the topic of this paper. To provide blanket coverage of the German-speaking regions, as many city chats as possible were analyzed. The channels in the Internet Relay Chat (IRC) seemed best suited to this purpose, as it offers the advantage of an automatic protocol of the chats while they are taking place. This means that at least theoretically large amounts of chat texts can be collected. In practice, however, there are certain limits:

- The number of participants on the channels is quite variable, resulting in corpora of unequal size.

- The principle of "participant observation" that ideally exists when the linguist is logged onto a channel can come to an abrupt close when one of the dominant chatters catches you being idle, called "ideln" in the German jargon. This usually results in being kicked out of the chat, or being "gekickt".

So far 26 city chats and two regional chats have been included in this study. The latter were considered because the IRC channels for Austria and Switzerland have proven to be very quiet or non-existent. The Swiss city channels were especially unfruitful, although commercial chats ("Swisschat", for example) have a high participation rate. The linguistic data for this analysis was recorded automatically, as explained above, and then examined for such linguistic units that must fulfil three criteria. These units are:

- highly recurrent,

- regionally identifiable,

- found in all corpora.

The analysis would, in the ideal case, represent the relative and absolute frequency of occurrence of the units. The absolute frequency was listed in a few cases that were relatively telling. In other instances, where only the occurrence or the lack of the feature was of importance, this was not listed. The geographical distribution of the observed linguistic units is demonstrated with the help of maps.

2 Results

It is important to remember that for every linguistic item that is examined and charted in the following analysis, this is by no means the only occurrence of this item, and the item does not occur exclusively in chat situations. Because of the situation described above, that participants in all channels can come from anywhere, it is to be expected that, on the one hand, certain forms can be found in places where they would be unacceptable on the grounds of a basis dialect study; on the other hand, the large number of deviations from the standard like syn- and apocope, anacoluths, repairs, particles, interjections, emoticons and comic words can be attributed to the influence of spoken speech, which has been described elsewhere (Kelle (2000), Jakobs (1998), Günther/Wyss (1996)).

2.1 Dialect features/expressions

Alongside the above mentioned features which can be viewed as features of the standard spoken variety (Schwitalla (1998)), there are also "dialectisms" that appear in varying frequency depending on the location of the channel; chats in major cities in the southern German-speaking regions show an increasing tendency toward the use of regional elements (cf. Kelle (2000)). In Bavaria and Austria long strings of conversation in dialect appear alongside single dialect words and short syntagms in a standard setting. Swiss chatters, however, when using dialect, tend to use only Schwyzerdütsch for whole conversation strings and replies. This increased use by participants of single regional expressions, clauses and conversation turns will not be considered in the following, because they appear too infrequently and are not widespread enough in comparison with the other channels. What will be considered are frequently used grammatical words, negations and the like; a look at the regional varieties of greeting forms will conclude the study. On the maps, the forms found to be most common are printed larger for emphasis. Rarer forms are listed on the side.

2.2 Map 1 *ich*

The personal pronoun *ich* shows the following variants:

ich / isch / i

The main variant is *ich* with the exception of *i*, the central form in Austria. As the numbers show, *isch* is represented only marginally, but appears, as we can see when comparing it to map "ich" from the Deutscher Sprachatlas (c.f. König (1978), 162), in the strip between the *ik* area in the north and the *i* area in the south, where the Sprachatlas has *ich* as the central form. The fact that *isch* is missing in the Sprachatlas may be explainable by the indirect method used to collect the material. *ik* could not be found in the chats at all. Thus map one, with respect to the language use in chats, deviates considerably from the (historical) map in the Sprachatlas.

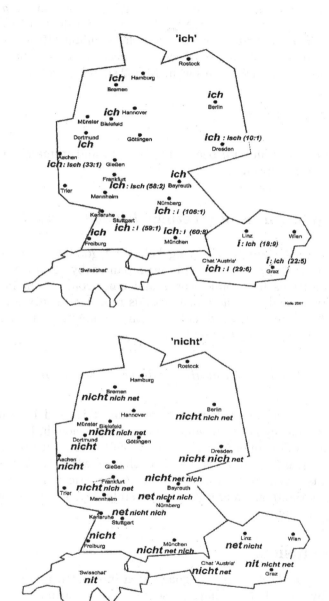

2.3 Map 2 *nicht*

The map for *nicht* shows a similar distribution to that of *nein*. For this example, the *nicht*-map from the Wortatlas der deutschen Umgangssprachen can be consulted for comparison (Eichhoff (1978), Map 116). It shows a north-south differentiation between *nicht/nich/nischt* in the north and *nit/it/ned/ed* in the south. Map 2 shows the following variants:

nicht / nich / net / nit

South of Frankfurt *net/nit* begins to show up and in many cases it becomes the central form.

2.4 Map 3, Forms of greeting: *Hi/Moin/Servus*

Chatting consists largely of saying hello and goodbye. Especially the greeting rituals are extensive and accompanied by several relationship building additions like comic words and emoticons. Seen in terms of conversational analysis, these chat rituals represent a mixture of greeting/reply to greeting in combination with introductory small talk. The following greeting forms can be found:

Hi / Moin / Tag-Tach / Hoy-Hey / Morgen / Servus-Sers

Hi has become the most dominant form, as it is used internationally. Second in frequency is *Moin*, which, surprisingly enough, has not simply persisted in its Frisian home (cf. König (1996), 242), but instead has become the central form in central and southern Germany. In Austria *Servus* dominates, as is to be expected, with its phonetic variants *Sers/Seass*. The other variants are marginal and possibly dependent on the time of day (*morgen/Tag*).

3 Conclusion

The division of the German language area into north and south that is indicated by several of the maps presented here has also been detected in other studies (König (1998), 233, Durell (1989)). König writes: "While in the dialects the border of the Old High German consonant shift generally forms the main rift between north and south, this division is much farther south in the colloquial varieties. The line popularly known as the "Mainlinie" seems to be documented in the language as well." (König (1994), 233, my translation)

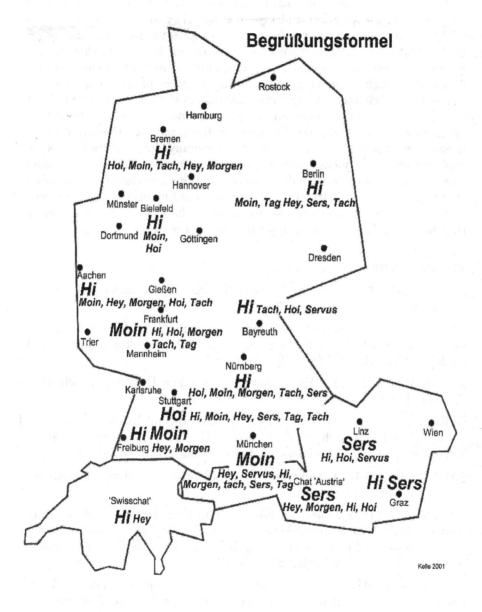

Begrüßungsformel

Kelle 2001

288

Chats, then, show the typical distribution of regional features in the highly frequent elements charted in these maps. The less frequent lexical units, as the above examples show, are much more in line with regional style or regional dialect. It must be pointed out, however, that city chats are not a source for basis dialects. Rather, they are reliable indicators of regionality in language use – and that despite the fact that the origin of the individual chatters cannot be determined. In spite of this heterogeneity of users, the linguistic characteristics of individual chat regions do show through in the corpus, providing evidence of the competence of the respective chatters. Only those chatting in the south use *i* instead of *ich*, though the laws of economy in writing would make it plausible for northern chatters to shorten the word in the same way, thereby making it easier on themselves. But language economy does not suffice as an explanation in every case: *isch* is not easier to type. Therefore, it must have a great deal to do with demonstrating linguistic identity. And when we observe the degree to which the group-building effects that are generally attributed to dialects also show up in chats, then it is no wonder that new linguistic norms of appropriateness are being formed.

References

BELLMANN, G. (1994ff.): Mittelrheinischer Sprachatlas. Niemeyer, Tübingen.

DURELL, M. (1989): Die „Mainlinie" als sprachliche Grenze. Putschke, W. and Veith, W. and Wiesinger, P. (eds.): Dialektgeographie und Dialektologie, Elwert, Marburg, 89–109.

EICHHOFF, J. (1978): Wortatlas der deutschen Umgangssprachen, 2. Francke, Bern.

GÜNTHER, U. and WYSS, E. L. (1996): E-Mail-Briefe – eine neue Textsorte. Hess-Lüttich, E. W. B. and Holly, W. and Püschel, U. (eds.): Textstrukturen im Medienwandel, Lang, Frankfurt/Main, 61–86.

JAKOB, K. (1984): Dialekt und Regionalsprache im Raum Heilbronn. Elwert, Marburg.

JAKOBS, E. (1998): Mediale Wechsel und Sprache. Entwicklungsstadien elektronischer Schreibwerkzeuge und ihr Einfluß auf Kommunikationsformen. *Holly, W. and Biere, B. U. (eds.): Medien im Wandel, Westdeutscher Verlag, Opladen, 187–209.*

KELLE, B. (2000): Regionale Varietäten im Internet – Chats als Wegbereiter einer regionalen Schriftlichkeit. *Deutsche Sprache, forthcoming.*

KÖNIG, W. (1.1978): dtv-Atlas zur deutschen Sprache. dtv, München.

KÖNIG, W. (12.1998): dtv-Atlas zur deutschen Sprache. dtv, München.

SCHWITALLA, J. (1998): Gesprochenes Deutsch. Schmidt, Berlin.

The Navigation Problem in the World-Wide-Web *

M. Levene

Department of Computer Science
University College London
Gower Street, London WC1E 6BT, U.K.
email: mlevene@cs.ucl.ac.uk

Abstract: Herein we build statistical foundations for tackling the navigation problem users encounter during web interaction, based on a formal model of the web in terms of a probabilistic automaton, which can also be viewed as a finite ergodic Markov chain. In our model of the web the probabilities attached to state transitions have two interpretations, namely, they can denote the proportion of times a user followed a link, and alternatively they can denote the expected utility of following a link. Using this approach we have developed two techniques for constructing a web view based on the two interpretations of the probabilities of links, where a *web view* is a collection of relevant trails. The first method we describe is concerned with finding frequent user behaviour patterns. A collection of trails is taken as input and an ergodic Markov chain is produced as output with the probabilities of transitions corresponding to the frequency the user traversed the associated links. The second method we describe is a reinforcement learning algorithm that attaches higher probabilities to links whose expected trail relevance is higher. The user's home page and a query are taken as input and an ergodic Markov chain is produced as output with the probabilities of transitions giving the expected utility of following their associated links. Finally, we characterise typical user navigation sessions in terms of the entropy of the underlying ergodic Markov chain.

1 Introduction

The World-Wide-Web (known as the web) has become a ubiquitous tool, used in day-to-day work, to find information and conduct business, and it is revolutionising the role and availability of information. (Currently the web contains over a billion web pages; see LG99 for a recent analysis of the amount of information on the web and its distribution.) Although current search engines have access to large off-line databases that are frequently updated with new online data, they are still deficient in narrowing down the list of "hits" to a manageable number and in ranking the results in a meaningful way by using contextual knowledge. In addition, search engines do not address the problems encountered during *navigation* (colloquially known as "surfing") which often lead users to "getting

---

*Invited lecture

lost in hyperspace" meaning that when following links users tend to become disoriented in terms of the goal of their original query and the relevance to the query of the information they are currently browsing; we refer to this problem as the *navigation problem*. Moreover, current search technology does not make adequate use of past knowledge about the individual user who is using the system or of past experience gained by the group of users he belongs to; such knowledge can be used to adapt the system to the user's goal.

Herein we concentrate on the navigation step which is not adequately dealt with in current browser technology. In particular, we summarise our recent work which addresses the navigation problem in the context of a probabilistic model of the web. The rest of the paper is organised as follows. In Section 2 we give a brief overview of hypertext and present our formal model of hypertext where initially we view a hypertext database as a finite automaton and then extend this view to that of a probabilistic finite automaton. In Section 3 we introduce the notion of a *web view* which is a subgraph induced by a collection of trails within the topology of the hypertext database. In Subsection 3.1 we detail our first technique for constructing a web view, which is in the area of web data mining, whose transition probabilities correspond to our first interpretation in terms of the proportion of times a user followed a link. In Subsection 3.2 we detail our second technique for constructing a web view, based on a reinforcement learning algorithm, whose transition probabilities correspond to our second interpretation in terms of the expected utility of following a link. In Subsection 3.3 we utilise our view of a hypertext database as an ergodic Markov chain by characterising typical user navigation sessions in terms of the entropy of the Markov chain. We summarise in Section 4.

2 Hypertext as an Underlying Model for Web Navigation

The foundations of the web are rooted in the area of *hypertext* Nie90, which breaks from the traditional organisation of text as a linear sequence of words dictating to the reader the order in which the text should be read; we often refer to the reader of a hypertext as the user. Hypertext organises documents in a nonsequential (or nonlinear) order. It presents the reader with several different options of reading a document, the choice of how to read the document being made at the time of reading. Let us call a textual unit of information a *page*. A *hypertext database* consists of a set of pages which are *linked* together according to the authors' specifications, i.e. a hypertext database is a directed graph (digraph), where the nodes are the pages and the arcs are the links. Every link connects two nodes, the starting node which is called the *anchor* node (or simply the anchor) and the finishing node which is called the *destination* node (or simply the destination).

The web is undoubtedly the largest hypertext database available providing readers with an almost unlimited source of data. Without going into any detail, each unit of information on the web is known as a resource, and each resource has a unique identifier, i.e. a URL, describing where the resource resides and how to retrieve it. Every web user has a *home page*, which is a hypertext page authored by the user, providing information and links created by the user. Thus the home page essentially connects the information provided by the user to the larger body of information available on the web, via the links that can be followed from the home page. Any other user *visiting* this home page can also follow these links.

Apart from querying the database users are most often browsing through pages of the hypertext database while traversing links. This process of following a *trail* of information in a hypertext database is called *navigation* (or alternatively *link following*). During the navigation process users may become "lost in hyperspace", meaning that they become disoriented in terms of what to do next and how to return to a previously browsed page. This is one of the main unsolved problems confronting hypertext, which is known as the *navigation problem*. It is the problem of having to know where you are in the database digraph representing the structure of a hypertext database, and knowing how to get to some other place you are searching for in the database digraph.

As stated at the beginning of this section a hypertext database is a digraph whose nodes are the pages and arcs are the links. We give semantics to a hypertext database in terms of a class of finite automata HU79, which we call *Hypertext Finite Automata* (HFA). The alphabet of the HFA is in a one-to-one correspondence with the page set of the hypertext database, and to each state of the HFA there corresponds a single page. We will assume for now that the state set of the HFA and the page set of the hypertext database are also in a one-to-one correspondence. In addition, all the states of the HFA are both initial and final, due to the fact that we can start our navigation at any page and finish at any page. The state transitions of the HFA occur according to the links of the digraph of the hypertext database, namely the state transition from state s_i to state s_j, labelled by symbol (page) P_i, is given by

$$s_i \xrightarrow{P_i} s_j$$

and corresponds to a link from page P_i to page P_j. Our interpretation of this state transition is that a user browsing P_i decides to follow the link leading to page P_j. At the end of the navigation session, after some further state transitions, the user will be in state, say s_k, browsing page

P_k. A word that is accepted by a HFA, which we call a *trail* of the HFA, is a sequence of pages $P_1, P_2, \ldots, P_n$, which were browsed during a navigation session, starting at page P_1, then following links according to the state transitions of the HFA and ending at page P_n. The language accepted by a HFA is the set of trails of the HFA. In other words, the language accepted by a HFA is the set of all possible trails a user could follow, which are consistent with the topology of the hypertext database.

Let xy denote the concatenation of the words x and y. Then a word y is a *subword* of a word w if $w = xyz$ for some words x and z, and a word w is the *join* of words xy and yz if $w = xyz$ and y is not the empty word.

In LL99c we provide a characterisation of the set of languages accepted by a HFA, as the subset of regular languages closed under the operations of subwords and join. This result is intuitive in terms of web navigation since subwords correspond to subtrails, and the join of two words corresponds to the join of two navigation trails, where the second trail completes the first one.

We now formulate simple queries over HFA as follows. A *trail query* (or simply a query) is an expression of the form

$$k_1 \text{ AND } k_2 \text{ AND } \ldots \text{ AND } k_n,$$

where the k_i are keywords.

A trail, T, which is accepted by a HFA *satisfies* a trail query if for all the k_i there is a page P_j in T such that k_i is a keyword of P_j. (We omit to further specify the notion of a *keyword* and refer the reader to BR99 which discusses how keywords can be extracted from a page of text.)

In LL99b we show that checking whether a HFA accepts a trail satisfying a trail query is NP-complete. The proof of this result utilises a duality between *propositional linear temporal logic* Eme90 and a subclass of finite automata. In temporal logic terminology the condition that k_i is a keyword of page P_j is the assertion that "sometimes" k_i, viewed as a condition on P_j, is true. Therein we also defined a more general class of queries which supports the additional temporal operators "nexttime" and "finaltime", and more general Boolean conditions. In the context of hypertext the natural interpretation of "time" is "position" within a given trail. So, "sometimes" refers to a page at some position in the trail, "nexttime" refers to the page at the next position in the trail, and "finaltime" refers to the page at the last position in the trail.

In LL99b we have shown that only for restricted subclasses of queries is the problem of checking, whether a HFA accepts a trail satisfying a query, polynomial-time solvable. Such a subclass essentially prescribes a one-step at a time navigation session using the "nexttime" operator. Current navigation practice where links are followed one at a time conforms to this subclass. These time-complexity results have led us to investigate a probabilistic approach to navigation in hypertext by adding probabilities (or equivalently weights) to the automaton's state transitions (or equivalently links), resulting in *Hypertext Probabilistic Automata* (HPA).

We interpret the probabilities attached to links in two separate ways:

1. The HPA models a user's (or group of users) navigation behaviour patterns, and the transition probability denotes the proportion of times that the user (or group of users) followed the link from its anchor node.

2. Given a query the HPA models the expected trail relevance, and the transition probability denotes the expected utility of following the link.

We further develop the notion of HPA by viewing them as finite *ergodic Markov chains* KS60. We consider the user's home page as an artificial starting state of any navigation session and assume there is a positive probability (however small) of jumping to any other relevant web page. These probabilities can be viewed as the initial probabilities of the Markov chain. The user then follows links according to the topology of the web and the transition probabilities, eventually returning to his home page at the end of the navigation session. The probability of a trail T, denoted by $p(T)$, is thus defined as the product of the initial probability of the first page of the trail together with the transition probabilities of the links in the trail.

3 Web Views

We define a *web view* as a collection of trails which are either the result of user navigation sessions over a period of time, or are relevant trails that satisfy a user's trail query. Thus a web view is a subgraph of the digraph of the hypertext database induced by a collection of trails. We limit the trails in a web view by accepting into the web view only trails whose overall probability is above some *cut-point* $\lambda \in [0, 1)$.

Let $\mathcal{M}$ be an ergodic Markov chain modelling the semantics of the hypertext under consideration, in our case modelling the web. Then a web view over $\mathcal{M}$ constrained by λ is the set of all trails T in $\mathcal{M}$ such that $p(T) > \lambda$.

In the next two subsections we will describe two different techniques for constructing web views based on our two interpretations of the transition probabilities of the Markov chain $\mathcal{M}$.

3.1 Data Mining of User Navigation Patterns

Our first technique for constructing a web view is within the area of *web data mining*, which is concerned with finding frequent user behaviour patterns. In $\mathcal{M}$ the high probability trails, i.e. those having probability above the cut-point, correspond to the user's preferred trails.

We assume that we have at our disposal web log data; for example, collected by the user's browser, from which it is possible to infer user navigation sessions. It is customary to define a navigation session as a sequence of page visits (i.e. URL requests) by the user where no two consecutive visits are separated by more than a prescribed amount of time, which is normally not more than half an hour.

When sufficient such log data is available we pre-process this data into a collection of trails, each trail being represented as a sequence of URLs. Moreover, we assume that the start and end URL of all trails correspond to the user's home page. We note that a trail may appear more than once in this collection, since the user may follow the same trail on two or more different occasions. We then build an ergodic Markov chain (or equivalently HPA), say $\mathcal{M}$, whose initial probabilities correspond to the frequency the user visited a page present in any one of the input trails, and whose transition probabilities correspond to the frequency that a link was followed in any one of the input trails. We observe that the states of $\mathcal{M}$ are the pages the user visited and the topology of $\mathcal{M}$, i.e. its underlying digraph, is induced by the links the user followed. In constructing $\mathcal{M}$ we have implicitly assumed that when the user chooses a link to follow he/she does not base his decision on the previous pages visited during the navigation session. That is, we have assumed that $\mathcal{M}$ is a first-order Markov chain. This assumption can be relaxed so that N (with $N \geq 1$) previous pages including the current one are taken into account; the case with $N = 1$ is the first-order case when the user bases his decision only on the page currently being browsed.

Once the HPA $\mathcal{M}$ has been constructed from the collection of trails, which have been pre-processed from the log data, we employ a Depth-First Search (DFS) to find all the trails in $\mathcal{M}$ starting from the user's home page and having probability above the cut-point λ. We have run extensive experiments with synthetic and real data to test the performance of the DFS algorithm BL99. It transpires that for a given cut-point there is a strong linear correlation between the size of $\mathcal{M}$, measured by its number of states, and the running time of the algorithm, measured by the number of links it traverses. Moreover, for a given cut-point, the number of mined trails increases linearly with the size of $\mathcal{M}$. On the other hand, the number of mined trails increases exponentially with the decrease in the cut-point.

3.2 Automated Navigation from User Queries

Herein we view the specification of the goal of a navigation session in terms of a query, which normally would be a set of keywords. We also assume as before that the navigation session starts from a fixed web page, say the user's home page. Starting from the home page we are interested in constructing a web view of trails which are highly relevant to the query. To this end we construct a HPA whose link probabilities represent the expected relevance of a trail resulting from following those links. The relevance of a trail is calculated as the average of the relevances of the pages in the trail, where the relevance of an individual page in a trail is the score of the page with respect to the input query. We note that we may compute the relevance of a trail by functions other than the average, for example by eliminating or penalising duplicate pages in a trail, or by applying a discount factor to pages which are further away from the start page.

The method used to construct this web view is based on a *sample-credit-update* loop, a common concept in reinforcement learning. The generic algorithm is composed of the following three steps:

1. Starting from the user's home page a sample of trails is taken according to the topology of the web and the link probabilities of the HPA. (Initially the link probabilities are uniform random, i.e. the probability of choosing one link out of m out-links is $1/m$. We call a HPA with such uniform link probabilities a *random* HPA.)

2. Links are credited according to the relevance of the trails passing through these links and the probabilities of links are normalised.

3. The web view is updated according to a learning rate which is between zero and one, which combines the old and new link probabilities.

We have run extensive experiments with synthetic and real data to test the performance of the web view construction algorithm ZL99. Our results show that starting from a random HPA the expected trail relevance is significantly increased by the algorithm until the final HPA is output, once the link probabilities have converged within a small error.

3.3 Computing the Entropy of User Navigation

Herein we utilise the view of a HPA as a finite ergodic Markov chain, say $\mathcal{M}$, where all user navigation sessions start from the user's home page and eventually return to this page. Over a period of time we assume that the empirical distribution of the Markov chain probabilities, induced by the user navigation sessions, stabilises in accordance with the actual transition probabilities. The entropy of the Markov chain is central to this approach, since once the empirical distribution stabilises, the entropy of a *typical* trail is "close" to the entropy of the Markov chain as a consequence of the *Asymptotic Equipartition Property* (AEP) CT91. Such a typical trail can then be seen to represent the user's navigation behaviour over a period of time.

In LL99a we developed an iterative method for computing this entropy by considering a long navigation session, which can be viewed as the concatenation of shorter sessions each starting from the user's home page. Therein we show that the empirical entropy converges from below to the true entropy, i.e. the empirical entropy is always an underestimation of the true entropy. The empirical entropy of a navigation trail of length t is given by

$$H(\mathcal{M}, t) = -\sum_{i=1}^{n} \sum_{j=1}^{n} \frac{m_{i,j}}{t} \log \frac{m_{i,j}}{m_i},$$

where n is the number of states of $\mathcal{M}$, $m_{i,j}$ is the number of times the link from the ith page to the jth page was followed, and m_i is the number of visits to the ith page.

4 Concluding Remarks

We have presented a statistical foundation for navigation in the web and hypertext structures based on a formal model in terms of hypertext probabilistic automata and ergodic Markov chains. Using this approach we have developed two techniques for constructing a web view. The first technique utilises web log data to construct a web view of user navigation trails, where a trail having higher probability is considered to be more relevant. The second technique utilises the user query in order to construct a web view of automatically generated trails, where a link having higher probability leads to a trail whose average relevance is higher.

We are currently working on combining the two interpretations of probability as the frequency of user traversal and the relevance to a given query. For this purpose, after a web view is constructed with respect to a user query, the transition probabilities, representing the expected relevance of following the corresponding links, can be modified to take into account the user's navigation behaviour according to a web view which is constructed from user web log data.

References

J. BORGES and M. LEVENE. Data mining of user navigation patterns. In *Proceedings of Workshop on Web Usage Analysis and User Profiling (WEBKDD), in conjunction with ACM SIGKDD International Conference on Knowledge Discovery and Data Mining*, pages 31–36, San Diego, Ca., 1999. Long version submitted for publication.

R. BAEZA-YATES and B. RIBEIRO-NETO. *Modern Information Retrieval*. ACM Press and Addison-Wesley, Reading, Ma., 1999.

T.M. COVER and J.A. THOMAS. *Elements of Information Theory*. Wiley Series in Telecommunications. John Wiley & Sons, Chichester, 1991.

E.A. EMERSON. Temporal and modal logic. In: J. Van Leeuwen, ed.: *Handbook of Theoretical Computer Science*, volume B, chapter 16, pages 997–1072. Elsevier Science Publishers, Amsterdam, 1990.

J.E. HOPCROFT and J.D. ULLMAN. *Introduction to Automata Theory, Languages and Computation*. Addison-Wesley, Reading, Ma., 1979.

J.G. KEMENY and J.L. SNELL. *Finite Markov Chains*. D. Van Nostrand, Princeton, NJ, 1960.

S. LAWRENCE and C.L. GILES. Accessibility of information on the web. *Nature*, 400:107–109, 1999.

M. LEVENE and G. LOIZOU. Computing the entropy of user navigation in the web. Research Note RN/99/42, Department of Computer Science, University College London, 1999.

M. LEVENE and G. LOIZOU. Navigation in hypertext is easy only sometimes. *SIAM Journal on Computing*, 29:728–760, 1999.

M. LEVENE and G. LOIZOU. A probabilistic approach to navigation in hypertext. *Information Sciences*, 114:165–186, 1999.

J. NIELSEN. *Hypertext and Hypermedia*. Academic Press, Boston, Ma., 1990.

N. ZIN and M. LEVENE. Constructing web views from automated navigation sessions. In *Proceedings of ACM Digital Library Workshop on Organizing Web Space (WOWS)*, pages 54–58, Berkeley, Ca., 1999.

Mining Web Usage Data for Automatic Site Personalization *

Bamshad Mobasher[1]

[1]School of Computer Science, Telecommunications, and Information Systems, Depaul University, Chicago, Illinois, USA

Abstract: The ability to collect detailed usage data at the level of individual mouse clicks, provides Web-based companies with a tremendous opportunity for personalizing the Web experience of clients. Most current approaches to Web personalization include using static profile of users obtained through registration, and approaches based on collaborative filtering. These approaches suffer from the problems of the profile data being subjective, as well as getting out of date as the user preferences change over time. We present an approach to Web personalization based on Web usage mining, taking into account the full spectrum of data mining techniques and activities. We describe and compare Web usage mining techniques, based on *transaction clustering* and *pageview clustering*, to extract usage knowledge for the purpose of Web personalization. We also discuss how the extracted knowledge can be effectively combined with the current status of an ongoing Web activity to perform real-time personalization. This approach allows personalization to be achieved based on objective aggregate "usage profiles" representing how users actually tend to use a site rather than based on subjective ratings or registration-based information.

1 Introduction

Web personalization can be described, as any action that makes the Web experience of a user customized to the user's taste or preferences. Existing approaches to Web personalization for e-commerce, rely heavily on getting human input for determining the personalization actions. These include rule-based systems which use static profiles of users obtained through a registration process, as well as collaborative filtering systems, such as NetPerceptions, which generally rely on user ratings of objects. The drawbacks of this are, (a) the input is often a subjective description of the users by the users themselves, and thus prone to biases, and (b) the profile is static, and thus good for personalization for some time after it is collected; but its performance degrades over time as the profile ages. Furthermore, collaborative filtering techniques (Herlocker et al (1999), Shardanand and Maes (1995)), which match user records with those of similar users in real time, often do not scale well as the number of items and users increase. Other approaches to personalization are based on content-based filtering technologies which use personal profiles of users

---

*Invited lecture

to and recommend other items (e.g., pages) based on content similarity. (Joachims et al (1997), Lieberman (1995)). However, techniques based on content similarity may miss other types of semantic relationships among objects (e.g., products often purchased together).

Recently, a number of approaches have been explored dealing with specific aspects of Web usage mining for the purpose of automatically discovering user profiles or business intelligence. For example, Perkowitz and Etzioni (1998) proposed the idea of optimizing the structure of Web sites based on co-occurrence patterns of pages within usage data for the site. Schechter et al (1998) have developed techniques for using path profiles of users to predict future HTTP requests, which can be used for network and proxy caching. Spiliopoulou et al (1999), Cooley et al (1999), and Buchner and Mulvenna (1999) have applied data mining techniques to extract usage or navigational patterns from Web logs, for the purpose of deriving marketing intelligence. Shahabi et al (1997) and Nasraoui et al (1999) have proposed clustering of user sessions to predict future user behavior. Srivastava et al (2000) provide an up-to-date survey of Web usage mining techniques, including applications of usage mining to personalization.

In this paper we describe an approach to usage-based Web personalization taking into account the full spectrum of Web mining techniques and activities. Our approach is described by the architecture shown in Figure 1, which heavily uses data mining techniques, thus making the personalization process both automatic and dynamic, and hence up-to-date. Specifically, we have developed techniques for preprocessing of Web usage logs and grouping *pageviews* into sets called *user transactions* which represent units of semantic activity suitable for performing data mining. We describe and compare Web usage mining techniques, based on *transaction clustering* and *pageview clustering*, to extract usage knowledge for the purpose of Web personalization. We also propose techniques for combining this knowledge with the current status of an ongoing Web activity to perform real-time personalization. Finally, we provide an experimental evaluation of the proposed techniques using real Web usage data.

2   A General Framework for Personalization Based on Web Usage Mining

Principal elements of Web personalization include modeling of Web objects (pages, etc.) and subjects (users), categorization of objects and subjects, matching between and across objects and/or subjects, and determination of the set of actions to be recommended for personalization. Figure 1 depicts a general architecture for Web personalization based on usage mining. The overall process is divided into two components: the

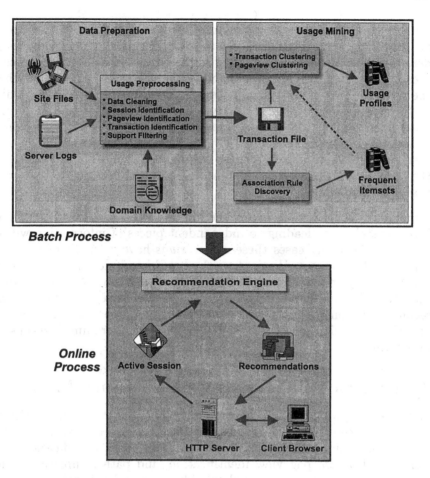

Figure 1: A General Architecture for Automatic Personalization based on Web Usage Mining

offline component which is comprised of the data preparation and specific Web mining tasks, and the online component which is a real-time recommendation engine. The data preparation tasks result in aggregate structures containing the preprocessed usage data to be used in the mining stage. These structures include a user transaction file capturing meaningful semantic units of user activity. Only relevant pageviews are included in the transaction file. Each pageview represents a collection of HTTP requests contributing to a single display in the user browser.

In the online component of the system, the Web server keeps track of the active server session as the user's browser makes HTTP requests. The recommendation engine considers the active user session in conjunction with the discovered profiles to provide personalized content. The personalized content can take the form of recommended links or products, or targeted advertisements tailored to the user's perceived preferences as determined by the matching usage profiles. If the data collection procedures in the system include the capability to track users across visits, then the recommendation set can represent a longer term view of potentially useful links based on the user's activity history within the site. If, on the other hand, profiles are derived from anonymous user sessions contained in log files, then the recommendations provide a "short-term" view of user's navigational history. These recommended objects are added to the last page in the active session accessed by the user before that page is sent to the browser.

Maintaining a history depth may be important because most users navigate several paths leading to independent pieces of information within a session. In many cases these *sub-sessions* have a length of no more than 2 or 3 references. We capture the user history depth within a sliding window over the current session. The sliding window of size n over the active session allows only the last n visited pages to influence the recommendation value of items in the recommendation set. The notion of a sliding session window is similar to that of N-grammars discussed in [Cha96].

3   Preprocessing Tasks for Web Usage Mining

When dealing with server-side data collection, the major difficulties in usage preprocessing are due to the incompleteness of the available data. The required high-level tasks are data cleaning, user identification, session identification, pageview identification, and path completion. The latter may be necessary due to client-side or proxy level caching. Transaction identification can be performed as a final preprocessing step prior to pattern discovery in order to focus on the relevant subsets of pageviews in each user session. The difficulties involved in identifying users and sessions depend greatly on the server-side technologies used for the Web site. For Web sites using cookies or embedded session IDs, user and session identification is trivial. Web sites without the benefit of additional information for user and session identification must rely on heuristics methods. We use the heuristics proposed in Cooley et al (1999) to identify unique user sessions form anonymous usage data and to infer cached references.

Pageview identification is the task of determining which page file accesses contribute to a single browser display, and is heavily dependent on the intra-page structure, and hence requires detailed site structure information. Furthermore, among the relevant pageviews some may be more significant than others. The significance of a pageview may depend on usage, content and structural characteristics of the site, as well as prior domain knowledge specified by the site designer. For example, in an in an e-commerce site pageviews corresponding to product-oriented events (e.g., shopping cart changes) may be considered more significant than others. In order to provide a flexible framework for a variety of data mining activities a number of attributes must be recorded with each pageview. These attributes include the pageview id (normally a URL uniquely representing the pageview), duration, static pageview type (e.g., content, navigational, product view, index page, etc.), and other meta-data.

The goal of transaction identification is to dynamically create meaningful clusters of references for each user, based on an underlying model of the user's browsing behavior (Cooley et al 1999). This allows each page reference to be categorized as a *content* or *navigational* reference for a particular user. Content references can be further classified according to page types or the type of user activity (e.g., product purchases). Finally, the transaction file can be further filtered by removing very low support pageview references, i.e., references to those pageviews which do not appear in a sufficient number of transactions. This type of *support filtering* can be useful in eliminating noise from the data, such as that generated by shallow navigational patterns of "non-active" users, and pageview references with minimal knowledge value for the purpose of personalization.

The above preprocessing tasks ultimately result in a set of n pageview records appearing in the transaction file, $P = \{p_1, p_2, \cdots, p_n\}$, with each pageview record uniquely represented by its associated URL, and a set of m user transactions, $T = \{t_1, t_2, \cdots, t_m\}$, where each $t_i \in T$ is a subset of P. To facilitate various data mining operations such as clustering, we view each transaction t as an n-dimensional vector over the space of pageview references, $t = \langle w(p_1, t), w(p_2, t), \ldots, w(p_n, t) \rangle$, where $w(p_i, t)$ is a weight, in the transaction t, associated with the pageview represented by $p_i \in P$. The weights can be determined in a number of ways, for example, binary weights can be used to represent existence or non-existence of a product-purchase or a documents access in the transaction. On the other hand, the weights can be a function of the duration of the associated pageview in order to capture the user's interest in a content page. The weights may also, in part, be based on domain-specific significance weights assigned by the analyst.

4 Automatic Personalization Based on Aggregate Usage Profiles

The transaction file obtained in the data preparation stage can be used as the input to a variety of data mining algorithms such as the discovery of association rules or sequential patterns, clustering, and classification.

However, the discovery of patterns from usage data by itself is not sufficient for performing the personalization tasks. The critical step is the effective derivation of good quality and useful (i.e., actionable) "aggregate profiles" from these patterns. Ideally, profiles capture an aggregate view of the behavior of subsets of users based their interests and/or information needs. In particular, aggregate profiles must exhibit three important characteristics:

1. they should capture possibly overlapping interests of users, since many users may have common interests up to a point (in their navigational history) beyond which their interests diverge;

2. they should provide the capability to distinguish among pageviews in terms of their significance within the profile; and

3. they should have a uniform representation which allows for the recommendation engine to easily integrate different kinds of profiles (e.g., profiles based on different pageview types).

We represent *usage profiles* as overlapping weighted collections of pageview records. Each item in a usage profile is a URL representing a relevant pageview, and can have an associated weight representing its significance within the profile. The profile can be viewed as an ordered collection, if the goal is to capture the navigational path profiles followed by users (Spiliopoulou et al 1999), or as unordered, if the focus is on capturing associations among specified content or product pages. Based on the information contained in each pageview record, other types of constraints can also be imposed on profiles. An advantage of this representation is that profiles can be viewed as pageview vectors, thus facilitating the task of matching a current user session with similar profiles using standard vector operations. In the following sections, we present two techniques for discovering overlapping usage profiles based on clustering of transactions and clustering of pageviews, respectively.

4.1 Discovery of Usage Profiles from Transaction Clusters

Traditional collaborative filtering techniques (e.g., Shardanand and Maes (1995)), are based on matching, in real-time, the current user's profile against similar records (nearest neighbors) obtained by the system over time from other users. However, as noted in recent studies (O'Conner and Herlocker (1999)), it becomes hard to scale collaborative filtering techniques to a large number of items (e.g., pages or products), while maintaining reasonable prediction performance and accuracy. One potential solution to this problem is to first cluster user records with similar characteristics, and focus the search for nearest neighbors only in the matching clusters. In the context of Web personalization this task involves clustering user transactions identified in the preprocessing stage.

Given the mapping of user transactions into a multi-dimensional space as vectors of pageview, standard clustering algorithms, such as k-means, generally partition this space into groups of transactions that are close to each other based on a measure of distance or similarity. Such a clustering will result in a set $TC = \{c_1, c_2, \cdots, c_k\}$ of transaction clusters, where each c_i is a subset of the set of transactions T. Support filtering technique discussed earlier can provide an effective dimensionality reduction method while actually improving clustering results. Ideally, each cluster represents a group of users with similar navigational patterns. However, transaction clusters by themselves are not an effective means of capturing an aggregated view of common user patterns. Each transaction cluster may potentially contain thousands of user transactions involving hundreds of pageview references. Our ultimate goal in clustering user transactions is to reduce these clusters into weighted collections of pageviews which, as noted earlier, represent aggregate usage profiles.

Preliminary results (Mobasher 1999) have identified one potentially effective method for the derivation of pageviews from transaction clusters. For each cluster $c \in TC$, we compute the mean vector m_c. The mean value for each pageview in the mean vector is computed by finding the ratio of the sum of the pageview weights across transactions to the total number of transactions in the cluster. To obtain the usage profile, the weights are normalized so that the maximum weight in each usage profile is 1, and low-support pageviews (i.e. those with mean value below a certain threshold μ) are filtered out. Given a transaction cluster c, we construct a usage profile pr_c as a set of pageview-weight pairs:

$$pr_c = \{\langle p, weight(p, pr_c)\rangle \,|\, p \in P, weight(p, pr_c) \geq \mu\},$$

where the significance weight, $weight(p, pr_c)$, of the pageview p within the usage profile pr_c is:

$$weight(p, pr_c) = \frac{1}{|c|} \cdot \sum_{t \in c} w(p, t),$$

and $w(p, t)$ is the weight of pageview p in transaction $t \in c$. Each profile, in turn, can be represented as vectors in the original n-dimensional space.

4.2 Discovery of Usage Profiles from Pageview Clusters

Another approach we consider is to directly compute clusters of pageview references based on how often they occur together across user transactions (rather than clustering transactions, themselves). Preliminary results based on this technique were initially discussed in Mobasher et al

1999. The profiles obtained by reducing transaction clusters group together pages that co-occur commonly across "similar" transactions. On the other hand, pageview clusters tend to group together frequently co-occurring items across transactions, even if these transactions are themselves not deemed to be similar.

However, traditional clustering techniques, such as distance-based methods, generally cannot handle this type clustering. The reason is that instead of using pageviews as features, the transactions must be used as features, whose number may be in hundreds of thousands in a typical application. Furthermore, dimensionality reduction in this context may not be appropriate, as removing a significant number of transactions as features may result in losing too much information. We have found that the Association Rule Hypergraph Partitioning (ARHP) technique (Han et al 1998) is well-suited for this task since it can efficiently cluster high-dimensional data sets without requiring dimensionality reduction as a preprocessing step. The ARHP has been used successfully in a variety of domains, including the categorization of Web documents (Han et al 1999).

Using association rule discovery methods such as the Apriori algorithm (Agrawal and Srikant (1994)), initially find groups of items (pageviews appearing in the preprocessed log) occurring frequently together in many transactions (*frequent item sets*). Association rules, derived from these itemsets, capture relationships among pageviews based on the navigational patterns of users. The set I of frequent itemsets are used as hyperedges to form a hypergraph $H = < V, E >$, where $V \subseteq P$ and $E \subseteq I$. A hypergraph is an extension of a graph in the sense that each hyperedge can connect more than two vertices. The weights associated with each hyperedge are computed based on the confidence of the association rules involving the items in the frequent itemset. The hypergraph H is then partitioned into a set of clusters C. Each cluster $c_i \in C$ represents a group of items (pageviews) which are very frequently accessed together across transactions. The similarity among items is captured implicitly by the frequent item sets. Each cluster is examined to filter out vertices that are not highly connected to the rest of the vertices of the partition. The connectivity function of vertex v (a pageview appearing in the frequent itemset) with respect to a cluster c is defined as:

$$conn(v, c) = \frac{|\{e \mid e \subseteq c, v \in e\}|}{|\{e \mid e \subseteq c\}|}$$

The vertices with connectivity measure greater than a given threshold value are considered to belong to the partition, and the remaining vertices are dropped from the partition. Once the stopping criteria has been reached for all of the partitions of a hypergraph, vertices can be "added back" to clusters depending on a user defined overlap parameter. For each partial edge that is left in a cluster, if the percentage of vertices from the original edge that are still in the cluster exceed the overlap percentage, the removed vertices are added back in. This will allow some vertices to belong to more than one cluster. The connectivity value of an item (pageviews) defined above is used as the weight associated with that item for the cluster. As noted in the case of transaction clustering, the weights associated with pageviews in each cluster are used as part of the recommendation process when clusters are matched against an active user session.

4.3 From Usage Profiles to Recommendations

In our proposed architecture, usage profiles obtained using either of the clustering techniques are represented as collections of pageview-weight pairs. This will allow for both the active session and the profiles to be treated as n-dimensional vectors over the space of pageviews in the site. Thus, given a usage profile C, we can represent C as a vector $C = \langle w_1^C, w_2^C, \cdots, w_n^C \rangle$, where

$$w_i^C = \begin{cases} weight(p_i, C), & \text{if } p_i \in C \\ 0, & \text{otherwise} \end{cases}$$

Similarly, the current active session S is also represented as a vector $S = \langle s_1, s_2, ..., s_n \rangle$, where s_i is a significance weight associated with the corresponding pageview reference, if the user has accessed pi in this session, and $s_i = 0$, otherwise. We can compute the profile matching score using a similarity function such as the normalized cosine measure for vectors:

$$match(S, C) = \frac{\sum\limits_{k} w_k^C \cdot S_k}{\sqrt{\sum\limits_{k} (S_k)^2 \times \sum\limits_{k} (w_k^C)^2}}.$$

Note that the matching score is normalized for the size of the clusters and the active session. This corresponds to the intuitive notion that we should see more of the user's active session before obtaining a better match with a larger cluster representing a user profile. Given a profile C and an active session S, a recommendation score, $Rec(S, p)$, is computed for each pageview p in C as follows:

$$Rec(S, p) = \sqrt{weight(p, C) \cdot match(S, C)}.$$

If the pageview p is in the current active session, then its recommendation value is set to zero. We obtain the usage recommendation set, $UREC(S)$, for current active session S by collecting from each usage profile all pageviews whose recommendation score satisfies a minimum recommendation threshold ρ, i.e.,

$$UREC(S) = \{w_i^C \mid C \in UP, \text{and } Rec(s, w_i^C) \geq \rho\},$$

where UP is the collection of all usage profiles. Furthermore, for each pageview that is contributed by several usage profiles, we use its maximal recommendation score from all of the contributing profiles.

5 Experimental Results

We used the access logs from the University of Minnesota Computer Science Web server to test the three methods discussed earlier. The preprocessed log (for February of 1999) was converted into a session file comprising 14294 user transactions and a total of 4001 pageviews, before support filtering (each represented by a unique URL corresponding to that pageview). We provide a summary of these results.

For the pageview clustering technique we used the hypergraph partitioning algorithm as modified in Clifton and Cooley (1999) to take frequent itemsets as the input. Each pageview serves as a vertex in the hypergraph, and each edge represents a frequent itemset. For the recommendation process we chose a session window size of 2, since the average session size was 2.4. The recommendation results are given for the sample path /research $\Rightarrow$ /grad-info $\Rightarrow$ /registration-info. Each table in Figure 2 corresponds to one step in the user navigation through the path. In each case the current active session window is given along with the top recommendations. A cut-off value of 0.30 was used for the recommendation score. In each case the recommendation set is composed of pageviews from a number of matching clusters. When /research page is requested, the pageviews for a number of popular research groups in the department are added to the set. When /grad-info is requested some of the frequently visited pageviews associated with that page as well as related class registration pages rank higher.

For the transaction clustering technique, the same transaction file was clustered using multivariate k-means clustering. The transaction clusters were converted to usage profiles using the method discussed earlier. Again a cut-off recommendation value of 0.30 was used in the resulting recommendation sets. These results are summarized in Figure 3. In comparing the results with those obtained by usage clustering, we observe that these results (as well as results from other experiments with a variety of usage data), support our intuition that the usage clustering method can capture overlapping interests of different types of users, even if the associated transaction profiles are not considered similar enough. For example, in the first reference to the /research page, the usage clustering method, in

Session Window	Recommendation	Score
/research	/newsletter/newfaculty.html	0.73
	/newsletter	0.65
	/faculty	0.55
	/research/cnmrg	0.55
	/research/softeng	0.55
	/research/airvl	0.51
	/research/mmdbms	0.48
	/personal-pages	0.37
	/registration-info	0.35
	/registration-info/spring99.html	0.32
	/grad-info	0.30
	/registration-info/schedule99-00.html	0.30
	/grad-research	0.30

Session Window	Recommendation	Score
/research	/faculty	0.59
/grad-info	/personal-pages	0.52
	/newsletter/newfac.html	0.52
	/newsletter	0.46
	/grad-info/grad-handbook.html	0.45
	/grad-info/course-guide.html	0.45
	/grad-info/prospective-grads.html	0.40
	/registration-info	0.39
	/research/cnmrg	0.39
	/research/softeng	0.39
	/research/airvl	0.36
	/registration-info/spring99.html	0.35
	/research/mmdbms	0.34
	/registration-info/schedule99-00.html	0.33

Session Window	Recommendation	Score
/grad-info	/faculty	0.51
/registration-info	/personal-pages	0.45
	/grad-info/grad-handbook.html	0.45
	/grad-info/course-guide.html	0.45
	/grad-info/prospective-grads.html	0.40
	/registration-info/spring99.html	0.36
	/registration-info/schedule99-00.html	0.34

Figure 2: Recommendations Based on Pageview Clusters

addition to the core set of recommendations, also provided recommendations for users (mainly graduate students) who may be interested in registering for courses, as well users who may be interested in finding out about research areas of new faculty. Similar observations can be made about the other steps in the sample path.

On the other hand, the transaction clustering technique seems to provide a narrower aggregated view of usage activity more directly centered around the a core set of pageviews. Which of these methods is more suitable as part of Web personalization may depend on the structure and content of a particular site, as well as the goals of the site designers and operators.

Session Window	Recommendation	Score
/research	/faculty	0.62
	/grad-info	0.56
	/grad-research	0.53
	/personal-pages	0.47
	/tech-reports	0.44
	/research/cnmrg	0.40
	/research/mmdbms	0.40
	/research/airvl	0.37
	/grad-info/grad-handbook.html	0.30

Session Window	Recommendation	Score
/research /grad-info	/grad-info/grad-handbook.html	0.60
	/faculty	0.48
	/grad-research	0.41
	/personal-pages	0.37
	/tech-reports	0.34
	/grad-info/course-guide.html	0.32
	/research/cnmrg	0.31
	/research/mmdbms	0.31
	/registration-info/spring99.html	0.30

Session Window	Recommendation	Score
/grad-info /registration-info	/grad-info/grad-handbook.html	0.61
	/registration-info/spring99.html	0.60
	/grad-info/course-guide.html	0.33
	/registration-info/schedule99-00.html	0.32
	/personal-pages	0.30

Figure 3: Recommendations Based on Transaction Clustering

6 Conclusions

Most current approaches to personalization rely heavily on human participation to collect profile information about users. This suffers from the problems of the profile data being subjective, as well getting out of date as the user preferences change over time. We have provided several techniques in which the user preference is automatically learned from Web usage data, by using data mining techniques. This has the potential of eliminating subjectivity from profile data as well as keeping it up-to-date. We have described a general architecture for automatic Web personalization based on the proposed techniques, and discussed solutions to the problems of usage data preprocessing, usage knowledge extraction, and making recommendations based on the extracted knowledge. Our experimental results indicate that the techniques discussed here are promising, each with its own unique characteristics, and bear further investigation and development.

References

AGRAWAL, R. and SRIKANT, R. (1994): Fast Algorithms for Mining Association Rules. Proceedings of the 20th VLDB conference, pp. 487-499, Santiago, Chile.

BUCHNER, A. and MULVENNA, M. D. (1999): Discovering Internet Marketing Intelligence through Online Analytical Web Usage Mining. *SIGMOD Record*, (4) 27.

CLIFTON, C. and COOLEY, R. (1999): TopCat: Data Mining for Topic Identification in a Text Corpus. Proceedings of the 3rd European Conference of Principles and Practice of Knowledge Discovery in Databases, Prague, Czech Republic.

CHARNIAK, E. (1996): Statistical Language Learning. MIT Press.

COOLEY, R., MOBASHER, B. and SRIVASTAVA, J. (1999): Web Mining: Information and Pattern Discovery on the World Wide Web. Proceedings of the IEEE International Conference on Tools with Artificial Intelligence, pages 558-567, Newport Beach.

HAN, E-H., BOLEY, D., GINI, M., GROSS, R., HASTINGS, K., KARYPIS, G., KUMAR, V., MOBASHER, B. and MORE, J. (1999): Document Categorization and Query Generation on the World Wide Web Using WebACE. *Journal of Artificial Intelligence Review*, to appear.

HERLOCKER, J., KONSTAN, J., BORCHERS, A. and RIEDL, J. (1999): An Algorithmic Framework for Performing Collaborative Filtering. Proceedings of the Conference on Research and Development in Information Retrieval.

HAN, E-H., KARYPIS, G., KUMAR, V. and MOBASHER, B. (1998): Hypergraph Based Clustering in High-Dimensional Data Sets: A Summary of Results. *IEEE Bulletin of the Technical Committee on Data Engineering*, (21) 1.

JOACHIMS, T., FREITAG, D. and MITCHELL, T. (1997): Webwatcher: A Tour Guide for the World Wide Web. Proceedings of the 15th International Conference on Artificial Intelligence, Nagoya, Japan.

LIEBERMAN, H. (1995): Letizia: An Agent that Assists Web Browsing. Proceedings of the 1995 International Joint Conference on Artificial Intelligence, Montreal, Canada.

MOBASHER, B., COOLEY, R. and SRIVASTAVA, J. (1999): Creating Adaptive Web Sites through Usage-Based Clustering of URLs. Proceedings of the IEEE Knowledge and Data Engineering Workshop (KDEX'99).

MOBASHER, B. (1999): A Web Personalization Engine Based on User Transaction Clustering. In Proceedings of the 9th Workshop on Information Technologies and Systems (WITS'99).

NASRAOUI, O., FRIGUI, H., JOSHI, A. and KRISHNAPURAM, R. (1999): Mining Web Access Logs Using Relational Competitive Fuzzy Clustering. Proceedings of the Eight International Fuzzy Systems Association World Congress.

O'CONNER, M. and HERLOCKER, J. (1999): Clustering Items for Collaborative Filtering. Proceedings of the ACM SIGIR Workshop on Recommender Systems, Berkeley.

PERKOWITZ, M. and ETZIONI, O. (1998): Adaptive Web Sites: Automatically Synthesizing Web pages. Proceedings of Fifteenth National Conference on Artificial Intelligence, Madison, WI.

SPILIOPOULOU, M. and FAULSTICH, L. C. (1999): WUM: A Web Utilization Miner. Proceedings of EDBT Workshop WebDB98, Valencia, Spain, *LNCS 1590*, Springer Verlag, 1999.

SRIVASTAVA, J., COOLEY, R., DESHPANDE, M. and TAN, P-T. (2000): Web Usage Mining: Discovery and Applications of Usage Patterns from Web Data. *SIGKDD Explorations*, (1) 2.

SCHECHTER, S., KRISHNAN, M. and SMITH, M. D. (1998): Using Path Profiles to Predict HTTP Requests. Proceedings of 7th International World Wide Web Conference, Brisbane, Australia.

SHARDANAND, U. and MAES, P. (1995): Social Information Filtering: Algorithms for Automating Word of Mouth. Proceedings of the ACM CHI Conference.

SHAHABI, C., ZARKESH, A., ADIBI, J. and SHAH, V. (1997): Knowledge Discovery from Users Web-Page Navigation. Proceedings of Workshop on Research Issues in Data Engineering, Birmingham, England.

Integrating Combinatorial Relationships in a Cartography for Web Site Promotion

F. Velin[1,2], P. Kuntz[1,3], H. Briand[1,3]

[1]IRIN (Institut de Recherche en Informatique de Nantes), Nantes, France

[2]Lnet Multimedia, Saint-Herblain, France

[3]Ecole polytechnique de l'université de Nantes, Nantes, France

Abstract: This paper proposes a two-dimensional representation of semantic (based on site contents) and combinatorial (based on the hyperlinks) relationships between Web sites. It describes an approach for the visualization of combinatorial relationships coming from a scaling method in a l_1-metric space and presents experimental results on real data.

1 Introduction

The recent explosion of e-commerce has led to the creation of many trading Web sites. However, to date, few of them are really successful. To attract net surfers, it is necessary to take care of the design of a site (Siegel (1997)) as well as its promotion (Sweeney (1999)). The latter requires on the one hand use of marketing skills and on the other hand good knowledge of how the Internet works. But, while much work has been done about how to author attractive pages (computer-human interaction, Web design, ...), the promotion part of "webmarketing" has been little investigated so far. Promoting a site consists in advertising it in such a way that numerous Internet users know it exists and visit it. On the Web, that means creating —or asking for the creation of— hyperlinks to the site in question; the place and look of these links must be suitable for their purpose.

In order to choose promising pages in regard to link creation, decision-makers must have information about a group of candidate pages. There exist software tools to download the contents of a site. But the problem then consists in handling effectively a great mass of information and giving legible results to the decision-maker. In our context, dealing with the information comes down to a clustering problem: partitioning the set of potentially interesting sites so that sites with many semantic relationships (based on the contents) and many combinatorial links (based on the hyperlinks) are put together while sites without common characteristics are placed in distinct classes. And the visualization problem consists in finding an intelligible representation mode of classes that highlights the main relationships. This paper proposes a representation as a bi-dimensional map and describes an approach for the visualization of combinatorial relationships coming from a scaling method in a l_1-metric space. We present experimental results obtained with real data taken from a case study in the field of Cognac.

2 Integrating relationships on a map

We suppose the existence of a reference —or target— site s^* in the considered domain for the site promotion. Such a site is characterized by a numerous and targeted audience. In the context of e-commerce, having a link on the home page of s^* is the ideal situation. However, this may be extremely expensive and it can be more interesting, with regard to the expected results, to ask for the creation of links on sites semantically and combinatorially "close" to the target site. So it is necessary to supply a decision-maker with a representation that shows what those sites are and how they are related to the target site and connected with one another. Hence, the set of sites S considered here includes the reference site s^* and the so-called satellite sites $s_1, \ldots, s_n$, i.e. sites that have at least one page referred to by a page from s^*.

2.1 Common visualizations of Web ressources

There exist numerous types of visual representations of Web resources, from plans of the underlying networks to artistic visions of the "cyberspace" (Anders (1998)). They may be distinguished by the type of object they deal with: groups of pages, single Web site or site sets. In the first case, trees or hyperbolic trees represent pages that are directly or indirectly linked to a given page. They usually aim at making exploration and navigation easier. At a higher abstraction level, information found on pages may be visualized on "conceptual maps" used for searching and data retrieval. For a single site, maps whose general form is a tree describe links between sections and subsections. They make it possible to browse effectively, but also give relevant overviews of the contents of sites.

It seems that representations which consider sites as the basic units to handle are less commonly used. Terveen et al. (1999) interestingly define a site as an "organized collection of pages on a specific topic maintained by a single person or group". Handling sites then means taking both structural and conceptual characteristics into account, and for visualization, it is necessary to have sophisticated maps that give all the relevant information in an appropriate way. In particular, Bray (1996), Terveen et al. (1999) have developed representations which show groups of sites along with information which can be deduced from intra-site (size, topics, ...) or inter-site (graph of hyperlinks between sites) characteristics. But the examples treated by these authors deal with relatively small site sets (some dozens) while we are frequently confronted with cardinalities greater than 100 in our application. It is then necessary to make use of very specific techniques for site classification and placing, to have representations with varying levels of detail.

2.2   Structure of the map

Circular or semicircular representations are often used to show how far from a central object other objects are. In particular, they can be found for the representation of sites whose contents are further and further removed from a given topic (Terveen et al. (1999)), or for the visualization of generic-specific relationships between terms in a thesaurus (Chaumier (1982)). To preserve interpretation habits, we have decided to give a map the look of a target on which the reference site s^* is the bull's-eye and where satellite sites are placed according to their distance from s^* (figure 1a). That distance depends on the number of hyperlinks that exist between a satellite site s_i and the reference one s^*.

Besides the distance from the center, our representation integrates semantic aspects which aim at grouping in a same area sites that are associated with a same topic. We restrict ourselves to the lexical analysis of textual information, which is sufficient to draw a cartography of relationships at a "macroscopic scale" and, for now, we associate each site with a list of concepts c_i described by keyword conjunctions. But this difficult problem of text mining is far beyond the scope of this article and we refer to Velin et al. (2000) for details.

To make site topology more legible, the representation also integrates combinatorial relationships based on the existence of links between satellite sites. Our target is divided into a number of angular sectors, each corresponding to a semantic concept c_i. And, in a zone bounded by two concentric circles, sites are positioned according to the characteristics of the connections they share with one another.

3   Integration of combinatorial relationships

For the problem of site promotion, measuring the communication streams between sites is highly relevant. Unfortunately, because of its strategic importance, this type of information is very rarely publicized. Measures based on random walks on the Web graph can be used to estimate popularity score (e.g. Brin and Page (1998)). However, due to their probabilistic nature, they may induce an important error and are difficult to apply with sufficient reliability in the context of webmarketing. To deal with this lack of information, we only consider combinatorial relationships defined by the number of links connecting pairs of sites. This allows us to better understand the general topology of sites dealing with common topics.

3.1 Relationships between satellite sites

In our representation, we are concerned not only with relationships between each satellite site and the reference site —as it can often be seen— but also with relationships between satellite sites. The network of hyperlinks between those sites can be modeled by a multigraph $G = (S, E)$ where $S = \{s_1, \ldots, s_n\}$ is the set of satellite sites of the reference site s^* and where every edge in E is associated with the existence of a hyperlink between two sites in S. For the representation on the map described in section 2.2, G can be partitioned into subgraphs

$$G_{1,1}, G_{1,2}, \ldots, G_{1,j}, \ldots, G_{p,q}, \ldots, G_{k,l}$$

where the vertex set of each $G_{p,q}$ is associated with a semantic concept c_p and a distance interval I_q. The problem consists in placing vertices on the map in such a way that their relationships are highlighted: "strongly connected" vertices must be placed close to one another while those which are weakly connected or not connected at all can be placed separately.

A pragmatic approach to take these constraints into account is to measure the strength of linkage between vertex pairs by a dissimilarity coefficient $d : S \times S \to R^+$ so that d_{ij} is small when sites s_i and s_j are strongly connected and large in the inverse case. Hence, the placing problem can be set as an embedding problem. Let (E, δ) be the underlying metric space in which the placing is done. It is a question of finding a set of points $X = \{x_1, \ldots, x_n\}$ in E so that every point x_i is an unambiguous representation of vertex s_i in S and, the distance δ_{ij} between each pair of points in X best coincides with the dissimilarity d_{ij} on S. This scaling problem depends on the respective choice of d and (E, δ) and on the adequacy criterion between d and δ.

3.2 Choice of a dissimilarity on the site set

When dealing with graphs, a common measure for d is the length of the shortest path (number of edges) between pairs of vertices. Experiments have shown this can be used for the representation of small and well-balanced graphs (Littman et al. (1992)). However, that is less suitable for the representation of relationships in the very heterogeneous graphs we meet here. That is why we prefer a local measure: the dissimilarity between two vertices is only a function of the neighborhood of every vertex in $G_{p,q}$. Numerous measures developed in numeric taxonomy for binary data like graph adjacency matrices can be used here; further to comparative results (Kuntz (1992)), we chose the following measure. Let $N(s_i)$ be the vertex set incident to vertex s_i union s_i: $N(s_i) = \{s_j \in S; \ (s_i, s_j) \in E\} \cup \{s_i\}$. The dissimilarity d aims at gathering vertices which have many common neighbors and few different ones: $d_{ij} = |N(s_i) \vartriangle N(s_j)| / (|N(s_i)| + |N(s_j)|)$. The singleton $\{s_i\}$ is added in order to emphasize the existence of an edge between s_i and s_j by taking it into account twice in the symmetric difference between $N(s_i)$ and $N(s_j)$.

Another definition can be given from the $n \times n$ adjacency matrix $A = [a_{ij}]$ of G with a_{ii} set to 1 for the equivalence. Let n_{ij} be the number of k such that $a_{ik} = 1$ and $a_{jk} = 1$, and $n_i = \sum_{k=1,n} a_{ik}$. With this formulation, d can be recognized as the well-known Czekanovski-Dice coefficient (Dice (1945)) originally defined to evaluate differences between binary data in ecology: $d_{ij} = 1 - 2 \cdot n_{ij}/(n_i + n_j)$.

3.3 Choice of the embedding metric space

In order to produce an easily understandable display of the relationships between sites on a plane, three embedding spaces based on the most familiar Minkowski metrics can be considered:

1. the rectilinear plane: $E = R^2$ and δ is the l_1-metric defined by $\delta_{ij} = \left| x_i^1 - x_j^1 \right| + \left| x_i^2 - x_j^2 \right|$ with x_i^1 and x_i^2 the coordinates of x_i;
2. the rectilinear grid: $E = Z^2$ with the l_1-metric;
3. the Euclidean plane: $E = R^2$ and δ is the usual Euclidean distance.

The dissimilarity d is known to be l_1-embeddable in a rectilinear space (e.g. Fichet (1987)), but unfortunately, it is easy to deduce from a recent characterization of particular rectilinear embedding spaces that the dimension of the space should be greater than 2 for d.

Indeed, Bandelt et al. (1998) have shown that the maximum number of equidistant points that can be placed in the m-dimensional rectilinear space is $2m$ for $m \leq 3$. We conclude that (S, d) is not embeddable in the rectilinear space in the general case as all the vertices which are not adjacent and which have no common neighbours are at the same distance of one. Moreover, several authors have shown that d is not Euclidean (e.g. Gower and Legendre (1984)) and, a "good" approximation based on the spectral decomposition of the Torgerson matrix very often requires more than two dimensions for real data sets (e.g. Kuntz and Hénaux (2000)). So, the placing problem comes down to an approximation problem: minimizing $e(d, \delta)$ with e a function measuring the error of approximation and δ chosen here as an l_1-metric appropriate for display on a computer screen.

One of the simplest approximations consists in minimizing $\sum_{i,j} \left(\delta_{ij} - \left| x_i^1 - x_j^1 \right| + \left| x_i^2 - x_j^2 \right| \right)^2$. But, Hubert and Arabie (1992) have underlined the difficulties of obtaining adequate solutions with a simple gradient-based strategy and proposed an alternative heuristic that first constructs "good" object orders along each dimension and then, resorts to non-negative least-squared to re-estimate the coordinates for the objects based on the object orders. But, due to the complexity of the problem of order construction, their tests are based on relatively small sets of data only. As a matter of simplication and because of technical requirements for our implementation, we here focus on an iterative method developed at AT&T Bell Labs (Swayne et al. (1998)). The error criterion is $e^2(d, \delta) = 1 - \left(\sum_{ij} d_{ij}.\delta_{ij} \right)^2 / \left(\sum_{ij} d_{ij} \right) \left(\sum_{ij} \delta_{ij} \right)$. The optimization is performed with an iterative algorithm based on a series of gradient descents with different step sizes (see figure 1b for an illustration of the process).

4 Experimental results

A map generator implementing the approach expounded above has been written in Java and tested on real data. Here, we present a case study of a Cognac producer who wants to create a trading Web site that will let Internet users discover and buy his products. This site must be adequately promoted, that is being referenced on sites which will invite a great number of prospects to visit it.

Preliminary search sessions on the Net lead us to find one of the main reference sites in the field of Cognac ($s^* =$ http://www.swfrance.com). To be able to study the sites connected with s^* and then to estimate the appropriateness of choosing one or more of them to create links, we will draw a map. The considered set of sites S, which was built by an offline browsing utility, contains 158 elements.

Following to the lexical study of the contents of those sites, we retained 10 semantic concepts ("Wines and Spirits", "Tourism and Travel", ...), plus one additional "Unknown" concept for the sites whose contents cannot be retrieved. For each concept represented on the map by an angular sector, we computed the dissimilarity d between the satellite sites s_i whose number of links with the reference site is of the same order (i.e. in a same interval bounded by two circles). And we apply the embedding on each of these subsets (figure 1).

Experimental results confirm the validity of our approach for the site promotion problem. We are currently carrying out additionnal experiments on two directions: the comparison of our results with a recent approach for multidimensional scaling based on integral transformations of the objective function (Bennani, 1999), and the study of the influence of different metrics for the representation of combinatorial relationships.

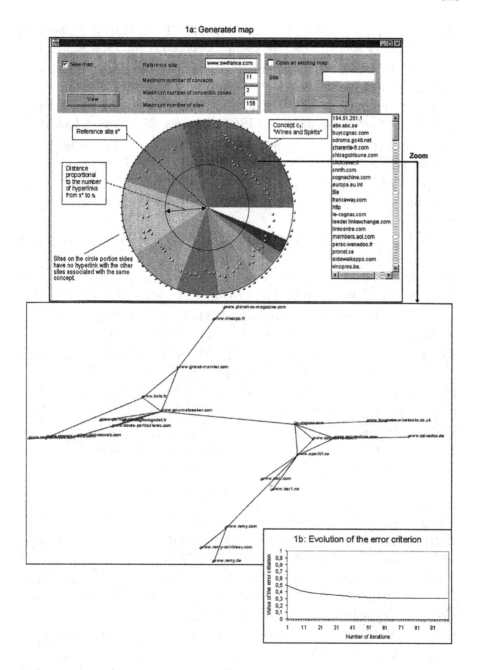

Figure 1: Illustration of the approach with data taken from a real case

References

ANDERS, P. (1998): Envisioning Cyberspace: Designing 3D Electronic Space. New York: McGraw Hill.

320

BANDELT, H.-J., CHEPOI, V. and LAURENT, M. (1998): Embedding into rectilinear spaces. *Discrete Comp. Geometry*, vol. 19, n°4, 595–604.

BENNANI, M. (1999): Global minimization for metric multidimensional scaling. Vereniging v. Ordinatie en Classification Spring Meeting.

BRAY, T. (1996): Measuring the Web. Proc. of the 5th World Wide Web Conf., *Comp. Network and ISDN Systems*, 28, Elsevier, 993–1005.

BRIN, S. and PAGE, L. (1998): The Anatomy of a Large-Scale Hypertextual Web Search Engine. Proc. of the 7th WWW Conf., Elsevier.

CHAUMIER, J. (1982): Analyse et langages documentaires : le traitement linguistique de l'information documentaire. Paris: Entreprise moderne d'édition.

DICE, L. (1945): Measures of the amount of ecologic association between species. *Ecologie*, vol. 26, 297–302.

FICHET, B. (1987): The role played by L_1 in data analysis. *Stat. Data Analysis Based on the $l_1$norm and Related Methods*, Elsevier, 185–193.

GOWER, J.-C. and LEGENDRE, P. (1984): Metric and Euclidean properties of dissimilarity coefficients. *J. of Classification*, vol. 3, 5–48.

HUBERT, L. and ARABIE, P. (1992): Multidimensional scaling in the city-block metric: a combinatorial approach. *J. of Classif.*, 9, 211–236.

KUNTZ, P. (1992): Euclidean representation of an abstract graph for its partitioning (in French). PhD thesis, EHESS, Paris.

KUNTZ, P. and HENAUX, F. (2000): Numerical Comparisons of two Spectral Decompositions for Vertex Clustering. *Data Analysis, Classification and Related Methods*, Springer Verlag, 113–119.

LITTMAN, M., SWAYNE, D., DEAN, N., and BUJA, A. (1992): Visualizing the Embedding of Objects in Euclidian Space. *Computing Science and Statistics: Proc. of the 24th Symp. on Interfaces*, 208–217.

SIEGEL, D. (1997): Secrets of Successful Web Sites : Project Management on the World Wide Web. Simon & Schuster Macmillan.

SWAYNE, D., COOK, D., and BUJA, A. (1998): XGobi: Interactive Dynamic Data Visualization in the X-Window System. *J. of Comp. and Graphical Statistics*, vol. 7, 125–140.

SWEENEY, S. (1999): 101 Ways to Promote Your Web Site. Maximum.

TERVEEN, L. G., HILL, W. C., and AMENTO, B. (1999): Constructing, Organizing, and Visualizing Collections of Topically Related Web Resources. *ACM Trans. Comp.-Hum. Interaction*, vol. 6, n°1, 67–94.

VELIN, F., PETER, P., and BELLEIL, C. (2000): Exploitation of textual data in the context of Web mining (in French). Proc. of EGC'2001, Hermes (to appear).

Part 5

Applications in Management Science, Finance, and Marketing

Common Due Date Scheduling
- Straddling Jobs and Due Windows -

Martin Feldmann

Lehrstuhl für Betriebswirtschaftslehre und Unternehmensforschung
Universität Bielefeld, D-33501 Bielefeld, Germany

Abstract: This paper deals with two important NP-hard JIT-scheduling problems. First, the restrictive single machine common due date scheduling (CDDS) with individual earliness and tardiness penalties is analysed. Second, the question is extended to the more general case of the restrictive common due window scheduling (CDWS). Along with local search different meta-heuristics may be of interest - but at any rate primarily an appropriate problem representation has to be found. For the CDDS and CDWS some very beneficial properties of optimal solutions exist that submit a classification of these solutions in three or rather seven cases. In contrast to techniques, already developed a new problem-representation with dummy jobs, given in this paper, does not exclude some optimal solutions a priori. It has become possible to map the complete space of optimal solutions for restrictive CDDS and CDWS instances with minimal effort; furthermore, different local search operators, which could generate reasonable neighbourhoods are conceivable.

1 Introduction and survey

In JIT-scheduling earliness of job completion as well as its tardiness has negative consequences. In an intramanufacturing situation starving or blockage can occur if intermediate goods are not completed on time. In an intermanufacturing situation avoidable logistic expenditure, e.g. holding cost, additional transportation etc., may be incurred. In the long run this leads to dissatisfied customers as well as the loss of goodwill and reputation. This type of situation fits traditional due date models, where each job has its own, individual due date, perfectly (KRÄMER/LEE 1993).

Instead of individual due dates, common due dates or common due windows regularly occur, if for example batch delivery is stipulated or parts have to be assembled on a subsequent production unit. Even from a practical point of view, common due date problems are relevant in many applications: A customer orders a bundle of easy perishable goods which has to be delivered at a specified time; in a chemical mixture some ingredients have a short halflife period etc. In all of these cases, the jobs have to follow the identical time restriction of a common due date or window.

A large number of papers concerning scheduling against due dates, common due dates and due windows have appeared during the last two decades, see for instance: KANET 1981 and BAKER/ SCUDDER 1990 for an excellent review of fundamental results in scheduling against due dates. In literature two kinds of due dates or due windows, namely restrictive and unrestrictive ones, are distinguished: a due date or a due window is called restrictive if it influences the optimal job-sequence. With regard to the complexity status two classes of common due date problems have proven to be NP-hard, namely if a restrictive common due date is given or if different jobs incur different penalties, see the survey in BISKUP/FELDMANN 2000. Even the unrestrictive common due date problem becomes NP-hard if arbitrary earliness and tardiness penalty rates are considered; the proof is given by HALL/POSNER 1991. Hence heuristic approaches for the CDDS are preponderant see LEE/KIM 1995, JAMES 1997 and FELDMANN/BISKUP 1999.

The next section introduces important properties of optimal solutions and takes advantage of them by the development of an appropriate mapping of optimal solutions. This procedure overcomes the underlying weakness of the parallel Genetic Algorithm given by LEE/KIM 1995 and the Tabu Search approach presented by JAMES 1997. After a detailed description of the new approach, computational experiments with a problemsize of up to 1000 jobs are briefly reviewed. A comparison to the results of JAMES 1997 confirms the high efficiency of the new representation in combination with different meta-heuristics (cp. FELD-MANN/BISKUP 1999). In the third section the problem is extended to the CDWS. Again properties of optimal solutions allow a classification of all potential optimal solutions, where seven cases have to be distinguished. A new 2-phase problem representation for the CDWS is provided that benefits from the seven cases of optimal solutions by an extension of the representation procedure of the CDDS.

2 Properties of optimal solutions of the CDDS

In the following a short description of the CDDS is given:

d := common due date
n := number of jobs
p_i := processing time of job i
α_i := earliness penalty of job i per time unit
β_i := tardiness penalty of job i per time unit
C_i := completion time of job i
E_i := earliness of job i, $E_i := \max\{d - C_i, 0\}$
T_i := tardiness of job i, $T_i := \max\{C_i - d, 0\}$
B := set of jobs scheduled to finish early or in time, $B = \{i|C_i \leq d\}$
A := set of jobs scheduled to begin in or after d, $A = \{i|C_i - p_i \geq d\}$

All jobs are assumed to be available at time zero and each of them needs exactly one operation. They have to be processed on a single machine or a production unit. The production times p_i are deterministic and known in advance, preemption of jobs is prohibited and a common due date d is given. Since the restrictive case (d influences the optimal job sequence) is the more realistic and difficult one, the problems dealt with in this paper are assumed to be restrictive. The objective of the CDDS is to find a feasible schedule S which jointly minimizes the sum of earliness and tardiness penalties

$$f(S) = \sum_{i=1}^{n} \alpha_i E_i + \sum_{i=1}^{n} \beta_i T_i \qquad (1)$$

In the following, three properties of optimal solutions for the CDDS that are essential for the development of the problem representation are presented:

Property 1: In an optimal schedule there is no idle time between the processing of consecutive jobs; a general proof is given by CHENG/ KAHLBACHER 1991.

Property 2: An optimal schedule has the so-called v-shaped property: the jobs $i \in B$ are ordered according to non-increasing ratios p_i/α_i and the jobs $j \in A$ are ordered in non-decreasing ratios p_j/β_j. The proof can be done by an interchange argument, see for instance BAKER/ SCUDDER 1989.

Despite this property in an optimal schedule a so-called straddling job - not belonging to the sets A and B - may emerge. The processing of this job is started before and finished after the due date. If in an optimal schedule a straddling job s exists, no statement of its ratios p_s/α_s and p_s/β_s can be made, see HOOGEVEEN/VAN DE VELDE 1991.

Property 3: An optimal schedule exists in which either the processing of the first job starts at time zero or one job is completed at the due date; the proof is similar to that of HOOGEVEEN/VAN DE VELDE 1991.

Considering Property 3, the search for an optimal schedule should not be restricted to schedules starting at time zero as a leading idle time may occur. Additionally this property implies the possibility that in an optimal schedule the first job starts at time zero and the completion time of one job coincides with d.

The weakness of the parallel genetic algorithm (LEE/KIM 1995) is that it neglects Property 3 and limits the search space to schedules in which the first job starts at time zero, although this might exclude optimal schedules a priori. The weakness of the tabu search approach (JAMES 1997) is that he does not allow an arbitrary job to be the straddling one, since he always chooses the job of set A with the smallest ratio of processing time and penalty (JAMES 1999).

3   Representation of CDDS with dummy jobs

Choosing an appropriate problem representation is amongst the most important tasks in the design-process of any heuristic search procedure. The representation can be seen as a mapping which transfers a feasible solution of the problem into a specific, suitably coded, represented solution. As a matter of principle the problem representation should fulfil the following requirements: it has to be complete, i.e. all possible solutions must be representable and none of the represented solutions may be infeasible. In the ideal case each given solution should be unequivocally represented and the mapping should only contain redundancies if the search process can take distinct advantage of them. Further it has to be guaranteed that the entire solution space can be reached by specific search operators: each solution must be attainable independently of the starting point, see FELDMANN 2000.

For the CDDS problem the representation has to take into account that the starting point of the first job is not known in advance. Furthermore a straddling job violating the v-shaped property might exist. In figure1 all possible optimal solutions are classified by the three disjunctive cases - assuming that the jobs in set B and set A are ordered according to the v-shaped property. In the first case, one job starts in time zero and the last job of B is finished exactly in d. Leading idle time occurs in case number two, as the first job is delayed and the last job of B finishes exactly in d. In the third case, a straddling job s exists: the first job of set B starts in time zero, the last job of B is completed prior to d and the start of the first job of set A is late.

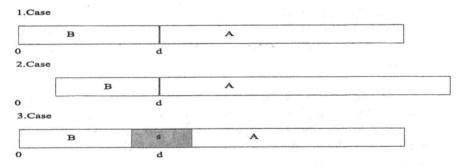

Figure 1: Classification of all optimal solutions of the CDDS

If we assume the jobs to be indexed according to the shortest processing time (SPT) rule, it is possible to calculate the maximum number of non-tardy jobs $|B|_{max}$ for which the following inequalities hold:

$$\sum_{i=1}^{|B|_{max}} p_i \leq d \text{ and } \sum_{i=1}^{|B|_{max}+1} p_i > d \tag{2}$$

For the problem-representation a permutation with dummy jobs is used: $|B|_{max}$ dummy jobs - each with $p_i = 0$ - are added to the permutation of the n given jobs of the problem i.e. the permutation contains $n + |B|_{max}$ jobs. The procedure for assigning the permutation unequivocally into an optimal schedule can be described as follows. Let [i] be the job that occupies the i-th position of the permutation and $p[i]$ be the processing time of this job.

Step 1: $P_{sum} := 0$; i:= 1; $A := \{1, 2, .., n, .., n + |B|_{max}\}$; $B := \emptyset$
Step 2: $P_{sum} := P_{sum} + p[i]$
Step 3: **If** $P_{sum} \leq d$ **Then** $B := B \cup [i]$; $A := A \setminus [i]$
       Else [i] is the straddling job; $A := A \setminus [i]$
Step 4: **If** $((i < |B|_{max} + 1)$ **And** $(P_{sum} < d))$
       Then i := i +1; **Goto** Step 2
       Else A and B are ordered according the v-shaped property; End

Interpretation procedure

The processing times $p[i]$ are summed up according to the order given in the permutation. The first case of figure 1 occurs if at some point (with $i \leq |B|_{max} + 1$) P_{sum} exactly equals d. The second case occurs if the sum of the processing times of the first $|B|_{max} + 1$ jobs of the permutation is smaller than d (since some of the dummy jobs are among the first positions). In this case the completion of the last job of the set B coincides with d and the processing of the jobs in the set A is followed immediately. The third case occurs if at some point (with $i \leq |B|_{max} + 1$) P_{sum} exceeds the due date d. The job s that occupies the i-th position of the permutation is the straddling one. If a straddling job exists the first job of the set B is started in time zero. After the last job of set B the straddling job s and afterwards the jobs belonging to set A are scheduled.

With the determination of the starting time of the first job and the construction of the sequence (according to the v-shaped property) the objective function value (see formula 1) can easily be calculated. To demonstrate the procedure in detail and show how solutions belonging to the third case of figure 1 can be constructed, the following small example with 10 jobs is given:

328

#	1	2	3	4	5	6	7	8	9	10
p_i	20	6	13	13	12	12	12	3	12	13
α_i	4	1	5	2	7	9	5	6	6	10
β_i	5	15	13	13	6	8	15	1	8	1

If a common due date $d = 46$ is assumed, at most 5 non-tardy jobs can occur. Therefore $|B|_{max} = 5$ dummy jobs: 11, 12, 13, 14, 15 - each with the processing time zero - are added to the above given 10 jobs. Every permutation of these 15 numbers can be unequivocally interpreted as a solution of the CDDS problem instance. Let us further assume that the following permutation is given: 3 7 2 4 9 11 6 1 15 10 5 12 14 8 13. The procedure sums up the processing times of the jobs according to the order given in the permutation. As the sum of the processing time of the first four jobs is $44 < d = 46$ and the sum of the first five jobs is 56 $> d = 46$, the job number 9 is identified as being the straddling one. It will start in time point 44 and will finish in 56. The jobs 3, 7, 2 and 4 are assigned to set B. Set A includes $\{1, 5, 6, 8, 10\}$. The jobs in set A and B are ordered according to the v-shaped property, so the following schedule (belonging to the third case of figure 1) is given:

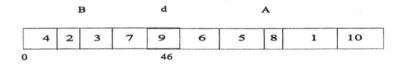

Figure 2: Solution of the example CDDS instance with $f(S) = 1025$

Starting with a randomly chosen permutation, different (local search) operators are thinkable to generate a neighbourhood of the given solution to find new solutions. For instance a tardy job might be shifted from a position j, $j \in |B| + 1, |B| + 2, ..., |B|_{max} + n$ in the permutation to a position k, $k \in 1, 2, ..., |B|$, while the jobs occupying the positions k, k + 1, ..., j - 1 are shifted right by one position etc.

There are several advantages to this problem representation: a) All feasible schedules can be represented. b) Different local search operators are suitable. c) It is at most necessary to interpret the first $|B|_{max} + 1$ positions to unequivocally define the represented schedule. d) Computational results show high efficiency as with little computational effort in 16 of 20 instances (problem-size: 250 jobs) better solutions than those of JAMES 1997 are obtained. Details and comparisons of the metaheuristic approaches are given in FELDMANN/BISKUP 1999. Further is was possible to attain improvements of the CDDS benchmarks - given in http://www. ms.ic.ac.uk/info.html - up to 5% solving altogether 140 instances with sizes of 20, 50, 100, 200, 500 and 1000 jobs.

4 Two-phase representation of CDWS

In contrast to the CDDS the problem of scheduling against a common due window (CDWS) is more recent. Emphasising the results of HALL/POSNER 1991, AZIZOGLU / WEBSTER 1997 state that the CDWS is NP-hard even for the case of an unrestricted common due window. If we suppose job-individual earliness and tardiness penalties and the type of penalty function given by BAKER/SCUDDER 1990, only one approach need be mentioned: in 1997 AZIZOGLU/WEBSTER considered the problem of scheduling around an unrestricted common due window with arbitrary earliness and tardiness penalty rates. They proposed a two-step branch and bound algorithm that can find optimal solutions for small problem instances up to a size of 30 jobs. To the best of our knowledge no procedure for the restrictive CDWS - with respect to this restrictions - exists.

For a brief description of the CDWS, some additional notation is needed:

e := start of the due window
d := end of the due window
E_i := earliness of job i, $E_i := \max\{e - C_i, 0\}$
B := set of jobs scheduled to finish early or in time, $B = \{i | C_i \le e\}$
A := set of jobs scheduled to begin in or after d, $A = \{i | C_i - p_i \ge d\}$
W := set of jobs that start and finish in the due window

The objective of the CDWS equals the objective of the CDDS: a feasible schedule S, which jointly minimizes the sum of earliness and tardiness penalties, has to be found. In this paper the following type of penalty function is stated:

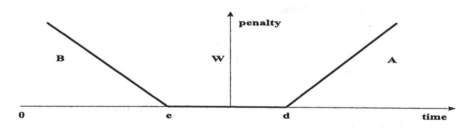

Figure 3: Type of the penalty function due to BAKER/SCUDDER 1990

The properties of optimal solutions for the CDDS must be modified: Property 1 and 2 still hold for the CDWS. Property 3 is extended: if in an optimal schedule the first job does not start in time zero, one job will finish in e or in d. The proof can easily be given by a comparison of the cost reduction effect causes by shifting all jobs to the left or to the right until either one job is finished exactly in e and/or in d or the first job starts in time zero. In other words: leading idle-time can only occur, if one of the jobs finishes in e and/or in d. According to the existence of straddling jobs this property permits: if in an optimal schedule the first job does not start in time zero only one or no straddling job can occur. Two straddling jobs may only occur if the first job starts in time zero. These three properties allow a classification of all optimal solutions of the CDWS in the following seven disjunct cases:

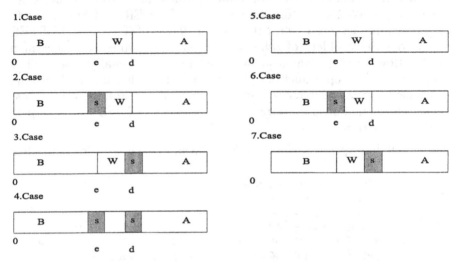

Figure 4: Classification of all optimal solutions of the CDWS

To find an appropriate mapping for these solutions, we use the permutation with $|B|_{max}$ dummy jobs introduced above. Additionally $|W|_{max}$ is calculated, which gives the maximum number of jobs that can be produced completely in the time interval $(d - e)$:

$$\sum_{i=1}^{|W|_{max}} p_i \leq (d - e) \text{ and } \sum_{i=1}^{|W|_{max}+1} p_i > (d - e) \tag{3}$$

The 2-phase procedure of assigning the permutation unequivocally to a schedule can be described as follows:

Phase I:
Step 1: $P_{sum} := 0; i := 1; A := \{1, .., n, .., n + |B|_{max}\}; B := \emptyset; W := \emptyset;$ hold $:=$ false
Step 2: $P_{sum} := P_{sum} + p[i]$
Step 3: **If** $P_{sum} \leq e$ **Then** $B := B \cup [i]; A := A \setminus [i]$
           Else $[i]$ straddles $e; A := A \setminus [i]$; hold $:=$ true   [2; 4]
Step 4: **If** $((i= |B|_{max} + 1)$ **And** $(P_{sum} < e))$
           Then leading idle time: $e - P_{sum}$ occurs; hold $:=$ true   [5;6;7]
      If $((i= |B|_{max} + 1)$ **And** $(P_{sum} = e))$
           Then the last job of set B finishes in e; hold $:=$ true   [1;3]
      If $((i< |B|_{max} + 1)$ **And** $(P_{sum} < e))$

Then i := i +1
Step 5: **If** hold = false **Then Goto** Step 2; **Else Goto** Step 6

Phase II:
Step 6: j := i ; w := 0; hold := false
Step 7: **Repeat**
    j := j +1
    If $p[j] = 0$ **Then** j := j + 1; **Else** $P_{sum} := P_{sum} + p[j]$; w := w + 1
    If $((w < |W|_{max})$ **And** $(P_{sum} < d))$ **Then** $W := W \cup [j]; A := A\setminus [j]$
    If $((w < |W|_{max})$ **And** $(P_{sum} = d))$
        Then $[j]$ finishes in d; $W := W \cup [j]$; $A := A\setminus [j]$; hold := true   [2;1;5]
    If $((w < |W|_{max})$ **And** $(P_{sum} > d))$
        Then $[j]$ straddles d; $A := A\setminus [j]$; hold := true   [4;3;7]
    If $((w = |W|_{max})$ **And** $(P_{sum} = d))$
        Then $[j]$ finishes in d; $W := W \cup [j]$; $A := A\setminus [j]$; hold := true   [2;1;5]
    If $((w = |W|_{max})$ **And** $(P_{sum} > d))$
        Then $[j]$ straddles d; $A := A\setminus [j]$; hold := true   [7]
    If $((w = |W|_{max})$ **And** $(P_{sum} < d))$
        Then $[|B|_{max} + 1]$ straddles e; $[j]$ finishes in d;
        $W := W \cup [j]$; $A := A\setminus [j]$; $A := A\setminus[|B|_{max} + 1]$; hold := true   [6]
    Until (hold = true)
Step 8: Jobs in set A and B are ordered according the v-shaped property; **End**

Interpretation procedure for CDWS solutions

The numbers in squared brackets arranged in the left part of the interpretation procedure denote the seven cases given in figure 4. Phase I
preselects three different groups of cases: either the represented solution
is upon [2;4] or [1;3] or [5;6;7]. The purpose is to decide which jobs belong to set B, tag the job that straddles e (if one exists) and identify
leading idle-time. The goal of phase II is to classify the jobs belonging
to set W and to identify the job straddling d (if one exists). Note that
in phase II dummy jobs are passed over, as it is not reasonable to insert
idle-time in the common due window. The above mentioned advantages
of the representation with dummies still hold for the CDWS.

5 Conclusion

Important properties of optimal solutions of the CDDS and the CDWS
permit a classification of all potential optimal solutions and the development of their appropriate mapping – by a representation with dummy
jobs – that overcomes the underlying weakness of already existing approaches.

References

AZIZOGLU, M. and WEBSTER, S. (1997): Scheduling about an unrestricted common due window with arbitrary earliness/tardiness penalty
rates. IIE Transactions, 29, 1001-1006.

BAKER, K.R. and SCUDDER, G.D. (1989): On the assignment of optimal due dates. Journal of the Operational Research Society, 40, 93-95.

BAKER, K. R. and SCUDDER, G. D. (1990): Sequencing with earliness and tardiness penalties: a review. Operations Research, 38, 22-36.

BISKUP, D. and FELDMANN, M. (2000): Benchmarks for scheduling on a single-machine against restrictive and unrestrictive common due dates. To appear in Computers & OR.

CHENG, T.C.E. and KAHLBACHER, H.G. (1991): A proof for the longest-job-first policy in one-machine scheduling. Naval Research Logistics, 38, 715-720.

FELDMANN, M. and BISKUP, D. (1999): Single-machine scheduling for minimizing earliness and tardiness penalties by meta-heuristic approaches. To appear in Applied Intelligence.

FELDMANN, M. (2000): A Development framework for Nature Analogic Heuristics. In: Gaul, W. and Decker, R. (eds.) Classification and Information Processing at the turn of the Millenium, Springer, Heidelberg, 192-200.

HALL, N.G. and POSNER, M.E. (1991): Earliness-tardiness scheduling problems, I: Weighted deviation of completion times about a common due date. Operations Research, 39, 836-846.

HOOGEVEEN J. A. and VAN DE VELDE, S. L. (1991): Scheduling around a small common due date. European Journal of Operational Research, 55, 237-242.

JAMES, R.J.W. (1997): Using tabu search to solve the common due date early/tardy machine scheduling problem. Computers & OR, 24, 199-208.

JAMES, R.J.W. (1999): personal communication.

KANET, J.J. (1981): Minimizing the average deviation of job completion times about a common due date. Naval Research Logistics Quarterly, 28, 643-651.

KRÄMER, F.-J. and LEE, C.-Y. (1993): Common Due-Window Scheduling. Production and Operations Management, 2, 262-275. LEE C.-Y. and S. J. KIM (1995): Parallel genetic algorithms for the earliness-tardiness job scheduling problem with general penalty weights. Computers & Industrial Engineering, 28, 231-243.

Currency Derivatives in German Non-financials: Empirical Evidence on Theoretical Approaches

D. Mahayni[1]

Institut für Gesellschafts- und Wirtschaftswissenschaften,
Universität Bonn, D-53113 Bonn, Germany

Abstract: According to the wellknown results of Modigliani and Miller, corporate risk management is redundant in perfect capital markets. By constructing models of a more realistic setting of imperfectness using different information and transaction costs, such as those related to agency and insolvency problems, taxes and exposure, several authors justify the use of derivative instruments on the corporate level. Based on annual reports of German public non-financial corporations 1998, simple proxies for measuring the connection of theory and the use of currency derivatives are established and tested. In a line with evidence from US corporations reported by e.g. Géczy et al. (1997), transaction cost-related arguments are quite important, although company size is *not* a determinant of the decision whether to use currency derivatives or not. Also, leverage and growth options show some significance by hinting at a benefiting use of derivatives to reduce underinvestment problems.

1 Introduction

The use of derivatives has continued its rapid growth during the past years as can be seen by the increase in the notional amount of exchange-traded derivatives to more than 387 trillion US-$ in 1998. The significant rise in interest in the corporate application of derivatives is largely due to the growing importance of small and medium-sized shareholders, the internationalization of capital markets as well as a number of testily discussed corporate failures blaming derivatives. As a consequence of this development, the quality and quantity of derivatives disclosure in annual German business reports has also risen in recent years, even without sound legal regulation. Although reporting practices are still far from satisfactory, they enable a basic classification of a sample of enterprises into users vs. non-users. They even allow a subsample to be taken by which to investigate more closely existing levels of derivatives use. In the following sections, an attempt is made to identify patterns of currency derivatives use and company characteristics and, even more importantly, to find empirical evidence on the basis of theoretical justifications.

---

[1]The author would like to thank Antje Dudenhausen for valuable discussions and Anne Ruston for English language comments.

2 Theoretical foundations and measurement

The remainder of this section briefly deals with the principal arguments supporting the use of derivatives in an imperfect market setting and presents a simple proxy for the respective strand of justification, based on German accounting standards.

2.1 Financial agency costs

Debt financing is more expensive than sole equity provision. To some extent this is due to information asymmetries between different parties involved in the decision-making process, e.g. shareholders, bondholders and management. Owner managers who are basically risk neutral will act with risk aversion because of the privileged claims of debtholders. This leads to disadvantageous consequences that differ from those resulting from a first best solution. In the context of the asset substitution problem (Jensen, Meckling (1976)) riskier projects will be carried out while in the underinvestment problem (Myers (1977)), projects with a positive net present value will not be executed. Derivatives can be favorably used by lowering the incentive to counteract an optimal decision (cp. e.g. Breuer (1997)). With growing debt more importance is attached to both problems, expressed by leverage (LEV) as the percentage of debt on all liabilities. The asset substitution problem becomes more relevant the higher the probability of financial distress, because the payoffs for the owner manager will less likely be positive. Thus, an insolvency proxy (INS) as the ratio of assets to equity and long-term debt is created to approximate the solidity of the financial (time) structure of assets and liabilities. It increases with the probability of financial distress and is consequently positively related to derivatives use. Underinvestment situations intensify with the availability of potentially valuable projects. The larger the set of growth opportunities, the larger the potential agency conflicts and the merit of derivatives. Growth options (GRO) are quantified in a simplified Tobin's q measure.[2] Finally, Froot et. al. (1993) show the potentially benefiting effect of derivatives to smooth internal cash flows. The "interest" (INT) paid on debt, calculated as the total interest expense divided by total debt, serves as a proxy for companies facing higher costs of external financing. As a substitute for the coordination of cash flows, a high level of liquidity can make hedging superfluous. Liquidity (LIQ) is measured as the sum of cash and marketable securities.

---

[2] As market capitalization plus book value of debt divided by book value of assets. This number tends to be too large compared to the interpretation of Tobins q due to German accounting rules. However, the number is not interpreted in absolute terms.

2.2 "Economic" agency problems

Conflicts that arise from principal-agent problems with management acting on its own behalf can be attributed to compensation and reputation causes if risk aversion of the management is assumed. Arguments with regard to **compensation** have a bearing on the wealth position of management. Managers as a rule are poorly diversified due to the fact that all their human capital is invested in one company. Therefore they tend to smooth the volatility of cash flows. The higher their stake in the company measured as quota of management shares on all shares (MGT), the higher their level of derivatives use. For reasons of their comparatively superior qualification, good managers can utilize derivatives to suppress price risks such as the currency risk to show their good performance concerning core business risks, thereby building **reputation** (Breeden, Viswanathan (1998)). As good management is supposed to be more successful in terms of corporate earnings, earnings per share (EPS) are used as a proxy for management quality.

2.3 Financial distress

A company faces a rise in expected costs of financial distress with increasing probability of insolvency. Such costs originate from direct costs incurred by insolvency settlements as well as from indirect costs due to the deterioration of stakeholder relationships. Hedging lowers the probability of insolvency, thus reducing expected costs of financial distress. As a simple proxy for the probability of insolvency, the above sketched INS is used. An application of LIQ and LEV, INT could also be possible in this context as a low level of liquidity and high debt obligations make insolvency more likely. Moreover, a high "cost of capital" INT points to a riskier undertaking.

2.4 Tax arguments

Corporations facing a convex tax schedule can profit by a lower expected tax payment for subsequent tax periods by volatility reduction of the tax basis (Smith, Stulz (1984)). In Germany, the corporate income tax rate is constant with different rates for retained earnings and distributed dividends. In this linear (direct) tax schedule, an indirect progression is induced by several effects on the tax assessment basis, e.g. investment credits, loss carry forwards and other tax credits. The average tax rate (TAX), calculated as taxes on income divided by profit before taxes on income, serves as proxy for the progression of the tax tariff. The lower the average tax rate, the higher the progression, the higher the potential benefit of derivatives use.

2.5   Transaction costs

Economies of scale and scope in implementation and maintenance of a risk management program as well as market access and transaction costs increase with established respectively large companies, lowering the hurdle to use (currency) derivatives. Company size (SIZ) is measured by the sum of market capitalization plus the book value of debt. The same line of argument might hold when not the corporate size but the size of exposure, approximated by the quota of foreign sales to total sales (EXP), is the underlying influence. Additionally, an individual hedging of exposure by investors might be impossible or undesirable since the complexity of the exposure position is increasingly difficult to communicate or for reasons of competition not disclosed (DeMarzo, Duffie (1991)).

3   Descriptive statistics

3.1   Sample and derivatives use

Starting point of the sample are the annual reports of enterprises of the German stock indices DAX100 and SDAX for the fiscal year ending in 1998. These indices comprise the 200 largest German corporations principally selected by market capitalization and liquidity characteristics. Added were 83 firms in the German start-up market segment "Neuer Markt" per June 1999, totaling 283. If banks, insurers and other financials as well as companies consolidated in others also included in the sample are deducted, the number reduces to 213 approximately evenly spread among the 3 market segments. 111 make an explicit statement concerning derivatives decisions, 81 % of them in the DAX segments. Indirect information can be drawn from qualitative statements in the annual reports of the remaining companies. This enlarges the sample to 161 elements. Due to their initial public offering in 1999, 23 companies cannot make available consistent financial data for the independent variables. This leads to a final reduction to 138. While 70 % do make use of currency derivatives for hedging purposes, 30 % do not.[3] Again, the major fraction of users, i.e. 78 %, stems from the two size segments. Of the 97 users, 59 quantify the notional amount of their currency derivatives.

---

[3]It is assumed that currency derivatives are solely used for hedging purposes and not for speculation. Evidence for this assumption is the explicit exclusion of speculation (in a broad definition) in most annual reports describing the aims of derivatives usage. Apart from this observation, the majority of enterprises speculating is most likely not to give any information at all, and automatically excluded here.

Industry	DAX100	SDAX	NEMAX	total	(of 138)
Automotive	5/5	0/1	0/1	5/7	5,1%
Raw materials	3/3	2/2	0/0	5/5	3,6%
Chemistry	4/4	1/1	0/0	5/5	3,6%
Construction	5/6	2/7	0/1	7/14	10,1%
Consumer goods	6/6	3/4	0/0	9/10	7,3%
Food	1/2	0/2	0/0	1/4	2,9%
Industrial	2/2	2/3	0/0	4/5	3,6%
Engineering	13/13	2/2	0/1	15/16	11,6%
Media	0/1	0/0	3/4	3/5	3,6%
Pharmaceutical	9/10	1/4	0/1	10/15	10,9%
Wholesale	4/7	9/10	0/0	13/17	12,3%
Software	1/1	0/0	4/13	5/14	10,1%
Technology	4/4	3/3	3/6	10/13	9,4%
Telecommunication	1/1	0/0	1/4	2/4	2,9%
Transportation	2/2	0/0	0/2	2/2	1,5%
Utilities	1/2	0/0	0/2	1/2	1,5%
total	61/69	25/39	11/30	97/138	100%

Table 1: Derivatives usage by industries and market segments

Currency derivatives are particularly used by engineering and consumer goods companies, industries rather typical for international trade, whereas the software and food business are more nationally orientated. Regarding the market segments, 88% in the DAX, 64% in the SDAX and only 37% in the Neuer Markt use currency derivatives. This may indicate a strong influence of enterprise size.

3.2 Firm characteristics

The following table provides descriptive statistics for the independent variables,[4] i.e. the company characteristics.[5]

proxy	notation	mean	st.dev.	median	minimum	maximum
LEV	%	60,419	17,356	64,526	11,870	95,369
GRO		2,684	3,318	1,419	0,832	20,134
INT	%	2,962	1,973	2,514	0,038	15,385
LIQ	Mio DM	14,814	16,536	8,888	0,019	85,955
MGT	%	30,385	33,019	12,4	0	100
EPS	DM/share	3,235	3,005	2,825	-2,7	18,3
TAX	%	33,201	18,012	38,326	0	69,388
INS		0,868	0,626	0,750	0,005	4,784
SIZ	Mio DM	16205	45743	1828,730	46,99	369330
EXP	%	39,341	31,255	41,555	0	98,537

Table 2: Descriptive statistics of firm characteristics

[4]Under consideration of data mining problems, some substitutive and additional variables have been investigated. However, results cannot be displayed here for the sake of space. In general, the central results are quite robust to different specifications.

[5]MGT can be 100 % because a few companies publicly trade only preferred stock.

338

Using a partial correlation analysis to correct the potential bias of company size (results differ especially with respect to LEV and EPS), the Spearman correlation coefficients of the independent variables are well below $|0,5|$, except for $\rho_{INS-LIQ} = -0,55$ and $\rho_{INS-LEV} = 0,57$, hinting at the quality of the insolvency measure INS.

4 Analysis

4.1 Univariate test: users vs. non-users

When mean values are compared in the subsamples of users vs. non-users, statistically significant[6] differences in the presumed direction are found for the transaction arguments EXP and SIZ, the agency-related influence of outside capital LEV and the hedging substitute LIQ which also may represent insolveny reasons, and finally management quality orientated EPS. Regarding our hypothesis, GRO and MGT signal statistical ambiguities induced by the only modest use of currency derivatives in the Neuer Markt featuring both high growth options and management stakeholdings.

variable	notation	user (N = 97)	non-user (N = 41)	hypothesis ☺≙ correct etc.	level of significance
LEV	%	63,76	52,51	$U > NU$ ☺	***
GRO		2,49	3,14	$U > NU$ ☺	***
INT	%	2,74	3,48	$U > NU$	
LIQ	Mio DM	12,71	19,8	$U < NU$ ☺	*
MGT	%	25,41	42,17	$U < NU$ ☺	***
TAX	%	34,09	31,1	$U < NU$	
EPS	DM/share	3,63	2,3	$U > NU$ ☺	***
INS		0,83	0,96	$U < NU$	
SIZ	Mio DM	22418	1508	$U > NU$ ☺	***
EXP	%	51,38	10,86	$U > NU$ ☺	***

Table 3: Mean comparison of currency derivative users vs. non-users

4.2 Multivariate analysis: Probit and Tobit

Coefficients are interpreted only with regard to their respective sign and statistical significance as in this context only the relative importance of the underlying theories is of interest and not the absolute influence on the currency derivative decision. The Probit estimates inform about the influence of the proxies on the probability of using currency derivatives or not, whereas the Tobit estimates contain additional information, that is the *book value* of derivatives on date of balance. Due to its higher information content, the latter is in general preferable. However, the

---

[6]Level of significance for *** = 0, 01, ** = 0, 05 and * = 0, 1, respectively. Results are similar in a t-test and a non-parametric test.

former deals with 38 more cases thus making the results more reliable. Testing the Probit model with the 100 observations of the Tobit sample does not change the results of the larger Probit sample. For the same reason, the following interpretation contains the Probit results as an influence on the decision of whether to use currency derivatives or not. The Tobit results differ insofar as they are influenced by the volume of currency derivatives used.[7] The following table shows the estimations of the β-coefficients for the Probit and Tobit models.[8]

Var.	Probit (N = 138) β-coeff.	sign. (z-test)	Tobit (N = 100) β-coeff.	sign. (t-test)	Probit	Tobit
LEV	0,0338	0,036	130,99	0,041	☺**	☺**
GRO	0,2574	0,013	-467,89	0,17	☺**	
INT	-0,1248	0,11	-411,19	0,261		
LIQ	-0,0268	0,061	-82,16	0,174	☺**	
MGT	-0,0034	0,515	2,403	0,91		
EPS	0,0818	0,359	587,22	0,038		☺**
TAX	0,0059	0,529	-34,53	0,35		
INS	-0,8151	0,02	-9056,9	0,000	☺**	☺***
SIZ	0,000036	0,491	0,1149	0,000		☺***
EXP	0,0311	0,000	55,43	0,011	☺***	☺**
const	-1,973	0,129	-3644,9	0,454		

Table 4: Probit and Tobit results for currency derivatives usage

5   Conclusions

1. The **transaction** cost hypothesis is statistically significant in both models. As a refinement of earlier studies producing the same result in either binary models or other restricted regression approaches, enterprise size is *not* a determinant of the utilization, *but* the volume decision for currency derivatives. This result is intuitively appealing since hardly any barriers exist preventing the purchase of derivative instruments, i.e. even the smallest company is able to take a position in the currency derivative markets. However, economies of scale and scope grow with the increase in company size, thus increasing the amount of derivatives used, e.g. small companies still find it difficult to access the use of financially engineered products. That foreign currency derivatives usage is a consequence of "exposure" does not seem remarkable. Still, this result shows foreign sales that underlie this measure to play a dominant role in conducting a risk management program, hinting primarily at hedging transaction exposure and not economic or translation exposure.[9]

---

[7]For an application of other limited dependent regression models the sample seems to be too small.

[8]The ancillary term in the Tobit estimate is not reported here. The *prob* $> \chi^2$ is in both models 0,0000. The Probit model classifies 83,3% of cases correctly.

[9]This view is supported by explicit remarks in most annual reports.

2. The explanation based on **insolvency costs** is statistically significant in *opposite* direction to the hypothesis, i.e. the "term structure" of assets and liabilities is indicating a more stable manner of financing as a characteristic of a hedging enterprise. This observation is insofar ambiguous as two other proxies implying a higher probability of insolvency, i.e. leverage and liquidity, are in a line with the predictions.

3. Leverage as a proxy for all **financial agency problems** stemming from outside capital represents in both models a statistically significant influence as it implies suppositions made in 2.1.[10] For the second influence (INS) approximating the asset substitution problem, statements similar to those in the above paragraph apply. Companies possessing larger growth options are more likely to use currency derivatives. This fact together with LEV alludes to the underinvestment hypothesis although an inconsistence is observable in the univariate analysis. Evidence for the use of currency derivatives in the context of the coordination problem is rather weak. However, the statistically significant negative association of derivatives with liquidity could explain a missing connection owing to the substitutive character of liquidity for investment purposes.[11]

4. The indications for **economic agency problems** as a motivation are quite weak. The only hint stems from the significant relevance of earnings per share in the Tobit model. A cautious interpretation is that those motives are not the *predominant* factors for using currency derivatives. However, they allow good managers, once the decision to use derivatives is determined by other factors such as exposure or leverage, to reveal their superior performance by using higher volumes of hedging instruments. The significant opposite sign of MGT in the univariate analysis might hint at a speculative use of derivatives by management.

5. No evidence for the validity of **tax**-caused motives can be identified.[12]

With the steadily increasing quality of derivatives disclosure in the annual reports of German non-financials, further research will be able not only to broaden the sample, but also to conduct intertemporal studies. This is important for making statements concerning the stability of the results

---

[10]Derivatives might also have an influence on capital structure as they allow under certain tax and debt conditions a higher leverage and reduced tax payment. Here we observe a higher leverage, but no systematic lower average tax rate.

[11]This might also explain the relatively small use of derivatives in the Neuer Markt. However, the volume decision should be of relevance in this case.

[12]This is confirmed by the survey results of Gebhardt, Ruß (1999).

over time and will, in addition, provide reliable info concerning the effect of derivatives on corporate cash flow volatility. This has not been possible in this study. Moreover, an exact separation of participation and volume decision will leave ample scope for further investigation, in particular for evidence concerning non-US companies.

References

BREEDEN, D. and VISWANATHAN, S.(1998): Why Do Firms Hedge? An Asymmetric Information Model. Working Paper, Duke University.

BREUER, W. (1997): Unternehmerische Investitions- und Finanzierungsentscheidungen bei Verfügbarkeit von Devisenforwardgeschäften. *Zeitschrift für betriebswirtschaftliche Forschung, 49, Sonderheft 38, 191–225.*

DeMARZO, P. M. and DUFFIE, D. (1991): Corporate Financial Hedging with Proprietary Information. *Journal of Economic Theory, 53, 261–286.*

FROOT, K. A., SCHARFSTEIN, D. S. and STEIN, J. C. (1993): Risk Management: Coordinating Corporate Investment and Financing Policies. *Journal of Finance, 48, 1629–1658.*

GEBHARDT, G. and RUß, O. (1999): Einsatz von derivativen Finanzinstrumenten im Risikomanagement deutscher Industrieunternehmen. *Zeitschrift für betriebswirtschaftliche Forschung, 51, Sonderheft 41, 23–83.*

GECZY, C., MINTON, B. A. and SCHRAND, C. M. (1997): Why Firms use Currency Derivatives. *Journal of Finance, 52, 1323–1354.*

JENSEN, M. C. and MECKLING, W. H. (1976): Theory of the Firm: Managerial Behavior, Agency Costs and Ownership Structure. *Journal of Financial Economics, 3, 305–360.*

MYERS, M. C. (1977): The Determinants of Corporate Borrowing. *Journal of Financial Economics, 5, 147–175.*

SMITH, C. W. Jr. and STULZ, R. (1985): The Determinants of Firms' Hedging Policies. *Journal of Financial and Quantitative Analysis, 20, 391–405.*

Data Visualization and Preparation by Separating Sales Force Data

Matthias Meyer

Seminar für Empirische Forschung und Quantitative Unternehmensplanung,
Ludwig-Maximilians-Universität München, D-80539 München, Germany

Abstract: This article presents the so called "separation" as a method for the preparation and visualization of customer data. The suitability and potential of this method is shown by an example of the pharmaceutical industry.

1 Introduction and Data Description

Many firms, such as pharmaceutical companies, are deeply dependent on their sales forces to inform consumers (here: physicians) about their products.

There are about 65.000 physicians (practitioners, internists) in Germany who are visited by sales representatives. Typically, each pharmaceutical company has about 150-300 sales representatives, so that each of them pays visits to 200-600 physicians in a defined district.

Usually the salary of the sales representatives has a fixed and a variable portion where the amount of the variable portion depends on the achieved market share or the changes of the market share in the sales representatives' district.

Besides visiting the physicians, sales representatives have the possibility to invite them to workshops and conferences. Theoretically these marketing activities can be used and combined arbitrarily for all physicians. It should be noticed that the time of each sales representative is restricted and, in addition, sales force activities are relative expensive. For those reasons sales representatives cannot pay several visits to all physicians in their districts. Generally, they have two possibilities to influence the market share in their districts (cf. Meyer 2000):

1. Customer classification and identification of target customers in order to optimize the effects of marketing activities.

2. Estimation of response functions in order to identify effective (combinations of) marketing activities.

Both alternatives complement one another, since specific combinations of marketing activities for target groups can be determined. However, the main problem is the identification of suitable (combinations of) activities.

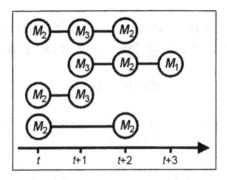

Figure 1: Possible contact combinations

In the following contact data for 50.000 physicians (in sum 190.000 visits during one year) is examined. The visits were paid to the physicians by 150 sales representatives of a pharmaceutical company.

2 Data Preparation by Separating Data

2.1 Some Notes on the Data

In detail we have information about the sum of visits per physician per quarter but we do not know the distribution of the visits within a quarter.

A first analysis of the data showed that only half of the physicians were visited. One third of those physicians got exactly one visit per quarter, another third got two visits per quarter and the last third got three and more than three visits per quarter. That is why we created three new variables : M_1 = one visit , M_2 = two visits, M_3 =three and more than three visits). It can be assumed that the costs and the effects of one visit, two visits and three visits per quarter are quite different. For this reason M_1, M_2 and M_3 can be seen as three different marketing activities which can be arbitrarily combinated over different quarters but not within a quarter.

Then the problem was to find the combinations which have an influence on the market share or sales of the product. Figure 1 shows some of all possible combinations of marketing activities (cf. Meyer 1999).

2.2 Idea of Separating Data

The evaluation of the effects of marketing activities is typically done by using market response functions. In general those functions contain special terms for modelling interactions between different marketing activities. For many different marketing activities this results in a large number of possible interaction terms. This led us to the idea of identifying frequent and relevant combinations of marketing activities that should be represented by interaction terms. In order to identify these combinations, we developed the so called "separation" of the contact information (Meyer 1998, Meyer 1999).

There are two ways to identify frequent combinations:

1. The basic idea is to generate every theoretical possible combination and to determine its frequency.

2. The second idea is to determine the number of individuals with the same contact combination. In contrast to the first possibility we take a look at the combination of marketing activities of each observation and determine if the combination is already known. If not we define a new counter for this combination, in the other case we increase the corresponding counter by 1.

Both alternatives can be optimized by reducing the number of scans through the database. In general the second alternative needs considerable less scans than the first way.

2.3 Differences between Separating Data and Sequence Mining

In this section we describe the type of problem concerning sequence mining in order to show similarities and differences to the given problem.

The problem of sequence mining is to discover all sequential patterns with a user-defined minimum support in a database of sequences (Agrawal/ Srikant 1995). Firstly, Srikant / Agrawal generalized the problem by adding time constraints in order to specify a minimum and/or maximum time period between adjacent elements in a pattern. Secondly, they relaxed the restriction that the items in an element of a sequential pattern must come from the same transaction by allowing user-specified time windows (Srikant/Agrawal 1996). Thirdly, they introduced so called taxonomies which are less important for our problem.

Different researchers developed algorithms for the problem of sequence mining which can be divided into generate-and-test-algorithms and structure-based-algorithms:

1. Generate-and-test-algorithms, e.g. AprioriAll, GSP (Generalized Sequential Patterns) (cf. Agrawal/Srikant 1995, Srikant/Agrawal 1996)

2. Structure-based-algorithms, e.g. SPADE (SPADE=Sequential Pattern Discovery Using Equivalence Classes, cf. Zaki 2000), WAP-mine-algorithm (WAP=Web Access Pattern, cf. Pei/Han et al. 2000)

Each algorithm has been developed and succesfully tested for special purposes (Joshi/Karypis et al. 1999). In the past, the improvement of the efficiency of algorithms had the highest priority. Especially the researchers were looking for efficient procedures to generate these patterns. This is where our type of problem differs from the problem of sequence mining. For our type of problem we have the following assumptions and simplifications:

1. The marketing activities take place in a fixed period of time.

2. We do not use time windows.

3. We have a maximum of different marketing activities within a quarter, i.e. in contrast to the analysis of market basket data or web access data we have a limited number of theoretical possible combinations.

It can be stated that the separation is adaquate for our type of problem. Compared with sequence mining algorithms the main purpose of the separation is to identify frequent combinations of a limited number of activities within a fixed period of time.

3 Visualization of Separated Data

In order to simplify the identification of frequent combinations, a special visualization tool was developed. It allows to figure the separated combinations by graphical objects. As shown in Figure 2, every marketing activity corresponds to a colored rectangle. Several contacts over the time then form a sequence of rectangles (Figure 2). The height of the rectangles bases on the amount of individuals with the corresponding combination. In Figure 3, the labeled combination has a relatively high percentage/share. In addition to contact and sales data, data describing e.g. age and gender of physicians should be taken into account. The present example only distinguishes whether a physician belongs to the target group (=1) or not (=0). This additional information is shown by the right boxes of Figure 4. The left boxes represent the share of physicians in the target group within the corresponding contact combination. The right boxes show the share of all physicians of the target group in that combination.

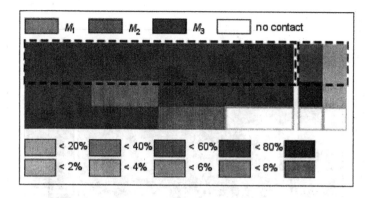

Figure 2: Visualization of contact combinations

By separating sales force contact data of a pharmaceutical firm we obtained useful insights (cf. Meyer 1999, Meyer 2000). In detail we examined contact data from 150 sales representatives over a period of four quarters. In addition we examined the product's sales data for each of the districts.

Figure 3 shows the separated contact data and the sales data (time series of the market shares) for one district. The sales representative visited about half of the 262 physicians in his district. A major part of the physicians was paid three and more than three visits per quarter. On another part of physicians the activities were increased. During the examined time period the market share increased clearly. Compared with other districts, this sales representative works very successfully. We suppose that the concentration on physicians of the target group was another reason for this success. Of course such statements always have to be seen in relation to the products and activities of competitors. Therefore, additional statistical analyses are required.

But we can conclude, that separating the data and visualization of the separated data leads to useful insights.

4 Conclusion

In this article we presented the so called "separation" as a new method for data preparation which especially allows deeper insights into the effects of marketing activities. In order to show the usefulness of the method we described an example of the pharmaceutical industry. By separating sales force data interesting hypotheses about the effects of different and combined contacts were generated.

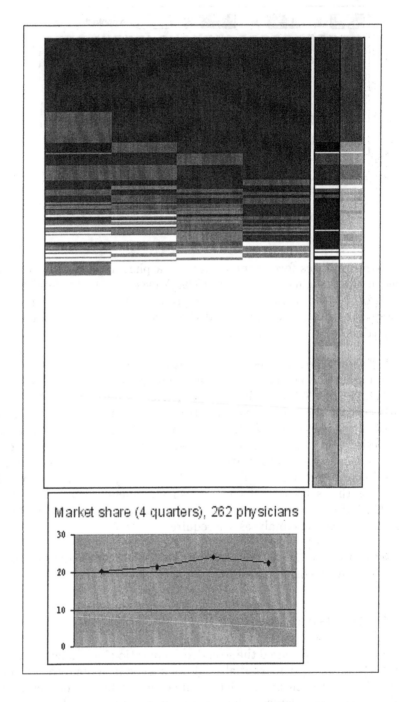

Figure 3: Visualization of contact combinations

References

AGRAWAL, R. and SRIKANT, R. (1995): Mining Sequential Patterns, in Proc. of the Int'l Conference on Data Engineering (ICDE), Taipei, Taiwan, March 1995.

JOSHI, M., KARYPIS, G. and KUMAR, V. (1999): A Universal Formulation of Sequential Patterns. Technical Report No. 99-21, University of Minnesota, Minneapolis.

MEYER, M. (1998): Ermittlung von Marktreaktionsfunktionen auf regionaler Ebene – Grundlagen und empirische Ergebnisse, in Kischka, Lorenz, Derigs, Domschke, Kleinschmidt, Möhring (eds.): Operations Research Proceedings 1997, Springer, Berlin.

MEYER, M. (1999): Regionale Marketingbudgetierung – Ansätze zur Entscheidungsunterstützung. DUV, Wiesbaden.

MEYER, M. (2000): Visualisierung und Wirkungsmessung im Außendienst- und Direktmarketing mit separierten Daten, will appear in Hippner, Küsters, Meyer, Wilde (eds.): Handbuch Data Mining im Marketing 2000, Vieweg/Gabler, Braunschweig/Wiesbaden.

PEI, J., HAN, J., MORTAZAVI-ASL, B. and ZHU, H. (2000): Mining Access Patterns Efficiently from Web Logs, in Proc. Pacific-Asia Conference on Knowledge Discovery and Data Mining (PAKDD'00).

SRIKANT, R. and AGRAWAL, R. (1996): Mining Sequential Patterns: Generalizations and Performance Improvements, in Proc. of the Fifth Int'l Conference on Extending Database Technology (EDBT), Avignon, France.

ZAKI, M.J. (2000): SPADE: An Efficient Algorithm for Mining Frequent Sequences. *Machine Learning, 0, 1-31*.

Fuzzy Scenario Evaluation

M. Missler-Behr

Institut für Statistik und Mathematische Wirtschaftstheorie
Universität Augsburg, D-86135 Augsburg, Germany

Abstract: The task of scenario analysis is to choose selectively some scenarios of the total scenario space, which are representative, consistent and without contradictions, stable and quite different to each other. Because the total scenario space contains often several million elements, a systematic approach is needed. In this paper a new approach is described, which uses fuzzy rule bases to evaluate the desired attributes of scenarios. The rule bases are stated in a general manner, therefore they can be used for every scenario analysis independent of the examined topic. The specific reference to the actual topic is drawn by constructing empirical membership functions out of the specific data.

1 Scenario Analysis

Scenario analysis is an instrument of strategic controlling, which has the task to develop possible, quite suitable pictures of the future called scenarios. Not only the pictures themselves but the logical process of the scenarios from today to a future timepoint are the main aspects in scenario analysis. An advantage of this method in contrast to other wellknown forecasting methods is the possibility to use quantitative and qualitative variables to enlighten the future. Not to predict the future but to think of possible, different futures in advance is the main task of scenario analysis (Gausemeier et al. (1995)).

The scenario process can roughly be divided in five steps: (1) The investigated subject is exactly defined, delimitated and analysed. (2) The most important environmental areas and their critical key items are determined. (3) The critical key items are analysed and their possible future developments are described. (4) All possible feature combinations of the complete set of key items are created. They constitute the total scenario space. We are looking now for few, different, consistent, stable and representative scenarios out of the total scenario space. (5) The selected scenarios are integrated in strategic planning. A detailed description of scenario analysis can be found in Gausemeier et. al. (1995) or von Reibnitz (1991).

2 Evaluation Criterions

Most time the evaluation criterions used to direct the scenario selection are orientated on the special selection method but not on the problem itself. Scenario probabilities or frequencies, consistency, stability or polarity are used as evaluation criterions for example. Evaluation methods are for example equation systems, optimization models or simulations, Branch and Bound-methods, heuristics or methods of cluster analysis. An overview of the different methods and criterions is given by Mißler-Behr (1993). It is characteristic for all methods just to use only one evaluation criterion but not more criterions at the same time.

It seems reasonable to evaluate scenarios by consistency, stability and polarity parallel at the same time. All attributes should have equal weight. A scenario is called consistent if the items of the scenario variables fit well together. No contradictions are in a consistent scenario. A scenario is called stable if the consistency of the scenario does not or just slightly change if only few items in the scenario description change. Stable scenarios are mostly robust and are normally valid for a longer time period. Polarity of two or more scenarios means, that the regarded scenarios are most different.

3 Databasis

As input data we need judgements about the relation of the items of two scenario variables. The pairwise judgements are given as common, subjective consistency estimations. They are ordinal scaled, mostly at a five point scale. A consistency estimation of -2 means, that the regarded scenario items contradict each other strongly. -1 means that the items are slightly contradictory. If the items are independent and neutral, the consistency estimation will be 0. Do they favour each other, the estimation will be +1. If they even cause each other, +2 is the appropriate value for the consistency estimation. If we have m scenario variables we need approximatly m(m-1)/2 consistency estimations.

4 Fuzzy Rule Based Scenario Evaluation

4.1 Main Idea

- Out of the total scenario space we exclude all scenarios which contain at least one strongly contradiction. These scenarios contain at least one consistency estimation of -2. Empirical examinations have shown that these scenarios will not be jugded as consistent. The main aspect of the exclusion is the reduction of the number of scenarios which will be considered in further examinations.

- Consistency, stability and polarity of all remaining scenarios will now be judged. These three attributes seem essential and sufficient to describe representative elements of the total scenario space. Consistency, stability and polarity will be modelled as linguistic symbols (see Zimmermann 1996). First of all we have to clarify how the three qualitative attributes can be measured. The measuring variables are linguistic variables which explain the linguistic symbols. For all linguistic variables we state two terms: low and high. The three attributes of the scenarios can be judged with the help of generally accepted rule bases, underlying the experience of scenario managers. With the help of empirical membership functions we judge the linguistic variables and their terms. The membership functions are constructed using quantiles, which are determined with the help of the measuring variables of all remaining scenarios.

- For the collective, common evaluation of the applicability as center by the linguistic symbols consistency, stability and polarity we use a further rule base.

4.2 Linguistic Variables, Rule Bases And Membership Functions

Figure 1 shows the linguistic variables and symbols as well as the total hierarchy which are used to evaluate the scenarios for their applicability as first or second scenario center.

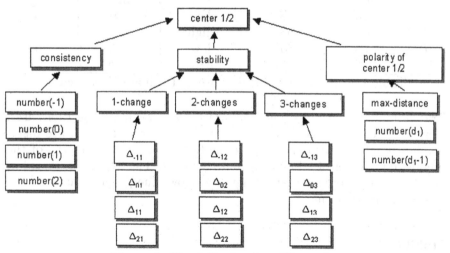

Figure 1: Total Evaluation Hierarchy

The linguistic symbols and variables are explained now:

Consistency

To evaluate consistency we use the frequencies of the values of consistency estimations contained in a scenario. As a result we get four linguistic variables named number(-1), number(0), number(1) and number(2). number(-1) correspondes to the absolute frequency of the consistency estimations with value -1 in the actual scenario. The other variables are explained in an equivalent way. Using this way of evaluation has the advantage, that positive and negative consistency estimations can not be balanced as this is done when using the sum of consistency estimations.

The rule base to evaluate consistency contains 16 elements. Table 1 shows an extract. Rule 2 states that the consistency of a scenario is evaluated high, if the number of strong favouring consistency estimations is high and the numbers of light contradictions, of neutral and light favourable estimations are low. In rule 5 mainly neutral consistency estimations occur. This constellation does not support consistency, therefore consistency will be judged as low. Rule 7 shows in contrary a smooth positive influence. In rule 10 the positive and negative influences compensate each other. Consistency is here not supported. But rule 12 shows a slightly positive influence compared to rule 10. More than two terms for the linguistic variables are not suitable. In that case the rule bases would be extremly enlarged.

No.	number(-1)	number(0)	number(1)	number(2)	consistency
2	low	low	low	high	high
5	low	high	low	low	low
7	low	high	high	low	high
10	high	low	low	high	low
12	high	low	high	high	high

Table 1: Extract of the Rule Base to Evaluate Consistency

Trapezoidal membership functions are used to evaluate the rule bases. Empirical research has shown that we can construct appropriate membership functions with the help of the 0, 0.2, 0.8 and 1-quantils of the linguistic variables of all investigated scenarios. The linguistic terms low and high are complementary. Figure 2 shows the general shape of the membership functions.

Stability

The effect of one, two or three changes in the scenario variables is used to evaluate stability of scenarios. The effects are measured by the number of changes in consistency estimations.

First we are looking at one change. A given scenario is compared to all other scenarios which differ in just one scenario variable. All consistency estimations of the given scenario are compared of those of a changed scenario. The number of changes of each consistency value -1, 0, +1 and

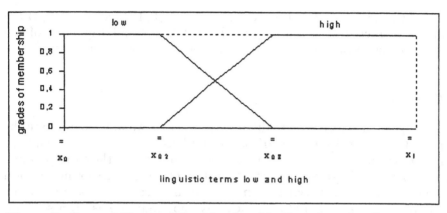

Figure 2: General Shape of the Membership Functions for Consistency Evaluation

+2 are notified. Considering all compared scenarios the maximal number of changes is modelled as linguistic variable for each consistency value: Δ_{j1}. The index j represents the possible consistency values, the index 1 symbolizes one change. The same idea is transfered to the situation with two or three changes in the scenario variables of the compared scenarios. We get equivalent linguistic variables Δ_{j2} and Δ_{j3}. The middle branch of Figure 1 shows the evaluation hierarchy of stability. First the effects of one, two and three changes are evaluated separately. Then these linguistic symbols are used to evaluate total stability.

The rule bases to evaluate one, two or three changes are the same. Each contains 16 rules. Table 2 shows an extract of the rule bases. As soon as three of four linguistic variables are judged high also the corresponding linguistic symbol is judged high. Some rules to evaluate total stability is given in Table 3. If two or three changes are judged high total stability is judged low.

No.	Δ_{-1i}	Δ_{0i}	Δ_{1i}	Δ_{2i}	1-change 2-changes 3-changes
18	low	low	low	high	low
22	low	high	low	high	low
28	high	low	high	high	high

Table 2: Extract of the Rule Bases to Evaluate Stability with One, Two and Three Changes (i=1, 2, 3)

No.	1-change	2-changes	3-changes	stability
66	low	low	high	high
71	high	high	low	low

Table 3: Extract of the Rule Base to Evaluate Total Stability

The 12 membership functions of Δ_{ji} ($j = -1, 0, 1, 2$ and $i = 1, 2, 3$) are also constructed with the help of the 0, 0.2, 0.8 and 1-quantils of the used linguistic variables of all investigated scenarios (see Figure 2).

Polarity

To judge polarity we have to distinguish whether we want to evaluate the polarity of the extreme scenarios, the third scenario or the third and the fourth scenario in common. To describe the polarity of the corresponding scenarios we orientate on the ideal position of these scenarios in the total scenario space. Polarity between two scenarios can be measured by the number of scenario variables which have not equal items. If a scenario is described by m variables, the index to state the distance between to scenarios can have values between 0 and m.

Polarity of the extreme scenarios

The extreme scenarios should have maximal distance. The actual maximal distance of a scenario is measured by the variable max-distance. On the other side the extreme scenarios should not exist of isolated elements, they should represent a whole class of scenarios. This fact can be measured by the frequencies of the theoretically maximal distance (number(d_1)) and the second highest distance (number($d_1 - 1$)).[1] Because the distributions of these two variables can be quite extreme, the membership functions have to be constructed for each scenario analysis seperately. The shape of the membership functions has to reflect the shape of the distributions.

Polarity of the third scenario center

If we are looking for three scenario centers, we first determine the two extreme scenarios as described before and then the third center. The third center has to be placed in the middle of the total scenario space. Therefore the actual maximal distance should be as low as possible and the frequencies of distance values around the median distance should be quite high. Table 4 shows an extract of the rule base to evaluate the polarity for the third center. It contains in total 16 rules. The membership functions are constructed with the help of the 0, 0.7, 0.9 and 1-quantils of the corresponding variables out of all investigated scenarios.

Polarity of the third and fourth scenario center

If we have to determine four scenario centers, we first determine the extreme scenarios and then the third and fourth center together at the

---

[1]The used manner of writing orientates on the style of writing quantils. The theoretically maximal distance is the 1-quantil of the distance values. It is denoted by d_1. The second highest distance value is equal to the theoretically maximal distance minus 1: $d_1 - 1$.

No.	number $(d_{0.5} - 1)$	number $(d_{0.5})$	number $(d_{0.5} + 1)$	max-distance	polarity of center 3
87	low	high	high	low	high
88	low	high	high	high	high
91	high	low	high	low	high
92	high	low	high	high	low

Table 4: Extract of the Rule Base to Evaluate Polarity of the Third Center

same time. The determination of a third center, as described before, is skipped.

The third and fourth center should be placed with equal distances between the extrem scenarios. Therefore the frequencies around the 0.33 and 0.66-quantils of the theoretical possible distance values are used to decribe the ideal positions of these scenarios. Also in this case the actual maximal distance should be as low as possible. The rule base to describe the polarity of the third and fourth center contains 128 rules in total. The membership functions are constructed with the help of the 0, 0.4, 0.6 and 1-quantils of the corresponding variables out of all investigated scenarios.

4.3 Collective Evaluation

For the final collective evaluation the results of evaluating consistency, stability and polarity are analysed at the same time. We need three rule bases to judge the applicability of the scenarios as first or second center, as third center or as third and fourth center. The left and middle branches of Figure 1 stay the same in all three rule bases. Just the right branch differs from case to case. It describes the polarity of the different centers. Therefore all three rule bases contain the same 8 rules. The applicability as a center is only judged high if all three attributes are judged high.

4.4 Operators

As aggregation operator we use the minimum operator. In this way we use a strong evaluation scale because we use the weakest attribute. But this procedure seems reasonable because we have to choose just few scenarios out of a very large set. The implication operator has no influence because all rules have the same weight of one. As accumulation operator we choose the algebraic sum, which means that the results of all rules can influence the final evaluation result.

If two scenarios are evaluated for their applicability as centers then the final selection will be based on a comparison of distances between the highest graded scenarios.

5 Conclusions

In the described fuzzy rule based approach of scenario evaluation the fuzzyness in the data, caused by the ordinal input data itself and the plenty of data, is systematically taken into considerationen and worked out. Generally accepted rule bases are formulated, which can be applied to all subjects treated with scenario analysis on principle. The rule bases are independent of their context. The complete rule bases contain 248 rules in total and can be found in Mißler-Behr (1998). The actual scenario topic itself is refered to by the membership functions, which are empirically constructed. The approach judges the three attributes consistency, stability and polarity equivalently and parallel at the same time. In this way this appoach is superior to the typically used methods of scenario evaluation. Limitations of the number of variables which are used in the scenario analysis do not exist.

References

GAUSEMEIER, J.; FINK, A. and SCHLACKE, O. (1995): Szenario-Management: Planen und Führen mit Szenarien. Hanser, München, Wien

MISSLER-BEHR, M. (1993): Methoden der Szenarioanalyse. DUV, Wiesbaden

MISSLER-BEHR, M. (1998): Merkmalskatalog und komplettes Regelwerk zur Szenariobewertung. Arbeitspapiere zur Mathematischen Wirtschaftsforschung, Nr. 163, Institut für Statistik und Mathematischen Wirtschaftstheorie, Universität Augsburg

REIBNITZ, VON U. (1991): Szenario-Technik: Instrumente für die unternehmerische und persönliche Erfolgsplanung. Gabler, Wiesbaden

ZIMMERMANN, H.-J. (1995): Datenanalyse: Anwendungen von Data-Engine mit Fuzzy Technologien und Neuronalen Netzen. VDI, Düsseldorf

ZIMMERMANN, H.-J. (1996): Fuzzy Set Theory and its Applications. Kluwer, Bosten, Dordrecht, London

Fair Stock Risk Premiums under Firm-specific Price Jumps

B. Nietert

Department of Finance
Passau University, 94030 Passau, Germany

Abstract: A CAPM under firm-specific jumps of only one stock yields a security market plane with (market) factors: risk premium of the market portfolio and risk premium of the correction portfolio against that jumps. Pursuing a variance decomposition based on these results, we will demonstrate that the firm-specific jump of stock j is completely systematic risk. The unsystematic risk component solely stems from "normal" risk.

1 Preliminaries

1.1 Introduction to the problem

Combined jump and diffusion processes are nowadays a widely accepted model of stock prices (see Beinert (1997) and Nietert (1999) for a survey of empirical studies supporting this statement). Therefore, it is not surprising that pricing theory – for option pricing theory see e.g. Merton (1976) and Bates (1991), for the determination of stocks' risk premiums see e.g. Ahn/Thompson (1988) and Aase (1993) – has been concerned with the effects of jumps. A closer look at the literature, however, reveals a hidden contradiction: Merton (1976: 133) regards firm-specific jumps as completely unsystematic risk, whereas Ahn/Thompson (1988: 159) consider them to contain systematic components. Both statements are clearly incompatible.

The resolution of this contradiction draws some theoretical interest but is by no means restricted to theory; it has in addition practical implications: If jumps exert influence on stocks' risk premiums, the "classical" CAPM will send wrong buy and sell signals for stocks. Yet, knowing the correct risk premium is especially valuable in an environment of large price movements. Moreover, the exact nature of firm-specific jump risk has consequences to the correct selection of an option pricing model. In the case of unsystematic jump risk we can rely on Merton (1976), in the case of systematic jump risk, we will have to choose a totally different class of models (e.g. Bates (1991)). Thus, theoretical and practical considerations call for a clarification of the nature of firm–specific jump risk.

To that end, we have to decompose stocks' return variances into their systematic and unsystematic parts. The prerequisite for this is a model of the stocks' returns, that in turn is based on a CAPM under jumps. Surprisingly, this jump CAPM is missing in the literature.

Consequently, it is the objective of our paper to identify the nature of firm-specific jump risk by developing a CAPM under firm–specific jumps and by decomposing stocks' variances into systematic and unsystematic parts.

1.2 Starting point of the analysis

To derive the CAPM, we have to analyze investors' portfolio decisions, aggregate their demand and use the market equilibrium assumption. Since this was partially done by Ahn/Thompson (1988), we can use their results as a starting point to advance their outcome with respect to the CAPM under jumps and a variance decomposition. Therefore, at least the setup of our model does not follow Merton (1976). For, he assumes that the "classical" CAPM still holds in a jump environment and starts his quest for the nature of firm–specific jump risk based on this belief. Yet, according to Jarrow/Rosenfeld (1984), we know that this will only be true if jump risk is unsystematic. Merton's assumption thus directly determines his results.

To illustrate our points and to avoid unnecessary complexities, we will focus on the case where only stock j is subject to firm–specific jumps and "normal" price movements are governed by a geometric Brownian motion. The model's setup can be generalized easily. Thus, the risk premiums under firm-specific jumps of stock j read:

$$\alpha - 1r = -\underbrace{\frac{\overbrace{J_{WW}W(t)}^{A}}{J_W}\Omega \mathbf{w}_M(t)}_{\text{1st term}} \tag{1}$$

$$-\underbrace{\frac{\overbrace{E_t\{\tilde{\varphi}_j J_W[(1+w_{Mj}(t)\tilde{\varphi}_j)W(t),t]\}}^{B_j}}{J_W}\frac{\lambda_j}{KK_j}\Omega \mathbf{H}_j}_{\text{2nd term}}$$

$\alpha - \mathbf{1}r$ $n \times 1$ vector of risk premiums per unit time

$J[W(t), t]$ expected utility of the optimum consumption/portfolio strategy from t to T (indirect utility function)

$W(t)$ wealth in t

$\mathbf{w}_M(t)$ $n \times 1$ vector of portfolio weights

Ω $n \times n$ variance/covariance matrix per unit time

$E_t\{\}$ expectation conditional on information in t

λ_j intensity, that is mean number of jumps per unit time, of stock j's Poisson process

$\tilde{\varphi}_j$ random variable denoting stock j's jump amplitude in t, where: $E_t\{\tilde{\varphi}_j(t)\} \neq 0$

$\begin{pmatrix} 0 \\ 1 \\ 0 \end{pmatrix}$ $n \times 1$ vector with one as jth component and zero as other elements

$$\mathbf{H}_j \equiv \frac{1}{\mathbf{1}^T \Omega^{-1} \begin{pmatrix} 0 \\ 1 \\ 0 \end{pmatrix}} \cdot \Omega^{-1} \begin{pmatrix} 0 \\ 1 \\ 0 \end{pmatrix} = KK_j \Omega^{-1} \begin{pmatrix} 0 \\ 1 \\ 0 \end{pmatrix}$$ correction portfolio against a jump of stock j

With the help of equation (1) we are able to demonstrate that risk premiums under firm–specific jumps are not only dependent on the covariance with the market portfolio like in the "classical" CAPM (1st term), but also on a jump term (2nd term). This is turn means that we have different risk premiums under firm-specific jumps combined with diffusion risk compared to a situation of purely diffusion risk.

There is one problem with equation (1), however. Since it contains investors' unobservable (indirect) utility function, it is not a CAPM. – The CAPM is based on observable market factors only. Therefore, we have to calculate these unknowns to turn the simple risk premium formula into the CAPM.

2   Derivation of the CAPM under firm-specific jumps

To express the unknown indirect utility function through observable market factors, we multiply equation (1) with the market portfolio $\mathbf{w}_M(t)$ and the correction portfolio against stock j's jumps, $\mathbf{H}_j$, and end up with the following equation system:

$$\begin{aligned} E_D^*\{R_M - r\} &\equiv \mathbf{w}_M^T(t)(\alpha - \mathbf{1}r) \\ &= A \cdot \mathbf{w}_M^T(t)\Omega\mathbf{w}_M^T(t) - B_j \cdot \mathbf{w}_M^T(t)\Omega\mathbf{H}_j \end{aligned} \tag{2}$$

and

$$E_D^*\{R_{H_j} - r\} \equiv \mathbf{H}_j^T(t)(\alpha - \mathbf{1}r) \tag{3}$$

$$= A \cdot \mathbf{H}_j^T \Omega \mathbf{w}_M(t) - B_j \cdot \mathbf{H}_j^T \Omega \mathbf{H}_j$$

$E_D^*\{\cdot\}$ per unit time expectation of return's diffusion component
$*$ marks per unit time expressions
R_M return of the market portfolio within period dt
R_{H_j} return of the correction portfolio $\mathbf{H}_j$ within period dt

From this point on, the derivation of the CAPM is just routine business: We have to solve the above equation system with respect to A and B_j, substitute the solution back into the risk premium equation (1) and simplify. Thus, we get – according to the jump CAPM – for the risk premium of the jumping stock j:

$$\alpha_j - r = \frac{\mathrm{var}_D^*(R_{H_j}) \cdot \mathrm{cov}_D^*(R_j, R_M) - \mathrm{cov}_D^*(R_M, R_{H_j}) \cdot \mathrm{cov}_D^*(R_j, R_{H_j})}{\mathrm{var}_D^*(R_M) \cdot \mathrm{var}_D^*(R_{H_j}) - \mathrm{cov}_D^{*2}(R_M, R_{H_j})}$$
$$\cdot E_D^*\{R_M - r\} \tag{4a}$$

$$+ \frac{\mathrm{var}_D^*(R_M) \cdot \mathrm{cov}_D^*(R_j, R_{H_j}) - \mathrm{cov}_D^*(R_M, R_{H_j}) \cdot \mathrm{cov}_D^*(R_j, R_M)}{\mathrm{var}_D^*(R_M) \cdot \mathrm{var}_D^*(R_{H_j}) - \mathrm{cov}_D^{*2}(R_M, R_{H_j})}$$
$$\cdot E_D^*\{R_{H_j} - r\}$$

the risk premiums of all other stocks i:

$$\alpha_i - r = \frac{\mathrm{var}_D^*(R_{H_j}) \cdot \mathrm{cov}_D^*(R_i, R_M)}{\mathrm{var}_D^*(R_M) \cdot \mathrm{var}_D^*(R_{H_j}) - \mathrm{cov}_D^{*2}(R_M, R_{H_j})} \cdot E_D^*\{R_M - r\}$$
$$\tag{4b}$$

$$+ \frac{-\mathrm{cov}_D^*(R_M, R_{H_j}) \cdot \mathrm{cov}_D^*(R_i, R_M)}{\mathrm{var}_D^*(R_M) \cdot \mathrm{var}_D^*(R_{H_j}) - \mathrm{cov}_D^{*2}(R_M, R_{H_j})} \cdot E_D^*\{R_{Hj} - r\}$$

$\mathrm{var}_D^*(\cdot) \equiv \frac{\mathrm{var}_D(\cdot)}{dt}$ variance of return's diffusion component per unit time

$\mathrm{cov}_D^*(\cdot) \equiv \frac{\mathrm{cov}_D(\cdot)}{dt}$ covariance between the diffusion components of two returns per unit time

Equation (4) clarifies that all stocks' risk premiums are a function of two (market) factors: the risk premium of the market portfolio and the risk premium of the correction portfolio against jumps of stock j. In the case of stock j subject to jumps only we therefore have a security market plane as opposed to the "classical" CAPM, where we have a security market line.

These market factors are combined with weights taking into account the characteristics of each stock, namely differences in "normal" risk: $\text{cov}_D^*(R_i, R_M)$ and differences in jump risk: $\text{cov}_D^*(R_j, R_{H_j})$. Since the latter covariance is only unequal to zero for the jumping stock j, it is exactly this divergence that determines the price difference between the jumping and the non jumping stocks.

One last point is worth mentioning. Equation (4) uses the diffusion component of the market and the correction portfolio, not their jump/diffusion component. Hence, data processing to eliminate the jump components from the observable factors is necessary before we can use the jump CAPM. This in turn means that a naive adaptation of the "classical" CAPM to jumps fails to work.

3 Variance decomposition

Due to our CAPM (equations (4a) and (4b)) we do not only understand how to calculate risk premiums, but we also know that firm–specific jump risk has a price influence.

What we are not fully aware of, however, is the exact extent to which the jump risk is relevant to pricing. The sole way to figure this out is to pursue a variance decomposition, which in turn builds upon a return model. At exactly this point the CAPM comes into play: It made clear that the return of every stock is a linear function of the return of the market portfolio and the return of the correction portfolio.

Based on this information, we decompose the variances as follows: The total (jump and diffusion) return variance of each stock k shall be explained best possible by the variance of the sum of market and correction portfolio. This yields a breakdown of total variance into two uncorrelated parts: The first part can be explained by the variance of the sum of the market and the correction portfolio and thus is contained in both portfolios. Therefore, this explainable part is solely relevant to pricing (systematic risk). The second part, the stocks' residual risk, cannot be explained by the combined risk of the market and the correction portfolio because it is not included therein. Thus, it is irrelevant to pricing and we call it unsystematic risk.

Technically speaking, we regress the combined jump/diffusion return of each stock k on the combined jump/diffusion return of the market portfolio and the combined jump/diffusion return of the correction portfolio, i.e.

$$R_k = E\{R_k\} + \beta_{Mk}(R_M - E\{R_M\}) + \beta_{H_jk}(R_{H_j} - E\{R_{H_j}\}) + h_k \quad (5)$$

R_k	total (that is jump and diffusion) return of stock k in the period dt
R_{H_j}	total (that is jump and diffusion) return of portfolio H_j in the period dt
β_{Mk}, β_{H_jk}	regression coefficient of stock k due to a linear two factor regression of R_k on R_M and R_{H_j}
h_k	part of stock k's return that cannot be explained

to pursue based on the above return model the following variance decomposition

$$
\underbrace{\text{var}^*(R_k)}_{\text{total risk}} = \underbrace{\beta_{Mk}^2 \text{var}^*(R_M) + \beta_{H_jk}^2 \text{var}^*(R_{H_j}) + 2\beta_{Mk}\beta_{H_jk}\text{cov}^*(R_M, R_{H_j})}_{\text{systematic risk}}
$$
$$
+ \underbrace{\text{var}^*(h_k)}_{\text{unsystematic risk}} \tag{6}
$$

All we have to do now is to compute the variances/covariances in the above equation using the definition of the regression coefficients β. After tedious simplifications, we arrive at the following risk decomposition

for the jumping stock j

$$
\text{syst. } R_j = \frac{\text{var}_D^*(R_M)KK_j - 2 \cdot KK_j w_{M_j}\text{cov}_D^*(R_j, R_M) + H_{jj}\text{cov}_D^{*2}(R_j, R_M)}{\text{var}_D^*(R_M)H_{jj} - KK_j w_{M_j}^2}
$$
$$
+ \lambda_j E\{\varphi_j^2\} \tag{7a}
$$

for all other stock i

$$
\text{syst. } R_i = \frac{H_{jj}\, \text{cov}_D^{*2}(R_j, R_M)}{\text{var}_D^*(R_M)H_{jj} - KK_j w_{M_j}^2} \tag{7b}
$$

According to equations (9a) and (9b), firm-specific jump risk is completely systematic, the unsystematic part of the total risk solely stems from stocks' "normal" price movements. This result is surprising. Not the fact that firm-specific jumps contain systematic risk. This was clear from Ahn/Thompson's formula and our jump CAPM. But the exact extent is astonishing. So the question arises: Why is firm-specific risk fully systematic?

Key to understanding this outcome is the fact that both the market portfolio and the correction portfolio contain stock j. Thus, a jump in the return of stock j leads to a jump in the return of the market and the correction portfolio. However, under firm–specific jumps no other stock is subject to a jump at the same time as stock j thereby preventing any diversification effect. – The story is different with "normal" risk because all stocks are subject to "normal" risk at the same time. A portfolio of stocks has, for that reason, a risk reducing effect so that the variance of the sum of the market and the correction portfolios does not contain the whole amount of "normal" risk.

4 Conclusion

We started from the observation that there is a controversy in the finance literature between Merton (1976) and Ahn/Thompson (1988) concerning the systematic nature of firm–specific jump risk. Resolving this conflict not only is of theoretical interest, but also has practical implications for stock and option pricing.

Our analysis has produced the following results: It is not possible to obtain fair stock risk premiums under firm–specific jumps of stock j by simply inserting the combined jump/diffusion parameters into the "classical" CAPM. Instead, we have to advance the "classical" security market line to a security market plane with (market) factors: risk premium of the market portfolio and risk premium of the correction portfolio against jumps of stock j. – A variance decomposition confirms the pricing influence of firm-specific jumps: The firm–specific jump of stock j is completely systematic risk, the unsystematic risk component solely stems from "normal" risk. This is simply due to the fact that jump risk, contrary to "normal" risk, does not allow any diversification.

Just one remark on the case of more than one stock subject to firm–specific jumps: In principle, we have the same framework as in the case of one firm–specific jump. Firm-specific jumps cannot occur at the same time, therefore a diversification of jump risk is impossible, whereas "normal" risk permits diversification. – However, firm-specific jumps are no longer completely systematic risk. For, both stock i and j can cause a jump of the market and the correction portfolio. Since the examined stock is subject to merely one jump risk, a market/correction portfolio combination, that is subject to several jumps, loses explanatory power.

Equipped with this theoretical background, we are able to tackle our initial problem: Referring to the question of the systematic nature of firm–specific jumps, we agree with Ahn/Thompson (1988): Firm–specific jumps contain systematic risk. Thus, stock analysts have to take care of the different structure of risk premiums under firm-specific jumps. Moreover, in option pricing we have to rely on a formula that can cope with systematic jump risk (e.g. Bates (1991)). By no means we are allowed to use Merton (1976).

References

AASE, K. K. (1993): A Jump/Diffusion Consumption Based Capital Asset Pricing Model and the Equity Premium Puzzle. *Mathematical Finance, 3, 65-84.*

AHN, C. M. and THOMPSON, H. E. (1988): Jump–Diffusion Processes and the Term Structure of Interest Rates. *The Journal of Finance, 43, 155-174.*

BATES, D. S. (1991): The Crash of '87: Was it Expected? The Evidence from Options Markets. *The Journal of Finance, 46, 1009-1044.*

BEINERT, M. (1997): Kurssprünge und der Wert der deutschen Aktienoption. Deutscher Universitäts–Verlag, Wiesbaden.

JARROW, R. A. and ROSENFELD, E. R. (1984): Jump Risks and the Intertemporal Capital Asset Pricing Model. *The Journal of Business, 57, 337-351.*

MERTON, R. C. (1976): Option Pricing when Underlying Stock Returns are Discontinuous. *Journal of Financial Economics, 3, 125-144.*

NIETERT, B. (1999): Dynamische Portfolio Selektion unter Berücksichtigung von Kurssprüngen. *Zeitschrift für betriebswirtschaftliche Forschung, 51, 832-866.*

What Components Determine Stock Market Returns in the 1990's?

M. Pojarliev, W. Polasek

University of Basel
Institute of Statistics and Econometrics,
Bernoullistrasse 28, CH-4051 Basel, Switzerland

Abstract: Stock market returns reflect influences from many sources, such as local and global financial variables, exchange rates, the business outlook and macroeconomic policy variables. How much forecasting ability is contained in these variables?
We examine the stock index returns of the US, UK, German and Japanese markets and apply a principal components (PC) analysis to find out if various sources of information can be combined into a few factors. We also include proxy variables for volatility in the PC model. The data suggest that about 5-6 factors can be used to approximate the predictive power of the original regression model. We find some similar factors in the models of the different countries. We show that PC models for stock returns can explain about 50% of the variation measured by R^2.

1 Introduction

Despite the debate on the efficiency of stock markets, there exists a demand for portfolio managers to forecast future returns for portfolio decisions. Previous research has shown that multi-factor models have supplanted the traditional CAPM in explaining an asset's returns. The driving force behind the multi-factor models has been the development of the arbitrage pricing theory (APT), (Ross, 1976). The idea of the APT model was to find a few factors that could explain the returns of a collection of stocks in a portfolio. Thus, we will try to explain in this paper the monthly returns of the Dow Jones, FTSE, DAX and Nikkei indices with principal components regression models.

We will concentrate on the following research questions. First, how much of the predictability (R^2 measure) of stock index returns can be explained by a principal components model? We will use the squared returns of certain variables as proxies for the volatility component, since it was shown in Polasek and Ren (1999) that multiple VARCH-M models can improve the predictability considerably. Second, which sources of economic risk are most important for explaining the predictability of stock returns? And third, are there differences in the component structures between the countries?

The paper is organized as follows: First of all, in Section 2, we develop the basic principal components (PC) regression model and the method of extracting factors from the regression. In Section 3 we apply the PC model to the stock returns of four countries. In a final section we summarize our findings.

2 Principal components regression

Principal components analysis can be used to reduce the number of regressors in the regressor matrix. This is particularly useful in regressions with many variables. Let us consider a normal linear regression model with centered variables, i.e. $\bar{y} = 0$, $\bar{x} = 0$, for $i = 1, .., p$, where we have an $n \times 1$ vector $\mathbf{y}$ of dependent variables and an $n \times p$ regressor matrix $\mathbf{X}$:

$$\mathbf{y} = \mathbf{X}\beta + \epsilon, \epsilon \sim \mathbf{N}[\mathbf{0}, \sigma^2 \mathbf{I}_n]. \tag{1}$$

Consider now a principal components transformation of the regressors in $\mathbf{X}$:

$$\mathbf{W} = \mathbf{X}\mathbf{G} \quad or \quad \mathbf{W}\mathbf{G}' = \mathbf{X}, \tag{2}$$

where the covariance matrix of $\mathbf{X}$, with $\mathbf{G}$ the principal components loading matrix, is given as

$$\boldsymbol{\Sigma} = Var(\mathbf{x_t}) = \mathbf{X}'\mathbf{X}/n \tag{3}$$

and has an eigenvalue decomposition of the form

$$\boldsymbol{\Sigma} = \mathbf{G}\boldsymbol{\Lambda}\mathbf{G}' \tag{4}$$

with $\boldsymbol{\Lambda} = diag(\lambda_1, ..., \lambda_p)$ a diagonal matrix with the eigenvalues of $\boldsymbol{\Lambda}$, and $\mathbf{G}$ the matrix of eigenvectors having the property $\mathbf{G}'\mathbf{G} = \mathbf{I}_p$. Inserting the principal components regression into the regression model we obtain

$$\mathbf{y} = \mathbf{W}\mathbf{G}'\mathbf{G}\beta + \epsilon \quad or \quad \mathbf{y} = \mathbf{W}\alpha + \epsilon \tag{5}$$

with the new coefficient vector $\alpha = \mathbf{G}'\beta$. Since the columns of $\mathbf{W}$ are orthogonal, i.e. $\mathbf{W}'\mathbf{W} = \mathbf{G}'\mathbf{X}'\mathbf{X}\mathbf{G} = n\boldsymbol{\Lambda}$, the least squares estimator of α does not change if only a subset of the variables in $\mathbf{W}$ is selected. The OLS estimate of α is given by

$$\hat{\alpha} = (\mathbf{W}'\mathbf{W})^{-1}\mathbf{W}\mathbf{y} \tag{6}$$

With w_i the ith of p column vectors of $\mathbf{W}$ we can calculate the OLS estimates in (5) for each component simply as

$$\hat{\alpha}_i = \frac{\mathbf{w}_i\mathbf{y}}{n\lambda_i} \tag{7}$$

where λ_i is the ith eigenvalue of $\mathbf{X}'\mathbf{X}/n$. Because the $\mathbf{W}$ matrix is orthogonal we have a simple ANOVA decomposition of $\mathbf{y}'\mathbf{y}$, the total sum of squares:

$$\mathbf{y}'\mathbf{y} = \sum_{i=1}^{p} \hat{\alpha} \mathbf{w}_i' \mathbf{w}_i + \hat{\varepsilon}'\hat{\varepsilon} \qquad (8)$$

with the OLS residual vector being $\hat{\varepsilon} = \mathbf{y} - \mathbf{W}\hat{\alpha}$. This decomposition implies also a nice decomposition of the R^2 into p sub R^2 contributions (denoted by $R_{\alpha i}^2$) measures of the principal components regression:

$$R^2 = \frac{\mathbf{y}'\mathbf{y} - \hat{\varepsilon}'\hat{\varepsilon}}{\mathbf{y}'\mathbf{y}} = \sum_{i=1}^{p} n\lambda_i \hat{\alpha}_i^2 / \mathbf{y}'\mathbf{y} = R_{\alpha 1}^2 + ... + R_{\alpha p}^2. \qquad (9)$$

We define $R_{\alpha i}^2 = \frac{\lambda_i \hat{\alpha}_i}{Var(y)}$ as the proportion of the variance of $\mathbf{y}$ (note that $nVar(\mathbf{y}) = \mathbf{y}'\mathbf{y}$ since $\bar{y} = 0$) which can be explained by the ith principal components regressor. Note that OLS estimates $\hat{\alpha}_i$ can be tested for significance with the ordinary t-test:

$$t_{\alpha_i} = \frac{\hat{\alpha}_i}{s.e.(\alpha_i)} \sim t_{n-p-1}$$

with the standard error of the estimator

$$s.e.(\alpha_i) = \frac{n\lambda_i(n-p-1)}{\hat{\varepsilon}'\hat{\varepsilon}}.$$

There are as many principal components as there are original variables. Several criteria show which components should be retained (see Mardia et al., 1992).

The *principal components loadings* $\mathbf{G}$ are shown in the next chapter for the US model. The loadings are the coefficients of the principal components transformation. They provide us with a convenient summary of the influence of the original variables on the new components and form a basis for interpreting factors.

3 Country models

A linear regression model using the variables from table 1 (from October 1994 until March 1999) and the standardized monthly returns of the Dow Jones index (from November 1994 until April 1999) as the dependent variable yields a multiple R^2 of 0.6511. Thus, the simple regression model was able to predict about 65% of the fluctuation in the next month's return. To reduce the number of variables in the regressor matrix, we apply *principal components analysis*. We are using the first five principal components in the PC regression according to Kaiser's criteria (see

Symbol	Description
I10y	10 year Treasury bond
E	100/(price-earnings ratio)
X	returns of trade weighted currency index, 1990=100
I3m	middle rate of the three month Treasury bill
SM	RSI for the returns of the Dow Jones index, basis 1993
BM	RSI for the yields of the 10 year Treasury bond, bas.1993
EAR	aggregate earnings revisions, 6 m. moving average, in %
CPI	returns of the consumer price index less food
DAX	returns of the DAX index
USDDM	exchange rate of the US \$ to the DM
MSCIE	returns of the MSCI Europe 15
vI3m	$I3m^2$: volatility of I3m
vEAR	$EAR.^2$ volatility of EAR
vDAX	DAX^2: volatility of DAX
vCPI	CPI^2: volatility of CPI
vMSCIW	$MSCIW^2$: volatility of MSCI World

Table 1: List of the standardized, monthly time series from October 1994 until March 1999 which are used for the US principal components model (source: Datastream).

Mardia et al., 1992): only components with eigenvalues over the average (0.98) should be retained as "factors". These factors explain 80% of the variance of the original exogenous variables. Using the R^2 decomposition we can calculate the R^2 of the PC regression by summing the first five proportions.

As opposed to the factors in the APT, our components are statistical constructs. The advantage of this methodology is that the principal components loadings help us to interpret the factors and see which sources of information are most important for forecasting returns. In the APT type of models, the factors have to be chosen a priori and the importance of information is not empirically quantified.

Table 2 lists the loadings of the five components for the Dow Jones returns. We have chosen factor names so that they are useful for interpretation. In the first factor, which is most important (as it explains 41% of the variance of the original variables), only the term structure of interest rates has influence. The rest of the variables have weights less than 0.05, thus they don't play a significant role for the factor decomposition. Therefore we called this factor "*Term Structure*" (TS). The second factor is called "*Volatility*" because the largest weights are from the squared returns of the MSCI world index, the DAX index and the consumer price index. This result confirms previous research (Polasek and Ren, 1999)

name	TS	Volatil.	World inf.	Inflation.	P/E
I10y	**0.45**	0.13	-0.03	-0.09	0.08
E	-0.04	-0.07	0.08	0.08	**-0.79**
X	-0.01	0.12	-0.28	-0.31	0.03
I3m	**0.55**	0.13	0.10	-0.15	0.00
SM	-0.05	-0.08	0.21	0.05	-0.01
BM	**0.43**	-0.15	0.07	0.09	-0.19
EAR	0.02	-0.03	0.16	-0.13	0.17
CPI	0.00	0.36	-0.05	**0.56**	-0.12
DAX	0.00	0.19	**0.44**	-0.24	-0.05
US$DM	0.00	-0.24	0.14	0.24	**0.51**
MSCIE	0.01	-0.31	**0.69**	0.18	0.00
vI3m	**-0.55**	0.12	0.10	-0.14	-0.02
vEAR	0.05	0.04	-0.05	0.17	-0.04
vDAX	0.00	**0.44**	0.15	-0.09	0.09
vCPI	0.01	**0.37**	-0.01	**0.53**	0.13
vMSCIW	-0.01	**0.50**	**0.33**	-0.18	0.00
$R^2_{\alpha i}$ in %	16.86	11.32	10.23	8.04	7.03

Table 2: The factor loadings of the principal components analysis for the returns of the Dow Jones index (bold values emphasizes important variables). The last row shows the R^2 decompositions.

that volatilities play an important role in determining the stock returns. The name "World information" refers mainly to European returns and the volatility of the MSCI world index. The largest weights in the factor "CPI" or "Inflation" are the relative increases of the consumer price index and its squared returns. The CPI is often used to measure inflation. The largest weight in the last factor "P/E" stems from the price-earnings ratio (see Table 1) i.e. the earning-price ratio. Table 3 gives the summary of the principal components regression for the returns of the Dow Jones index.

The PC models for the other countries yield 6 factors and an R^2 of 0.74 for the UK model, 7 factors and an R^2 of 0.52 for the German model and 5 factors and an R^2 of 0.44 for the Japanese model. In contrast to the US model a factor "Exchange rate" is present in all other countries models which indicates the importance of the US$. Now we write the orthogonal decomposition in (5) for the five components of the PC analysis of the Dow Jones index as

$$\hat{y}_t = \hat{\alpha}_1 w_{1t} + ... + \hat{\alpha}_5 w_{5t}, \quad t = 1, ..., 54 \tag{10}$$

Figure 1 plots the estimated returns $\hat{y}_t$ and 5 contributions $\hat{A}_{it} = \hat{\alpha}_i w_{it}$ for $i = 1, ..., 5$. for each time point by a shaded barplot. It is interesting

	coef.	std.err	t.stat	p.value
TS	-13.5763	3.0965	-4.3844	0.0001
Volatility	-0.3400	0.0939	-3.6212	0.0007
World inf.	0.3281	0.0809	4.0586	0.0002
CPI	0.2409	0.0666	3.6180	0.0007
P/E	-1.5961	0.5473	-2.9162	0.0054
Residual St. Err. = 0.6916, Multiple R^2 =0.5578				
N = 54, F-stat. = 12.3618 on 5 and 49 df, p-value = 0				

Table 3: Principal Components (PC) regression for Dow Jones returns

to note that the largest deviation (those of observations 47 and 49) can be explained by only 3 factors.

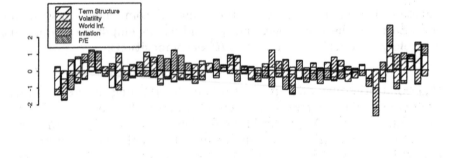

Figure 1: Estimated factor contributions of the US model. The upper panel shows the estimated returns $\hat{y}_t$ of the Dow Jones index by the 5 factors. The second panel plots the actual returns (standardized) from November 1994 until April 1999.

4 Conclusions

Applying principal components regression to stock returns, we have reduced the number of variables in the regressor matrix from 14-16 to 5-7 components. To interpret these factors, we have used names of the variables with the largest weights in the factor loadings. The analysis shows that the Dow Jones index influences all other markets and the factor *"World information"* determines strongly the stock market fluctuations of the UK, Germany and Japan. Recall that the MSCI North America index has more than 50% weight in the MSCI World index.

There are some differences in the country models: the UK stock market is more sensitive to local information than the German and the Japanese stock markets. The term structure of interest rates in the USA has a big influence on the returns of the Dow Jones index. The exchange rate of local currency to the US $ seems to influence the local stock market. It will be interesting to see whether the US $ has such an influence on the other stock markets after the establishment of the Euro. The factor *"Volatility"* is present in all four models. There are differences in the predicting performance for the different stock markets. The returns of the FTSE index are better to forecast ($R^2 = 0.74$) than the returns of the Nikkei index ($R^2 = 0.44$).

In general we can say that in the second half of the 1990's the stock market returns were determined by the term structure of the interest rates, the exchange rate of local currency to the US $, influences of other stock markets, the volatility of fundamental variables and inflation.

Our research confirms previous research of Ferson and Harvey (1991), which found that significant predictability for stock returns exists. A related paper will report on the use of principal components models for active portfolio management.

References

FERSON, W. and HARVEY, C. (1991): Sources of Predictability in Portfolio Returns. *Financial Analysts Journal, May-June, 49–56.*

MARDIA, K. V. and KENT, J. T. and BIBBY, J. M. (1992): Multivariate Analysis. Academic Press, London

POJARLIEV, M. and POLASEK, L. (2000): Portfolio construction using multivariate time series forecasts. *University of Basel, ISO, Working paper.*

POLASEK, W. and REN, L. (1999): Volatility analysis during the Asia crisis: A multivariate GARCH-M model for stock returns in the US, Germany and Japan. *To appear in Applied Stochastic Models in Business and Industry, 2001*

ROSS, S. (1976): The Arbitrage Theory of Capital Asset Pricing. *Journal of Economic theory, 13, 341–360.*

A Comparison of Estimators for Multivariate ARCH Models

W. Polasek, S. Liu

University of Basel
Institute of Statistics and Econometrics,
Bernoullistrasse 28, CH-4051 Basel, Switzerland

Abstract: Multivariate or vector autoregressive conditional heteroskedastic (VARCH) models have become increasingly important for applications in several fields of economics and finance. This paper compares the method of scoring for maximum likelihood estimation (MLE) of Liu and Polasek (1999) with currently used alternative estimators. We estimate a bivariate VAR-VARCH model with a simulated data set and compare the method with classical and Bayesian methods which are available in econometric program packages.

1 Introduction

Univariate autoregressive conditional heteroskedastic (ARCH) models have been used in econometrics since Engle (1982) and are successfully applied in many fields of economics. A recent monograph of univariate and multivariate ARCH models in finance can be found in Gourieroux (1997). Most current estimation of the multivariate ARCH models uses the numerical techniques based on the BHHH method of Berndt et al. (1974) for maximum likelihood (ML) estimation. Using the scoring method as in Fomby et al. (1984) for ML estimation we expect to obtain better estimates in small samples since we use the exact information matrix.

The plan of the paper is as following. Section 2 reviews the ML estimation procedure and section 3 describes the special VAR(1)-ARCH(1) model that we use in the numerical example of section 4. Section 5 concludes.

2 MLE for heteroskedastic time series

Consider a multivariate time series y_t, $t = 1, ..., T$, of dimension M, which is independently and identically distributed and specified by the conditional moment structure: the $M \times 1$ conditional mean vector is $E(y_t \mid \psi_{t-1}) = \mu_t$ and the $M \times M$ conditional variance matrix $Var(y_t \mid \psi_{t-1}) = V_t$, where ψ_{t-1} indicates the information set available at time $t - 1$.

The general multivariate conditional heteroskedastic model can be written as

$$y_t = \mu_t + u_t, \qquad t = 1, ..., T, \tag{1}$$

or $y_t \sim (\mu_t, V_t)$ where we assume that $\mu_t = \mu_t(\theta)$ and $V_t = V_t(\theta)$ are functions of the $p \times 1$ vector of parameters θ. If the distribution of u_t is unknown, then we estimate the system by pseudo ML. For ML we assume that u_t is a $M \times 1$ disturbance vector which follow a normal distribution: The (conditional) mean vector is $E(u_t \mid \psi_{t-1}) = 0$ and the conditional variance matrix is $E(u_t u_t' \mid \psi_{t-1}) = V_t$ is positive definite.

The process (1) is stationary and the stability conditions can be found in Gourieroux (1997). The conditional log-likelihood function of $y = (y_1, ..., y_T)'$ in (1) is given by

$$
\begin{aligned}
L(y, \theta) &= \sum_{t=1}^{T} L_t(y, \theta) \\
&= -\sum_{t=1}^{T} \frac{1}{2} \log | V_t | - \sum_{t=1}^{T} \frac{1}{2} u_t' V_t^{-1} u_t, \quad t = 1, ..., T. \quad (2)
\end{aligned}
$$

To apply the scoring method for MLE, we define the $p \times 1$ gradient vector $g = g(\theta)$ by

$$
g = \sum_{t=1}^{T} \frac{\partial L_t(y, \theta)}{\partial \theta'}, \quad (3)
$$

and the $p \times p$ Hessian matrix $H = H(\theta)$

$$
H = \sum_{t=1}^{T} \frac{\partial^2 L_t(y, \theta)}{\partial \theta \partial \theta'}. \quad (4)
$$

If E indicates the mathematical expectation with respect to y, then the $p \times p$ information matrix $F = F(\theta)$ is defined as

$$
F = -E(H). \quad (5)
$$

In the following two lemmas, we describe the gradient vector and the information matrix of the ARCH time series model (1).

Lemma 1: The gradient vector of model (1) is

$$
g(\theta) = \frac{1}{2} \sum_{t=1}^{T} \left(\frac{\partial \text{vech} V_t}{\partial \theta'} \right)' D' D \text{vech} P_t + \sum_{t=1}^{T} \left(\frac{\partial \mu_t}{\partial \theta'} \right)' V_t^{-1} u_t, \quad (6)
$$

where

$$
P_t = V_t^{-1} u_t u_t' V_t^{-1} - V_t^{-1}, \quad (7)
$$

vech denotes the vectorisation operator which eliminates all supra-diagonal elements of the matrix, vechV_t is a $N \times 1$ vector and D is the $M^2 \times N$ duplication matrix ($N = M(M+1)/2$).

Lemma 2: The information matrix F for model (1), defined as

$$F = E(R), \qquad (8)$$

where $R = R(\theta)$ is the second order derivative given by

$$R = \frac{1}{2} \sum_{t=1}^{T} \left(\frac{\partial \text{vech}V_t}{\partial \theta'}\right)' D'(V_t^{-1} \otimes V_t^{-1})D \frac{\partial \text{vech}V_t}{\partial \theta'}$$
$$+ \sum_{t=1}^{T} \left(\frac{\partial \mu_t}{\partial \theta'}\right)' V_t^{-1} \frac{\partial \mu_t}{\partial \theta'}, \qquad (9)$$

where D is the $M^2 \times N$ duplication matrix and $\otimes$ is the Kronecker product. The proofs of lemma 1 and 2 can be found in Liu and Polasek (1999).

Model (1) with the pseudo ML estimation is proposed by Gourieroux (1997): if the underlying distribution is not known we use the conditional normal likelihood function. If the error distribution is assumed to be normal, then the pseudo ML estimates is the same as MLE. Note that Lemma 1 and 2 are also valid for the pseudo MLE approach. The rules for vech, D and Kronecker products can be found in e.g. Magnus and Neudecker (1999). We demonstrate the estimation procedure for a bivariate VAR(1)-ARCH(1) model with diagonal coefficient matrices using simulated data. The ML estimation based on the scoring method is implemented by the following iteration procedure (now R replaces the unknown F):

$$\theta_{j+1} = \theta_j + \lambda_j R_j^{-1} g_j, \qquad (10)$$

where $\lambda_j \leq 1$ controls the step size and j is the current iteration index.

For the estimation comparison we use the GARCH module 'S+GARCH' of the statistical software package Splus from MathSoft (1996) and for the MCMC estimation the BASEL package of Polasek et al. (2000). The BHHH algorithm for MLE of the S+GARCH module follows the iteration procedure in (10) and replaces R_j by $\sum_t g_{jt} g'_{jt}$.

The MCMC algorithm in the BASEL package determines the posterior distribution of the parameters by an iterative simulation procedure, i.e.

by drawing random variates from the conditional posterior posterior distribution which are obtained by the joint distribution $p(y, \theta)$. The joint distribution of the VAR-GARCH model for $y = (y_1, ..., y_T)$ and $\theta = (\theta_1, ..., \theta_M)$ is given by

$$p(y, \theta) \propto \prod_{t=1}^{T} \prod_{m=1}^{M} N[y_t^m \mid \mu_t(\beta^m), V_t^m] \; p(\theta^m), \tag{11}$$

where $N[.]$ denotes the multivariate normal distribution, (β^m are the regression coefficients of the mth equation $m = 1, ..., M$. For the parameters $\theta^m = (\beta^m, \alpha^m)$ we assume the informative prior distribution independence between the equations, i.e. $\prod_{m=1}^{M} p(\theta^m)$.

(a) For $B = (\beta^1, ..., \beta^M)$, we find as full conditional posterior distribution

$$p(B \mid y, \alpha^m) = N[B_{**}, D_{**}],$$

where B_{**} and D_{**} are the mean and covariance hyper-parameters of the multivariate normal distribution conditional on the α^m parameters of the variance equation.

(b) The ARCH coefficients α^m are simulated (conditional on β^m) by a Metropolis-Hastings step using an iterative proposal distribution.

3 Diagonal VAR(1)-ARCH(1) model

Consider the following bivariate VAR(1)-ARCH(1) model ($M = 2$), which is the "dvec" model of S+GARCH:

$$\begin{pmatrix} y_{1t} \\ y_{2t} \end{pmatrix} = \begin{pmatrix} \mu_{1t} \\ \mu_{2t} \end{pmatrix} + \begin{pmatrix} u_{1t} \\ u_{2t} \end{pmatrix}, \quad t = 1, ..., T, \tag{12}$$

where $y_t = (y_{1t}, y_{2t})'$ is the tth 2×1 vector of observations of the time series $\{y_1, ..., y_T\}$. The mean $\mu_t = (\mu_{1t}, \mu_{2t})'$ is specified by the diagonal VAR(1) equation

$$\begin{pmatrix} \mu_{1t} \\ \mu_{2t} \end{pmatrix} = \begin{pmatrix} \beta_{10} \\ \beta_{20} \end{pmatrix} + \begin{pmatrix} \beta_{11} & 0 \\ 0 & \beta_{22} \end{pmatrix} \begin{pmatrix} y_{1t-1} \\ y_{2t-1} \end{pmatrix}, \tag{13}$$

where $\beta_{10}, \beta_{20}, \beta_{11}$ and β_{22} are scalar parameters. The conditional variance matrix of $u_t = (u_{1t}, u_{2t})'$ is the 2×2 diagonal positive definite matrix V_t:

$$V_t = \begin{pmatrix} v_{11t} & v_{12t} \\ v_{12t} & v_{22t} \end{pmatrix}$$

which is vectorised as $\operatorname{vech}V_t = (v_{11t}, v_{12t}, v_{22t})'$ and is parameterised as

$$
\begin{pmatrix} v_{11t} \\ v_{12t} \\ v_{22t} \end{pmatrix} = \begin{pmatrix} \alpha_{10} \\ \alpha_{20} \\ \alpha_{30} \end{pmatrix} + \begin{pmatrix} \alpha_{11} & 0 & 0 \\ 0 & \alpha_{22} & 0 \\ 0 & 0 & \alpha_{33} \end{pmatrix} \begin{pmatrix} u_{1t-1}^2 \\ u_{1t-1}u_{2t-1} \\ u_{2t-1}^2 \end{pmatrix} \tag{14}
$$

with $\alpha_{10} > 0$, $\alpha_{20} > 0$, $\alpha_{30} > 0$, $\alpha_{11} \geq 0$, $\alpha_{22} \geq 0$ and $\alpha_{33} \geq 0$ such that $V_t > 0$ exists.

The parameter vector is partitioned as $\theta = (\beta', \alpha')'$, where the AR coefficients are $\beta = (\beta_{10}, \beta_{20}, \beta_{11}, \beta_{22})'$ and $\alpha = (\alpha_{10}, \alpha_{20}, \alpha_{30}, \alpha_{11}, \alpha_{22}, \alpha_{33})'$ contains the coefficients for the variance equation. The gradient vector $g(\theta)$ and the Hessian $R(\theta)$ can be analytically determined using the Lemmas 1 and 2.

4   Two Examples

For the first example we use S-PLUS to simulate a bivariate ARCH model. We generate a time series of $T = 200$ observations for the VAR(1)-ARCH(1) model (12)-(14) with the parameter vector of (14):

$$
\begin{aligned}
\theta &= (\beta', \alpha')' \\
&= (\beta_{10}, \beta_{20}, \beta_{11}, \beta_{22}, \alpha_{10}, \alpha_{20}, \alpha_{30}, \alpha_{11}, \alpha_{22}, \alpha_{33})'.
\end{aligned}
$$

We fix the following values for the AR coefficients in (12):

$$
\beta_{10} = 0.10, \quad \beta_{11} = -0.4, \quad \beta_{20} = 0.30, \quad \beta_{22} = 0.05
$$

are for the ARCH equation in (13) we choose

$$
\begin{aligned}
\alpha_{10} &= 0.15, & \alpha_{11} &= 0.01, \\
\alpha_{20} &= 0.05, & \alpha_{22} &= 0.07, \\
\alpha_{30} &= 0.10, & \alpha_{33} &= 0.05,
\end{aligned}
$$

Based on $g(\theta)$ and $R(\theta)$, we write a MLE program to find estimates by using the method of scoring. The iteration process of (10) is conditioned on the first two observations. The criterion to check the convergence of the iteration is

$$
\frac{\hat{\theta}_{j+1} - \hat{\theta}_j}{\hat{\theta}_j} \leq 0.005 \tag{15}
$$

and we use the step size $\lambda_j = 1/10j$, It takes about 100 iterations for the S+GARCH package (MathSoft 1996)to achieve convergence. If the relative errors in (14) is set to 0.01 instead of 0.005, then the coefficients converge at about 25 iterations. The MCMC simulation of the BASEL package also converges quite fast within a few thousand iterations.

Parameters	True Values	S+GARCH Estimates	BASEL Estimates	MLE Estimates
β_{10}	0.10	0.1223657	0.1086234	0.13972
β_{20}	0.30	0.2004163	0.2678540	0.2855772
β_{11}	-0.40	-0.5246969	-0.5083313	-0.5427349
β_{22}	0.05	0.0493810	0.0158123	0.0404794
α_{10}	0.15	1.0107307	0.0505836	0.2498541
α_{20}	0.05	-0.0001644	0.0519461	0.1158166
α_{30}	0.10	0.6928885	0.1056807	0.2946794
α_{11}	0.01	-0.1427515	0.0304871	0.1397502
α_{22}	0.07	-0.0180374	0.0378279	0.1243003
α_{33}	0.05	0.1011727	0.0279547	0.0774030
MSE				
AR coeff.		0.0259668	0.1400330	0.0222498
ARCH coeff.		1.1435582	0.0127414	0.0708833
Total MSE		1.1695250	0.1527744	0.0931331

Table 1: MSE comparisons of estimates: The S+GARCH, BASEL and ML estimates

We compute the simple mean squared error (MSE) by $||\hat{\theta} - \theta||^2 = \sum(\hat{\theta}_i - \theta_i)^2$, the squared distances between the estimates and known values of the parameters. In Table 1 we compute the squared distances for the mean equation (AR coefficients) and for the variance equation (ARCH coefficients) separately. The sum of the two parts is called 'Total MSE' and is listed in the last row of Table 1.

Among all three methods, the S+GARCH estimates turn out to be worst. Instead of e.g. $\alpha_{10} = 0.15$ S+GARCH estimates $\hat{\alpha}_{10} = 1.01$. Since ARCH coefficients in S+GARCH are not constrained to be positive, α_{11} and α_{22} are estimated to be negative while their true values are positive.

As a second example we estimate the bivariate diagonal VAR-VARCH model (12) for the exchange rates of German Mark and British Pound both against the US Dollar (where we use weekly log-differenced data from 2 Jan. 1985 until 21 Jan. 1998).

The comparison of the coefficient estimates in Table 2 shows that both MLE estimates produce similar results, only the signs of the β_{11} coefficient and two α coefficient differ. The standard deviations of the parameter estimates are the smallest for the 'scoring' ML estimates. The Bayesian posterior means of the BASEL package deviate quite substantially from the ML estimates and seem to be more plausible. The difference between the estimation methods for the exchange rates is quite surprising if we compare them with the rather similar results of the sim-

θ	S+ GARCH Estim.	S+ GARCH Std.Err.	BASEL Estim.	BASEL Std.Err.	MLE Estim.	MLE Std.Err.
β_{10}	-0.00210	5.448e-04	-0.40244	0.09383	-0.00083	1.869e-04
β_{20}	0.00304	3.610e-04	-0.32309	0.06922	0.00056	1.863e-04
β_{11}	-0.17065	2.116e-02	-0.20243	0.08380	0.00537	1.165e-02
β_{22}	-0.26104	1.281e-02	0.05307	0.02966	0.02258	1.198e-02
α_{10}	0.00018	7.898e-06	0.05549	0.02050	0.00181	9.934e-06
α_{20}	-0.00011	4.271e-06	0.03679	0.02828	0.00024	6.787e-06
α_{30}	0.00011	2.761e-06	0.06631	0.02591	0.00178	9.605e-06
α_{11}	0.54405	6.776e-02	0.04009	0.02614	0.04434	1.850e-02
α_{22}	0.53076	5.132e-02	0.10918	0.08216	-0.01115	1.414e-02
α_{33}	0.51261	4.233e-02	0.08627	0.05999	0.16051	1.774e-02

Table 2: Comparison of Estimates: Mean and Std. Errors from the S+GARCH, the BASEL package and the 'scoring' MLE

ulation example in Table 1.

5 Conclusions

This paper has compared 2 classical and a Bayesian estimation method for a special multivariate conditional heteroskedastic time series models. The 'diagonal' VAR(1)-ARCH(1) model was fitted to a simulated example and an economic example involving weekly exchange rates. For the simulated VAR-VARCH model, the method of scoring turned out the best results in terms of the mean squared error in comparison to the other two methods. We found that the BHHH algorithm performs overall quite badly while the MCMC algorithm gives the best results for the ARCH parameters. Further simulation results are needed to give a more detailed picture of the performance of the MLE in high dimensional VAR-VARCH models.

References

BERNDT, E., HALL, B., HALL, R. and HAUSMAN, J. (1974) Estimation and inference in nonlinear structural models, *Annals of Economic and Social Measurement*, 3, 653-665.

ENGLE, R.F. (1982) Autoregressive conditional heteroskedasticity with estimates of the variance of United Kingdom inflation, *Econometrica*, 50(4), 987-1006.

FOMBY, T., HILL, R.C. and JOHNSON, S.R. (1984) *Advanced Econometric Methods*, Springer, New York.

GOURIEROUX, C. (1997) *ARCH Models and Financial Applications*, Springer, New York.

LIU, S. and POLASEK, W. (1999) Maximum likelihood estimation for the VAR-VARCH model: A new approach, in *Modelling and Decisions in Economics, Essays in Honor of Franz Ferschl*, Leopold-Wildburger, U., Feichtinger, G. and Kistner, K.-P., eds, Physica-Verlag, Heidelberg, pp. 99-113.

MAGNUS,J.R. and NEUDECKER, H. (1999) *Matrix Differential Calculus with Applications in Statistics and Econometrics*, revised edition, John Wiley and Sons, Chichester, UK.

MathSoft (1996) S+GARCH User's Manual, Version 1.0, Data Analysis Products Division, MathSoft, Seattle.

POLASEK, W. et al. (2000) The BASEL package: A Bayesian Sampling Environment Language, PC-Version, University of Basel, Switzerland.

Pricing of a New Integrated Risk Reinsurance Product

Hato Schmeiser

Dr. Wolfgang Schieren-Lehrstuhl für Versicherungs- und Risikomanagement,
Humboldt-Universität zu Berlin, D-10178 Berlin, Germany

1 Introduction

In the following paper, we want to make some considerations on pricing
of a specific integrated risk reinsurance contract form called "double-
trigger" from the viewpoint of a reinsurance company.[1] Double-trigger
reinsurance contracts, which up to now have not really been focussed
in the scientific literature[2], can be classified in the area of *Alternative
Risk Transfer* ("ART")[3]. They differ from other protection strategies of
(primary) insurance companies in that, along with a defined claim result,
additional realizations from the investment side[4] are integrated in such a
way that only a specific combination of events will result compensation
payments by the reinsurer. Accordingly, the objective of these kinds of
contracts is that they (only) pay in situations in which poor underwriting
results can not be compensated by good capital investment returns and
vice versa.

The starting point for our analysis is to assume, that the cash flow characteristics of trigger contracts - especially because of the individuality of
traditional reinsurance products - can't be reproduced by financial securities traded on the capital market (the so-called spanning condition[5] is
not fulfilled). Therefore, an arbitrage-oriented preference-free valuation
of such a contract is not possible. We plead for an actuarially motivated
preference-dependent procedure under *explicit consideration* of *diversification effects*. In contrast to the arbitrage-theoretical duplication assessment as well as to traditional actuarial models, which only consider

---

[1] A differing double-trigger conception with respect to the following assessment is
considered in SCHMEISER, GRÜNDL (2000).

[2] cf. i.e. CANTER et al. (1996), CUMMINS, GEMAN (1995), HAN, LAI (1995),
HASEKAMP (2000), KIELHOLZ, DURRER (1997), SMITH et al. (1997), WAGNER
(1998).

[3] Among these belong, in particular, risk securitization, derivative financial
instruments for insurance index positions (e.g. PCS-Options) and reinsurance swaps
(CATEX).

[4] For moral hazard reasons this "trigger" is typically based on one or more capital
market indices.

[5] cf. ROSS (1978), p. 456, WILHELM (1985), p. 101.

384

in isolation the probability distribution of the compensation payments by the reinsurer, the interrelations to the existing portfolios of the reinsurer become central for the determination of pricing limits for trigger contracts.

Within the framework of deducting a price limit, we assume that the risk transferred by the cedent remains entirely with the reinsurer. To this extent we don't get either a (partial) risk transfer of the double trigger contract (i.e. via traditional reinsurance or securitization), nor are hedging strategies - of whatever kind - carried out on the part of the focussed reinsurer.

Knowing a price limit for a certain contract calculated in this manner makes it possible for us to distinguish between the following cases: if a *market price* exists, or the primary insurer has made a concrete offer for the trigger contract which is *higher* than the calculated price limit, it is recommended that the reinsurer sign the contract even without concurrently incorporating further transformation and/or hedging strategies. In the other case, the risk transfer must be seen in the context of taking additional risk management steps. In both cases we can understand the value of further risk management measures by observing the lowering of the price limits that it produces. From this, the determination of price limits that we set forth serves not only in the decision of whether to sign the contract, but it also establishes a starting point for measuring the increase in value that occurs from the risk management instruments that the reinsurer takes with regard to the trigger product.

2 The Pricing Model

In the following section, we want to limit ourselves to the valuation of *one* special double trigger arrangement. We focus a stop-loss whole account coverage with full risk transfer[6], which is based on a loss ratio modified by changes of a capital market index (or several indices).[7]

If $\hat{P}$ indicates the premium income of the cedent before concluding the trigger contract and S the corresponding *whole account* claim distribution (*after* traditional reinsurance) of the period under consideration, the loss ratio X can be derived from $X = S/\hat{P}$.[8] If $\hat{I}_0$ stands for the value of the observed capital market index in t $= 0$ and I_1 for the index level

---

[6]In case of a stop-loss whole account contract, the obligation to pay for the reinsurer comes up when the annual loss ratio of the primary insurer exceeds a previously agreed upon priority (typically defined in percent of the entire original premium $\hat{P}$ of the cedent).

[7]From now on we will only consider one capital market index.

[8]In order to separate deterministic from stochastic values, we want to designate the former with the index "^".

at $t = 1$, the effects of a change in the index (e.g. Euro Stoxx 50) on the investment returns of the focused asset portfolio (e.g. European stocks) of the primary insurer can be approximately modeled with help of the factor $\hat{\beta}$.[9] We now define with $\tilde{X}$ the *modified loss ratio* with the relation

$$\tilde{X} := \frac{\tilde{S}}{\hat{P}} := X - \frac{(I_1 - \hat{I}_0)}{\hat{P}} \cdot \hat{\beta}. \tag{1}$$

If we assume $\hat{P}$ as a constant value (and therefore, in particular, independent of S), we can now turn to an absolute formulation, i.e. to a consideration of the modified loss distribution $\tilde{S}$. Now if $\hat{M}$ depicts the agreed upon *absolute* priority[10], the following equation applies for the compensation payments of the reinsurer S_{DT} in the case of our focused double-trigger contract[11]

$$S_{DT} = max(\tilde{S} - \hat{M}, 0). \tag{2}$$

According to equation (2), the basis of the stop-loss contract forms the aggregate loss distribution $\tilde{S}$ (= the sum of the net loss distributions for the individual lines of businesses, where for their part both the number and the size of each claim are generally stochastic) of the primary insurer, modified by changes of a capital market index. It is almost certain, that in practical applications $\tilde{S}$ does not have a explicit analytical expression.[12] Thus to determine $\tilde{S}$, it is in general necessary to turn to suitable approximation procedures, which are (in the risk-theoretical literature) roughly systemized into analytical[13] and numerical[14] methods.[15] Should - in the course of a concrete application - the assumption of independence of the different components be violated, $\tilde{S}$ may often only be approximately determined with (stochastic) simulation methods.[16] For instance, if the result of a simulation were that $\tilde{S}$ is *approximately* lognormal distributed (with parameters μ and σ), we would get for the mean and variance of S_{DT}

---

[9]The level of factor $\hat{\beta}$, for which we want to assume it is generally > 0, is principally subject to the agreement between cedent and reinsurer. For the objectification of $\hat{\beta}$, econometric methods can be obtained.

[10]At the same time it should be pointed out that this double-trigger formulation - in contrast to the contract form considered in SCHMEISER, GRÜNDL (2000) - doesn't define any priority for losses on the one hand and for the capital market index on the other, but the priority $\hat{M}$ refers instead to the *aggregate* distribution $\tilde{S}$.

[11]In order to make our derivations not too complicated, we are not going to introduce further reinsurance layers.

[12]cf. CUMMINS (1991) with further proofs.

[13]cf. i.e. the Edgeworth or the Normal Power approximation.

[14]cf. i.e. the Recursion method by *Panjer* or the Fast Fourier approach.

[15]cf. i.e. DAYKIN et al. (1994), pp. 125-136 or SCHRÖTER (1994), pp. 254-436.

[16]cf. in depth i.e. DAYKIN et al. (1994), pp. 137-154.

$$E(S_{DT}) = e^{\mu + \frac{1}{2}\sigma^2} \cdot (1 - \Phi(\hat{M}_{Ln} - \sigma)) - \hat{M}(1 - \Phi(\hat{M}_{Ln})) \qquad (3)$$

and

$$
\begin{aligned}
Var(S_{DT}) \;=\; & e^{2\,(\mu + \sigma^2)} \cdot (1 - \Phi(\hat{M}_{Ln} - 2\,\sigma)) \\
& - 2\,\hat{M}\,e^{\mu + \frac{1}{2}\sigma^2} \cdot (1 - \Phi(\hat{M}_{Ln} - \sigma)) \\
& + \hat{M}^2(1 - \Phi(\hat{M}_{Ln})) - E(S_{DT})^2, \qquad (4)
\end{aligned}
$$

where $\hat{M}_{Ln} = (ln\,\hat{M} - \mu)/\sigma$ and Φ denotes the distribution function of a standard normal distribution.[17]

Aside from the distribution structure of S and I_1 as well as the (deterministic) values $\hat{I}_0$, $\hat{\beta}$ and $\hat{M}$, the probability distribution of the compensation payments for the reinsurer S_{DT} are determined by the existing correlation between S and I_1.[18]

In the reinsurance practice, it is usual to carry out an isolated valuation based on the distribution structure of S_{DT}. We can mention here e.g. the expectation value principle, the standard deviation principle, or the percentile principle[19], with which we typically get different results for the safety loading on the mean $E[S_{DT}]$. However from a theoretical viewpoint such a procedure should not be used as it does not take any diversification effects in the portfolio of the reinsurer into account. In other words: it is fundamentally important for valuation which contribution to the total risk of our focussed reinsurer the trigger contract makes. We want to study this in the following section.

To clarify our argumentation, we want to develop a simple one-period stochastic model of a reinsurance company, which can be brought in to evaluate the special double-trigger reinsurance form that we're considering here. In order to keep the analysis clear, we make a few simplifying assumptions:

- The premium income for the period under consideration are paid at t = 0, the corresponding claims are paid at t = 1.

- There are no operating costs in the observed period (in particular no additional transaction costs for the trigger contract).

- Only claims and returns are stochastic.

---

[17] cf. i.e. SCHRÖTER (1994), p. 46 and the example at the end of the chapter.

[18] Even so the primary insurer under consideration could be an "index company", it can be assumed that *in general* there will be no heavy interaction (at least) between S and I_1.

[19] An overview can be found in i.e. HEILMANN (1988), pp. 110-123.

For the derivation of the price limit, we differentiate two constellations: the situation of the reinsurer *before* and the situation of the reinsurer *after* signing the trigger reinsurance contract.

If $\hat{E}C_0$ designates the equity capital at t = 0, $\hat{P}_{Re}$ the premium income, S_{Re} the loss distribution *before* signing the trigger contract and r the yield of the entire capital investment, the equity capital EC_1 at t = 1 is given by the equation

$$EC_1 = (\hat{E}C_0 + \hat{P}_{Re}) \cdot (1 + r) - S_{Re}. \tag{5}$$

If $\hat{P}_{DT}$ stands for the premium of the double-trigger contract, the equity capital EC_1^* in t = 1 after contract signing is given by

$$
\begin{aligned}
EC_1^* &= (\hat{E}C_0 + \hat{P}_{Re} + \hat{P}_{DT}) \cdot (1 + r) - S_{Re} - S_{DT} \\
&= EC_1 + \hat{P}_{DT} \cdot (1 + r) - S_{DT}. \tag{6}
\end{aligned}
$$

For further investigation we now suggest the following procedure: for the absolute price limit of the trigger contract from the point of view of the reinsurer, it must be such that the expected gains $E(EC_1) - \hat{E}C_0$ may not be lowered after contract signing. Furthermore, we will include a second restriction on a "Value-at-Risk" basis: specifically we want the (one-period) ruin probability $\Psi = prob(EC_1 < 0)$ not to be increased by the closing of the trigger contract.[20]

In a formal sense, we retain a stochastic optimizing program for fixing the price limit with $\hat{P}_{DT} \to$ min! subject to (I) $E(EC_1) \leq E(EC_1^*)$ and (II) $\Psi \geq prob(EC_1^* < 0)$. Because of restriction (II), the optimizing assessment is termed a "chance-constrained program", that in general can only be approximately solved by means of numerical methods.[21/22]

Our procedure draws its rationale from the following considerations: we assume the reinsurance company to be risk-neutral, i.e. it only observes the expected gain (this is reflected in (I)). The ruin restriction (II) could in this respect either

- formalize a required solvency margin by the insurance regulators or

- be included as a means of avoiding costs of financial distress from the viewpoint of the stockholders.[23]

---

[20]cf. also ALBRECHT (1990), p. 242.

[21]cf. also the example at the end of the chapter.

[22]cf. KALL, WALLACE (1994), pp. 231–275 with further proofs and ALBRECHT (1986), esp. p. 355–358 and the primary literature cited there. For specific distribution assumptions for EC_1^* the above program can be converted into an equivalent deterministic (typically non-linear) program; see moreover e.g. CHARNES, COOPER (1963), pp.18–39.

[23]cf. GRINBLATT, TITMAN (1998), pp. 715–718.

- In a further interpretation of financial distress costs, the retention of a high security level $(1 - \Psi)$ can also serve in getting premium payments at a level of $\hat{P}_{Re}$ (the solidity of the reinsurer - particularly communicated by ratings - has great importance for the primary insurer).

In the view of the reinsurance company the level of the price limit $\hat{P}_{DT}$ is - apart from the size and structure of the portfolio on hand and the compensation distribution S_{DT} of the trigger contract - strongly determined by the interrelations between EC_1, r and S_{DT}. It can be assumed, that in reality a (small) negative correlation between EC_1 and S_{DT} exists, as S_{DT} may be positively correlated with the loss distribution S_{Re} of the reinsurer and negatively with the investment rate of return r.

In case of a binding shortfall restriction (II) in the stochastic optimization problem, it could happen that we get a considerable safety loading on the net risk premium $E(S_{DT})$. The calculated lower price limit $\hat{P}_{DT}$ may then be so high, that we may have only a limited demand on the side of the cedent.

We want to illustrate this with a short sample calculation: let $\tilde{S}$ follow a lognormal distribution with $E(\tilde{S}) = 80{,}000{,}000$ €, $\sigma(\tilde{S}) = 6{,}000{,}000$ € and let the agreed upon priority $\hat{M}$ be 90,000,000 €; from equations (3) and (4) we get $E(S_{DT}) \approx 157{,}418$ € as well as $\sigma(S_{DT}) \approx 904{,}641$ €. Now assume that the equity capital in $t = 1$ before closing the double-trigger contract EC_1 is normal distributed with $E(EC_1) = 100{,}000{,}000$ € and $\sigma(EC_1) = 30{,}390{,}711$ €, which leads to a ruin probability Ψ of about 0.05%. Suppose the absolute price limit $\hat{P}_{DT}$ for the trigger contract was invested at a risk-free rate $\hat{r}$ of 4%, and as restrictions on the upper stochastic optimization program we have (I) $100{,}000{,}000$ € $\leq E(EC_1^*)$ and (II) $0.05\% \geq prob(EC_1^* < 0)$, the following dependencies between the correlation coefficient $corr(EC_1, S_{DT})$ and the $\hat{P}_{DT}$ can be derived:

$corr(EC_1, S_{DT})$	0	-0.1	-0.2
$\hat{P}_{DT}$	≈ 209.000 €	≈ 788.000 €	$\approx 1.722.000$ €

3 Conclusion

Central in our essay was the investigation and pricing of a special double-trigger arrangement; it concerns a stop-loss whole account coverage with full risk transfer based on a loss ratio modified by the change in a capital market index.

The question is to what extent such contracts represent a meaningful complement to traditional protection strategies for primary insurance companies, or will even replace them one day. As our analysis shows, this depends particularly on to what extent the reinsurer is able to reduce the absolute lower price limit through further risk transformation or hedging measures, with the goal to enlarge (or create) the potential area of agreement between him and the primary insurance company.

References

ALBRECHT, P. (1986): Konstruktion und Analyse stochastischer Gesamtmodelle des Versicherungsgeschäfts auf der Grundlage risiko- und finanzierungstheoretischer Ansätze, Habilitation (unpublished), Mannheim.

ALBRECHT, P. (1990): Zur Anwendung der Deckungsbeitragsrechnung in der Schadenversicherung. *Zeitschrift für die gesamte Versicherungswissenschaft, 79, 205–250.*

CANTER, M. and COLE, J. and SANDOR, R. (1996): Insurance Derivatives: A new Asset Class for the Capital Markets and a new Hedging Tool for the Insurance Industry. *The Journal of Derivatives, 5, 89–104.*

CHARNES, A. and COOPER, W. (1963): Deterministic Equivalents for Optimizing and Satisficing Under Chance Constraints. *Operations Research, 2, 18–39.*

CUMMINS, J. (1991): Statistical and Financial Models of Insurance Pricing and the Insurance Firm. *Journal of Risk and Insurance, 261–302.*

CUMMINS, J. and GEMAN, H. (1995): Pricing Catastrophe Insurance Futures and Call Spreads: An Arbitrage Approach. *The Journal of Fixed Income, 5, 46–57.*

DAYKIN, C. and PENTIKÄINEN, T. and PESONEN, M. (1994): Practical Risk Theory for Actuaries, London 1994.

GRINBLATT, M. and TITMAN, S. (1998): Financial Markets and Corporate Strategy. Irwin/McGraw-Hill, Boston.

HAN, L. and LAI, G. (1995): An Analysis of Securitization in the Insurance Industry. *Journal of Risk and Insurance, 62, 286–296.*

HASEKAMP, U. (2000): Finanzinnovationen im Versicherungskontext: Securitization und börsengehandelte Derivate. Verlag Versicherungswirtschaft, Karlsruhe.

HEILMANN, W. -R. (1988): Fundamentals of Risk Theory. Verlag Versicherungswirtschaft, Karlsruhe.

KALL, P. and WALLACE, S. (1994): Stochastic Programming. Wiley, Chichester.

KIELHOLZ, W. and DURRER, A. (1997): Insurance Derivatives and Securitization: New Hedging Perspectives for the US Cat Insurance Market. *The Geneva Papers on Risk and Insurance, 82, 3–16.*

ROSS, S. (1978): A Simple Approach to the Valuation of Risky Streams. *Journal of Business, 51, 453–475.*

SCHMEISER, H. and GRÜNDL, H. (2000): On the Pricing of Double-Trigger Reinsurance Products. *Discussion Papers in Business No. 2a,* published by the Department of Business and Economics, Humboldt University Berlin.

SCHRÖTER, K. (1994): Verfahren zur Approximation der Gesamtschadenverteilung - Systematisierung, Techniken und Vergleiche. Verlag Versicherungswirtschaft, Karlsruhe.

SMITH, R. and CANCELO, E. and DI DIO, A. (1997): Reinventing Reinsurance Using the Capital Markets. *The Geneva Papers on Risk and Insurance, 82, 26–37.*

WAGNER, F. (1998): Risk Securitization - An Alternative Risk Transfer of Insurance Companies. *The Geneva Papers on Risk and Insurance, 89, 574–607.*

WILHELM, J. (1985): Arbitrage Theory - Introductory Lectures on Arbitrage-Based Financial Asset Pricing, Springer, Berlin.

A Multiple Method Approach for Discrimination and Classification in Marketing Research

T. Temme

Business Administration and Marketing
University of Bielefeld, D-33501 Bielefeld, Germany

Abstract: This proposal suggests the complementary use of multiple methods in marketing research. In particular, the results obtained from the CHi-square Automatic Interaction Detector (CHAID) are both combined and integrated with several techniques of discrimination and classification. The approach is demonstrated by an empirical example from the automotive industry.

1 Introduction

Most marketing and business research studies to date treat different methods of discrimination and classification as competing techniques rather than complementary ones (Malhotra et al. (1999)). The common practice is to recommend instructions to marketing decision makers exclusively on the basis of a unique, i.e. the 'best' method. Consequently, results provided by methods performing only slightly worse are wasted. However, this wasted information may imply other marketing decisions than the results of the best method. In this case the use of a single technique can increase the risk of management decisions instead of decreasing it. Therefore, marketing researchers should always ask themselves whether they have missed some important part of the information available. Furthermore, especially in the field of discrimination and classification, finding a best method is not at all an easy task, because "different problems have different features and [...] what is regarded to as good often varies from problem to problem" (Hand (1997, p. 3)).

An alternative to the utilization of a single technique of data analysis is the support of marketing decision making by the use of multiple methods. The basic idea of this approach is that different methods "could complement each other in providing further insights into the phenomenon under study" (Malhotra et al. (1999, p. 2)). Hence, the aim is to integrate the results obtained by different methods in order to provide a more reliable decision support for marketing managers. The main objective of this proposal is to answer the question to what extent the uncertainty of marketing decisions can be reduced by the integrated use of multiple methods of discrimination and classification. In addition to the study of Malhotra et al. (1999), who dealt with the mutual assistance of several classification results, the present approach is extended to the task of discrimination, i.e. the computation of variable contributions. Because of its suitability for handling vast amounts of objects and variables the current approach is applied to a variety of combinations of the CHi-square Automatic Interaction Detector (CHAID) (Kass (1980)) with other methods, in particular discriminant analysis, logistic regression and neural networks. The idea of using the results obtained by classification trees as inputs for other methods of discrimination and classification has been proposed by Green (1978) and more recently by Kuhnert et al. (2000). Thus, a further feature of the approach is the combination of results provided by different methods.

2 A typical problem of marketing research

A motor car manufacturer may be confronted with the task of carrying out a target group specific restyling of his 4 product brochures with subsequent distribution via mailing. This a priori problem of segmentation leads to the data analytical question how potential purchasers of the 4 motor car versions A, B, C, and D (dependent variables) differ with regard to several aspects of buying behavior (independent variables). These aspects were covered by a survey of roughly 800 customers. With respect to the selection of the mainly categorical predictors two different sets of variables are considered: The first one is labelled 'subjective' variables. These concern primarily psychodemographic product qualities and are measured dichotomously. Hence, subjective variables can serve as a basis for the restyling of the brochures. In order to do so the main task is one of discrimination, i.e. the determination of the subjective variables' contributions to group separation. The second type of variables are mainly sociodemographic data, which can be obtained not only by questioning customers but also from internal and/or other external database supplies. Therefore, they are called 'objective' variables and are suitable for the brochure-sending decision. This decision corresponds to the classical task of supervised classification, i.e. the assignment of individuals with unknown group memberships to one of the four car versions.

3 Preceding CHAID analyses

For processing the given problems of discrimination and classification CHAID was used first because of its general suitability for a segment oriented analysis of large qualitative data bases. When using the subjective variables within a CHAID analysis the psychographic profiles of the resulting segments may be used for a version specific restyling of the brochures, which will not be discussed here in detail. See Decker, Temme (2001) for further discussion. With respect to the subjective variables' contribution to group separation it should merely be mentioned that the aspects of spaciousness (PLATZ) and quality (QUALI) seem to have great discriminative power. These qualities are followed by those of progressive technology (TECHN) and styling (STYLI) as well as of technology, again, comfort (KOMFO), and sportiness (SPORT). This ranking was derived by the variable specific chi-square values computed at each branch of the CHAID analysis and listed in table 1. However, thanks to the CHAID algorithm we have two results for the variable TECHN. So one might ask, What is the 'true' discriminative power of this variable? This leads to the more general question, Can we rely on the findings when using only a single method?

Rank	Variable	χ^2	DF	α	n
1	PLATZ	96.74	3	0.001	780
2	QUALI	50.72	3	0.001	672
3	TECHN	25.88	3	0.001	362
4	STYLI	17.68	3	0.001	310
5	TECHN	12.29	3	0.006	228
6	SPORT	11.56	3	0.009	163
7	KOMFO	8.45	3	0.038	199

Table 1: Subjective variables' chi-square values obtained by CHAID

In the second step of the preceding CHAID analyses we will pursue the question, Which of the potential new customers should get which type of brochure when analyzing objective variables? The classification result of this analysis is shown in table 2 in the usual form of a confusion matrix. The hit rate of correct assignments is 65.51 % and outdoes rates to be expected when random assignments are made. But unfortunately, not a single individual is assigned to car version D. Again, the questions arise, Can our results serve as a reliable basis for marketing decisions? and, Have we considered all available information?

Actual	Predicted A	B	C	D	Total
A	267	33	4	0	304
B	101	167	24	0	292
C	9	28	77	0	114
D	6	11	53	0	70
Total	383	239	158	0	780

Table 2: Objective variables' classification obtained by CHAID

As a first result, we can sum up that the CHAID analyses lead to quite satisfactory results from a statistical point of view. But nevertheless as mentioned above, from a marketing decision maker's standpoint some uncertainties concerning the reliability of the results still remain. In order to reduce these uncertainties other methods should be added to the solution process. As a result, the following investigations should gain some insights into whether the results obtained from multiple methods can mutually assist each other in providing more reliable marketing decision support.

4 Use of multiple methods

If the results obtained from CHAID are combined with discriminant analysis (based on a dummy recoding of predictors), a neural network (supervised classification via a three-layered perceptron), and logistic regression (generalized logits model), the following methodological modules can be constructed:

- CHAID/DISCRIM
- CHAID/NEURAL
- CHAID/LOGISTIC

Within these modules the resulting CHAID segments constitute the categories of an independent variable, while the individual car versions are used again as levels of the dependent variable. Hence, the interaction information uncovered by CHAID is used completely in the form of the terminal nodes. By contrast, in the methodological modules DISCRIM, NEURAL, and LOGISTIC the preliminary results of the CHAID analyses are only used to suggest the independent variables to be included and the categories relevant for each of these variables. In this way the interaction information is not included within these modules and CHAID is used as a screening procedure only.

4.1 Investigation of variable contributions

In order to deal with different methods of discrimination in a suitable manner the variables' contributions to group separation were computed by the use of 'relevancy ratios'. These ratios were determined by relating a variety of goodness of fit measures corresponding to each methodological module disregarding a given variable to the measures of corresponding complete modules. Closely related approaches to this procedure stem from model and/or variable selection strategies within neural networks (Anders (1997, p. 122)), logistic regression (Hosmer, Lemeshow (1989, p. 15)), or (stepwise) discriminant analysis (Huberty (1994, p. 232)). If the resulting ratio of a variable is smaller than 1, the contribution of this variable to group discrimination can be judged as 'negative'; if it is greater than 1, the contribution is 'positive'. The relevancy ratios resulting from the analysis of subjective variables are given in table 3.

In this tabulation the entries represent the relevancy ratios of the variables listed in the columns w.r.t. the goodness of fit criteria listed in the rows. In addition, the resulting variable rank orders are given in brackets. For example, with regard to *Roy's Maximum Root (RMR)* within the module DISCRIM, the variable concerning spaciousness (PLATZ) has

Goodness of fit criterion	QUALI	SPORT	STYLI	KOMFO	TECHN	PLATZ
CHAID						
• Pearson Chi-Square	1.563 (2)	1.109 (4)	1.091 (5)	1.036 (6)	1.273 (3)	1.687 (1)
• Likelihood Ratio Chi-Square	1.423 (2)	1.052 (5)	1.057 (4)	1.040 (6)	1.229 (3)	1.717 (1)
• Phi Coefficient	1.250 (2)	1.053 (4)	1.045 (5)	1.018 (6)	1.128 (3)	1.299 (1)
• Contingency Coefficient	1.195 (2)	1.041 (4)	1.034 (5)	1.013 (6)	1.099 (3)	1.233 (1)
• Cramer's V	1.250 (2)	1.053 (4)	1.045 (5)	1.018 (6)	1.128 (3)	1.299 (1)
CHAID/DISCRIM						
• Pillai-Bartlett Trace	1.563 (2)	1.109 (4)	1.091 (5)	1.036 (6)	1.273 (3)	1.687 (1)
• Hotelling-Lawley Trace	1.605 (2)	1.111 (4)	1.100 (5)	1.040 (6)	1.311 (3)	1.785 (1)
• Roy's Maximum Root	1.227 (2)	1.004 (6)	1.125 (4)	1.023 (5)	1.215 (3)	1.568 (1)
• Bartlett's V	1.579 (2)	1.110 (4)	1.095 (5)	1.037 (6)	1.289 (3)	1.733 (1)
• Wilks' Lambda	1.136 (2)	1.035 (4)	1.031 (5)	1.013 (6)	1.081 (3)	1.158 (1)
DISCRIM						
• Pillai-Bartlett Trace	1.272 (2)	1.074 (5)	1.129 (4)	1.015 (6)	1.150 (3)	1.653 (1)
• Hotelling-Lawley Trace	1.291 (2)	1.075 (5)	1.139 (4)	1.019 (6)	1.167 (3)	1.755 (1)
• Roy's Maximim Root	1.133 (2)	1.014 (6)	1.095 (4)	1.027 (5)	1.111 (3)	1.846 (1)
• Bartlett's V	1.281 (2)	1.074 (5)	1.133 (4)	1.016 (6)	1.158 (3)	1.700 (1)
• Wilks' Lambda	1.071 (2)	1.022 (5)	1.037 (4)	1.005 (6)	1.043 (3)	1.137 (1)
CHAID/NEURAL						
• Schwarz's Bayesian Criterion	0.997 (5)	0.998 (3)	1.011 (2)	0.996 (6)	0.998 (4)	1.023 (1)
• Akaike's Information Criterion	1.014 (2)	1.002 (5)	1.010 (3)	1.001 (6)	1.010 (4)	1.026 (1)
• Sum of Squared Errors	1.037 (2)	1.007 (5)	1.019 (4)	1.004 (6)	1.027 (3)	1.051 (1)
• Mean Squared Error	1.031 (2)	1.005 (5)	1.019 (4)	1.002 (6)	1.023 (3)	1.049 (1)
• Final Prediction Error	1.006 (2)	1.001 (5)	1.005 (3)	1.000 (6)	1.005 (4)	1.012 (1)
NEURAL						
• Schwarz's Bayesian Criterion	1.018 (2)	1.002 (5)	1.009 (4)	1.000 (6)	1.014 (3)	1.025 (1)
• Akaike's Information Criterion	1.021 (2)	1.006 (5)	1.013 (4)	1.004 (6)	1.017 (3)	1.028 (1)
• Sum of Squared Errors	1.043 (2)	1.013 (5)	1.027 (4)	1.011 (6)	1.035 (3)	1.056 (1)
• Mean Squared Error	1.041 (2)	1.012 (5)	1.025 (4)	1.010 (6)	1.033 (3)	1.054 (1)
• Final Prediction Error	1.010 (2)	1.003 (5)	1.006 (4)	1.002 (6)	1.008 (3)	1.013 (1)
CHAID/LOGISTIC						
• Likelihood Ratio Chi-Square	1.423 (2)	1.052 (5)	1.057 (4)	1.040 (6)	1.229 (3)	1.717 (1)
• Likelihood Ratio Index	1.423 (2)	1.052 (5)	1.057 (4)	1.040 (6)	1.229 (3)	1.717 (1)
• -2 Log-Likelihood	1.041 (2)	1.007 (5)	1.007 (4)	1.005 (6)	1.026 (3)	1.060 (1)
• Akaike's Information Criterion	1.026 (2)	1.003 (5)	1.007 (4)	1.002 (6)	1.015 (3)	1.050 (1)
• Schwarz's Bayesian Criterion	0.987 (5)	0.994 (3)	1.007 (2)	0.992 (4)	0.986 (6)	1.040 (1)
LOGISTIC						
• Likelihood Ratio Chi-Square	1.674 (2)	1.076 (5)	1.142 (4)	1.019 (6)	1.164 (3)	1.674 (1)
• Likelihood Ratio Index	1.674 (2)	1.076 (5)	1.142 (4)	1.019 (6)	1.164 (3)	1.674 (1)
• -2 Log-Likelihood	1.058 (2)	1.010 (5)	1.018 (4)	1.003 (6)	1.020 (3)	1.058 (1)
• Akaike's Information Criterion	1.053 (2)	1.006 (5)	1.014 (4)	0.999 (6)	1.016 (3)	1.053 (1)
• Schwarz's Bayesian Criterion	1.040 (2)	0.997 (5)	1.004 (4)	0.990 (6)	1.006 (3)	1.040 (1)

Table 3: Subjective variables' relevancy ratios and rank orders

a relevancy ratio of 1.846, which can be judged as positive; furthermore, according to the corresponding ratios in the same row the resultant rank order of this variable is 1. By a close inspection of table 3 one can see that most of the modules reproduce the results of the CHAID pre analysis, i.e. the variables' rank order. Hence, the 'true' rank of the variable TECHN seems to be 3. However, from a more statistical point of view, the computation of confidence intervals e.g. by bootstrap procedures should be added to this kind of 'eyeballing' in order to realize a statistical quantification of the reliability of the results.

4.2 Investigation of group assignments

A summary of the correct assignments by the methodological modules based on the analysis of the objective variables is displayed in table 4. Groupwise and total hit rates are given in brackets. The analysis was carried out on a validation sample of about 200 objects.

Module	A	B	C	D	Total
(1) CHAID	62	46	20	0	128
	(0.816)	(0.630)	(0.690)	(0.000)	(0.653)
(2) CHAID/DISCRIM	62	46	0	14	122
	(0.816)	(0.630)	(0.000)	(0.778)	(0.622)
(3) DISCRIM	64	45	17	8	134
	(0.842)	(0.616)	(0.586)	(0.444)	(0.684)
(4) CHAID/NEURAL	62	46	20	0	128
	(0.816)	(0.630)	(0.690)	(0.000)	(0.653)
(5) NEURAL	54	51	20	0	125
	(0.711)	(0.699)	(0.690)	(0.000)	(0.638)
(6) CHAID/LOGISTIC	62	46	20	0	128
	(0.816)	(0.630)	(0.690)	(0.000)	(0.653)
(7) LOGISTIC	54	50	20	0	124
	(0.711)	(0.685)	(0.690)	(0.000)	(0.633)

Table 4: Correct assignments obtained by analyzing objective variables

If we take a look at total hit rates, the result seems clear: The performances of all modules are largely similar, so without a loss of information we would choose DISCRIM for our sending decision, because this technique (slightly) outperforms all other modules. However, by taking into account groupwise allocations, it becomes obvious that no one module completely dominates the others across all groups. Due to this finding, which corresponds to that of Malhotra et al. (1999, p. 9), the question arises, How (dis)similar are the results of the methodological modules really? To answer this question Kuncheva (2000) uses Yule's coefficient Q (Bock (1974, p. 62)) as a measure of association between the performance of two classifiers. These are shown in table 5 for the present example.

Q varies between -1 and 1; it has a value close to 1, if the classifiers tend to recognize the same objects correctly; methods which commit errors on different objects will render Q negative (Kuncheva (2000, p. 243)). For example, the modules CHAID and CHAID/DISCRIM are very

Module	(1)	(2)	(3)	(4)	(5)	(6)	(7)
(1) CHAID	1.000	0.908	0.989	1.000	0.981	1.000	0.979
(2) CHAID/DISCRIM	0.908	1.000	0.959	0.908	0.753	0.908	0.742
(3) DISCRIM	0.989	0.959	1.000	0.989	0.949	0.989	0.955
(4) CHAID/NEURAL	1.000	0.908	0.989	1.000	0.981	1.000	0.979
(5) NEURAL	0.981	0.753	0.949	0.981	1.000	0.981	1.000
(6) CHAID/LOGISTIC	1.000	0.908	0.989	1.000	0.981	1.000	0.979
(7) LOGISTIC	0.979	0.742	0.955	0.979	1.000	0.979	1.000

Table 5: Pairwise Yule's coefficients

similar, because they classify exactly the same individuals correctly. By contrast, CHAID and NEURAL assign many objects to different classes, so they are quite dissimilar. A cluster analysis of the modules based on the dissimilarities $1 - Q$ using Ward's method reveals the following three groups of similar modules:

Cluster 1:   CHAID, DISCRIM, CHAID/NEURAL, and CHAID/LOGISTIC

Cluster 2:   NEURAL, and LOGISTIC

Cluster 3:   CHAID/DISCRIM

As a result, one can state that it does not matter which module we would choose within these clusters, but between them there is a certain dissimilarity. Hence, the results of modules coming from different clusters, e.g. CHAID/DISCRIM and NEURAL, are not as similar as one might have assumed when taking into acount total hit rates only. Therefore, by using only one method from one of the three clusters for the support of marketing management w.r.t. the sending decision, we would have missed information available by using methods from one of the other clusters, respectively. In order not to waste information in sitations outlined above a vast amount of approaches concerning the combination of multiple learned models has recently been suggested (Chan et al. (1999)). Thus, the previous remarks can also be taken as a 'pre detector' analysis, by which one can explore in a decriptive manner whether a classifier combination is promising or not; so for the present example we can say, it is. For this reason among other approaches a renewed classification based on an optimal scaling of the individuals is attempted. To realize this a correspondence analysis of the indicator matrix containing the assignments of the seven modules and the actual classification is performed within the framework of a leaving-one-out validation. This means, the unclassified individuals are mapped into the correspondence space by assigning a frequency weight of zero to these, respectively. Subsequently, the resulting coordinates of the left out individuals are used to re-classify these by using a nearest neighbour procedure on the basis of a further cross validation. A similar approach of classifier combination has been proposed by Merz (1999). The results of the procedure described above

398

are documented in table 6. By comparing it to the results summarized in table 4 we can see that the renewed assignment completely dominiates the original modules across all groups. Hence, due to the use of complete information supplied by multiple methods the re-classification result is more suitable w.r.t. the present problem of marketing decision making. Furthermore, brochures can be sent out now to potential new purchasers of all car versions.

Actual	Predicted				Total
	A	B	C	D	
A	74	2	0	0	76
B	0	72	0	1	73
C	0	0	29	0	29
D	1	0	1	16	18
Total	75	74	30	17	196

Table 6: Re-classification based on an optimal scaling of individuals

5 Summary

A multiple method approach involving the complementary use of several techniques of discrimination and classification was demonstrated by means of a typical example of marketing research. In order to compute suitable measures for psychodemographic variables' contributions to group discrimination the use of relevancy ratios was suggested. Using these, the rank order of variables obtained in a preceding CHAID analysis was reproduced by a variety of methodological alternatives. In this way, a confirmation of the preceding CHAID results was achieved w.r.t. the aspect of discrimination. A (dis)similarity investigation based on pairwise Yule's coefficients revealed that the same variety of multiple methods leads to different results if classification is the objective in analyzing sociodemographic variables. Furthermore, it was possible to resolve the problem of group separation occurring in a preceding CHAID analysis of these variables by means of a renewed classification based on an optimal scaling of individuals. Basically, for the given problem the integrated use of multiple methods of discrimination and classification leads to an appreciable improvement in the quality of marketing decisions, because far more reliable decision support is reached than in the case of applying a single method. However, the general suitability of the approach presented here for marketing research should be tested by other data examples in the future. Furthermore, a consideration of computational aspects, like training time and memory requirements, is advised.

Acknowledgements. The author wishes to thank Professor R. Decker for helpful comments during the research process as well as Professor L. Fahrmeir for graciously providing the data.

References

ANDERS, U. (1997): Statistische neuronale Netze, Vahlen, München.

BOCK, H.-H. (1974): Automatische Klassifikation, Vandenhoeck & Ruprecht, Göttingen.

CHAN, P. K.; STOLFO, S. J.; WOLPERT, D. (1999): Guest editors' introduction to special issue on integrating multiple learned models, *Machine Learning, 36, 5–7.*

DECKER, R.; TEMME, T. (2001): CHAID als Instrument der Werbemittelgestaltung und Zielgruppenbestimmung im Marketing, to appear in: Wilde, K.; U. Küsters; H. Hippner; M. Meyer (Hrsg.): Handbuch Data Mining im Marketing, Vieweg, Braunschweig.

GREEN, P. A. (1978): An AID/Logit procedure for analyzing large multiway contingency tables, *Journal of Marketing Research, 15, 132–136.*

HAND, D. J. (1997): Construction and assessment of classification rules, Wiley, Chichester.

HOSMER, D. W.; LEMESHOW, S. (1989): Applied logistic regression, Wiley, New York.

HUBERTY, C. J. (1994): Applied Discriminant Analysis, Wiley, New York.

KASS, G. V. (1980): An exploratory technique for investigating large quantities of categorical Data. *Applied Statistics, 29, 119–127.*

KUHNERT, P. M.; DO, K.-A.; McCLURE, R. (2000): Combining non-parametric models with logistic regression: an application to motor vehicle injury data, *Computational Statistics & Data Analysis, 34, 371–386.*

KUNCHEVA, L. I. (2000): Fuzzy classifier design, Physica, Heidelberg.

MALHOTRA, K. K.; SHARMA, S.; NAIR, S. S. (1999): Decision making using multiple models, *European Journal of Operational Research, 114, 1–14.*

MERZ, C. J. (1999): Using correspondence analysis to combine classifiers, *Machine Learning, 36, 33–58.*

Goodness-of-Fit Measures for Two-mode Cluster Analyses

Andreas Unterreitmeier, Manfred Schwaiger

Seminar für Empirische Forschung und Quantitative Unternehmensplanung,
Ludwig-Maximilians-Universität München, D-80539 München, Germany

Abstract: Two-mode cluster analyses take pleasure in increasing distribution
not only in psychological but also in management applications, for example in
the controlling of advertising effects (Schwaiger 1997a). Until today, only a few
index numbers exist that are able to measure the goodness-of-fit of a two-mode
classification, like VAF, TIC and CCC.
This paper is meant to consider how heterogeneity within a two-mode cluster
can be quantified by referring to intramode similarity relations. An approach
by Schwaiger (1997a, p. 122 f.) calculates the square deviations between an
original matrix and matrices of cluster-centroids that originate by relating elements of one mode (combined in a two-mode cluster) in each case to the vector
of the mode-specific class-centroid. In the strict sense, this index number can
only be used to compare two classifications with an identical number of clusters.
The subject of the discussion will be a suggestion that extends this procedure.
Moreover, it is able to compare partitions with different numbers of clusters.

1 Introduction

Classification methods represent a crucial part of exploratory data analysis. Their value for practical business tools appears especially in the
context of interpreting results. A typology does not arise to life nor
does a two-mode dendrogram become helpful for decisions before resulting clusters are interpreted. A researcher's scepticism about exploratory
results is generally considered important, because the number crunching
of data may cause misleading conclusions in the interpretation, one of
the reasons being that not every detailed information can be taken into
consideration. Questions such as how a present classification can be evaluated basically arise in the analyses of classification results. The answer
to this question is mainly dependent on the criterion of the goodness used.
Therefore we want to discuss the few available goodness-of-fit-measures
for the two-mode cluster analysis in Chapter 2 and furthermore present
an adaption of the criterion of variance (e.g. Opitz 1980, p. 76) for two-
mode clusters and its application in Chapter 3.

In the two-mode cluster analysis row- and column-elements of a data
matrix are classified simultaneously. As an input for the two-mode cluster
analysis, a data matrix $\mathbf{X} = \left(x_{ij}\right)_{(n \times m)}$ must be used. For that purpose,
any two-mode matrix serves as a data matrix $\mathbf{X}$ if created by relating

numerical values x_{ij} to the elements $O_i \in O$, $M_j \in M$ of the cartesian product $O \times M$ ($O = \{O_1, \ldots, O_n\}$, $M = \{M_1, \ldots, M_m\}$). Possibilities of application in economic and social sciences are described in DeSarbo (1982), De Soete (1984), Both/Gaul (1986), Eckes (1993 and 1995) and Schwaiger (1998).

To illustrate our explanations we use an association matrix obtained by forming the average of the ratings of 53 students, who were asked to evaluate eight (more or less) famous persons by relating to given attributes on a six-step, bipolar scale.

Two-mode cluster analysis now is meant to unite prominent persons and the attributes primarily associated with them in two-mode clusters. Different algorithms are available for that purpose (cf. Schwaiger 1997a, p. 96ff.). We will focus on hierarchical methods creating a dendrogram as a result and, at the same time, showing the process of fusion in contrast to non-hierarchical methods. The methods used are the Centroid-Effect-Method CEM (Eckes/Orlik 1991, 1993), the Missing-Value-Algorithm (Espejo/Gaul 1986, p. 123) in Average-Linkage-Variant (MVAL), and the ESOCLUS-Algorithm (Schwaiger 1997a, p. 113ff.) in the Complete- and Average-Linkage form (ESOCLUS CL resp. ESOCLUS AL).

The classification results differ, so we have to decide on which results to rely on considering a goodness-of-fit index.

2 Goodness-of-Fit Indicators for Two-Mode Classification Results

A qualitative evaluation of two-mode cluster analysis is basically possible with representative methods like factor analysis, MDS and correspondence analysis if their goodness of fit is at least sufficient. The positions of objects and attributes resp. the attribute-vectors in the graphic representations suggest similarities or dissimilarities that should occur in the cluster analyses as well. But it has already been proved that these methods of representation fail on numerous constellations of data (Schwaiger 1997b, 1998) and therefore can contribute only little to the clarification of the question of which criteria of evaluation the user can refer to, if the goodness of graphical representation is insufficient, thus especially if two-mode cluster analyses are very helpful as methods to uncover and visualize structures.

2.1 Goodness-of-Fit Measures for Dendrograms

If hierarchical methods are applied, the process of fusion can be shown by means of a tree-diagram. Analyzing such a two-mode dendrogram, the viewer essentially perceives the spatial distances between elements.

These distances are determined by the length of the way from element i along the branches of the tree-diagram to element j. Short distances are intuitively associated with great similarity, although technical insufficiencies of this implicit interpretation are sometimes problematic.

Consequently, one may compare the similarity between an object i and an attribute j, given by x_{ij}, with the spatial proximity of i and j in the tree-chart.

For this purpose we calculate the spatial distances δ_{ij} ($i = 1, \ldots, n$, $j = 1, \ldots, m$) by assigning δ_{ij} to the level of fusion (to be read on the x-axis in the tree-charts) of object i and attribute j.

In this way, we get $\Delta = (\delta_{ij})_{n \times m}$ that we bring in relation to matrix $D_{(n \times m)}$ containing association data from X transformed according to

$$d_{ij} = \max_{i,j} x_{ij} - x_{ij}, \quad i = 1, \ldots, n, \ j = 1, \ldots, m. \tag{1}$$

by calculating the Cophenetic Correlations Coefficient (Sokal/Rohlf 1962):

$$\mathrm{CCC} = \frac{\sum\limits_{i=1}^{n}\sum\limits_{j=1}^{m}(d_{ij} - \bar{d})(\delta_{ij} - \bar{\delta})}{\sqrt{\sum\limits_{i=1}^{n}\sum\limits_{j=1}^{m}(d_{ij} - \bar{d})^2 \cdot \sum\limits_{i=1}^{n}\sum\limits_{j=1}^{m}(\delta_{ij} - \bar{\delta})^2}} \in [-1; 1] \quad \text{with} \tag{2}$$

$$\bar{d} = \frac{1}{mn}\sum_{i=1}^{n}\sum_{j=1}^{m} d_{ij} \quad \text{and} \quad \bar{\delta} = \frac{1}{mn}\sum_{i=1}^{n}\sum_{j=1}^{m} \delta_{ij} \ .$$

We receive another, somewhat problematic goodness-of-fit-measure by modifying the concept of the Variance-Accounted-For to distances (cf. Gaul/Baier 1993). It is

$$\mathrm{VAF_D} = 1 - \frac{\sum\limits_{i=1}^{n}\sum\limits_{j=1}^{m}(d_{ij} - \delta_{ij})^2}{\sum\limits_{i=1}^{n}\sum\limits_{j=1}^{m}(d_{ij} - \bar{d}_{ij})^2}, \tag{3}$$

whereas by addition of an appropriate constant to matrix Δ it must be guaranteed that $\bar{\delta} = \bar{d}$ is valid. The fact that VAF_D values can also adopt negative values in individual cases has to be criticized seriousely. In this case an interpretation of the goodness-of-fit measure is no longer possible.

Based on the goodness-of-fit measures CCC und VAF_D the dendrograms can be compared (Table 1).

Method	Variant	VAF$_D$	CCC
ESOCLUS	Complete Linkage	0,85	0,66
	Average Linkage	0,93	0,70
MV-Algorithm	Average Linkage	0,56	0,75
Centroid-Effect-Method		0,28	0,71

Table 1: Evaluation of goodness

Table 1 does not show a steady best method. Furthermore, it has to be pointed out that even if CCC und VAF$_D$ values are good, it may happen that class structure and original data do not match.

From that we derive the recommendation to use VAF$_D$ and CCC merely as a hint instead of a decision rule. We now turn to the evaluation of class structure.

2.2 Goodness-of-Fit Measures for the Evaluation of Classifications

Whereas the one-mode cluster analysis gives us numerous indices for the evaluation of a classification (cf. Opitz 1980), there are only two index numbers in the two-mode area. Besides, they can only be applied to non-hierarchical methods. Strictly speaking, they are useful for algorithms that try to reproduce, according to the one-mode ADCLUS-principle, the data matrix $\mathbf{X}$ by a new estimated matrix $\hat{\mathbf{X}}$ according to $\hat{\mathbf{X}} = \mathbf{PWQ}^T + \mathbf{C}$ with $\mathbf{P}$ and $\mathbf{Q}$ containing class memberships and $\mathbf{W}$ expressing the matrix of cluster weights. With the goodness-of-fit criterion VAF or with the Theil Inequality Coefficient (cf. Theil 1970) we determine the goodness of reproduction.

Until today, there have been no indices for the evaluation of **any** two-mode class structure. An appropriate suggestion will be presented in the next section.

3 The Squared Deviation of Mode-Specific Class Centroids

The following explanation is based on the vital assumption that a decision maker perceives objects which are combined in one cluster as homogenous relative to the criteria used for the classification. Therefore it is advisable to figure out how far the single elements of a cluster deviate from the class centroid. Besides, it has to be noted that a definition for the centroid of a two-mode class does not exist. Consequently, we build the (known) object-specific centroid $\mathbf{c}_s^{(1)}$, $s = 1, \ldots, S$ for a classification with S (one- or two-mode) classes on the one hand by building the average over all row objects of a class relative to all attributes. On the other hand, we calculate a (fictitious) attribute-specific centroid $\mathbf{c}_s^{(2)}$, $s = 1, \ldots, S$ by building the average of the column vectors in $\mathbf{X}$ of all column objects in class s.

If we put every row object of the original matrix $\mathbf{X}$ equal to the corresponding centroid, we get $\mathbf{C}_{(n \times m)}^{(1)} = \left(c_{ij}^{(1)} \right)$ with $c_{ij}^{(1)} = \frac{1}{|O_s|} \sum_{i \in s} x_{ij}$, with $|O_s|$ being the number of row objects of cluster $\mathcal{K}_s$ containing i and $\mathbf{C}_{(n \times m)}^{(2)} = \left(c_{ij}^{(2)} \right)$ with $c_{ij}^{(2)} = \frac{1}{|M_s|} \sum_{j \in s} x_{ij}$, with $|M_s|$ denoting the number of column objects of cluster $\mathcal{K}_s$ containing j.

Now we compute the mode-specific squared deviations from the centroid with $\text{QCD}^{(1)} = \sum_{i=1}^{n} \sum_{j=1}^{m} (c_{ij}^{(1)} - x_{ij})^2$ and $\text{QCD}^{(2)} = \sum_{i=1}^{n} \sum_{j=1}^{m} (c_{ij}^{(2)} - x_{ij})^2$ and aggregate it to $\text{QCD} = \text{QCD}^{(1)} + \text{QCD}^{(2)}$.

We obtain an index number normed on the interval $[0; 1]$ and rated the better the closer it is to zero, by dividing QCD by the maximum possible value $\text{QCD}_{\max}$ in the last step of fusion, i.e. exactly whenever there is only one two-mode cluster left containing all row and column objects: $\text{QCD}_{\text{norm}} = \frac{\text{QCD}}{\text{QCD}_{\max}}$.

QCD_{norm} can be interpreted as the degree of exhaustion of the maximum possible heterogeneity. But attention has to be paid to the fact that the ideal value of zero is also adopted if there is no cluster left containing more than one element of a mode, thus in general distinctively before the last step of fusion.

3.1 The Use of QCD to Determine a Proper Number of Classes

Let us exemplarily study the results of the ESOCLUS AL-Algorithm. We receive the QCD-values listed in Table 2.

Number of classes	$\text{QCD}^{(1)}$	$\text{QCD}^{(2)}$		QCD	QCD_{norm}
1	31,666	37,005	($\text{QCD}_{\max} =$)	68,672	1,0000
2	12,137	24,666		36,803	0,5359
3	9,423	19,342		28,765	0,4189
4	7,723	13,163		20,886	0,3041
5	5,531	13,163		18,694	0,2722
6	3,635	11,075		14,710	0,2142
7	1,362	3,912		5,274	0,0768
8	0,000	3,912		3,912	0,0570
9	0,000	2,069		2,069	0,0301
10	0,000	2,069		2,069	0,0301
11	0,000	1,276		1,276	0,0186
12	0,000	0,536		0,536	0,0078
≥ 13	0,000	0,000		0,000	0,0000

Table 2: QCD-values to ESOCLUS AL

If we plot the values $QCD^{(1)}$ and $QCD^{(2)}$ in dependence on the number of classes (which should be very small in order to gain clarity) in a system of co-ordinates, it is possible to determine a proper number of classes analogous to the known elbow-criterion.

Based on accumulated inter- and intramode interclass distances (listed in the grand-matrix), two or six clusters are useful whereas according to QCD two, four or seven clusters seem to be more reasonable.

3.2 The Comparison of Two Classifications with the Help of QCD

Up to the present, we could only use the goodness-of-fit measures shown in Table 1 for choosing a method. Depending on the subjective preference, either the Missing-Value-Algorithm or ESOCLUS (both in the average linkage variant) is preferred. According to the elbow-criterion it is recommended for the Missing-Value-Algorithm to use either 2 or 5 classes and for ESOCLUS AL 2, 3 or 6 classes (for CEM and ESOCLUS complete linkage 2,3,4 and 5 classes are useful).

Now we would like to put the resulting class structures in opposition and check them with the QCD criterion. CEM and Missing-Value Algorithm show identical clusters in the relevant range and therefore have been combined. One- and two-class-solutions are identical for all inspected variants, restricting further investigation to the 3-, 4- and 5-class-solutions. If we confront QCD values with the corresponding class structure we receive Table 3 in which the result best according to QCD is marked with an asterisk.

3 clusters	CEM resp. MVAL	ESOCLUS AL	ESOCLUS CL
$QCD^{(1)}$	6,5747	9,4225	6,5747
$QCD^{(2)}$	20,3358	19,3420	38,0449
QCD	26,9105*	28,7646	44,6196
4 clusters	CEM resp. MVAL	ESOCLUS AL	ESOCLUS CL
$QCD^{(1)}$	4,8464	7,7230	11,7817
$QCD^{(2)}$	20,3358	13,1633	24,7792
QCD	25,1822	20,8863*	36,5609
5 clusters	CEM resp. MVAL	ESOCLUS AL	ESOCLUS CL
$QCD^{(1)}$	3,4890	5,5309	4,0424
$QCD^{(2)}$	20,3358	13,1633	6,5536
QCD	23,8248	18,6941	10,5960*

Table 3: Goodness of different classification solutions

CEM and MVAL prove to be best choice for the 3-class-solution, although especially this partition is suggested by the classical elbow-criterion only for CEM, but not for MVAL. On the other hand, ESO-CLUS AL for the 4-class-solution and ESOCLUS CL for the 5-class-solution are clearly superior, which we could not infer on by using the elbow-criterion, either.

The above listed statement that even good CCC and VAF$_D$ do not necessarily mean a great compatibility of the classification with the original data has become obvious by this example.

4 Conclusion

Because of the sensibility of algorithms in two-mode cluster analyses not only a goodness-of-fit measure to evaluate the process of fusion should be applied but also a measure for the evaluation of class structure.

The declaration of a **proper** goodness-of-fit measure for the evaluation of a two-mode process of fusion and/or a given two-mode classification proves to be difficult altogether, because it is dependent on user preferences. It always has to be established which dimension of goodness (fit of dendrogram, homogeneity of clusters etc.) will be on focus.

We advocate a simultaneous use of CCC and QCD while neglecting VAF$_D$ because of the possible interpretation problems for the following reasons:

- The concept of QCD presented in Chapter 3 may enhance the less extensive range of available goodness-of-fit measures as a plausible index. The CCC expresses how strongly calculated distances correlate with empirically ascertained intermode distances and complements the QCD as far as the CCC reflects intermode homogeneity – understood as the grade of association between row- and column-objects in a two-mode cluster – whereas QCD expresses intramode homogeneity.

- Results of methods that belong to different groups of methods (for example classifications based on hierarchical and non-hierarchical algorithms) can be compared in an evaluating sense with the help of QCD.

References

BOTH, M. and GAUL, W. (1986): Ein Vergleich zweimodaler Clusteranalyseverfahren. *Methods of Operations Research, 57. Jg., 1986, 593–605.*

DE SOETE, G. (1984): Ultrametric Tree Representations of Incomplete Dissimilarity Data. *Journal of Classification, Vol. 1, 1984, 235–242.*

DESARBO, W.S. (1982): GENNCLUS: New Models for General Non-hierarchical Clustering Analysis. *Psychometrika, Vol. 47, Nr. 4, 1982, 449–475.*

408

ECKES, T. and ORLIK, P. (1991): An Agglomerative Method for Two-Mode Hierarchical Clustering, in: Bock, H. and Ihm, P. (eds.): Classification, Data Analysis and Knowledge Organisation, Amsterdam 1991, 3–8.

ECKES, T. and ORLIK, P. (1993): An Error Variance Approach to Two-Mode Hierarchical Clustering. *Journal of Classification, Vol. 10, 1993, 51–74.*

ECKES, T. (1993): Multimodale Clusteranalyse: Konzepte, Modelle, Anwendungen, in: Montada, L. (ed.): Bericht über den 38. Kongreß der Deutschen Gesellschaft für Psychologie in Trier 1992, Vol. 2, Göttin-gen 1993, 166–176.

ECKES, T. (1995): Recent Developments im Multimode Clustering, in: Gaul, W. and Pfeiffer, D. (eds.): From Data to Knowledge, Theoretical and Practical Aspects of Classification, Data Analysis and Knowledge Organisation, Berlin et al. 1995, 151–158.

ESPEJO, E. and GAUL, W. (1986): Two-Mode Hierarchical Cluste-ring as an Instrument for Marketing Research, in: Gaul, W. and Schader, M. (eds.): Classification as a Tool of Research, Amsterdam 1986, 121–128.

GAUL, W. and BAIER, D. (1993): Marktforschung und Marketing Management: computerbasierte Entscheidungsunterstützung, München 1993.

OPITZ, O. (1980): Numerische Taxonomie, Stuttgart, New York, 1980.

SCHWAIGER, M. (1997a): Multivariate Werbewirkungskontrolle – Konzepte zur Auswertung von Werbetests, Wiesbaden 1997.

SCHWAIGER, M. (1997b): Ein methodischer Ansatz zur Auswertung von Recall-Daten, in: Jahrbuch der Absatz- und Verbrauchsforschung, hrsg. von der GfK-Nürnberg, 43. Jg. 1997, Heft 4, 440–453.

SCHWAIGER, M. (1998): Wirkungskontrolle kommunikationspoliti-scher Maßnahmen, in: Reincke, S.; Tomczak, T.; Dittrich, S. (eds.): Marketingcontrolling, THEXIS Fachbuch für Marketing, St. Gallen 1998, 200–213.

SOKAL, R. R. and ROHLF, F. J. (1962): The Comparison of Dendrograms by Objective Methods. *Taxon, Vol. 11, 1962, 33–40.*

THEIL, H. (1970): Economic Forecasts and Policy, Amsterdam, London 1970.

On Volatility Transfers During the Asia Crisis in 1997-1998

Edy Zahnd

Department of Quantitative Economics,
University of Fribourg, CH-1700 Fribourg, Switzerland

Abstract: To test the heat wave or meteor shower hypothesis, like Booth et al. (1997), we build a vector autoregressive (VAR) model for the conditional variances of the 5 variables, later for 11 variables. With 5 or 11 variables, standardmethods available for 3 dimension-cases do not work (multivariate vector AR-GARCH models do not work). Therefore, we use an ad hoc method. The period for estimation is from 1994 to 1998. We estimate univariate MA-GARCH, AR-GARCH or ARMA-GARCH models for the volatilities and we try to find out which volatilities might be the causes for others.

1 Introduction

To study the Asian crisis and the spillovers or, in other words, the transfer of volatilities from one market to another, we use univariate GARCH(1,1) or more complicated AR-GARCH, MA-GARCH or ARMA-GARCH models to compute volatilities, vector autoregressive (VAR) models for the volatilities of different markets (Engle et al. (1990), Booth et al. (1997)). These VAR models can show the nature of the change in volatility: when the impact of a shock coming from the same market is much bigger than the impact of shocks transfered from other markets, it's a heat wave. When on one market the impact of shocks transfered from other markets is dominant, it's a meteor shower.

On July 2, 1997, the Thai monetary authorities gave up the fight for the parity of the Thai baht with the US dollar. One arising question is if this decision has any connection with the turn over of Hong Kong to China on July 1, 1997. Investors sold the currency and the stocks fell sharply. The crisis spread further to the Indonesian rupia and to the Malaysian ringgit. In this framework, we try to show which markets have had a significant impact on the US and Swiss markets and we use the analytic asymptotic kind of impulse response functions based on the VAR model as in Hamilton (1994, p.339).

2 GARCH models for 5 series of returns

To estimate the conditional variances of the series over the period from May 3, 1994 to April 17, 1998, we built one univariate MA-GARCH or AR-GARCH(1,1) model for each series on the following model:

$$y_t = c + \varepsilon_t, \text{ where } \varepsilon_t \sim N(0, h_t), \text{ with } h_t = \omega + \alpha \varepsilon_{t-1}^2 + \beta h_{t-1}. \quad (1)$$

For a stationary GARCH(1,1) model, it is necessary that $\alpha + \beta < 1$ with $\alpha > 0$ and $\beta > 0$ to insure that the conditional variance is always positive. Table 1 gives the values of c, ω, α and β for the SMI, DJ, Hang Seng and Nikkei returns y_t (defined as log differences multiplied by 100).

Returns	c	ω	α	β
SMI	0.105 (3.9)	0.053 (4.0)	0.110 (5.5)	0.827 (26.3)
DJ	0.095 (3.2)	0.014 (3.2)	0.085 (10.2)	0.897 (68.7)
Hang Seng	0.089 (2.28)	0.070 (5.0)	0.121 (8.5)	0.849 (53.9)
Nikkei	0.023 (0.64)	0.053 (6.1)	0.089 (6.4)	0.882 (53.1)

Table 1: Estimation of the GARCH(1,1) model for 4 markets (with the corresponding t statistics).

Trying to model the Jakarta index the same way, we note that the returns are autocorrelated of order 1. An attempt to use a GARCH(1,1) fails by lack of stationarity of the model, because the sum $\alpha + \beta$ is slightly higher than 1. Instead, the following threshold GARCH-in-mean model is estimated:

$$y_t = 0.032 + 0.218h_t - 2.510D_t + u_t, \text{ with MA(2)-GARCH residuals} \quad (2)$$

$$u_t = \varepsilon_t + 0.353\varepsilon_{t-1} + 0.171\varepsilon_{t-2}, \text{ with } \varepsilon_t \sim N(0, h_t) \text{ and} \quad (3)$$

$$h_t = 0.304 + 0.103\varepsilon_{t-1}^2 + 0.278\varepsilon_{t-1}^2 d_{t-1} + 0.359h_{t-1} + 0.000123t + 3.273D_t \quad (4)$$

where the trend variable t is an increment equal to zero for August 1, 1997, positive afterwards and negative before, d_t, the threshold, is 0 if $\varepsilon_t > 0$, 1 if $\varepsilon_t < 0$ and D_t is the dummy for the Asia crisis, equal to 1 from August 1, 1997 on, 0 before. All the t statistics for this model are significant at the 0.05 level except the constant in (2). Note that in this model, the sum of $\alpha + \beta$ is smaller than 1, showing that the model is stationary. However, there is a problem with this model: In an ADF unit root test with many lagged differences (more than 12, which can be explained by a lower AIC and a higher log likelihood in the test equation) in the test equation, we cannot reject the hypothesis of a unit root, meaning that the Jakarta volatility computed with this model is not stationary, even if the model is stationary. This is due to the use of a dummy variable for the Asia crisis. As a volatility cannot keep on rising over a very long period and has to return to a mean value sooner or later, we accept to introduce this volatility in the VAR model for the volatilities. Finally, as the stationarity can be questioned here, a further study may include fractionnally integrated models and long memory processes (Mills, 1997, p. 83, Maddala and Kim, 1998, p. 296–300).

In a pairwise Granger causality test with 2 lags, the following null hypotheses were accepted: SMI does not Granger-cause DJ, Nikkei does not

Granger-cause SMI, SMI does not Granger-cause Nikkei, Jakarta does not Granger-cause DJ, Nikkei does not Granger-cause DJ, Nikkei does not Granger-cause Hang Seng, Jakarta does not Granger-cause Nikkei. We note that with 3 lags, the null hypothesis that SMI does not cause Dow Jones and the null that Dow Jones does not cause Nikkei are rejected (unlike in the case with 2 lags). Further, we have to remember that Granger himself warned that the omission of other relevant variables could result in spurious causality (Maddala and Kim, 1998, p. 189).

3 VAR model for the 5 conditional variances

We use the previous 5 conditional variances in a vector autoregressive (VAR) model (VAR model properties: see Canova (1995), Hamilton (1994, p. 257), Pesaran (1997)) over the period from May 6, 1994, to April 17, 1998 (1031 observations). For this two-step procedure, see Booth et al. (1997). In our VAR(2) of the form:

$$X_t = A_0 + \sum_{j=1}^{2} A_j X_{t-j} + u_t \tag{5}$$

with $t = 1, 2, ..., n$, where X_t is a $k \times 1$ vector of variables, we order the 5 variables (conditional variances) with their two lags as follows in the 5 equations: SMI, DJ, Hang Seng, Nikkei, Jakarta. In the unilateral t test (critical value for a high number of d.f. is 1.645, asymptotically equivalent to the normal), the following coefficients (indicated by their rank of occurrence in the equation) were significant at the 0.05 significance level:

SMI: coefficients 1+, 2+, 3+, 4−, 5−, 6−, 7−, 11− (constant),

DJ: coefficients 3+, 4−, 5+, 7−, 8+, 10−, 11+ (constant),

Hang Seng: coefficients 1+, 2−, 3+, 4−, 5+, 6−, 9+, 10−,

Nikkei: coefficients 3+, 4−, 7+, 8−, 10+, 11+ (constant),

Jakarta: coefficients 3+, 4−, 5−, 6+, 8+, 9+, 11− (constant),

where + is for positive effects and − is for negative effects. In an impulse response function for 5 conditional variances, based on the previous VAR, we note that apparently, the heat waves observed on the main diagonal are dominant, whereas the DJ has a significant impact on the Hang Seng and the SMI, while the Hang Seng has a smaller impact on the Dow Jones. We now examine the case of 6 additional markets.

For India, we get the following AR(1)-GARCH(1,1) model:

$$y_t = -0.0479 + u_t, \text{ where } u_t = 0.334u_{t-1} + \varepsilon_t \text{ with } \varepsilon_t \sim N(0, h_t) \tag{6}$$

$$\text{and } h_t = 0.0689 + 0.145\varepsilon_{t-1}^2 + 0.811h_{t-1}. \tag{7}$$

There are no more autocorrelations in the correlogram of the standard-ized residuals, the p-values for the lags 2 to 25 from the Ljung-Box Q-statistics are all higher than 0.05. For the squared standardized residuals, all the p-values for the lags 4 to 25 are bigger than 0.05. An ARCH-test with 5 lagged standardized residuals squared cannot reject the null hypothesis that there are no significant autocorrelations in the 5 lagged standardized residuals squared.

For Korea,

$$y_t = -0.038 + u_t \tag{8}$$

where u_t follows an ARMA process with one AR(1) parameter and one MA(12) parameter:

$$u_t = 0.149u_{t-1} + \varepsilon_t - 0.081\varepsilon_{t-12} \tag{9}$$

where the unique root of the characteristic AR polynomial (equal to the inverse of the AR coefficient for an AR(1) process) and all the roots of the characteristic MA polynomial lie outside the unit circle. We have $\varepsilon_t \sim N(0, h_t)$ with

$$\log(h_t) = -0.076 + 0.945 \log(h_{t-1}) + 0.113 \left| \frac{\varepsilon_{t-1}}{h_{t-1}} \right| - 0.083 \frac{\varepsilon_{t-1}}{h_{t-1}} + 0.134 D_t \tag{10}$$

with the D_t dummy variable equal to one from October 1, 1997, to April 17, 1998 and 0 otherwise. This EGARCH model (Nelson, 1991) is better than a TGARCH model (Ding et al. (1993), Rabemananjara and Zakoian (1993)) we estimated, because the likelihood is higher and the Akaike criterion lower.

For Malaysia, we also note that in a simple AR(1)-GARCH(1,1) model, the GARCH parameters are $\alpha = 0.134$ and $\beta = 0.864$, such that $\alpha + \beta = 0.998$. When we apply a Wald test for the null hypothesis that $\alpha + \beta = 1$, we see that we cannot reject it even at the 10% significance level. If we consider the returns, it seems that the increase in volatility began as late as, and not before, in August 1997. We use a dummy variable equal to 1 from August 1, 1997, to April 17, 1998, like for Jakarta, and to 0 before. We note that the third moment plays a role in the mean equation here, and that the level is significant in the variance equation, in association with the Asian crisis dummy variable. Trying to find an adequate model maximizing the log likelihood, we get the following one, providing the highest likelihood, the lowest AIC and the lowest standard error of residuals:

$$y_t = -0.0582 - 0.00443y_{t-1}^3 + 10.482D_t + u_t \tag{11}$$

where D_t is here an outlier dummy equal to 1 on May 1, 1995, and zero otherwise, and u_t follows an AR(1) process:

$$u_t = 0.252u_{t-1} + \varepsilon_t \tag{12}$$

where the unique root of the characteristic AR polynomial lies outside the unit circle. The estimation of the parameter of this equation is not done using the Cochrane Orchut procedure (Pesaran and Pesaran, 1997, p. 91). The Gauss-Newton method for MLE is used here, because of simplicity. Here also we have the $\varepsilon_t \sim N(0, h_t)$ with

$$h_t = 5.582 + 0.667h_{t-1} + 0.121\varepsilon^2_{t-1} - 0.770z_{t-1} + 1.197D_t - 0.148y_{t-1} \quad (13)$$

where z_t is the log of the Malaysia index in level and D_t is a dummy equal to 1 for the period from August 1997 to April 1998. The estimation of this model, estimated over the period from May 5, 1994, to April 17, 1998, is done in this case only with the Bollerslev-Wooldridge robust standard errors and covariance, because the conditional distribution was not Gaussian.

For the Singapore AR(1)-GARCH(1,1) model, the null hypothesis that $\alpha + \beta = 1$ can be rejected. We can use the simple following model over the period from May 3, 1994, to April 17, 1998, with a constant, an AR(1) parameter and GARCH(1,1) residuals:

$$y_t = -0.0158 + u_t, \text{ where } u_t = 0.163u_{t-1} + \varepsilon_t, \text{ with } \varepsilon_t \sim N(0, h_t) \quad (14)$$

$$\text{and } h_t = 0.0329 + 0.133\varepsilon^2_{t-1} + 0.841h_{t-1}. \quad (15)$$

For Thailand,

$$y_t = -0.0699 + u_t, \text{ where } u_t = 0.205u_{t-1} + \varepsilon_t, \text{ with } \varepsilon_t \sim N(0, h_t) \quad (16)$$

$$\text{and } h_t = 0.123 + 0.164\varepsilon^2_{t-1} + 0.795h_{t-1}. \quad (17)$$

Here also, the null hypothesis that $\alpha + \beta = 1$ can be rejected. The estimated volatility is stationary when tested with a Dickey Fuller test with any number of lags.

For Taiwan, we get

$$y_t = 0.0676 + \varepsilon_t, \text{ with } \varepsilon_t \sim N(0, h_t) \quad (18)$$

$$\text{and } h_t = 0.455 + 0.116\varepsilon^2_{t-1} + 0.653h_{t-1}. \quad (19)$$

Here also, the null hypothesis that $\alpha + \beta = 1$ can be rejected. When tested for autocorrelations, the standardized residuals show a Ljung-Box test statistic (with 9 or 12 lags) allowing to accept the null of no auto-correlations up to lag 9 or 12.

4 VAR model for 11 conditional variances – Stationarity of the model

The VAR models can be considered as a reduced form of a simultaneous equations model (see Deschamps, 1985) where all the predetermined variables are lagged endogenous variables or other variables (the latter can be simultaneous also, i.e. without lag). As we have already seen, the characteristic polynomial produced by setting the determinant of the system equal to zero, must have only roots outside the unit circle to insure that the VAR is stationary (Franses, 1998, p. 196). This means that the roots of the following polynomial in z: $|I_k - \phi_1 z - \phi_2 z^2 - ... - \phi_p z^p| = 0$ (where the ϕ_i are matrices and I_k is an identity matrix of dimension k) lie outside the unit circle (Hamilton (1994, p. 259 and p. 298), Pesaran and Pesaran (1997, p. 420)). Only when this condition is fulfilled will the process be covariance-stationary (Hamilton, 1994, p. 259). Also important is that the variables are stationary, or, at least, pairwise cointegrated (Canova (1995)).

Hereafter, we compare the AIC and SC approach to select the order of the VAR. We note that AIC is not the adequate criterion here, because it decreases continuously. On the other hand, SC selects order 2. We can also use the likelihood ratio test or the Wald test. If we compare the VAR(2) and the VAR(3) models at the light of LR test (Pesaran and Pesaran, 1997, p. 422 and p. 272), we note that with a 5% level of significance, the null hypothesis that VAR(3) and VAR(2) are identical is strongly rejected. However the LR test is biased, because the model is not parsimonious or because the covariance matrix of the residuals is not diagonal. Even with the degrees of freedom adjusted LR test statistic proposed by Pesaran and Pesaran (1997, p. 422), the result is the same. Another method had been proposed by Sims (1980, p. 17) (see also Hamilton, (1994, p. 297)), but the penalty for additional variables or lags is not important enough neither. An alternative method to determine the order of the VAR model is presented by Lütkepohl (1991, p. 308): he suggests to link the number of parameters in each equation to both the sample size (T) and the dimension of the time series (k) according to the rule: $kp = T^{1/3}$. In our case, $T^{1/3} = 10.08$ suggests that $p = 1$ would be high enough. Knowing that the Schwarz criterion, which selects a VAR(2), does not overestimate the order of the process, we keep the order 2. According to Canova (1995), the residuals have to be stationary and not autocorrelated, like in univariate AR or ARMA models. There should be no ARCH effect, meaning that the squared residuals should not show any autocorrelation. We checked these three points. To test for stationarity of the variables, we used ADF tests with a constant for the conditional variances, like in Canova (1995, p. 112). However, as mentioned previously, we used different numbers of lagged terms in the test equation. As for the squared residuals, the null hypothesis of no autocorrelation can be accepted only in five cases out of 11, denoting the presence of GARCH effects, leading to the conclusion that VAR-GARCH models (estimated by MLE) can also be used (see Polasek and Kozumi (1995) for a similar model).

As we have seen for the model for 5 variances, the impulse response function "traces the effect of a one standard deviation shock to one of the innovations on current and future values of the endogenous variables" (Hamilton, 1994, p. 318). The errors of the VAR model equations are orthogonalized by a Choleski decomposition so that the covariance matrix of the resulting innovations is diagonal. Thus changing the order of equations changes the impulse responses. According to Canova (1995, p. 92), and as noted by Sims, "examining the impulse response function may be the most effective way of checking for Granger non causality in multivariate framework". "...it is essential to transform the innovations of the system into a contemporaneously uncorrelated form". According to Pesaran and Pesaran (1997 p. 420-424), the VAR(p) model:

$$X_t = A_0 + \sum_{j=1}^{p} A_j X_{t-j} + u_t = A g_t' + u_t \qquad (20)$$

with $t = 1, 2, ..., n$, where X_t is a $k \times 1$ vector of jointly determined dependent variables and the vector of disturbances has a $k \times k$ variance-covariance matrix $\Omega = E(u_t u_t')$. The vectors of disturbances u_t are supposed to have a multivariate normal distribution, and the vector of observations is $g_t = (1, X_{t-1}, X_{t-2}, ..., X_{t-p})$ for $t = 1, 2, ..., T$. The orthogonalized impulse response function advanced by Sims (1980) relies on the transformation of the VAR(p) in an infinite order multivariate MA process:

$$X_t = \sum_{j=0}^{\infty} A_j u_{t-j}. \qquad (21)$$

We used the orthogonalized residuals for the 11 conditional variances to derive the impulse response function (Hamilton, 1994, p. 318).

5 Conclusion

Considering the analytical impulse response function, we note that: Malaysia had some impact on Korea, Singapore and the Hang Seng, the Dow Jones showed a sensitive impact on Hang Seng and SMI, some impact on Singapore, and an only very small impact on Japan, Thailand had a sensitive impact on Singapore, the Nikkei had some impact on Malaysia and Korea, Jakarta had some impact on Thailand and a sensitive impact on Singapore, Korea had almost no impact, Singapore had some impact on Thailand, India had a small impact on Switzerland, the SMI had only a small impact on Malaysia.

Impulse response functions based on a VAR(2) model for 11 markets

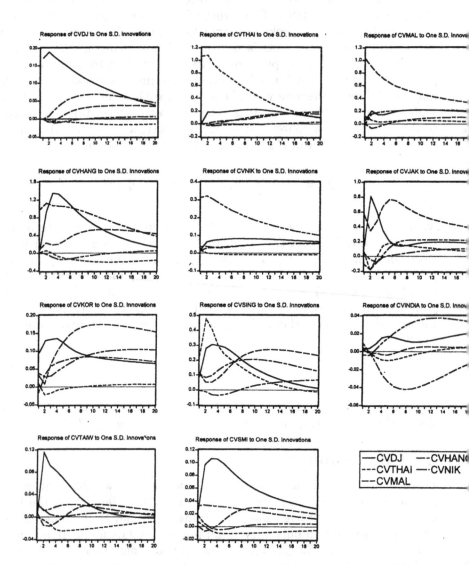

Considering the significance of the VAR model coefficients, we conclude that the volatility of the Dow Jones is explained by itself, by Hang Seng$_{t-1}$, Nikkei$_{t-1}$, Nikkei$_{t-2}$, Jakarta$_{t-2}$ in the 5 dimension VAR(2). In the 11 dimension VAR(2), it can be explained by itself, Malaysia$_{t-1}$, Malaysia$_{t-2}$, Hangseng$_{t-1}$, Nikkei$_{t-2}$, Jakarta$_{t-1}$, Singapore$_{t-1}$. The volatility of the SMI is explained by itself, Dow Jones$_{t-1}$, Dow Jones$_{t-2}$, Hang Seng$_{t-1}$, Hang Seng$_{t-2}$, Nikkei$_{t-1}$. In the 11 dimension VAR(2), it can be explained by itself, Dow Jones$_{t-1}$, Dow Jones$_{t-2}$, Malaysia$_{t-2}$, Hang Seng$_{t-1}$, Hang Seng$_{t-2}$, India$_{t-1}$, India$_{t-2}$.

Considering a test on several coefficients of each equation (heat wave hypothesis), we conclude that if the null hypothesis in a Wald test for a heat wave is that all the coefficients for the other markets in a given equation are equal to zero, then: in the 5-dimension VAR(2) for 5 variables, the heat wave hypothesis is rejected both for the SMI and for the Dow Jones.

Then, if we test the influence of the omitted variables Malaysia, India, Thailand, Taiwan, Korea and Singapore by an F-test or by a likelihood ratio test, the null of no influence is strongly rejected at a 5% probability level, indicating that it was correct to include more markets in the 5-dimension VAR(2) model.

References

BOOTH, G.G., CHOWDHURY, M., MARTIKAINEN, T. and TSE, Y. (1997): Intraday Volatility in International Stock Index Futures Markets. *Management Science, Vol. 43, No. 11, 1564–1576.*

CANOVA, F. (1995): Vector Autoregressive Models: Specification, Estimation, Inference, and Forecasting. In: Pesaran M. H. and Wickens W. (eds.), Handbook of Applied Econometrics, Macroeconomics. Blackwell, Oxford, 73–138.

DESCHAMPS, P. (1985): Cours d'économétrie, Université de Fribourg, Suisse.

DING, Z., GRANGER, C. W. J. and ENGLE, R. F. (1993): A Long Memory Property of Stock Market Returns and a New Model. *Journal of Empirical Finance, 1, 83–106.*

ENGLE, R. F., ITO, T. and LIN, W.-L. (1990): Meteor Showers or Heat Waves? Heteroskedastic Intra-Daily Volatility in the Foreign Exchange Market. *Econometrica, Journal of the Econometric Society, Vol. 58, No. 3, 525–542.*

FRANSES, P. H. (1998): Time Series Models for Business and Economic Forecasting. Cambridge University Press.

418

HAMILTON, J. D. (1994): Time Series Analysis. Princeton University Press, Princeton, New Jersey.

LUETKEPOHL, H. (1991): Introduction to Multiple Time Series Analysis. Springer, Berlin, New York.

MADDALA, G. S. and KIM, I.-M. (1998): Unit Roots, Cointegration, and Structural Change. Cambridge University Press.

MILLS, T. C. (1997): The Econometric Modelling of Financial Time Series. Cambridge University Press.

NELSON, D.B. (1991): Conditional Heteroskedasticity in Asset Returns: A New Approach. Econometrica, 59, 347–370.

PESARAN, H. M. and PESARAN, B. (1997): Working with Microfit 4.0, Interactive Econometric Analysis. Oxford University Press.

POLASEK, W. AND KOZUMI, H. (1995): The VAR-VARCH model: A Bayesian approach. University of Basel, Switzerland, WWZ-Discussion papers Nr. 9508.

RABEMANANJARA, R. and ZAKOIAN, J. M. (1993): Threshold ARCH Models and Asymetries in Volatility. *Journal of Applied Econometrics, 8, 31–49.*

SIMS, C. A. (1980): Macroeconomics and Reality. *Econometrica, Vol. 48, No. 1, 1-48.*

Applications in Medicine, Biology, Archaeology, and Others

Part 6

Applications in Medicine, Biology, Archaeology and Others

QTL Mapping in Plant Populations

K. Emrich

Fachbereich für Statistik der Universität D-44221 Dortmund, Germany

Abstract: The author derived explicit expressions for the maximum likelihood estimates of genetic parameters when the iterative EM algorithm is applied. These explicit formulas enable a comparison between new computed parameter estimates with ones that are calculated using the ECM algorithm, which is implemented in standard software (e. g. QTL-Cartographer) for the analysis of quantitative traits. Finally the calculation of the variance covariance matrix of maximum likelihood estimates enables us to determine a confidence interval for the location of a quantitative trait locus.

1   Introduction

The investigation of genes affecting economically important agronomic traits has a long tradition in statistics. Along with rapid developments in molecular marker technologies, biometrical models have been constructed, refined and generalized for detecting, mapping and estimating the effects of genes that control quantitative traits. Loci of quantitative genes are called 'Quantitative Trait Loci' (QTLs).

A wide range of models and methods have been developed for the investigation of effects of quantitative trait loci. Jansen (1996) explains a Monte Carlo expectation maximization algorithm for fitting multiple QTLs to incomplete genetic data. Stephens and Fisch (1998) employ reversible jump Markov chain Monte Carlo methodology to compute posterior densities for the parameters and the number of QTLs. Interval mapping methods estimate the parameters of a model for all putative QTL positions of a part of the genome. Likelihood ratio test statistics are computed for these QTL positions and build a likelihood ratio (or an equivalent Lod Score) profile whose maximum is an estimate of a QTL position. Kao and Zeng (1997) presented an interval mapping method that applied an ECM (Expectation/ Conditional Maximization) algorithm in order to derive maximum likelihood estimates and they determined asymptotic variance-covariance matrices for the estimates. In this article the author proposes a similar design to derive explicit expressions for parameter estimates employing the EM algorithm.

We consider experimental populations derived from a cross between two parental inbred lines P_1 and P_2, differing mainly in a quantitative trait of interest. This allows for investigating the realizations of alleles of marker loci of a marker interval that contains a putative QTL. The marker loci and the QTL are diallelic. If the F_1 individuals are selfed or intermated, a F_2 -population is produced with nine observable marker genotypes. The realizations of the alleles of the QTLs are *not observable*. Conditional probabilities of the QTL genotypes given the marker genotypes are derived straightforwardly, if the recombination frequencies between the marker loci and the QTL are known (see Emrich and Urfer (1999)). These conditional probabilities are referred to as p_{ji} (with j=1,2,...,n for a sample of n plants and i=1,2,3 for the three QTL genotypes). They are functions of the parameter p for the location of the QTL. p is considered as *fixed* in the following model building and parameter estimation process. The aim is to find maximum likelihood estimates of QTL effects including their estimated standard errors.

2 F_2-Generation Model

The genetic model for one QTL represents the relation between a 'genotypic value' G and some genetic parameters β_0, a and d:

$$G = \begin{pmatrix} G_2 \\ G_1 \\ G_0 \end{pmatrix} = \begin{pmatrix} 1 \\ 1 \\ 1 \end{pmatrix} \beta_0 + \begin{pmatrix} 1 & -\frac{1}{2} \\ 0 & \frac{1}{2} \\ -1 & -\frac{1}{2} \end{pmatrix} \begin{pmatrix} a \\ d \end{pmatrix} \qquad (1)$$

β_0 is a joint value of the genetic model and a and d are additive and dominance effects of QTL in the F_2-population. Unique solutions of the genetic parameters exist in dependence of the genotypic values and frequencies of genotypes Q_1Q_1, Q_1Q_2 and Q_2Q_2 of the QTL.
Consider QTL mapping data, where y_j (j=1,2,...,n) is the investigated trait value of plant j and X_j (j=1,2,...,n) is a vector that contains data for the genetic markers and other explanatory variables.
We have to assume that:

- it exists no interaction (that is no epistasis) between QTLs

- consider no interference in crossing over

- there is not more than one QTL in the testing interval

A statistical composite interval mapping model is constructed on the basis of the genetic model:

$$y_j = ax_j^* + dz_j^* + X_j\beta + \varepsilon_j \qquad (2)$$

y_j is the trait value of the plant j (j=1,2,...,n), a and d are additive and dominance effects of the putative QTL, β is a partial regression coefficient vector of dimension k that contains the joint value β_0 of the genetic model, X_j is a subset of matrix that contains chosen marker and variable information, $\varepsilon_j \sim N(0, \sigma^2)$ and x_j^* and z_j^* (with j=1,2,...,n) are discrete random effects with

$$x_j^* = \begin{cases} 1 \\ 0 \quad \text{if the QTL is} \\ -1 \end{cases} \begin{matrix} Q_1Q_1 \\ Q_1Q_2 \\ Q_2Q_2 \end{matrix} \text{and } z_j^* = \begin{cases} \frac{1}{2} & \text{for QTL } \quad Q_1Q_2 \\ -\frac{1}{2} & \text{otherwise} \end{cases}$$

$$(3)$$

The realizations of the putative QTL in plant j are not observable. Thus only the probability distribution of the realizations of the discrete random effects are defined in dependence of the conditional probabilities of the QTL genotypes given marker genotypes for plant j (called p_{ji}, with j=1,2,...,n, i=1,2,3):

$$g_j(x_j^*, z_j^*) = \begin{cases} p_{j1} & \text{if } x_j^* = 1 \text{ and } z_j^* = -\frac{1}{2} \\ p_{j2} & \text{if } x_j^* = 0 \text{ and } z_j^* = \frac{1}{2} \\ p_{j3} & \text{if } x_j^* = -1 \text{ and } z_j^* = -\frac{1}{2} \end{cases}$$

$$(4)$$

This is the distribution of the QTL genotype specified by x_j^* and z_j^* (with j=1,2,...,n).

A Likelihood function is obtained for a sample of n individuals and for the parameter vector $\theta = (a, d, \beta, \sigma^2)$ as:

$$L(\theta|Y, \mathbf{X}) = \prod_{j=1}^{n} [\sum_{i=1}^{3} p_{ji} f(y_j; \mu_{ji}, \sigma^2)]$$

$$(5)$$

with

$$\mu_{j1} = a - \frac{d}{2} + X_j\beta, \quad \mu_{j2} = \frac{d}{2} + X_j\beta, \quad \mu_{j3} = -a - \frac{d}{2} + X_j\beta$$

$$(6)$$

and f is the normal density of y_j with expectation value μ_{ji} (i=1,2,3 and j=1,2,..,n) and variance σ^2.

3 Parameter Estimation by EM algorithm

The QTL genotypes are considered as missing values. Define a data set $Y_{mis} = (y_{(mis,j)})$, (with j=1,2,...,n) of "missing data" for the QTL genotypes, and a data set $Y_{obs} = (y_{(obs,j)})$ (with j=1,2,...,n) for the observed values y_j and the marker information (cofactor vectors X_j , j=1,2,...,n). We contemplate a hypothetical complete-data set called $Y_{com} = (Y_{obs}, Y_{mis})$. In such a situation the EM algorithm can be applied for maximum likelihood estimation of the parameters of the statistical model. Consider the random variable vector Y_{com} of the complete-data set with density function $f(Y_{com}|\theta)$ and $\theta \in \Theta \subseteq \Re^d$. If Y_{com} contained only observed values, the objective way estimating the parameters would be to maximize the complete-data log-likelihood function of θ:

$$l(\theta|Y_{com}) \propto ln f(Y_{com}|\theta) \tag{7}$$

Unfortunately, Y_{com} contains the not observable missing values Y_{mis}. If we assume that the missing data in Y_{mis} are missing at random, than the log-likelihood for θ is:

$$l_{obs}(\theta|Y_{obs}) \propto ln \int f(Y_{com}|\theta)dY_{mis} \tag{8}$$

In most practical applications (including the here described situation), it is very complicated to maximize this log-likelihood function. The EM algorithm solves this problem of maximizing l_{obs} by *iteratively maximizing* $l(\theta|Y_{com})$. For each iteration, the EM algorithm has two steps, the **E-step** and the **M-step**. Using appropriate starting values for $\theta^{(0)}$,

- the (t+1) **E-step** finds the conditional *expectation* of the complete data log-likelihood with respect to the conditional distribution of Y_{mis} given Y_{obs} and the parameter $\theta^{(t)}$:

$$Q(\theta|\theta^{(t)}) = \int l(\theta|Y_{com})f(Y_{mis}|Y_{obs}, \theta = \theta^{(t)})dY_{mis} \tag{9}$$

This is a function of θ for fixed Y_{obs} and fixed $\theta^{(t)}$.

- The (t+1)-st **M-step** calculates a *maximum* $\theta^{(t+1)}$ for $Q(\theta|\theta^{(t)})$, so that

$$Q(\theta^{(t+1)}|\theta^{(t)}) > Q(\theta|\theta^{(t)}) \; \forall \; \theta \in \Theta \tag{10}$$

Under certain restrictions (Dempster et al. (1977)), the sequence of estimates of the iterations steps of the EM algorithm converges against a (global or local) maximum of l_{obs}. Obviously, depending on the chosen starting values (and the used restrictions) in some applications a saddle-point of l_{obs} is found, but very often the EM algorithm is able of finding a maximum.

For the F_2-generation situation and the models (1) and (2) the observed data $(y_{(obs,j)})$ given the missing data $(y_{(mis,j)})$ are normally distributed:

$$f(y_{(obs,j)}|\theta, X_j, x_j^*, z_j^*) \sim N(ax_j^* + dz_j^* + X_j\beta, \sigma^2) \tag{11}$$

The conditional density of missing data given specified observations is the above defined density of QTL genotypes $g_j(x_j^*, z_j^*)$. The density of the complete data set $(y_{(com,j)})$ is considered as the likelihood-function and defined as:

$$L(\theta|y_{(com)}) = \prod_{j=1}^{n} f(y_{(obs,j)}|\theta, X_j, x_j^*, z_j^*)g_j(x_j^*, z_j^*) \qquad (12)$$

$\theta = (a, d, \beta_0, \ldots, \beta_{k-1})^T$ is the parameter vector. One computes the conditional *expectation* of the complete data log-likelihood with respect to the conditional distribution of Y_{mis} given Y_{obs} and the parameter $\theta^{(t)}$ in the **E-step of the EM algorithm** as:

$$\begin{aligned}
Q(\theta|\theta^{(t)}) &= \int lnL(\theta|Y_{mis})f(Y_{mis}|Y_{obs}, \theta = \theta^{(t)})dY_{mis} \\
&= \int ln[\prod_{j=1}^{n} f(y_j; \mu_{ji}, \sigma^2)g_j(x_j^*, z_j^*)]f(Y_{mis}|Y_{obs}, \theta = \theta^{(t)})dY_{mis} \\
&= \sum_{j=1}^{n}\sum_{i=1}^{3} ln[f(y_j; \mu_{ji}, \sigma^2)p_{ji}]\pi_{ji}^{(t)} \qquad (13)
\end{aligned}$$

where $\pi_{ji}^{(t)} = \dfrac{p_{ji}f(y_j;\mu_{ji}^{(t)},\sigma^{2(t)})}{\sum_{v=1}^{3}p_{jv}f(y_j;\mu_{jv}^{(t)},\sigma^{2(t)})}$ is the posterior probability of the QTL genotype.

For the **M-step of the EM algorithm** Q is *maximized*: Setting the partial derivatives of Q equal to zero, the matrix equation follows explicitly as:

$$\mathbf{A}\theta^{*(t+1)} = b, \text{ with } \theta^{*(t+1)} = (a^{(t+1)}, d^{(t+1)}, \beta_0^{(t+1)}, \ldots, \beta_{k-1}^{(t+1)})^T \qquad (14)$$

For the models (1) and (2), the matrix $\mathbf{A} = (A_1, A_2, \cdots, A_{k+2})^T$ is derived as

$$A_1 = (\sum_{j}(\pi_{j1}^{(t)} + \pi_{j3}^{(t)}), \frac{1}{2}\sum_{j}(\pi_{j3}^{(t)} - \pi_{j1}^{(t)}), \cdots, \sum_{j}(\pi_{j1}^{(t)} - \pi_{j3}^{(t)})X_{jk}) \qquad (15)$$

$$A_2 = (\frac{1}{2}\sum_{j}(\pi_{j3}^{(t)} - \pi_{j1}^{(t)}), \frac{1}{4}\sum_{j}(\pi_{j1}^{(t)} + \pi_{j2}^{(t)} + \pi_{j3}^{(t)}), \cdots, \frac{1}{2}\sum_{j}(-\pi_{j1}^{(t)} + \pi_{j2}^{(t)} - \pi_{j3}^{(t)})X_{jk})$$

$$(16)$$

$$A_{k+2} = (\sum_{j}(\pi_{j1}^{(t)} - \pi_{j3}^{(t)})X_{jk}, \frac{1}{2}\sum_{j}(-\pi_{j1}^{(t)} + \pi_{j2}^{(t)} - \pi_{j3}^{(t)})X_{jk}, \cdots, \frac{1}{2}\sum_{j}X_{jk}X_{jk}) \qquad (17)$$

and b is calculated as

$$b = (\sum_{j=1}^{n}(\pi_{j1}^{(t)} - \pi_{j3}^{(t)}))y_j, \frac{1}{2}\sum_{j=1}^{n}(-\pi_{j1}^{(t)} + \pi_{j2}^{(t)} - \pi_{j3}^{(t)})y_j, \cdots, \sum_{j=1}^{n}X_{jk}y_j)^T \qquad (18)$$

The partial derivative for σ is dependent from the other parameters, but the linear equation system of the other partial derivatives (set equal to zero) does not contain σ. Therefore in a $(t+1)$-th iteration step the first $(k+1)$ parameters are estimated by solving the linear equation system and then used for calculating the estimate of the last parameter:

$$\sigma^{2(t+1)} = \sum_{j=1}^{n} \sum_{i=1}^{3} [(y_j - \mu_{ji}^{(t+1)})^2 \pi_{ji}^{(t)}] \tag{19}$$

The parameter estimate vector of the $(t+1)$-th iteration step of the EM algorithm is $\theta^{(t+1)} = (a^{(t+1)}, d^{(t+1)}, \beta_0^{(t+1)}, \ldots, \beta_{k-1}^{(t+1)}, \sigma^{2(t+1)})^T$. The EM algorithm is widely used in different applications. Selinski and Urfer (1998) applied this method for the estimation of toxicokinetic parameters for the risk assessment of potential harmful chemicals.

4 The Asymptotic Variance-Covariance Matrix and Confidence Intervals

Kao and Zeng (1997) described a method to calculate an asymptotic variance-covariance matrix for the specified model. The result of the iterative algorithm to estimate the parameters of the model is

$$\theta = (a, d, \beta_0, \beta_{k-1}, \sigma^2)^T.$$

The parameter p is set as earlier estimated (or "known", e. g. from a lod score analysis). The a posteriori probabilities of the parameter estimation were calculated in the prior application of the EM algorithm. For cases where the EM algorithm is used, a method is derived to acquire the asymptotic variance-covariance matrix. This is equivalent to extracting the observed information of the incomplete problem. The likelihood function of the (hypothetically) complete data set can be found by making the following considerations: The complete data problem is regarded as a two stage hierarchical model. The QTL genotypes are the realizations of a two dimensional random variable (x_j^*, z_j^*) $(j=1,2,\ldots,n)$, which are randomized from a trinomial experiment. Each realization of the random variable is assigned to one of the QTL genotypes. The observations are normally distributed with a mean depending on the realization of the QTL genotype. Then the likelihood function of the (hypothetical) complete data set is:

$$\lambda(Y_{com}|p, a, d, \beta, \sigma^2) = \prod_{j=1}^{n} \sum_{i=1}^{3} [p_{ji} f(y_j; \mu_{ji}, \sigma^2)^{\eta_i(x_j^*, z_j^*)}] \tag{20}$$

The exponents in these formula realize to one or zero in dependence of the QTL genotypes. (see Emrich and Urfer (1999)). Now, for a *fixed* sample the log-likelihood function is described as:

$$ln(\lambda) = \sum_{j=1}^{n} \sum_{i=1}^{3} [p_{ji} - ln(\sqrt{2\pi\sigma^2}) - \frac{1}{2}(\frac{y_j - \mu_{ji}}{\sigma})^2] \tag{21}$$

For independent observations the information matrices are derived as:

$$I_{obs}(\theta|Y_{obs}) = I_{com} - I_{mis} \tag{22}$$

$$\text{with } I_{com} = \sum_{j=1}^{n} E[-\frac{\partial^2 \ln(\lambda(y_{(com,j)}|\theta))}{\partial \theta^2}|y_{(obs,j)}, \theta]_\theta \tag{23}$$

$$I_{mis} = \sum_{j=1}^{n} E\{[\frac{\partial \ln(\lambda(y_{(com,j)}|\theta))}{\partial \theta}][\frac{\partial \ln(\lambda(y_{(com,j)}|\theta))}{\partial \theta}]^T|y_{(obs,j)}, \theta\}_\theta$$

$$- \sum_{i=1,i\neq j}^{n} E[\frac{\partial \ln(\lambda(y_{(com,i)}|\theta))}{\partial \theta}|y_{(obs,j)}, \theta]_\theta E[\frac{\partial \ln(\lambda(y_{(com,j)}|\theta))}{\partial \theta}|y_{(obs,j)}, \theta]_\theta^T \tag{24}$$

And the asymptotic variance covariance matrix is computed as the inverse of the observed information matrix:

$$Cov(\theta) = (I_{obs})^{-1} \tag{25}$$

For example the information of the parameter for the location of the QTL is calculated with:

$$I_{obs}(p,p) = -\sum_{j=1}^{n}\sum_{i=1}^{3} p_{ji}^{(2)}\pi_{ji} - \frac{1}{\sigma^2}\sum_{j=1}^{n}\sum_{i=1}^{3}(p_{ji}^{(1)})^2\pi_{ji} - \frac{1}{\sigma^2}\sum_{\substack{j,m=1\\m\neq j}}^{n}[\sum_{i=1}^{3}p_{mi}^{(1)}\pi_{mi}][\sum_{i=1}^{3}p_{ji}^{(1)}\pi_{ji}] \tag{26}$$

Here, the $p_{ji}^{(1)}$ are the first derivatives of the p_{ji}. For the other parts of I_{obs} see Emrich and Urfer (1999). Now, especially the confidence interval for the parameter of the location of the QTL can be determined.

5 Outlook

In this work a method is described for the estimation of genetic parameters in a F_2-population and for calculating standard errors. In a forthcoming paper examples will be published showing that the EM algorithm and the so called ECM algorithm as described by Kao and Zeng may or may not converge against a different maximum. A calculation of first examples seemed to indicate that for some starting points the ECM algorithm has a tendency to find a saddlepoint instead of a maximum, which of course is not a maximum likelihood estimate. On the other hand, there exists no mathematical proof for both algorithms that they

428

find a maximum instead a of saddlepoint. For most practical applications, the EM algorithm is known to find a maximum.

Melchinger et al. (1998) investigated plant height measurements of a F_2-population of maize, which were genotyped for a total of 89 marker loci. They provided this data set for a detailed statistical analysis. The aim of our further statistical approach is to find maximum likelihood estimates for QTL locations and effects including their estimated standard errors using the described and further methods. Recently, Kao et al. (1999) presented a new statistical approach for interval mapping, called multiple marker interval mapping (MIM). It uses multiple marker intervals simultaneously to fit multiple putative QTLs directly in the model for mapping QTLs. Here the ECM algorithm is used as well. To integrate our estimation procedure in this approach seems to be a promising field for further statistical research.

References

DEMPSTER, A. P., LAIRD, N. M. and RUBIN, D. B. (1977): Maximum Likelihood from Incomplete Data via the EM Algorithm. *J. R. Statist. Soc. B 39, 1-38.*

EMRICH, K. and URFER, W. (1999): Estimation of genetic parameters using molecular markers and EM algorithms. *Technical Report 48/1999. Department of Statistics, University of Dortmund. Available from the world wide web: http://www.statistik.uni-dortmund.de/sfb475/sfblit.htm*

JANSEN, R. C. (1996): A general Monte Carlo method for mapping multiple quantitative trait loci. *Genetics 142, 305-311.*

KAO, C.- H. and ZENG, Z.- B. (1997): General formulas for obtaining the MLE's and the asymptotic variance-covariance matrix in mapping quantitative trait loci when using the EM algorithm. *Biometrics 53. 653-665.*

KAO, C.- H., ZENG, Z.- B. and TEASDALE, R. D. (1999): Multiple Interval Mapping for Quantitative Trait Loci. *Genetics 152, 1203-1216.*

MELCHINGER, A. E., UTZ, H. F. and SCHÖN, C. C. (1998): Quantitative trait locus (QTL) mapping using different testers and independent populaton samples in maize reveals low power of QTL detection and large bias in estimates of QTL effects. *Genetics 149, 383-403.*

SELINSKI, S. and URFER, W. (1998): Interindividual and interoccasion variability of toxicokinetic parameters in population models. *Technical Report 38/1998, University of Dortmund.*

STEPHENS, D. A. and FISCH, R. D. (1998): Bayesian analysis of quantitative trait locus data using reversible jump Markov chain Monte Carlo. *Biometrics 54, 1334-1347.*

Robust Multivariate Methods in Geostatistics

Peter Filzmoser[1], Clemens Reimann[2]

[1]Department of Statistics, Probability Theory, and Actuarial Mathematics,
Vienna University of Technology, A-1040 Vienna, Austria

[2]Geological Survey of Norway, N-7491 Trondheim, Norway

Abstract: Two robust approaches to principal component analysis and factor analysis are presented. The different methods are compared, and properties are discussed. As an application we use a large geochemical data set which was analyzed in detail by univariate (geo-)statistical methods. We explain the advantages of applying robust multivariate methods.

1 Introduction

In regional geochemistry an advantage could be that instead of presenting maps for 50 (or more) chemical elements only a few maps of the principal components or factors may have to be presented, containing a high percentage of the information of the single element maps. Additionally, it might be possible to find effects which are not visible in the single element maps. Especially factor analysis is used in different kinds of applications to detect hidden structures in the data.

Geochemical data sets usually include outliers which are caused by a multitude of different processes. It is well known that outliers can heavily influence classical statistical methods, including multivariate statistical methods. Even one single (huge) outlier can completely determine the result of principal component analysis. For that reason it is advisable to use robust multivariate methods for detecting the multivariate structure. Section 2 treats two methods of robust principal component analysis. Two different versions of robust factor analysis which have recently been proposed, are considered in Sections 3 and 4. Section 5 gives an example with a real geochemical data set.

2 Robust Principal Component Analysis

Let x be a p-dimensional random vector with $E(x) = \mu$ and $\mathrm{Cov}(x) = \Sigma$. The covariance matrix can be decomposed as $\Sigma = \Gamma A \Gamma^\top$, where the columns of $\Gamma = (\gamma_{.1}, \dots, \gamma_{.p})$ are the eigenvectors of Σ and A is a diagonal matrix with the corresponding eigenvalues (arranged in descending order) of Σ. The principal components of x are defined by $z = \Gamma^\top(x - \mu)$. Classically, μ is estimated by the sample mean $\bar{x}$, and Σ by the sample covariance matrix S, which is decomposed into eigenvectors and -values. $\bar{x}$ as well as S are highly sensitive with respect to outlying observations.

Hence, for seriously analyzing geochemical data, a robust version of principal component analysis (PCA) has to be applied.

PCA can easily be robustified by estimating the covariance matrix Σ in a robust way, e.g. by taking the Minimum Covariance Determinant (MCD) estimator of Rousseeuw (1985). The robustly estimated covariance matrix is not influenced by outliers, and hence the eigenvector/eigenvalue decomposition is also robust. Since the MCD additionally gives a robust estimation of μ, the whole PCA procedure is robust. We will discuss the usage of the MCD estimator in more detail in the context of factor analysis (Section 3).

Another way for robustifying PCA was introduced by Li and Chen (1985). The method is based on the projection pursuit technique. PCA can be seen as a special case of projection pursuit, where the variance of the projected data points is to be maximized. Let $X = (x_1^\top, \ldots, x_n^\top)^\top$ be a data matrix with observation vectors $x_i \in I\!\!R^p$ ($i = 1, \ldots, n$). Now, let us assume that the first $(k-1)$ projection directions $\widehat{\gamma}_{.1}, \ldots, \widehat{\gamma}_{.(k-1)}$ are already known. We define a projection matrix

$$P_1 = I_p, \qquad P_k = I_p - \sum_{j=1}^{k-1} \widehat{\gamma}_{.j} \widehat{\gamma}_{.j}^\top. \qquad (1)$$

P_k corresponds to a projection onto the space spanned by the first $(k-1)$ projection directions. We are interested in finding a projection direction a which maximizes the function

$$a \quad \longrightarrow \quad S(XP_k a) \qquad (2)$$

under the restrictions $a^\top a = 1$ and $P_k a = a$ (orthogonality to previously found projection directions). Defining S in (2) as the classical sample standard deviation would result in classical PCA. The method can easily be robustified by taking a robust measure of spread, e.g. the *median absolute deviation* (MAD)

$$\mathrm{MAD}(y) = \operatorname*{med}_i |y_i - \operatorname*{med}_j(y_j)|. \qquad (3)$$

Since the number of possible projection directions is infinite, an approximative solution for maximizing (2) is as follows. The k-th projection direction is only searched in the set

$$A_{n,k} = \left\{ \frac{P_k(x_1 - \widehat{\mu}_n)}{\|P_k(x_1 - \widehat{\mu}_n)\|}, \ldots, \frac{P_k(x_n - \widehat{\mu}_n)}{\|P_k(x_n - \widehat{\mu}_n)\|} \right\} \qquad (4)$$

where $\widehat{\mu}_n$ denotes a robust estimation of the mean, like the L_1-median or the component-wise median.

The algorithm outlined above was suggested by Croux and Ruiz-Gazen (1996). It is easy to implement and fast to compute which makes the method quite attractive to use in practice. Furthermore, this robust PCA method has a big advantage for high-dimensional data (large p) because it allows to stop at a desired number $k < p$ of components, whereas usually all p components are to be extracted by the eigenvector/eigenvalue decomposition of the (robust) covariance matrix. Moreover, the method still gives reliable results for $n < p$, which is important for a variety of applications. The computation of the MCD estimator requires at least $n > p$.

3 Robust Factor Analysis using the MCD

The aim of factor analysis (FA) is to summarize the correlation structure of observed variables $x_1, \ldots, x_p$. For this purpose one constructs $k < p$ unobservable or latent variables $f_1, \ldots, f_k$, which are called the *factors*, and which are linked with the original variables through the equation

$$x_j = \lambda_{j1} f_1 + \lambda_{j2} f_2 + \ldots + \lambda_{jk} f_k + \varepsilon_j, \tag{5}$$

for each $1 \leq j \leq p$. The error variables $\varepsilon_1, \ldots, \varepsilon_p$ are supposed to be independent, but they have *specific variances* $\psi_1, \ldots, \psi_p$. The coefficients λ_{jl} are called the factor *loadings*, and they are collected into the matrix of loadings Λ.

Using the vector notations $x = (x_1, \ldots, x_p)^\top$, $f = (f_1, \ldots, f_k)^\top$, and $\varepsilon = (\varepsilon_1, \ldots, \varepsilon_p)^\top$, the usual conditions on factors and error terms can be written as $E(f) = E(\varepsilon) = 0$, $\mathrm{Cov}(f) = I_k$, and $\mathrm{Cov}(\varepsilon) = \Psi$, with Ψ a diagonal matrix containing on its diagonal the specific variances. Furthermore, ε and f are assumed to be independent.

From the above conditions it follows that the covariance matrix of x can be expressed by

$$\Sigma = \Lambda \Lambda^\top + \Psi. \tag{6}$$

In classical FA the matrix Σ is estimated by the sample covariance matrix. Afterwards, decomposition (6) is used to obtain the estimators for Λ and Ψ. Many methods have been proposed for this decomposition, of which maximum likelihood (ML) and the principal factor analysis (PFA) method are the most frequently used.

Similar to the previous section, the parameter estimates can heavily be influenced when using a classical estimation of the scatter matrix. The problem can be avoided when Σ is estimated by the MCD estimator, which looks for the subset of h out of all n observations having the smallest determinant of its covariance matrix. Typically, $h \approx 3n/4$.

Pison et al. (1999) used the MCD for robustifying FA. They have shown that PFA based on MCD results in a resistant FA method with bounded influence function. It has better robustness properties than the ML-based counterpart. The empirical influence function can be used as a data-analytic tool. The method is also attractive for computational reasons since a fast algorithm for the MCD estimator has recently been developed (Rousseeuw and Van Driessen (1999)).

4 FA using Robust Alternating Regressions

A limitation of the MCD-based approach is that the sample size n needs to be bigger than the number of variables p. For samples with $n \leq p$ (which occur quite frequently in the practice of FA), a robust FA technique based on alternating regressions, originating from Croux et al. (1999), can be used.

For this we consider the sample version of model (5):

$$x_{ij} = \sum_{l=1}^{k} \lambda_{jl} f_{il} + \varepsilon_{ij} \qquad (7)$$

for $i = 1, \ldots, n$ and $j = 1, \ldots, p$. Suppose that preliminary estimates for the factor scores f_{il} are known, and consider them as constants for a moment. The loadings λ_{jl} can now be estimated by linear regressions of the x_j's on the factors. Moreover, by applying a robust scale estimator on the computed residuals, estimates $\hat{\psi}_j$ for ψ_j can easily be obtained (for example by computing the MAD of the residuals).

On the other hand, if preliminary estimates of the loadings are available, linear regression estimators can again be used for estimating the factor scores. Indeed, if we take i fixed in (7) and suppose that the λ_{jl} are fixed, a regression of x_{ij} on the loadings λ_{jl} yields updated estimates for the factor scores. Since there is heteroscedasticity, weights proportional to $(\hat{\psi}_j)^{-1/2}$ should be included.

Using robust principal components (Section 2) as appropriate starting values for the factor scores, an iterative process (called alternating or interlocking regressions) can be carried out to estimate the unknown parameters of the factor model. To ensure robustness of the procedure we use a weighted L_1-regression estimator since it is fast to compute and very robust. More details about the method and the choice of the weights can be found in Croux et al. (1999). Note that in contrast to the method described in Section 3, the factor scores are estimated *directly*.

5 Example

We consider a data set described and analyzed by univariate methods in Reimann et al. (1998). From 1992-1998 the Geological Surveys of

Finland (GTK), and Norway (NGU) and the Central Kola Expedition (CKE), Russia, carried out a large multi-element geochemical mapping project, covering an area of 188,000 km^2 between 24° and 35.5°E up to the Barents Sea coast. One of the sample media was the C-horizon of podzol profiles, developed on glacial drift. C-horizon samples were taken at 605 sites, and the contents of more than 50 chemical elements was measured for all samples. Although the project was mainly designed to reveal the environmental conditions in the area, the C-horizon was sampled to reflect the geogenic background.

In the following we will apply the alternating regression-based FA approach (Section 4). Robust PCA and MCD-based FA was used in Filzmoser (1999) for the upper layer, humus, of the complete data set.

For the investigation of the C-horizon data we only considered the elements Ag, Al, As, Ba, Bi, Ca, Cd, Co, Cr, Cu, Fe, K , Mg, Mn, Na, Ni, P, Pb, S, Si, Sr, Th, V and Zn. These variables have been transformed to a logarithmic scale to give a better approximation to the normal distribution. In order to put everything to a common scale we first standardized (robustly) the variables to mean zero and variance one. We want to analyze the data by using non-robust least squares (LS) regression and robust weighted L_1-regression in the alternating regression scheme. We decided to extract 6 factors which results in a proportion of total variance of 75% for both cases. The loadings of factors $F1$ to $F6$ are shown in Figure 1. We just printed the elements with an absolute value of the loadings larger than 0.3 to avoid confusion. The percentage of explained variance is printed at the top of the plots. Figure 1 shows that for the first factor $F1$ there is just a slight difference between the non-robust (a) and the robust (b) method. However, for the subsequent factors this difference grows. Especially the loadings of factors $F4$ and $F6$ are strongly changing.

It is also interesting to inspect the factor scores which are directly estimated by our method. Because of space limitations we only show the scores of the second factor $F2$ (Figure 2), which is interesting because it nicely reflects the distribution of alkaline intrusions in the survey area. Figure 2 shows the whole region under consideration. The dark lines are the borders of the countries Russia (east), Norway (north-west), and Finland (south-west). The gray lines show rivers and the coast.

At a first glance the two results presented in Figure 2, the non-robust (a) and the robust (b) scores of factor $F2$ seem to be very similar. But already the ranges of the estimated scores are different ($[-3.08, 4.98]$ for the non-robust and $[-3.82, 5.13]$ for the robust method (in the maps we used the same scaling). The smaller range is typical for LS-based methods because *all* data points, including the outliers, are tried to be fitted. Robust methods fit the majority of "good" data points which

434

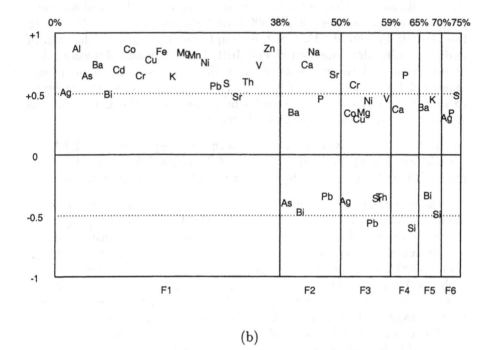

(a)

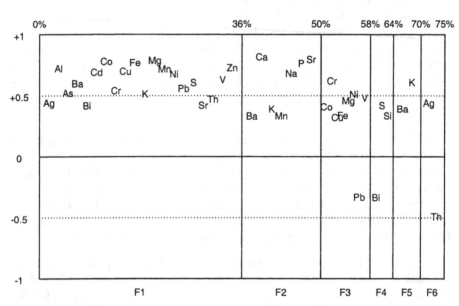

(b)

Figure 1: Loadings of the alternating regression based FA method using (a) LS-regression and (b) weighted L_1-regression.

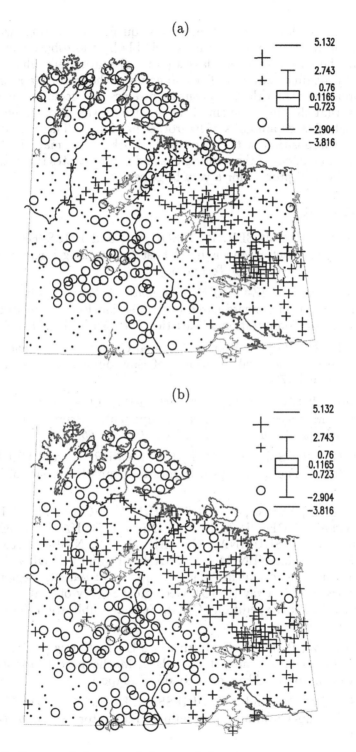

Figure 2: Scores of the second factor of the alternating regression based FA method using (a) LS-regression and (b) weighted L_1-regression.

leads to a reliable estimation. As a consequence, the regions with high and low outliers are presented more reliable by the robust method. In the map the two uppermost classes (crosses) mark areas which are underlain by alkaline bedrocks. The anomalies in the factor maps are much more prominent than the intrusions themselves in a geological map. The reason is that the emplacement of the intrusions was accompanied by the movement of large amounts of hydrothermal fluids. These changed the chemical composition of the intruded bedrocks. The map thus reflects the alteration haloes of these intrusions and demonstrates the importance of the geological process for a very large region.

References

CROUX, C., FILZMOSER, P., PISON, G., and ROUSSEEUW, P. J. (1999): Fitting Factor Models by Robust Interlocking Regression. Preprint, Vienna University of Technology.

CROUX, C. and RUIZ-GAZEN, A. (1996): A Fast Algorithm for Robust Principal Components based on Projection Pursuit, in Prat (ed.): Proceedings in Computational Statistics, Physika-Verlag, Heidelberg.

FILZMOSER, P. (1999): Robust Principal Component and Factor Analysis in the Geostatistical Treatment of Environmental Data. *Environmetrics, 10, 363-375.*

LI, G. and CHEN, Z. (1985): Projection-Pursuit Approach to Robust Dispersion Matrices and Principal Components: Primary Theory and Monte Carlo. *J. Amer. Statist. Assoc., 80, 759-766.*

PISON, G., ROUSSEEUW, P. J., FILZMOSER, P., and CROUX, C. (1999): Robust Factor Analysis. Preprint, Vienna University of Technology.

REIMANN, C., ÄYRÄS, M., CHEKUSHIN, V., BOGATYREV, I., BOYD, R., CARITAT, P. DE, DUTTER, R., FINNE, T. E., HALLERAKER, J. H., JÆGER, Ø., KASHULINA, G., LEHTO, O., NISKAVAARA, H., PAVLOV, V., RÄISÄNEN, M. L., STRAND, T., and VOLDEN, T. (1998): Environmental Geochemical Atlas of the Central Barents Region. Geological Survey of Norway (NGU), Geological Survey of Finland (GTK), and Central Kola Expedition (CKE), Special Publication, Trondheim, Espoo, Monchegorsk.

ROUSSEEUW, P. J. (1985): Multivariate Estimation with High Breakdown Point, in Grossmann et al. (eds.): Mathematical Statistics and Applications, Vol. B, Akadémiai Kiadó, Budapest.

ROUSSEEUW, P. J. and VAN DRIESSEN, K. (1999): A Fast Algorithm for the Minimum Covariance Determinant Estimator. *Technometrics, 41, 212-223.*

Resampling Methods in Physical Mapping

S. Heber[1,2], J. Stoye[2], M. Frohme[1], J. Hoheisel[1], M. Vingron[2]

Deutsches Krebsforschungszentrum (DKFZ)
[1]Funktionelle Genomanalyse (H0800), [2]Theoretische Bioinformatik (H0300)
Im Neuenheimer Feld 280, D-69120 Heidelberg, Germany

Abstract: We describe an approach to physical mapping based on the evaluation of replicates of a standard physical mapping algorithm. This way probe contigs are assembled dividing the original problem into smaller and easier subproblems while excluding dubious data. The probe contigs are further processed by computing a confidence value for putative local probe orders derived from bootstrap replicates. Based on these confidence values we define a neighbourhood of the original probe order. This neighbourhood is supposed to contain the correct solution and allows to detect and visualize 'weak' points in the probe order. It is also a helpful tool for designing further experiments to improve the quality of the physical map.

1 Introduction

The sequence of a genomic DNA molecule cannot be determined directly. Instead, smaller pieces of DNA need to be generated. This leads to the major goal of physical mapping: ordering a library of cloned fragments of DNA according to their position in the genome.

Here we focus on a physical mapping protocol based on hybridization experiments (Hoheisel et al. (1993)). We start with a clone library C of clones which correspond to subintervals of a larger contiguous piece of DNA G, all having approximately the same size. From C we select a subset $P \subset C$ of probes. Each probe $p_i \in P$ is labeled and tested against the clone library. If a clone contains DNA complementary to the probe sequence, the probe will hybridize to this clone and a positive hybridization signal can be detected. The result of these experiments is a binary *clone/probe hybridization matrix* $A = (a_{ij})$ where

$$a_{ij} := \begin{cases} 1 & \text{if probe } p_j \text{ hybridizes to clone } c_i; \\ 0 & \text{otherwise.} \end{cases}$$

The physical mapping problem is to find the order of the probes P that corresponds to their real position in G. (A subsequent problem would be to extend this order to the whole clone library. Here we do not deal with this problem.) The physical mapping problem can be translated into the following combinatorial problem (Greenberg, Istrail (1994)): Given a hybridization matrix, find a permutation of the columns (probes) such that the reordered matrix has the *consecutive ones property*, i.e., every row has at most one block of consecutive ones.

Unfortunately, physical mapping by hybridization experiments is vulnerable to errors and ambiguities, and the physical mapping problem under such conditions is supposed to be ill-defined and NP-hard.

The major practical problems of hybridization mapping are the management and visualization of large data sets, the efficient selection of probes to minimize the number of hybridization experiments, and the detection and resolution of inconsistencies in the hybridization data.

In our approach we divide the problem into smaller and easier subproblems by partitioning the probe set into independent parts (probe contigs). This is done by a clustering approach based on the reliability of certain probe configurations in replicates of the original physical map. For each probe contig, we apply bootstrap resampling to asses the quality of the solution and to define a confidence neighbourhood.

The confidence neighbourhood can be used for visualization, data cleaning, and to design further experiments, improving the quality of the physical map.

2 Algorithms

In the following we describe the algorithms used for contig construction and confidence neighbourhood construction.

To compute an approximation to the true solution of the physical mapping problem we use a vector-TSP formulation as described in Cuticchia et al. (1992). In this approach a Hamiltonian cycle of minimal weight in a complete graph with the extended probe set $\widetilde{\mathcal{P}} := \mathcal{P} \cup \{p_0\}$ as nodes and the Hamming distance between the columns of the extended clone/probe hybridization matrix $\widetilde{A}$ as edge weight is computed by simulated annealing. For further details we refer to Cuticchia et al. (1992).

While 'contig' is normally defined as an ordered set of overlapping clones representing a contiguous stretch of DNA we introduce here the somewhat differently defined *probe contigs* which are based on the repeated occurrence of probe stretches in multiple probe permutations. Let Π be a family of probe permutations (for example the results of different simulated annealing runs or bootstrap replicates). Then $C = \{p_{i_1}, \ldots, p_{i_m}\} \subset \mathcal{P}$ is a *probe contig* if it is a maximal set of probes that occurs contiguously, ordered in one of the two orientations $\overrightarrow{C} := (p_{i_1}, \ldots, p_{i_m})$ or $\overleftarrow{C} := (p_{i_m}, \ldots, p_{i_1})$ in all permutations of Π.

Using probe permutations derived from experimental data, one hardly finds stretches of probes that re-occur in exactly the same order in all permutations. Therefore we use a distance function between probes that averages the rank distances of probes in the different permutations.

Let $\mathrm{rk}_\pi(p_i)$ denote the position of probe p_i in permutation π. Given Π, the *averaged rank distance* (ARD) between two probes p_i and p_j is defined as

$$ARD_\Pi(p_i, p_j) \ := \ \frac{1}{|\Pi|} \sum_{\pi \in \Pi} |\mathrm{rk}_\pi(p_i) - \mathrm{rk}_\pi(p_j)|.$$

In the following we list two properties of the ARD for an idealized family of probe permutations $\widetilde{\Pi}$ where each position and orientation of different probe contigs occurs with the same frequency. These properties make the ARD suitable for contig selection. For proofs and further details see Heber et al. (2000).

Property 1: Within a probe contig $\overrightarrow{C} = (p_1, p_2, \ldots, p_m)$ we have

$$ARD_{\widetilde{\Pi}}(p_i, p_j) \ = \ |i - j|.$$

Property 2: For a given probe set $\mathcal{P}$, let C_1, C_2 be two probe contigs, $C_1 \neq C_2$. Then for all $p \in C_1, q \in C_2$, we have

$$ARD_{\widetilde{\Pi}}(p, q) \ = \ \frac{2|\mathcal{P}| + |C_1| + |C_2|}{6} \ \geq \ \frac{|\mathcal{P}| + 1}{3}.$$

For two ordered probe contigs $\overrightarrow{C_1} = (p_1, \cdots, p_k)$ and $\overrightarrow{C_2} = (q_1, \cdots, q_l)$, $N := |C_1||C_2|$ and a family of probe permutations Π, we consider all four possible concatenations $\widetilde{C} := \{\overrightarrow{C_1}\overrightarrow{C_2}, \overrightarrow{C_1}\overleftarrow{C_2}, \overleftarrow{C_1}\overrightarrow{C_2}, \overleftarrow{C_1}\overleftarrow{C_2}\}$ and define the *contig distance* of C_1 and C_2 as

$$d(C_1, C_2) \ := \ \min_{C \in \widetilde{C}} \left\{ \frac{1}{N} \sum_{\substack{p \in C_1 \\ q \in C_2}} (ARD_\Pi(p, q) - |\mathrm{rk}_C(p) - \mathrm{rk}_C(q)|)^2 \right\}.$$

Our contig construction algorithm is a modification of a greedy clustering algorithm, combined with a stopping criterion based on Properties 1 and 2 of the ARD. In an ideal case, neighbouring probes within a probe contig should have an ARD distance of 1 while probes of different probe contigs should show ARD distances larger than $\frac{|\mathcal{P}|+1}{3}$. This gives us an criterion to stop the merge loop at contig borders.

Algorithm:

1. Initialize the contig set such that each single probe corresponds to a contig.

2. Repeat while further merges are possible:

(a) Search the contig pair with the smallest contig distance where merging is not forbidden by the stopping criterion.

(b) If such a pair is found, merge the contigs.

3. Output the contig set.

The resulting probe contigs are used to divide and clean the hybridization data. To asses the quality of the contigs we perform a subsequent bootstrap analysis. The approach is similar to Wang et al. (1994), but with the roles of clones and probes exchanged. We create B pseudosamples of the original data by selecting $|C|$ times with replacement from the rows of the hybridization matrix A. This mimics repeating the hybridization experiment, each time using the same set of probes $\mathcal{P}$ but a different clone library.

For each of these pseudosamples, we compute a corresponding probe order π^* using the above described algorithm for physical map construction. Let Π^* be the set of these permutations.

Then, for each pair of probes (p, q) with $p, q \in \widetilde{\mathcal{P}}$ and $p \neq q$, we define the bootstrap value $b((p, q)) \in [0, 1]$ as the relative frequency of their consecutive occurence. Using the fact that each $p \in \widetilde{\mathcal{P}}$ has exactly two different neighbours in each $\pi^* \in \Pi^*$, we obtain for each $p \in \widetilde{\mathcal{P}}$ that

$$\sum_{q \in \widetilde{\mathcal{P}}} b((p, q)) = 2.$$

We represent these bootstrap values in a weighted, complete *bootstrap graph* $GB = (\widetilde{\mathcal{P}}, E, b)$. In GB a probe order π corresponds to a Hamiltonian cycle – we use $E(\pi) \subseteq E$ to indicate the corresponding edge set.

To represent the variability of a solution π of the map construction algorithm in a compact way, we define a neighbourhood N of π in the bootstrap graph GB. Given π, the bootstrap graph $GB = (\widetilde{\mathcal{P}}, E, b)$, and a confidence level $\gamma \in [0, 1]$, we construct for each probe $p \in \widetilde{\mathcal{P}}$ a set of adjacent edges $CI(p, \gamma) \subseteq E$ which comprises the edges $e_1, e_2 \in E(\pi)$ of the original solution π and a minimal number of the heaviest edges adjacent to p such that

$$\sum_{e \in CI(p, \gamma)} b(e) \geq 2\gamma.$$

We set $N(\gamma) := \bigcup_{p \in \widetilde{\mathcal{P}}} CI(p, \gamma)$. By definition,

$$N(\gamma_1) \subseteq N(\gamma_2) \quad \text{for} \quad \gamma_1 \leq \gamma_2 \quad \text{and} \quad \gamma_i \in [0, 1].$$

Thus we have a monotonically increasing parametrized candidate set for the true solution with $N(0) = E(\pi)$ and $N(1) = E(\pi) \cup \{e \in E : b(e) > 0\}$.

3 Applications and Simulations

In order to show the performance of our algorithms we applied them to a physical mapping data set (Frohme et al. (2000)) from the bacterial genome of *Xylella fastidiosa* (Silvestri et al. (2000)) and to several simulations.

3.1 Application to *Xylella fastidiosa* Data

In order to demonstrate the advantages of the ARD over the popular Hamming distance we show in Figure 1 visualizations of the corresponding distance matrices using the same probe order. The ARD distance matrix shows a clear cluster structure that correlates well with the contigs in the hybridization data matrix (data not shown) while in the Hamming distance matrix no such structure can be seen. (This still remains true if one applies other thresholds for the visualization.)

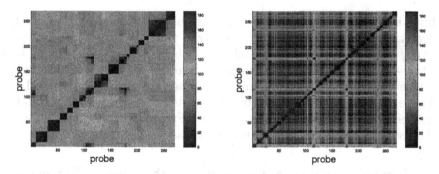

Figure 1: Left: ARD distance matrix of the *Xylella fastidiosa* data set based on 200 bootstrap replicates. Right: The Hamming distance matrix of the *Xylella fastidiosa* data set.

3.2 The Bootstrap Values as a Confidence Measure

In order to evaluate the bootstrap value as a confidence measure, we created 50 artificial raw data sets mimicking the parameters of previous mapping projects: a linearized genome of size 2000kb, a clone library consisting of 1000 clones of size 40kb, a probe set consisting of 200 clones selected from the clone library, false positives occurring at a rate of 1%, and false negatives occurring at a rate of 5.5%. For these data sets we computed the bootstrap graphs with a resampling rate of $B = 1000$. Their edges were partitioned into 11 bins according to their bootstrap value. An edge $e = (p, q)$ was classified as 'true' if p and q were neighbours in the 'true' physical map and 'false' otherwise. Averaged over 50 independent simulations, the vast majority of the false edges fall into the

bootstrap bin	true	false
$b = 0$	0.06	19351.98
$0.0 < b \leq 0.1$	5.02	429.72
$0.1 < b \leq 0.2$	6.24	40.92
$0.2 < b \leq 0.3$	7.00	22.70
$0.3 < b \leq 0.4$	7.32	14.34
$0.4 < b \leq 0.5$	12.48	13.50
$0.5 < b \leq 0.6$	11.38	9.40
$0.6 < b \leq 0.7$	12.24	5.68
$0.7 < b \leq 0.8$	16.80	4.86
$0.8 < b \leq 0.9$	24.72	3.94
$0.9 < b \leq 1.0$	97.74	1.96

Figure 2: Left: Average number of true and false edges in the bootstrap bins. Right: Mean and standard deviation of the *error rate* in the different bootstrap value bins. The bin consisting of edges with bootstrap value 0 is omitted.

bin with bootstrap value 0. In the other bins, the number of false edges decreases monotonically as the bootstrap value increases. On the other hand, most of the true edges fall into the high-scoring bootstrap bins, while only 0.06 (0.03%) true edges fall into the bin with bootstrap value 0 (see Figure 2, left). We define the *error rate* of a bin as the relative frequency of false edges in the bin. There is a strong negative correlation between error rate and bootstrap value (Figure 2, right). This supports the usage of the bootstrap values as a measure of 'quality' for a physical map.

An alternative quality measure, described in the context of STS-mapping is the *double-linkage* strategy (Arratia et al. (1991)). Here one only takes marker pairs into account that hybridize simultaneously to more than $M \geq 2$ clones. We investigated this approach on our simulations (Figure 3, left) and compared the rate of edges of the 'true' solution in the highest scoring edge set with the corresponding rate for the bootstrap values (Figure 3, right). We found that the bootstrap values are better suitable to restrict the search space for the correct probe order: For a given number of highest scoring edges, bootstrapping always yielded more 'true' edges than the linkage approach.

3.3 Confidence Neighbourhood

In order to investigate the relation among the confidence level γ, the size of the confidence neighbourhood $N(\gamma)$, and the number of true edges contained in $N(\gamma)$, we plotted the number of true edges contained in $N(\gamma)$ versus the size of $N(\gamma)$ (Figure 4, left). The curve shows a steep ascent until a value of γ around 0.95. Intuitively, this indicates the price, measured in false edges, one has to pay for the delineation of an increas-

linkage bin	true	false
$l = 0$	0.10	7999.24
$0 < l \leq 4$	0.14	10553.94
$4 < l \leq 8$	0.80	205.62
$8 < l \leq 12$	1.62	166.34
$12 < l \leq 16$	4.30	154.82
$16 < l \leq 20$	9.22	139.04
$20 < l \leq 24$	20.18	141.30
$24 < l \leq 28$	32.52	134.48
$28 < l \leq 32$	43.76	103.08
$32 < l \leq 36$	42.44	62.64
$36 < l$	43.92	40.50

Figure 3: Left: Average number of true and false edges in the linkage bins. Right: Average number of 'true' edges in the highest scoring edge set for the bootstrap approach and the linkage approach, respectively.

ing number of true edges. Upon increasing γ, the size of the confidence neighbourhood increases, slowly collecting all true edges although gradually including more and more false edges as well.

A visualization of a confidence neighbourhood $N(0.95)$ of a probe contig of *Xylella fastidiosa* is shown in Figure 4, right.

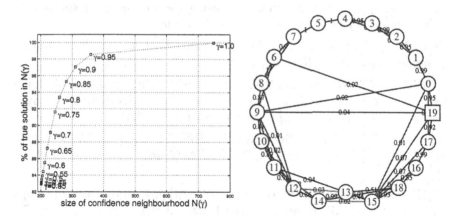

Figure 4: Left: Average number of true edges in the confidence neighbourhood $N(\gamma)$ plotted against the size of $N(\gamma)$. The data points are labelled by their confidence level γ. Right: Visualization of the confidence neighbourhood $N(0.95)$ of a probe contig of *Xylella fastidiosa*. The nodes are orderd on the circle according to their occurence in the original solution. The square denotes the dummy node representing p_0.

4 Discussion

We presented a method to divide the physical mapping problem into sub-problems by partitioning the probe set into independent probe contigs. This reduces the problem to a size where exact optimization is feasible. The probe contigs could be used to clean up the hybridization data by discarding isolated probes that cannot be assembled into a probe contig and which are supposed to be error prone. A further improvement could be obtained by fitting the hybridization fingerprints of single clones to a probe contig and eliminating the hybridization signals with other probe contigs. For each of the remaining probe contigs we computed bootstrap replicates of the probe order and used them to define a confidence neighbourhood. This neighbourhood is a helpful tool to detect and visualize the weak points and ambiguities in the probe order. Additionally it can be used to generate alternative probe orders and to determine putative probe contig ends. These are important to design further experiments which could improve the quality of the physical map.

References

ARRATIA, R., LANDER, E. S., TAVARE, S. and WATERMAN, M. S. (1991): Genomic Mapping by Anchoring Random Clones: A Mathematical Analysis. *Genomics, 11, 806–827.*

CUTICCHIA, A., ARNOLD, J. and TIMBERLAKE, W. E. (1992): The Use of Simulated Annealing in Chromosome Reconstruction Experiments Based on Binary Scoring. *Genetics, 132, 591–601.*

FROHME, M. et al. (2000): Mapping Analysis of the *Xylella fastidiosa* Genome. *Nucl. Acids Res., 28, 3100–3104.*

GREENBERG, D. and ISTRAIL, S. (1994): The Chimeric Mapping Problem: Algorithmic Strategies and Performance Evaluation on Synthetic Genomic Data. *Computers Chem., 18, 207–220.*

HEBER, S., STOYE, J., FROHME, M., HOHEISEL, J. and VINGRON, M. (2000): Contig Selection in Physical Mapping. *J. Comp. Biol., 7, 395–408.*

HOHEISEL, J. et al. (1993): High Resolution Cosmid and P1 Maps Spanning the 14 Mb Genome of the Fission Yeast *S. pombe. Cell, 73, 109–120.*

SILVESTRI, M. L. et al. (2000): The Genome Sequence of the Plant Pathogen *Xylella fastidiosa. Nature, 406, 151–157.*

WANG, Y., PRADE, R. A., GRIFFITH, J., TIMBERLAKE, W. E. and ARNOLD, J. (1994): ODS_BOOTSTRAP: Assessing the Statistical Reliability of Physical Maps by Bootstrap Resampling. *CABIOS, 10, 625–634.*

Validating Dialect Comparison Methods

Wilbert Heeringa[1], John Nerbonne[1], Peter Kleiweg[1]

[1]University of Groningen, Faculty of Arts, Alfa-Informatica,
P.O.Box 716, 9700 AS Groningen, The Netherlands

Abstract: The range of dialectometric methods suggests the need for validation work. We propose a gold standard, based on the consensual classification
of a well-studied area. Fidelity to the gold standard is assessed via matrix overlap measures (Rand and Fowlkes/Mallows). Word-based techniques in which
varieties are compared to each other directly emerge as superior.

1 Introduction

Séguy (1971) and Goebl (1982, 1984) were among the first to advocate
extensive deployment of statistical classification techniques in dialectology. This paper focus on methods which aim at measuring the phonetic
distance between varieties at an aggregated level, Hoppenbrouwers and
Hoppenbrouwers's (1988), Kessler's (1995) and Nerbonne et al's (1996).
The techniques should generalize straightforwardly to lexical distance
measures such as Séguy's (1971).

1.1 Comparison Methods

A great number of alternative methods have been proposed for comparing
and classifying dialects. Many of the alternatives are refinements of one
other, leading to the question which methods are most suitable in general.
The present paper examines the performance of a range of methods on a
well-understood area, The Netherlands.

We examine dialect distance measurements varying several dimensions.

1. Unit of measurement: word vs. corpus.
   Hoppenbrouwers and Hoppenbrouwers (1988) attain respectable
   results in holistic measures of corpora. Kessler (1995) and others
   measure differences per word.
2. Direct comparison vs. comparison via standard language.
3. Phonetic representation: phones vs. phonetic features.
   PHONES are letter-like units which can be described via a small
   number of phonetic properties, their FEATURES.
4. In feature-based measures: feature system.
   We compare a system developed for measuring the accuracy of
   phonetic transcription (Vierregge) to a phonologically motivated
   system (Hoppenbrouwers's)

5. In feature-based measures: distance measure between feature bundles, which can be determined via Euclidean distance, Manhattan (city-block) distance, or via a measure based on Pearson's r.

6. Order sensitivity: Levenshtein distance vs. feature/phone bags. Levenshtein distance counts *on* and *no* as different, while other measures simply count phones or features.

7. In Levenshtein measures: value of insertions and deletions. These values may be determined either with respect to a logical maximum or with respect to maxima in existing material.

8. Sensitivity of measure to frequency (Information Gain Weighting).

9. Representation of diphthongs (complex vowels) as one vs. two segments.

Although not all of the nine dimensions combine with one another, we nonetheless examine 334 combinations. The variety reinforces the need for validation techniques.

2 "Gold Standard" Validation

The leading idea in our validation is that dialectometric methods ought to agree with expert consensus in well-studied cases, which we take to be a "Gold Standard." A gold standard provides therefore a classification of language varieties with which (nearly) all experts agree. When expert dialectologists disagree on a well-studied variety (which often happens near area borders, for example), then that variety cannot be part of the gold standard. In this way the gold standard is incomplete, but it represents consensus.

Our research is based on 104 local varieties, for which the data is taken from the *Reeks Nederlands(ch)e Dialectatlassen* (Blancquaert & Peé (1925–1982)). From the transcriptions in the atlas we chose 100 words as being representative of the dialect. The gold standard was defined with respect to these 104 varieties from the RND, and their phonetic data was input to the distance procedures.

Two authoritative dialect maps were taken as starting points, namely the map of Van Ginneken (1913) which we took from Weijnen (1966), and the map of Daan, found in Daan & Blok (1969). The map of Van Ginneken is based on objective linguistic criteria, together with the judgement of the dialectologist (Goossens (1977)). The map of Daan is based on the "arrow" method. Dialects which are judged (nearly) equal by the speakers are connected by arrows. Connected dialect points are dialect areas, and borders emerge as small strips which are not crossed by arrows.

Both maps are criticized (legitimately or not), but this does not disqualify them from use in our project. We found three levels of comparability:

partitions of three, five and twelve areas. We regard the sum of errors in these divisions as a comprehensive error.

2.1 Distance Validation

We examine various methods from two perspectives derived from distance. The first perspective emphasizes that varieties within the gold-standard groups ought to be relatively close to each other as compared to varieties outside the gold-standard group. We check whether the distances within groups ("within") are much smaller than distances between groups ("without"). We choose this terminology to emphasize the similarity between this calculation and the well-known F distribution. For each group g_k in the gold standard we calculate the ratio between the mean squared within-group distance and the mean squared without-group distance. Let d_{ij} be the distance between dialect i and dialect j:

$$within_{g_k} = \frac{\sum_{i \in g_k} \sum_{j \in g_k} d_{ij}^2}{|d_{i \in g_k, j \in g_k}|} \qquad (1)$$

$$without_{g_k} = \frac{\sum_{i \in g_k} \sum_{j \notin g_k} d_{ij}^2}{|d_{i \in g_k, j \notin g_k}|} \qquad (2)$$

$$F\ ratio = \sum_{k=1}^{c} \frac{within_{g_k}}{without_{g_k}} \qquad (3)$$

The last equation determines an overall value for the assignment in a gold standard with c groups. The lower the F-ratio, the better the distance assignment corresponds with the gold standard. We normalize F-ratio by dividing it by c.

A second perspective derived directly from distance is that of discrimination. A distance assignment discriminates well if the (gold standard) groups emerge clearly. To operationalize this idea, we regard a dialect as a point in n-space fixed by its distance to the n dialects in the sample. We then expect gold standard groups to occupy relatively small regions (compared to non groups), with minimal overlap among groups, and thus maximal discrimination. Fisher's Linear Discriminant measures the discrimination between two groups (Schalkoff (1992)). The idea is that group means should differ maximally with respect to group variances. We calculated group discrimination for each dimension. If the gold standard has c groups among n varieties, the total discrimination between all group pairs over all dimensions is:

$$D = \sum_{d=1}^{n} \sum_{i=2}^{c} \sum_{j=1}^{i-1} \frac{(\mu_{di} - \mu_{dj})^2}{\sigma_{di}^2 + \sigma_{dj}^2} \qquad (4)$$

where i, j ranges over dialect groups. We normalize D by dividing it by the number of group pairs $\binom{c}{2}$ and dimensions n. Larger values indicate better discrimination.

2.2 Validation via Classification

We clustered distance matrices to obtain classifications. We examined seven clustering techniques: single link, complete link, group average, weighted average, unweighted centroid, weighted centroid and minimum variance, also known as Ward's method (Jain & Dubes (1988)).

In validation, we use a gold standard which is specified as a partition. Therefore the dialect distances we calculated were converted to a partition as well so that the one partition could be compared to the other. From the dendrogram we could derive a partition of k groups, where k is equal to the number of groups in the gold standard ($2 \le k \le n - 1$). Note that we don't use the most detailed hierarchical information in the dendrogram, only the highest level divisions.

Rand Index

Having two partitions we compare them with each other by using the Rand index (Rand (1971)) which Hubert & Arabie (1985) recommend as "one of the most popular alternatives for comparing partitions..." Given n dialects, suppose we have a partition M, based on the distances of the method we want to validate, and a partition G which is the gold standard. Both partitions consist of k groups. Each of the $\binom{n}{2}$ dialect pairs belongs to one of the following types:

1. M and G assign the dialects to the same group;
2. M and G each assign the dialects to different groups;
3. M assigns the dialects to different groups but G to the same; or
4. M assigns the dialects to the same group, but G to different ones;

1 and 2 are agreements, while 3 and 4 represent disagreements. We construct a matrix, where the rows correspond with the groups of M, and the columns correspond with the groups of G. Let n_{ij} be the number of dialects in group i of M and group j of G, $n_{i.}$ the total number of dialects in group i of M and $n_{.j}$ the total number of dialects in group

j, and g be the number of groups in the partitions under comparison, $g = |G| = |M|$. The number of agreements R_k is:

$$\binom{n}{2} + 2\sum_{i=1}^{g}\sum_{j=1}^{g}\binom{n_{ij}}{2} - \left[\sum_{i=1}^{g}\binom{n_{i.}}{2} + \sum_{j=1}^{g}\binom{n_{.j}}{2}\right] \qquad (5)$$

The number of disagreements is equal to $\binom{n}{2} - agreements$. The error rate is expressed as the probability of a disagreement: $disagreements/\binom{n}{2}$.

Fowlkes and Mallows Index

An other method for comparing partitions was developed by Fowlkes & Mallows (1983). A brief description can be found in Hubert & Arabie (1985). Their measure of association B_k is defined as:

$$\sum_{i=1}^{n}\sum_{j=1}^{n}\binom{n_{ij}}{2} / \sqrt{\sum_{i=1}^{g}\binom{n_{i.}}{2} * \sum_{j=1}^{g}\binom{n_{.j}}{2}} \qquad (6)$$

If each group in M perfectly matches with a group in G, B_k is 1. If each group in M is equally distributed over all groups in G, B_k is 0.

3 Consistency

In the case of word-based methods, we can check on consistency using Cronbach's α, which is derived from the inter-item correlation of the words. Each of the more than 5×10^3 dialect pairs is assigned a separate distance based on each of the 100 words. We calculate the correlation r between words $w1$ and $w2$ in the usual way, for each pair of words. This is summarized in the average correlation $\bar{r}$. Cronbach's α is calculated as follows:

$$\alpha = \frac{n_w\bar{r}}{1 + (n_w - 1)\bar{r}}, \text{ where } n_w \text{ is the number of words} \qquad (7)$$

4 Which Validation Methods?

Both the F ratio and Fisher's Linear Discriminant tend to select techniques which maximize the contrast between groups. The F emphasizes group coherence with respect to contrast to other groups (reflected in dendrograms), and Fisher's Linear Discriminant emphasizes contrast, but relative to the variance of the distance measures. Only the second validation technique was able to identify methods which were "linguistically successful"—ones which led to successful classifications after clustering

	Rand	F & M	Cronbach
Comparison method			
corpus frequency	0.64	1.51	
frequency per word	0.54	1.81	0.94
Levenshtein indel from corpus	0.55	1.79	0.93
Levenshtein indel theoretically	0.52	1.79	0.91
Levenshtein indel variable	0.60	1.73	0.95
Phone representation			
phones	0.56	1.79	0.90
features Hoppenbrouwers redundant	0.55	1.76	0.88
features Vieregge	0.53	1.77	0.88
features Hoppenbrouwers not redundant	0.54	1.78	0.88
Representation diphthongs			
as two segments	0.55	1.76	0.88
as one segment	0.54	1.78	0.88
Comparison feature histograms/bundles			
Manhattan	0.54	1.77	0.88
Euclidean	0.55	1.77	0.89
'Pearson'	0.54	1.76	0.88
Frequency weighting of features			
no weighting	0.54	1.78	0.88
weighting	0.55	1.76	0.88
Direct or indirectly comparison			
direct	0.55	1.78	0.93
indirect	0.51	1.82	0.83
Cluster methods			
single link	0.78	1.50	
complete link	0.34	1.99	
group average	0.36	1.94	
weighted average	0.39	1.91	
unweighted centroid	0.89	1.40	
weighted centroid	0.85	1.43	
minimum variance	0.20	2.23	
Totals			
worse	0.98	1.20	0.79
best	0.07	2.56	0.96

Table 1: Mean method scores using Rand, Fowlkes/Mallows (F & M) and Cronbach's α (Cronbach). All word methods are very reliable with 100 words (Cronbach). Minimum variance clustering, direct comparison (without reference to standard language) and word-based methods are clearly superior. Frequency Weighting leads to slightly worse results; two-segment representation of diphthongs is slightly better, and feature-comparison schemes are roughly equivalent. There appear to be dependencies among these choices — the best don't simply use all the best (average) choices. See text for further details.

according to our gold standard. The methods which scored optimally according to the F ratio emphasized contrast and seemed to underassess group-internal diversity. When we examined dendrograms produced by these methods, there tended to be virtually no group-internal distance, something which the best methods consistently recognize. We found this surprising, and had expected the F ratio to be more useful.

Fisher's Linear Discriminant is much more successful than the F ratio; in general, methods which score well here led to clusterings which were close to the gold standard. Details were often wrong, however, particularly in cases with larger numbers of groups.

Both the Rand index and the Fowlkes and Mallows index work very well, and, furthermore, they tended to agree most on the best methods. On the basis of 104 dialects and summarized over all three levels of the gold standard, both indexes judges the same method as the best.

These results are perhaps not surprising if one recalls that the gold standard is essentially nominal. The distance measures are of course metric, which is why metric criteria such as Fisher's Linear Discriminant apply at all, but the nominal matrix-overlap criteria (Rand and Fowlkes/Mallows) measure most directly what the gold standard wants: a classification of dialects.

5   Which Dialectometric Methods?

Table 1 shows results for the Rand index, the Fowlkes and Mallows index and Cronbach's α. We average results' scores in order to address questions of choice separately. See the caption for a summary of results.

The same method came out as optimal according to both the Rand index and the Fowlkes/Mallows: Levenshtein using unweighted Vieregge features with 1-segment diphthongs, in which varieties were compared directly (rather than through standard Dutch), and in which feature vector distance was assayed via $1 - r$. The value of insertions and deletions was determined with reference to a null vector, which might be interpreted as silence, and which also worked best on average among Levenshtein methods.

References

BLANCQUAERT, E. and PEÉ W. (1925–1982): *Reeks Nederlands(ch)e Dialectatlassen*, De Sikkel, Antwerpen.

DAAN, J. and BLOK D. P. (1969): *Van Randstad tot Landrand; toelichting bij de kaart: Dialecten en Naamkunde*, Noord-Hollandsche Uitgevers Maatschappij, Amsterdam.

FOWLKES, E. B. and MALLOWS, C. L. (1983): 'A Method for Comparing Two Hierarchical Clusterings', *Journal of the American Statistical Association* **78**, 553–569.

GOEBL, H. (1982): *Dialektometrie: Prinzipien und Methoden des Einsatzes der Numerischen Taxonomie im Bereich der Dialektgeographie*, Österreichische Akademie der Wissenschaften, Wien.

GOEBL, H. (1984): *Dialektometrische Studien. Anhand italoromanischer, rätoromanischer und galloromanischer Sprachmaterial aus AIS und ALF*. 3 volumes, Niemeyer, Tübingen.

GOOSSENS, J. (1977): *Inleiding tot de Nederlandse Dialectologie*, Wolters-Noordhoff, Groningen.

HOPPENBROUWERS, C. and HOPPENBROUWERS, G. (1988): 'De featurefrequentiemethode en de classificatie van nederlandse dialecten', *TABU: Bulletin voor taalwetenschap* **18**(2), 51–92.

HUBERT, L. J. and ARABIE, P. (1985): 'Comparing Partitions', *Journal of Classification* **2**, 193–218.

JAIN, A. K. and DUBES, R. C. (1988): *Algorithms for Clustering Data*, Prentice Hall, Englewood Cliffs, New Jersey.

KESSLER, B. (1995): Computational Dialectology in Irish Gaelic, *in* 'Proceedings of the European Association for Computational Linguistics', EACL, Dublin, pp. 60–67.

NERBONNE, J. et al. (1996): Phonetic Distance between Dutch Dialects, *in* G. Durieux, W. Daelemans and S. Gillis, eds, 'CLIN VI, Papers from the sixth CLIN meeting', University of Antwerp, Center for Dutch Language and Speech, Antwerp, pp. 185–202.

RAND, W. M. (1971): 'Objective Criterion for Evaluation of Clustering Methods', *Journal of the American Statistical Association* **66**, 846–850.

SCHALKOFF, R. (1992): *Pattern Recognition: Statistical, Structural and Neural Approaches*, John Wiley & Sons, Inc., New York.

SÉGUY, J. (1971): 'La relation entre la distance spatiale et la distance lexicale', *Revue de Linguistique Romane* 35, 335-357.

VAN GINNEKEN, J. (1913): *Handboek der Nederlandsche taal. Deel I: De sociologische structuur der Nederlandsche taal*, Nijmegen.

VIEREGGE, W. H. (1987): Basic Aspects of Phonetic Segmental Transcription, *in* A. Almeida and A. Braun, eds, 'Probleme der phonetischen Transkription, *Zeitschrift für Dialektologie und Linguistik*, Beihefte', Franz Steiner Verlag Wiesbaden GMBH, pp. 5–55.

WEIJNEN, A. (1966): *Nederlandse dialectkunde*, Van Gorcum, Assen.

Rater Classification on the Basis of Latent Features in Responding to Situations

M. Meulders[1], P. De Boeck[1], I. Van Mechelen[1]

[1]Department of Psychology,
University of Leuven, Belgium

Abstract: The present paper investigates to what extent several expansions of probability matrix decomposition models may be used to capture qualitative differences between raters. The models are applied to a specific data set about raters who indicate whether they would display hostile responses in frustrating situations.

1 Introduction

Probability matrix decomposition models (PMD; Maris et al. (1996)) may be used to analyse repeatedly observed binary associations between two sets of elements. In a specific application, the two sets may, for instance, contain patients and symptoms (Maris et al. (1996)), facial expressions and emotions (de Bonis et al. (1999)), situations and responses (Meulders et al. (1999)), etc. In most applications of PMD models, different raters judge whether pairs of elements are associated. However, the models may also be used to analyse associations that are recorded with the same rater at different time points and so on.

To explain observed associations, PMD models assume a twofold process: First, it is assumed that raters covertly classify elements (e.g., situations and responses) by indicating whether or not they have a certain feature. Second, it is assumed that these latent classifications are combined according to a prespecified mapping rule. More specifically, the latent feature classifications are formalized as realizations of latent Bernoulli variables. Furthermore, the mapping rule may be chosen to reflect the theory one has about the process that generated the data. For instance, one may assume that elements are associated if they have at least one element in common. Maris et al. (1996) labeled this rule a disjunctive communality rule.

As an illustration consider raters p $(p = 1, \ldots, P)$ who judge whether they would display hostile responses r $(r = 1, \ldots, R)$ (e.g., feel irritated, become tense, curse, want to strike someone) in frustrating situations s $(s = 1, \ldots, S)$ (e.g., someone told lies about you, someone opened your personal mail). When applying a classical PMD model (which we will further label $M1$) to these judgments, the following assumptions are made:

1. It is assumed that raters attribute features f $(f = 1, \ldots, F)$ to a situation with a certain probability. These features refer to the nature of the frustration in a particular situation. For instance, a feature may reflect that the frustration in the situation is perceived as being intentionally caused, or that showing aggression in the situation is seen as highly undesirable. Formally, the attribution of features to situations is considered the realization of a Bernoulli variable, $X_{pr}^{sf} \sim \text{Bern}(\sigma_{sf})$, with $X_{pr}^{sf} = 1$ if rater p attributes feature f to situation s when he/she judges the pair (s, r), and 0 otherwise.

2. It is assumed that responses are linked to features with a certain probability. A link between a feature and a response means that the attribution of that feature to a situation is a sufficient condition for the response to occur. For instance, the feature that the frustration in a situation is perceived as "being intentionally caused", may be a sufficient condition for the person to curse. Formally, the links between features and responses are represented by the realization of latent Bernoulli variables $Y_{ps}^{rf} \sim \text{Bern}(\rho_{rf})$ that equal 1 if response r is linked to feature f when rater p judges the pair (s, r), and 0 otherwise.

3. It is assumed that a rater's judgment about whether he/she would display a certain response in a certain situation is determined by the features that are linked to the situation and the response. In particular, it is assumed that a rater will display a response if that response is linked to at least one feature that is attributed to the situation. Defining the observed variable B_p^{sr} to equal 1 if a rater p indicates that he/she would display response r in situation s, and 0 otherwise, this rule may be formally stated as follows:

$$B_p^{sr} = \oplus_f X_{pr}^{sf} Y_{ps}^{rf}, \tag{1}$$

with $\oplus$ denoting the boolean sum.

From the above assumptions it follows that all raters have the same probability to display response r in situation s. In particular, Maris et al. (1996) show that:

$$P(B_p^{sr} = 1 | \sigma, \rho) = 1 - \prod_f (1 - \sigma_{sf} \rho_{rf}). \tag{2}$$

In addition, the assumption that the latent variables are independently realized for each triple (s, r, p) implies that all observed judgments are statistically independent. In other words, the classical PMD model $(M1)$ assumes raters to be replications of one another. As such, the model does not take into account any systematic differences between raters. As this assumption may be untenable in several substantive contexts, it is a challenge to formulate new extensions of PMD models that take rater differences explicitly into account. An important aspect of this endeavour is to evaluate whether rater differences in the observed data are adequately captured by the model.

In the following paragraphs we will first consider some extensions of the classical PMD model ($M1$), that allow to capture qualitative rater differences (Section 2). Next, we will describe measures to evaluate whether observed rater differences are adequately captured by these model extensions (Section 3). Subsequently, we describe how to evaluate the significance of the proposed measures in a Bayesian framework (Section 4). Finally, we apply the models to real situation-response data (Section 5). In this application, we will not discuss the specific interpretation that results from the parameter estimates (Meulders et al. (1999)), but rather we will focus on the capacity of the different model extensions to capture different measures of rater differences.

2 Extensions of PMD models to capture rater differences

A first way to include qualitative rater differences in PMD models is to modify the latent structure assumption of the model (Maris (1999), Meulders et al. (1999)). More specifically one may assume that raters have a fixed opinion about the features that are attributed to a specific situation and that the features that are linked to a response are random (which means that they are renewed at each new judgment). This model, labeled M_2, may be expressed as follows:

$$B_p^{sr} = \oplus_f X_p^{sf} Y_{ps}^{rf} \qquad (3)$$

Contrary to the classical PMD model $M1$, the fact that raters now have a fixed opinion about the features that are attributed to a situation can be expressed as $X_{p1}^{sf} = ... = X_{pR}^{sf}$, for each p, s, f. Hence, for each pair of persons and situations (s, p), 2^F latent classes are defined containing pairs (s, p) so that for each pair belonging to a certain latent class, the pattern of features attributed by the person to the situation is the same across response judgments. Similarly, one may consider a model that assumes links between features and a response vector for each rater to be fixed, and the attribution of features to situations to be random. This model, labeled M_3, may be expressed as follows:

$$B_p^{sr} = \oplus_f X_{pr}^{sf} Y_p^{rf} \qquad (4)$$

In other words, for the pairs of persons and responses (r, p), 2^F latent classes are defined so that for each pair (r, p) belonging to a certain latent class, the pattern of features linked to the response for the person is the same across situations.

We notice that a model in which raters have a fixed opinion both about which features are attributed to a situation and which features are linked to a response, is problematic. First, with a specific number of features F and a specific mapping rule $C(\cdot)$, it may be the case that no latent data $(\mathbf{x}_p, \mathbf{y}_p)$ exist for which $\mathbf{b}_p = C(\mathbf{x}_p, \mathbf{y}_p)$; (with $\mathbf{x}_p$ and $\mathbf{y}_p$ denoting the latent data vectors pertaining to person p, and $\mathbf{b}_p$ denoting the observed data vector pertaining to person p). Second, even if the previous problem would not occur in a specific analysis, estimation of the model would still be problematic from a practical point of view because the number of latent classes $2^{(S+R)F}$ is too large to handle.

A second way to include qualitative rater differences is to assume latent classes that contain raters who use the same subset of features when making the judgments (Meulders et al. (2000)). Defining the latent variable Z_p^f to equal 1 if rater p uses feature f and 0 otherwise, the model, labeled M_4, may be expressed as follows:

$$B_p^{sr} = \oplus_f Z_p^f X_{pr}^{sf} Y_{ps}^{rf}. \tag{5}$$

The probability to display response r in situation s given that one uses a certain pattern of features $\mathbf{z}$ now equals:

$$P(B_p^{sr} = 1 | \boldsymbol{\sigma}, \boldsymbol{\rho}, \mathbf{z}) = 1 - \prod_f (1 - \sigma_{sf}\rho_{rf})^{z_p^f}. \tag{6}$$

Defining γ_k as the probability that a person uses the feature pattern $\mathbf{z}_k$, that is, $P(\mathbf{Z} = \mathbf{z}_k | \boldsymbol{\gamma}) = \gamma_k$ $(k = 1, \ldots, 2^F; \sum_k \gamma_k = 1)$, the probability to display a response r in a situation s equals:

$$P(B_p^{sr} = 1 | \boldsymbol{\sigma}, \boldsymbol{\rho}, \boldsymbol{\gamma}) = \sum_k P(B_p^{sr} = 1 | \boldsymbol{\sigma}, \boldsymbol{\rho}, \mathbf{Z} = \mathbf{z}_k) P(\mathbf{Z} = \mathbf{z}_k | \boldsymbol{\gamma}). \tag{7}$$

3 Measures to evaluate whether rater differences are captured by the model

In order to evaluate whether rater differences in the observed data are adequately captured by the model two types of correlational measures will be used (Meulders et al. (1999)). The first type are correlations between pairs of situations s and s^*, for a specific response r:

$$T_{rss^*}(\mathbf{B}) = \text{cor}_p(B_p^{sr}, B_p^{s^*r}). \tag{8}$$

This kind of measure may be used to evaluate whether there are differences across situations in the features that are linked to a specific response. The second type are correlations between pairs of responses r and r^*, for a specific situation s:

$$T_{srr^*}(\mathbf{B}) = \mathrm{cor}_p(B_p^{sr}, B_p^{sr^*}). \tag{9}$$

This kind of measure may be used to investigate whether there are differences across responses in the pattern of features attributed to a situation.

Besides the correlational measures, we also investigate whether the variability due to raters, as defined in a classical analysis of variance, is captured by the model. The present application can be formalized as a randomized block factorial design (Kirk (1982, p. 441)), each block containing one rater, and the two factors referring to the situation variable and the response variable, respectively. The sum of squares due to raters may be expressed as follows:

$$T(\mathbf{B}) = SR\sum_{p}(\bar{B}_{p}^{..} - \bar{B}^{..})^2, \tag{10}$$

with $\bar{B}_{p}^{..}$ being the mean of the judgments of rater p and $\bar{B}^{..}$ being the mean of all judgments.

4 Model checking in a Bayesian framework

To investigate whether the presented PMD models capture the rater differences measured by the three statistics (8), (9) and (10), we compare the observed value of these statistics with their reference distribution under the model. In this respect, we will use the *posterior predictive reference distribution* of future datasets $\mathbf{B^{rep}}$ that could have been observed under the model if the actual experiment were replicated with the same parameter values that generated the observed data. This distribution is formally defined as follows (Rubin (1984)):

$$p(\mathbf{B^{rep}}|\mathbf{B}) = \int p(\mathbf{B^{rep}}|\theta)p(\theta|\mathbf{B})d\theta, \tag{11}$$

θ being a vector that comprises all the parameters of the model. To compute the posterior predictive distribution we first use a data augmented Gibbs sampling (DAGS) algorithm (Gelfand, Smith (1990), Tanner, Wong (1987)) to compute a sample of the posterior $p(\theta|\mathbf{B})$ and afterwards we use the draws of this sample to simulate replicated data sets under the model.

5 Illustrative application

As an illustration of the presented PMD models we analyse situation-response data that were collected by Vansteelandt (1999). In this study

316 raters indicated to what extent they would display each of 4 hostile responses in each of 14 frustrating situations (0=not, 1=limited, 2=large). To apply the PMD model the raw data were dichotomized (0 vs. 1 or 2).

In this section we will not discuss the parameter estimates that are obtained with a specific model; rather we will focus on the way different models using four features capture different measures of rater differences. The reason to consider this particular number of features is because the four-feature model M_1 is a saturated model for the $S \times R$ frequencies $\sum_p B_p^{sr}$. Yet, it is not a saturated model for the $S \times R \times P$ binary data array; as will be seen, it may still be rejected because it does not capture any differences between raters.

In the estimation procedure, the DAGS algorithm is used to simulate, for each model, four chains with random starting points. The algorithm is stopped if the convergence diagnostic $\hat{R}^{\frac{1}{2}}$ (Gelman, Rubin (1992)) computed on the second halves of the chains, is smaller than 1.1 for each parameter. For models $M1$, $M2$, $M3$ and $M4$ this turned out to be the case after 4100, 4500, 5000 and 11000 iterations, respectively. Finally, for each model, a sample of 2000 draws is constructed by taking evenly spaced draws from the second halves of the four chains.

The sample of the posterior is used to simulate the reference distribution of the statistics (8), (9) and (10) for each model. Figure 1 displays the 364 observed correlations between $91 = (14 \times 13)/2$ pairs of situations, computed for each of the 4 responses (left panel) and the 84 observed correlations between $6 = (4 \times 3)/2$ pairs of responses computed for each of the 14 situations (right panel) within the corresponding 95% posterior interval (PI). In each plot, the correlations are ordered along the x-axis according to the mean of their 95% PI. Furthermore, to indicate this interval, the 2.5-th and 97.5-th quantiles of different correlations are connected with a line. For models M_1, M_2, M_3 and M_4, 9%, 8%, 88% and 67% of the observed correlations between pairs of situations are within the 95% PI; for the correlations between responses this is the case for 44%, 92%, 43% and 70% of the correlations, respectively. Hence, correlations between pairs of situations are best explained by assuming that raters have a fixed pattern of features linked to each response (M_3) and, as shown in Figure 1, they are mostly underestimated when a random pattern of features is assumed (M_1 and M_2). An intermediate position is taken by model M_4. In the same way, correlations between pairs of responses are best explained by assuming that raters have a fixed pattern of features attributed to each situation (M_2), whereas Figure 1 shows that they are often underestimated when a random pattern of features is assumed (M_1 and M_3). Finally, model M_4 here also takes an intermediate position.

Using classical ANOVA, the value of the rater sum of squares statistic

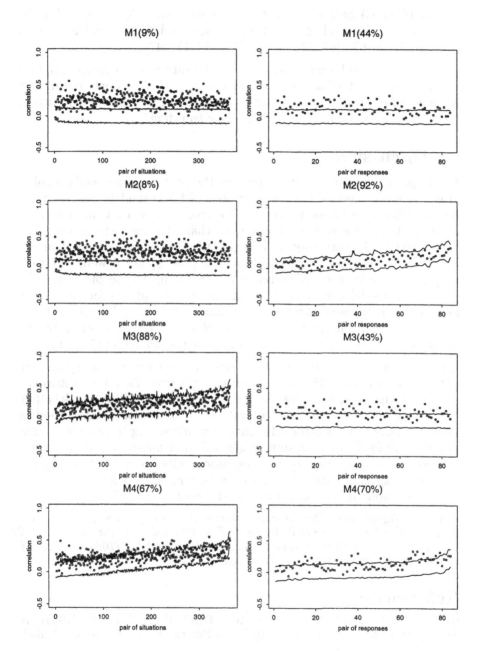

Figure 1: Correlations between pairs of situations (left panel) and correlations between pairs of responses (right panel) plotted in the corresponding 95% posterior interval simulated under models M_1, M_2, M_3 and M_4

for the observed data equals 386. For models M_1, M_2, M_3 and M_4 the 95% posterior interval of this statistic evaluated at the replicated data sets equals $[46, 63]$, $[61, 84]$, $[172, 247]$ and $[217, 347]$.

Thus, the observed sum of squares due to raters is underestimated by all the models. Furthermore, of all models, M_1 fits worst because it assumes no rater differences at all, and model M_4 comes closest in fitting this particular measure of differences due to raters.

6 Discussion

In the present paper we investigate, in the context of a specific application, to what extent different extensions of PMD models capture qualitative differences between raters. The results show that models using a different latent structure assumption than the one used in the classical PMD model may help to fit correlations between pairs of elements pertaining to one set (e.g. situations, responses) fairly well, but that they have problems to fit correlations pertaining to the other set. In contrast, a model assuming different subsets of features for each rater explains both types of correlations in a moderate way. Furthermore, in the present application, the latter model better allows to capture the differences due to raters as defined in a classical analysis of variance.

It is important to note that in the present application, a substantial part of the observed rater differences is left unexplained. Therefore, future research may focus on building alternative extensions of PMD models that do capture all differences between raters. In this respect, PMD models involving quantitative rater differences are interesting to consider. Such models may for instance assume a general rater parameter, indicating a tendency to display more or less responses. Alternatively, they may assume rater-specific parameters for each feature, indicating that features may be of more or less importance to different raters (Maris (1996)).

Acknowledgements. The research reported in this paper was partially supported by the Fund for Scientific Research-Flanders (Belgium) (project G.0207.97 awarded to Paul De Boeck and Iven Van Mechelen) and GOA/2000/02 awarded to Paul De Boeck and Iven Van Mechelen)

References

DE BONIS, M., DE BOECK, P., PÉREZ-DIAZ, F., NAHAS, M. (1999): A Two-process Theory of Facial Perception of Emotions. *Life Sciences, 322, 669-675.*

GELFAND, A. E., SMITH, A. F. M. (1990): Sampling Based Approaches to Calculating Marginal Densities. *Journal of the American Statistical Association, 85, 398-409.*

GELMAN, A., RUBIN, D. B. (1992): Inference from Iterative Simulation using Multiple Sequences. *Statistical Science, 7, 457-472.*

KIRK, R. E. (1982): Experimental Design: Procedures for the Behavioral Sciences (Second Edition), Brooks/Cole Publishing Company, Pacific Grove, California.

MARIS, E., DE BOECK, P., VAN MECHELEN, I. (1996): Probability Matrix Decomposition Models. *Psychometrika, 61, 7–29.*

MARIS, E. (1999): Estimating Multiple Classification Latent Class Models. *Psychometrika, 64, 187-212.*

MARIS, G. (1996): Probabiliteits Matrix Decompositie Modellen voor Trichotome Data [Probability Matrix Decomposition Models for Trichotomous Data]. *Unpublished Masters Thesis.*

MEULDERS, M., DE BOECK, P., VAN MECHELEN, I. (1999): A Taxonomy of Latent Structure Assumptions for Probability Matrix Decomposition Models. *Unpublished Manuscript, Department of Psychology, Leuven, Belgium*

MEULDERS, M., DE BOECK, P., VAN MECHELEN, I. (2000): Probability Matrix Decomposition Models Including Rater Differences. *Unpublished Manuscript, Department of Psychology, Leuven, Belgium*

RUBIN, D. B. (1984): Bayesianly Justifiable and Relevant Frequency Calculations for the Applied Statistician. *Annals of Statistics, 12, 1151–1172.*

TANNER, M. A., WONG, W. H. (1987): The Calculation of Posterior Distributions by Data Augmentation. *Journal of the American Statistical Association, 82, 528–540.*

VANSTEELANDT, K. (1999): A Formal Model for the Competency-demand Hypothesis. *European Journal of Personality, 13, 429–442.*

Results of Automatic Conversion of Diagnoses from ICD-9 to ICD-10 for Cancer Registration

Martin Meyer, M. Franzkowiak de Rodriguez

Population based Cancer Registry Bavaria, Registration Office
D-91052 Erlangen, Germany

Abstract: The 10th revision of the International Classification of Diseases (ICD-10) is intended to be used in all German medical units since 1.1.2000. Because former patient records have been stored with diagnosis codes of the 9th revision (ICD-9), the problem of a mixed-standard database arises for a long term registry like the Population based Cancer Registry Bavaria. Validated conversion tables are existing (Zaiss et al (1996)), but due to structure incompatibilities between ICD-9 and ICD-10 it is not possible to find a unique match for each entry of the catalogs. For time series analysis it is necessary to get consistent coding over all records without the break between the 9th and 10th revision. We examined the results of an automatic conversion routine included in the registry's database. Using additional information from the complete cancer record like morphology and topography allows to find a conversion decision for problematic codes. With this method we were able to convert all diagnoses codes of an empiric sample of 1719 ICD-9 codes.

1 Introduction

An important task of a population based cancer registry is monitoring cancer incidences over time. If any classification standard changes during the period of observation, problems with the creation of time series could appear.

Documentation standards of the Bavarian Population based Cancer Registry follow recommendations of international and national organizations, e.g. International Agency for Research on Cancer IARC (Parkin et al (1994)), Arbeitsgemeinschaft Deutscher Tumorzentren ADT (Dudeck et al (1999)). The World Health Organization (WHO) provides a family of classification systems within the International Classification of Diseases (ICD): For the classification of diseases the ninth revision of ICD was used in Germany until 1999. The tenth revision is effective since January 1, 2000 in all German medical units. To reach the aim of a consistent cancer registry database it is necessary to translate older diagnoses from ICD-9 to the new standard ICD-10. As far as possible this conversion should be done automatically, the extent of manual conversion should be minimized. Due to protection of personal data the cancer registry is not able to access the original patient files. Only the values of the cancer record may be used to handle the conversion problem.

Problems are caused by those ICD-9 codes which point to a set of more detailed ICD-10 entries. Problematic cases within the complete catalog have been reported by Zaiss et al (1996).

ICD-O-2 is used to classify topography and morphology information of a tumor. The upgrade from ICD-O-1 to ICD-O-2 happened in the year 1990. Actually no conversion problem is existing, because the data collection of the Population based Cancer Registry Bavaria started 1998.

2 International Classification of Diseases

The ninth revision of the International Classification of Diseases (ICD-9) was published 1976 and introduced 1979 in all member countries of the World Health Organization. ICD-9 consists of 17 chapters (chapter II: neoplasms). Due to a lack of codes regarding *reasons of injury and poisoning* and *influencing health status* two add-on classifications (E-/V-classification) established after introduction of ICD-9. 989 categories for diseases - represented as 3-digit-codes - are included in ICD-9 and add-ons. To enable a more detailed level of documentation 5711 subcategories (4-digit-codes) are provided.

The tenth revision of ICD was published 1992 (German version 1994). A long period of discussion and some modifications followed until the usage of ICD-10 became mandatory for all medical units in Germany. One new feature of this revision is the leading character (A...Z) to identify the different chapters. 21 chapters contain 2036 3-character codes for disease categories and 12166 subcategories with 4-character codes. Former add-on classifications were integrated into the ICD-10 scheme, the former chapter *Diseases of the nervous system and sense organs* was split into three new chapters. General a higher grade of detail was achieved with the tenth revision, but also some categories were dropped or merged with similar diseases.

3 Problems converting from ICD-9 to ICD-10

3.1 Conversion table

A conversion table was created and maintained by A. Zaiss et al (1996). In Germany it is distributed through the German Institute for Medical Documentation and Information (DIMDI, Cologne). The latest version (3.0 from September 21, 1999) is available at
http://www.dimdi.de/germ/klassi/fr-klassi.htm.

The table contains possible 14278 pairs of matching ICD-9 and ICD-10 codes plus 60 unconvertible entries (either ICD-9 or ICD-10 is undefined). For ICD-10 codes, which point to more than one ICD-9 code, the preferred code is marked, if possible.

Though the ICD-10 catalogue consists of more detailed codes than

ICD-9, it would be more easy to translate codes from ICD-10 to ICD-9. This way would not be practicable for our cancer registry, because it is necessary to preserve comparability with national and international ICD-10 based incidence and mortality statistics. We expect that the majority of diagnoses codes sent to the registry will be written in ICD-10 notation, therefore it is more economic to translate the remaining items from ninth to tenth revision.

Five matching situations are possible (Table 1). For a conversion direction from ICD-9 to ICD-10 the 1:1-situation and the n:1-situation lead to a unique match of an ICD-10 code. Only 53% of ICD-9 codes belong to these both categories. In the opposite direction (ICD-10 to ICD-9) for 73% of ICD-10 codes a unique ICD-9 code can be found. This is one reason that the authors of the conversion table do not recommend the conversion from from ICD-9 to ICD-10.

ICD-9 : ICD-10	codes ICD-9	codes ICD-10
1 : 1	2104 (35.9%)	2104 (22.3%)
1 : n	494 (8.4%)	4764 (50.6%)
n : 1	976 (16.7%)	90 (1.0%)
n : m	2265 (38.6%)	2425 (25.7%)
no match	25 (0.4%)	35 (0.4%)

Table 1: Matching situations (3- and 4-character-codes)

3.2 Neoplasms vs. other diagnoses

In the special case of cancer registration it is sufficient to focus on the ICD chapter II "neoplasms". During the development of ICD-10 there were not as many structural changes from 9th to 10th revision in this chapter as in other chapters like *mental disorders*. This situation leads to much better rates of unique convertible codes and is the base of good conversion results in the field of cancer diagnoses (Table 2). The rate of automatically convertible codes increases from 53% (overall ICD) to 74% (neoplasms only). Applying the conversion to empirical patient records leads to much better results (87%), because the cancer findings with high incidence can be converted without any problems. Unconvertible codes (no match) cannot be found in the chapter "neoplasms".

Typical chapters with a good rate of unique convertible codes (see table 3) are those with minor structural changes (e.g. *Neoplasms*) or the younger chapters of former add-on classifications (e.g. *Influencing health status and contact with health services*).

ICD-9:ICD-10	overall ICD-9	neoplasms (140.0-239.9)
1 : 1	2104 (35.9%)	375 (64.7%)
1 : n	494 (8.4%)	60 (10.3%)
n : 1	976 (16.7%)	56 (9.7%)
n : m	2265 (38.6%)	89 (15.3%)
no match	25 (0.4%)	0 (0.0%)

Table 2: Matching situation for the ICD chapter *neoplasms* (3- and 4-character-codes)

chapter	unique conversion possible
Infectious and parasitic diseases	34.6%
Neoplasms	**74.3%**
Mental disorders	33.5%
Injury and poisoning	30.1%
Influencing health status and contact with health services	79.2%

Table 3: Rate of unique conversion (1:1, n:1) from ICD-9 to ICD-10 for selected chapters

4 Results of conversion of empiric cancer diagnoses

We examined the first 1719 cancer records sent 1998/1999 to the cancer registry. In the empiric sample not all diagnoses codes appear with identical frequency. More frequently used codes represent cancer findings with a high incidence. Nearly all of them can be converted without any ambiguity.

Example: The ICD-9 code 174.4 "Malignant neoplasm of female breast, upper-outer quadrant" can be unique converted to ICD-10 C50.4 "Malignant neoplasm of breast, upper-outer quadrant".

The distribution of codes favors good conversion results.

If there are two possibilities to translate an ICD-9 code to ICD-10 and one of the destination codes would be very unspecific (e.g. C80 "Malignant neoplasm without specification of site"), we marked the more specific item (C43.9 "Malignant melanoma of skin, unspecified") as preferred code. In the conversion table of Zaiss et al (1996) this is done only in the opposite direction from tenth to ninth revision. Diagnoses with preferred destination codes can be converted automatically, too.

Often the classification rules of ICD-10 provide useful information to handle conversion problems. For example the category C45 may be used only for those cases whose morphology code starts with 905 and whose behavier code is 3. By this way a new conversion rule can be created:

> **If** morphology code = 905x/3 **then**
>> convert 164.9 to C45.7
> **else**
>> convert 164.9 to C38.3

Some classification rules of this type are explicitly printed in the ICD-10 books, others had to be generated by the cancer registry. Though the cancer registry does not receive just diagnoses alone but a complete cancer record, it is possible to solve many conversion problems using additional information. Morphology and topography are the mainly used items, celltype can be analyzed in some cases to force a conversion decision. In our empiric sample (n=1719) all codes, which were not unique convertible by application of the conversion table, could be translated by that method. In the future - after collection of more data records - we expect that only very few cases need to be sent back to the tumour centres to classify them new from the original patient documents.

Conversion type	Cancer records
Automatic conversion (1:1, n:1)	1502 (87.4%)
Automatic conversion after rule modification (preferred codes)	20 (1.2%)
Conversion with additional information (Morphology)	101 (5.9%)
Conversion with additional information (Morphology + Celltype)	44 (2.6%)
Conversion with additional information (Topography)	44 (2.6%)
Conversion with additional information (Morphology + Topography)	8 (0.5%)
No conversion	0 (0.0%)

Table 4: Conversion of 1719 empiric cancer records

A different approach to reduce the number of unconvertible diagnoses codes is to limit the destination codes to three characters. For most cancer incidence analyses this level of differentiation would be sufficient. ICD-9 codes with two or more corresponding ICD-10 subcategories within the same disease category could be converted to the unique 3-character code of this category. For the results see table 5.

	unique match 4-character code	unique match 3-character code
Overall ICD-9	53%	75%
Neoplasms	74%	85%
Empiric sample	87%	92%

Table 5: Conversion to ICD-10 (3/4-character codes)

We decided not to apply this approach: The win of some more unique convertible codes is not balanced with the loss of information by truncation of the 4th digit of all ICD-10 diagnoses.

5 Conversion procedure

The conversion process is mainly based on a relational database table containing all matching pairs of ICD-9/ICD-10 codes (table 6).

ICD-9	ICD-10	unique	preferred code
...	...	...	...
172.9	C43.9	No	Yes
172.9	C80	No	No
173.0	C44.0	Yes	-
173.1	C44.1	Yes	-
173.2	C44.2	Yes	-
...	...	...	...

Table 6: Rows of the conversion table

The automatic part of the conversion procedure is realized by a single SQL command:

```
select ICD10 from CONVERSIONTABLE
    where ICD9=:CODE_TO_CONVERT
    and (UNIQUE='Yes' or PREFERRED='Yes');
```

If a definite conversion cannot be found after this step, but additional information like morphology is available, then some special rules are applied in a second step (compare preceeding chapter). Only the cases remaining unconverted after both steps have to be handled manually.

6 Conclusions

For the chapter neoplasms of the International Classification of Diseases a good rate of convertible ICD-9 codes can be achieved. ICD-9 codes matching exactly one ICD-10 code can be converted automatically. For the neoplasms the number of these codes is much higher than for other chapters like mental disorders or injury and poisoning.

In many cases conversion problems are associated with bad documented cancer records (.9 - codes: "unspecified"). Good documentation quality reduces the number of bad documented records and prevents conversion problems.

Cancer records remaining unconverted can be handled using additional information from the complete cancer record like topography and morphology. Again a good documentation quality with a low rate of missing data items helps to receive good conversion results.

The efforts of conversion must be done only once for records stored before January 2000. Time series analysis will be possible on the full data acquisition period with consistent diagnoses codes without a break between ICD-9 and ICD-10 codes.

Acknowledgements. This work was partially supported by the Deutsche Krebshilfe e.V.

References

DUDECK, J., WAGNER, G., GRUNDMANN, E., HERMANEK, P. (eds.) (1999): Basisdokumentation für Tumorkranke: Prinzipien und Verschlüsselungsanweisungen für Klinik und Praxis, 5. rev. Auflage, Zuckschwerdt München, Bern, Wien, New York

PARKIN, D.M., CHEN, V.W., FERLAY, J., GALCERAN, J., STORM, H.H. and WHELAN, S.L. (1994): Comparability and Quality Control in Cancer Registration. IARC Technical Report, Lyon

ZAISS, A., SCHULZ, S., GRAUBNER, B. and KLAR, R. (1996): Conversion Table between ICD-9 and ICD-10. Brender, Christensen, Scherrer, McNair (eds.): Medical Informatics Europe 1996, IOS Press Amsterdam

Exploring Roman Brick and Tile by Cluster Analysis with Validation of Results

H.-J. Mucha[1], H.-G. Bartel[2], J. Dolata[3]

[1]Weierstrass Institute for Applied Analysis and Stochastics (WIAS),
Mohrenstraße 39, D-10117 Berlin, Germany
(e-mail: mucha@wias-berlin.de)

[2]Institut für Chemie,
Humboldt-Universität zu Berlin, Hessische Straße 1-2, D-10115 Berlin,
Germany
(e-mail: hans-georg=bartel@chemie.hu-berlin.de)

[3]Landesamt für Denkmalpflege Rheinland-Pfalz, Abt. Archäologie,
Amt Mainz, Große Langgasse 29, D-55116 Mainz, Germany
(e-mail: Dolata@em.uni-frankfurt.de)

Abstract: Mathematical methods of classification are suited to support archaeological interpretation (Ihm (1978)). Especially clustering techniques are frequently used data mining tools for finding structure in the data set. They aim at the partition of a generally huge set of unarranged high-dimensional objects (observations) into homogeneous subsets (clusters). Usually the starting point is data without hypotheses about the data. Here a sample of Roman brick and tile is collected which is characterized by 19 chemical elements (variables). The sample size is 613 (Dolata (1999a)). An adaptive clustering algorithm is applied which can handle different scaling of the variables automatically. The number of clusters is investigated by using a simulation technique. Furthermore the importance of the variables is quantified in the same way. Afterwards this knowledge is used for both hierarchical clustering and the visualization of data and clusters by principal component analysis.

1 The archaeological data

It is well known that roofing with tiles and underfloor heating with brick-constructed hypocausis are the most numerous uses of brick and tile in the north-western provinces of the Roman Empire. These architectures are really common in the Transalpine area because of the rougher climates compared to the Mediterranean area. Not only the commander's residence, but even all functional buildings and the barracks in the major military camps in the Rhine area – e.g. Nijmegen, Vetera, Neuss, Mainz and Strassburg – were tiled at the middle of the first century A.D. Even in the winter half-year hot tub-baths, heated by hypocausis, were in full action. Figure 1 shows an example which is investigated here (for a detailed explanation see Dolata (1998)).

Heavy clay products are important findings in archaeological excavations, particularly if they are marked with stamps of the manufacturing firm.

Figure 1: Landesmuseum Mainz ZS 1982.

These are references concerning their chronology and function. The evaluation of stratigraphic-documented excavations is possible by systematic and comparative investigation of brickstamps.

Brick and tile making was done by working vexillations of all military units stationed in a Roman province. Especially in the northern part of *provincia Germania superior* large military brickyards were set in Strassburg-Königshofen, Rheinzabern, Frankfurt-Nied, Gross-Krotzenburg and Worms; two further places are not yet identified. These brickworks belonged to different legions and were run in different periods.

Chemical analysis (X-Ray Fluorescence Analysis) of large quantities of stamped Roman bricks and tiles from different sites in South-Western Germany resulted in new sources of archaeometrical kind for historical and archaeological investigation (Dolata (1998, 1999b)). Methods of utilization of these engineering-sources have to be developed. Traditionally in Germany archaeology is part of the Arts. Therefore archaeologists must be assisted to recognize the value of these sources. Mathematical methods of classification are suited to support the archaeological interpretation (Dolata and Werr (1998), Mucha et.al (1999)).

2 Adaptive clustering technique

Let us explore the structure of row points of a $(I*J)$-data table $\mathbf{X}$ $=(x_{ij})$, $i = 1, 2, \ldots, I$, $j = 1, 2, \ldots, J$ assuming K different subpopulations (clusters) and a Gaussian model. When the covariance matrices of the clusters are constrained to be diagonal, the well-known sum of squares criterion

$$V_K = \sum_{k=1}^{K} tr(\mathbf{W}_k), \tag{1}$$

is to be minimized (Bock (1974), Späth (1985), Banfield and Raftery (1993)). Herein $\mathbf{W}_k = \sum_{i \in C_k} (\mathbf{x}_i - \bar{\mathbf{x}}_k)(\mathbf{x}_i - \bar{\mathbf{x}}_k)^T$ is the sample cross-product matrix for the k-th cluster C_k , and the expected value of variable j in cluster C_k is estimated by

$$\overline{x}_{kj} = 1/n_k \sum_{i \in C_k} m_i x_{ij}, \tag{2}$$

where n_k and m_i denote the mass of cluster C_k and the mass of observation i, respectively. Usually the mass is proportional to the number of observations. Like in this application in archaeology, the variables are often measured in quite different scales. For that reason appropriate weights of the variables q_j have to be chosen. Then criterion (1) has the form

$$V_K = \sum_{k=1}^{K} \sum_{i \in C_k} m_i d_Q^2(\mathbf{x}_i, \overline{\mathbf{x}}_k), \tag{3}$$

where $d_Q^2(\mathbf{x}_i, \overline{\mathbf{x}}_k) = (\mathbf{x}_i - \overline{\mathbf{x}}_k)^T \mathbf{Q}(\mathbf{x}_i - \overline{\mathbf{x}}_k)$ is the squared weighted Euclidean distance with $\mathbf{Q}$ diagonal. We recommend adaptive weights like diagonal elements proportional to the inverse pooled within-cluster variances $q_{jj} = 1/\overline{s}_j^2$, where $\overline{s}_j$ is the pooled standard deviation of the variable j

$$\overline{s}_j^2 = 1/M \sum_{k=1}^{K} \sum_{i=1}^{I} \delta_{ik} m_i (x_{ij} - \overline{x}_{kj})^2. \tag{4}$$

The indicator function δ_{ik} is defined in the usual way: $\delta_{ik} = 1$, if observation i comes from cluster k, or $\delta_{ik} = 0$ otherwise. Because of simplicity one can use M equals the sum of all weights m_i of the observations i, $i = 1, 2, ..., I$, i.e. M becomes independent from the number of clusters K. The weights can be estimated in the adaptive K-means method in an iterative manner (Mucha (1992)).

Figures 2 and 3 show the result of the adaptive K-means clustering using inverse pooled within-cluster variances into eight clusters. Clusters with quite different numbers of observations are detected. Near to the bottom of this projection using principal components of the covariance matrix concerning the adaptive weights $q_{jj} = 1/\overline{s}_j^2$, the small cluster 4 looks near to the cluster 3 at the right hand side. In reality, i.e., taking the true distances instead of the approximate ones in the plot, the cluster 8 on the left hand side is the nearest neighbour of cluster 4. Moreover the plot stretched by the principal components 3 and 4 shows the cluster 1 well separated from the clusters 2, 3 and 8.

Considering eight clusters, the weights $\sqrt{q_{jj}}$ of the variables are estimated. In order to appraise the importance of the variables standardized weights $s_j^2/\overline{s}_j^2$ (with total variances in the numerator) are to be preferred: 6.658 (SiO_2), 8.191 (TiO_2), 1.38 (Al_2O_3), 1.116 (Fe_2O_3), 3.723 (MnO),

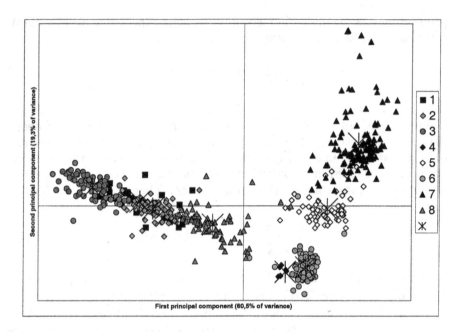

Figure 2: Principal component plot of eight clusters which are obtained by the adaptive K-means method. The cluster centers are marked by *.

Cluster	#	MTM	Place of military brickyard	Found in	Brickstamp
1	31	H505	not yet identified 1A	Niederbieber	*legio XXII Primigenia*
2	101	H294	Rheinzabern A	Speyer	*PORTIS*, type *Altrip 1a*
3	87	G111	not yet identified 1B	Mainz	*legio XXII Primigenia*
4	7	G087	not yet identified 3	Mainz	*cohors XXIIII Voluntariorum*
5	73	G105	Gross-Krotzenburg	Mainz	*cohors IIII Vindelicorum*
6	116	H240	Strassburg-Königshofen	Saalburg	*legio VIII Augusta*
7	124	G100	Frankfurt-Nied	Mainz	*legio XXII Primigenia*
8	74	H174	Rheinzabern B	Rheinzabern?	*antefix*

Chemical composition (selected contents) of Most Typical Members (MTM) of clusters										
Cluster	MTM	TiO_2	MnO	MgO	CaO	Na_2O	Cr	Zn	Sr	Zr	Nb
1	H505	0,5	*0,104*	2,22	*14,82*	0,64	115	72	287	143	13
2	H294	0,67	*0,073*	2,47	*11,24*	0,71	96	101	263	138	15
3	G111	0,59	*0,102*	2,9	*16,49*	0,59	121	90	383	121	11
4	G087	0,64	0,024	1,68	1,11	0,62	88	*273*	100	342	7
5	G105	0,81	0,015	1,06	0,42	0,24	85	42	117	205	19
6	H240	0,63	0,03	1,12	0,65	*1,03*	84	65	106	298	13
7	G100	*1,69*	0,023	0,89	0,68	0,17	*177*	59	115	307	*37*
8	H174	0,67	*0,067*	2,31	*6,31*	0,75	107	109	200	149	16

Figure 3: Description of clusters of Figure 2.

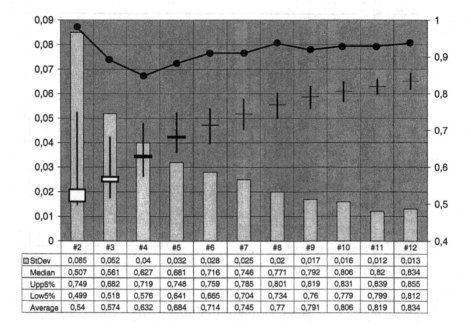

	#2	#3	#4	#5	#6	#7	#8	#9	#10	#11	#12
☐ StDev	0,085	0,052	0,04	0,032	0,028	0,025	0,02	0,017	0,016	0,012	0,013
Median	0,507	0,561	0,627	0,681	0,716	0,746	0,771	0,792	0,806	0,82	0,834
Upp5%	0,749	0,682	0,719	0,748	0,759	0,785	0,801	0,819	0,831	0,839	0,855
Low5%	0,499	0,518	0,576	0,641	0,665	0,704	0,734	0,76	0,779	0,799	0,812
Average	0,54	0,574	0,632	0,684	0,714	0,745	0,77	0,791	0,806	0,819	0,834

Figure 4: Statistics of the baseline distribution of Rand's measure for different number of clusters.

8.56 (MgO), 18.394 (CaO), 6.556 (Na_2O), 1.825 (K_2O), 1.152 (V), 2.683 (Cr), 1.633 (Ni), 1.867 (Zn), 1.47 (Rb), 8.889 (Sr), 2.135 (Y), 4.712 (Zr), 3.857 (Nb), and 2.327 (Ba). These weights are suitable for interpretation of the clustering result from chemical point of view.

3   Finding the number of clusters

Obviously, there is a cluster structure in Figure 2. More generally the stability of clusters as well as the number of clusters can be investigated by simulations. Many measures are developed in order to validate cluster analysis results by comparing partitions. One of the most popular measures is Rand's index (Rand (1971)). The Rand's index equals 1 at most (two partitions correspond to each other) and 0 at least. For a detailed description of this topic in the context of simulation studies, see Mucha (1992). Figure 4 presents some statistics of the baseline distribution for comparing partitions of adaptive K-means clustering of random multivariate normals (i.e., data without structure). The number of clusters investigated here ranges from 2 until 12. In order to investigate the stability of clustering the masses m_i of the observations in (3) are changed randomly in the interval (0, 2). This is a kind of soft sampling. There are figured out 200 partitions for each number of clusters. At the right hand

476

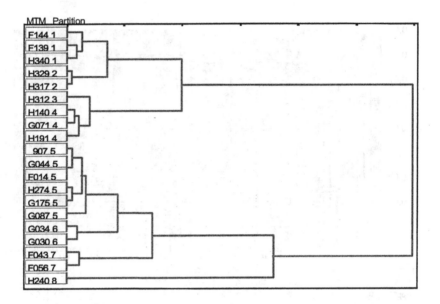

Figure 5: The sub-dendrogram of hierarchical clustering.

side of Figure 4 the scale for the Rand's index is drawn. The candlestick visualizes the median and average (box length) as well as the 95- and 5-percentiles. At the opposite site the scale for the bars of the standard deviation of Rand's index is given. The upper line in the picture gives the medians of the Rand's index for comparing partitions of adaptive K-means clustering of the Roman brick and tile data. These values are obtained by using the same sampling technique. At least two clusters are highly significant at the chosen significance level. From archaeological point of view eight clusters are reasonable, and this is supported by the simulation study (Figure 4) and also by hierarchical clustering results (see Figure 5 in: Mucha et al. (1999)).

4 Visualization of clusters and data

Once adaptive weights of variables are obtained they can be used in hierarchical clustering or in principal components analysis. Figure 5 shows a dendrogram of hierarchical cluster analysis minimizing the logarithmic trace criterion

$$V_K = \sum_{k=1}^{K} n_k log\ tr(\mathbf{W}_k\ /n_k) \qquad (5)$$

at each stage of merging clusters. Here n_k denotes the mass of k-th cluster C_k. It is allowed that the volume can vary from cluster to cluster. The sub-dendrogram can be obtained by cutting the dendrogram of the 613

MTM Place of brickyard

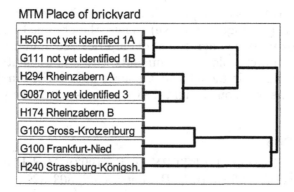

Figure 6: Dendrogram of the clusters of Figure 2.

samples (terminal nodes) at 20 clusters and denoting each cluster by the Most Typical Member (MTM) of the cluster. From the statistical point of view MTM of a cluster is the object with minimum distance to the center of the corresponding cluster. (The notation of all 613 objects and therefore the notation of the MTMs is of no archaeological meaning, it is that one of the sample in the corresponding series of chemical analyses.)

5 Archaeological interpretation

The result of clustering obtained by the described adaptive K-means algorithm is shown in Figures 2 and 3. In Figure 3, chemical contents (rounded values) are selected with respect of their effect of separating cluster centers (see the bold italic printed values).

In comparison with an archaeological empirical, but computer aided classification result (Mucha et al. (1999), Bartel et al. (2000)) the clustering obtained here is quit similar to the previous one. There are two kinds of slight disagreements: (a) The previous found clusters "Rheinzabern" (= place of Roman brickyard) and "not yet identified 1" are now separated into two clusters "Rheinzabern A/B" and "not yet identified 1A/1B", respectively, (b) The small empirical clusters "Mainz/Rheinhessen" (4 objects), "Worms" (= previous "not yet identified 2") (19 objects), and "unable for reference" (11 objects) are particularly not identified as clusters, but contained in some of the larger ones. Therefore, one of the further tasks of investigations will be to minimise these slight discrepancies varying both mathematical and archaeological models. Using hierarchical cluster analysis (Ward's method), it can be shown (see Figure 6) that the originally separated clusters "Rheinzabern A/B" and "not yet identifies 1A/1B", respectively, are immediately combined in one of the next steps of fusion. Indeed, the only remarkable difference between the two clusters "Rheinzabern A/B" is, for instance, the content of CaO:

478

"Rheinzabern A" has a high, "Rheinzabern B" a medium value of this oxide content (see Figure 3 above). Thus, the obtained results are both a first approximation of agreement of empirical, computer aided classification based on archaeological arguments with a mathematical one based on a cluster analysis model and a source of effective further tasks for minimising the mentioned slight disagreements which are yet consisting.

References

BANFIELD, J. D. and RAFTERY, A. E. (1993): Model-Based Gaussian and Non-Gaussian Clustering. *Biometrics, 49, 803–821.*

BARTEL, H. -G., DOLATA, J., and MUCHA, H. -J. (2000): Klassifikation gestempelter römischer Ziegel aus Obergermanien. *Archäometrie und Denkmalpflege 2000, 86–88.*

BOCK, H. H. (1974): Automatische Klassifikation. Vandenhoeck & Ruprecht, Göttingen.

DOLATA, J. (1998): Archäologische und archäometrische Untersuchung an römischer Baukeramik und Ziegelstempeln. *Archäometrie und Denkmalpflege 1998, 93–95.*

DOLATA, J. (1999a): Referenzmaterialien für die Herstellungsprovenienzen römischer Baukeramik im nördlichen Obergermanien. *Mainzer Arch. Zeitschr., 6, forthcoming.*

DOLATA, J. (1999b): Ingenieurtechnische Untersuchung an antiken Ziegelsteinen aus Mainz: Interdisziplinäre Erforschung römischer Baukeramik und Ziegelstempel. *Ziegel Zeitschrift, 6, 421–423.*

DOLATA, J. and WERR, U. (1998): Wie gleich ist derselbe? Homogenität eines römischen Ziegels und Aussagegrenzen geochemischer Analytik aufgrund von Meßtechnik und Materialvarietät. *Mainzer Arch. Zeitschr., 5, forthcoming.*

IHM, P. (1978): Statistik in der Archäologie. Archäo-Physika, Bd. 9, Köln.

MUCHA, H. -J. (1992): Clusteranalyse mit Mikrocomputern. Akademie Verlag, Berlin.

MUCHA, H. -J., DOLATA, J., and BARTEL, H. -G. (1999): Klassifikation von 613 Proben als Referenzen für die Herstellungsprovenienzen römischer Baukeramik im nördlichen Obergermanien. *Mainzer Arch. Zeitschr., 6, forthcoming.*

RAND, W. R. (1971): Objective criteria for the evaluation of clustering methods. *Journal of the American Statistical Association, 66, 846–850.*

SPÄTH, H. (1985): Cluster Dissection and Analysis. Ellis Horwood, Chichester.

Relief Intensity and the Formation of the Archaeological Record

Thomas Saile

Seminar für Ur- und Frühgeschichte, Universität Göttingen, Nikolausberger Weg 15, 37075 Göttingen, Germany

Abstract: The influence of relief intensity on the distribution of archaeological sites depends on the prevailing constellation of geofactors in the area of investigation. In hilly relief regions without change of substrata relief intensity proves a suitable size to describe areas of favourable archaeological record. In flat relief regions with frequent and small scale changes of substrata the explanation potential of relief intensity is reduced.

1 Introduction

Spatial distribution patterns displayed on archaeological maps are essentially determined by two factors: favoured choice of sites and selective archaeological record. With regard to the historic record of a site processes of relief levelling are decisive. Therefore interpretation of distribution maps should be preceded by extensive criticism of sources proving present day site record to be of historic origin. In this connection geoarchaeological views are gaining increasing importance (Waters, Kuehn (1996)).

Relief intensity is expressed by the maximum altitude difference measured in meters between the highest and lowest point of a surface unit. Corresponding to the different values various types of relief are identified. For example elevation differences varying between 0–10 m per km^2 are referred to by Scholz (1990, 41 Tab. 11) as flat relief, hilly relief is identified by variations of 11–100 m, whereas mountain relief is characterized by an altitude difference higher than 100 m per km^2. However, relief intensity proves to be a relatively rough measure as the spatial basic components are of considerable extent.

2 Hypothesis

Discovery of archaeological sites, invisible on the surface, requires prior exposure. In agriculturally utilised hill slope regions erosion increases the possibility of exposing archaeological sites with the result that relief zones of greater dynamics tend to be over represented on distribution maps. Furthermore, regions with increased probability of exposure and discovery are often found in apparently favoured prehistoric choice of settlement areas. Significant overemphasis of archaeological sites of particular relief zones, caused by erosion, would result in far reaching consequences with regard to interpreting distribution maps and prehistoric cultivated areas.

Favoured settlement areas seem to appear frequently in slope sections endangered by erosion, and are often located in ecotope border regions (Skorupinski (1991)). Little awareness exists today of settlement sites which are to be expected under alluvial deposits, respectively under forest or grassland thus greatly reducing their chances of exposure and observation. Essentially influenced by environmental and social factors, the pattern of prehistoric settlement behaviour in general appears to be biased as in its parts it is recognised at varying degrees of intensity.

Confirmation, respectively rejection, of the hypothesis follows in an empirical manner in two steps: Initially it is to be examined whether the distribution pattern observed does deviate significantly from the theoretically expected frequency, resulting from the spatial extent of the different areas of relief intensity. If this is the case it remains to be discussed whether a causal link exists between relief intensity and site distribution.

3 Model Regions

Research is conducted in two typical Central European landscapes. A map of relief intensity by Sabel is available for an area covering 557 km^2 in the northern region of the Wetterau (Saile (1998, 64 Fig. 65)). The loess landscape of the Wetterau is characterized by hill relief. Sabel differentiated four levels of increasing relief. Besides an epoch-spanning overall statement we present a description of the conditions in periods of Earliest and Later Linear Pottery culture (LBK).

The second research area is a section of the North German old morainic landscape, spanning both sides of the lower mid-watercourse of the River Elbe. Covering an area of 1430 km^2 the land surveying office of Lower Saxony provided data of its digital elevation model, DGM 50, from which the relief intensity data was derived. The concentration of sites dating between the 6th–12th century AD in the region of Höhbeck–Lenzen (276 km^2) and in the vicinity of Karstädt (144 km^2) was studied on a large scale. Apart from ranges of terminal moraines with hill relief this region is characterized essentially by low relief.

4 Results and Significance Test

A comparison of relief categories and the corresponding distribution of sites in the Wetterau research area produced a striking result: Considerably fewer sites are known in low relief compared to intensified relief regions than the theoretically expected frequency distribution revealed. Considering the 19 localizable Earliest LBK sites alone, such tendency is shown even more clearly. Later LBK also reveals a similar pattern of

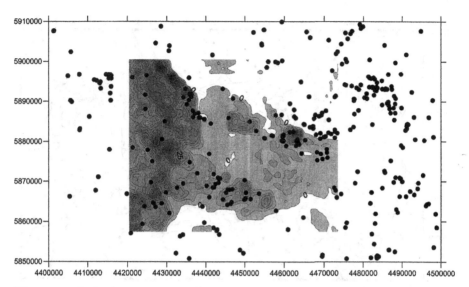

Figure 1: Relief intensity zones and distribution of sites from Early to High Middle Ages within the range of DGM 50 data 'NE-Lower Saxony'. Method of calculation: Kriging (smoothed contour lines).

distribution. The lowest relief region spanning 80 km^2 (14 %), covers only 7 % ($n = 8$) of the sites whilst the region with the highest relief intensity (210 km^2; 38 %) covers 50 % ($n = 55$) of localizable sites (Saile (1998, 64 ff. Fig. 66–70)).

Within the range of the DGM 50 data 'NE-Lower Saxony', sites, whose surroundings belong to the relief category of 10–14 m per km^2 , are clearly over represented. Lower relief zones do not reveal any significant deviation of distribution and high relief regions recede proportionately (Fig. 1; 5d). The smoothed contour lines of the relief map were determined by *Kriging* (Burrough (1987, 222 ff.)), presenting a well adjusted surface to the relevant data. In the northern, eastern and southern marginal zones of the DGM data, characterised by few data, the method is forced to extrapolate with the emergence of partly absurd data; this is a well known problem (Zimmermann (1995, 56 ff.)). However, figure 1 also reveals that larger concentrations of sites are outside, respectively, in the marginal zone of the DGM data. The two areas with the largest concentration of sites are situated in the Höhbeck–Lenzen region and in the vicinity of Karstädt (Fig. 2). Whilst areas of increased relief intensity in the Höhbeck–Lenzen region revealed an extra proportional number of sites (Fig. 3) such tendency was not quite as clearly marked in the vicinity of Karstädt (Fig. 4). In fact it is rather conspicuous that the southern region is predominantly vacant of sites which evidently do not refer to the relief categories, whilst in the north the largest concentration of sites is discernible as a linear distribution pattern.

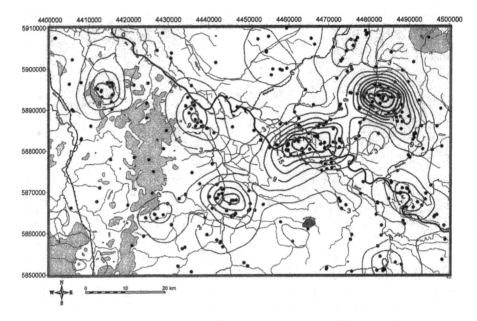

Figure 2: Density of sites dating from the Early to High Middle Ages spanning both sides of the lower mid-watercourse of the River Elbe (measured as number of neighbouring sites in a 5 km radius). Method of calculation: Kriging (smoothed contour lines)

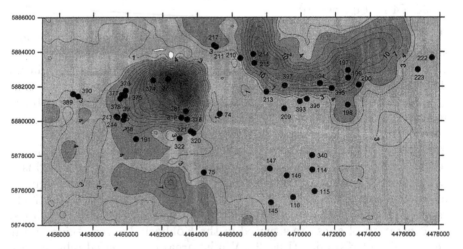

Figure 3: Relief intensity zones and Early to High Middle Ages distribution of sites in the Höhbeck-Lenzen region. Method of calculation: Kriging (smoothed contour lines).

For an interpretation of these observations (Fig. 5) it is crucial whether differences in distribution were due to random or attributable to differ-

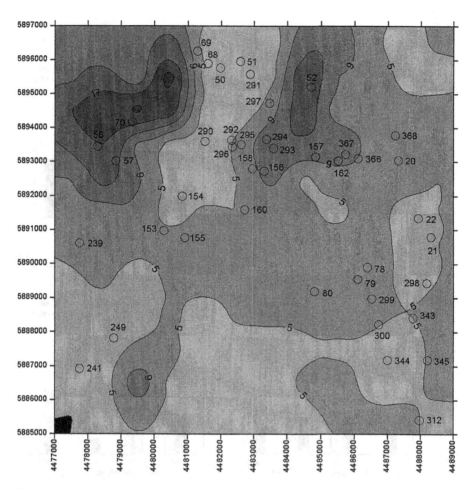

Figure 4: Relief intensity zones and Early to High Middle Ages distribution of sites in the Karstädt (Prignitz) region. Method of calculation: Kriging (smoothed contour lines).

ent probabilities of characteristics in the population. Nominal scaled frequency distribution may be compared with the test statistic χ^2. The chi-squared goodness of fit test compares a sample to a specified theoretical population and the test is made of how good the correspondence 'fits' between these two distributions (Sachs (1984, 320 ff.)).

The chi-squared goodness of fit test of diachronic distribution in the northern Wetterau revealed a significant deviation at 0.1% level of the observed sample from the theoretically expected frequency (Table 1a). Synchronic distribution of 110 Later LBK sites in the different relief categories also deviates significantly from the theoretical frequency (Table 1b). If the Later LBK deviation is still significant at 5% level an appro-

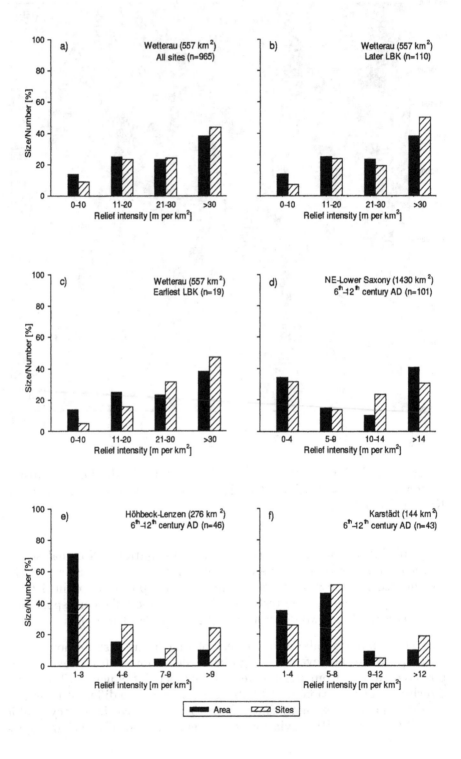

Figure 5: Distribution of sites in regions of varying relief intensity

priate statistical affirmation for the Earliest LBK cannot be made (Table 1c). Although the same tendency is clearly marked in the bar chart (Fig. 5c), the extent of the sample is low at $n = 19$.

Within the range of DGM data the observed distribution at 0.1% level reveals itself as significantly divergent from the theoretically expected frequency (Table 1d). The same applies to the distribution of sites in the Höhbeck–Lenzen region which reveals the most marked differences already in the bar chart (Fig. 5e; Table 1e). Yet an entirely different picture emerges in the vicinity of Karstädt. Here observed distributions react within the random limit as the theoretically expected (Table 1f). Alteration of categories or spatial reference units do not lead to significant deviations. In so far the result reveals itself as stable and there is no reason to doubt the null hypothesis.

5 Discussion

Although the chi-squared tests have usually produced significant deviations from the theoretically expected frequency the question remains, whether definite links exist between relief intensity and site density or if it is merely fictitious correlation. Is it possible to explain site distribution on the model?

Case Model 1: In the Wetterau Sabel presupposed that a serious, evidence distorting gap in site distribution may probably be discounted. He observed that Early Neolithic settlements are situated preferably in today's luvisol regions. Here, czernozem was apparently degraded in post-Neolithic times whereas in more wet locations with inflow of carbonates such degradation did not take place. According to Sabel Early Neolithic farmers avoided such allegedly wet areas. This would support the fact that today's czernozem regions were obviously less densely populated during the Neolithic period as were today's luvisol regions. But this statement would impute LBK settlers unjustly that they had avoided the most fertile agricultural sites although it is well known they also settled on less fertile soil and in part even in border areas and certain favourable highland regions.

An explanation deviating from the previously mentioned concept, however appears to be much more plausible: In the northern Wetterau, regions of low relief meet, to a large extent, the distribution centres of the czernozem. Not only is Holocene erosion in low relief areas very low but also possible exposure of sites. The resulting low discovery frequency may lead to apparently settlement free zones. No varying degrees of collecting activities are discernible between western and eastern sections of the Wetterau (Saile (1998, 49 ff. esp. Fig. 46 and 48)).

Thus the following may be established for the northern Wetterau: The different relief intensity is crucial to the frequency of sites. Regions of

a)

Wetterau, all sites

Relief intensity [m per km^2]	Area (557 km^2)	O_i (observed)	E_i (expected)	$O_i^2 \cdot E_i^{-1}$
0 – 10	14%	87	135	56.1
11 – 20	25%	222	241	204.5
21 – 30	23%	232	222	242.5
> 30	38%	424	367	489.9
?	100%	965	965	993.0

$?^2_{calc} = 993 - 965 = 28$
$?^2_{table}(3; 0.1\%) = 16.27$
$?^2_{calc} > ?^2_{table} \Rightarrow H_1$(significant deviation at 0.1% level)

b)

Wetterau, Later LBK

Relief intensity [m per km^2]	Area (557 km^2)	O_i (observed)	E_i (expected)	$O_i^2 \cdot E_i^{-1}$
0 – 10	14%	8	15	4.3
11 – 20	25%	26	28	24.1
21 – 30	23%	21	25	17.6
> 30	38%	55	42	72.0
?	100%	110	110	118.0

$?^2_{calc} = 118 - 110 = 8$
$?^2_{table}(3; 5\%) = 7.81$
$?^2_{calc} > ?^2_{table} \Rightarrow H_1$(significant deviation at 5% level)

c)

Wetterau, Earliest LBK

Relief intensity [m per km^2]	Area (557 km^2)	O_i (observed)	E_i (expected)	$O_i^2 \cdot E_i^{-1}$
0 – 10	14%	1	3	0.3
11 – 20	25%	3	5	1.8
21 – 30	23%	6	4	9.0
> 30	38%	9	7	11.6
?	100%	19	19	22.7

$?^2_{calc} = 22.7 - 19.0 = 3.7$
$?^2_{table}(3; 5\%) = 7.81$
$?^2_{calc} \leq ?^2_{table} \Rightarrow H_0$(no significant deviation at 5% level)

Table 1: Chi-squared goodness of fit tests of observed distribution to theoretically expected frequency.

d)

NE-Lower Saxony, sites of 6th-12th century AD

Relief intensity [m per km^2]	Area (1430 km^2)	O_i (observed)	E_i (expected)	$O_i^2 \cdot E_i^{-1}$
0 – 4	34%	32	34	30.1
5 – 9	15%	14	15	13.1
10 – 14	10%	24	10	57.6
≥ 15	41%	31	42	22.9
?	100%	101	101	123.7

$?^2_{calc} = 123.7 - 101.0 = 22.7$
$?^2_{table}(3; 0.1\%) = 16.27$
$?^2_{calc} > ?^2_{table} \Rightarrow H_1$(significant deviation at 0.1% level)

e)

Höhbeck-Lenzen, sites of 6th-12th century AD

Relief intensity [m per km^2]	Area (276 km^2)	O_i (observed)	E_i (expected)	$O_i^2 \cdot E_i^{-1}$
1 – 3	71%	18	33	9.8
4 – 6	15%	12	7	20.6
7 – 9	4%	5	2	12.5
> 9	10%	11	4	30.3
?	100%	46	46	73.2

$?^2_{calc} = 73.2 - 46.0 = 27.2$
$?^2_{table}(3; 0.1\%) = 16.27$
$?^2_{calc} > ?^2_{table} \Rightarrow H_1$(significant deviation at 0.1% level)

f)

Karstädt, sites of 6th-12th century AD

Relief intensity [m per km^2]	Area (144 km^2)	O_i (observed)	E_i (expected)	$O_i^2 \cdot E_i^{-1}$
1 – 4	35%	11	15	8.1
5 – 8	46%	22	20	24.2
9 – 12	9%	2	4	1.0
> 12	10%	8	4	16.0
?	100%	43	43	49.3

$?^2_{calc} = 49.3 - 43.0 = 6.3$
$?^2_{table}(3; 5\%) = 7.81$
$?^2_{calc} \leq ?^2_{table} \Rightarrow H_0$(no significant deviation at 5% level)

Table 1: continued

low relief are zones neither disadvantaged by substrata nor collecting activities. Furthermore, palynological studies also make prehistoric settlements in these regions likely.

Case Model 2: In the north-east of Lower Saxony medium relief intensity regions revealed an over proportionately large number of sites (Fig. 1). These are essentially settlements from marginal zones of ground moraines. In contrast to the loessic landscape of the Wetterau regions of medium relief intensity are overlapping with change of substrata resulting from glacial processes. To a large degree such mutual increase of favoured choice of settlement sites and selective archaeological record may serve to explain the distribution of sites in the region of Höhbeck–Lenzen deviating markedly from the proportion of relief zones (Fig. 3; 5e; Table 1e).

If, within the scope of the DGM data and the region of Höhbeck–Lenzen, one concedes a certain degree of importance as to the influence of relief intensity for selective archaeological record, it appears as if the situation in the vicinity of Karstädt may differ entirely. Compared to the remaining research areas this region is characterised by relatively low relief, ranging between 1 and 22 m per km². No obvious deviation is discernible between distribution of sites and categories of relief intensity (Fig. 4; 5f; Table 1f).

The distribution pattern of sites could thus be determined by collecting activities or geological factors. Indeed, the number of sites dating from the Early and High Middle Ages, in the area searched systematically by local researcher E. Lüders of Karstädt, is clearly higher than in the adjacent regions (Lüders (1966)). For the distribution of archaeological sites geological conditions are of secondary importance only. The linear structure in the northern region of the map (Fig. 4) reveals itself as a pearl-strand type arrangement of Slav settlements along a watercourse. It is noteworthy that in the south obviously fewer sites are known despite the fact that geological conditions are similar to the northern region.

Whilst in the north-east of Lower Saxony, in areas of small scale change of substrata, the effects of relief intensity and favoured choice of settlement sites are overlapping, and thus increasing the impact, relief intensity among the shallow undulating old morainic landscape around Karstädt is obviously not decisive for the exposure of archaeological sites. This area is dominated by specific collecting activities.

References

BURROUGH, P. A. (1987): Spatial aspects of ecological data. In: Jongman, R. H., ter Braak, C. J. F. and van Tongeren, O. F. R. (eds.), Data analysis in community and landscape ecology. Pudoc, Wageningen, 213–251.

LÜDERS, E. (1966): Archäologische Gemarkungsaufnahmen im Gebiet um Karstädt, Kreis Perleberg. Informationen des Bezirksarbeitskreises für Ur- und Frühgeschichte Schwerin, 6, 11–22.

SACHS, L. (1984): Applied Statistics. Springer, New York.

SAILE, T. (1998): Untersuchungen zur ur- und frühgeschichtlichen Besiedlung der nördlichen Wetterau. Selbstverlag des Landesamtes für Denkmalpflege Hessen, Wiesbaden.

SCHOLZ, E. (1990): Reliefansprache. In: Barsch, H. and Billwitz, K. (ed.), Physisch-geographische Arbeitsmethoden. Haack, Gotha, 34–45.

SKORUPINSKI, T. (1991): Historische Bodenerosion in der Gemarkung Nieder-Wöllstadt, Wetteraukreis. In: Rupp, V. (ed.), Archäologie der Wetterau. Verlag der Bindernagelschen Buchhandlung, Friedberg, 47–55.

WATERS, M.R. and KUEHN, D.D. (1996): The Geoarchaeology of Place: The Effect of Geological Processes on the Preservation and Interpretation of the Archaeological Record. American Antiquity, 61, 483–497.

ZIMMERMANN, A. 1995: Austauschsysteme von Silexartefakten in der Bandkeramik Mitteleuropas. Habelt, Bonn.

Spatio-Temporal Modeling of Cancer Mortality Rates

Ulrike Schach

Fachbereich Statistik
Universität Dortmund, 44221 Dortmund, Germany
uschach@statistik.uni-dortmund.de

Abstract: The distribution of stomach cancer mortality data in Germany reveals clusters at different locations, in this case "Regierungsbezirke". It is common practice to classify the rates in quintiles and color them in order to find neighboring sites with extreme rates. Statistical methods can help to model the spatial and temporal autocorrelation structure within the data. This paper is about modeling data dependent on space and time with two different approaches. A classical linear model, based on an innovation process will be introduced and parameters for the temporal and the spatial autocorrelation can be estimated using ML methods. On the other hand, corresponding parameters are estimated through a Bayesian modeling of the data. The results of both methods are then compared theoretically and numerically.

1 Introduction and Description of the Data

When modeling spatio-temporal phenomena, it is necessary to account for the complex dependence structure within the data. The data set underlying this analysis are stomach cancer mortality rates of men. The data are provided by the German Cancer Institute, Heidelberg. Spatially, the data are spread on an irregular lattice over the 30 regions of former West Germany, called "Regierungsbezirke". In contrast to common linear modeling, where the observations must be independent, a stochastic dependence structure of the data on the lattice is assumed here. In order to model it, a definition of neighborhood must be chosen. For the following analysis, two regions are considered as neighbors, if they share a common border. For a different definition of neighborhood, based on geostatistics, see Markus et al. (1999). Additional to the spatial distribution, there is a temporal structure, as the data are available for the time period from 1976 to 1990 on a yearly basis.

1.1 Standardization

The raw stomach cancer mortality counts have been standardized with respect to 5 year age group and gender. An indirect standardization with a mixture of an internal and external standard population has been chosen. The standard population is based on the sum over the years from 1976 to 1990 for every region, as with an internal standardization for every year, the temporal trend within the data would not have been preserved. The indirect method of standardizing is reasonable, as the standardized mortality ratio (SMR) can be calculated. It equals the quotient of the mortality in the study population divided by the expected mortality of the study population, if it had the same mortality as the standard population. Having calculated the SMR's in the described way, they show a strong linear dependence of the standard deviation on the mean. Therefore, a logarithmic transformation has been chosen, in order to remove this trend.

1.2 Descriptive Statistics

Figure 1 shows the temporal trend of the logged SMR's for male stomach cancer.

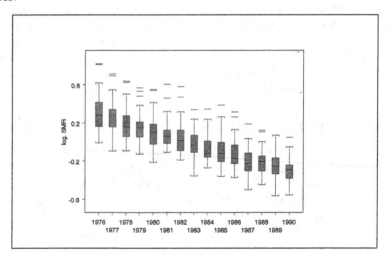

Figure 1: Temporal distribution of logged stomach cancer SMR's of men aggregated over the 30 regions of Germany

Clearly visible is the downward temporal trend of the data. The spatial distribution of the data is displayed in figure 2. The years of 1976, 1983 and 1990 have been chosen as examples.

Figure 2 shows that the mortality ratios are clustered, i.e. that adjacent regions are more similar, than would be expected under the assumption of independence. The standardized rates are classified in quintiles. Obviously, there are relatively high rates in the south of Germany in the three selected years. All maps of the years in between show a similar pattern. According to cancer specialists, no reasons for this are known yet. Additionally, one can see the relative increase of cancer deaths in the north of Germany.

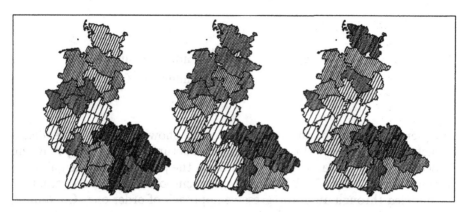

Figure 2: Spatial structure of stomach cancer mortality rates for the
years 1976, 1983 and 1990

2 Spatio-Temporal Models

As it is the aim of the analysis to model the dependencies as described
above, two models will be introduced now that account for the spatial
and the temporal structures. The first is based on a classical frequentist,
the second one on a Bayesian approach. A transformation of a Markov
type dependence for the spatial structure is especially important for both
models. With respect to a specified spatial definition of neighborhood,
the time series definition of the Markov property can be described as
follows: the outcome of region i, $i = 1, \ldots, N$, given the outcome of its
adjacent regions does not depend on the outcomes of all non neighboring
regions on the lattice. A model based on this assumption is conditionally
autoregressive (CAR). A different approach, which is not persued here,
uses the simultaneous distribution of the data on the lattice (SAR), as
described by Besag (1974).

2.1 Frequentist Approach based on an Innovation Process

Let Z_t be a multivariate stochastic process with the following characteristics:

i) $\{Z_1, \ldots, Z_t\} \sim \text{Gau}(0, \tilde{\Sigma})$,

ii) $\{Z_t\}$ has the Markov property,

iii) $\{Z_t\}$ is second order stationary.

Using the characteristics of multivariate normally distributed random
vectors, an innovation process ϵ_t and a matrix C can be defined with the
following properties

$$Z_t = C \, Z_{t-1} + \epsilon_t \qquad \epsilon_1, \epsilon_2, \ldots \text{ iid. } \sim \text{Gau}(0, \Sigma_0) \qquad (1)$$
$$\epsilon_t \text{ independent of } Z_1, \ldots, Z_{t-1}$$
$$t = 1, \ldots, T.$$

As mentioned before, the underlying data show a spatial dependence structure. We model this dependence structure by assuming that the process at location i and time t depends on the process at the neighboring regions of i at time $t-1$. Additionally, the temporal dependence structure is modeled through an autoregressive approach of order one. Combining these two ideas, we obtain the following structure

$$Z_t = \alpha \, Z_{t-1} + \beta \, B \, Z_{t-1} + \epsilon_t \qquad t = 1, \ldots, T. \qquad (2)$$

B is the neighborhood matrix of the following form: the (i, j)-th element of B is zero, if the regions i and j have no common border, or if $i = j$. Otherwise, $b_{ij} = \frac{1}{n_i}$, where n_i is the number of neighbors of region i. α is the parameter of the temporal and β of the spatial autocorrelation. If we define $C := \alpha \, I + \beta \, B$, equation (2) is a special case of (1). $\text{Cov}(Z_t)$, which is time invariant due to the second order stationarity of the process, is denoted by Σ. On the basis of the innovation term ϵ_t and suitable regularity conditions, the process Z_t can be expressed recursively through the constant matrix C, based on the initial distribution at time $t = 1$, plus an innovation term ϵ_t

$$Z_t = \sum_{j=0}^{t-1} C^j \, \epsilon_{t-j} + C^t \, Z_0 \qquad t = 1, \ldots T. \qquad (3)$$

It can be shown, that the Markov process Z_t converges as $t \to \infty$, if α and β, i.e. matrix C satisfy certain conditions. A sufficient condition is that the spectral norm, i.e. the square root of the maximum eigenvalue of $C \, C'$ is less than one.

Likelihood Function and ML Estimation

After having set up the model, the unknown parameters α and β can be estimated using the likelihood function and ML method, see Cressie (1993), p. 477 ff. Due to the Markov property of the stochastic process Z_t, the likelihood function can be written as a product of conditional transition probabilities. The only unknown matrix before setting up the likelihood is Σ. Based on equation (3), Σ can be expressed by

$$\Sigma = \mathrm{cov}(Z_t) = \sum_{j=0}^{\infty} C^j \, \Sigma_0 (C')^j. \tag{4}$$

If ϵ can be considered as noise, which acts on the components of the process, it is reasonable to assume that all components have the same variance and are independent of each other. Hence the assumption $\Sigma_0 = \sigma_0^2 I$ is plausible. Given starting values for α, β and σ_0, and a stopping rule for the infinite series of equation (4), terminated by a condition on the spectral norm of C, matrix Σ will be obtained. So the likelihood function can be expressed as

$$l(\alpha, \beta, \sigma_0 \mid Z_1, \ldots, Z_T) \quad = \quad \frac{1}{(2\pi)^{\frac{N}{2}} \sqrt{\det \Sigma}} \exp\{-\frac{1}{2} Z_1' \, \Sigma^{-1} \, Z_1\} \tag{5}$$

$$\prod_{t=2}^{T} \frac{1}{(2\pi)^{\frac{N}{2}} (\sigma_0^2)^{\frac{N}{2}}} \exp\{-\frac{1}{2} \frac{1}{\sigma_0^2} \|Z_t - C \, Z_{t-1}\|^2\}.$$

It is easy to show that the likelihood function can be extended to the case of covariates or a temporal trend. For this analysis, the temporal trend of the standardized and logged SMR's, as visible in figure 1, will be estimated within the model. The ML estimator has been chosen for this problem, since it has good asymptotic behaviour for ergodic Markov chains under relatively weak regularity conditions. According to Hall & Heyde (1980), p.156, it can be shown that the ML estimator is asymptotically normal, consistent and sufficient, even in the case of dependent observations. Hence statistical tests and confidence intervals can be built, based on the normal distribution.

Results of the Classical Approach

The unknown parameters of the likelihood function so far are α, β, and σ_0. Additionally, the linear time trend parameter θ is included. Using a modified quasi-Newton method, the likelihood function has been maximized with respect to these parameters. Table 1 displays the results.

α	:	(0.6913	$\pm$	0.080)
β	:	(0.1968	$\pm$	0.090)
σ_0	:	(0.1187	$\pm$	0.012)
θ	:	(-0.0046	$\pm$	0.001)

Table 1: Estimated 95% confidence intervals for the estimated parameters

The results of table 1 are reproducible, independent of the starting values for the unknown parameters. Therefore it can be assumed that the results define a global instead of a local maximum of the likelihood function. The average number of iterations is 6 in this case.

2.2 Bayesian Approach

In contrast to classical models, the Bayesian approach allows for variation of the unknown parameters, which are modeled in the prior distribution. The model is given by $f(x \mid \nu)$ and the prior by $f(\nu)$. Taking the data into account, the a posteriori knowledge about the parameter ν can be written as $f(\nu \mid x) \propto f(\nu) f(x \mid \nu)$, which is well known as the Bayes theorem. The actual calculation of the a posteriori distribution is rather difficult, especially if it is not a known distribution type. In recent years, computer intensive methods based on Markov Chain Monte Carlo algorithms have become more and more important. They allow for drawing a sample from the unknown a posteriori distribution instead of calculating it. The parameter estimates are then based on mean and standard deviation of a sample that is reliably large enough. Usually, the chains are given a so called "burn in" period, after which the observations for the unknown parameters are drawn. The following three-stage spatio-temporal Bayes model is based on the normality assumption and the CAR-approach, as described in section 2.1 for the classical model.

3-Stage Model Representation

Stage 1: Prior distributions

$$\alpha \sim \text{Gau}(0, 1E-4)$$
$$\beta \sim \text{Gau}(0, 1E-4)$$
$$\tau \sim \text{Gamma}(1E-3, 1E-3)$$
$$\theta \sim \text{Gau}(0, 1E-4)$$

Stage 2: Modeling of the spatial dependence at time $t = 1$

$$b_i \mid \bar{b}_i, \tau \sim \text{CAR}, \text{Gau}(\bar{b}_i, \tau)$$

Functional relation:

$$\bar{b}_i = \text{mean of the adjacent regions of } i$$
$$\tau = \text{precision}$$

Stage 3: Modeling of the SMR's

$$R_{t,i} \mid \mu_{t,i}, \tau \sim \text{Gau}(\mu_{t,i}, \tau)$$

Functional relation:

$$\mu_{t,i} = \alpha \, R_{t-1,i} + \beta \bar{b}_{t-1,i} + \theta \, t$$
$$\sigma_0 = 1/\sqrt{\tau}$$

All following simulations have been carried out with the WinBUGS software, based on the Gibbs sampler. Due to the complex dependence structure of the data in this analysis, with conditional independence assumptions as described in the introduction of this section, directed acyclic graphs cannot be used here. Instead, so called chain graphs as described by Spiegelhalter et al. (1996) need to be applied. Again, as in the classical model, a parameter for the temporal trend has been included.

Parameter Estimates of the Bayesian Approach

After a burn in period of 2,500 iteration steps and based on a sample of 2,000, the following parameter estimates and confidence intervals are obtained.

α	:	(0.6906	$\pm$	0.066)
β	:	(0.1970	$\pm$	0.077)
σ_0	:	(0.0909	$\pm$	0.006)
θ	:	(-0.0047	$\pm$	0.001)

Table 2: Estimated 95% confidence intervals for the estimated parameters

Again, different starting values have been used, in order to see, whether the parameter estimates are dependent on them. In the Bayesian model it turns out that for different combinations of starting values after the first hundred iterations, all four parameters have converged perfectly already.

3 Discussion

As tables 1 and 2 show, the classical linear model and the Bayes approach lead to approximately the same parameter estimates. Especially for the autocorrelation parameters α and β, and the temporal trend θ, both methods obtain nearly identical results. However, taking a closer look, great differences between the approaches can be found. As mentioned, the parameter estimates of the classical linear model are based on an average of 6 iterations. Computing times are relatively long and take even longer, when calculating the variance-covariance matrix in order to test for significance of the parameters. In the Bayesian approach, hundreds of samples can be drawn within seconds of time, including the generation of confidence intervals, autocorrelation functions, etc. automatically. As stated above, the independence of the parameter estimates of the starting values is almost "visible", when looking at the chains of the first samples. In the classical approach, there even need to be conditions on the parameters α and β to guarantee convergence. A carefully designed simulation study could be used to compare the two approaches more systematically. Future research has to be undertaken in the direction of covariates. When including covariates in both models, two cases can be formulated: either the matrix X of covariates is a constant matrix over time, or X has a temporal structure itself. Apart from the difficulty to obtain variables which have an influence on stomach cancer mortality with the required temporal and spatial resolution, the parameter estimates of the models described here could change, due to a so far unaccounted underlying process of these covariables. According to Becker et al. (1984), p.51 f., nutrition, personal and familial disposition, and typical occupations are risk factors. In the case that these risk factors as covariates are too difficult to obtain, Kafadar and Tukey (1993) propose how to find surrogates. Additionally, an alternative weighting of neighboring regions, e.g. a hierarchy of higher order would be worth examining. The models described in this analysis assume an autoregressive structure of order one, but models with higher orders can be thought of as well.

References

BECKER, N.; FRENTZEL-BEYME, R. and WAGNER, G. (1984): Atlas of Cancer Mortality in the Federal Republic of Germany. 2nd edition. Springer, Berlin

BESAG, J. (1974): Spatial Interaction and the Statistical Analysis of Lattice Systems. *Journal of the Royal Statistical Association B, 36, 192-225.*

CRESSIE, N. (1993): Statistics for Spatial Data. Wiley, New York

HALL, P. and HEYDE, C. (1980): Martingale Limit Theory and its Application. Academic Press, New York

KAFADAR, K. and TUKEY, J. (1993): U.S. Cancer Death Rates: A Simple Adjustment for Urbanization. *International Statistical Review 61, 259-281.*

MARKUS, L.; BERKE, O.; KOVACS, J. and URFER, W. (1999): Spatial Prediction of the Intensity of Latent Effects Governing Hydrogeological Phenomena. *Environmetrics 10, 633-654.*

SPIEGELHALTER, D.; THOMAS, A. and BEST, N. (1996): Computation on Bayesian Graphical Models. *Bayesian Statistics 5* (Bernardo, J.; Berger, J.; Dawid, A. and Smith, A., eds.). Oxford University Press, *407-425.*

The Classification of Critical Periods for Melanoma Development due to UV–Radiation

D. Schneider, A. Pfahlberg, O. Gefeller

Department of Medical Informatics, Biometry und Epidemiology,
University of Erlangen–Nuremberg, D–91054 Erlangen, Germany

Abstract: Sufficient epidemiologic evidence exists that exposure to ultraviolet light is related to the occurence of malignant melanoma. Especially intermittent intensive sunlight and sunburns are important risk factors. Elwood and Jopson (1997) presented in a meta–analysis of case–control studies an overall odds ratio (OR) of 1.91 (95%–confidence interval (CI): 1.69 – 2.17) for sunburns at all ages. Concerning the idea of a "critical period" for the relationship between sunburn episodes and malignant melanoma there is substantial heterogeneity in the published literature. This analysis is based on data of 603 melanoma patients and 627 population controls from 11 participating centers in seven European countries. The results confirm the increase in melanoma risk for an increasing number of sunburns during childhood and adulthood in the same magnitude of risk. The maximum OR for the highest exposure category of more then five painful and blistering sunburns during the childhood was 2.0 (95%–CI: 1.2 – 3.5) and during the adulthood 2.1 (95%–CI: 1.4 – 3.3), respectively. Thus there exists equivalent risk for both periods of life and our data do not support the presence of a "critical period".

1   Introduction

Cutaneous malignant melanoma (CMM) incidence and mortality rates are increasing in white populations worldwide more rapidly than any other cancer (Swerdlow (1990)). There is sufficient epidemiologic evidence that exposure to ultraviolet light is an important risk factor for developing malignant melanoma (Koh (1991)). Especially intermittent intensive sunlight and sunburns play an essential role. Elwood and Jopson (1997) presented in a meta–analysis of melanoma case–control studies an overall OR of 1.91 (95%–confidence interval (CI): 1.69 – 2.17) for sunburns at all ages. In general it is largely irrefutable that sunburns increase the risk for melanoma. In contrast, there is heterogeneity in the published studies concerning the classification of a "critical period" during lifetime with an exceptional risk for malignant melanoma. Out of 13 retrospective studies comparing the history of sunburns for different ages, four major studies support the idea of a "critical period" in early life. Particularly two case–control studies suggest that sunburn experience in childhood causes the highest risk on melanoma development. Zanetti et al. (1992) found that painful and blistering sunburns during

500

childhood were associated with increased risk (OR=6.5; 95%–CI: 3.4 –
12.3), while there was no significant effect of severe sunburns in lifetime
when adjusting for type of skin reaction to sun exposure and history of
sunburns in childhood. Østerlind et al. (1988) have pointed out that the
"critical period" is before the age of 15 with an OR of 3.7 (95%–CI: 2.3
– 6.1) for more than four sunburn episodes.

Migration studies comparing domiciles close and far from the equator
during different time periods in an individual´s life comprise another indirect method to investigate the age relationship between development
of malignant melanoma and sunburn episodes. Studies on immigrants,
mainly from the British Isles to Australia, showed that migration in the
first decade of life led to a risk of melanoma similar to that of native–born
populations while migration at later ages was associated with a lower risk
(Holman (1986); Khlat (1992)).

In this paper, a brief description of the results of the epidemiologic study
FEBIM ("Effect of febrile infectious diseases and vaccinations on malignant melanoma") devoted to the evaluation of the relationship between
the frequency of sunburns in childhood and adulthood, respectively, and
the occurence of malignant melanoma of the skin is given.

2 Study Design

From March 1994 to August 1997 a population–based case–control study
within the framework of the European Organization for Research and
Treatment of Cancer (EORTC) was conducted by 11 participating centers in seven European countries. A total of 603 patients with newly
diagnosed CMM, confirmed by histopathology, and 627 randomly chosen
neighbourhood–controls were interviewed at their homes by means of
a standardized questionnaire by the same pretrained person per center
(see Table 1). To avoid major imbalances in the age/sex/ethnical origin
distribution between the cases and controls, a frequency–matching for
sex/age (three broad categories: < 40 years, 40 – 59 years, > 59 years)
and ethnic origin was carried out within each collaborating center. For
the consideration of the exposure factors for cases and controls the study
focused mainly on the history of febrile infectious diseases and vaccinations (Kölmel et al. (1999)). Also particular attention was paid to sun
exposure and sun susceptibility. Individual sunlight exposure was carefully assessed by asking about painful episodes of sunburn, past residence
in a sunny country, exposure to sunlight during holidays and during the
year outside the holiday period and outdoor work. With regard to the
classification of a "critical period" between sunburn episodes and malignant melanoma two periods of life, until 15 and older than 15 years were
chosen.

The importance of sunburn frequencies in these two periods were statistically analysed separately as well as jointly by means of a logistic

	Cases	Controls
Göttingen	53	52
Berlin	6	6
Tallin	101	101
Vienna	45	45
Sofia	115	115
Tel Aviv	47	54
Padova	55	60
Verona	44	44
Dijon	55	59
Hamburg	11	11
Dresden	71	80
Total	603	627

Table 1: Distribution of the eligible study subjects among the collaborating centers

regression model. Variables like center, sex, age and ethnical origin were included in the model as adjustment factors. The results of the age relationship between development of malignant melanoma and sunburn episodes were quantified by adjusted ORs and their corresponding 95%–CIs obtained by the profile likelihood method. All statistical analyses were performed using SAS software (Version 6.12, SAS Institute Inc., Cary, NC, USA).

3 Results

Table 2 shows the results of a separate analysis of the relationship between CMM and history of sunburns during childhood and adulthood. Generally, there is a continuous increase of melanoma risk for an increasing number of sunburns during childhood and aduldhood in the same magnitude of risk elevation. The maximum OR for the highest exposure category, defined as more than five sunburns, was 2.0 (95%–CI: 1.2 – 3.5) during the childhood and 2.1 (95%–CI: 1.4 – 3.3) during the adulthood, respectively.

To examine the possible joint influence of child and adult sun exposure on melanoma risk we cross–tabulated the sunburn influence during childhood and adulthood (see Table 3). The reference group is defined by the subcollective of persons with no sunburn episodes in both lifetime periods. The pooled analysis shows that within rows for a fixed column, respectively for the columns within a fixed row, the ORs increase at almost the same rate. Thus both childhood and adulthood

Risk factor	Cases (n=603) %	Controls (n=627) %	adjusted OR	95% CI
number of sunburns I) during childhood				
0	60.4	64.7	1.0	
1 – 2	20.8	21.8	1.1	0.8 – 1.4
3 – 5	12.0	9.6	1.4	0.9 – 2.0
≥ 6	6.8	3.9	2.0	1.2 – 3.5
II) during adulthood				
0	43.4	47.8	1.0	
1 – 2	30.8	32.3	1.1	0.8 – 1.4
3 – 5	14.1	12.8	1.4	1.0 – 2.0
≥ 6	11.7	7.1	2.1	1.4 – 3.3

Table 2: Separate analyses concerning the influence of sunburns during childhood and adulthood

sunburn frequencies have nearly independent effects in both lifetime categories, whereas the corresponding melanoma risks more or less add their effects for the separate periods.
A further increase in risk for frequent sunburns in adulthood can be seen for those without sunburn in childhood as for those with sunburn in childhood.

4 Discussion

The results of the present case–control study FEBIM confirm the known increase in melanoma risk for an increasing number of sunburns. Also the magnitude of risk elevation of more than five sunburns during childhood and adulthood resembles those of the literature (Elwood and Jopson (1997)).
However, as concerns the hypothesis of an exceptional risk for sunburns during childhood, there is incongruity. Already Whiteman and Green (1994) pointed out in a review of the literature that only two case–control studies suggested that sunburn experience in childhood causes higher risk on melanoma development. Other investigations found no or just small risk evaluations for childhood compared to other lifetime periods. Also our data show that there exists nearly equivalent melanoma risk for both periods of life with independent effects for sunburn episodes during childhood and adulthood. Therefore we can not support the presence of a "critical period" which is playing a crucial role.

The interpretation of results concerning the relationship between sun-

sunburns during adulthood	sunburns during childhood		
	0	1 – 2	≥ 3
0	1.0	1.2	1.9
		(0.8 – 1.8)	(1.0 – 3.6)
1 – 2	1.2	1.1	1.4
	(0.8 – 1.7)	(0.7 – 1.8)	(0.8 – 2.5)
≥ 3	1.6	1.8	2.1
	(1.1 – 2.4)	(0.9 – 3.5)	(1.3 – 3.5)

Table 3: Joint analyses concerning the influence of sunburns during childhood and adulthood (adjusted OR accompanied by 95%–CI)

burn episodes and melanoma development is complicated by the fact that there exist other cutaneous, endogenous and exogenous factors which are most probably associated to the occurrence of melanoma. The presence and number of common acquired and dysplastic melanocytic nevi is a major constitutional risk factor. The analysis of a prospective cohort–study of 631 children showed that the number of raised nevi is subject to sunlight–exposure (Autier et al. (1998)). These results confirm findings from earlier cross–sectional studies (Gallagher et al. (1990); Dennis et al. (1996)) and case–control studies (White et al. (1994); Breitbart et al. (1997)) which presented that intensive sun–exposure is important for development of melanocytic nevi and, therefore, indirectly for CMM. In addition for instance genetic disposal (familial melanoma), blue color of eyes, red hair and fair-skin phototype as well as causes for an immunosuppression can influence malignant melanoma risk. Thus the inherent mixture of risk factors for CMM does not allow to disentangle the different contributions in a retrospective study as ours.
Probably the most difficult problem in determining the effect of sunburns in different periods during life is the problem of how to design a study which is able to asses this question accurately. The present knowledge is based on retrospective studies relying on self–reported sun–exposure habits. Therefore the greatest threat to validity of case–control studies is misclassification of sunburn exposure. Does an individual really remember what happened, for instance in childhood? Alternatively, is it possible that painful events in childhood, like severe sunburns are more easily remembered than in later life?
It has also been supposed that melanoma patients tend to overreport past sun–exposure habits in an attempt to explain to themselves why they have the diagnosis of malignant melanoma. Also, is it possible that cases want to differentiate lifetime periods in that way that their parents

504

are responsible for their childhood and for that they report more sunburns for this phase and otherwise they suppress the history of sunburns during adulthood.

A quantitative assessment of these different misclassification scenarios and their effect on risk estimates has not performed until now since data from validation studies are lacking. An urgent need for such studies is obvious and has recently been articulated by Autier and Doré (1998) and La Vecchia (1999).

In conclusion, our results underline the hypothesis that there is no convincing evidence for a "critical period" during lifetime with an exceptional risk for malignant melanoma. Therefore, sun protection throughout all periods of life will remain the most important device of melanoma prevention.

Acknowledgements. The study was supported by the Cancer Research Institute, New York, and the Deutsche Krebshilfe, Bonn, FRG.

References

AUTIER, P. and DORÉ, JF (1998): Influence of sun exposures during childhood and during adulthood on melanoma risk. *International Journal of Cancer, 77, 533–537.*

AUTIER, P.; DORÉ, JF; CATTARUZZA, M. S. et al. (1998): Sunscreen use, wearing clothes, and number of nevi in 6- to 7-year-old European children. *Journal of National Cancer Institute, 90, 1873–1880.*

BREITBART, M.; GARBE, C.; BÜTTNER, P et al. (1997): Ultraviolet light exposure, pigmentary traits and the development of melanocytic nevi and cutaneous melanoma. A case-control study of the German Central Malignant Melanoma Registry. *Acta Dermatologica, 77, 374–378.*

DENNIS, L. K.; WHITE, E.; LEE, J. A. et al. (1996): Constitutional factors and sun exposure in relation to nevi: a population–based cross–sectional study. *American Journal of Epidemiology, 143, 248–256.*

ELWOOD, J. M. and JOPSON, J. (1997): Melanoma and sun exposure: an overview of published studies. *International Journal of Epidemiology, 19, 801–810.*

GALLAGHER, R. P.; MCLEAN, D. I.; YANG, C. P. et al. (1990): Anatomic distribution of aquired melanocytic nevi in white children. A comparison with melanoma: the Vancouver Mole Study. *Archives of Dermatology, 126, 466–471.*

HOLMAN, C. J. D.; ARMSTRONG, B. K.; HEENAN, P. J. et al. (1986): The causes of malignant melanoma: results from the West Australien Lions Melanoma Research Project. *Recent Results in Cancer Research, 102, 18–37.*

KHLAT, M.; VAIL, A.; PARKIN, M. et al. (1992): Mortality from melanoma in migrants to Australia: variation by age at arrival and duration of stay. *American Journal of Epidemiology, 135, 1103–1113.*

KOH, H. K. (1991): Cutaneous melanoma. *New England Journal of Medicine*, *325(3), 171–182.*

KÖLMEL, K. F.; PFAHLBERG A.; MASTRANGELO G. et al. (1999): Infections and melanoma risk: results of a multicentre EORTC case–control study. *Melanoma Research, 9, 511–519.*

LA VECCHIA, C. (1999): Sunscreens and the risk of cutaneous malignant melanoma. *European Journal of Cancer Prevention, 8(4), 267–269.*

ØSTERLIND, A.; TUCKER, M. A.; STONE B. J. et al. (1988): The Danish case–control study of cutaneous malignant melanoma. *European Journal of Cancer, 42, 319–324.*

SWERDLOW, A. J. (1990): International trend in cutaneous melanoma. *Annals of the New York Academy of Science, 609, 235–251.*

WHITEMAN, D. and GREEN, A. (1994): Melanoma and sunburn. *Cancer Causes Control, 5, 564–572.*

WHITE, E.; KIRKPATRICK, C. S. and LEE, J. A. (1994): Case–control study of malignant melanoma in Washington state. I. Constitutional factors and sun exposure. *American Journal of Epidemiology, 139, 857–868.*

ZANETTI, R.; Franceshi, S.; Rosso S. et al. (1992): Cutaneous melanoma and sunburns in childhood in a Southern European population. *European Journal of Cancer, 28A, 1172–1176.*

Classification in the Prescription of Medicaments

R. Schuster, D. Melcher,

Biometrisches Zentrum NORD beim Medizinischen Dienst der
Krankenversicherung Schleswig-Holstein,
Katharinenstr. 11a, 23554 Lübeck, Germany
Tel.: 0451-4803-306; Fax: 0451-4803-300;
E-Mail: reinhard.schuster@mdk-sh.de

1   Introduction

At the North German Biometrical Centre 50 million data records of medicine prescribed in charge of the health insurance determined by law ("Gesetzliche Krankenversicherung GKV") were analysed (data with respect to paragraph 300 SGB V, only prescriptions taking place outside hospitals were considered, time of data collection: 1998-1999). In contrast to the health report of Germany which is based on a small sample, our data include nearly all prescribed medicines of certain regions (for GKV patients). Besides the scientific point of view one has to know that there are demands and restrictions by law.

In Germany there are more than 50,000 drugs (in a more restricted sense) and over 250,000 medicines determined by so-called " pharmacological central numbers" (PZN). The amount of substance, the form of application, the package size and so on are given by the PZN. The financial volume of the mentioned medicines in Germany is over 35 billion DM per year. The yearly rising payments in connection with stable insurance premiums of the GKV in the present time imply the urgency of the realization of reserve potentials.

In order to ensure a high quality of prescriptions while providing patients with drugs under budget conditions one has to use classifications as a result of a combination of pharmacological data bank information, market information and therapeutic standards.

Different levels of aggregation are needed, starting with central indices down to details of the individual situation. In the common interest of doctors, patients and health insurances much more transparency, structured advises and discussions are necessary. In the process of drug examination studies it is essential to bring together all participants active in the pharmaceutical sector, to discuss and agree on common goals, and to define priorities for action. Irrational drug use has both a medical and an economic impact. Medically it leads to suboptimal, ineffective or even dangerous therapy. It may lead to higher cost caused by longer diseases or additional hospital admissions. Economically it leads to enormous waste of resources.

2 The ATC system

In the Anatomical Therapeutic Chemical (ATC) classification system, the drugs are divided into groups according to the organ or system on which they act and their chemical, pharmacological and therapeutic properties. The purpose of the ATC classification system is to serve as a tool for drug utilisation research in order to improve quality of drug use.

The Nordic Council on Medicines established the ATC system in 1975, further developments were done in cooperation with the Norwegian Medical Depot. In 1981 the WHO Regional Office for Europe recommended the ATC system for international drug utilisation studies. In 1996 the WHO Centre for drug Statistics Methodology was linked to the WHO Headquarter in Geneva. A major aim of the Centre is to maintain stable ATC codes over time to allow trends in drug consumption to be studied without the complication of frequent changes to the system.

Using seven code positions, drugs are classified in groups of five different levels. At the first level one has: A: Alimentary tract and metabolism, B: Blood and blood forming organs, C: Cardiovascular system, D: Dermatologicals, G: Genito-urinary system and sex hormones, H: Systemic hormonal preparations, excl. sex hormones, I: Immunologicals, J: General antiinfectives for systemic use, L: Antineoplastic and immunomodulating agents, M: Musculo-skeletal system, N: Nervous system, P: Antiparasitic products, insecticides and repellents, R: Respiratory system, S: Sensory organs, V: Various.

The 2nd and 3rd level divide into therapeutic/pharmacological subgroups. The 4th level is a therapeutic/pharmacological/chemical subgroup. The 5th level identifies the chemical substrate.

Medical products are classified according to the main therapeutic use of the main active ingredient. A medical product can have more than one ATC code if it is available in different strengths or formulations with clearly different therapeutic uses. It can also be used for different important indications and the use of the drug may differ from one country to another. Even in Germany there are minor differences in dependence of the used data bank.

We will give one classification example:

A	Alimentary tract and metabolism
A10	Drugs used diabetes
A10B	Oral blood glucose lowering drugs
A10BF	Alpha glucosidase inhibitors
A10BF01	Acarbose

On a next level of classification one has all drugs with Acarbose as the main active ingredient: in Germany the product name is "Glucobay" in 19 different versions (defined as PZN) distributed by six companies.

Not for all drugs defined by the PZN an ATC code is available. But in Germany there exists an additional product classification (Lauer-Taxe or similar data banks), which contains (with minor differences) extensions of the ATC-Classification up to the 3rd level. This completeness of classification we do not find in the " Red List" (" Rote Liste") which is widely used by doctors, especially in the field of generica. There also exist complete indication related classifications of all drugs (in the larger sense of the 250.000 PZN) with more levels.

The results given by the German " Arzneimittelverordnungsreport" (drug prescription report) are linearly ordered lists on several levels of aggregation. In contrast we prefer tree constructions in the sense of mathematical graph theory (or more general graphs) as appropriate representations. The knots of the graphs may be given by the transfer to the next level of ATC classification. Another possibility to construct different paths form the knots is given by the differentiation in dependence of the doctor, the medical speciality (i.e. ophthalmologist), patient or patient group. The knots can be realized as link structures in a HTML document. One can find such an example in " www.mdk-sh.de" using the path BZN, PLATO.

One can use the given information in order to identify special situations in the individual practice of a doctor. It has large implications for budget negotiations in the current situation.

3   Aut-idem-potentials of coast reduction

The doctor has the possibility to allow the pharmacist (on his prescription formula) to give the patient " nearly the same" drug. It must have the same similar substrates, the same dosage and pharmaceutical form in a much stronger form as given by the ATC classification, which is well defined and called " aut idem". In the mathematical sense it is a subclass of the equivalent class of PZN given by the ATC classification (in the 5th level). Usually the doctor will take this decision by himself. There are difficulties as a consequence of the very large number of drugs in Germany, the influence of the pharmaceutical companies, different therapeutic opinions (established at universities) and so on.

We want to give an example (prices based on a certain date using the acceptance of the drugs in a German region):

The table should not indicate that the drug with the lowest cost is a reference drug. The use of positive and negative lists is on the one hand not a stable and scientifically orientated way and on the other hand there are judgements by German laws not to use some lists produced in the past.

Nevertheless one can construct measures of cost reduction under basis of aut idem tables as mean values over large groups of patients which can

drug	prescriptions	price
CAPTO CORAX 50 Tabl.	116	31,84 DM
CAPTO 50 mg ABZ Tabl.	1675	31,84 DM
CAPTO 50 1A Pharma Tabl.	53	31,84 DM
CAPTOPRIL AL 50 Tabl.	8943	31,84 DM
...		
ACE HEMMER ratiopharm 50 Tabl.	41348	36,60 DM
SANSANAL 50 Tabl.	115	36,63 DM
CAPTOPRIL BASICS 50 mg Tabl.	135	36,83 DM
CAPTOPRIL 50 HEUMANN TAbl.	2902	36,86 DM
...		
CAPTOPRIL VERLA 50 Tabl.	43	47,99 DM
CAPTO PUREN 50 Tabl.	1903	49,50 DM
...		
ACENORM 50 Tabl.zu 50 mg	18974	86,49 DM
ESPARIL 50 Tabl.	301	92,39 DM
...		
LOPIRIN 50 Tabl.	1606	130,98 DM
TENSOBON 50 Tabl.	6032	130,98 DM

be used as a statistical orientation and one single index of a group of relevant parameters in order to develop a realistic drug policy.

In order to reach the mentioned goal, one has to go one step back from the viewpoint of informatics. If one has constructed a widely accepted measure as a result of the aut idem lists (the discussion process is on the way in different directions in different regions of Germany), one has to integrate these parameters in the mentioned ATC structure in order to be able to identify the components with high financial potentials and the components with high need for medical and pharmacological discussion.

On the basis of the mentioned data we want to give some details of the potentials of reduction of the chemical substrates of high importance (related to the above mentioned German region):

chemical substrate	ATC code	cost
Captopril	C09AA01	4.384.003 DM
Nifedipin	C08CA05	3.962.308 DM
Theophyllin	R03DA04	3.536.198 DM
Isosorbid mononitrat	C01DA14	2.462.028 DM
Ranitidin	A02BA02	2.169.658 DM

If we go further into detail and differentiate with respect to the amount of active substance, the form of application, and the package size, we get

Captopril Tab.		
reduction potential	size	substance amount
1.510.431 DM	100ST	25.0 mg
1.429.399 DM	100ST	50.0 mg
1.064.029 DM	100ST	12.5 mg
112.714 DM	50ST	25.0 mg
106.650 DM	50ST	50.0 mg
96.025 DM	50ST	12.5 mg
15.457 DM	100ST	75.0 mg
15.382 DM	100ST	100.0 mg
11.733 DM	20ST	25.0 mg
8.808 DM	20ST	50.0 mg
8.071 DM	20ST	12.5 mg

We can see that only three positions are of major interest. Parts of the related aut idem list for the first combination line are listed above.

4 Further screening criteria: Lorenz curve, Gini coefficient, innovation potential and information distribution systems

In economic considerations the Lorenz curve and the Gini coefficient are tools to describe inequality of consumption of resources(BOSCH 1992). In our case we define a linearly ordered structure by the financial volume of the medicines prescribed as cumulative values (percental values starting with the lowest costs) in relation to the percental part of patients included to that point. As an example: 80% of the patients induce 20% of the costs. Usually one uses an interpolation to smooth curves. Although one does not need any individual information of patients for this analysis, an anonymous identification label is necessary for this procedure. Of course, subgroups are interesting on both scales (subgroup of patients and subgroups of drugs i.e. on the basis of the ATC code). The area between the described curve and the diagonal is called the Gini coefficient.

It is also useful to use the drug (more precisely the PZN) as an identification value instead of the patients (there are different prices for drugs as well as for prescriptions for patients). In a large range of situations a small Gini coefficient (nearly the same resources used for all individuals) may be a hint for a deficit of differentiation of therapeutic procedure. In special situations the same result can be induced by high specialisation. In that sense screening parameters could be used for preselection and as one single coordinate in a parameter space. As an example for an additional parameter we can use the degree of realization of the aut idem potential mentioned above.

Innovative drugs also play an important role, especially in connection with new therapeutic possibilities. In budget negotiations they are regularly mentioned in a favourite position, although a further differentiation with respect to the degree of innovation shows a much higher amount of pseudo-innovations. The classification of the health report mentioned above uses the following categories

- A: new active substrate or new application of therapeutic relevance
- B: improvement pharmacodynamic or pharmacokinetic qualities of known application principles
- C: analogous drug with no or marginal differences with already introduced drugs
- D: therapeutic principle with insufficient evaluation

A regional example gives the following percental values within the medicament classified by A to D:

- A: 1%
- mixed A/B, A/C, A/D: 14%
- B: 18%
- C: 65%
- D: 0%

Only 6% of all drug are innovative in the sense of a A to D classification, and nearly two third of them are "pseudo-innovations" (more precisely: class C innovations). One can conclude that real innovations are not a central problem for health insurances. This part of financial volume is less than the increase from 1998 to 1999 (in the mentioned region) of all drugs.

Another interesting parameter is the proportion of drugs for severe diseases determined in discussions between doctors and health insurances.

Only a set of central parameters (at least 10) may be sufficient for a realistic preselection of an evaluation of economic and qualitative prescription behaviour of a doctor in comparison (in a medical and in a statistical sense) with his relevant group. After this first preselection step one has detailed information of different aggregation levels to verify or falsify the first presumption with medical and pharmacological expert information. The preselection reduces the cost of included experts or may reach at least a realistic amount of work for a specialist.

In the project PLATO (Pharmakologische Listen und Auswertungen für die Transparenz in der Ordination, pharmacological lists and evaluations for transparence in prescription) we have a software tool for a dynamic construction of 10 thousands of HTML documents (Internet or intra-net structure). The related navigation structure is able to reach the relevant point of resolution beginning from mentioned parameters down to details of each prescription. It is in use by certain health insurances for advising discussions and budget evaluations. In present time there are talks to reach possibilities to provide such informations to doctors, patients and health insurances using the Internet.

References

BOSCH, K. (1992): Statistik-Taschenbuch, R. Oldenbourg-Verlag, München, pp 36–41.

Effects of Independent Non–differential Misclassification on the Attributable Risk

C. Vogel, M. Land, O. Gefeller

Department of Medical Informatics, Biometry and Epidemiology,
University of Erlangen–Nuremberg, D–91054 Erlangen, Germany

Abstract: Misclassification affects the estimation of measures of association in epidemiologic studies. The paper investigates the situations of non–differential misclassification of exposure *or* disease, of independent non–differential misclassification of exposure *and* disease and misclassification in the presence of covariates and the resulting effects on the attributable risk. Of special interest is the situation where a dichotomous covariate is misclassified.

1 Introduction

Misclassification affects the estimation of epidemiologic measures of association between exposure and disease. Previous methodological work has concentrated on the effects of misclassification on the relative risk (e.g. Flegal et al. (1986)). The effects of misclassification on the attributable risk, however, cannot be derived directly from these results as the attributable risk is a function of the relative risk and the prevalence of exposure. Walter (1983) and Hsieh and Walter (1988) examined the effects of non–differential exposure misclassification on the attributable risk, the effects of non–differential disease misclassification are presented by Hsieh (1991). In practice, both exposure and disease can be misclassified simultaneously. In addition, the attributable risk, adjusted for confounding and effect–modification, is affected by effects of misclassification of the covariate(s).

After briefly outlining the basic concepts of attributable risk and misclassification in the following section, the effects of misclassification of exposure and/or disease on the attributable risk are discussed in the third section. Finally, the situation where a dichotomous covariate is misclassified is examined in the fourth section.

2 Basic Concepts

2.1 Attributable Risk

Levin (1953) introduced the attributable risk which represents the fraction of disease that might be avoided if the entire population contracted

disease at the rate of those unexposed to a risk factor. Its original definition is equivalent to

$$AR = \frac{P(D=1) - P(D=1|E=0)}{P(D=1)} , \tag{1}$$

where $P(D=1)$ and $P(D=1|E=0)$ represent the probabilities of
disease among the entire population and the unexposed, respectively.
Note that the applicability of risk attribution is restricted to situations
in which the exposure is associated with an increased risk of disease, i.e.
the relative risk exceeds 1.

An adjusted measure of attributable risk taking into account the effects
of confounding and/or effect–modification has been introduced by Whittemore (1982) in the following form:

$$AR_{adj} = 1 - \sum_{k=0}^{K} \frac{P(C=k) \cdot P(D=1|E=0 \wedge C=k)}{P(D=1)} , \tag{2}$$

where $P(C=k)$ is the fraction of the population in the k-th stratum of
the covariable(s) C, and $P(D=1|E=0 \wedge C=k)$ is the stratum–specific
disease rate among the unexposed. The adjusted attributable risk can
be rewritten as a weighted sum of the stratum–specific attributable risks
AR_k:

$$AR_{adj} = \sum_{k=0}^{K} P(C=k|D=1) \cdot AR_k , \tag{3}$$

where $P(C=k|D=1)$ is the fraction of diseased in the k-th stratum.
A review of methods of adjustment has been provided by Gefeller (1992)
and Coughlin et al. (1994).

2.2   Misclassification — Basic Definitions

In order to define the concepts of non–differentiality and independence
characterizing the misclassification situations to be analyzed let the variables E' and D' indicate the observed exposure and disease status, respectively.

Misclassification of exposure is called *non–differential* if it is independent
of true disease status, i.e. for every $i, j, k \in \{0, 1\}$:

$$P(E'=i|E=j \wedge D=k) = P(E'=i|E=j) . \tag{4}$$

Similarly misclassification of disease is called *non–differential* if it is independent of true exposure status, i.e. for every $i, j, k \in \{0, 1\}$:

$$P(D'=i|D=j \wedge E=k) = P(D'=i|D=j) . \tag{5}$$

In the context of joint misclassification of exposure and disease the concept of independence is of particular interest. Misclassification of exposure and disease is called *independent* if observed exposure and disease variables are stochastically independent given true exposure and disease variables, that is, if and only if for every $i, j, k, l \in \{0,1\}$ we have:

$$P(D' = i \wedge E' = j|D = k \wedge E = l) =$$
$$P(D' = i|D = k \wedge E = l) \cdot P(E' = j|D = k \wedge E = l) . \quad (6)$$

3 Effects of Misclassification in 2×2–Tables on the Attributable Risk

The goal of this section is to analyze the situations of (i) non–differential exposure misclassification, (ii) non–differential disease misclassification, (iii) independent non–differential misclassification of exposure and disease and their effects on the attributable risk.

For every $i, j \in \{0,1\}$ we define the true/observed state probability $p_{ij} := P(D = i \wedge E = j) \,/\, p'_{ij} := P(D' = i \wedge E' = j)$, i.e. the probability that the true/observed status of disease is i and the true/observed status of exposure is j and their representations as vectors $\vec{p} := \begin{pmatrix} p_{11} & p_{10} & p_{01} & p_{00} \end{pmatrix}^{T} /$ $\vec{p}' := \begin{pmatrix} p'_{11} & p'_{10} & p'_{01} & p'_{00} \end{pmatrix}^{T}$.

Sensitivity Se_E and specificity Sp_E of exposure classification denote the probabilities for correct classification of exposure status among the exposed and the unexposed, respectively. Similarly sensitivity Se_D and specificity Sp_D of disease classification are defined.

3.1 Non–Differential Exposure Misclassification

Under non–differential exposure misclassification we can express the observed state probabilities as a linear function of the true state probabilities

$$\vec{p}' = M_E \cdot \vec{p} , \quad (7)$$

where the so–called exposure misclassification matrix M_E is given by:

$$M_E := \begin{pmatrix} Se_E & 1 - Sp_E & 0 & 0 \\ 1 - Se_E & Sp_E & 0 & 0 \\ 0 & 0 & Se_E & 1 - Sp_E \\ 0 & 0 & 1 - Se_E & Sp_E \end{pmatrix} . \quad (8)$$

Replacing the true state probabilities in the formula

$$AR = \frac{p_{11} \cdot p_{00} - p_{10} \cdot p_{01}}{p_{1.} \cdot p_{.0}} \quad (9)$$

by the observed state probabilities according to (7) we get the observed attributable risk

$$AR' = \frac{(Sp_E + Se_E - 1) \cdot (p_{11} \cdot p_{00} - p_{10} \cdot p_{01})}{p_{1.} \cdot [(1 - Se_E) \cdot p_{.1} + Sp_E \cdot p_{.0}]} . \tag{10}$$

Using equations (9) and (10) one can show that the difference and the ratio of the true to observed attributable risk are

$$AR - AR' = \frac{(p_{11} \cdot p_{00} - p_{10} \cdot p_{01}) \cdot (1 - Se_E)}{p_{1.} \cdot p_{.0} \cdot [(1 - Se_E) \cdot p_{.1} + Sp_E \cdot p_{.0}]} , \tag{11}$$

$$\frac{AR}{AR'} = 1 + \frac{(1 - Se_E)}{(Sp_E + Se_E - 1) \cdot p_{.0}} . \tag{12}$$

The factor $p_{11} \cdot p_{00} - p_{10} \cdot p_{01}$ is greater than 0, if and only if the relative risk is greater than 1, which is a natural condition in the context of attributable risk. Thus, the difference between the true and observed attributable risk (11) is positive. Consequently, under non–differential exposure misclassification the attributable risk is biased toward the null. Given perfect sensitivity the attributable risk is unbiased. The ratio of the true to observed attributable risk (12) is isotone in the prevalence of exposure. Therefore high prevalence of exposure leads to severe bias.

3.2   Non–Differential Disease Misclassification

Similar to the previous subsection in the situation of disease misclassification the observed state probabilities are a linear function of the true state probabilities: $\vec{p}' = M_D \cdot \vec{p}$, where the so–called disease misclassification matrix M_D is given by:

$$M_D := \begin{pmatrix} Se_D & 0 & 1 - Sp_D & 0 \\ 0 & Se_D & 0 & 1 - Sp_D \\ 1 - Se_D & 0 & Sp_D & 0 \\ 0 & 1 - Se_D & 0 & Sp_D \end{pmatrix} . \tag{13}$$

The observed attributable risk, the difference and the ratio of the true to observed attributable risk

$$AR' = \frac{(Sp_D + Se_D - 1) \cdot (p_{11} \cdot p_{00} - p_{10} \cdot p_{01})}{p_{.0} \cdot [Se_D \cdot p_{1.} + (1 - Sp_D) \cdot p_{0.}]} , \tag{14}$$

$$AR - AR' = \frac{(p_{11} \cdot p_{00} - p_{10} \cdot p_{01}) \cdot (1 - Sp_D)}{p_{1.} \cdot p_{.0} \cdot [Se_D \cdot p_{1.} + (1 - Sp_D) \cdot p_{0.}]} , \tag{15}$$

$$\frac{AR}{AR'} = 1 + \frac{(1 - Sp_D)}{(Sp_D + Se_D - 1) \cdot p_{1.}} \tag{16}$$

are easily derived. The formulas (15) and (16) can be interpreted as follows: under non–differential disease misclassification the attributable risk is biased toward the null. Given perfect specificity the attributable risk is unbiased. Low prevalence of disease leads to severe bias.

3.3 Independent Non–Differential Misclassification of Exposure and Disease

The situation of non–differentiality and independence, i.e. the situation, where (i) misclassification of exposure is independent of true disease status, (ii) misclassification of disease is independent of true exposure status, (iii) the observed exposure and disease variables are independent given the true exposure and disease variables, can be described by the following theorem.

Theorem 4 : *Misclassification of exposure and disease is independent and non–differential if and only if the following conditions hold:*

1. *Exposure misclassification is independent of true and observed disease status, that is, if and only if for every i, j, k, l ∈ {0,1}:*

$$P(E' = i | E = j \wedge D = k \wedge D' = l) = P(E' = i | E = j) \ . \tag{17}$$

2. *Disease misclassification is independent of true and observed exposure status, that is, if and only if for every i, j, k, l ∈ {0,1}:*

$$P(D' = i | D = j \wedge E = k \wedge E' = l) = P(D' = i | D = j) \ . \tag{18}$$

Under independent non–differential misclassification of exposure and disease we can express the observed state probabilities as a linear function of the true state probabilities, where the linear link is defined by the product of the commutative misclassification matrices for exposure M_E and disease M_D: $\vec{p}\,' = M_E \cdot M_D \cdot \vec{p} = M_D \cdot M_E \cdot \vec{p}$. Thus, the effects of joint misclassification are derived multiplicatively from the marginal effects of exposure and disease misclassification. Therefore the effects of simultaneous misclassification of exposure and disease can be understood by sequentially analyzing the respective effects of exposure and disease misclassification. Due to commutativity of the matrices, it is not relevant, however, in which order the misclassification effects are taken into account.

4 Effects of Misclassification in the Presence of Covariates

4.1 Non–Differential Misclassification of Exposure

In the presence of covariates misclassification of exposure is called *non–differential* if it is independent of true disease and covariate status. In the weighted sum representation (3) of the adjusted attributable risk the weights are unbiased and the stratum–specific attributable risks are biased toward the null. Thus, non–differential misclassification of exposure tends to bias the attributable risk toward the null as long as exposure classification is better than random:

$$AR'_{adj} \;=\; \sum_{k=0}^{K} P(C = k | D = 1) \cdot AR'_k \leq AR_{adj}.$$

4.2 Non–Differential Misclassification of Disease

In the situation of non–differential disease misclassification, i.e. where disease misclassification is independent of true exposure and covariate status, both the weights and the stratum–specific attributable risks are biased in the weighted sum representation (3) of the attributable risk. Nevertheless using the results of section 3.2 it is easy to show that the attributable risk is again biased toward the null:

$$AR'_{adj} = \underbrace{\frac{(Sp + Se - 1) \cdot P(D = 1)}{(Sp + Se - 1) \cdot P(D = 1) + (1 - Sp)}}_{\leq 1} \cdot AR_{adj} \leq AR_{adj} \ . \quad (19)$$

4.3 Non–Differential Misclassification of a Dichotomous Covariate

We define the probabilities for the correct classification of the stratum 0 and 1 of the dichotomous covariate:

$$a_{00} := P(C' = 0 | C = 0) \qquad a_{11} := P(C' = 1 | C = 1) \ . \quad (20)$$

Note that non–differentiality describes the situation, where the probabilities for the correct classification of the stratum 0 and 1 of the covariate are independent of true exposure and disease variables. Again we assume that $a_{00} + a_{11} - 1 > 0$, which means that classification is better than random.

The observed adjusted attributable risk depends on a_{00}, a_{11} and $\vec{p}$:

$$AR'_{adj} = 1 - \frac{1}{p_{1..}} \cdot$$

$$\left\{ \frac{[a_{00} \cdot p_{100} + (1 - a_{11}) \cdot p_{101}] \cdot [a_{00} \cdot p_{..0} + (1 - a_{11}) \cdot p_{..1}]}{a_{00} \cdot p_{.00} + (1 - a_{11}) \cdot p_{.01}} \right.$$

$$\left. + \frac{[(1 - a_{00}) \cdot p_{100} + a_{11} \cdot p_{101}] \cdot [(1 - a_{00}) \cdot p_{..0} + a_{11} \cdot p_{..1}]}{(1 - a_{00}) \cdot p_{.00} + a_{11} \cdot p_{.01}} \right\} \cdot$$

The partial derivatives are given by $\frac{\partial AR'_{adj}}{\partial a_{00}} = \alpha(\vec{p}) \cdot f(a_{00}, a_{11}, \vec{p})$ and $\frac{\partial AR'_{adj}}{\partial a_{11}} = \alpha(\vec{p}) \cdot g(a_{00}, a_{11}, \vec{p})$, where f and g are positive functions and $\alpha(\vec{p}) = (p_{..1} \cdot p_{.00} - p_{..0} \cdot p_{.01}) \cdot (p_{100} \cdot p_{.01} - p_{101} \cdot p_{.00})$. The derivatives are not explicitly outlined here. Consequently, the partial derivatives have the same sign, the sign itself only depends on the true distribution.

In the situation of random classification, i.e. $a_{00} + a_{11} - 1 = 0$, observed adjusted and true non–adjusted attributable risks are equal. The adjusted attributable risk as a function of a_{00}, a_{11} is either isotone or antitone in both variables. Thus, the observed adjusted attributable risk is positioned between the adjusted and the non–adjusted true attributable risk. In the case of positive confounding, i.e. $AR > AR_{adj}$, which is equivalent to $\alpha(\vec{p}) < 0$, the observed adjusted attributable risk tends to overestimate the true adjusted attributable risk. In the case of negative confounding, i.e. $AR < AR_{adj}$, which is equivalent to $\alpha(\vec{p}) > 0$, the observed adjusted attributable risk tends to underestimate the true adjusted attributable risk. Positive confounding is given if and only if the stratum–specific disease rate among the unexposed is lower in the stratum with the higher prevalence of exposure.

5 Discussion

The matrix–based method presented above shows that in all investigated situations the direction of the misclassification bias is the same as for the relative risk. Under non–differential misclassification of exposure or disease — in the presence or absence of covariates — the observed attributable risk tends to underestimate the true attributable risk. The effect of independent non–differential misclassification of exposure and disease can be derived multiplicatively from the marginal effects of non–differential exposure and disease misclassification. Thus, the attributable risk is again biased toward the null. Misclassification of a dichotomous covariate leads to a partial loss of ability to control for confounding. Nevertheless as long as classification of a dichotomous confounder is better than random control for this confounder leads to an improved measure of association.

The results of these methodological considerations concerning the effects of misclassification of the attributable risk have direct implication for the epidemiological practice. The insights into the direction of bias in the case of independent non–differential misclassification offer the opportunity to consider observed attributable risks in epidemiological studies fulfilling the underlying conditions as lower bounds for the true ones when interpreting the findings. Furthermore, the formulae derived in this paper relating the observed to the true attributable risk given the misclassification probability distribution allow some kind of post-hoc sensitivity analysis in epidemiological studies: for a range of reasonable misclassification scenarios in the specific context of the study the true attributable risk can now be directly computed.

Acknowledgements. This work has been supported by a grant of the Deutsche Forschungsgemeinschaft (grant no. Ge 637/4-1).

References

COUGHLIN, S. S., BENICHOU, J. and WEED, D. L. (1994): Attributable risk estimation in case–control studies. *Epidemiologic Reviews, 16, 51–64.*

FLEGAL, K. M., BROWNIE, C. and HAAS, J. D. (1986): The effects of exposure misclassification on estimates of relative risk. *American Journal of Epidemiology, 123, 736–751.*

GEFELLER, O. (1992): Comparison of adjusted attributable risk estimators. *Statistics in Medicine, 11, 2083–2091.*

HSIEH, C. C.(1991): The effect of non–differential outcome misclassification on estimates of the attributable and prevented fraction. *Statistics in Medicine, 10, 361-373.*

HSIEH, C. C. and WALTER, S. D. (1988): The effect of non–differential exposure misclassification on estimates of the attributable and prevented fraction. *Statistics in Medicine, 7, 1073-1085.*

LEVIN, M. L. (1953): The occurrence of lung cancer in man. *Acta Unio Internationalis Contra Cancrum, 9, 531-541.*

WALTER, S. D. (1983): Effects of interaction, confounding and observational error on attributable risk estimation. *American Journal of Epidemiology, 117, 598-604.*

WHITTEMORE, A. S. (1982): Statistical methods for estimating attributable risk from retrospective data. *Statistics in Medicine, 1, 229-243.*

A New Approach to Discriminant Analysis with Longitudinal Data

K.-D. Wernecke

Institut für Medizinische Biometrie,
Charité, Humboldt-Universität zu Berlin, D - 13344 Berlin, Germany

Abstract:

Experimental designs in medicine are often characterized by repeated observations on the same patient. In an approach of analysis of variance, you may analyse such data with the help of multivariate analysis of variance for repeated measurements (Timm (1980)).

On the other hand, if the aim is an individual allocation of patients into one of different groups (diagnoses) a discriminant analysis has to be applied. In a first attempt, Tomasko et al. (1999) modified the well-known linear discriminant analysis using the mixed model ANOVA for the estimation of fixed effects (covariates) and for a determination of various structures of covariance matrices including unstructured, compound symmetry and autoregressive of the first order. We extended the approach and applied this analysis to medical data.

1 Introductory Example

Diagnostic parameters were investigated from a multicentre study on International Investigation of Breast MRI (IIBM). By evaluation of contrast-enhancement, breast MRI promises additional pathophysiological information that is not available from conventional breast imaging. An increasing number of authors have confirmed the value of contrast-enhanced (CE) MRI for certain indications. However, accuracy data in the literature vary, and concern exists that a widespread use of CE MRI combined with insufficient standards might cause unsatisfying results.

Therefore, the purpose of our investigations consisted in:

- Investigation whether - based on enhancement and morphologic characteristics - a statistically founded distinction between benign and malignant lesions is possible,

- Development of a rule that allows optimum retrospective discrimination of benign from malignant lesions at sensitivity and specificity levels that are clinically useful.

2 Analysis of Variance (ANOVA)

In univariate analysis of variance for repeated measures we assume

$$y_{kjh} = \mu + \beta_k + \tau_{kh} + \delta_{kj} + \epsilon_{kjh} \; ; \; k = 1, \ldots, K \; ; \; j = 1, \ldots n_k \; ; \; h = 1, \ldots q$$

with μ: the overall mean, β_k: fixed group effects, τ_{kh}: interactions between groups and repetitions ($\sum_{h=1}^{q} \tau_{kh} = 0 \; \forall k$), δ_{kj}: random effects with $\delta_{kj} \in N(0, \sigma_b^2)$, independent among each other and with respect to errors $\epsilon_{kjh} \in N(0, \sigma^2)$. The model supposes equal correlations in the repetitions (so-called compound symmetry) which is not fulfilled in medical practice. In contrast, with serial measurements the correlations would decrease as the distance between two measurements increases.

2.1 Specified Models for Serial Measurements

We regard a covariance structure of an autoregressive process of order 1 (Hearne et al. (1983))

$$\Omega^{het} = \frac{1}{1 - \rho^2} \begin{bmatrix} \sigma_1^2 & \rho\sigma_1\sigma_2 & \cdots & \rho^{q-1}\sigma_1\sigma_q \\ \rho\sigma_2\sigma_1 & \sigma_2^2 & \cdots & \rho^{q-2}\sigma_2\sigma_q \\ \vdots & \vdots & \ddots & \vdots \\ \rho^{q-1}\sigma_q\sigma_1 & \rho^{q-2}\sigma_q\sigma_2 & \cdots & \sigma_q^2 \end{bmatrix} \; ; \; |\rho| < 1$$

Azzalini (1995) proposed a further modification in the form

$$\Sigma = \Omega^{het} + \sigma_b^2 \mathbf{11}'_{q \times q} \text{ or } \Sigma = \Omega^{hom} + \sigma_b^2 \mathbf{11}'_{q \times q} \text{ , if } \sigma_h^2 = \sigma^2 \; \forall h$$

(Ω^{hom} for $\sigma_h^2 = \sigma^2 \; \forall h$ accordingly).

2.2 Models with Mixed Effects

In a mixed model approach every observation $\mathbf{y}_j = (y_{j1}, \ldots, y_{jq_j})'$ is represented by

$$\mathbf{y}_j = \begin{bmatrix} y_{j1} \\ y_{j2} \\ \vdots \\ y_{jq_j} \end{bmatrix} = \mathbf{X}_j \begin{bmatrix} \beta_1 \\ \beta_2 \\ \vdots \\ \beta_m \end{bmatrix} + \mathbf{Z}_j \begin{bmatrix} \delta_{j1} \\ \delta_{j2} \\ \vdots \\ \delta_{jp} \end{bmatrix} + \begin{bmatrix} \epsilon_{j1} \\ \epsilon_{j2} \\ \vdots \\ \epsilon_{jq_j} \end{bmatrix} \tag{1}$$

with $\beta_1, \ldots, \beta_m$ fixed effects, $\delta_{j1}, \ldots, \delta_{jp}$ random effcts and

$$\mathbf{X}_j = \begin{bmatrix} x_{j11} & x_{j12} & \cdots & x_{j1m} \\ x_{j21} & x_{j22} & \cdots & x_{j2m} \\ \vdots & \vdots & \ddots & \vdots \\ x_{jq_j1} & x_{jq_j2} & \cdots & x_{jq_jm} \end{bmatrix} \quad \mathbf{Z}_j = \begin{bmatrix} z_{j11} & z_{j12} & \cdots & z_{j1p} \\ z_{j21} & z_{j22} & \cdots & z_{j2p} \\ \vdots & \vdots & \ddots & \vdots \\ z_{jq_j1} & z_{jq_j2} & \cdots & z_{jq_jp} \end{bmatrix}$$

with $\mathbf{X}_j$ design-matrix of fixed, $\mathbf{Z}_j$ design-matrix of random effects. Under the suppositions

$$Cov[\delta_{jl}, \epsilon_{kh}] = 0 \; ; \; Cov[\delta_{jl}, \delta_{ks}] = 0 \; \forall l \neq s \; ; \; Cov[\epsilon_{jh}, \epsilon_{kt}] = 0 \; \forall j \neq k$$

$$E\begin{bmatrix} \delta_j \\ \epsilon_j \end{bmatrix} = \begin{bmatrix} 0 \\ 0 \end{bmatrix} \quad \text{and} \quad Var\begin{bmatrix} \delta_j \\ \epsilon_j \end{bmatrix} = \begin{bmatrix} \Delta & 0 \\ 0 & \mathbf{V}_j \end{bmatrix}$$

we get the expectations and covariance matrix in the form of

$$E[\mathbf{y}_j] = \mathbf{X}_j \underline{\beta} \quad \text{und} \quad Cov[\mathbf{y}_j, \mathbf{y}_j'] = \Sigma_j = \mathbf{Z}_j \Delta \mathbf{Z}_j' + \mathbf{V}_j \tag{2}$$

with the special cases $(\mathbf{Z}_j = \mathbf{1}_j = 1)$

$$\Delta = \delta_{11} \; ; \; \mathbf{Z}_j \Delta \mathbf{Z}_j' = \delta_{11} \mathbf{11}' = \sigma_b^2 \mathbf{11}' \; ; \; \mathbf{V}_j = \sigma^2 \mathbf{I} \tag{3}$$
$$\mathbf{Z}_j \Delta \mathbf{Z}_j' = \sigma_b^2 \mathbf{11}' \; ; \; \mathbf{V}_j = diag(\sigma_1^2, \ldots, \sigma_{q_j}^2)$$
$$\Delta = 0 \; ; \; \mathbf{V}_j = \Omega_j^{het} \text{ or } \mathbf{V}_j = \Omega_j^{hom} \text{ , if } \sigma_h^2 = \sigma^2 \; \forall h$$

3 Discriminant Analysis with Longitudinal Data

To simplify matters, we regard only $K = 2$ and suppose $\Sigma_1 = \Sigma_2 = \Sigma$. In linear discriminant analysis (LDA) we use

$$D(\mathbf{y}) = [\mathbf{y} - \frac{1}{2}(\hat{\mu}_1 + \hat{\mu}_2)]' \hat{\Sigma}^{-1} (\hat{\mu}_1 - \hat{\mu}_2) \tag{4}$$

($\hat{\Sigma}$ "suitable" estimation of Σ; $\hat{\mu}_1, \hat{\mu}_2$ estimations of the true expectations) and allocate an observation $\mathbf{y}$ into group (class) 1, if

$$D(\mathbf{y}) > \log \frac{\pi_2}{\pi_1} \; ,$$

otherwise into group (class) 2 (π_1, π_2 priors). Basic idea in Tomasco et al. (1999): Use as "suitable" estimation of the covariance matrix $\Sigma_j = \mathbf{Z}_j \Delta \mathbf{Z}_j' + \mathbf{V}_j$ one of the variants from equation (3) and apply the linear discriminant analysis as usual. Unfortunately, they did not take into account, that a covariance structure with autoregressive of first order (alone) may not appropriate in medical applications because of the high individual component which is usually present. Therefore, we prefer the approach

$$\mathbf{Z}_j \Delta \mathbf{Z}_j' = \sigma_b^2 \mathbf{11}' \; ; \; \mathbf{V}_j = \Omega_j^{het} \text{ or } \mathbf{V}_j = \Omega_j^{hom} \text{ , if } \sigma_h^2 = \sigma^2 \; \forall h \tag{5}$$

in our applications (Azzalini (1995)).

3.1 Estimation of the Discrimination Error

We use always the "π–method" which estimates the so-called "actual or true error rate" and judges the discrimination result with a choosen sample discriminator for those patients not belonging to the training sample.

3.2 Feature Selection

Using the amount of the discrimination error as selection criterion, we perform always a cross-validated feature selection (Wernecke (1993)). Thereby the given sample is reduced repeatedly by a certain number of observations and with the remaining rest, the feature selection process is carried out. In every step, the removed objects are allocated using the decision rule obtained and the wrong allocations are counted (cross-validated error rate).

In the end we select those features for a discrimination rule which appear most frequently in the validation steps. If certain features show up again and again in the validation steps they can be considered as particularly stable. Exactly the most frequent features were recommended to the medical doctors and for those a new error estimation is accomplished (recommended error rate).

4   Results of the IIBM-Study

The study resulted in findings of more than 500 patients (more than 800 tissues). The analyses were performed with the signal intensities to 6 consecutive times (SIG_k, $k = 1, \ldots, 6$ with $SIG_1 = SIG_{base}$ as baseline-value). In a first step we applied the well-known linear discriminant analysis to the data. The differentiation between "Malignant" und "Benign" was made on the basis of histological classes (Table 1).

Malignant	132 lesions
from there:	129 from histol.cl. I : malignant neoplasm invasive
	3 from histol.cl. VII : other
Benign	63 lesions
from there:	9 from histol.cl. IV : proliferative lesion
	30 from histol.cl. V : benign lesion, tumorous
	22 from histol.cl. VI : benign lesion, non-tumor
	2 from histol.cl. VII : other

Table 1: Differentiation between "benign" and "malignant" lesions

For each lesion all together 21 parameters were calculated from the MRI signal intensities:

$$ENH_{k-1} = (SIG_k - SIG_1)/(SIG_1) \times 100 \; ; \; k = 2, \ldots, 6$$

$$MSLP = \max_{k=1}^{2} ENH_k \; ; \; ENHMAX = \max_{k=1}^{5} ENH_k$$

$$SAT = (SIG_2)/(\max_{k=2}^{6} SIG_k) \times 100$$

$$WO = (\max_{k=2}^{6} SIG_k - SIG_6)/(\max_{k=2}^{6} SIG_k)$$

$$ENHi\_j = ENH_i - ENH_j \; ; \; SIGi\_1 = SIG_i - SIG_1$$

and others.

4.1 Results with the Linear Discriminant Analysis

Taking all the 21 features into account, the following characteristics were most frequently choosen in the selection procedure (Table 2). This resul-

Feature	Linear Discriminant Analysis										
	Selection in valid. as i-th feature										
	1	2	3	4	5	6	7	8	9	10	11
SAT	1	1	1	1	1	1	1	1	1	1	1
$ENH4\_3$	3	0	0	3	4	3	3	2	2	3	0
WO	0	2	4	0	0	0	7	0	4	2	0
$ENHMAX$	0	3	0	0	5	0	8	0	0	0	4

Table 2: Selected features in 11 validations

ted in the discrimination errors 15.90% (cross-validated error rate) and 16.92% (recommended error rate), respectively, and we got the classific-ation Table 3 (in Table 3 means: Row [%]: 1st row, column: Sensitivity;

Freq. Row [%] Col. [%]	In class		Total
From class	1	2	
1	123 93.2% 88.5%	9 6.8% 16.1%	132
2	16 25.4% 11.5%	47 74.6% 83.9%	63
Total	139	56	195

Table 3: Classification table using the "plain" LDA

528

2nd row, column: Specificity; Col. [%]: 1st row and column: Pos. Prediction; 2nd row and column: Neg. Prediction).

4.2 Results with the New Discrimination for Longitudinal Data

All together we investigated the following variants:

1. LDA with altered expectation value structure by removing interactions (residual analysis),

2. LDA, covariance structure modelled as heterogeneous or homogeneous compound symmetri,

3. LDA, covariance structure modelled as heterogeneous or homogeneous autoregressive of order 1,

4. LDA, covariance structure identical to 2. and 3. with an additional random component (patient impact).

In contrast to the first calculation with LDA, we now took the pure original signal values into consideration, related to the baseline. In particular we regarded only the variables

$$DIFF_{k-1} = (SIG_k - SIG_1) ; \ k = 2,\ldots,6$$

or

$$RELDIF_{k-1} = (SIG_k - SIG_1)/(SIG_1) ; \ k = 2,\ldots,6$$

Without feature selection, the discrimination rule with covariance structure modelled as homogeneous autoregressive of order 1 and additional patient's random component was best and resulted in 18.46% (R–method – resubstitution), 19.49% (π–method), resp., using only the features $RELDIF$. The following classification tabels for π-error rate (left) and R-error (right) were obtained (Table 4).

A feature selection in building-up steps using the same covariance structure resulted in $RELDIF_3$ as redundant. The estimation of the discrimination error with the remaining 4 features yielded: 17.44% (R-method), 18.97% (π–method), respectively. To judge the results, you have to keep in mind, that the first discrimination with "plain" LDA were performed with 21 features and the last with only 4 pure original signal intensities. Therefore, the new approach confirmed the results firstly obtained and seems to be very promising in future.

The main advantages of the new approach are:

Freq. Row [%] Col. [%] From cl.	Into class 1	Into class 2	Total
1	109 82.6% 87.9%	23 17.4% 32.4%	132
2	15 23.8% 12.1%	48 76.2% 67.6%	63
Total	124	71	195

Freq. Row [%] Col. [%] From cl.	Into class 1	Into class 2	Total
1	109 82.6% 89.3%	23 17.4% 31.5%	132
2	13 20.6% 10.7%	50 79.4% 68.5%	63
Total	122	73	195

Table 4: Classification tables with the new approach of LDA

- Use of all available longitudinal data, regardless of completeness, i.e. no case-wise deletion of patients with "missing values",

- Various possibilities of structuring the covariance matrix Σ,

- Determination of a modified covariance matrix for every patient under a reduced number of parameters to estimate,

- For these reasons particular advantageous in small samples.

References

AZZALINI, A. (1995): Topics in repeated measurements analysis: ANOVA with correlated data. University of Padua Press, Padua.

HEARNE, E.H., G.M. CLARK and J.P. HATCH (1983): A Test for Serial Correlation in Univariate Repeated Measures Analysis. Biometrics, 39, 239-243.

TIMM, N.H. (1980): Multivariate Analysis of Variance of Repeated Measurements. In: Krishnaiah, P.R. (ed.): Handbook of Statistics. North Holland Publ. Comp. Amsterdam, New York, Oxford.

TOMASKO, L., R.W. HELMS and S.M. SNAPPINN (1999): A discriminant analysis extension to mixed models. Statistics in Medicine, 18, 1249-1260.

WERNECKE, K.-D. (1993): Jackknife, Bootstrap und Cross-Validation: Eine Einführung in Methoden der wiederholten Stichprobenziehung. Allgemeines Statistisches Archiv, Vol. 77 (1), 32-59.

Author Index

Subject Index

Printing: Strauss GmbH, Mörlenbach
Binding: Schäffer, Grünstadt